W9-BXP-862

THE WAY OF JESUS CHRIST

Other books by Jürgen Moltmann

THE CRUCIFIED GOD
THEOLOGY OF HOPE
THE CHURCH IN THE POWER OF THE SPIRIT
THE TRINITY AND THE KINGDOM
GOD IN CREATION

JÜRGEN MOLTMANN

The Way of Jesus Christ

CHRISTOLOGY IN MESSIANIC
DIMENSIONS

HarperSanFrancisco
A Division of HarperCollins*Publishers*

Translated by Margaret Kohl from the German
Der Weg Jesu Christi: Christologie in messianischen Dimensionen
published by Christian Kaiser Verlag, Munich, 1989.

THE WAY OF JESUS CHRIST: Christology in Messianic Dimensions. English translation copyright © 1990 by Margaret Kohl. All rights reserved. Printed in the United States of America. No part of this book may be used or reproduced in any manner whatsoever without written permission except in the case of brief quotations embodied in critical articles and reviews. For information address HarperCollins Publishers, 10 East 53rd Street, New York, New York 10022.

FIRST HARPERCOLLINS EDITION PUBLISHED IN 1990.

Library of Congress Cataloging-in-Publication Data

Moltmann, Jürgen.
    [Weg Jesu Christi. English]
    The way of Jesus Christ : christology in messianic dimensions / Jürgen Moltmann.
      p.   cm.
    Translation of: Weg Jesu Christi.
    Includes bibliographical references and indexes.
    ISBN 0–06–065910–6 (alk. paper) :
    1. Jesus Christ—Person and offices.   2. Jesus Christ—Messiahship.
I. Title.
BT202.M55213   1990
232—dc20   89–46471
                                                CIP

---

90 91 92 93 94 RRD(H) 10 9 8 7 6 5 4 3 2 1

This edition is printed on acid-free paper that meets the American National Standards Institute Z39.48 Standard.

*Cordially dedicated
to my colleagues Hans Küng and Eberhard Jüngel
and our longstanding and always enjoyable
Tübingen table round*

CONTENTS

PREFACE

In accordance with the intention I expressed in 1985, this third volume in my series of systematic contributions to theology is devoted to christology. And because I have ventured to call the whole of my theology 'messianic theology', the dimensions of this christology are messianic. Within these dimensions, I do not wish to talk solely about 'the Christ of hope' in the form of an eschatological christology (although characterizations of that kind are not of course wrong). But the future hope of Israel and Judaism is already messianic; and it was from this that the Christian faith proceeded. For if we take the word 'Christian' literally, the Christian faith is a messianic faith. The messianic hope binds Christianity and Judaism, and divides them. In order to bring out the enduring link with Judaism, which nothing can ever destroy, I have tried in chapter I to clarify the dimensions of the messianic idea in dialogue with Jewish philosophers of religion.

I considered a whole series of titles before I decided on the one finally chosen. I thought of 'Christ – the Hope of the World'; 'Christ – the Coming One'; 'Christ on the Way'; and 'Christ in Becoming'. This shows that I am trying to think of Christ no longer statically, as one person in two natures or as a historical personality. I am trying to grasp him dynamically, in the forward movement of God's history with the world. What I wanted was not an eternal christology for heaven, but a christology for men and women who are on the way in the conflicts of history, and are looking for bearings on that way. Of course the one does not exclude the other. But the only possible beginning is the point one has reached oneself. In a liturgical doxology of Christ we contemplate in wonder the God who has become human, and the human Christ who is deified, and we formulate the christological dogma as they did in Nicaea and Chalcedon. But men and women who are living in the exile of history, and who are searching for life, need a christology for pilgrims (*christologia viatorum*). That means a christology of the way (*christologia viae*), which points beyond itself and draws people towards the future of Christ, so that they remain on Christ's path, and move forward along that path. In this sense the knowledge of Christ remains a provisional knowledge. It has to be formulated as a promise, which can only thrust forward to the seeing face to face. Properly understood, doxological christology and this eschatological christology complement and intensify one another. Yet every word of thanks is based on some positive experience, and every word of praise is founded on something in life. So doxological christology would be left in the air if it were not grounded on the experience of the men and women who follow the path of Jesus Christ.

I finally decided to call this book 'The Way of Jesus Christ'; and for this I had three reasons.

1. The symbol of the way embodies the aspect of process, and brings out christology's alignment towards its goal. This symbol can comprehend Christ's way from his birth in the Spirit and his baptism in the Spirit to his self-surrender on Golgotha. It also makes it possible to understand the path of Christ as the way leading from his resurrection to his parousia – the way he takes in the Spirit to Israel, to the nations, and into the breadth and depth of the cosmos.

2. The symbol of the way makes us aware that every human christology is historically conditioned and limited. Every human christology is a 'christology of the way', not yet a 'christology of the home country', a christology of faith, not yet a christology of sight. So christology is no more than the beginning of eschatology; and eschatology, as the Christian faith understands it, is always the consummation of christology.

3. Finally, but not least important: every way is an invitation. A way is something to be followed. 'The way of Jesus Christ' is not merely a christological category. It is an ethical category too. Anyone who enters upon Christ's way will discover who Jesus really is; and anyone who really believes in Jesus as the Christ of God will follow him along the way he himself took. Christology and christopraxis find one another in the full and completed knowledge of Christ. In this christology I have linked dogmatics and ethics in closer detail than in the previous volumes.

A christology of the way of Jesus Christ has to tell, and has to argue. It has once again to work through the history of the christological symbols, metaphors and ideas, as a way of arriving at new christological concepts. Consequently I have not based this christology on the christological dogma of the patristic church but – as far as I was able – have cast back historically and exegetically to the histories of the biblical tradition, in order with their help to arrive at new interpretations of Christ which will be relevant for the present day. So this christology is also a narrative christology, and image thinking, which seeks to link remembrances of Christ with expectations of him.

A christology of the way of Christ will always interpret his way in the light of his goal. This already follows from the roots of christology in Jewish messianology. A christology of the way becomes by its very nature a christology against the horizon of eschatology. But today the concept of eschatology has become blurred. It can mean various different orientations towards the future, and it can also mean the dimension of eternity. I have therefore broken the subject up, fanning it out into its different aspects. I have presented the historical mission of Christ (chapter III) in the framework of the messianic hope in history, the sufferings of Christ (chapter IV) against the horizon of the apocalyptic expectation of the End-time, and the resurrection of Christ (chapter V) in the light of the eschatological vision of the new creation of all things. My additional purpose here is to define the categories 'messianic', 'apocalyptic' and 'eschatological' in Christian terms, relating them to the way of Christ.

I originally envisaged that chapter VI would be 'The Presence of Christ'. But in *The Church in the Power of the Spirit* I already dealt in some detail with the apostolic presence of Christ in the church, and with the hidden presence of Christ in the poor; and since a new German edition of this book will appear in 1989, I have dispensed with this subject here. But I should like to draw explicit attention to the relevant chapters in that earlier book.

This christological outline is linked with a claim which I believe stands, even if I myself should not have been able to do it full justice. In the first volume of this messianic theology I tried to free the Christian doctrine of God from the confines of the ancient metaphysics of substance, and from the framework of the modern metaphysics of transcendental subjectivity, in order to develop a social doctrine of the Trinity in the different context of a metaphysics of community, process and relation. In the second volume, on the doctrine of creation, I took further steps to escape from the paradigm

of the modern world, which can be summed up under the headings
'subjectivity', 'materialization' and 'history', my purpose being to
prepare a theology which will be in a position to relate human
history to the nature of the earth, and to reconcile the two. Broadly
speaking, therefore, this christology implies the transition from the
metaphysical christology of the 'ancients' to the historical christology of modern times, and makes the now necessary transition from
the historical christology of modern times to a post-modern
christology, which places human history ecologically in the
framework of nature. Modern 'historical thinking' pushed out the
older 'metaphysical thinking'; and this was true of modern Protestant christology too. But newer thinking takes up the old
metaphysical thinking again, under the conditions of 'historical
thinking', and in a cosmological perspective. A transition does not
have to be a breach. Transitions can also place traditions within
wider horizons, and preserve older perceptions by translating them
into new situations. Modern historical thinking set human history
over against a nature without history. Newer thinking integrates
human history in the natural conditions in which it is embedded.
Modern christology therefore directs its attention towards Christ's
bodily nature and its significance for earthly nature as a whole,
because embodiment is the existential point of intersection between
history and nature in human beings.

For a long time one of the important questions in modern
christology was the transition from 'the Jesus of history' to 'the
Christ of faith'. I discussed this question in the *Theology of Hope*
(1964; ET 1967) and *The Crucified God* (1972; ET 1974). But since
then I have come to find another question more important still,
because it is more 'down to earth' – more 'embodied'. This question
is the path leading from the Jewish Jesus to the Christian Jesus, and
the rediscovery of the Jewish Jesus in the Christian Jesus. In this
christology, therefore, I wanted the Christian–Jewish dialogue to be
continually present. But because christology is felt to be a stumbling
block by many Jews (and nowadays by some Christians too), the
open dialogue is today unfortunately hindered and marred by a
number of prejudices and false judgments. People who restrict the
Christian faith to 'the historical Jesus' or – more recently – to 'Rabbi
Jesus', dispensing with the allegedly 'high christology' of Paul, John
and the ancient church, do not only lose the Christian faith in the
resurrection. At the same time they cast away the faith in God that is

specifically Christian. And they do not surmount all possible theological anti-Judaism just by doing so. I should therefore already like to point out here that not everyone who recognizes and acknowledges the unique nature of Jesus is an 'anti-Judaist'. That epithet can be applied only to those who stress Jesus' unique nature by belittling Judaism and at its cost, so that the uniqueness of Jesus is used as a way of denying 'unbelieving Jews' their right to existence. On the other hand, not everyone who stresses Jesus' Jewish origin, and the things he has in common with the Judaism of his time, is 'anti-Christian'. That can be said only of people who intend to use this as a way of watering down the uniqueness of Jesus, so as to deprive the Christian faith of its foundation, and in order to deny Christians *their* right to existence. These two prejudices and misjudgments are certainly not comparable historically speaking, for from Constantine to 'Auschwitz' the first of them has etched into history appalling traces of blood and tears. The second judgment, on the other hand, was probably as a rule no more than the conjecture of Christian insecurity and anxiety. Christian–Jewish dialogue today must be a tentative dialogue – especially in Germany – for it is a dialogue between the sufferers and the guilty; and it should be kept free from the prejudices and misjudgments I have described.

My own findings in christology have been enriched and also relativized by the publications of feminist theology. Continual discussion with my wife, Elisabeth Moltmann-Wendel, opened my eyes to many things which I should probably otherwise have overlooked. It also made me conscious of the psychological and social limitations of my male point of view and judgments. I am particularly indebted to her for the third chapter of this christology. But of course I alone am responsible for everything that I have said or have not said.

The literature on christology as a whole, and on its individual questions, has become so vast that I must ask all writers for their indulgence if I cite only the contributions that are important for the train of thought I have put forward here, and do not try to offer encyclopaedic surveys. This request for indulgence is also addressed to all those who have written theses, essays or books on my theology. It was impossible for me to enter here into their expositions and critical questions. I reserve for myself a self-examination in the light of the discussions set on foot by my theological work.

The Volkswagen Foundation accorded me an academy grant for the period from 1 April, 1988, to 31 March, 1989, in order that I might write this book. I should like here to express my thanks for this generous help, which gave me the liberty and peace to concentrate on the work.

Part of this christology was presented in the Keene Lectures in Chelmsford Cathedral in 1986, in the Ferguson Lectures at Manchester University in 1989, and in the G. P. Kaye lectures at the Vancouver School of Theology.

I should like to thank my assistants Claudia Rehberger, Thomas Kucharz and Carmen Krieg for their critical co-operation over this book, and want to express my deep gratitude to, and admiration for, my translator Margaret Kohl.

Jürgen Moltmann

ABBREVIATIONS

ATD	*Das Alte Testament Deutsch,* Göttingen
BiLe	*Bibel und Leben,* Düsseldorf
BSRK	Bekenntnisschriften und Kirchenordnungen der nach Gottes Wort reformierten Kirche, ed. W. Niesel, Zürich 1985
BZ NF	*Biblische Zeitschrift,* Neue Folge, Paderborn
CD	K. Barth, *Church Dogmatics,* ET Edinburgh and Grand Rapids 1936–69
CSEL	Corpus Scriptorum Ecclesiasticorum Latinorum, Vienna 1866
EK	*Evangelische Kommentare,* Stuttgart
EKK	Evangelisch-katholischer Kommentar zum Neuen Testament, Zürich
ESL	*Evangelisches Soziallexikon,* Stuttgart 1954, 6th ed. 1970
EStL	*Evangelisches Staatslexikon,* Stuttgart 1966
ET	English translation
EvErz	*Evangelische Erziehung,* Frankfurt
EvTh	*Evangelische Theologie,* Munich
FRLANT	Forschungen zur Religion und Literatur des Alten und Neuen Testaments, Göttingen
GCS	Griechischen christliche Schriftsteller der ersten drei Jahrhunderte, Berlin 1897ff.
HThK	Herders theologischer Kommentar zum Neuen Testament, Freiburg 1953ff.
HZ	*Historische Zeitschrift,* Tübingen
JBL	*Journal of Biblical Literature,* Philadelphia
JDTh	Jahrbücher für deutsche Theologie, Stuttgart
JSSt	*Journal of Semitic Studies,* Manchester
KT	Kaiser Traktate
KuD	*Kerygma und Dogma,* Göttingen

NT	*Novum Testamentum*, Leyden
NTD	Das Neue Testament Deutsch, Göttingen 1932ff.
PG	J. P. Migne, Patrologia Graeca, Paris 1857ff.
PL	J. P. Migne, Patrologia Latina, Paris 1844ff.
QD	Questiones Disputatae, Freiburg
*RE*³	Realencyklopädie für protestantische Theologie und Kirche, Leipzig, reprint Graz
*RGG*³	Die Religion in Geschichte und Gegenwart, 3rd ed., Tübingen 1957–1965
STh	Aquinas, *Summa Theologiae*
StZ	*Stimmen der Zeit*, Freiburg
TDNT	Theological Dictionary of the New Testament, ed. G. Kittel and G. Friedrich, trans. G. W. Bromiley, Grand Rapids 1964–76
ThEx	Theologische Existenz heute, Munich
ThExNF	Theologische Existenz heute, neue Folge, Munich
ThQ	*Theologische Quartalschrift*, Tübingen
ThSt	*Theologische Studien*, Zürich
WUNT	Wissenschaftliche Untersuchungen zum Neuen Testament
ZAW	*Zeitschrift für die alttestamentliche Wissenschaft*, Berlin
ZEE	*Zeitschrift für evangelische Ethik*, Gütersloh 1957–
ZNW	*Zeitschrift für die neutestamentliche Wissenschaft*, Berlin
ZThK	*Zeitschrift für Theologie und Kirche*, Tübingen

Translator's Note

Biblical quotations have as a rule been taken from RSV, except where changes of wording were necessary to bring out the author's point. Where English translations of books referred to exist, references to these have been given as far as possible, but in many cases quotations have been translated direct from the German. The absence in the relevant note of a page reference to the English translation will make this clear.

A very few minor changes have been made to the German text for the sake of the English-speaking reader. These were made in consultation with Professor Moltmann, to whom I should like to express my gratitude for his co-operation and patient help.

Margaret Kohl

I

The Messianic Perspective

There is no such thing as a christology without presuppositions; and its historical presupposition is the messianic promise of the Old Testament, and the Jewish hope which is founded on the Hebrew Bible. We can only truly and authentically understand Jesus if we perceive him and his history in the light of the Old Testament promises and the history of hope of Israel today. What does christology mean except messianology? 'The Christ' is Israel's messiah. Israel's messiah is 'Yahweh's anointed one', and to think of him means hoping for him and his redeeming rule. Of course Christian messianology takes its impress from the unique figure of Jesus, his message and his special divine history. But we must always have in mind the Old Testament and Israel's history, in which Jesus lived and which is the source of his theological significance as 'the Christ'. Here, therefore, we shall not think of 'Christ' as a proper name (although the early Hellenistic congregations of course already did so). We shall see it as the title for his function – his function for the men and women who are to be redeemed and his function for the coming God. This means that we shall continually have to translate the name 'Christ' back into the title 'messiah', so that we can take in what it originally meant: Jesus is the messiah; the church is the messianic community; being a Christian means being human in the messianic sense. The name Christian is not the designation of a party. It is a promise. It is what is messianic.

In this chapter we shall ask what the word 'messianic' meant for Judaism. What were the Jewish categories? From these we shall be able to develop the categories for the special christology of Jesus in the context of fundamental theology. Here the term messianic is intended to comprehend both the messiah as person, and the messianic kingdom, the messianic era and the messianic land, the messianic signs and the messianic people in history. Of course I am developing the concept 'messianic' in the light of Jesus' person and history. What else can a 'Gentile Christian' do? But my purpose is to unfold the concept in so open a way that it respects the Jewish messianic hope, and is interpreted in continual dialogue with Jewish philosophers of religion. I am not presupposing that the Old Testament messianic hope points simply of itself to Jesus of Nazareth (which was what the theology of the prophetic proofs maintained). But I am assuming that Jesus understood himself and his message in the expectation categories of this messianic hope, and that his followers saw him in these categories, so that Jesus is linked with the messianic hope in a primal and indissoluble sense.

Christian christology has divided Christians and Jews. That is true. But it does not have to degenerate into a Christian anti-Jewish ideology, since hope for the messiah also links Christians with Jews, and this link is stronger than the division. Community in contradiction is often stronger than community in agreement. For that reason, no Christian christology must ever attempt to obliterate the Jewish hope for the messiah: Jesus is not 'the end of the messiah'.[1] And for the same reason, no Christian christology must purpose to inherit the Jewish hope for the messiah, thereby – consciously or unconsciously – declaring that the testator is now dead: Jesus is not 'the fulfilment' of the messianic hope which puts an end to Israel.[2] Finally, no Christian christology must surrender the hope for the messiah. Without it Christianity will be paganized. It will be anti-Jewish through indifference.[3] Christian christology is a particular form of Israel's hope for the messiah, and it is still related to, and dependent on, the Jewish forms of the messianic hope that anteceded Christianity and run parallel to it.

'Messianism is the most profoundly original idea in Judaism', claimed Martin Buber, rightly.[4] 'Messianism is the idea which Israel gave the world', affirmed Gershom Scholem.[5] This is not merely one Old Testament idea among others: the Old Testament as a whole is 'the book of a continually growing expectation' (von Rad's phrase), pointing beyond itself, and beyond every historical fulfilment. According to the prophetic interpretation, an explosive power builds up in Israel's history, and when 'the explosion comes, it is not revolutionary; it is messianic'.[6] The mission of Christianity is to be seen as the way in which Israel pervades the world of the Gentile nations with a messianic hope for the coming God. Christianity loses nothing by recognizing that its hope springs from this enduring Jewish root. Judaism surrenders nothing by recognizing what Martin Buber felt to be the 'mysterious' spread of the name, commandments and kingdom of its God by way of Christianity. This was the insight of the great Maimonides, in the Middle Ages, when he saw the phenomenon of Christianity as a *praeparatio messianica* of the nations for the world-wide coming of the kingdom of the God of Abraham. On the basis of this common messianic hope, we shall try here to develop a christology in Christian–Jewish dialogue.

By taking the messianic promise as the point of departure for christology, I am proceeding further along the path on which I started out in 1964 with the *Theology of Hope* (ET 1967). There I set the revelation of God in the event of Jesus' crucifixion and resurrection against the horizon of the expectation opened up by the Old Testament history of promise.[7] I summed up this viewpoint in the following concise theses: '1. It was *Yahweh*, the God of Abraham, of Isaac and of Jacob, the God of the promise, who raised Jesus from the dead. Who the God is who is revealed in and by Jesus emerges only in his difference from, and identity with, the God of the Old Testament. 2. *Jesus was a Jew*. Who Jesus is, and what the human nature is which is revealed by him, emerges from his conflict with the law and the promise of the Old Testament.' At that time, however, I was primarily concerned with Jesus' resurrection and the eschatological horizon which the resurrection opened up. Here I am beginning with the Spirit–christology which apprehends Jesus as the messianic prophet of the poor.[8] I shall therefore stress even more strongly than I did in 1964 *the continuity* between the Christian gospel and the Jewish history of promise found in the Old Testament.

I am also taking up the eschatological direction of christology through which in *The Crucified God* (1972; ET 1974)[9] I confronted the metaphysical 'christology from above' and the anthropological 'christology from below' with a christology that points forwards.

In those earlier books, however, I concentrated solely on the resurrection and the cross of Christ. This focus was partly due to the time at which the books were written, and their context in the history of theology. I am now surrendering this standpoint in order to set 'the eschatological history' of Jesus in a holistic christology. The title which suggests itself for the Christ of an integral christology of this kind is not 'true God' or 'true human being', but 'the One who will come'. This was John the Baptist's question to Jesus and, as the answer shows, Jesus' whole proclamation and ministry stands under this sign: it makes the coming God messianically present. Through his resurrection from the dead, Jesus' death on the cross is moved into the apocalyptic light of the coming judgment; and his raising to become 'the leader of life' makes him the bearer of hope, quintessentially and *per se*, for the eschatological future. 'A christology that is really moulded by the scriptural testimony of Old and New Testaments will have an eschatological hallmark. By circling round the mystery of the One who *has* come, it will in everything it sees inevitably point towards the One who *will* come'.[10] But 'the One who will come' is simply and solely the code word for the messiah who prepares the way for 'the coming God', and takes to meet him his people and his earth.

Unfortunately, from early on Christian theology split up the unity of Old Testament messianology into christology on the one hand, and eschatology on the other.[11] As a result, many Christians have lost sight of the inner link between the two. The sermons preached at the end of the church year, in Germany at least, on All Souls' Day, Repentance Day and 'the Sunday of the Dead', are seldom radiant with the hope of resurrection and with Easter jubilation. Christian theology has overstressed the christology, which it cut away from eschatology; and the eschatology has been neglected. This came about because the incarnational christology of the patristic church presented the descent and ascent of the Redeemer in the vertical perspective of eternity, and moved the divine sonship of Jesus into the centre. The horizontal history of the *ruach* – the Holy Spirit – 'who spake by the prophets', as the Nicene Creed says, and who shaped the proclamation and ministry of the earthly Jesus, ceased to be noticed. As a result christology also lost the eschatological future horizon of Christ's parousia. The theme of this truncated christology became the person of the divine human being who came into the world to save sinners. In addition, in the early rivalry and dispute with the synagogue, a whole sector of futurist eschatology was vilified and excluded as what Article XI of the *Confessio Helvetica* describes as 'the Jewish dream'. This was the sector generally termed 'chiliastic eschatology'. Once that had been eliminated, eschatology lost its futurist orientation, and all that remained was its eternal aspect, in which all moments of time are equally present, and equally remote. Historical times were literally 'in-different'. The Last Days gave way to a timeless next world, and the Last Judgment of world history was replaced by the hour of death of the individual person. In this way the Old Testament hope for the messiah was pushed out of christology and eschatology alike. We shall rediscover the essential connection between the two only when we find our way back to the common roots of both, in the messianology of the Old Testament. The lamentable cleavage between faith in Christ and hope for the future can be healed in an eschatological christology which leads on to a christological eschatology. This means that when we perceive Jesus as the Christ, we do so in remembered hope. It is this recollection of hope that is practised in every eucharist.

§1 THE GENESIS OF THE MESSIANIC HOPE

The way in which something comes into being usually already determines its potentialities and limits, its merits and its inherent obstacles and deadlocks. So we shall begin by asking about the historical origins of the messianic hope in Israel.[12] Its roots are political, and Martin Buber believes that they can be found in the institution and decline of Israel's hereditary monarchy.

The story of Samuel and Saul as I Sam. 8 tells it has a clearly anti-monarchical colouring. Israel had been a twelve-tribe amphictyony, led by charismatic prophets and ordered or governed by appointed 'judges'. The fact that the ark of the covenant, as Yahweh's throne, was carried into war, shows that the people tried to live under a direct theocracy: 'Yahweh is king'. From time to time Yahweh's *ruach* fell upon charismatic rulers. But at the assembly in Ramah there was a kind of spontaneous plebiscite against Samuel: 'Appoint for us a king to govern us like all the nations' (v. 5). This wish displeased the prophet, but 'the Lord said to Samuel, "Hearken to the voice of the people in all that they say to you; for they have not rejected you, but they have rejected me from being king over them"' (v. 7). In a moving speech, Samuel urges upon the people the evils of a hereditary monarchy, through which they will be plundered, exploited and enslaved (vv. 10–18). But the people wish to be 'like all the nations' and demand a king. God installs a king over his people Israel, at their request – but according to the account in Book of Samuel, probably also as a punishment. The first king, Saul, then accordingly counted as a castaway. It is only the second king, David, who is described as 'the anointed of the God of Jacob' (II Sam. 23). In David's 'last words', the Davidic kingship already takes on messianic features: 'the Spirit of the Lord' has spoken through him; he rules 'as a just man among men in the fear of the Lord'. He 'dawns on them like the morning light, like the sun shining forth upon a cloudless morning'; Yahweh's covenant with the king is 'an everlasting covenant'; his salvation will 'grow' and the 'godless men . . . will be utterly consumed with fire' (II Sam. 23.2–7).

Glory descends on David for a special reason. He has brought the ark of the covenant to Zion, so that the God who pilgers with his people is given a permanent dwelling place – the Shekinah – in the land of promise. 'When the ark is brought to Zion God takes possession of a piece of earth as divine dwelling, the sanctuary on Zion.'[13] Through conquest, Mount Zion had become the heritable land of the Davidic kings. When God chose Zion, it was the equivalent of choosing the house of David for the kingdom. Ever since the ark had been brought there, God himself is Zion's true Lord. So the king of Israel who reigns from Zion is declared 'son of God' (Ps. 2.7, 89.27f.). The Davidic king rules on behalf of God and is supposed to represent God's kingship: 'Sit at my right hand, till I make your enemies your footstool', says the ancient enthronement oracle (Ps. 110.1), which recurs in Paul's eschatological christology (I Cor. 15.25). When the sanctuary was established on Zion, the tradition of the Melchizedek priesthood was taken up at the same time. According to this tradition, Mount Zion, as the centre of the cosmos, is the throne of 'the most high God'. Anyone who rules from Zion rules in the name of the most high God, and therefore has a universal claim. Nathan's prophecy to David (II Sam. 7.3–16) includes the charge to build the temple on Zion, and it points to the future of the house of David in a way that is messianic through and through: 'When your days are fulfilled and you lie down with your fathers, I will raise up your offspring after you, who shall come forth from your body, and I will establish his kingdom. He shall build a house for my name, and I will establish the throne of his kingdom for ever. I will be his father, and he shall be my son' (vv. 12–14).

At the latest after the ark had been brought to Zion, the Davidic kingdom was at the same time a priesthood. Royally anointed with Yahweh's *ruach*, the Davidic ruler became both king and priest. But because prophets like Samuel and Nathan confronted these priestly kings from the very beginning, the Israelite monarchy was subjected to prophetic criticism as well as prophetic assent. The prophets abandoned the direct, charismatic theocracy of the early period, but remained the custodians of Israel and her kings; for Yahweh was 'the true king of Israel' and hence the prototype and judge of the earthly kings on Zion (I Sam. 2.10). Because Yahweh had compassion on his unhappy people in Egypt, his justice and righteousness always means 'giving deliverance to the needy' (Ps. 72; Isa. 11.4). Kingly rule in the name of this God therefore can only mean defending the rights of the poor, having mercy on humble, unimportant people, protecting the weak, and liberating the oppressed. What must be expected of the king in Yahweh's name is in crass contrast to the tyrannical portrait of the king which Samuel warningly held up to the people (I Sam. 8).

So we already find discrepancies, even in the story of how Israel's monarchy came into being; and from these discrepancies emerged the hope for a messiah king who would be well pleasing to God.

1. The first discrepancy – according to Martin Buber – is to be found in the transition from the direct, charismatic theocracy of the early period to a theocracy mediated through a priestly king. The theocracy that is mediated by human beings – and which is now mediated dynastically, moreover, instead of charismatically – can hardly meet the claims of a direct theocracy. 'The history of the kings is the story of how those who had been anointed failed to live up to that anointing. It is this fact alone that can explain the rise of messianism: belief in the anointed one who will fulfil his anointing.'[14]

2. We find the second discrepancy, in my view, in the particular content of Yahweh's direct charismatic theocracy, and in the general content of the theocracy mediated through the monarchy. For Yahweh's kingship is not merely 'charismatic'. As the first commandment says, it is rule that is grounded on liberation from slavery, liberation for the freedom of the divine covenant. But if general dynastic rule is to remain enforcible, it is bound to be directed towards the legitimation, safeguarding and increase of its own power. A kingship like the kingship of 'all the other nations' consists of judging and 'fighting battles' (I Sam. 8.20). But a monarchy in Yahweh's name, imbued with his Spirit, ought to mean defending the rights of the poor, having compassion on the humble, and liberating the oppressed.

So it was not merely the all-too-human failure of the kings to meet the claim of the divine unction which led to the messianic hope. It was the very constitution of a monarchy that was set up to save, in the name of the compassionate God. In the arena of power politics, kingship in the name of the God who promises mercy can hardly be implemented. Any such monarchy must by its very nature lead to a hope which reaches out beyond all experienced political reality, and which no political reality can ever satisfy. Yet for all that, this hope remains realistic; for what it expects is not a religious redeemer of souls, but the 'theopolitical messiah' (Buber's phrase) of people and country.

Under the onslaught of the Assyrian armies, Israel's brief political independence ended. Her kings were too weak, too corrupt, and too incapable to stand up to the great Assyrian power. Yet 'whereas everywhere else in Syria the royal ideologies behind the state structures disappeared with the coming of Assyrian hegemony, in Israel the image of the king actually acquired new depths: it was transformed into the image of the messiah'.[15] Through this 'transformation' the defeated people were able to assimilate and come to terms with these annihilating experiences of the sufferings of history. That was probably only possible because Israel was able to compare and confront the priestly king with the prophet led by the Spirit. It was thanks to the voice of the prophets in the second half of the eighth century that, although Israel lost its identity as state, it preserved its religious identity by learning to understand its political catastrophes as the judgments of its God. The transformation of the image of the king into the image of the messiah is part of this dramatic process. Of course, no image of hope is ever born out of pure disappointment and mere defeat. No real hope has its genesis in 'creative despair'.[16] Hope must always be preceded by some positive remembrance. We discovered a specific form of this positive remembrance in the early constitution of the theo-political monarchy, and especially in the David/Zion tradition. And viewed more generally, Siegmund Mowinckel is surely right: 'Israel's unique conception of God as the God of history is the root of eschatology.'[17]

§2 THE GROWTH OF THE MESSIANIC FIGURE

1. *The Messiah*

We shall first of all follow the text in the book of Isaiah, looking at the promises in 7.10ff., 9.2ff. and 11.1ff. Afterwards we shall draw on corresponding texts from Micah 4 and Zechariah 9.

In the Assyrian war, the losing king Ahaz is given a prophetic sign (*'ot*): 'Behold, a young woman shall conceive and bear a son, and shall call his name Immanuel. He shall eat curds and honey when he knows how to refuse the evil and choose the good' (Isa. 7.14–15). With this 'Immanuel' Isaiah announces to God's faithless and incapable representative the coming of the faithful and true king who will meet the claims of his anointing. Whether the 'young woman' refers to the queen or to some far-off relative is not clear, but when we look at Isa. 9.7, we see that the 'Immanuel' belongs to the house of David. 'Immanuel' is undoubtedly an antitype to the reigning king, Ahaz; the one conforms to God's conception, the other gainsays it. But he is not merely an antitype in the spiritual sense; for 'even the fulfilling, messianic kingdom is a real political kingdom, though a theopolitical one, a kingdom furnished with political power for the political implementation of God's will . . .'[18] 'Immanuel' is 'the king of the remnant, out of whom the nation is to be renewed'. In the desert, where nothing can be prepared, he will be fed with the divine food of poverty, the symbolic matriarchal food, 'milk and honey'. Even as a child he already knew how to reject evil and choose good.

Isaiah 9.2–7 develops the picture of hope which this 'Immanuel' represents. He is the true David and 'like the sun shining forth upon a cloudless morning' (II Sam. 23.4). 'The people' that now 'walks in darkness' sees in him 'the great light'. He brings the kingdom of peace and burns the weapons of war. He brings the kingdom of justice and righteousness. He will fulfil that for which David and Zion were chosen. His kingdom will have no end, but will endure to eternity. According to Isa. 8.17 and 21ff. the 'people' in the dark country (9.2) are the people who have been forsaken by God, for God has 'hidden his face' from them. They are the defeated, homeless, hungry people in tribulation. They are of course Israel – though no longer Israel as a national, political entity, but as 'the poor' who experience and endure God's judgment.[19] Immanuel is the saviour king who 'defends the bowed-down among the people, delivers the sons of the needy and crushes the oppressor' (Ps. 72.4).

Isaiah 11.1–9 goes a step further, giving this picture of the messiah a new depth. The coming messiah, who springs from the house of Jesse, is the true 'anointed one'. Yahweh's *ruach* will 'rest' on him, and will equip him with wisdom, understanding, counsel and strength, and with 'the fear of the Lord' (cf. II Sam. 23.2). His legitimation depends on the divine righteousness, not on his Davidic origin. He will bring justice to the poor and an equitable judgment to the miserable, and he will defeat the wicked – the oppressors. So the kingdom of his righteousness does not merely embrace poor human beings. He brings peace to the whole of creation, peace between man and beast, and peace among the beasts themselves (vv. 6–8). This kingdom will reach out from his holy place Mount Zion, so that 'the earth shall be full of the knowledge of the Lord' – a vision which no doubt corresponds to Isaiah's vision at his call (6.3): 'the whole earth is full of his glory'.

The figure of the messiah therefore evolves out of a remembrance of David. But in the prophetic counter-stroke to Assyria's military destruction of the political independence of Israel's monarchy, this messianic figure assumes forms of hope which go far beyond any reminiscence of the historical David. What expands and deepens the specific recollection of David so greatly are the dimensions of hope for the final, and therefore enduring, coming of the God of promise himself, the God of compassionate justice and righteousness. Isaiah's messiah is the king of the future who will be filled with the Spirit – 'the fulfilling king' as Buber calls him.[20] He is 'God-like' because he represents the archetypal divine rule. Yet he is also God's counterpart, in the way that 'the son' is a counterpart to his father, and 'the counsellor' to the judge. But he is not a superman. He is 'the messianic human being'.[21]

But between the remembrance of the historical David and hope for the divine messiah-king on the throne of David there are interruptions; and these forbid the idea of a linear continuity. The external interruption is the defeat and destruction of Israel's political independence by the Assyrian empire in 722/721. For Israel, things will never be the same again. The inward interruption is 'the new beginning' which the prophets sense God is going to make with the miserable remnant of Israel, by way of the messiah-king. The new beginning awakes the happiest memories of the past, but it does not lead back into that past. It transforms the remembrance into a still greater hope. There is more in the new messianic David than there ever was in the historical David of old. So to transform the image of the king into the image of the messiah is not to idealize the past. The transformation is not designed to rouse nostalgia. On the contrary, it mobilizes the people to set forward afresh, hoping in God. This difference between past and future is constitutive for the messianic hope; and out of it is born what we have to call 'eschatological' hope.[22]

The picture of the messiah of the poor and his messianic kingdom of peace is complemented by his entry into Jerusalem as Zechariah 9.9–10 paints it: 'Lo, your king comes to you, made righteous and saved.[23] He is humble and riding on an ass. . . . He will do away with the chariots from Ephraim and the war horses from Jerusalem, and the battle bows shall be destroyed, and he shall speak peace to the nations; and his dominion shall be from sea to sea, and from the River to the ends of the earth.' Micah 4.1–4 draws a similar picture. In the kingdom where Zion's messiah of peace reigns, the nations 'shall beat their swords into ploughshares, and their spears into pruning hooks; nation shall not lift up sword against nation, neither shall they learn war any more; but they shall sit every man under his vine and under his fig tree'. This is to happen 'in the last days' – that is, in the days of the messiah. But it will happen in the Spirit of the God of Israel, in whose name we walk 'now' (Micah 4.5). So this is not an eschatological vision of a world beyond history. It is a messianic vision of *history in the future* which, in anticipation, throws its light on the 'walking', or conduct, of the present – that is to say, its politics.[24]

At this point we must consider the theological question which Martin Buber asked, and for which he found his own answer. Does God give this promised messiah, or does God wait for his coming? 'YHWH, who in the primal era waited for an answer from a human race, who in the era of charismatic rule waited for an answer from a people, now waits for the answer from one of the anointed – has waited for it ever since he granted Israel the hereditary monarchy on condition that the king observe its guiding principle: the fulfilment of his commission. . . . The waiting God is the promise that the one awaited will come.'[25]

Buber would like to let this paradox stand; but he does say that the messianic prophecy 'is an offer, not a forecast'.[26] This leaves a number of possibilities open: God awaits the messiah, and the messianic human being responds; or God awaits the messiah, and himself finds the messianic human being; or God awaits the messiah and God gives the messiah; or God awaits the messiah and Yahweh's *ruach* brings the messiah. The categories of his 'dialogistic principle' have made Buber shrink back before the messianic secret, so that he makes contradictory assertions. On the one hand, for him the messianic hope is not an 'eschatological hope' because the specific thing about it is its 'practical historical core'.[27] It is a 'theopolitical hope'. On the other hand, he calls messianism 'the most profoundly original idea in Judaism',[28] because it projects the outline of its images of hope into 'an absolute future'. 'We must remember: in the future, in the sphere that is eternally, archetypically far, eternally, archetypically near, fleeting and enduring like the horizon, in the kingdom of the future in which no more than iridescent, shifting, fleeting dreams else venture, the Jew has dared to build a house for humanity, the house of true life.' But this 'absolute future' is no longer historical. It is the eschatological future. And it is the eschatological future because it is the eternal future, which is always future and never becomes present.[29] But if this is the future of the messianic hope, then the 'practical historical core' is abandoned. It can no longer play any part. And because this absolute future can never enter into history without surrendering its absolute character, Buber then has to declare that 'co-operative power is given to all humanity, all time is immediate to redemption, all action for God's sake may be termed messianic'.[30] But in this case, is messianism not simply another word for moral idealism?

The idea of the God who is the God of promise in his awaiting of the messiah is a splendid idea, because here God is no longer thought of in merely active terms. He is passive too. God does not only give. He also receives. Buber likes to quote an apocryphal saying about Jesus: 'God says: "In all the prophets have I awaited thee, so that thou mayst come and I may rest in thee. For thou art my rest."' If we wished to interpret this more actively, we should have to say: through his waiting, God lets the messiah come. He allows him his time. Yet the messiah comes in order to prepare the way for God himself, the way to his rest in creation. So the coming of the messiah also expresses 'the zeal of the Lord' (Isa. 9.7), not merely his waiting patience. The coming of the messiah heralds the coming of God himself (Isa. 35.4).

Who is the subject of the messianic hope? The dialogistic principle is a good one for free people. But free people do not really need a messiah to save them. They can help themselves. But how can 'the people who dwell in darkness' create the 'great light' all by themselves? How can alienated people beget the messianic human being? The messianic hope was never the hope of the victors and the rulers. It was always the hope of the defeated and the ground down.[31] The hope of the poor is nothing other than the messianic hope.

2. The Son of Man

The expectation of the Son of man belongs to the Jewish apocalyptic that is associated with the prophet Daniel. Historically speaking, whether this universal figure of hope grew up out of Israel's hope for the messiah, or whether it has different roots, is disputed. But in the tradition that followed, hope for the messiah and the expectation of the Son of man were fused into a single, unified vision of the future. This, then, does in fact point to common roots, and to an associated group of transmitters. It is true that Gerhard von Rad considered it 'quite impossible' for apocalyptic to be interpreted as a 'child of prophecy',[32] because the way it looked at history was irreconcilable with the interpretation of the prophets. Yet even Daniel is not totally outside the complex of Israelite and prophetic tradition. The forms taken by his 'sense of history',[33] at least, can be seen as 'an inheritance from the great prophets'. Here we shall look first at the figure of the Son of man in Daniel 7, a text belonging to the second century BC.[34]

In the first vision, 7.1–8, the vision of the four beasts (later known as 'image of the monarchies'), Daniel sees four beasts rising one after another from the sea, the symbol of the powers of chaos. Each rules for a certain time and then falls. The gryphon, or winged lion, symbolizes the Babylonian empire, the voracious bear the empire of the Medes, the winged leopard the Persian empire, and the pulverizing monster with the ten horns the Macedonian empire. These empires, which fight for universal power, represent the forces of chaos. They are godless and inhuman because they are contrary to creation. At the same time, 'dominion is given' them (v. 6) and they have their preordained eras in world history. In contrast to this picture of history as a chaotic tussle for power, the second vision (vv. 9–14) shows God's Last Judgment. The judgment thrones are placed. The judge appears, an old man with garment and hair gleaming white in glory. He sits on the fiery wheeled throne (cf. Ezek. 10). In his power is the 'stream of fire' which burns up the last bestial kingdom. In the third vision, 'one like a son of man' appears from the clouds of heaven (v. 13). To him God gives the kingdom, the power and the glory. The nations serve him, and his kingdom will have no end.

In verse 15 the interpretation of these visions begins. Here 'the saints of the Most High' take the place of 'the son of man' as judge and ruler. These 'saints' are probably Israel – the true Israel which has stood fast in persecution. The kingdom and the dominion and the power are given to 'the holy people of the Most High, whose kingdom is an everlasting kingdom' (v. 27). The shift from the son of man to the people of the Most High is a remarkable one, but the notion of representation makes it possible.

Who is 'the son of man'? Initially he was quite simply 'the son of a human being', a particular example of the human species, but one who represents the whole *pars pro toto*, an individual who fulfils the destiny of human beings, which is to be the image of God, and who hence manifests the God with the human face (Ezek. 1.26). Since the inhuman, bestial empires of the Babylonians, Medes, Persians and Macedonians are contrasted with the kingdom of 'the son of man', this kingdom clearly means 'the human kingdom of the true human being', the kingdom which makes true humanity possible, in righteousness and universal peace. The kingdom of the son of man does not evolve out of the succession of world empires. It breaks out of the transcendence into the history of human struggles for power, as something utterly new: 'The son of man brings with him the End-time turn of events, through which human beings are liberated for their real destiny.'[35] But this means that 'the human kingdom' is not the immanent 'goal of history'; it is history's end. For this kingdom is God's foreordained goal for humanity; it is not the goal of the powers of chaos *within* history.

If we can call Israel's messiah-king the messianic human being, then the son of man is certainly the true human being, long awaited, but always impeded by the bestial empires of the world. He brings God's righteousness and justice into the world. That is why his kingdom is the kingdom of freedom, and has no end. When the son of man comes out of 'the clouds', this symbolizes the inaccessible sphere of God (as it does with Moses: Ex. 24.18). When 'all power' is given him, he is installed as earthly representative of God's rule over the world. If all nations are to serve him, this universality is a reminder of the messianic hope in Isa. 9 and 11.

If we exclude the possibility that 'the saints of the Most High' are the angels,[36] and interpret them as the true Israel,[37] then we are struck by the fact that in the present form of the text no contradiction seems to be felt between the rule of a 'son of man' and the rule of 'the people of the Most High'. Is the individual figure of the 'man' simply being collectively interpreted here, as von Rad supposes?[38] Or does the collective idea also perhaps help to bridge the difference between the 'son of man' and 'the saints', as Mowinckel argued?

In the visions of the son of man in Daniel 7.1–14, Israel does not appear – neither historical Israel, nor 'true' Israel. 'The Ancient of Days' has none of the features of the God of Abraham, Isaac and Jacob; nor is the countenance of the son of man an Israelite countenance. The vision is not a historical vision. It is a speculative one. That is to say, we cannot detect the seer's point of vantage. Apparently he is gazing from the end of history at the history of the world, seeing it as the struggle of the empires for universal power. Politically unimportant as it was, Israel was not a factor in world history, and does not appear. So the end of this history of terrors is not the kingdom of the messiah, which extends from Zion, and the pilgrimage of the nations to Zion. The end is the transcendent, eschatological kingdom of the son of man. When the writer talks about the coming One as 'the son of man', it is as if he is going back beyond Israel's remembered history of promise to the history of creation, and is thinking of the true human being, who was created to be 'the image of God'. In the apocalyptic hope, Israel's messianic hope apparently becomes so universal that her special promise and her own history disappear, and the original horizon of creation is reached. In other words: in the universal apocalyptic desolation, where power politics heap up crime and horrors without end, the power of chaos seems to be victorious. In the perils of this catastrophe, only the remembrance of God's faithfulness as Creator to men and women, his image, permits any hope for 'the kingdom of the truly-human human being'.

When, in the interpretation of the vision, 'the son of man' is replaced by 'the people of the Most High', this is evidently intended to introduce Israel's special hope once more into the universal hope for humanity. But now 'the son of man' is no longer mentioned in the interpretation at all. According to v. 14, 'all people serve him'; according to v. 27, the particular 'people of the Most High' takes his place. According to v. 14, the son of man alone represents God's rule over the world; according to v. 27, the representative is 'the people

Son of Man = God's ruler for people / Israel is the people / messianic

of the Most High'. This makes the concept of the messiah relevant again: the messiah cannot be understood without his special messianic people; but the son of man takes in all people, belonging to all nations.

If the two traditions are conflated as they are in chapter 7, tensions make themselves felt between Israel's messiah and humanity's son of man, between the messianic human being and the truly-human human being. These are of course the tensions between a universal charge and a particular existence, and they already arise from the historical election of Israel to be a light to the Gentiles. But in the vision of the future they have to be reconciled.

The Book of Enoch and IV Ezra try to achieve this harmonization. According to Daniel 7, God judges, and after the judgment the son of man rules. According to Enoch 62, the son of man judges and rules in his heavenly kingdom. In the Book of Enoch, the son of man is called the anointed one (48.10), and like the messiah in Isaiah 11, he is equipped with Yahweh's *ruach*. In IV Ezra 13.32, God calls the son of man 'my son', giving him the royal Davidic title. The son of man is also going to appear on Zion (13.35f.). Since he is filled with 'the spirit of Wisdom' through whom God has created all things, in the End-time son of man we see again the primal Wisdom of creation. So the figure of the son of man 'embraces' Davidic messianism; the two do not exist side by side, isolated from one another.[39]

Admittedly, it may be doubted whether one can go as far as Hartmut Gese, and talk about an organic transformation process 'which expands Davidic messianology into the messianology of the son of man, without invalidating the older form, or even divesting it of its significance'.[40] The tensions between the two ideas are very strong. It seems to me that the link in eschatology between hope for the messiah and the expectation of the son of man, corresponds to the link between the creation of mankind and Israel's particular history of promise. This would mean that the Israel-centric messianic hope is the preliminary stage to humanity's hope for the son of man, and that historical and prophetic messianism is the immanent side of the apocalyptically transcendent expectation of the son of man. We should then arrive at the picture of a two-stage messianology: the messiah is the immanent side of the transcendent son of man, and the son of man is the universal side of Israel's particular messiah. Messianism is the historical side of apocalyptic, and apocalyptic is the transcendent side of messianism. For the messianic kingdom is not itself already the kingdom of God; it is no more than its historical preparation. The messianic kingdom will be set up in 'the last days' of this aeon, but the kingdom of God will be established in the eternity of an aeon that is new. It is only if these two strata are preserved that messianism is not dissolved in apocalyptic, or apocalyptic in messianism. The theopolitical character of the messiah is maintained, without being spiritualized or caught up and absorbed eschatologically. But apocalyptic universalism becomes the horizon which lends meaning to the messiah's intervention in history. The two strata preserve Israel's historical mission and the messianic promise given to her, but they set these against a universal horizon which is the world-wide perfecting of humanity.

Any dispersion of the messianic hope in the apocalyptically universal expectation of the son of man would mean a disastrous dissolution of Israel. And the converse is also true: any transformation of the apocalyptically universal expectation of the son of man into Israel's messianism would put an excessive and destructive strain on Israel. The messianic human being is on the way to the truly-human human being, but he cannot as yet, in these present days, be that human being himself. In an estranged world, even the Redeemer in his visitation still bears the form of the strange land. So it is surely inevitable that in Daniel 7 it should at one time be 'the son of man' who is to rule in justice and righteousness, and at another 'the people of the Most High'.

If we try to sum up, we might oversimplify and say the following. The messiah is a historical figure of hope belonging to nation, space and time. The son of man is a figure of expectation for all nations; he is above the world, because he overcomes the world. Both figures are transparent for the kingdom of God in its direct, unmediated glory. It is this which the two figures represent in history, and which they have to mediate to human beings who are estranged from God. That is why both figures are also provisional and passing. In them, and through their rule, *the coming God himself* announces his coming (Isa. 35.4). They must not themselves get in the way of this divine future, or give it a fixed form through any conceptions to which they themselves give rise. Their purpose is to make people open for God's own future. That is probably the reason why in Old Testament messianology the messiah and the son of man are figures of hope which ultimately remain shadowy,[41] and why the messianic and the apocalyptic hopes always bar themselves against fulfilment through any existent tangible forms. A historical, personally defined and definable messiah or son of man conflicts with the openness of the messianic and apocalyptic hope, which is related to God himself, and therefore transcendent. These hopes do not permit any personal cult. It is only when God himself comes with the messiah and the son of man that this openness will be filled and the longing of men and women which matches it assuaged. Then this hope will be satisfied and its scepticism overcome.

How shall we recognize this? We shall see God himself come when we see justice for the poor, and healing for the sick, when we see that the oppressed are freed, and that tears are wiped away. We shall see his coming, that is, from the new creation of all things (Isa. 25.8; Rev. 21.5). Looked at from the opposite direction, the messiah and the son of man are figures on the way to God's rest in his creation. They are formations and personifications of the eschatological history of the world's redemption. In the perspectives of Wisdom, they are stages of God's indwelling in his creation (his shekinah), before he arrives at his eternal sabbath rest in the happiness of his perfect indwelling (cf. Ecclus. 24; Rev. 21).

The messiah/son of man development is undoubtedly the most important line of tradition in Old Testament messianology, but it is not the only one that touches the promises and hopes of Israel taken up in the New Testament. The line of tradition dealing with the king-messiah line is parallelled by others, in which the messiah is seen as priest or prophet.[42]

Since the Davidic promise talks about a priestly king, we have already looked at the priestly tradition to some extent. But it has an origin of its own in the prayer for Levi, in Moses' blessing (Deut. 33.8–11). Just as in Jacob's blessing Judah is declared the royal tribe, in Moses' blessing Levi is designated the priestly one. The lots to be cast (Urim and Thummim), the transmission of divine revelation and the law, as well as the rituals to be performed at the cultic celebrations, are all Levi's special responsibility. When the monarchy is established, priestly functions pass to Zion's ruler, and he can then delegate them to his priests. Psalm 110.4 enthrones the king himself as priest 'after the order of Melchizedek'. But after the exile, hope for the messiah king evidently faded. Instead the figure of the priest came to the fore again. In the prophet's vision in Zechariah 4, 'two olive trees' stand on the right and on the left of the lamp (v. 3), and the interpretation explains that 'These are the two anointed who stand by the Lord of the whole earth' (v. 14). 'The splendour of the ancient image of the messiah is now distributed between the two',[43] the anointed king and the anointed priest. We find a corresponding vision in Zechariah 3.1–7, where the high priest Joshua, who is accused by Satan, stands before God.

The prophetic line is more important, however, and also stronger, for it goes back to Moses, who is the prototype of all prophets, and according to Deuteronomy 18.9–22 the criterion of all prophecy: 'The Lord your God will raise up for you a prophet like me from among you, from your brethren – him you shall heed.' This prophetic office is based on the divine revelation on Sinai, which Moses received 'face to face' and which was sealed by the glory of God itself. For Israel, this Mosaic prophecy was the primal and essential mediation between God and the people, not the monarchy. The promise to Moses is the promise that Israel will never lack prophets or a prophetic communication of God's will. The promise was also understood as the assurance that 'at the end of days' God would raise up a new Moses, for the End-time exodus from the slavery of history into the land of the eternal home country. This tradition was passed down in the Qumran community. The king of Israel is 'chosen' by God; the Levite is 'appointed' to serve in the sanctuary; but the prophet in the succession of Moses will be 'raised up' – that is through a special, personal and direct call. It is this that gives prophecy its 'charismatic' character. But no one is a prophet unless he is in the succession of Moses and remains faithful to the revelation given on Sinai. This lends prophecy in Israel continuity.

When Jerusalem was destroyed, Israel's monarchy ended, and for a time the priestly ministry in the temple ceased as well. Only the prophets accompanied the people into exile. They preserved Israel's identity by interpreting its history and awakening its hope. It is therefore not surprising that the prophetic office in the succession of Moses should have been the matrix out of which the hope for the 'new servant of God' grew. This hope is expressed in the Servant songs in Deutero-Isaiah (Isa. 40–55).[43a] Moses is 'God's servant' *par excellence* (Ex. 14.31 and frequently), and the prophets in general are similarly understood as 'God's servants (Isa. 44.26; Amos 3.7, and frequently). Like them, the new 'Servant of God' is fashioned by Yahweh, called from his mother's womb, and chosen out of God's good pleasure. He is forced to fulfil his mission because Yahweh's *ruach* has seized him (Isa. 42.1; 61.1). His people are the poor and

The scattered, blind
and Poor are the people

The suffering
Servant
is the vicarious
suffering of
God

the mourners, the blind and the prisoners, the weary, and those who
have been scattered. He will bring the people to repentance. Then
God will gather his people, and lead them out to the 'new exodus'.
He will bring justice among the nations. Heaven and earth will
rejoice. His redemption will ripple out from Israel, by way of the
nations, to the whole creation.

But the new Servant of God redeems in a priestly way, through his
vicarious* suffering (Isa. 53). He is ill-treated, humiliated, assailed,
abandoned by God, and dies a violent death 'for us' and 'for many'
(53.6 and 12). Through the vicarious suffering of his servant, God
brings about the salvation of sinners and the poor. 'Through his
wounds we are healed.' He is victorious through his pain, he
convinces through his suffering. Because of this, in the end he
appears as the one justified and exalted by God himself (53.11), the
one to whom the world belongs. This figure of the new Servant of
God who is promised, and who is victorious through his suffering,
gathers up Israel's whole prophetic movement. Through his vicarious suffering for the people, he excels even the first of all the
prophets, Moses, and his intercession for the people before God. The
Suffering Servant of God is the image of the messianic completion of
Israel's prophecy.

Who is this 'Servant of God'? Deutero-Isaiah's text leaves this
open, probably deliberately open, so that we continually have to ask
this question, and are forced to live with it.[44] Because of the
parallelism to suffering Israel, who is also called 'God's servant', we
may think of a personification of the people. That would be in line
with Israelite representation thinking. But if the Servant of God is the
corporate person of Israel itself, who suffers for Israel's redemption?
If the people is the redeemer, who redeems the people? In order to
conceive of the people's redemption, we have to think of a future
figure, chosen by God from Israel and raised up for this purpose.[45]
This hope for the 'Suffering Servant of God' who will redeem Israel
and the many, probably grew up in a similar way to the messianic
hope. In the new slavery in Babylon, the remembrance of Moses and
the exodus came alive again, and became a present ground for a new
hope in God. Since Jerusalem had been destroyed and the people had
been driven out of the land of promise, the breach with that ancient

*The German word *stellvertretend* comprehends all the nuances covered by the two
English words 'vicarious' and 'representative', and this should be borne in mind in the
present text [Trans.].

exodus tradition could not be bridged. But the remembrance of the earlier tradition was a reason to hope for God's creative faithfulness in the future. That is why the new 'Servant of God' excels even the first prophetic leader, Moses. He is to be at once the prophet of the exodus, the priest of reconciliation, and the sacrifice that will bring about redemption.

The promise of the suffering servant of God and the promise of the messiah/son of man stand side by side in the Old Testament and Jewish messianology, curiously unrelated to one another.[46] There is never any mention of expiatory suffering on the part of the messiah. At the same time, it may be assumed that a messianic understanding of the songs of the Suffering Servant preceded Jesus' ministry. Otherwise that understanding could hardly have become the normal pattern for a theological interpretation of Jesus' history.

§3 MESSIANIC CATEGORIES

The phenomena of Old Testament, Jewish and Christian messianism are so motley and equivocal that it is impossible to construct any 'system' out of them.[47] But because these phenomena have a central importance in the legacy of the Old Testament, it is useful to discover some of messianism's essential characteristics.

In discussing Martin Buber's contradictory interpretation of the messianic concept, we already said that the messianic hope has to be understood historically; that we must not detach it from its practical historical core, or lose sight of its specific historical subject, and that we must not disregard the temporally meant future towards which it is directed. The heart of messianism is to be found in political experiences for which a theological interpretation had to be found, if the people were to survive as God's people. The subject of the messianic hope is this beset people. The future of the messiah is to be found in its future history, even if it is only 'the Last Days'. If, using Buber's phrase, we term the messianic future 'the absolute future', then it does not belong within time at all, not even future time. It then loses its practical historical core in a particular experience, and loses its particular people as well. Unlike Buber, we are therefore distinguishing between the messianic future *in* history, or at the end of history, and the eschatological future *of* this whole history – that is between 'the Last Days' and the new eternal aion.[48] Of course the transitions are fluid. The early fusing of hope for the messiah and hope for the son of man make that plain. But it is none the less useful to distinguish the two. This distinction between 'messianic' and 'eschatological' then makes it possible to distinguish – and also to relate to one another – the special group which transmitted the messianic hope in Israel (the remnant of Israel, or its poor), and the general group of those involved in the expectation of the son of man (all human beings, humanity as a whole).

In the modern discussion, the words 'messianic' and 'eschatological' have been used loosely and in very varying senses. Often no more was meant than a general orientation towards the future, progression, or a utopian goal. But that is certainly just as wrong as it is to press so-called 'Hebrew historical thinking' into the service of the modern faith in historical progress. We must therefore look more closely at the practical historical core.

Gershom Scholem and Walter Benjamin have pointed to the extraordinary experience of the historical breach out of which the messianic idea was born, and to which it again points. 'Jewish messianism is by origin and nature – and this cannot be too much stressed – a theory about a catastrophe. This theory stresses the revolutionary, subversive element in the transition from every historical present to the messianic future.'[49] But here Scholem puts together two quite different revolutions: on the one hand the downfall; on the other the uprising. The first is a catastrophe, the second the deliverance. Both are leaps, as Scholem suggests: transitionless transitions. And the leap into the messianic future presupposes the downfall into the misery of the historical present. Let us look back at the origin of Israel's messianic hope. It was not simply born out of a historical disappointment (which was Buber's psychological interpretation). It emerged quite specifically from the conquest of Israel by the Assyrian empire, the subjugation of the people, and their enslavement.

Gerhard von Rad emphatically stressed this theopolitical experience of the breakdown of the traditions and institutions by which up to then Israel had been sustained, and he therefore put his 'Theology of Israel's Prophetic Traditions' under the motto of Isaiah 43.18: 'Remember not the former things nor consider the things of old. For behold, *I* purpose to do a new thing.' The demolition of the old is the precondition for the new, and what is prophetically new 'is – to use the controversial but unavoidable term – the eschatological'.[50] To be more precise, and using my own terminology: it is the messianic in the eschatological. The theological and political rupture of the old is a catastrophe. The catastrophe turns into 'the old' what has hitherto been the sustaining pillar, and so divides the times of history into a 'before' and an 'after', divides them so radically that past and future can no longer appear on the same continuous temporal line. They have become two different eras or epochs. After the catastrophe, Israel in some sense arrived at zero point. It was threatened with self-dissolution, and in danger of paying homage to the victorious gods of those who had proved stronger. For its own catastrophe was at the same time the catastrophe suffered by its trust in God, and was thus even the catastrophe of its God himself. Is it possible still to be 'Israel' at all after a catastrophe such as this? Apparently the people never saw themselves as faced with this choice. Because God had chosen them, the choice was not open. The awareness of election must have been so strong that it preserved the people's identity.

This was 'the hour of the prophets', and the hour in which the messianic hope was born. By virtue of the hope for the new beginning which the electing God was going to give his people through his messiah, the old traditions which had sunk and been forgotten in the cataclysm became remembrances pointing to the future.

Of course this can be judged the idealization of a past time that can never be brought back. But before one makes any such judgment, it should be realized this is a quite normal process of perception. It is in the foreign country that we first come to cherish home. It is only when we have been driven out of paradise that we know what paradise is. Every perception requires detachment and 'alienation'. That is why all self-knowledge is always a little too late, or a little too soon. In the pressure of events we are blind to what these events are. So it is the messianic hope which makes clear for the first time what past history has to say about Yahweh's anointed, and about David. Hope for the new Jerusalem gives a present awareness of what the Jerusalem of old really was. Walter Benjamin said about this kind of historical perception: 'To articulate historically what is past does not mean knowing "what really happened". It means taking possession of a memory as it flashes up in the moment of danger.'[51] But this 'hermeneutics of danger' (as J. B. Metz described it) is only the one side, and the beginning: 'It is only redeemed mankind that can call up and claim its past at every one of its moments.'[52]

The past can only be very generally described as past time. The victors suppress the real, specific past of the vanquished until their memories disappear, their sense of history has been snuffed out, and their identity extinguished. But in present *danger*, what is past, and therefore repressed, is made present as remembered identity. And the future redemption will liberate the whole past, and will make it present, freeing it from its suppression, and its repression. Just as the catastrophe ends history, condemning it to be something past, so, conversely, redemption gives history a new beginning, and redeems the past, making it the eternal present. Where the catastrophe represses memories, redemption will bring them back again. History understood as a continuum, as development and progress, can only be the history of the victors, who wish to secure and expand their own power. History as it is experienced by the defeated, the subjugated and the enslaved is the experience of catastrophe and the hope for redemption, the experience of an enforced end and a longed-for new beginning, a downfall suffered and a new dawn hoped for. The catastrophe permits hope only for the overthrow of conditions as they have come to exist. This may be called the revolutionary element in the messianic hope.

Because of this, the question: when will the messiah come? does not receive a reply that has anything to do with time in its linear sense. It is answered through the qualification of the situation (kairos) which makes the messianic intervention possible and necessary. The conditions for his coming are named, but no date is given. 'The messiah will come when all his guests have sat down at table.' 'The messiah will come when the whole of Israel keeps a single sabbath – or when the whole of Israel keeps none.' 'The messiah will come like a thief in the night.' The 'transitionless transition' into the messianic era is incalculable, in the way that a miracle or a leap into another quality of history is incalculable. 'Three things come without warning', writes a Talmudic teacher in the third century, not without irony: 'The messiah, a find, and a scorpion.'[53]

This permits two possible conclusions:

1. *The messiah will come when he is necessary.* When the need is greatest, and people have given up hope, he will come. Because the messianic redemption is a response to the historical catastrophe, this catastrophe theory, which we have to call apocalyptic, has a good deal in its favour. Admittedly it deprives the messiah of the liberty to come when he thinks best. It extorts his coming, so to speak, through

its opposite: when the world plunges, and is plunged, into calamity, redemption will come *e contrario*. This apocalyptic catastrophism meets us again in our modern nuclear age. But its Armageddon theology is a miscalculation, and nothing other than a justification for the crime of the nuclear inferno.[54]

2. *The messiah will come when it is possible* because the way has been prepared for him. This is the advice of the prophets (Isa. 40). Prepare the way for the Lord! Repent! Arise, shine! Lift up your heads! The messiah does not come unheralded. He lets the gospel, through which he announces himself, go ahead of his coming. In this sense Buber may be right when he says that 'all time is immediate to redemption, all action for God's sake may be termed messianic'.[55] This does not mean that good deeds bring the messianic redemption any closer; still less does it mean that good deeds are themselves the messianic redemption. But it does mean that hope for the coming of the messiah will already be messianically active here and now. That is what the Jewish Alenu prayer calls 'the betterment of the world for the kingdom of God': 'To mend the world'[56] by bringing a *tikun* into the world, a repair where the world is in need of one.[57] But of course the *tikun* is more than a 'repair' to the world, because the completion of all *tikun* is the kingdom of the messiah and, following the messiah's path, the kingdom of God itself. Since every *tikun* is the realization of an objective possibility, the splinters of the messianic era must already be exploded into the historical time of the present. In this sense every moment can be a messianic moment, 'every second can be the little door through which the messiah can enter'.[58] To prepare the way for the messiah means living in the light of Advent and, together with this world, becoming open for his coming. It means anticipating his coming in knowing and doing. It means 'now already' putting forth all our powers, in order, if we can, to let something become visible of the redemption of all things, which the messiah will perfect in his days.

Is this importunity? Does it mean 'pestering' the end to come, and 'compelling' the messiah to appear? It is certainly true that, as Scholem says, 'the allurement of action, the call to implement, to "bring it about"',[59] is inherent in the utopian elements of Jewish messianism. Christian messianism too is familiar enough with the upsurges of eschatological impatience for the implementation of what is hoped for. It is not merely the chiliastic and revolutionary movements of the Taborites, the Anabaptists and the Puritans that are subject to this temptation. On the contrary, from Constantine onwards, the Christian empire itself and the clerical theocracy of the middle ages were viewed as the anticipatory vanguard of the promised eternal kingdom; and they perished on the rock of this idea. The difference between importuning the messiah by deepening the catastrophe, and importuning him by way of a high-handed establishment of his kingdom is not as great as Scholem thinks. The apocalyptists and the revolutionaries belong to the same family. Between them runs the line of a serenely unhurried passion for messianic action, active hope, and the expectant liberation of the poor and oppressed – the line, that is, of the messianic *tikun* ethic.

Scholem movingly describes as 'the price of messianism' the great danger to which messianic thinking and living is subjected: 'To live in hope has a greatness, but it is also something profoundly unreal . . . The messianic idea in Judaism has enforced *a deferred life*, in which nothing can be done and accomplished in a way that is final.'[60]

The messianic hope can act in two opposite directions. It can draw the hearts of men and women away from the present into the future. Then it makes life in the present empty, and action in the present empty – and of course suffering over present oppression too. But it can also make the future of the messiah present, and fill that present with the consolation and happiness of the approaching God. In this case what the messianic idea enforces is the very opposite of 'deferred life'. It is life in anticipation, in which everything must already be done and accomplished in a way that is final, because the kingdom of God in its messianic form is already 'nigh'.

What Scholem does not mention is the situation of the people who live with the messianic hope because with this hope they have survived the catastrophes. For the people who 'dwell in darkness' – the slaves, the prisoners, the exploited and oppressed – this hope is not something unreal and remote. It is their only present reality. If they have self-respect and human dignity, then only in this hope and because of it. The messianic hope for a future which will change everything is the reason why prisoners do not come to terms with their prisons, and slaves do not submit to the slave-owners. Because of the messianic hope, they live with 'uplifted heads', in spite of the reality of life in the present. If it were not for this hope they would come to terms with this situation of slow death. They would bend down to the dust until the dust no longer mattered.[61] But they do not come to terms with the present; they feel its injustice in pain, and rebel against it. And the reason is their unquenchable hope. 'A people only dies when its hope dies', says a Brazilian proverb, rightly.

Yet there is one unambivalent anticipation of the messianic era in the midst of the eras of history, and that is the sabbath. The weekly sabbath makes the feast of creation present in the divine rest, in which human beings and animals are to find rest also. Then 'Queen Sabbath' comes to the oppressed and the exhausted, and raises them up. But this means that the sabbath also anticipates the messianic era. The songs at 'the third meal', on the afternoon of the sabbath, are 'heady with the intoxication of the certainly approaching future of the messiah'.[62] In the present of the sabbath, the feast of creation, the feast of liberation and the feast of redemption are all simultaneously celebrated. In terms of redemption, the sabbath can be called 'a sixtieth part of the coming world'.[63] The sabbath represents an advance pledge, an 'anticipatory payment' of the messianic time, just as the messianic time to come is conceived as 'an endless sabbath'. It is said that 'when the whole of Israel keeps a single sabbath, the messiah will come'. That means that to keep the sabbath, truly and together, is the messianic time; and the reverse is also true. But it means also that in every true sabbath celebration the messiah enters the present through this little door, and with 'Queen Sabbath' comes among those who are his. The weekly sabbath points beyond itself to the sabbath year, the sabbath year points beyond itself to the year of jubilee, the year of jubilee points towards the sabbath of the messianic era, and the sabbath of the messianic era points towards God's own eternal sabbath. The sabbath day is a kind of messianic intermezzo in the era of history, and the celebration of the sabbath is a kind of messianic 'sacrament of time'. Through the succession of sabbath days and sabbath years, 'the One who will come' moves time into the rhythms of messianic expectation. The sabbath does not belong within the continuum of working days. It interrupts them, as human beings come to rest, and as nature is allowed to rest. In this way the sabbath opens human beings and nature for the coming of the wholly-other time of the messiah. It makes them ready for the messiah's coming, in the midst of what is transitory. Beside the noisy messianism of the apocalyptic of catastrophe, and the wild messianism of revolutionary utopianism, the sabbath is a still but steady, and thus lasting, messianism. It comes in everyday life, and brings the dream of redemption into the unnoticeable ordinariness of life as it is lived.

§4 CHRISTOLOGY IN JEWISH–CHRISTIAN DIALOGUE

At the centre of all Jewish–Christian dialogue is the inexorable
messianic question: 'Are you he who is to come, or shall we look for
another?' The messianic hope leads us to Jesus, but it also hinders
Jews from seeing Jesus as the expected messiah who has already
come.[64] Jesus replies to John the Baptist's messianic question
through his proclamation, and his signs and wonders. The gospels
understand his whole coming and ministry in the contexts of Israel's
messianic hope. Yet it is the very same messianic hope which
apparently makes it impossible for 'all Israel' to see Jesus as being
already the messiah. Because earliest christology grew up in this field
of tension, every Christian christology is forced to come back to this
conflict, and has to struggle and come to terms with the Jewish
'no'.[65] This is the fundamental question at the centre of Christian
christology: Is the Jewish 'no' anti-Christian? Is the Christian 'yes'
anti-Jewish? Are the 'no' and the 'yes' final or provisional? Are they
exclusive, or can they also dialectically acquire a positive meaning
for the people who feel compelled to utter them?

Martin Buber formulated the Jewish objection to the messiahship
of Jesus in his discussion with the New Testament scholar Karl-
Ludwig Schmidt on 14 January 1933, in the Jewish school in
Stuttgart, and formulated it in such classic terms that it has been
continually repeated by other Jews ever since: 'The church rests on
its faith that the Christ has come, and that this is the redemption
which God has bestowed on mankind. We, Israel, *are not able* to
believe this.' It is not a question of unwillingness, or hard-hearted
defiance. It is an 'inability to accept'. Buber had a profound respect
for Jesus, and even for Christianity; but his admission of this
inability was determined by a still more profound experience: 'We
know more deeply, more truly, that world history has not been
turned upside down to its very foundations – that the world is not yet
redeemed. We *sense* its unredeemedness. The church can, or indeed
must, understand this sense of ours as the awareness that *we* are not
redeemed. But we know that that is not it. The redemption of the
world is for us indivisibly one with the perfecting of creation, with
the establishment of the unity which nothing more prevents, the
unity which is no longer controverted, and which is realized in all the
protean variety of the world. Redemption is one with the kingdom of
God in its fulfilment. An anticipation of any single part of the

completed redemption of the world – for example the redemption beforehand of the soul – is something we cannot grasp, although even for us in our mortal hours redeeming and redemption are heralded. But we can perceive no caesura in history. We are aware of no centre in history – only its goal, the goal of the way taken by the God who does not linger on his way.'[66]

Schalom Ben-Chorin adopted this argument early on: 'The Jew is profoundly aware of the unredeemed character of the world, and he perceives and recognizes no enclave of redemption in the midst of its unredeemedness. The concept of the redeemed soul in the midst of an unredeemed world is alien to the Jew, profoundly alien, inaccessible from the primal ground of his existence. This is the innermost reason for Israel's rejection of Jesus, not a merely external, merely national conception of messianism. In Jewish eyes, redemption means redemption from all evil. Evil of body and soul, evil in creation and civilization. So when we say redemption, we mean the whole of redemption. Between creation and redemption we know only one caesura: the revelation of God's will.'[67] So according to Ben-Chorin there is after all one Jewish caesura in the history of this unredeemed world: the revelation of the Torah on Sinai, given to the people of Israel through Moses.

Gershom Scholem, finally, also reiterates this reason for the Jewish 'no': 'It is a completely different concept of redemption which determines the attitude to messianism in Judaism and Christianity. . . . In all its shapes and forms, Judaism has always adhered to a concept of redemption which sees it as a process that takes place publicly, on the stage of history and in the medium of the community; in short, which essentially takes place in the visible world, and cannot be thought of except as a phenomenon that appears in what is already visible. Christianity, on the other hand, understands redemption as a happening in the spiritual sphere, and in what is invisible. It takes place in the soul, in the world of every individual, and effects a mysterious transformation to which nothing external in the world necessarily corresponds. . . . The reinterpretation of the prophetic promises of the Bible which applies them to the sphere of "the heart" . . . has always seemed to the religious thinkers of Judaism an illegitimate anticipation of something which could at best come about as the inward side of an event which takes place essentially in the outward world; but this inward side could never be separated from that event itself.'[68]

So can there be an anticipation or 'advance payment' of redemption in some particular sectors, before the final, total and universal
redemption of the world? Can the Redeemer himself have come into
the world before the redemption of the world has become a real
happening? This is the question of Christian existence: can one
already be a Christian in this unredeemed world, and therefore exist
as a messianic person?

But before we try to answer this critical challenge to Christian
existence, we have to put the counter-question; for the argument
about the unredeemed world reflects on Jewish existence too. As a
'Gentile Christian' one must therefore put this 'Gentile question' to
Israel: even *before* the world has been redeemed so as to become the
direct and universal rule of God, can God already have a chosen
people, chosen moreover *for the purpose of this redemption*? Does
Israel's election not destroy Israel's solidarity with unredeemed
humanity, even if the election is meant in a representative sense? And
if this world is so totally unredeemed, is the Jewish caesura, the
revelation of God's will on Sinai, not an impossible possibility, in the
midst of all this evil? And is it not asking too much of Israel to expect
her to obey that revealed will? To put the question in simpler and
existential terms: can one already be *a Jew* in this Godless world?
After all the cruel persecutions of human beings, and in forsakenness
by God, can one still be a Jew? But is not Israel, the people of God's
will and election, something quite unique in the world of the nations
– something that could never have been deduced? In the context of
the messianic hope for the redemption of the world, we will be
grateful for the miracle of Israel's prophetic existence. For if
redemption did not throw its light ahead of it, and if there were no
anticipation of redemption in this world, why should we consider the
world to be 'unredeemed' at all? The hard fact of 'the unredeemed
world' does not only speak against Christians. It speaks against Jews
too. And it does so in both cases just because, and in so far as, both
Christians and Jews, each in their own mode of existence, controvert
the unredeemed world and contravene its evils.

The picture which Buber, Ben-Chorin and Scholem paint of
Christianity is certainly true to a particular kind of historical
Christianity; but it does not fit Jesus himself; nor is it essentially
applicable to the authentic acknowledgment of Jesus as the Christ
which is prepared for discipleship. For all these writers call in
question only what they suppose to be the Christian 'concept' of

redemption. But in what historical era do we find this concept, which internalized redemption into the redemption of the saved soul? There is no doubt at all that we find it in the historical Christendom which abandoned the real futurist eschatology of the New Testament and internalized human salvation, at the same time banishing the future of God to a world beyond this one, so that redemption is no longer seen in the kingdom of God, the 'new heaven and the new earth', but now only in the saving of the individual soul for the heaven of the blessed.

Scholem rightly points to the fateful role played by Augustine in this development. This reduction of eschatology is generally explained by the alleged experience of disappointment over the delay of the parousia. And it is to Albert Schweitzer, the theologian of this disappointment, and to his school of 'consistent eschatology' that Buber and Ben-Chorin appeal. But the historical process was in fact quite different.[69] What internalized eschatological redemption was not *disappointment over the course of history*. It was the *political realization* of Christ's messianic kingdom in the Christian imperium of the emperors Constantine, Theodosius and Justinian. If this Christian imperium is interpreted as the 'thousand-year-Reich', then the saints must reign with Christ and judge the nations. In the millennium, resistance to Christ cannot be tolerated. So in the Christian *imperium sacrum* there was no justice for dissidents, people of other beliefs – and Jews. Enforced political Christianization solved the problem of the heathen. The mission to the Jews was supposed to solve 'the Jewish problem'. Later on the Inquisition was designed to solve the problem of the heretics. The appalling 'final solution' of the Jewish question was projected by 'the thousand-year-Reich' under Hitler's pseudo-messianic leadership. If the church exists in a chiliastically interpreted Christian empire of this kind, then it is bound to interiorize salvation and leave everything external to the Christian emperors: the church looks after people's souls and their salvation; the emperor claims their bodies, and provides for the welfare of the empire.

This ancient chiliastic political theology has assumed continually new forms in the history of Christendom. But down to the present day, it still dominates all notions about 'the Christian West', 'Christian civilization' and 'the age of Christendom'.[70] The christologies that are developed in theocracies like this are anti-Jewish, because these political theocracies themselves are anti-Jewish. It is not in the christologies for Jesus' sake that we find anti-Judaism, as the other side of the coin. It is in the chiliastic christologies of empire and domination. The more the European churches free themselves today from their ancient role as established or state churches, the more the Christian congregations find themselves in contradiction to the ideologies and conditions of power that sustain the empires and the 'redeemer nations' in which they exist; the more they open themselves for Israel and Jewish existence; and the more acutely they suffer, together with the Jews, for the sake of God's righteousness and justice, over the unredeemed condition of the world.

This means that all presentative chiliasm and all 'fulfilment' enthusiasm must be banished from the christology of the church as it exists in the world of history. Jesus of Nazareth, the messiah who has come, is the suffering Servant of God, who heals through his wounds and is victorious through his sufferings. He is not yet the Christ of the parousia, who comes in the glory of God and redeems the world, so that it becomes the kingdom. He is the Lamb of God, not yet the Lion of Judah. What has already come into the world through the Christ who has come and is present, is the justification of the godless and the reconciliation of enemies. What has not yet come is the redemption of the world, the overcoming of all enmity, the resurrection of the dead, and the new creation. The love of God has become manifest through Christ. But the glory of God has not yet broken forth out of its hiddenness. That is why the life of Christians here and now is 'hid with Christ in God' by virtue of the hope that 'when Christ appears, then you also will appear with him in glory' (Col. 3.3–4). But just because men and women 'now already' have peace with God through Christ, they are 'no longer' prepared to make terms with this peace-less world. Because they are reconciled with God, they suffer from this 'unredeemed world' and 'sigh' with the whole enslaved creation (Rom. 8) for the coming glory of God.

Even the raised Christ himself is 'not yet' the pantocrator. But he is already on the way to redeem the world. The Christian 'yes' to Jesus' messiahship, which is based on believed and experienced reconciliation, will therefore accept the Jewish 'no', which is based on the experienced and suffered unredeemedness of the world; and the 'yes' will in so far adopt the 'no' as to talk about the total and universal redemption of the world only in the dimensions of a future hope, and a present contradiction of this unredeemed world. The Christian 'yes' to Jesus Christ is therefore not in itself finished and complete. It is open for the messianic future of Jesus. It is an eschatologically *anticipatory and provisional* 'yes' – 'maranatha. Amen, come Lord Jesus' (Rev. 22.20). This means that it cannot be an excluding and excommunicating 'yes', not even when it is uttered with the certainty of faith. Anyone who confesses Jesus as 'the Christ of God' is recognizing the Christ-in-his-becoming, the Christ on the way, the Christ in the movement of God's eschatological history; and that person enters upon this way of Christ in the discipleship of Jesus.[71] The earthly Jesus was on the way to the revelation of his messiahship. This is what people call Jesus' 'messianic secret'. The risen Lord is on the way to his rule, which merely begins here, and is by no means universal, and his purpose is at the end to hand over the completed rule to God, who will then be 'all in all' (I Cor. 15.28) and will arrive at what Buber calls his 'direct theocracy'.[72]

The earthly – the crucified – the raised – the present – the coming One: these are the stages of God's eschatological history with Jesus. It is these stages which the title 'Christ' gathers together, and it is these which should interpenetrate christology and provide its framework. If we take this Christ-in-becoming, this Christ on the road, seriously, then we can take up an eschatological distinction that was made in the theology of an earlier time, and say that there can already be a *christologia viae* here and now, but there cannot yet be a *christologia patriae*. Until Christ's parousia, there can only be a historical christology, not yet a chiliastic one. This shuts out of christology all forms of ecclesiastical and political triumphalism, for the *christologia viae* is *theologia crucis*, and nothing else. The coming One is in the process of his coming and can be grasped only in that light: as on the road, and walking with us. But for that very reason every confession of Christ in the history of this unredeemed world has to be understood as a reaching out, an anticipation of the new creation in which every tongue will confess him in the glory of the Father (Phil. 2.11). Every confession of Christ leads to the way, and along the way, and is not yet in itself the goal.

Jesus the Lord as the early community of Christians acknowledged him is on the way to his rule, not merely through the coming *times*, but through present *spaces* as well. He takes the road from Jerusalem to the ends of the earth (Acts 1.8), from Israel to the Gentiles, from the Gentiles to Israel again, and back to Jerusalem (Rom. 11.26). He takes the road from the church to the poor, and from the poor to the church. The way of Christ comes into being under the feet of the person who walks it. To tread the way of Christ means believing in him.[73] Believing in him means going with him along the part of the road he is taking at the present moment. 'I am the way', says Jesus about himself according to one of the old Johannine sayings (John 14.6). We understand this as a signpost pointing the road to 'the Father', which is the road of the gospel through the world's history to the eternal kingdom.

If the Jewish 'no' to Jesus' messiahship is due to 'inability', as Buber said, and not to unwillingness or ill-will, then there is no reason for Christians to deplore this 'no' or to make it a reproach. Israel's 'no' is not the same as the 'no' of unbelievers, which is to be found everywhere. It is a special 'no' and must be respected as such.[74] In his Israel chapters, Romans 9 to 11, Paul saw God's will in Israel's 'no'. It is not because it says 'no' that Israel's heart has been hardened. It is because God hardened its heart that it cannot do anything but say 'no'.[75] Hardness of heart is not the same thing as rejection, and has nothing whatsoever to do with a moral judgment. To harden the heart is a historically provisional act on God's part, not an eschatologically final one. It is an act performed for a particular purpose, as the story of Moses and Pharaoh shows.

We therefore have to ask: what is the purpose? Why does God impose on the whole of Israel an 'inability' to say the 'yes' of faith to Jesus? The answer is: in order that the gospel may pass from Israel to the Gentiles, and that 'the last' may be first. 'Blindness has come upon part of Israel, until the full number of the Gentiles come in' (Rom. 11.25). Without Israel's 'no', the Christian church would have remained a messianic revival movement within Judaism itself. But because of the Jewish 'no', the Christian community had a surprising experience. It discovered that the Spirit of God comes upon Gentiles so that they are seized by faith in Christ directly, without becoming Jews first of all.[76] The mission to the Gentiles which Paul himself began is an indirect fruit of the Jewish 'no'. Paul emphasizes this to the Christian congregation in Rome, which was made up of both Jews and Christians: 'As regards the gospel they are enemies of God for your sake; but as regards election they are beloved for the sake of their forefathers' (11.28). It is therefore perfectly correct to say that 'We shall only put antisemitism behind us when we succeed theologically in making something positive out of the Jewish "no" to Jesus Christ'.[77] The 'something positive' is the mission to the Gentiles, out of which the church emerged. It is not just a matter of extracting something positive out of something negative – a 'making the best' of what is really in itself bad. According to Paul, it is God's will which is manifested in the Jewish inability to accept the gospel of Christ. That is why Paul, the Jewish Christian, can certainly deplore the Jewish 'no', and grieve over his own people (9.2–5), yet at the same time he can also praise the divine 'yes' which manifests itself out of this 'no': 'Their failure means riches for the world' (11.12), 'their rejection is the world's reconciliation' (11.15).

There can be no question of God's having finally rejected the people of his choice – he would then have to reject his own election (11.29) – and of his then having sought out instead another people, the church. Israel's promises remain Israel's promises. They have not been transferred to the church. Nor does the church push Israel out of its place in the divine history. In the perspective of the gospel, Israel has by no means become 'like all the nations'. Finally, Israel's 'no' does not make it a witness in history to God's judgment, so that it now exists merely as a warning to the community of Christ not to fall away from faith.[78] Just because the gospel has come to the Gentiles as a result of the Jewish 'no', it will return – indeed it must return – to Israel. 'The first shall be last.' Israel is 'the last' towards which everything else draws.

For Paul this was an apocalyptic 'mystery': 'Blindness has come upon a part of Israel, until the full number of the Gentiles come in, and so all Israel will be saved; as it is written, "The Deliverer will come from Zion, he will banish ungodliness from Jacob"' (11.25–26). For Paul, Israel's 'Deliverer' is the Christ of the parousia, the messiah who will come in the glory of God and whose name is Jesus. The Jewish 'no', which as Saul he maintained so zealously against the early Christian congregations, was overthrown through a call vision of the crucified and glorified Jesus. That is why Paul puts his hope for his people in the Deliverer 'from Zion', who is going to come in visible glory. He does not expect of this Deliverer the Jews' conversion, and that they will arrive at Christian faith. What he expects is Israel's redemption, and that she will be raised from the dead: 'What will their acceptance mean but life from the dead?' (11.15).[79] Israel will be delivered because she sees glory; and this will not happen merely to the final generation. Cutting right through the times of history, it will happen to all the dead at once, 'in a moment'. The apostle's hope of redemption therefore embraces all

Israel at all times. His practical answer to the Jewish 'no' is not anti-Judaism but the evangelization of the nations. For him, this brings the day of her redemption closer for Israel also.

The same Christ Jesus is not the same for everyone, because people are different. He has one profile for the poor and another for the rich, one profile for the sick and another for the healthy. Accordingly the same Christ Jesus has one particular profile for Jews and another for Gentiles: 'For I tell you that Christ became a servant to the Jews to show God's truthfulness, in order to confirm the promises given to the patriarchs, and in order that the Gentiles might glorify God for his mercy . . .' (Rom. 15.8–9a). According to this, Jesus is Israel's messiah, the one who finally affirms and fulfils the promises given to her; and he is at the same time the one who has pity on the Gentiles and is their saviour, the saviour who brings them to the praise of God. And in each case he is the one for the sake of the others:

– As *Israel's messiah* he becomes *the saviour of the Gentiles*. In Jesus, *Israel herself encounters the Gentiles* – Israel with her whole history, in a nutshell and in messianic form. That is why Matthew tells the story of Jesus, not as an individual history, but as the collective biography of Israel, from the flight into Egypt, the call out of Egypt, the days of temptation in the wilderness, to the story of the passion. Israel's messiah is at the same time Israel's representative. In Jesus Christ, Israel herself encounters believers from the nations in messianic form. Because Christ opens Israel to the Gentiles, the Gentiles for their part are gathered into the divine history of promise and faithfulness towards Israel.

– On the other hand, *Jesus encounters Israel as the saviour of the nations*, believed and worshipped by the many from all peoples. In this form – not directly but indirectly – he reveals himself to Israel as her messiah. In the risen Lord of the church of the nations, the peoples look towards Israel and remind Israel of the promise to Abraham and of Abraham's faith. The only justifiable Gentile Christian 'mission to the Jews' is the reminder to the Jews of their own gracious election, and its promise for humanity. This is surely what Paul means by 'making Israel jealous' for the faith that saves (Rom. 11.14). The faith that is meant is the faith whose 'father' is Abraham (Rom. 4.16), and which Paul proclaims as the justifying, saving faith in Christ. In the name of Abraham's faith, Christians and Jews can already become one here and now; for, just like Jewish faith, Christian faith desires to be nothing other than the faith of Abraham.

If, then, the Christian 'yes' has to be looked for in this direction – if it is the 'yes' which discovers in the Jewish 'no' what is positive, and God's will – then this must also be the approach of a 'Christian theology of Judaism' in a christology which is pro-Judaistic, not anti-Judaistic. But this is possible for Christian theology only if Jewish theology tries on the basis of the Jewish 'no' to understand what Buber calls 'the mystery' of Christianity. After Auschwitz, that is asking a very great deal. But believing Jews too might nevertheless perhaps also ask the theological question: what divine will is really expressed in the mission and spread of Christianity? Since the name of the Lord is made known to the ends of the earth through the mission of the gospel, Christians throughout the world pray daily with Israel for the sanctification of God's name, the doing of his will, and the coming of his kingdom. Cannot Israel, in spite of its own observance of the Jewish 'no', view Christianity as the *praeparatio messianica* of the nations, and thus recognize in it the way which its own hope for the messiah takes to the nations?[80] The messianic preparation of the nations for the coming of redemption would be without any basis if it did not proceed from the messiah himself. In the light of his future he comes into the present through his gospel, and opens men and women through faith for the redemption of this unredeemed world.

But this vista throws the question back to Christianity: would it not have first of all to be so lovely to look upon, that Israel would be able to see it as just such a *praeparatio messianica* of the world of the nations? The answer requires a profound renewal of the church and a fundamental revision of its theological tradition, for Jesus' sake.

II

Trends and Transmutations in Christology

§1 THE IDENTITY OF CHRISTOLOGY AND ITS RELEVANCE

In this chapter we shall look at the historical trends and transmutations of christology, down to the difficulties and deadlocks of the present day; and we shall begin by commenting on its biblical identity, its present position, and its therapeutic relevance in each of its phases.[1] We shall consider the theme and pattern of the orthodox christology of the ancient church, exploring what it has to say about the constitution of the person of Christ, and looking at its soteriological relevance in a world that was metaphysically interpreted. The 'turn to anthropology' in modern European times engendered a fundamentally different christological paradigm – the paradigm of modern liberal 'Jesuology', which is christology from an anthropological viewpoint. We shall look at this as we find it in Friedrich Schleiermacher and Karl Rahner, seeing how this new approach views the constitution of Christ's person, and considering its soteriological relevance in a world that is now reduced to human dimensions. We shall then try to develop the principles of an eschatological christology under the end-time conditions of our present scientific and technological civilization, which this outline hopes to develop. In the past, christology became dogmatically fixed. We shall try to throw it open once more for interpretations of Christ which are related to the present.

Of course no contemporary christology is ever completely new. Every christology is part of a grateful and critical dialogue with the christologies of predecessors and other contemporaries, setting its own tiny accents in this great dialogue about the messianic secret of Jesus Christ. In this chapter we can do no more than consider a few connections in the tradition, points at which the christological paradigm underwent a fundamental alteration. Changes of this kind come about when the soteriological relevance of christology changes; and that changes because the question of men and women about salvation has been recast. Christology which in this sense enters soteriologically into the questionings of its contemporaries, and therapeutically into the cultural situation in which the church exists, must always enter into the 'underside' of this history as well. The 'underside' of modern European cultural history is the barbarity which has bred the Third World, the ecological crisis and the system of nuclear deterrent.[2] Finally, a christology in eschatological perspective will have to be continually aware that it is historically conditioned; for without that, it would cease to be eschatologically provisional.

1. Christology as a Biblical Theme

Since it is a reflection about the subject, function and real-life situation of Christian faith (its *Sitz im Leben*), every christology presupposes *belief* – an *account* of Christ presupposes a living *faith* in him. Christian faith is alive where men and women confess that Jesus of Nazareth, 'crucified under Pontius Pilate', is Israel's messiah, the reconciler of the nations, the deliverer of the cosmos, the Son of the Father, and whatever the other statements about Christ have to say. Wherever people confess that Jesus is the Christ of God, there is living faith. Where this is doubted or denied or rejected, there is no faith. Christianity is alive as long as there are people who confess with the disciples and the women – with Martha (John 11) and Peter (Matt. 16) – 'You are the Christ, the Son of the living God', people who in his discipleship spread and live the gospel.

Believing and thinking inevitably belong together. The one has to light up the other. Faith in Christ is not a blind faith, and christology is not a neutral, detached science. The two come together and are one in *perception*: 'We have believed *and come to know*', says Peter in his acknowledgment of Christ (John 6.69). The First Epistle of John (1.1) stresses even more strongly that Christ is perceived with all the senses: 'That which we have *heard*, which we have *seen* with our eyes, which we have looked upon and *touched* with our hands, the word of life . . .' Christology does not merely presuppose belief in the sense of knowledge about Jesus Christ, and sincere trust in him. Its premise is also that Christ is *totally perceived*, with all the senses, and it takes into account this holistic perception as it is found in the living community with Christ.[3]

The theme of the acknowledgment 'Jesus is the Christ, Jesus is the Lord' is not merely the mystery of Jesus' person. From the very beginning, and quite essentially, this acknowledgment has always been at the same time a statement about the mystery of God. Paul is quoting an early Christian creed when he writes (Rom. 10.9): 'If you confess with your lips that Jesus is Lord and believe in your heart that God raised him from the dead, you will be saved.' To confess Jesus as the Lord is at the same time to confess the God who raised him from the dead; and the reverse is also true. The confession of faith in Christ is a confession of faith in God, and this confession of faith in the God who has raised Jesus from the dead is simultaneously a confession of faith in Jesus the Lord. This means in the first place that Christians believe in God for Jesus' sake, and in Jesus for God's sake. For Jesus' sake they believe in the Father, the living God who raises the dead; and for the sake of this God they believe in Jesus, who was his Christ. In the Christ they confess, they do not merely perceive that Jesus is 'theo-form'; they also discern that God is 'christo-form'. This further means that Jesus *is* the Lord because God *has raised* him from the dead. His *existence* as the Lord is to be found in God's eschatological *act* in him, which we call raising from the dead. Jesus' identity is this eschatological identity. He is not the Christ apart from this act of God. He is the Christ in the eschatological history of God, which brings about the end of this world of death and the beginning of the new creation. As 'the first-born of the dead' (Rev. 1.5) and 'the author of life' (Acts 3.15), he is God's Christ for the world. Jesus 'is' the Christ in this eschatological sense.

The subject of christology cannot therefore be cut down to the earthly person of Jesus of Nazareth, who was killed round about the year 33.[4] Nor does it have to do with the private person of the Galilean, or the historical personality of the Nazarene, who came on the scene as one human being among others, and disappeared from the stage again. The theme of christology extends to his resurrection and his presence in the Spirit of the coming God. This is already made plain by the earliest Christian creeds, which say that he was crucified and raised, died and rose again, was humiliated and exalted, is past, present and to come. Anyone who pares the theme of christology down to 'the Jesus of history', anyone who reduces the eschatological person of Christ to the private person of Jesus, and anyone who historicizes his presence to the time of his life on earth, must not be surprised to discover that christology is no longer a subject that has any relevance at all. For who could still get up any interest after 2,000 years in a historical Jesus of Nazareth who lived a private life and then died?

In this outline we shall assume that there are three dimensions to christology, and its biblical identifiability: 1. that Jesus is recognized as the Christ of God; 2. that God is believed to be the Father of Jesus Christ, who raised him from the dead; and 3. that the presence of Christ is experienced in the Spirit who is the giver of life.[5] This does not mean that we are laying down any rules about what has to be believed, as a way of setting up a kind of orthodox maximalism, over against a liberal christological minimalism. What it does mean is that these are the three aspects of the one Christ event to which faith owes its origin and its living force.

2. The Present Position of Christology

The premise of christology is Christian faith; so it also presupposes christopraxis, in the broadest sense of the word; for christopraxis is the source from which christology springs. Christology is not some remotely withdrawn theory, without any particular situation.[6] To confess faith in Christ goes together with discipleship. Even if reflection about the history of christological dogma creates a certain detachment, compared with immediate experience and direct praxis, christology nevertheless remains related to its practical situation, its *Sitz im Leben* in the community of Christ. The form-critical analyses of the christological creeds of the church in earlier times have made this clear. But these analyses are incomplete if they do not lead on to a critical awareness of the ideology underlying present-day christology too, where its social situation, its psycho-social function, and its practical relevance are concerned. Theory and practice cannot be separated even in christology. Their intertwinings are so complex that they resist the imposition of any simple pattern. Christological theory is not a reflection of a Christian praxis. Christian praxis is not the application of a christological theory. The christological theory which is concerned with the knowledge of Christ in his meaning for us today is itself a praxis, and we have to answer for it as such. And the Christian praxis of faith has already in itself cognitive significance, as we can see and recognize if we start from that total perception of Christ in the lived community of Christ about which we have already spoken. Christ is the foundation for salvation and new life. And for that reason christology and Christian ethics cannot be separated.

The *Sitz im Leben* for christology – its situation in life – is *the community of Christ*, with its elemental functions for living, and its tasks for the world surrounding it. That is why christology is related to *the gospel* of Christ which the congregation hears, and to which it witnesses. The proclamation and the daily witness of believers show who Christ really is for the community of his people today. At the centre of the gathered congregation is christology in its relation to *Christ's eucharist*; for in the praxis of the eucharist the congregation 'proclaims Christ's death till he comes' (I Cor. 11.26). The 'memorial of Christ' in the eating and drinking of his feast is essential for theological christology, because there the presence of Christ can be experienced, and because the eucharist binds his presence organically with his past – that is, his death – and with his future – that is, his parousia. Theological christology will take its bearings from this special eucharistic experience of time. The way the past is made present in the eucharist is different from a historical actualization. Theologically speaking, the historical analysis of 'the historical Jesus' always remains related to the eucharistic *anamnesis*. Otherwise it would literally 'escape the memory', and historicize Jesus in order to bury him once and for all, and to get free of him. And when the future of Jesus Christ is made present in the eucharist, the same may be said. Eucharistic theology also implies the *ecclesiological christology* of Jesus, the head of the fellowship that gathers round the Lord's table. Just as bread and wine are shared as the body and blood of Christ, so his community also experiences itself as Christ's body, and as his brotherhood and sisterhood. Theological christology is always related to this fellowship, and to the experiences of fellowship in this community.

Christopraxis in the narrower sense must be understood as the life of the community of Christians in the discipleship of Jesus. 'The way of Jesus' or 'the politics of Jesus' are phrases which describe the participation of the community of Christ in Jesus' own messianic mission to the poor and the sick, and to sinners.[7] The guideline of this christopraxis was, and still is, the messianic interpretation of the Torah in Jesus' Sermon on the Mount. But this praxis too is not the application of a theory about Christ. It is a way of life, a way in which people learn who Jesus is, learn it with all their senses, acting and suffering, in work and prayer. To know Jesus does not simply mean learning the facts of christological dogma. It means learning to know him in the praxis of discipleship. Theological christology remains related to this christopraxis, and has to absorb its experiences, and open people for again new experiences along this way. Christology emerges from Christian living and leads into Christian living. A mere theory about Christ is insufficient, because purely theoretical knowledge about him is inappropriate. Consequently christological theory has to point beyond itself, and paradoxically away from itself, to the doing of God's will, in which 'knowing Jesus' as the Lord really becomes whole and entire.

Christopraxis inevitably leads the community of Christ to the poor, the sick, to 'surplus people' and to the oppressed. Like the messiah himself, the messianic community is sent first of all to unimportant people, people 'of no account': 'Preach: the kingdom of God is at hand. Heal the sick, cleanse lepers, raise the dead, cast out demons. You received without paying. Give without pay too' (Matt. 10.7–8; cf. also Matt. 11.5–6). Christ's community belongs for Christ's sake to the fellowship of 'the least' of his brothers and sisters (Matt. 25) As the Christ for all human beings, Jesus takes hold of our divided and peaceless human society at its lowest point, among the miserable, the despised and the unimportant.[8] Because the community of Christ has its social and political place there, christology too will have to accept that place as its own, and will have to build this fact into its reflections.

3. The Therapeutic Relevance of Christology

Through its criterion 'in accordance with Scripture', Protestant theology established the Christian identity of the church's christology. This criterion means that christological statements have to be verified as originating historically and substantially in the Bible. But if christology were to confine itself to this 'origin' hermeneutics, it could rapidly become sterile, however much it was 'in accordance with Scripture'. It would then test all its statements against the biblical testimony about Jesus' person and history; but it would no longer be able to relate these statements therapeutically to people in the wretchedness of their present situation. The hermeneutics of christology's origin must therefore be complemented by the hermeneutics of its effects. Of course if we were so one-sided as to look solely at the effects, we could easily find ourselves in an identity crisis, however therapeutically topical our christological statements were. Here we shall relate the identity and relevance of christology to one another mutually;[9] and this brings us face to face with a double question: Is Jesus really the Christ? Who really is Jesus Christ for us today?

In the course of history, this second question has been answered in two ways, one of them apologetic, the other therapeutic. *Apologetic christology* was supposed to put people in a position to 'make a defence to anyone for the hope that is in you' (I Peter 3.15). It gathers together proofs for Jesus's messiahship and his resurrection, in order to clear away doubts and make faith possible. *Therapeutic christology* is soteriological christology. It confronts the misery of the present with the salvation Christ brings, presenting it as a salvation that heals.[9a] Healing power belongs to salvation; otherwise it could not save. These two kinds of relevance are not mutually exclusive. They complement one another.

In our present context we are stressing the unity of christology and soteriology. In the history of theology, the doctrine about the person of Christ has always provided the inner premise for the soteriology which is to be substantiated; while soteriology is the outward result of the christology. This unity between the christological foundation of soteriology and the soteriological explication of christology is never extinguished, even when christology is made the criterion for soteriology, so as to prevent soteriology from being delivered over to the caprice of people's own religious desires and anxieties, which would turn it into the religious wish-fulfilment of the moment.[10] Christian theology talks about *Christ's* salvation, not just any salvation. But it can talk about the salvation which Christ brings only as healing. It therefore has to be aware of the misery of the present – of any given present – and expose it for what it is. In the therapeutical circle of healing, it is the critical analysis of the misery, evil and suffering which first makes it possible for liberation and salvation to be experiencable at all, for the people affected. To put it in traditional theological language: the liberating and healing process of the forgiveness of sins involves both the exposure and the confession of sin, as well as the assurance of forgiveness, and the discovery of new life in the righteousness of God.

Admittedly, in the past the Christian doctrine of salvation was often applied solely to the eternal situation of human beings in God's sight, in order that eternal salvation might be related to the fundamental existential situation of men and women: their separation from God, their transience, finitude and mortality.[11] This meant that often enough this doctrine ignored the actual, practical human situation, in its real misery. To wipe out the metaphysical wretchedness of human beings does not automatically mean that their physical and moral, economic and social wretchedness is abolished too. If Christian soteriology confines itself to this metaphysical dimension, it can even actually contribute to physical affliction. In the theological sense, salvation is whole salvation and the salvation of the whole, or it is not God's salvation; for God is 'the all-determining reality'. It is therefore more appropriate to present the salvation which Christ brings in ever-widening circles, beginning with the personal experience of reconciliation and ending with the reconciliation of the cosmos, heaven and earth. In these contexts it is dangerous for the Christian doctrine of salvation, and senseless for human beings, if attention is devoted solely to 'the religious question' in any society, so as to demonstrate the salvation of Christ merely over against what is thought to be the religious wretchedness of men and women in that society; it is both dangerous and senseless because in an alienated society the religious sphere itself is alienated. In a society which has declared 'religion' to be 'a private affair', the salvation Christ offers can be presented as the private salvation of the individual soul if, and only if, Christianity assents to this confining of the religious question to 'the human heart', emancipated from social ties. But then the economic, social and political sins of human beings which have led to this personal isolation and spiritual loneliness are left without liberating criticism and without the saving hope of the gospel.

In discussing the christological soteriologies of tradition, we shall try here to arrive at a practical soteriology which enters into the real wretchedness of human beings, while keeping in view the eschatological horizon of the salvation of the whole. The End-time condition of world history today requires us to see the real misery of human beings as one with the growing universal misery of the earth. The deadly fear men and women are experiencing is fear of nuclear catastrophe in the present, and ecological catastrophe in the future, and the conflicts in social and economic life which are the result of both.[12] What was once presented as the general and timeless metaphysical wretchedness of human beings is now returning in the special form of the human miseries of the End-time: ever since Hiroshima, it is not only individual human beings that are mortal; the whole human race has become mortal too.[13] The ecological crisis can make the human race itself ephemeral, and can destroy all other living things on earth. The antinomies of modern civilization are drawing human beings and nature deeper and deeper into a common destiny. This forbids any reduction of salvation, whether it be personal or anthropological. In the danger of annihilation that is hanging over us, God's salvation is the healing and survival of the whole threatened earth and all individual created beings, in their common peril.

§2 THE THEME AND SCHEME OF COSMOLOGICAL CHRISTOLOGY

Compared with the modern world, the world of antiquity may be described as cosmocentric. Human beings saw themselves and their civilization as embedded in the orders of the cosmos, which wrapped them round. Correspondence and participation determined their lives: to live in accordance with nature was to live rightly. To participate in the laws of reason was to live in harmony with the gods. The individual was a member of his family, families were members of the *polis*, the community of the *polis* was a member of the cosmic community of all things. For agrarian societies, this harmony between human civilization and cosmic nature is typical and of vital importance. Even when people became aware of their special position in the cosmos, they continued to observe this harmony. The human being is a microcosm, a little world, which includes and reflects the larger world around, while the world is a macro-anthropos, designed to be the world of human beings. Nature cannot be thought of without human beings, and human beings cannot be thought of without nature. So whatever happens to human beings in the context of the divine, happens to the cosmos too.

The human being is aware of his humanity, compared with what is divine: 'Know thyself' was written on the temple at Delphi. And that meant: know that you are human, not divine. Know that you are mortal. When the human being is conscious of his *humanitas*, he is also aware that he derives from earth, not from heaven, and that he shares the fate of the earth. When he compares himself with the gods, the human being perceives the fundamental ontological difference between divine and earthly being: the divine being is eternal, one, infinite, immutable, immortal, impassible, and exists of itself; whereas what is human, like all earthly being, is temporal, manifold, finite, changeable, capable of suffering, mortal, and exists not of itself but out of something different from itself. The question of human existence is the question of all earthly being: how can finite being participate in the Being that is infinite, so that in eternal Being it may acquire a continuance that will resist transience in time and decay in death? Everything that is, and does not remain, asks unconsciously for a being that is, and remains eternally, a being that will give to what is fleeting, duration in the face of non-existence. But the human being asks this question consciously, on behalf of all earthly being. This is the question about God, and in a metaphysically interpreted, cosmocentric world, it is one with the question about salvation: 'God is the answer that is implicit in the finitude of human beings.' The question implicit in the existential finitude of human beings is the question about non-transience and immortality. Participation in the glory of the divine being that is eternal means receiving a life which knows no death but is unfading and immortal. It is not only the consciously questioning human being who will be possessed by this divine glory, by virtue of participation and correspondence. The whole cosmos will be drawn into the glory with him. The Fathers of the church saw this all-embracing goal of salvation as 'the deification of the human being' and 'the deification of creation'.[14]

In both its christology and its soteriology, the theology of the patristic church faced up to this fundamental question of a cosmocentric world. In its christology it worked out the doctrine of the two natures, which was brought to a provisional completion at the Council of Chalcedon in 451. In its soteriology it developed what the nineteenth century called 'the doctrine of physical redemption'. The two aspects correspond, although patristic christology is marked, not by soteriology alone, but by doxology too. We see this especially in the Nicene creed of 325 (381). From Irenaeus to Athanasius, the fundamental notion about the correspondence between christology and soteriology was formulated – in continually new variations – as follows: 'God became man so that we human beings should be gods, that is, should partake of the divine life.'[15] Put more precisely, this means that the eternal Son of God becomes human so that we human beings should receive the divine sonship. He manifests himself in flesh so that we fleshly beings may know the invisible Father, and by knowing him may become his: for to know confers community. The non-transitory and immortal Logos takes mortal, transitory human nature upon himself, so that transitory and mortal human beings may become non-transitory and immortal. For what is not assumed is not healed; but what God assumes is saved.

In these statements, the purposes behind soteriology illuminate the christology which is their premise and their *sine qua non*; while on the other hand the christology premised becomes relevant in the soteriology. The soteriology is broadly formulated. Its scope extends to the whole of human nature, not just to human personhood: transience and mortality, suffering and decay, impose on human beings wretchedness and lack of dignity. Non-transience and immortality through fellowship with God make human beings truly human, in their unimpeded dignity as God's image and God's children on earth. The wretchedness revealed and the salvation offered are certainly concentrated on men and women, but they do not merely affect them personally. The wretchedness and the salvation have to do with the very nature of human beings, and together with *their* nature, the nature of the cosmos too, of which they are members. The personally-related concepts of wretchedness and salvation (such as guilt and the forgiveness of guilt) are integrated into these other concepts, which are related to nature. 'If it were merely sin that existed, and not the resulting transience as well, contrition would be appropriate', said Athanasius, and goes on: 'But God becomes human and subjects himself to "the law of death" so as to take away death's power over human beings and his creation, and in order to bring immortality to light.'[16] The soteriological vision of *theopoiesis*, the deification of human beings and creation, presupposes that death has been vanquished through the death of the God who has become human, and through his resurrection.

The theological constitution of the person of Jesus Christ is consequently the constitution of the God-human being in the framework of the general metaphysical doctrine of the two natures; for this is the premise. We cannot trace here the history of the christology of the ancient church, and its development from the biblical beginnings down to the well-known Chalcedonian formulations.[17] 'Two-nature christology' has been subjected to considerable criticism, especially by nineteenth-century liberal Protestant theologians; but we must none the less remember that it developed out of the dual New Testament definitions to which we pointed at the beginning: crucified – raised; died – rose again; humiliated – exalted; past – present; and that it was in substance well able to retain the sense of these original definitions. Admittedly, the shift in christology's theme from Christ's cross and resurrection to the incarnation and birth of the divine human being is certainly something of a puzzle – that is to say, the way the centre shifts from Easter to Christmas. A christology which traces the path from Christ's death on the cross to his resurrection presents a kind of *'ascendence'* christology, from below upwards; whereas every incarnation christology pursues the path of the eternal Son of God from above downwards, and is a *'descendence'* christology.

This reversal of the perspective evidently came about very early on. Paul is already familiar with a hymn about Christ (quoted in Phil. 2) which begins 'at the top' and leads downwards, then going on to extol the great reverse movement of the story in God's exaltation of Christ. The early Christian community evidently deduced Christ's original sending *by* and *from* the Father from his eschatological exaltation *to* the Father. According to the logic of this deduction, the future reveals the origin. That is to say, Christ's descent is manifested in his resurrection. The process of incarnation is then merely the reversal of the process of resurrection, since what is last in perception is always first in being.[18] But this reversal of the christological picture is also conditioned by the fact that Jesus' resurrection from the dead was not understood merely as happening in time to the dead Jesus. It was simultaneously seen as the beginning of the eschatological era, when the dead will be raised. It therefore also meant the immediate presence of God's eternity. In time, Jesus is raised 'on the third day' after his death, but as the immediate presence of eternity his raising is simultaneous to all moments of his life. To adopt this standpoint is already to assume the perspective which looks from Jesus' divine to his human nature, and it is then possible to talk about his incarnation. But for Orthodox christology, Easter remained the centre, and the Easter liturgy was determinative, even through the incarnation christology of the ancient church was preserved unaltered.

We shall look at the detailed definitions of early Protestant orthodoxy where these bear on the theological constitution of the person of the incarnate God-human being, because from these we can see some of the impasses of metaphysical christology.[19]

The christology of Christ's single person in two natures is the condition which makes it possible to substantiate theologically the redemption of humanity through him. The fundamental concept here is the concept of incarnation. Incarnation is the movement in which the divine and human nature are united in the one person of the God-human being. This union (*unitio*) takes place in such a way that the eternal Logos, the second person of the Trinity, the eternal Son, assumes non-personal human nature in the womb of Mary, absorbing it into the unity and independence of his person, and into the fellowship of his divine nature. In the eternal Logos, the divine nature is a nature determined by personhood; the human nature that is assumed is a non-personal nature. The element in the God-human being that constitutes the person is the eternal Son of God. This is thought through in the symbol of the virgin birth: the eternal Son comes from the Father in the Holy Spirit and assumes human nature from the Virgin Mary. Because this human nature *ex Maria virgine* has no human father – i.e., is non-sexually conceived – it is excluded from original sin, and also from the consequence of original sin, which is death; and it is therefore immortal. The human nature assumed in the incarnation is hence an intact, unblemished human nature, without sin and without mortality, like the nature of Adam and Eve before the Fall. That is why the God-human being is called, not the 'real' human being, but the 'true' human being.[20] It is therefore solely of his own free will, out of compassion, not out of compulsion, that the God-human being then participates in the natural weaknesses of the flesh, to which existing human nature has been subjected ever since the Fall. The human nature which the eternal Son assumed in the incarnation is therefore 1. anhypostatic – i.e., non-personal, because the centre that constitutes its personhood is the eternal Son himself; 2. sinless and immortal; and 3. of that particular excellence of soul and body which is consequent on sinlessness. The result of the union of divine and human nature in the person of the God-human being is the full community or sociality of the two natures in him: *communio* or *communicatio idiomatum* (the communication of attributes). All statements about the person of Christ are based upon this full communion of his natures: God is human being – the human being Jesus Christ is God – God died – the human being Jesus is omnipresent – the son of Mary is the Son of the Highest; and so forth.

We do not need to go any further here into the individual
definitions of the various *status Christi* which were developed, in
early Protestant orthodoxy especially, as a way of differentiating the
communion of natures in the different statuses of Christ. For the
christology of the ancient church, the whole of salvation was in fact
already implicitly implemented when human nature was assumed by
the personally determined divine nature: 'The God-Logos united the
whole of human nature so that he might save the whole man; for
what is not assumed is not healed.' According to early Protestant
orthodoxy, on the other hand, the constitution of the person of the
God-human being through the assumption by the eternal Son of a
non-personal human nature was no more than the *presupposition*
for his saving work, not the saving work itself. For the saving work
itself, this theology then developed the familiar doctrine about
'Christ's threefold office'.

The impasses of two-nature christology have been described from
many different angles.[21] Here we shall mention only the questions
which are important for us.

1. If the eternal Logos assumed a non-personal human nature, he
cannot then be viewed as a historical person, and we cannot talk
about 'Jesus of Nazareth'. The human nature that was assumed
would then seem to be like the human garment of the eternal Son –
something which he put on when he walked on earth. It becomes
difficult to find an identity here between this human nature and our
own. Or has the eternal Son of God taken on 'human nature without
personhood' in the modern sense, so that he has assumed the human
being who is really a 'non-person'? Has he, that is, taken on deficient
human nature in its deepest humiliation? In this case the incarnation
itself would already be the assumption of the de-humanized, de-
personalized, oppressed human being who has been degraded to
mere 'brute matter'; and it would also mean the healing of this
dehumanized human being for eternal human dignity in God.[22] Or is
'true' human nature itself anhypostatically enhypostasized in the
divine person, as Paul suggests in his own language when he says: 'It
is no longer I who live, but Christ who lives in me' (Gal. 2.20)? But
then 'real', actual human personhood would in itself already have to
be termed the sin of egocentricism.[23]

2. If the eternal Logos has assumed a human nature without sin,
then he is immortal not merely in his divine nature but in his human
nature too, since mortality is a consequence of sin. But if he assumed

a human nature which was in itself immortal, then this cannot actually have been born either; for what is immortal has neither birth nor death. Here the image of the body of Christ which is 'transfigured' through the raising from the dead (Phil. 3.21) and which Rom. 6.9 says 'will never die again' is evidently projected back to the birth of this body from the Virgin Mary through the power of the Holy Spirit. Christ's human bodiliness is then already transfigured through the virgin birth. But this is an impossible possibility, because it is then impossible to talk even symbolically about either a 'virgin' or 'a birth'. Both the divine personal centre and the inherently immortal body of Christ must then be pre-existent and must have entered into Mary out of eternity. Finally, if the God-human being is inherently immortal not only in his divine nature but in his human nature too, then the dogmatic structure of reflection about his death and its meaning for salvation becomes questionable: for then Christ does not die his own death; he merely dies ours, out of compassion. In himself he would have remained immortal. But how can his death redeem, if it was not, and cannot have been, either the death of his divine nature or the death of his human one? The doctrine of the *communicatio idiomatum* can only transfer the attributes of the one nature to the other by reason of the unity of persons in Christ. But if the God-human being is in essence immortal not only in his divine nature but in his human nature too, in which capacity did Christ then die?

3. In the framework of the two-nature christology, all statements about 'the lowliness' of Jesus, his humanity, his suffering, and his death on the cross, are reduced, in favour of statements about his divinity, his exaltation and his triumph, and are integrated into these. The history of Christ is essentially the vertical history between God and human beings. It is 'the way of the Son of God into the foreign country', and 'the return home of the Son of man'.[24] If the history of Christ is essentially this vertical history, then it is a fundamentally 'eternal history'. What emerges as a whole is the picture of the triumphant Christ in the glory of God. It is no doubt due to this one-sided viewpoint that the prophetic proclamation of Jesus and his earthly ministry are not so much as mentioned in either the Apostles' or the Nicene creed. Between his birth from a virgin and his death under Pontius Pilate, the dogmatic history tells us *almost nothing*; and the same may be said of the traditional confessions of the Christian faith. The Nicene creed says 'and became man'; the Apostles' creed, merely 'suffered'.

4. The differentiation between the two natures bears the mark of incarnation christology, and does not derive from the particular history of Jesus himself. It is drawn from a general metaphysics of the world. Attributes are ascribed to the divine nature of Christ which the God of Abraham, Isaac and Jacob, 'the Father of Jesus Christ', never knew.[25] His faithfulness is transformed into a substantial immutability, his zeal, his love, his compassion – in short his 'pathos', his capacity for feeling – are supplanted by the essential apathy of the divine. The passion of his love and its capacity for suffering can no longer be stated. 'The God of history', 'the coming God', disappears in favour of the eternal presence of the heavenly Lord. And if the metaphysical distinction between God and the world which this presupposes is theologically equated with the distinction between Creator and creature (the equation made by Christian tradition), then the relation of the human to the divine nature can only be the relation of creature to Creator; it cannot be the relation of the Son to the Father. But this reduces christology to anthropology.

It is more appropriate, then, to start from Jesus' special relationship to God, whom he called Abba, dear Father, in order to elicit from this mutual relationship between the messianic child and the divine Father what is truly divine and what is truly human.[26] By first of all developing christology and the doctrine of God in specifically Christian – which means trinitarian – terms, we are not denying the task of christology in the framework of metaphysics in general. But the New Testament is not concerned about the relationship between Christ's human and his divine nature. It is concerned with Jesus' relationship as child to the Father, and with God's relationship as Father to Jesus. It is only the trinitarian concept of God which makes it possible to understand God for Jesus' sake in his relationship as Father, and Jesus for God's sake as the child and Son of the Father.

5. Finally, we must notice the political *Sitz im Leben* of patristic christology. This does not mean relativizing it historically or sociologically, but it does 'place' christology in both respects, and makes the bearing of its public function comprehensible. Nicaea (325) was the church's first Ecumenical or General Council. It was convened by the Emperor Constantine, who was greeted by the bishops as 'the thirteenth apostle'. It was in the imperial interest for the church to be dogmatically united, so that as a unified ecumenical organization it was in a position to guarantee the religious integra-

tion of the empire, which was made up of so many nations. The church's concern for orthodoxy in doctrine and liturgy, and for the exclusion of heresy, was entirely in line with the emperor's concern for a unified imperial religion. The struggle about christological orthodoxy was bound up with the struggle for the imperial church. All later ecumenical councils were convened by emperors, and ministered to the orthodoxy of the One Religion in the one Byzantine empire. The Orthodox Church lived in this 'Christian world' like the soul in the body, on the strength of the harmony between the ecclesiastical and the imperial power.[27] In its christology, Christ was not merely the head of the church. He was also the king of heaven and the pantocrator, thereby legitimating the Christian *imperator* and his empire. As 'the anointed of the Lord', the Orthodox emperor had a messianic charge to spread the kingdom of God on earth. For in the Christian empire God's plan in history was fulfilled.

This religious self-confidence always gave Byzantium and Moscow a special chiliastic sense of mission: this was the kingdom that redeems the world, and the nation that redeems the nations. In this way, theology aligned both the Christian church and the Christian state towards the kingdom of God; and in this respect it was 'an imperial theology', whether it is viewed in its transcendental or its eschatological configuration. Parallel to the church, the emperor was accepted as sacred representative of God's rule over the world.

This theocratic understanding of church and state has probably never been without chiliastic overtones and colourings: the saints of the Most High rule with Christ and judge the nations. In the kingdom of Christ, Satan is 'bound' for a thousand years, so that truth and goodness can spread without contradiction and without conflict. This Christ is the pantocrator of heaven and earth, the one who triumphs over evil and death – not to speak of his enemies on earth, the Jews, the heathen and the heretics. Christology in the 'eternal history' of fall and rise is *chiliastic christology*, christology in the thousand years' kingdom of Christ.

But what changes must christology undergo when this theocratic unity of church and Christian *imperium* crumbles, and the chiliastic dream vanishes, and the church has to live in a non-Christian, a-Christian and anti-Christian world? Is it not then wise to give up the untimely dream of the pantocrator and the imperial church in the thousand years' empire, and to turn back to the one crucified, and to live in his discipleship? Must not the chiliastically triumphing, eternal christology give way to *the christology of history*, which is a christology on the road, and a christology beneath the cross? In this world the church of Christ has as yet no social and political 'body' outside itself which it could interpenetrate as soul if it were once to surrender its own bodiliness. The church exists in contradictions and conflicts, and it must organize itself as the visible community of believers against the impeachments of this world of violence, so that it may show the world God's alternatives.

§3 THE THEME AND SCHEME OF ANTHROPOLOGICAL CHRISTOLOGY

Anthropological christology is simply Jesuology and nothing else. Jesuology is not the opposite of christology. The term is used for the modern christology which is also called 'christology from below'. The centre of this christology is the human being Jesus of Nazareth, not the exalted or pre-existent Christ. That is why we talk about Jesuology. And in doing so, we show the shift in christology that has taken place in modern times. The change-over from the old christological pattern to this new outline was a fundamental one. It began in European Protestantism at the time of the Enlightenment, but it is not confined to that context. It also took hold of Catholicism, Anglicanism and Orthodoxy, although the phases were not always simultaneous.

The christological disputes and discussions of the last two hundred years reflect a radical change in European theology as a whole; and this in its turn echoes a fundamental and general cultural revolution. This revolution has been called the modern era's 'turn to anthropology' (Martin Buber's phrase), modern man's revolt into subjectivity (Heidegger), the 'secularization' of society, the 'historicization' of history, the 'disenchantment' of nature, and so on. The modern world is an equivocal phenomenon, and the interpretations given to it are multifarious also. The people who talk about 'the secularized world' are comparing it with the sacral world of the middle ages. The people who describe the modern world view as anthropocentric are comparing it with the theocentricism of the middle ages. The people who define it as 'a historical world' are contrasting it with the ancient world of stable order, seeing in it the principle of permanent revolution at work.

The phenomenon of 'the modern world' is in fact unique and unparalleled in human history. For the first time, a world made by human beings has detached itself from the orders and rhythms of nature, and is now constructed solely according to human notions and interests. The fate of the human world is no longer determined by the forces of nature. It is determined by the will of human beings. Human beings are making themselves more and more independent of nature, and nature is more and more dependent on human beings. Men and women are becoming the determining subjects of their own history. The project 'scientific and technological civilization' has become the great universal human experiment,[28] and is increasingly becoming the fate of all human beings, whether they like it or not; for it is spreading inexorably. That is why the countries that have not yet been possessed by it are called 'development' or 'developing' countries. In all sectors of science and technology, developments have been set on foot for which there is no longer any realistic alternative, because the point of no return has already been passed. The old agrarian societies, which were kind towards nature, have been replaced by the industrial society which exploits and destroys nature, because human interests are its sole point of reference. A hundred years ago, most people lived in the country. In many countries today most of the population already lives in mass cities. The 'great trek' from the country to the town is still going on, and today it is a determining factor in the situation of the Third World as well. Later on we shall look further at the risks and contradictions of this civilization of ours, which is the major project of modern men and women.

Attentive Protestant theology was alive to the birth of the modern mind very early on, and entered into the inner problems involved. Hegel talked about a 'tremendous revolution in the Christian world . . . a totally different self-awareness of the true has come into being.'[29] This new awareness is the principle of human *subjectivity*. Through knowledge and will, human beings are now confronting nature. Nature is becoming their object. They are making themselves free, independent conscious subjects. Science and technology are making them the masters of a nature they have objectified. What this means for the build-up of the industrial world and for the demolition of nature has been described often enough. But modern theology asks initially only what it means for human beings. When the modern mind draws human beings out of their natural communities, individualizing them as conscious subjects, it makes them free and autonomous; but it also involves them in permanent identity crises. What is the human being, and what is truly 'human' – truly humane? This question is of vital importance for men and women in the modern world, because no natural limits are set to their inhumanity any longer. Ever since the Enlightenment this has been the main problem: the humanization of the hominized world, the humanization of the human beings who have made themselves the lords of the earth. Unless a humane humanity can be developed, it is inconceivable that human beings can survive, in the face of the power they have acquired. That is why European and American humanism grew up at the very time when these nations were subjugating nature by means of their industrial power: human dignity and human rights became the foundation of modern political constitutions. Modern Western democracy was established on the principle of subjectivity, and guarantees subjective liberties.

The theologian Herder was right when he said at the beginning of this era: 'Humanity is both Christ's nature and his work. What is divine in our race is its growth into humanity.'[30] But how can modern human beings find the way to their humanity – to their authenticity – to their human identity – if they are individually isolated, and grow lonely, and if neither the cosmos nor the gods give them any answer?

When the sense of truth became dominated by subjectivity, and the question of salvation thus came to be defined in anthropocentric terms, the old metaphysical incarnation christology became irrelevant. Behind the christological icons of the church, people discovered the earthly, human Jesus, who could be historically approached. In his life, and in the living influence of his personality, men and women found the primal image of the humanity well-pleasing to God (as Kant put it), and the pattern of moral perfection. Here, that is, they found the true and good human being *par excellence*. The christology determined by the principles of the modern mind transformed traditional christology fundamentally. Jesus was no longer understood against a theological background, as the God-human being. He was now viewed in an anthropological foreground, as God's human being. What was stressed now was not his incarnation and – as its physical sign – the virgin birth, but his human perfection in its correspondence to the divine and – as its sign – his sinlessness. Salvation was no longer to be found in the deification of human beings and creation. It was now seen in the inner identity of the self-divided human being, who had become a stranger to himself – an inner identity which would then make it possible to arrive at a moral humanity. Christ's incarnation and resurrection were now incomprehensible and impossible physical miracles of power which no longer fitted into the world picture of human domination over nature. But Jesus' human sinlessness was like a divine 'miracle of love' in the moral world, a miracle for which the modern human being yearningly waits.[31]

This change in the sense of truth is the reason why modern men and women no longer 'understand' what has no importance for them themselves. Their knowledge is no longer directed towards participation in what they perceive, and it has no interest in the community which perception confers. Knowledge is now aimed at subjective utility. What importance does it have for me? What use is it to me? These are the existential questions asked. Even the Protestant catechisms of the Reformation period have already ceased to ask the objective question 'What is Christ's resurrection?' They now enquire subjectively 'What are the benefits of Christ's resurrection for us?'[32] In putting this question they are conforming to the assertion of the young Melanchthon (although the consequences of his view only made themselves felt in nineteenth-century liberalism): 'Christum cognoscere hoc est beneficia eius cognoscere, non, quod isti docent, eius naturas, modos incarnationis contueri' ['To know Christ is to know his benefits, not, as those people teach, to contemplate his natures and the modes of his incarnation'].[33] To say this is to replace the question about essence (*essentia*) by the question about utility (*usus*). In earlier times reason had been participatory. The modern reason that replaces it has been made operational.

For Kant and the ethical theology that followed him, the theological question about fact and essence was therefore replaced by the enquiry about functional usefulness: 'can anything practical be deduced from it?' was his question to the dogmas of christology and to trinitarian doctrine. For 'by statements of faith we do not understand that which *ought* to be believed, but that which it is possible and useful to adopt for a practical (moral) purpose, even if these assertions are not actually demonstrable and *can* therefore only be believed'.[34] He found that 'for us, nothing whatsoever can be gained for practical purposes' from the doctrine of the Trinity or from christology. But as prototype of the humanity well-pleasing to

God, Kant revered Jesus of Nazareth. In his ethical exposition, the divine nature of Christ and the eternal Logos were replaced by 'the idea of mankind in its morally complete perfection', which Jesus embodied. Kant avoids using the name of Jesus, but since it was in Jesus that this 'Christ idea' was embodied, for him Jesus; as the prototype of true humanity, was also the mediator of the moral perfecting of the world, which was 'the second creation', the creation of the moral world. That is, to use traditional words, Jesus was 'the second Adam' or, as Kant himself preferred to say, 'the personified idea of the principle of Good'.[35]

In considering the constitution of the person of Christ according to this modern Jesuology, we shall look at Friedrich Schleiermacher's *Christian Faith* and Karl Rahner's transcendental theology.

For Schleiermacher, religion is situated in the 'feeling' of the human person. By this he means the fundamental tenor of human existence, not sentimental emotions. The subjective unity of life is to be found in the 'immediate self-consciousness', before human activities draw asunder from one another. In this matrix of the living being, theory and practice, ideal and real, being and the sense of being (i.e., consciousness), are one. Schleiermacher calls the primal religious experience of the self 'the feeling of absolute dependence', meaning by this nothing other than the anthropological equivalent of the concept of God as the all-determining reality. But when 'the absolute' takes the place of God, what is meant is only the correspondence to the concept of God in a person's inner self-experience. Objective religion becomes the religion of subjectivity.

According to the same method, Schleiermacher translates the theological definitions of traditional christology into modern anthropological terms: 'Everything individual in Christianity is related to the consciousness of redemption accomplished by the person of Jesus of Nazareth.'[36] 'The Redeemer is the same as all human beings, since human nature is everywhere the same; but he differs from all others through the unremitting potency of his God-consciousness,* which was the veritable existence of God in him.' Here the God-human being is replaced by the God-conscious human being, and Christ's divine nature becomes the existence of

---

*'God-consciousness' is the usual translation for Schleiermacher's *Gottesbewusst-sein*, and it does in fact convey the intimate link between the two halves of the term, although 'consciousness of God' would be normal English usage [Trans.].

God in Jesus' consciousness. The unchangeability of the divine
nature is now translated by the 'unremitting potency' of Jesus'
God-consciousness. This manifests itself in Jesus' 'essential sinlessness' – his absolute perfection,[37] which distinguishes him from all
other human beings, whose God-consciousness is clouded by sin.

If Jesus' God-consciousness takes over the function which was
earlier attributed to the divine nature of Christ, as the God-human
being, then that consciousness can have been subject to neither
development nor variation nor conflict. Jesus' purity is without any
traces and scars of struggle.[38] As a historical individual, Jesus is at
the same time the prototype of God's sinless, perfect humanity. The
redemptive efficacy which radiates from his life is to be found in his
communication of the potency of his God-consciousness, which is
simultaneously the communication of his sinless perfection. For
Schleiermacher, Jesus is the Redeemer because he is the 'productive
prototype' of the God-conscious human being.[39] This redeeming
efficacy rests on his prototypical character and issues from the
whole historical personality of Jesus of Nazareth, not especially from
his sufferings or his death. 'The disciples recognized in him the Son of
God without having any presentiment of his resurrection and
ascension.'[40] Even the passion does not add anything in particular to
the redeeming efficacy which emanates from the impression of his
person: 'The passion of Jesus is the perfect manifestation of the
God-consciousness which in very truth inheres in like fashion in
every aspect of his life.'[41] His suffering on the cross is the
corroboration of his God-consciousness. It has no special atoning
power, and no redemptive significance of its own. 'The Christ idea' is
the idea of the person who is wholly and entirely interpenetrated by
God-consciousness. Because God-consciousness, as the feeling of
absolute dependence, is inherent in every human being, in however
clouded and reduced a form, the Christ idea is inherent in every
human being too. As the perfect prototype of a humanity reconciled
with God, Jesus is the 'second Adam', the author and beginner of the
second creation, which is the perfecting of the physical creation
through the moral creation of a perfect, sinless humanity. 'The Being
of God' in Jesus is hence his perfect likeness to God. Jesus is what
every human being ought to be – what every human being longs to be
– what every human being can be, through faith in him. His 'God-
consciousness' must therefore be the consciousness of the creature
that is absolutely dependent on its Creator.

Following Schleiermacher's train of thought, modern nineteenth- and twentieth-century theologians tried to describe Jesus' sinless perfection more precisely, and to present it in the framework of his biography. Carl Ullmann described it as follows: 'His greatness is a greatness of inward being. His whole life is ruled by harmony. He is flooded round by peace and everywhere gives the impression of repose, tranquillity and assurance. His whole nature is cheerfulness and clemency, a pure symmetry of self-control.'[42] The image of 'the one who was completely pure' is a better proof of Christianity than all the miracles and healings.

But how can Jesus be the perfect human being when he was a man? Ullmann answers: 'We can call Jesus a man in the fullest sense of the word; but we must never see his unique character as resting upon his manliness, if manliness is opposed to womanliness. For he maintains equally all the gentleness, purity and tenderness of womanly nature.' And the romantic nineteenth-century portraits of Jesus do in fact display androgynous features. Right down to the present day, this modern Jesuology has made the human Jesus of Nazareth the projection screen for all the different fantasies of the true humanity which alienated men and women are seeking – men and women who have become strangers to themselves: Jesus offers pure personhood, absolute humanity, the faith that gives inner certitude, and so forth.

We find an analogous constitution given to the person of Christ in the later writings of Karl Rahner,[43] although his picture is sparser in content. In his ascendence christology he gives his earlier descendence christology a mystical reversal, and sets christology in the framework of anthropology, as its perfecting. The incarnation of God in Christ is God's communication of himself. We therefore have to say: the human being is the being which arrives at itself when God communicates himself to it. This statement is reversible: when human beings arrive at their true selves, God has communicated himself to them. The incarnation of God is therefore at the same time 'the uniquely supreme case of the actualization of man's nature in general'.[44] In Christ, God's self-immanence and human self-transcendence coincide. When God assumed human nature as his own, this 'simply arrived at the point to which it always strives by virtue of its essence'.[45] In the uncloseable openness of human self-transcendence 'the idea of Christ' is astir – this being the idea of human nature's fulfilment. Rahner discovers in the inward self-transcendence of human beings (or ascribes to it) a kind of 'anonymous' or 'seeking christology'.[46] If it were not for 'the idea of Christ' in the general make-up of human existence, no one would be in a position to recognize Jesus as 'the Christ', and to believe in him. By virtue of the seeking idea of Christ, everyone can recognize the Christ in Jesus, if they discover in Jesus the unique, supreme and perfect fulfilment of human existence in its complete commitment to God. With the help of this 'seeking christology', which Rahner ascribes to the general anthropology of inner self-transcendence, he is then able to talk about 'anonymous Christians'. A person who arrives at his essential nature and its true fulfilment is a 'Christian' whether he knows it or not, for 'he also accepts this revelation whenever he really accepts *himself completely*, for it already speaks *in* him'.[47] In true self-affirmation, human beings already accept the grace of their affirmation by God, whether they know it or not, and whether or not they give this name to it.

To be a Christian is accordingly for Rahner to be explicitly human, and to be human can mean being an anonymous Christian. 'The revelation of the Word in Christ . . . is simply the explicit form of that which we already are through grace.'[48] If through Christ the human being who surrenders himself to God, and the God who empties himself for human beings, both find expression, then the Christ event is the climax of both salvation history (from above) and evolution (from below). For 'self-transcendence' is the structural principle of the self-organization of matter and life. As spiritual beings men and women are the supreme 'self-transcendence of living matter', which in them attains to the mystery of God.[49] In this way, Rahner arrives at the cosmic horizon of biblical christology.

Rahner's reversal of incarnation christology into a christology of self-transcendence is in line with the new interpretation of metaphysical christology by way of anthropological categories which we find in Kant and Schleiermacher.[50] Rahner too ends up with Jesus, the perfect image of God, because he equates 'the idea of Christ' with fulfilled human existence.[51] But did tradition really mean no more by the redeeming God-human being than the prototypical 'man of God'? Is Jesus' relationship to God his Father really identical with the creature's relationship to his Creator? Is Jesus the Christ already 'the truly-human human being' or is he only 'the messianic human being' on the way to that redeeming future? Rahner's initial concern in his anthropological christology is an apologetic one: being a Christian is supposed to lose its peculiarly religious character in a humanistic world. But his concern is therapeutic as well: the home country of their identity in Christ is to be thrown open to alienated, searching human beings.

We have pointed to the identity crises of human beings in modern society which modern Jesuology hopes to solve. The point of reference of its soteriology is the self-divided human being – the human being who no longer knows what he is, and who has become a sinister figure even to himself and his fellows. The salvation about which modern christology speaks is therefore localized in 'the human heart'. The expression which people like to use here is 'existence', by which they mean a person's relation to himself, his subjectivity, his soul, his inner self-transcendence. Modern christology is soteriologically related to this existential experience of the individual self, but not to the external conditions of society which evoke these inner experiences and crises. In this respect, it has to be termed idealistic. This relegation of salvation to the inward realm of 'the heart' (and its presupposition in modern Jesuology) finds its sociological equivalent in the privatization of religion: 'religion is a private affair.'[52] A theology which with its christology goes along with the modern experience of subjectivity, and now conveys the content of the Christian doctrine of salvation only in as far as this is related to the individual subject of experience, is no longer willing – and no longer able – to call in question the social conditions and political limitations of this experience of subjectivity. This theology fits without any conflict into the requirements of the 'civil religion' of modern society. As the 'civil religion' of that society, it ministers to its educated and ruling classes, but not to its victims. Schleiermacher proclaimed the gospel of Christ to 'the cultured among Christianity's despisers', but not to 'poor sinners', remarked the poet Immermann, after hearing him preach.

§4 CHRISTOLOGY IN THE CONTRADICTIONS OF SCIENTIFIC AND TECHNOLOGICAL CIVILIZATION

1. *The Contradictions of Modern Civilization*

We have described 'the modern world' as the major project 'scientific and technological civilization'. Modern theology, with the modern principle that 'subjectivity is truth', has entered primarily into the inner self-experience of thinking human subjects in this civilization –

and more especially *male* subjects. We shall not consider merely what is allegedly 'incomplete' about this civilization, and its so-called 'residual risk'. We shall look at its fundamental contradictions, in order to align the soteriological aspect of christology towards the total misery of the present. Every theology has to enter into the changing conditions of the culture in which it is pursued, perceiving and developing its own concern in those conditions. And in this case our concern is christology. So the question is: *Who really is Christ for us today* (Bonhoeffer's formulation)? And who really are we today? But we shall not merely go into the rapid change in culture and awareness, and the increasing lack of orientation *in* this 'incomplete' civilization. We shall also look – and look first of all – at the other side of this civilization itself. For every civilization has its reverse side, which is a barbarism; every victorious history has its underside, which is the misery of the defeated; and all progress has its price. This other side is generally neither seen nor heard. Who bothers about the victims at whose expense he is living? But Christian theology would not be *Christian* and would not be *ecumenical* (in the proper sense of the word) if, in the civilization in which it has something publicly to say, it did not become the advocate of the people who are living 'on the other side'. It is not simply if it feels like it, that Christian theology concerns itself with the crises and contradictions of scientific and technological civilization, and the people who suffer under them. It *has to* make these things its concern.

(*a*) When scientific and technological civilization developed in Europe and North America, the Third World came into existence together with the First. From the very beginning, the vanquished countries and subjected peoples in America, Africa and Asia bore the largest share of the human and material costs of European progress. At the time of the Reformation, the destruction and exploitation of the American and Asiatic countries by Spain and Portugal began. At the time of the European Enlightenment, the French, and then the British, empire in Africa and India came into being, and also the slave trade. At the time of the bourgeois world of the nineteenth century, China was overshadowed by the opium war, and forced into inequitable treaties. At the moment we are living with the contradiction between the nations of the Third World, which are getting poorer and poorer, and deeper and deeper into debt, and the rapidly developing industrial nations of the First World. We see the growing North–South divide, the increasing debt gap, and however else we like to describe it. This is not the temporary crisis of a developing world civilization. It is a congenital defect of the civilization itself. The inequities and injustices in the world-wide economic system are not diminishing. They are increasing. But the community of the Christian church is made up of people in the Third World and in the First. So Christian theology cannot simply ask: who is Christ *for us* today? It has to ask: *Who really is Christ for the poor of the Third World?* and: Who is Christ for us, when we make use of their poverty for our own purposes? The great ecumenical challenge to Christian theology today is not the personhood of the people in the First World, who have become the 'determining subjects' of their own lives. It is the human dignity of the people in the Third World, who have been turned into non-persons.[53] The main problem for us here is not our own world – what Bonhoeffer termed 'the world that has come of age'. Our main problem is the world that we have made incapable of coming of age. If liberty is the central theme of modern European theology and philosophy, then for people in the Third World this means 'liberation' from oppression and apathy. Without their liberation, there cannot be any true liberty in the First World either. For true liberty is not a peculiar privilege. It is universal and indivisible.

The economic exploitation, racist humiliation and political subjugation of the peoples of the Third World are challenges to Christian theology today because these are the existential questions of the one church of Christ in this divided world. Third World theology, liberation theology, people's theology – these are developments of the greatest importance for theology in the First World. They make it impossible for that theology to dissipate itself in a theory of civil religion, which legitimates the First World's domination and privileges. The ecumenical community necessarily means seeing our own world with the eyes of its victims. It means developing a theology of conversion here which goes to meet the liberation theology of the victims there, and will correspond to that.[54] The crucified Christ has become a stranger to the civil religion of the First World and to that world's Christianity.

The Third World is not the only manifestation of the reverse side of the history of progress and the growth of economic and political power in the North Atlantic world. We discover this reverse side among 'the new poor' in the nations of the First World too.[55] Technological progress evidently benefits capital, not labour. The productivity of the economy is growing – and unemployment is not diminishing but increasing. A population is growing up which is living below the poverty line, people who are condemned to life-long unemployment, surplus people, who have no part in the wealth of the present, and have no future – people who are not needed. This contradiction too seems more than a passing crisis. It is inherent in the structure of technological development and in the market structure.[56] *Who is Christ for these 'surplus' masses of people today?*

(*b*) Technological civilization has brought incomparable progress in all sectors where the mastery of nature is concerned. But it has also produced the system of nuclear deterrent. It has been calculated that more than 50% of scientific intelligence and technical resources is at the disposal of the military and industrial complexes of the highly industrialized countries of the First World, for 'security' purposes. The possession and development of nuclear weapons promises a nation the status of a great power.[57] The dream of omnipotence can be fulfilled, if only negatively, through the ability to set off the universal nuclear inferno. With the atomic bomb, the final struggle for universal world hegemony has begun. That nation will win universal domination which can threaten all the other nations with nuclear annihilation, but which has made its own people invulnerable through a defence system in space (SDI). With the build-up of nuclear power, 'scientific and technological civilization' has reached its end-time – the time in which its own end and the end of all life on earth is possible at any moment.[58] It is not to be expected that mankind will ever forget what it has once learnt; so the struggle against the potential nuclear end will be an endless struggle for life – 'end-less' at best. For the first time in history, all the nations find themselves in a common situation: they are all of them together the single suffering object of the universal nuclear threat, even if some of them possess an atomic bomb and others do not. For the first time, a common world history is coming into being, even if only in a negative sense: the whole of humanity is in the same danger of nuclear extinction. In this universal deadly, end-time peril, life and survival would be conceivable only if humanity were to become a collective, active subject of its common survival, instead of the passive object of threat. Whether this speculative hypothesis ever turns into a real possibility that can be practically implemented, no one today knows. At least an international network in the awareness of political responsibility is beginning to make itself felt, in the form of security partnerships between potential enemies.[59]

From the very beginning, scientific and technological civilization was aimed at the human subjugation of nature, and the increase and consolidation of human power. So although people in this civilization are appalled by nuclear power, they are also fascinated by it. 'Nuclearism' has something religious about it, in both a positive and a negative sense, because it promises total power and total annihilation. The system of nuclear deterrent is in this respect a crypto-religion, for it makes the anxieties of men and women fathomless, and exploits their need for security to a limitless degree. It is the religion of nihilism, terminism, the perfected blasphemy, the self-made apocalypse of humanity.[60] Is the system of nuclear deterrent a temporary crisis of our civilization, or – as a built-in structural element – its destiny? What reversal of the system is required if we are to opt out of the system of nuclear deterrent? The Christian churches are challenged by nuclearism to the confession of faith which means renouncing 'the spirit, the logic and the practice of nuclear deterrent' and serving peace and life, in contradiction to this final product of scientific and technological civilization. They are challenged for their faith's sake, and by no means simply on the grounds of ethical and political judgments. *Who really is Christ for us today, threatened as we are by the nuclear inferno?*[61]

(*c*) As technological civilization expands and spreads, the ecological crisis grows with it:[62] the increasing destruction of the natural environment, the increasing annihilation of vegetable and animal species, the increasing exploitation of the earth's irreplaceable resources of energy, and the pollution of earth, water and air through poisonous waste and fumes. Because the ecological crisis grew up as a result of the human seizure of power over nature, it demonstrates particularly clearly the self-contradiction in which scientific and technological civilization – that major product of modern times – has become involved. The crisis is certainly *visible* in the natural environment; but it is actually a crisis of this modern system of domination itself. Human technology subjugates and exploits nature for human purposes. The sciences provide the dominating knowledge for nature's subjugation. The fundamental values of society which give birth to these sciences and technologies, and also govern them, are: the acquisition of power, the consolidation of power, and the pursuit of profit. Even if 'faith' in progress has been abandoned in the general mind of the public, modern industrial society is still programmed towards growth and expansion. The ancient values of pre-industrial, agrarian societies were equilibrium, harmony and a human society which found a home in a natural environment of self-regenerating natural forces. But these values have been pushed aside. The progress of modern civilization and the acquisition of still further power can be gained only at the cost and expense of nature. There are still short-term gains to be had. But in the long-term, the further progress of technological civilization in the direction it has taken up to now is driving us towards greater and greater environmental catastrophes, the end of which can only be universal ecological death – the break down of the system 'earth'. This is undoubtedly the third great challenge to Christian theology: *Who really is Christ for dying nature and ourselves today?*

The conference of the World Council of Churches in Vancouver in 1983 answered these three challenges to the Christian churches and theology with the call for a 'covenant for justice, peace, and the preservation of creation'.[63] We shall take up this objective and try to develop the soteriological aspect of christology in the context of these contradictions in modern civilization. Here we have to take account of the interdependence of the three different contradictions we have named; and we have also to remember the personal problems of the people who are forced to live with them, as objective facts. The inescapable political dimensions of this new paradigm for christology include the personal dimensions of modern Jesuology; and they also once more embrace the cosmological dimensions of the ancient church's christology – this time on an ecological level. But this can no longer be a christology that finds its correspondence in 'a Christian world'. It has to be a christology in the perils of the world, and a christology that challenges its destruction.

The distinction between a 'christology from above' and a 'christology from below' has come to be common coin in recent years, as a way of characterizing these two christologies.[64] Initially, this means no more than a difference of approach and method. One approach begins with the doctrine of God, and then develops a christology about the Son of God who has become a human being; the other approach starts with the human being Jesus of Nazareth, going on from that to develop his community with God. The first approach has a general metaphysical theology as premise, the second a general anthropology. In each case what is special and unique about Jesus Christ is presented in the framework of what is theologically, or anthropologically, generally held. But the general theological or anthropological concepts are not derived from the christology – that is, from the message and history of Jesus Christ; and they therefore lead to contradictions in the christological statements, which have then in the last resort to be presented in the form of paradoxes – 'the suffering of the impassible God', 'the presence of the dead Christ', and so forth.

The distinction 'from above' and 'from below' is in fact both superficial and misleading, because to know Jesus Christ practically and specifically can only be a matter of dialectical conditions: Jesus is known as the Christ of God for the sake of the God of promise, and in this process God is known as the Father of Jesus Christ for Jesus' sake. The nature and attributes of this God of Jesus Christ are therefore discerned from the history of Christ, from his passion and his raising from the dead; they cannot be perceived and premised from any other source. The same may be said about the knowledge of Jesus Christ's humanity and divinity: the earthly, human, and therefore historically knowable Christ is remembered and known in the light of his resurrection from the dead and his presence in the Spirit of God; and the raised and present Christ is perceived and known in the light of what was remembered and passed on about the life he lived. If this were not so, Jesus could not be identified with the Christ at all, or the Christ with Jesus. Here too, it is not a question of an alternative, but only of a dialectical perception of the mystery of Jesus Christ by way of remembrance, hope and experience.

If we wished to sum up, we should have to say: we have to look at Jesus' humanity in order to know his divinity, and we have to contemplate his divinity so as to know his humanity. Anyone who resolves this dialectical process of perception into dogmatic alternatives, is resolving – or dissolving – christology altogether. That person will end up with a theological christology without Jesus, or with an anthropological Jesuology without God. It is therefore high time that we abandoned the infelicitous phraseology 'from above' and 'from below' in christology, in order to turn to the more complex processes of coming to know Jesus Christ.

2. *The Theme and Scheme of Eschatological Christology Today*

As we have seen, the theme of *the christology of the ancient church* was too narrow in its definition – narrower than the christology of the New Testament. Christology's pre-history in the Old Testament's history of promise did not play any constitutive role in the christology of the patristic period. The proclamation and ministry of Jesus between his birth and his death are never mentioned in the christological dogmas. Finally, Christ's parousia – his coming in glory – disappears from the picture once the risen and exalted One is already worshipped as the glorified pantocrator. The christology of the ancient church is vertical, not horizontal: it focusses on the eternity of God, not on the history of the future of God's kingdom.

Modern *anthropological christology* takes as its subject the life and historical personality of Jesus. Everything which the christology of the ancient church saw in the Christ, the divine human being, modern christology expresses as the God-consciousness of the one and only sinless person, Jesus. But compared with the New Testament, the boundaries of this christology are also too narrow. Although its subject is the historical Jesus, no particular importance is ascribed to the Old Testament's history of promise; for as the perfect and true human being, Jesus could not well have been merely 'a Jew'. This christology is fraught with insoluble difficulties, because for it, the existence of Jesus finishes with his death. 'Resurrection' is given as reason for his presence today; but this presence cannot be the personal presence of Jesus Christ. It can be interpreted only as the continuing influence of his personality, or his 'concern'. In this case, however, his death has no special salvific meaning. If the christological theme is restricted to the historical person of Jesus, the very theme of christology evaporates.

Here we shall try to put forward the outline of a *christology in the eschatological history of God.* We are giving the name 'eschato-logical' to the coming redemption of the world, which is to be found in the universal messianic kingdom of peace, and in the perfecting of creation to become the kingdom of glory. By 'eschatological history' we mean the history which is aligned towards this future through God's calling and election, his promise and his covenant, and which is experienced and effected in the context of that future. It is history under the promise of life. It is in opposition to the history of death. The eschatological horizon which throws open this experience of history is God's horizon; and that means that it comprehends the history of both human beings and nature. The horizon of God the creator is a *cosmic* horizon. In it we see the history of nature too. All created things and conditions are true symbols and ciphers of this future. A christology of this divine eschatological history with the world discerns the person of Jesus as the Christ who is on the road, and in all the movements and changes of this history. God's eschatological history with the world is at heart God's history with Jesus, and Jesus' history with God. To be more precise: it is *the trinitarian history* of the Father, the Son and the Spirit.

Because history can only be *told*, in a sequence, we shall tell the different parts of this history one after another, and shall then try to reduce the tradition of ideas to a christological definition, so that we combine narrative elements with argumentative ones. We shall begin with the messianic mission of Jesus, the prophet of the poor, go on to the apocalyptic passion of Jesus, the Son of the Father, and then arrive at the transfiguring raising of Jesus from the dead. We shall devote particular attention to his reconciliation of the cosmos, as the Wisdom of creation. In the future of Christ in judgment and kingdom, we then find the completion of salvation in the glory of God, and the fulfilment of the promise of reconciliation in the redemption of the world. In accordance with the different situations of this divine eschatological history, the person of Jesus Christ changes and expands, until he is seen 'face to face'.

The second viewpoint which will be included and stressed in this outline is the relationship of Jesus Christ to other people, and his community with them. We are searching for an emphatically *social* christology. The traditional christologies have either focussed on his divine person – the divine Sonship – or on his historical personality – Jesus as a private person. Here we shall look at the 'social' person of Jesus, letting our understanding of his ministry be illuminated by his fellowship with the poor and the sick, with the people, with the women, and with Israel – a fellowship on which he himself was also dependent. This is also necessary when we consider the cross and the resurrection. If Jesus died as a private person, the significance of his death for salvation can only be ascribed to it subsequently. But he died as the brother of God-forsaken sinners, as head of the community of his followers, and as the Wisdom of the cosmos. If we wish to understand him, it is useful to start from his social relationships. Here the terms 'collective person' and 'representation person' which are used in the literature on the subject have to be defined more closely, so that we can also understand the processes of identification, solidarization and representation which confer community.

Not least among our concerns will be the shifting facets of the

divine person Jesus Christ which reflect his relationship to God –
Spirit, Son, Logos, Wisdom, Kyrios, and so forth. We understand
these, not as hypostases of the divine nature, but as trinitarian
relations in God; or in other words: divine self-relations in which
Jesus discovers and finds himself, and through which believers
delineate his divine mystery.

The individual chapters are designed in such a way that the
account of the ideas is followed by the conceptual interpenetration,
which enables us to understand the person of Jesus in his relation to
the future, in relation to his community with others, and in relation
to God. In order to make the unity of christology and christopraxis
clear, the account of the person of Christ is followed by an exposition
of his significance for salvation, and the meaning for ethics of the
way he chose.

III

The Messianic Mission of Christ

§1 SPIRIT CHRISTOLOGY

Jesus' history as the Christ does not begin with Jesus himself. It begins with the *ruach*/the Holy Spirit. It is the coming of the Spirit, the creative breath of God: in this Jesus comes forward as 'the anointed one' (*masi*ᵃ*h*, *christos*), proclaims the gospel of the kingdom with power, and convinces many with the signs of the new creation. It is the power of the creative Spirit: through this he brings health and liberty for enslaved men and women into this sick world. It is in the presence of the Spirit that God reveals himself to him with the name 'Abba', that Jesus discovers that he is the 'Son' of this Father, and that he lives out this intimate relationship in his community of prayer with God. The Spirit 'leads' him into the temptations in the desert. The Spirit thrusts him along the path from Galilee to Jerusalem. 'Through the eternal Spirit' (Heb. 9.14) he surrenders himself to death on the Roman cross. By the power of the Spirit, who gives new birth and new creation, God raises him from the dead. In word and meal, in community and baptism, Jesus is present in the Spirit 'for many', as the divine Kyrios. In the introductory chapters, we talked generally about 'the eschatological history of Jesus Christ'. We are now giving this a more specific designation, calling it the Spirit-history of Jesus Christ: the coming, the presence, and the efficacy of the Spirit in, through and with Jesus, is the hidden beginning of the new creation of the world.

We are starting with a *pneumatological christology*, because we discover that the efficacy of the divine Spirit is the first facet of the mystery of Jesus. In this way we are taking up Israel's messianic history of promise as the presupposition of every New Testament christology, and are developing christology out of the Jewish contours of the messianic promise.[1] This allows us to comprehend the messianic mission of the earthly Jesus, which was neglected in the christological dogma of Nicaea, and which has been passed down to us pre-eminently in the synoptic gospels. Spirit christology is also Wisdom christology; for in the Israelite tradition Spirit and Wisdom were initially closely related, and in later Wisdom literature they can even be used as interchangeable terms.[2] Spirit and Wisdom are incidentally feminine modes of the divine appearance. Spirit or Wisdom christology is the premise for every Son of God christology; for according to messianic tradition, the messiah who is anointed with the Spirit of God is 'the son of God'. Spirit christology and Wisdom christology express the messianic secret in different ways. But for that very reason, a Son of God christology is no substitute for either Spirit christology or Wisdom christology, and must not supplant them. Spirit christology is not set up in opposition to incarnation christology, for every doctrine of the incarnation begins with the statement 'conceived by the Holy Spirit'.[3] Nor is Spirit christology levelled at the doctrine of the two natures. But it does make it possible to absorb the exclusive christomonism of a christology of the God-human being into the fulness of trinitarian christology, with its wealth of relationships. The notion that there is an antithesis between an adoptionist and a pre-existence christology is a nineteenth-century invention.

When we are considering the New Testament testimony about the theological history of Jesus, it is impossible to talk about Jesus without talking about the workings of the Spirit in him, and about his relationship to the God whom he called 'Abba', my Father. The historical account of his life is from the very beginning a theological account, for it is determined by his collaboration – his co-instrumentality – with the Spirit and 'the Father'. His life history is at heart a 'trinitarian history of God'.[4] The complex dimensions of Jesus' life history are obscured if we talk about it only one of these dimensions – Jesus and God, or God and Jesus – so as to see him either as the heavenly God-man or as the earthly man of God. If christology starts by way of pneumatology, this offers the approach for a trinitarian christology, in which the Being of Jesus Christ is from the very outset a Being-in-relationship, and where his actions are from the very beginning interactions, and his efficacies co-efficacies.[5]

In this Spirit christology, we shall first of all look at the early traditions in the New Testament about Jesus' life – the Logion source (Q), the earliest form of Mark's Gospel (proto-Mark), and then the synoptic gospels and the Gospel of John. It looks as if by doing this we were coming close to 'the Jesus of history'. But this impression is deceptive. The gospels certainly recount the life-history of 'Jesus of Galilee'; and – because all counting begins with the first of a sequence – they start with Jesus' beginnings, either with John the Baptist, or with his being born of Mary. But they tell the story of his life in the light of his resurrection and his presence in the Spirit of God. This, I believe, may even be said of Q, which says nothing about Easter, but does not mention Jesus' death either, although its assumption is surely not that Jesus did not die. If the history of Jesus is made present through narrative in the light of his resurrection from the dead, what emerges is not a history in the modern sense of the word, but something new: 'the gospel of Jesus Christ'.[6] Here the *history* of the person who proclaimed to the poor the gospel of the kingdom of God actually itself becomes the *gospel*. The history of Jesus and his proclamation turns into the proclamation of Christ Jesus: Jesus' preaching of the kingdom is gathered up and made present in the apostolic preaching of the Christ.

In a reverse movement, the synoptic evangelists unfold this apostolic preaching of the Christ as they tell the life history of Jesus. They do not merely tell the history of a proclamation; they also tell the proclamation which this history itself is. The Jesus of the synoptic gospels is not the Jesus of the past – dead since Golgotha. By virtue of the eschatological raising from the dead, he is the One who is alive and present today.

The gospels therefore really do tell 'the history of a living person',[7] because they bring out the presence of the One past and the future of the One who has come. It is this that constitutes the unique character of the histories of Jesus in the gospels, compared with all the historicizations of his life.

In this making-present of past history, the salient point is the event of Jesus' death on the cross, and the experience of the presence of the risen One in the Spirit. The cross divides the community of Jesus' followers after Easter and their proclamation, from Jesus and his. But the Easter event also links the congregation with Jesus and his history – in what way, we shall see later. Here we are starting from the assumption that in the Easter appearances the risen One appeared as the One crucified, so that the resurrection witnesses could identify the living with the dead, the one present with the one past, the one to come with the one who had already come. It is the Easter event that prompts the confession of faith: 'Jesus is the Christ of God.' This event was called 'raising from the dead'. Raising from the dead is an eschatological symbol, and means that in the crucified Christ the future has already begun – the future of resurrection and eternal life, the annihilation of death and the new creation. But if the crucified Christ has been raised into the eschatological life of the new creation, then the raising of Jesus cannot be understood as simply one more event in his life, an event which took place historically, after his death. His death is a historical event and makes him a historical person. But his raising is much more: it is eschatological. The eschatological moment of his raising from the dead must therefore also be understood as God's eternal moment.[8] So the raising did not merely happen *synchronically* to the dead Jesus; it also happened *diachronically* to the whole Jesus in all the moments and aspects of his life and proclamation. That is why he is present in the power of the Spirit, not merely in his last moment on the cross but in all his moments from birth onwards. He is raised and present in the Spirit, not only as the one crucified, but also as the one baptized, as the healer, the preacher on the mount, the friend of sinners and tax-collectors, and the one whom the women accompanied to the moment of his death.

The *experience* of the presence of *the whole Christ* in the Spirit apparently reawakened *remembrances* of his whole life, and all his words and acts. Present experience and remembrance of his past correspond and must be kept in harmony. Nothing can be experienced of his presence which contradicts his history. Otherwise it would not be Jesus whose presence is experienced in the Spirit. To assume that Jesus' resurrection had a 'retroactive power' on his history, would be a violent assumption.[9] On the other hand, nothing can be remembered about Jesus' history which contradicts his experienced presence; for that presence would not then be the presence of the risen and exalted Lord.

Of course when the whole history of Jesus is made present in the light of his eschatological resurrection, something is introduced into the remembrances which must not absolutely have been part of them from the very outset: that is, the recognition of *who* Jesus really is. The remembrance of Jesus' openness for the revelation of the mystery of his person is recognizably reflected in the stories about what is known as 'the messianic secret'. If it is true that the Jesus described in the gospels is 'on the way to the One he will be',[10] then this fact must be understood in the light of his identification in the Easter appearances and in the presence of the Spirit. 'In the light of the resurrection' his past history is not merely made present and retrospectively interpreted; he himself is manifested in this past history in the light of his present future.

There are many different correspondences between the *experience* of the present Christ and the *remembrance* of the historical Jesus. These already took on the structure of a mirror image very early on: the One who is now raised from the dead to God is the One whom God once surrendered; the One who is now risen is the One who died; the One now exalted is the One who was once humiliated. The pre-Pauline hymn on Christ in Philippians 2 clearly shows the mirror-image correspondence between 'humiliated – exalted', but with a trinitarian difference: Christ humiliated himself – God the Father exalted him. It is therefore understandable that the idea of the *incarnation* of God's Son in Jesus of Galilee should be the inverted presupposition for the *exaltation* of Jesus of Galilee, and his installation as Son of God. The descendence and the ascendance match. Systematically, this must be understood to mean that Christ's exaltation and presence are the cognitive ground for his incarnation and his history; while the incarnation and history are the 'true' ground for his exaltation and presence. According to Aristotle, the first in the history of being is the last in the history of knowing, and vice versa. Consequently, the being of Jesus Christ is known in the light of his end, and his origin is known in the light of his future. In the light of the eschatological revelation in his raising from the dead, his history can be understood.

The experience of the Spirit evidently provides a differently supported logic of correspondence between the experience of Christ's presence and the remembrance of his history. If Christ is present now in the eternal Spirit of God, then his history must have been determined by this Spirit from the very beginning. One of the oldest confessional fragments, Rom. 1.3f., says: 'Born of the seed of David according to the flesh – proved to be Son of God with power according to the Spirit who sanctifies since the time when he rose from the dead.' I Tim. 3.16 also names these two stages: 'God is manifested in the flesh – vindicated in the Spirit.' According to this, the experience of the risen Christ is the experience of the Spirit. So in the history of the tradition, the process of the remembering making-present of the history of Christ apparently meant tracing the way back step by step: (1) His presence in the Spirit in the community of his people is presence 'since' his resurrection from the dead and his appearances in glory. (2) The presence of the Spirit in him personally dates 'from' his baptism by John, when he was about 30 years old (Mark 1.10). (3) He was strong in the Spirit 'from birth' (Luke 2.40). (4) He was actually conceived by the Holy Spirit (Luke 1.35). (5) He was in fellowship with the Father and the Spirit in eternity (John 1.1). (6) So the history of his Being presupposes the relationships of this Being to the Spirit and to the Father. Jesus grows into these relationships, and does so by way of the 'steps' we have cited, which are as it were the key junctures, or intersections, in the history of the Spirit with him.

The whole thrust of the experience of the presence of the Spirit of the risen Christ is towards presenting his whole history as the history of the Spirit with him. This is the point of approach for the pneumatological christology of the earthly life, ministry and way of Jesus Christ: the remembrance of the life-history of Jesus discerns Jesus' endowment with the Spirit and the workings of the Spirit in him. This is the sphere of pneumatological christology. Jesus appears as the messianic human being in the history of the Spirit of God with him and through him.

§2 CHRIST'S BIRTH IN THE SPIRIT

In this section we shall not talk about Jesus' virgin birth, as dogmatic tradition has done. We shall talk about the birth of Jesus Christ from the Holy Spirit; for what we are dealing with here is not a question of gynaecology; it is a theme of Christian pneumatology.

In the New Testament, Christ's 'virgin birth' is related only by Luke and Matthew. It was unknown, or considered unimportant, in wide areas of early Christian belief (the Pauline and Johannine sectors, for example). But from the third century onwards it became a firm component of the Christian creeds and theological christologies.[11] There is no special theological teaching about Mary in the New Testament, and no acknowledgment of her as 'mother of the Christ'. But when the christological conflicts began, mariology started to expand and to take on ever more elaborate forms in the ancient church. This mariology detached itself more and more from the New Testament testimony, and in certain Christian traditions was actually made the sustaining foundation of christology itself.[12] At no other point is the difference between the doctrine of the Orthodox and Roman Catholic churches and that of the New Testament as great as in the veneration of Mary, theological mariology, and the marian dogmas.[13] As this gap widened, the distance between the church's theology and Christianity's Jewish tradition grew with it. What does the Madonna with the Child Jesus in her arms – 'the Goddess and her hero' – have to do with the Jewish mother Miriam and her independent, self-willed son Jesus, who dissociated himself from her? Are the roots of the church's veneration of Mary and its mariology to be sought, not in Jewish Bethlehem, but in Ephesus, with its Diana cult?[14]

The third-century Roman baptismal creed runs: '. . . born of the Holy Spirit and the Virgin Mary . . .' In the Nicene creed the birth is linked with the incarnation: '. . . σαρκωθέντα ἐκ πνεύματος ἁγίου καὶ Μαριάς τῆς παρθένου . . .' (' . . . incarnate of the Holy Spirit and the Virgin Mary'; Latin: '. . . *incarnatus est de spiritu sancto ex Maria virgine* . . .'). In the Apostles' creed we read: '. . . *conceptus est de spiritu sancto, natus ex Maria virgine* ('. . . conceived by the Holy Spirit, born of the Virgin Mary . . .'). Are these confessional statements in accordance with the New Testament witness? Can they be shown to be a theologically necessary component of christology? Does this credal formula still have anything to say to us today? Is what it says today the same as what it once said?

1. *Christ's Birth in the Spirit from a Historical Perspective*

The virgin birth is not one of the pillars that sustains the New Testament faith in Christ. The confession of faith in Jesus, the Son of God, the Lord, is independent of the virgin birth, and is not based on it.[15] As we know, the faith of the New Testament has its foundation in the testimony to Christ's resurrection. It is only in Luke and Matthew that any link is forged with the nativity story. Moreover, we find the confession of faith in Christ in Christian traditions which know nothing of the virgin birth, or do not mention it. This indisputable fact alone allows us to draw the theological conclusion that the virgin birth does not provide the justification for confessing Christ. If there is a link at all, then the matter is reversed: the mariology does not sustain the christology; the christology sustains the mariology. It is for Christ's sake that his mother Mary is remembered and venerated.

The gospels mention Mary only in passing. She is not one of the group of disciples, women and men, who moved about with Jesus. Jesus' repudiation of his mother and his brothers and sisters (which was so scandalous and is therefore probably historically based: Mark 3. 31–35 par.), and Mary's absence, according to the synoptic passion narratives, from the group of women at the cross of her dead son, show how remote she was from Jesus and his message. It is only in the Jerusalem congregation after Easter (Acts 1.14) that we find Mary, and Jesus' brothers – but as believers, not relations. According to the gospels, Mary Magdalene played a central part in the group of women and men disciples, and for Jesus himself as well – not least as an eye witness of his death on the cross and his resurrection; in the middle ages she was therefore called 'the apostle of apostles'. But we look in vain to find a similar importance ascribed in the New Testament to Mary, the mother of Jesus.[16] Only on the fringe, in the nativity stories, does she acquire a christological importance, and then with a gesture which points away from herself, as it were, to Christ alone: '*fiat*' – 'so be it'. A biblically legitimated mariology can only be a christocentric one. This is what is meant by the statement which would otherwise be a truism: without Christ, no Mary.

Neither the nativity story in Matthew nor the (probably older) story in Luke are mariological in the church's sense. They are christocentric, for the concern of both is to proclaim the birth of the messianic child. According to Luke, the angel's announcement cites Isa. 7.14 and II Sam. 7.12f., but says nothing at all about a virgin birth. The messianic child is to be called 'Jesus'. He will be called 'Son of the Most High' and will become the Davidic messiah-king of Israel. It is only when Mary asks 'How?' that the interpretation follows, with its reference to her 'overshadowing' through the Holy Spirit, 'that power of the Most High', and its conclusion: 'Therefore the holy one to be born of you will be called the Son of God' (v. 35). The change of title between the announcement and the interpretation points to a Jewish-Christian congregation in a hellenistic environment. The Jews understood the messianic title, and it is lent familiarity and force through a prophetic proof. The title Son of God was understood even by Gentiles, and it is given a vindicatory explanation through the legend about the supernatural birth, which they knew from other contexts. Marvellous divine beings also have a marvellous divine birth. The story of the birth of Romulus was told in just the same way.

In Matthew the human centre is Joseph, not Mary. It is to him that the angel speaks, not to Mary. The theme is Joseph's 'justice'. Matthew 1.18–25 too is talking about an announcement, not about the nativity story itself. Life in the Spirit of God and Jesus as the child of God are thought of as being so intimately connected – even in Jesus' very beginnings, in his mother's womb – that this suggested the notion that Mary was pregnant through the Holy Spirit. What this idea is saying is: 'that which is conceived in her is of the Holy Spirit' (v. 20). According to v. 21 the divine child is given the name 'Jesus', which is said to mean that he is the Redeemer who saves his people from their sins. But according to v. 23 he is to be called 'Immanuel', 'God is with us'. This is in fact the impress which Matthew puts on the whole of his gospel, from its beginning to its end in 28.20: 'Lo, I am with you always, until the end of the world.' 'The presence of the exalted Lord among his people shows him to be the Immanuel, God with us.'[17] In Luke, the link found in the ancient creed (Rom. 1.3f.) between the Easter enthronement and the title of Son is projected into the birth of Jesus. In Matthew, it is Jesus' resurrection and his exaltation to be the Immanuel which are projected into the nativity story. In both Luke and Matthew, the promise of Jesus' birth is intended to say that he is the messianic Son of God and the Lord of the messianic kingdom not only since his resurrection from the dead, and not merely since his baptism by John the Baptist in Jordan, but by his heavenly origin and from his earthly beginnings. It was not only Jesus' ministry which was *in* the power of the Holy Spirit. He springs from the very beginning *from* the power of the Most High, the Holy Spirit. There was no time and no period of his life when Jesus was not filled with the Holy Spirit. Neither in Luke nor in Matthew nor anywhere else in the New Testament is there any link between the story of the virgin birth and the idea of the incarnation or pre-existence of the eternal son of God. But this link was then forged throughout the christology of the ancient church.[18]

In the literary sense, the stories about the announcement of the virgin birth are legends.[19] They are deliberately told in such a way that no mention is made of either witnesses or historical traditions. We are not told from whom the narrator heard the story. Neither Joseph nor Mary is named as guarantor. This distinguishes these stories so sharply from the testimonies of the men and women who witnessed the Easter appearances of the risen Christ, that it is impossible to talk about comparable miracles at the beginning of Christ's life-history and at its end.[20] But it will be permissible for us to assume that the nativity stories are secondary, retroactive projections of the experiences of the Easter witnesses with the risen Christ who is present in the Spirit; for they transfer to the pre-natal beginnings of Christ precisely that which has become manifest in the risen One who is present in the Spirit. In this way the narrators follow the logic that future and origin must correspond. If Christ has ascended into heaven, then he must have come down from heaven; and if he is present *in* the Spirit of God, who is the giver of life (I Cor. 15.45), then he must have come into life *from* this divine Spirit.

Because these narrators make no distinction between history and legend in the modern sense, but intend to relate a 'gospel', no objection can be made to the modern designation 'legend' for the stories about Christ's nativity. At that time the inherent truth of the nativity stories had to be expressed in the form of an aetiological myth. The truth is to be found precisely *in this mythical story* about Christ's origin, not in the biological facts. It is therefore factually inappropriate to call the virgin birth historical, let alone 'biological'; and modern positivist characterizations of this kind do anything but preserve the intention and truth of the story. In actual fact they destroy it. The narrators' aim is not to report a gynaecological miracle. Their aim is to confess Jesus as the messianic Son of God and to point at the very beginning of his life to the divine origin of his person.[21]

2. Christ's Birth in the Spirit from a Theological Perspective

In the history of the tradition there are evidently two different ideas about the way in which the origin of Jesus, as Son of God and Immanuel, can be told in mythical form.

The first idea suggests that God brought about the miracle of Mary's pregnancy through the Holy Spirit, that 'power of the Most High': 'Conceived by the Holy Spirit, born of the Virgin Mary.' This is a way of saying that *God alone is the Father of Jesus Christ,* and that he is his Father not merely according to Jesus' God-conscious-ness, but in his whole personhood, from the very beginning. God is to be declared the Father of Jesus Christ in so exclusive a way that the earthly fatherhood of Joseph has to be excluded. This corresponds in a very literal way to Jesus' saying: 'Call no man your father on earth, for you have one Father, who is in heaven' (Matt. 23.9). The patriarchal succession of generations is broken off for the sake of the history of the promise. According to this idea, God is the Father of Jesus Christ, the Holy Spirit is the male seed, and Mary, who is in the human sense a virgin, is his mother.[22]

The second idea sees behind the human motherhood of Mary *the motherhood of the Holy Spirit*. The ancient Roman baptismal creed therefore has the parallel formulation 'born from the Holy Spirit and the Virgin Mary'. Believers experience the motherhood of the Holy Spirit in their own 'miraculous birth' from the Spirit of God. That is why the Gospel of John directly precedes its statement about the incarnation of the eternal Word by saying: 'But to all who received him, who believed in his name, he gave power to become children of God; who were born, not of blood nor of the will of the flesh nor of the will of a man, but of God' (1.12, 13). If those who believe in Christ are 'born from the Spirit' to be God's children, as the metaphor says, then the Holy Spirit is the divine mother of believers – and of course the 'virgin mother'. The ancient Syrian and the more modern Moravian doctrine about 'the motherly office of the Holy Spirit' has its roots here, as well as in the function of the Paraclete, who comforts as a mother comforts.[23] The point of comparison for understanding the birth of Christ is not a human process of procreation and conception; it is the experience of the Spirit encountered by the men and women who are born again to become children of God. Because this experience of the Spirit is to be found in the community of Christ's people, through which Jesus Christ becomes 'the first-born among many brethren' (Rom. 8.29) and sisters, this first-born brother must himself be the archetype of the divine sonship and daughterhood in the Spirit. That is why the 'first-born brother' is called 'the only begotten Son of God'. The history of his primal and original birth from the Spirit of God merely brings out the difference that he is from the beginning and by nature that which believers become in his fellowship, through Word and Spirit: the messianic child of God. The Mary who in human and temporal terms is 'a virgin' must then be seen as a symbolic embodiment and as the human form of the Holy Spirit, who is the eternally virginal and divine mother of Christ. She should not be thought of as the human woman who becomes pregnant by the Holy Spirit, imagined in male terms. Looked at in this other light, the Holy Spirit would rather be the great virginal, life-engendering mother of all the living, and as such the divine archetype of Mary, the mother of Jesus Christ.[24] When we remember the feminine symbolism about the nature and activity of the Spirit which we find in Jewish, Syrian and Christian traditions, this idea is not wrong or inappropriate. In the Gospel of Thomas, Christ talks about the Holy Spirit as his 'mother'.[25]

Let us now try to discover the theological intention behind the two ideas about the virgin birth of Christ, and Mary's significance for salvation.

First of all, these nativity stories are trying to say that God is bound up with Jesus of Nazareth not fortuitously but essentially. From the very beginning, God is 'the Father of Jesus Christ'. His fatherhood does not merely extend to Christ's consciousness and his ministry. It embraces his whole person and his very existence. Consequently, the messiah Jesus is *essentially* God's Son. He does not become so at some point in history, from a particular moment in his life. He is from the very beginning the messianic Son, and his beginning is to be found in his birth from the Holy Spirit. Not only his consciousness but his physical being too bears the imprint of his divine sonship. This distinguishes the incarnation *from* or *out of* the Spirit from the indwelling of the Spirit *in* human beings. *Incarnation* has no presuppositions. *Inhabitation* presupposes human existence. If incarnation is identified with inhabitation, christology is dissolved in anthropology.

For the theologians of the patristic church, Christ's virgin birth was a sign, not so much of his divinity, as of his true humanity. It was gnostic theologians who, for the sake of Christ's divinity, allowed him only to 'appear' in the body, without really being there: the eternal Logos merely clothed himself in human form, in order to spiritualize human beings. Against this, the orthodox theologians of the ancient church stressed the reality of the incarnation of the Son of God by way of the virgin birth from Mary, just as they inserted 'the resurrection of the body' into the Apostles' creed; for 'what is not assumed cannot be redeemed either'. Consequently the eternal Logos assumed full and whole humanity and 'became flesh' through the Holy Spirit.[26]

If we wished to bring out this intention of the nativity story today, we should have to stress the *non*-virginal character of Christ's birth,[27] so as to 'draw Christ as deep as possible into the flesh', as

Luther said. He was a human being like us, and the addition 'without sin' in the Epistle to the Hebrews (4.15) does not refer to sexual reproduction. We find this unbiblical identification for the first time in Augustine's doctrine of original sin. In this context a different aspect should be stressed today: if the Son of God became wholly and entirely human, and if he assumed full humanity, then this does not merely take in human personhood; it includes human nature as well. It does not embrace adult humanity alone; it comprehends humanity diachronically, in all its phases of development – that is, it includes the being of the child, the being of the foetus and the embryo. The whole of humanity in all its natural forms is assumed by God in order that it may be healed. So it is 'human' and 'holy' in all its natural forms, and is prenatally by no means merely 'human material', or just the preliminary stage to humanity. That is why theologically the true and real birth of Christ has to be stressed. According to today's understanding of things, talk about Christ's 'virgin birth' through Mary dangerously narrows down his humanity, if the virgin birth is taken to mean that a supernatural-human process takes the place of a human-natural one. 'We [cannot] see any longer why Jesus as Son of God should come into the world in a different way from anyone else.'[28] If according to John 1.12 the point of comparison with the birth of the Son of God is to be found in the rebirth of believers from the Spirit into divine sonship and daughterhood, then, and then especially, we do not have to assume any supernatural intervention. We should rather view the whole process of the human begetting, conception and birth of Jesus Christ as the work of the Holy Spirit. Christ's birth from the Spirit is a statement about Christ's relationship to God, or God's relationship to Christ. It does not have to be linked with a genealogical assertion.

The other theological *motif* which led to the idea about Christ's virgin birth must be seen in the close link between the divine Spirit and the divine Sonship. According to Jewish expectation, the messianic son of God is the human being who is filled with the Spirit of God. In a reverse movement, in the messianic era the messianic human being brings about the pouring out of the Holy Spirit on all flesh. He comes in the Spirit of the Lord and brings the Spirit of the Lord, so that it fills the whole earth. If we now wished to say that Jesus was from the very beginning (and hence in his whole existence) the messianic child of God, we should also have to say that from the very beginning he was filled with the Spirit of God, and that his whole being is the warp and weft of the Spirit. He comes into existence from the Spirit, as the Nicene creed says. The descent of the Spirit of God and its indwelling in Mary must even precede the expectation of the messianic Son of God. Otherwise we should not be able to say that he came 'from the Spirit'. The Spirit does not 'create'; it 'engenders' and 'brings forth', as the birth metaphor says. If the messiah is called the Son of God, then to be consistent we have to talk about the Spirit as his divine 'mother'. He therefore comes into the world from the Father and from the Spirit, and with his coming God's Spirit takes up its dwelling in the world; first of all in the messianic Son, through his birth – then in the fellowship of the children of God, through their rebirth (John 3.6; I Peter 1.3, 23) – then through the rebirth of the whole cosmos (Matt. 19.28). The birth of the messianic Son of God 'from the Spirit' is the beginning and the sign of hope for the rebirth of human beings and the cosmos through God's Shekinah. That is why the indwelling of the Holy Spirit has to be told at the same time as the birth of Christ.

If we take the birth of Christ from the Spirit seriously, then much that the church has ascribed to 'the Virgin Mary' is transposed to God the Holy Spirit himself, and Mary can once again be that which she was and is: the Jewish mother of Jesus. The Holy Spirit, not Mary, is the source of life, the mother of believers, the divine Wisdom and the indwelling of the divine essence in creation, from which the face of the earth will be renewed. Mary is a witness, and in the form of the myth of Christ's origin she also embodies the indwelling of the life-giving Spirit. The so-called 'feminine' side of God, and the 'motherly mystery' of the Trinity, is to be sought for, not in Mary but in the Spirit. It is only after that, in a second stage, that it can be discovered in the story told about Mary. If the 'virgin birth' reflects the life-giving and engendering mystery of the Holy Spirit, then any possible mariology has to be part of pneumatology. If in the history of Christ Mary has this ministering function, a function that points away from herself, then and then especially she will arrive at her full significance in the history of the indwelling of the Holy Spirit. It is the Holy Spirit, not Mary herself, who is co-worker with the messianic Son of God, and who together with him will redeem the world. The history of Christ is a trinitarian history of the reciprocal relationships and mutual workings of the Father, the Spirit and the Son. Wide sectors of the church's later mariology must be viewed as a pneumatology narrowed down to the church. If we stop talking about Christ's virgin birth, and talk instead about his birth from the Spirit, we can then say: without the Holy Spirit there is no Mary, and without pneumatology there is no mariology which is sufficiently related to Christ.[29]

§3 CHRIST'S BAPTISM IN THE SPIRIT

1. *John the Baptist and Jesus of Galilee*

As far as we have any historical information on the subject, the public history of Jesus began when he was about thirty years old (Luke 3.23), with John the Baptist. The gospels take the story of John the Baptist first, following it witn the story of Jesus' ministry, their purpose being to show that Jesus emerged from the baptismal movement started by John, and that this provided the foundation for the Jesus movement. Here we are mainly following Q and Mark's Gospel. For both of them, the era of salvation that dawned with Jesus dates from John the Baptist, because it was through the baptism in Jordan that the Spirit of Yahweh/the Holy Spirit came upon Jesus and filled him with the power of his messianic commission. It is historically probable that Jesus was one of John's disciples at the Jordan, and was convinced by his apocalyptic message. It was only when John was thrown into prison by Herod for political reasons, and was silenced, that Jesus returned to Galilee and preached his gospel of the kingdom of God publicly (Mark 1.14). He took John's place in the eschatological history of the kingdom of God, to which John of course already belonged, since he too was 'filled with the Holy Spirit', as Luke says (1.15). John's cruel end was the hour of Jesus' public beginning. But Jesus 'way of righteousness' begins with his baptism (Matt. 3.15). The first question for christology therefore has to be: who was John the Baptist?[30]

John lived in the desert and preached baptism in the River Jordan for the forgiveness of sins and for repentance. He preached in the awareness that it was 'the final hour'. 'Even now the axe is laid to the root of the trees' (Matt. 3.10). God's judgment is immediately impending, and will begin with the house of God, Israel. Election will not protect her: 'I tell you, God is able from these stones to raise up children to Abraham' (Matt. 3.9). John proclaimed 'the future wrath of God' and called God's people to repent and return to the Torah: 'Do neither violence nor injustice to anyone' (Luke 3.14). Only those who turn back to God's way of righteousness have a chance in the coming divine judgment. John moved into the Judaean desert, living from the sparse provender that the desert provided – 'locusts and wild honey' – and dressed in beggar's garments. He called Israel to a 'new exodus': through the wilderness, over Jordan, into the promised land.

Everything John does is rich in symbolism and full of the remembrance of God's age-old history with Israel. He baptizes Israel's repentant people in the Jordan, in preparation for the new, final entry into 'the land of God'. John's message, symbolism and baptism constitute an 'eschatological sacrament of repentance'.[31] This baptism is different from ritual lustrations because of its eschatological finality. Nor is it the initiation rite for a new community. It is the eschatological sign of the conversion of all Israel. Although John had disciples, he evidently did not found any new sect. He proclaimed to the whole people a conversion in the awareness that all that was ahead was the free space of the imminent rule of God. John's eschatology was the expectation of God's imminent judgment, which opens the way for the kingdom of his justice and righteousness.

Jesus of Galilee recognized this message and the sign of conversion – the baptism of John – and he believed in John's divine mission. John's baptism was 'of God' (Mark 11.30). He brought 'the way of righteousness' – the true, end-time interpretation of the Torah (Matt. 21.32). He was 'more than a prophet' (Matt. 11.9) and 'the greatest of all human beings'. That is why Luke tells the story of John's birth parallel to Jesus' nativity story. John too was already 'filled with the Holy Spirit' in his mother's womb, and was 'strong in the Holy Spirit' (Luke 1.15, 80). These statements were made about Jesus as well, with the difference that Jesus was actually 'conceived' by the Holy Spirit, which Luke does not say of John. For Jesus and his disciples, John was the final summing up of the promises of the prophets and the Torah. For them he was the 'Elijah' who had come to usher in the end-time (Matt. 11.14). Jesus evidently did not see John merely as a 'forerunner', as 'an angel of God who prepares the way for him' (Mark 1.2); he actually took over John's message, and carried his eschatological mission further: 'Repent, for the kingdom of heaven is at hand.' This is the way Matthew sums up the message of both John (3.2) and Jesus (4.17). That is why we hear sayings of John on Jesus' lips – for example Matt. 7.19: 'Every tree that does not bear good fruit is cut down and thrown into the fire.' That is why we hear both from John and from Jesus the voice of 'the divine Wisdom' who is to return at the end-time (Luke 7.35; Matt. 11.19).[32]

If we compare John with the earthly Jesus, it looks as if Yahweh's self-same *ruach* and the self-same divine Wisdom speaks through them both and, after them, also through the company of their disciples, who called themselves 'prophets'. John and Jesus are 'God's prophets' and yet 'more than prophets'. Through both of them God's end-time finds words. Both suffered the same fate, being murdered for political reasons, the one by Herod, the other by Pilate. What are the differences between them?

The differences between Jesus and John are also still quite recognizable, historically speaking. John proclaimed the coming kingdom of God as a judgment of wrath on this unrepentant generation. But Jesus proclaims the coming kingdom of God as prevenient grace to the poor and to sinners. John left the civilized world and went to live in the desert. Jesus left the desert and went to the busy villages of Galilee. John lived on a starvation diet, from what the desert provided. But Jesus ate bread and drank wine with the poor and sinners of the people. John counted as an ascetic. Jesus was considered a 'glutton and a drunkard' (Matt. 11.19). John baptized for repentance. Jesus did not baptize anyone, but he forgave many people their sins. What is behind these external differences?

In my view, they are based on Jesus' unique baptismal experience. Of course we only hear about this at third or fourth hand. But we can draw certain conclusions from the agreements between the gospel accounts. Jesus was baptized together with a great number of other people (Luke 3.21); but what he evidently experienced was not 'the forgiveness of sins for conversion'. He experienced something different. The gospels call it the experience of the Spirit: 'The Spirit descended upon him like a dove' (Mark 1.10). 'God anointed Jesus of Nazareth with the Holy Spirit and with power', says the Acts of the Apostles (10.38).

Linked with this endowment with the Spirit is a vision of 'the open heavens' (Mark 1.10). This is a sign of salvation, for the image of 'the closed heavens' is a way of describing the affliction and the forsakenness of human beings, and the barrenness of the earth. The endowment with the Spirit is accompanied by a divine audition: either a personal one, to Jesus himself: 'Thou art my beloved Son, with whom I am well pleased' (Mark 1.11); or one addressed to the bystanders: 'This is my beloved Son, with whom I am well pleased' (Matt. 3.17). This is the enthronement pronouncement and the theological legitimation of Israel's kings which we find in Psalm 2.7. Jesus is uniquely endowed with the Spirit, his anointing is 'without measure' (John 3.34), and the Spirit 'rested' on him – that is to say, in him the Shekinah found its abiding dwelling place. According to the tradition of Israel's messianic promise, it is self-evident that all this leads to the divine Sonship of the one so anointed and endowed.[33] With the indwelling of Yahweh's *ruach*, Jesus' relationship to God becomes one of sonship, and he perceives that God's relationship to him is one of fatherhood. This too is entirely in accordance with Israel's messianic tradition.

But something unique is added: a new revelation of the name of God. Until the hour in Gethsemane, Jesus in his prayers always addressed God exclusively and with incomparable intimacy as 'Abba', my Father.[34] This suggests that the 'revelation' to Jesus about which Matt. 11.27 speaks should be related to his baptism:

> All things have been delivered to me by my Father;
> and no one knows the Son except the Father,
> and no one knows the Father except the Son
> and any one to whom the Son chooses to reveal him.

Otherwise it is only the Gospel of John in the New Testament that talks about so exclusive and reciprocal a knowing between Jesus and God the Father. But there is nothing to contradict the synoptic origin of this saying, or to gainsay its roots in Wisdom theology. This theology makes it understandable why Jesus does not merely proclaim as prophet the far-off, sovereign kingdom of God the Lord, but now proclaims as brother the imminent, loving kingdom of his Father. The 'Abba' name for God gives Jesus' proclamation of the kingdom a new quality, compared with John the Baptist, and with the prophets too: in the kingdom of Jesus' Father, what rules is *the justice of mercy* for all the weary and heavy-laden. In the kingdom of Jesus' Father, what reigns is *the liberty of the children of God* in the Spirit.

This allows us to draw the following conclusions: (1) When Jesus proclaims the 'imminent' kingdom of God (Mark 1.15), he is proclaiming the intimate nearness of God the Father, the nearness which is described through the name Abba; he is not proclaiming the coming of the wrathful judge of the world. (2) He demonstrates the nearness of the kingdom of God, not through threats and asceticism but through signs of grace to distraught men and women, and through miracles of health for life that has been sick. (3) According to his own understanding, the era in which he preached and ministered is not the 'last days' before the judgment, with their harassing distress. It is the liberating 'fulness of time' of the messiah (Gal. 4.4).

According to Luke 4.18ff., the endowment with the Spirit moves Jesus to proclaim in Nazareth the messianic sabbath year, which is the endless sabbath, the consummation of creation. That is why Matthew can describe the difference between Jesus and John by saying: 'He who is least in the kingdom of heaven is greater than he' (Matt. 11.11). It is the difference between the last time before the dawning of the kingdom of God, and the first time in that kingdom.

2. *The Kenosis of the Divine Spirit – Jesus' Endowment with the Spirit*

If the fullness of Yahweh's *ruach*/the Holy Spirit was alive in Jesus, then this energy is also the worker of all his works. Where the Spirit is not active, Jesus cannot do anything either. Dogmatic tradition has often set bounds to this energy of the Spirit which works through Jesus, in order to distinguish its workings, as something 'spiritual', from everything that might be called political. It cut off from earthly life the life which Jesus created in this power of the Spirit, calling it 'a heavenly life'.[35] As a result, this tradition maintained that the kingdom of Christ was 'not of this world' (John 18.36), in the sense that it was a purely spiritual kingdom, localized in heaven. This view was based on a spiritualistic misunderstanding of Yahweh's *ruach*/ the Holy Spirit. According to the Old Testament traditions (Gen. 1.2; Ps. 104.29f.), Yahweh's *ruach* is God's own power of creation, and the power of life which it communicated to all created things, in heaven and on earth. In considering Jesus' baptism and his endowment with the Spirit too, we have to understand the Spirit as *the creative energy* of God and *the vital energy* of everything that lives. In the Old Testament traditions, the Spirit is also the divine *saving power* through which God led Israel out of slavery into the land of freedom. In thinking about the power of the Spirit in Jesus as well, we have to proceed from this saving experience of Israel's, which was an experience of the divine Spirit. Yahweh's *ruach*/the divine Spirit is also, and not least, the Spirit who spoke through the prophets. In Jesus too he is *the prophetic Spirit*, who speaks through the messianic plenipotentiary (Isa. 61).

If we understand Yahweh's *ruach*/the Holy Spirit as the creative energy, the saving and the prophetic power of God, then the continuing presence of this Spirit implies the beginning of the end-time deliverance of men and women, the new creation and the manifestation of God's glory. The continuing presence of the Spirit in Jesus is the true beginning of the kingdom of God, and of the new creation in history. That is why in this power Jesus drives out demons, heals the sick and restores spoiled creation. This presence of the Spirit is the authority behind his proclamation. The Spirit gives it the power of conviction, and the Spirit causes the proclamation to be accepted in faith. The Spirit leads Jesus into the wilderness and accompanies him from Galilee to Jerusalem. In the first chapters of the synoptic gospels especially, the Spirit is presented as the divine determining subject of the way Jesus took. The divine Spirit who indwells Jesus, initiates and makes possible the relationship of the Father to the Son, and of the Son to the Father. In the Spirit, God experiences Jesus as the messianic child, and Jesus experiences God as 'Abba'. Jesus' relationship to God reflects God's relationship to Jesus. Because this last is theologically speaking the ground for the first, it is also the person-forming element in the mutuality of Jesus and God.

In the synoptic gospels, the story about Jesus' baptism and his full-filment with the Spirit is immediately followed by the story about the temptation in the wilderness (Mark 1.12,13; Matt. 4.1–11; Luke 4.1–13). Why? What are the gospel writers trying to say? The three accounts have the following features in common: (1) The Spirit led Jesus into the desert. (2) Satan tempted him. (3) The angels ministered to him. (4) He was among the beasts. According to Matthew and Luke, the devil, 'the tempter', assails Jesus' divine Sonship: 'If you are the Son of God, then . . .' What is in question here is not a metaphysical divine Sonship, but the messianic kingdom of Jesus, which is put to the test through temptations, and which is more precisely defined in these temptations; for the possibilities which the tempter offers Jesus are ways of seizing messianic power over Israel and the nations: bread for the hungry masses; universal power through the renunciation of God and the worship of Satan, who can give this power; the messianic sign for the liberation of Israel in the temple of the holy city. Matthew reverses the order of the second and third temptations, in order to stress that the climax is the tempter's promises of power to the messianic king.

We have to see this potential messianic 'seizure of power', which Jesus and the early Christians rejected, against the background of Jesus' helplessness in the story of the passion and his death on the cross. Filled with the Spirit, Jesus becomes the messianic Son of God; but through the temptations into which this same Spirit leads him, he is denied the economic, political and religious means for a 'seizure of power'. Here, that is to say, his passion in helplessness is prefigured: his victory comes through suffering and death. At his triumphal entry into Jerusalem he offers the people no bread, at his entry into the temple he does not perform the messianic sign, and before the Roman Pilate he does not call on the heavenly legions in order to win a military victory. From the story of the temptations the way to the cross follows. But the way to the cross is the way which God's Spirit 'leads' Jesus. The way of Jesus Christ through his passion is therefore also to be understood as the way of passion traced by God's Spirit, whose strength is made perfect in Jesus' weakness. The angels 'minister' to Jesus on this path, but in hiddenness, in the power of self-giving and suffering, not in the form of heavenly legions, against which the legions of the Romans are as nothing.

What being filled with the Spirit meant for Jesus' proclamation and his life is described on every page of the gospels. But they say nothing about what this 'descent' of the Spirit, and his indwelling in Jesus, means for God's Spirit itself. When the Spirit descends on Jesus 'like a dove', or 'in the form of a dove', the ancient symbol brings out God's tender commitment, which can best be grasped in feminine symbols – the commitment in which Jesus finds his identity and leads his life. If we talk about a 'condescending' of the Spirit, we have also to talk about a *kenosis of the Holy Spirit*, which emptied itself and descended from the eternity of God, taking up its dwelling in this vulnerable and mortal human being Jesus.[36] The Spirit does indeed fill Jesus with authority and healing power, but it does not make him a superman; it participates in his weakness, his suffering, and his death on the cross. Through its indwelling, the Spirit binds itself to Jesus' destiny. The Spirit proceeds from the Father and rests on Jesus, so that it goes forth from Jesus and comes upon men and women. In this way God's Spirit becomes *the Spirit of Jesus Christ*. It surrenders itself wholly to the person of Jesus in order to communicate itself through Jesus to other men and women. So the reverse side of the history of Jesus Christ is the history of the Spirit. The history of God's saving, creative and prophetic Spirit is indivisibly bound up with the history of Jesus Christ. It is the one single history of the mutual relationship between the Spirit and Jesus, Jesus and the Spirit. This is what Jesus' baptism means for the Holy Spirit.

The special feature of pneumatological christology is its openness for the activity of the self-same Spirit beyond the person and history of Jesus Christ. John the Baptist was full of the Spirit and driven by the Spirit. The Spirit spoke through the prophets. The creative Spirit is at work in the whole creation. Through Jesus Christ, the Spirit is sent upon the gathered community of his followers, so that its efficacy spreads. Liberal theologians liked to use this fact to relativize Jesus, as one bearer of the Spirit among many others. But by so doing they overlooked the unique character of Jesus' imbuement with the Spirit, which led to his divine Sonship and his special mission. On the other hand, Calvin already perceived that the Spirit of Jesus was given, not for himself alone, but for the whole community of his followers, whose head he is from the beginning.[37] This shows that Jesus was not baptized into the Spirit as a private person, but *pars pro toto*, representatively, as one among many, and as one for many. He received the Spirit for the sick whom he healed, for the sinners whose sins he forgave, for the poor whose fellowship he sought, for the women and men whom he called into his discipleship. He received the Spirit as the brother of men and women, as the friend of the poor, as the head of his gathered people, and as the messiah of God's new creation. So in a whole diversity of ways the Spirit constitutes the social person of Jesus as the Christ of God.

§4 THE GOSPEL OF THE KINGDOM OF GOD TO THE POOR

1. *The Gospel of Freedom*

The gospels present the history of Jesus in the light of his messianic mission, which was inaugurated through his baptism. His mission embraces his proclamation and his acts, his acts and his suffering, his life and his death. His proclamation of the imminent kingdom of God is part of his all-embracing mission. It brings out the meaning of his acts, just as, conversely, his acts accompany his proclamation. The two have to be seen together; but his mission must not be reduced to his charge to proclaim.[38] We shall begin here with the nature and content of his proclamation, and shall then go on to ask about the people to whom it was addressed. Before we look at the concept of the kingdom of God in Jesus' proclamation, we shall consider the concept of gospel, for the synoptic gospels – following the promise in Isa. 61.1 – show the proclaiming Jesus as God's messianic messenger of joy.[39]

In the Old Testament, to proclaim a gospel means bringing a message of joy, heralding a victory, announcing salvation.[40] Anyone who proclaims a joyful event is himself the bringer of joy, and is honoured accordingly. A divine victory over the enemies of the people is proclaimed and celebrated in the cult (Ps. 68.11; 40.9). A person who has been rescued from some necessity or distress proclaims in the congregation the marvellous act of God. The prophet Deutero-Isaiah poured a messianic content into the concept of *basar* (Greek εὐαγγελίζειν): the prophet promises the people in Babylonian captivity a new exodus – the end-time exodus out of slavery into the land of enduring freedom; for with his saving act Yahweh himself is going to ascend the throne and will establish his sovereignty without end. The new exodus into the freedom of the direct lordship of God is announced by the messenger: 'How beautiful upon the mountains are the feet of the messengers who proclaim peace, preach good, announce salvation, who say to Zion: your God is king' (Isa. 52.7). We can imagine the heralds who hurry ahead of the men and women who are returning home from Babylon, and who announce to the waiting people of Jerusalem Yahweh's final return home to Zion. This lends reality to their announcement of what is to come, for with their proclamation of Yahweh's royal rule, the time of salvation begins after the era of God's remoteness and the people's exile.

The gospel is the light which salvation throws ahead of itself. It is nothing less than the arrival of the coming God in the word. We have to put it in these emphatic terms in order to be able to discern the gospel's sacramental character: salvation runs ahead of itself and appears in the gospel; and the gospel is the beginning in word of the epiphany of the coming God.[41] In the very act of its announcement, the messianic era is already put into force. This means that the gospel is not a utopian description of some far-off future. It is the daybreak of this future in the pardoning, promising word that sets people free. This gives the word of comfort and claim the seal of the coming God and the authority of his future. It becomes the creative word which effects what it utters: 'For just as everything that has occurred in the world has a hidden beginning in the Word but a manifest end, so also are the times of the Most High: their beginning in Word and signs, their end in deeds and wonders' (IV Ezra 9.5f.). Deutero-Isaiah and Psalm 96 already see the messianic gospel in universal term: 'Yahweh is king' means more than the restoration of Israel and Zion; it is salvation for the nations too (96.2).

Isaiah 61.1ff. puts this gospel into the mouth of the end-time messianic prophet, who is filled with the Spirit of the Lord, and brings about salvation through his word. In relation to God, he proclaims the direct lordship of Yahweh without limits and without end, and in relation to human beings, justice, community and liberty. His message is addressed to the poor, the wretched, the sick and the hopeless, because these are the people who suffer most from God's remoteness and human hostility.

The message about the glory of God which is going to come upon his people, his land, and his whole creation is identical with the call to liberty: 'Loose the bonds from your neck, O captive daughter of Zion' (Isa. 52.2). Liberation is given a theological motivation and legitimation: 'The Lord will go before you' (52.12). The message 'God is king' makes the liberation of the people possible, and actually brings it about; and yet liberation is also the act of the prisoners, who liberate themselves, who break out of their imprisonment and return home on their own feet. The messianic message about the coming rule of God is not a reduction of human freedom. It actually makes freedom possible and sets it 'in a large room'. Nor is the message a compound of authority and freedom; it is the authority of freedom itself. The message of John the Baptist and Jesus also put the two together, as a single whole. 'The kingdom of God is at hand: be converted.' And for Paul the lordship of Christ is at the same time the kingdom of the liberty of God's children. The gospel of the kingdom of God is the gospel of the liberation of the people: the person who announces God's future brings the people freedom. Here the Protestant fear of Pelagianism is as misplaced as the atheistic assertion of human freedom in opposition to God.

2. *The Kingdom of God and New Creation*

The translation of the ἐγγύς of the kingdom of God is disputed. Does it mean 'the kingdom of God *is present?*' If it does, we are bound to ask: why is it not visibly present to every eye? And when is this general visible presence to be expected? If the kingdom is not visibly present, but only invisibly, then it is in heaven, not yet on earth. If the sentence means 'the kingdom of God *is at hand*' or *'near'*, we then have to explain how near it is. Luther translates the Greek as 'Das Himmelreich ist nahe herbeigekommen' – 'the kingdom of heaven has come close'. I shall adopt this translation, and say: it has come so close that the signs of the messianic era are already visible: the sick are healed, demons are driven out, the lame walk, the deaf hear, the poor have the gospel preached to them. It is so close that we can already pray to God as 'Abba', dear Father. It is so close that the Torah has to be messianically interpreted through the Sermon on the Mount, and can find its fulfilment in the discipleship of Christ.

The translations of βασιλεία τοῦ θεοῦ shift between the lordship or rule of God, and the kingdom of God.[42] These translations also reflect theological interpretations. Anyone who stresses *the lordship of God* means the rule of God in the present. Anyone who stresses *the kingdom of God* means the dimension and new order of all things according to God's precepts, and is talking about the future of this kingdom. If according to Jesus' gospel the kingdom of God is 'close', then it is already present, but *present* only as the *coming* kingdom. What can actually be experienced is the immediate lordship of God in the liberating of those who have been bound, and the healing of the sick, in the expulsion of devils and the raising up of the humiliated. But the conquest of death's power, and the experience of eternal life, are undoubtedly future. It would be one-sided to see the lordship of God only in his perfected kingdom, just as it is misleading to identify his kingdom with his actual, present rule.

In translating βασιλεία τοῦ θεοῦ we shall therefore use both terms, as complements to one another. In history God rules through Spirit and Word, liberty and obedience. But his rule comes up against conflict, contradiction and contention. It is a controversial rule, veiled in antagonism. It is therefore aligned towards a point beyond itself, which is its full perfecting in that future when God will rule uncontradicted, and in his glory will be all in all. For this future, the expression 'kingdom' is appropriate. God's present, liberating and healing activity points beyond itself to the kingdom of freedom and salvation. But through God's lordship, the coming kingdom already throws its light ahead of itself into this history of struggle. We therefore have to understand the liberating activity of God as the *immanence* of the eschatological kingdom of God, and the coming kingdom as the *transcendence* of the present lordship of God. If we transpose the concepts 'immanence' and 'transcendence' on to the historical level, we can say that the present lordship of God determines *the messianic era* and the future kingdom of God is the definition of *eschatological eternity*.

The double definition of βασιλεία τοῦ θεοῦ which we are proposing with our translation forbids us to banish the rule of God to a beyond which is totally unrelated to earthly, bodily and historical life; and this is what happens if 'the kingdom of heaven' is viewed as 'something purely spiritual' and 'not of this world'. The kingdom is then cut off from Jesus the messiah, through whom it is already present in the midst of this world, with its bodily sickness and political cruelty. But the double definition then forbids us equally to identify the kingdom of God in a chiliastic way with any existing state of affairs – the *imperium christianum,* for example – or with any utopian condition or 'golden age'. God's *lordship* is the *presence* of his kingdom, and God's *kingdom* is the *future* of his lordship.

In recent Protestant theology it has unfortunately become customary to interpret βασιλεία τοῦ θεοῦ solely as the present rule of God. And then it is all too easy to reduce it to moralistic terms: God's lordship reaches as far as men and women obey and do his will. But in this case it is helpless in the face of sickness and death. Earlier theological tradition always meant by 'the kingdom of God' 'the kingdom of glory', which was to follow on the present 'kingdom of grace'. But according to biblical tradition, the kingdom of glory is identical with *the new creation.* In order to avert and surmount both the moralization and the spiritualization of the concept of the present lordship of God, I am proposing in what follows sometimes to translate 'the kingdom of God' by 'new creation'. The lordship of God whose efficacy already reaches into this history of injustice and death, is accordingly to be understood as the newly creating, life-giving activity of God.

This gives us a new angle from which to view the ministry of Jesus. When Jesus expels demons and heals the sick, he is driving out of creation the powers of destruction, and is healing and restoring created beings who are hurt and sick. The lordship of God to which the healings witness, restores sick creation to health. Jesus' healings are not supernatural miracles in a natural world. They are the only truly 'natural' thing in a world that is unnatural, demonized and wounded. As parables of the kingdom, Jesus' parables are also parables of the new creation in the midst of the everyday life of this exhausted world. Finally, with the resurrection of Christ, the new creation begins, *pars pro toto*, with the crucified one.

3. The Dignity of the Poor

The gospel of the kingdom of God is proclaimed to 'the poor'. This is the stock term used in the synoptic gospels (Luke 4.18ff.; Matt. 11.5). On the one hand, the justice of God is presented as the right to have pity on the most pitiable; on the other hand the future of the kingdom of God begins among the people who suffer most from acts of violence and injustice – and that is the poor. The gospel assures the poor of God's life-giving, newly creating activity. The gospel is realistic, not idealistic. It does not bring new teaching; it brings a new reality. That is why what is most important for Jesus is his quarrel with poverty, sickness, demonism and forsakenness, not his quarrel with the teaching of the Pharisees and Sadducees.[43]

The collective term 'the poor' covers the hungry, the unemployed, the sick, the discouraged, and the sad and suffering. The poor are the subjected, oppressed and humiliated people (*ochlos*). The poor are sick, crippled, homeless (Luke 14.21–23). They are the beggars in the streets and on the country roads (Matt. 11.2–5). They are the sad (Luke 6.21). Their external situation is described with sufficient clarity: people want to take their very undergarment in pledge (Matt. 5.40). They are held liable for their debts to the extent of their own bodies (Luke 12.58) and their families (Matt. 18.23–35). Often enough they have to accept slavery and prostitution – which means a total loss of all their rights. The poor are 'non-persons', 'sub-human', 'dehumanized', 'human fodder'.

The counter-term for the poor is 'the man of violence', who makes someone else poor and enriches himself at the other's expense. We already find this antitype in the Old Testament.[44] 'The rich' have the power (Luke 1.46–54). They can hoard grain and force up prices so that they make the poor poorer. The tax-collector is rich because he cheats (Luke 19.1–10) and exploits his power at the cost of the powerless, who cannot defend themselves. The God of the rich is 'Mammon', and he is an unjust god. The rich therefore have to be exposed as the unjust and the men of violence. When Jesus and his disciples proclaim the gospel to the poor, they are explicitly or non-explicitly proclaiming to the rich God's judgment (Luke 6.24). This is not the slave's dream of revenge. It is the announcement of God's coming justice and righteousness, which will set the rich to rights as well – but as people, not as the rich.

Jesus and his disciples proclaim to the poor their future in the kingdom of God, because they have perceived that the kingdom of God already belongs to the poor: 'Blessed are the poor, for theirs *is* the kingdom of heaven' (Matt. 5.3). The gospel does not merely *bring* the kingdom of God *to* the poor; it also *discovers* the kingdom of the poor, which is God's kingdom.[45] The gospel does not merely call to conversion and faith. It also shows that the poor are God's fellow citizens, like the children to whom the kingdom of God already 'belongs' (Mark 10.14; Matt. 19.14). So anyone who proclaims the gospel to the poor belongs to the poor, and becomes poor himself, in community with them.

Sociologically speaking, the Jesus movement in Galilee was a movement of the poor;[46] the disciples are to go out barefoot, without any provisions, homeless and as beggars, and are to proclaim the gospel to the poor (Matt. 6.25–33). They put their trust entirely in God, so they have no worries. They live entirely from their hope for God's coming, so they take no account of either mammon or hunger. Their master himself lived as one of the poor, without the protection of a family, without a home country, without any income or provision for the future (Luke 9.58). They share with the people the little that they have, and as the poor they satisfy a great multitude (Luke 9.10ff.). The first Christian community in Jerusalem was still living so that 'they had everything in common' and 'there was not a needy person among them' (Acts 4.34–35). The movement of the poor which Jesus' gospel called into being in Galilee undoubtedly became a danger to the Jewish upper class and to the Roman occupying power with which that class collaborated. Jesus' execution on the Roman cross was apparently meant as a deterrent to social and political unrest of this kind. According to Philippians 2, Jesus died 'in the form of a slave'. He suffered the fate of many enslaved poor in the Roman empire, and especially in Palestine.

What does the gospel bring the poor? And when they are called blessed, as God's fellow citizens, what does this offer them? Certainly not the end of hunger, and the wealth of a richly blessed life. But it does bring *a new dignity*. The poor, the slaves and the prostitutes are no longer the passive objects of oppression and humiliation; they are now their own conscious subjects, with all the dignity of God's first children. The gospel brings them neither beans nor rice, but it does bring them the assurance of their indestructible dignity in God's sight.[47] With this awareness, the poor, slaves and prostitutes can get up out of the dust and help themselves. They no longer adopt the system of values of their exploiters, according to which it is only the rich who are real persons, whereas all those who are not rich are 'failures' who 'haven't made it' in life's struggle. The inward acceptance by the poor themselves of the values of the rich is a severe obstacle to their self-liberation. It makes poverty self-destructive, and produces self-hate in the poor themselves. The gospel about the kingdom of God which belongs to the poor, vanquishes this self-hate, and gives the poor courage, so that they can live with 'their heads held high' and can 'walk erect': *God* is on their side and *God's future* belongs to them. 'The men of violence' have shut them out of the pleasures of the present. But God has thrown open his future to them, and has made them the heirs of his coming kingdom.

If this hope spreads, then this future becomes the authority for their liberation and the source of their strength. The poor and the powerless are not offered some utopia or other, to console them for the lives they live in the present. On the contrary, through them the future of God comes into the present, because this future is already theirs. This is their authorization. The poor become God's children in this world of violence and injustice. The kingdom of God becomes 'the messianic kingdom of the poor'.[48] Jesus' promise does not put the poor on the way to becoming richer, which is a way that is always fraught with violence; it puts them on the way to community which, as the Feeding of the Five Thousand shows, is determined by 'the culture of sharing'.

The gospel is therefore one-sided and partisan in its commitment to the poor, and in the blessing it promises them; and it follows from this that according to Jesus' gospel the kingdom of God is already present among the poor and the sick, and among the children and slaves of the people (*ochlos*). If these are 'the least of the brothers and sisters' of the Son of man who is also the judge of the world (Matt. 25), then it is with them that the salvation or doom, eternal life or perdition of human beings is decided. It is only in community with the poor that the kingdom of God is thrown open to the others. If we look at the gospel of Jesus and the first beatitude together, then the kingdom of God dawns in the word proclaimed, and in the poor – that is, in the interplay between Jesus and the people. Jesus brings the gospel to the poor, and discovers the kingdom of God among the poor. The poor need him, and he depends on them. The messiah of the poor reveals the messianism of the poor – and kindles it. The One who proclaims the kingdom of God also represents the poor to whom the kingdom belongs. The poor are his family, his people, for they are the people of God's coming kingdom. He is one of them.

4. *Liberation through Conversion*

In a divided world destroyed by enmity, the one gospel has two faces, according to the group to which it turns. Jesus proclaims to the poor the kingdom of God without any conditions, and calls them blessed because the kingdom is already theirs. But the gospel of the kingdom meets the rich with *the call to conversion* (Mark 1.15 par.). We are using the word conversion instead of repentance in order to keep the idea free from the flavour of self-punishment. Conversion means turning round, the turn from violence to justice, from isolation to community, from death to life. According to John the Baptist, the compelling imminence of God's judgment made human conversion and the return to the way of justice and right-eousness *necessary*. The prevenient, pitying justice of God which Jesus proclaims makes conversion *possible*, and gives the strength for it. For Paul too, the approaching sunrise of the day of God makes it possible and necessary to lay aside 'the works of darkness' and to put on 'the armour of light' (Rom. 13.12ff.). The inviting proximity of the coming kingdom of God makes possible what was impossible before, and what is impossible without it. Conversion implements these new potentialities which God throws open. True life begins here and now, the true life which will come for the whole of creation with the kingdom of God. 'Conversion' is itself *an anticipation* of that new life under the conditions of this world. It is an anticipation lived in the possibilities which the gospel shows, and to which the Spirit of God gives effect. Conversion is life in anticipation of the kingdom of God, on the basis of the prevenience of this kingdom.

How far does this conversion go?

If God is the reality that determines everything, then his kingdom is the new creation that heals everything and puts everything straight. This means that the conversion to which the gospel about the nearness of God's kingdom calls, cannot be limited to either private or religious life. It is as all-embracing and holistic as the salvation of the new creation itself. Conversion takes hold of people, *and* the conditions in which people live and suffer. That is to say, it takes in personal life, life in community, and the systems which provide an order for these ways of living. In its trend and thrust, conversion is as all-embracing as the coming kingdom of God, whose proclaimed closeness makes conversion possible and necessary. Like the discipleship of Christ, conversion takes place totally, holistically, 'with all the heart and with all the soul and with all the strength', like the love of God (Deut. 6.5). If it does not happen like this it does not happen at all. If it is half-hearted and only touches part-sectors of reality, it is not a conversion that corresponds to the kingdom of God.

The call to conversion leads men and women into the discipleship of Jesus. The community which gathered round him, the men and women disciples, and the many whose names we do not know, are the preliminary form of the true Israel that turns to God. The community of those who are being converted and who follow Jesus are also the vanguard of the community of the messiah, the church. Again, we must see that this 'congregation' of Jesus' is to be found where Jesus is. It belongs to 'the people of the beatitudes'. As we can see from the catalogue of these beatitudes in Matthew and Luke as they were expanded after Easter, the 'people' of the passive and active beatitudes are the people and disciples who turn to the Sermon on the Mount: they are the poor and those who are hungry for justice and righteousness, the people who suffer and are persecuted for the sake of justice, the sad and the gentle. Here it becomes evident how those who are converted become a single people, one with the poor, and welded into the new messianic community.

Later on the Christian congregations shaped this new community of poor and rich in such a way that the rich gave alms, exercised the right to compassion by receiving strangers, clothing the naked, feeding the hungry, and visiting people in prison. As far as possible they renounced possessions, entrusting what they owned to the congregation, for the use of those who were in need. Before Constantine, the Christian congregations were communities with a social commitment.[49] Strangers were accepted, and new work was found for them. The poor in the congregations were fed, and even the city's own poor as well. Sick people who had been abandoned were taken in and cared for. The Christian congregations felt in duty bound to undertake the care of others. Until these independent congregations were absorbed into the parishes of the imperial church, many of them continued the struggle against real, practical poverty, hunger and sickness, acting in the name of Jesus, and following what he himself did. It was only with the Constantinian imperial church that there came to be an increasing tendency to spiritualize poverty, because the church had to leave 'welfare' to the emperor, and was forced to confine itself to the salvation of souls. If it had not been for this, the conflict which Jesus initiated with the gospel for the poor would have remained a living conflict, and spiritual and political power in the Christian empire would have remained unharmonized.

§5 THE HEALING OF THE SICK – THE EXPULSION OF DEMONS

The expulsion of demons and the healing of the sick are the mark of Jesus' ministry from the very beginning. They also belonged to the messianic mission of his disciples (Mark 3.15). What do they mean? Miraculous healings and exorcisms were common enough elsewhere in the ancient world as well. We find them in the ancient civilizations of Asia and Africa. They also exist beneath the surface of modern Western civilization. But in Jesus' case their context is unique; for this context is the dawn of the lordship of the divine life in this era of Godless death. The lordship of God drives out of creation the powers of destruction, which are demons and idols, and heals the created beings who have been damaged by them. If the kingdom of God is coming as Jesus proclaimed, then salvation is coming as well. If salvation comes to the whole creation, then the health of all created beings is the result – health of body and soul, individual and community, human beings and nature. That is why the people who gather round Jesus are shown to be not so much 'sinners' as sick. Suffering men and women come to Jesus because they seek healing. According to the gospel accounts, the expulsion of 'unclean spirits' and the healing of the sick among the people are not phenomena of the kind that was common coin in the ancient world, and which were conditioned by the time. Nor were they secondary phenomena attendant on Jesus' message which can just as well be dispensed with. They themselves are the message. In the discussion about Jesus' miracles, the connection between the healing of the sick and the expulsion of demons is often overlooked.[50]

1. Healing and Exorcism

Healing and exorcism must not be viewed in isolation, as way-out phenomena. They have to be seen in their relation to Jesus' messianic mission; for it is only when Jesus appears with his message that the sick and the possessed emerge from the darkness into which they had been banished, and press forward to him. This is not chance. When the doctor comes, the sick appear. When salvation approaches, disaster becomes manifest. When the kingdom of God is close, the forces that resist God are given a name and made to disappear. In the light of the imminent kingdom of God, this world which is in such need of redemption appears for what it is: truly possessed in its sicknesses.

Mark follows Jesus' first preaching in Capernaum immediately with a story about demons (1.2–28 par.), in order to show the ἐξουσία of Jesus' new teaching – its authority. He preaches with ἐξουσία, and with ἐξουσία commands the unclean spirits and they 'obey him'. His teaching is creative teaching, which effects what it says. Mark seems to find it even more important that after God has acknowledged Jesus at his baptism ('Thou art my beloved Son', 1.11), the 'unclean spirits' should be the first to recognize who Jesus is in God's eyes, and to confess him as 'the Christ': 'I know who you are, the Holy One of God' (1.24); 'You are the Son of God' (3.11; 5.7). According to Luke, when the people possessed by devils acknowledged Christ it was a mass phenomenon: 'Now when the sun was setting, all those who had any that were sick with various diseases brought them to him; and he laid his hands on every one of them and healed them. And demons also came out of many, crying, "You are the Christ, the Son of God!" But he rebuked them, and would not allow them to speak, because they knew that he was the Christ' (Luke 4.40–41). A wild scene, with a demonic confession of Christ! The demonic spirits evidently also know that with Jesus' coming their hour has struck. For when the messiah comes, the demons and idols have to disappear from the earth, because God himself desires to dwell in it. The gospels continually report the demons as saying: 'You have come to destroy us' (Mark 1.24). According to Matthew, they even cry: 'Have you come to torment us before the time?' (8.29). These spirits who torment human beings are evidently inwardly compelled on their own account to address the Son of man, because they feel 'tormented' by him. Whenever Jesus drives out demons from possessed people, these people are restored to health and reason, and are free to determine their own lives (Mark 5.15). The healing Jesus intervenes out of the compassion of God, who suffers with those he has created when they are sick, and desires them to be well. But Jesus himself, who has power over these spirits, comes to be suspected of having a pact with 'the prince of devils' (Mark 3.22), and of therefore 'casting out one devil with another', so that he too becomes unclean. Since at that time disease bore the stigma of impurity, the sick suffered from cultic and social discrimination. To put an end to this discrimination was an act of social criticism which was one side of Jesus' healings.

These demons are apparently forces, conceived of in personal terms, which are destructive of life and annihilate being itself. They enslave men and women, and make them dependent. They destroy the personality and derange the organism. They are characterized by their pleasure in 'tormenting'. They rouse the death-wish in human beings. Even if we do not imagine these forces of destruction in personal terms, to accept them permits us to interpret phenomena of torment between soul and body, between one human being and another, and in whole social systems. According to earlier personal imaginings about demons, they are 'fallen angels' under the rule of the Devil, who in relation to God is called Satan – that is, the Accuser – and in relation to the human world Diabolos – the Disorderer or Confuser. If angels are God's potencies of good in heaven, then 'fallen angels' are self-isolating and thus perverted potencies, which when they are cut off from God fall, pulling other creatures down with them into the abyss of annihilation: 'I am the spirit that always denies, for everything that is called forth is worth destroying', says Mephisto of himself in Goethe's *Faust*. According to the age-old hope, the 'demons' will disappear from the earth when the messiah comes. The messiah will redeem both human beings and demons. He will deliver human beings from the forces of destruction, so that they once again become free, whole and reasonable. And he will deliver these forces themselves from the service of destruction, putting them once more at the service of the Creator (Eph. 1.20–23; Col. 1.20).

The expulsion of demons and the healing of the sick go together, because the people bring their sick and their possessed to Jesus, and he heals both (Luke 6.18 par.). The 'power that goes out of him' has this double effect. It is identical with the lordship of God: 'But if it is by the finger of God that I cast out demons, then the kingdom of God has come upon you' (Luke 11.20). The gospels do not merely draw the portrait of the miracle-man, the θεῖος ἀνήρ, who is in possession of extraordinary powers; they paint the picture of God's messianic plenipotentiary, who de-demonizes the world, and through 'the powers of the age to come' (Heb. 6.5) makes the world whole and free and reasonable. When God sets up his rule over his world, and the Creator has compassion on his creation, it is not extraordinary that the sick should become well and devils should be expelled; it is a matter of course. Jesus' healings are simply what Christoph Blumhardt called 'miracles of the kingdom'. In the context of the new creation, these 'miracles' are not miracles at all. They are merely the fore-tokens of the all-comprehensive salvation, the unscathed world, and the glory of God. Without this eschatological context, indeed, they lose their meaning and become absurd marvels which can be forgotten. But in this context they speak their own language. They point to the bodily character of salvation and to the God who loves earthly life.

The lordship of God whose presence Jesus proclaims and discovers brings salvation. The particular characteristic of this salvation is 'healing power'.[51] But we must beware of turning σωτερία into an abstract general heading for all the different soteriological terms and concepts in the New Testament. It is better to start from the specific, practical processes which are called 'healing', 'cleansing', 'saving', 'delivering' and 'making well', and then to ask about the full perfecting of these acts and processes in salvation itself. Every sick person experiences healing in a different way, because diseases and possessions differ. And the same is true about the experience of deliverance from affliction and liberation from oppression. It is only the summing-up which says that Jesus 'healed', and that with the lordship of God 'salvation' has come.

Salvation, then, is the summing-up of all the healings. Since it is part of the lordship of God, it is as all-embracing as God himself and cannot be restricted to part-sectors of creation. It is not 'the salvation of the soul', although of course the sick person's soul also has to be healed. Nor can we exclude any particular earthly sphere from salvation, giving it the name of 'well-being' or 'welfare' and subtracting it from the influence of Jesus' lordship. 'Salvation is an entity which includes the wholeness and well-being of human beings. Salvation is for the *totus homo*; it is not merely salvation of soul for the individual.'[52] Salvation does not mean merely 'spiritual benefits'. It includes the health of the body. Jesus makes 'the whole human being' well (John 7.23).[53]

It is no less wrong to push salvation off into a world beyond this one, and to limit its effects to an invisible life of pure faith, outside empirical experience. Nor should we make the healings external signs of the inner process of the forgiveness of sins. The healing of the sick *and* the forgiveness of sins are necessary, and the one cannot be reduced to the other. At the same time, however much we stress the holistic nature of salvation, which is grounded in the power of God, there is a difference between salvation and healing which cannot be overlooked: *Healing* vanquishes illness and creates health. Yet it does not vanquish the power of death. But *salvation* in its full and completed form is the annihilation of the power of death and the raising of men and women to eternal life. Even the dead whom Jesus healed and raised – Lazarus, for example – were still subject to the power of death, and later died again. It is therefore correct when Paul (I Thess. 5.8; Rom. 8.24) sets salvation 'in the mode of hope' (as W. Schrage puts it). He does not assign salvation generally to a future for which we can only hope; we may put it more precisely, and say that he sets it in *the mode of hope for the resurrection*; for only this is the hope for the annihilation of death itself (I Cor. 15.28) and the liberation of the whole creation from that power of annihilation. Healings and salvation are related to one another in such a way that the *healings* are signs, this side of death, of God's power of resurrection or, as John says, signs of Christ's 'glory'; while *salvation* is the fulfilment of these prefigured real promises in the raising of the dead to eternal life. Just as healing overcomes sickness, so salvation overcomes death. Because every sickness is a threat to life, and is therefore a foreshadowing of death, every healing is a living foretoken of the resurrection.[54] The therapeutic significance of redemption lies in the healing of men and women in their essential being – that is, in the becoming whole of what has been separated by death, and in the universal elimination of the germ of decay and mortality.

Salvation in this sense has two sides to it, one personal and one cosmic. Paul calls the *personal* side of salvation 'the resurrection of the dead'. He calls the *cosmic* side 'the annihilation of death'. It is only if we see the two sides together that we understand that salvation also means 'the transfiguration of the body' (Phil. 3.21) and 'the new earth' (Rev. 21.4). These two aspects can also be perceived in Jesus' own healings: healing the sick is the personal side, driving out demons is the cosmic side. Sick people are subjectively healed; they are made free and well. At the same time the world is objectively de-demonized; the bacilli that cause these possessions are destroyed. Jesus heals the sick and symbolically liberates creation from the powers of destruction, which at that time were called 'demons'.

The *theological* problem raised by the stories of Jesus' healings has nothing to do with the modern scientific world view, and modern scientific medicine; for today too there are possessions and dependencies which rob men and women of their freedom, making them ill, and subjecting them to external compulsions. The 'demons' have simply been given other names. We do not have to believe in a particular, separate world of spirits in order to see how human life is destroyed by the powers of annihilation. The theological problem about Jesus' miracles is to be found rather in the threatening loss of hope for the kingdom of God which is summed up in the phrase 'the delay of the parousia'. Once this eschatological horizon disappears, the miracles cease to point to the beginning of the new creation of all things; and they then stand on their own as irritating marvels in an untransformed world. We do not look back to happenings which point forward eschatologically. It is only when this future becomes dark that these happenings turn into historical events which no longer have anything to say to us, because their day is past. The stories about the healings which the gospels tell will have something to say once more, to the degree in which we succeed in restoring the authentic, eschatological horizon of the messianic faith in Jesus.

The real theological difficulty of the stories about Jesus' healings, however, is raised by his passion and his death in helplessness on the cross. 'He saved others; let him save himself, if he is the Christ of God, his Chosen One' (Luke 23.35). But this is just what Jesus apparently cannot do. The healing powers that emanate from him, and the 'authority' which he has over the demons, are given him not for himself but only for others. They act through him, but they are not at his disposal. They issue from him but he cannot keep and use them for himself. There are no miracles on the road of his passion. On the cross he dies in forsakenness by God and man. Or is this the greatest of all the miracles, the all-embracing healing? 'He bore our sicknesses and took upon himself our pains . . . and through his wounds we are healed' (Isa. 53.4, 5). This was how the gospels saw it. So Jesus heals not only through 'power' and 'authority' but also through his suffering and helplessness.[55] In this wider sense of salvation as the overcoming of death and the raising to eternal life, people are healed not through Jesus' miracles, but through Jesus' wounds; that is, they are gathered into the indestructible love of God.

The *human* problem of Jesus' miracles of healing is to be found in the close link that was forged at that time and in that civilization between sickness and possession. Today this link would lead to a stigmatizing of the sick which would be in direct contradiction to Jesus' healings. When the sick are demonized – people with Aids for example – they are shut out of society and condemned to social death. Today it is precisely the de-demonization of diseases which would be the first step to the healing of the sick, if this means preserving their social relationships and continuing to recognize their human dignity. But there are also objective unjust circumstances which make people ill, as social medicine has shown. So it is often impossible to heal the sick without healing their relationships, the circumstances in which they live, and the structures of the social system to which they belong. The 'general spirit' which acquires objectified form in the circumstances which make people fall ill, has undoubtedly demonic features, because it oppresses people and destroys them. It therefore makes sense not to consider diseases solely in the isolation of their pathogenic causes, but to see those who are ill in the context of their life history, and to view their life history as part of their social history. The spiritist link between sickness and demons in the mythical and magical thinking of earlier times was an attempt in this direction. The healings of Jesus, and healings in his Spirit, are mindful of both the subjective and the objective factors which contribute to the illness of the person concerned.

2. Healing Faith

Whereas the gospels talk in general about Jesus' expulsion of demons and his healings as if the power emanated from Jesus alone (Mark 1.34, 39; 6.56), in nine stories about individual healings the faith of the people concerned is said to have been responsible. Jesus either sees the faith which comes to meet him, as in the healing of 'the man sick of the palsy' (Mark 2.5), or actually says: 'your faith has made you well', as in the case of the woman with the issue of blood (Mark 5.34).[56] In these stories Jesus always talks about faith in this way, absolutely and without any object.[57] Where there is faith, the power which goes out of Jesus 'works wonders'. Where faith is lacking – as in his home town, Nazareth – he cannot do anything. 'He marvelled because of their unbelief' (Mark 6.6). Faith has to be understood, not merely as sincere trust, but also as the urgent desire of the person concerned.[58] The woman with the issue of blood approaches Jesus from behind, out of the crowd, and defiles him through her touch. Jesus senses only 'that power had gone forth from him' (Mark 5.30). It is only when he sees what has happened to her, and what she has done to him, that he praises her belief that she will be healed, and blesses her with the 'peace' (Mark 5.34). The Canaanite woman runs after him in order to get help for her daughter (Matt. 15.21ff.). Jesus rebuffs her, because he believes that he has been sent only to Israel. She traps him with his own words – the words with which he has rejected her: 'The dogs eat the crumbs that fall from their masters' table.' He praises her obstinate will: 'Be it done for you as you desire' (Matt. 15.28).

It is evidently women especially who through their urgency call forth the power which is in Jesus. And Jesus himself grows from the expectation and faith of these women. He surpasses himself, as we say – he grows beyond himself. But it would be more exact to say: he grows into the One whom he will be, God's messiah.

The divine power of healing does not come from his side alone. Nor is it simply his own 'ministry', as and when he wishes to perform it. It is rather something that happens between him and the people who seek this power in him, and importune him. When Jesus and faith meet in this reciprocal activity, healing can happen. It is noticeable that many of the healings have to do with women, or are on behalf of daughters, who in a patriarchal society have few rights and a lower social standing. In Mark 5 and in Mark 7 a man and a

woman are healed in each case. Jesus always points the people who
have been healed away from himself to God, who is the One to be
thanked, and to their own faith, which has brought about the
healings. This is summed up in the story of the withered fig tree in
Mark 11.20–23, and the faith that moves mountains, about which
Paul talks in I Cor. 13.2. Faith is as strong as God himself. That is
why it is described in terms otherwise reserved for God alone: 'All
things are possible to him who believes' (Mark 9.23). This statement
about faith is unparalleled.[59] Its structure is similar to the structure
of the revelatory formula in Matt. 11.27: 'All things have been
delivered to me by my Father . . .' The healings are stories about faith
just as much as they are stories about Jesus. They are stories about
the reciprocal relationships between Jesus and the faith of men and
women. Jesus is dependent on this faith, just as the sick are
dependent on the power that emanates from Jesus.

§6 THE ACCEPTANCE OF THE OUTCASTS – THE RAISING UP OF THE HUMILIATED

Jesus proclaimed *the kingdom of God* to the poor and bestowed *the
power of God* on the sick; and in the same way he brought 'sinners
and tax-collectors' *the justice of God*, which is the justice of grace.[60]
He demonstrated this publicly by sitting down at table with them. In
the eschatological context of his own message, this shared meal is an
anticipation of the eating and drinking of the righteous in the
kingdom of God.

After calling the tax-collector Levi into his discipleship, Jesus
entered his house, and 'many tax collectors and sinners sat down at
table with Jesus and his disciples' (Mark 2.15). Either the calling of
Levi gave them courage, or they came anyway, simply of their own
accord. In response to the reproachful question of 'the scribes and
Pharisees': 'Why does he eat with tax collectors and sinners?', Jesus
gives the interpretative answer: 'Those who are well have no need of
a physician, but those who are sick; I came not to call the righteous,
but sinners to repentance' (2.16f.). Although it was the tax collectors
and sinners who had joined him at table on their own initiative, the
conclusion was comprehensive: 'This man receives sinners and eats
with them' (Luke 15.2).

In the stories about Jesus the term 'sinner' is not yet defined
theologically and universally as it is in Paul (Rom. 3.23). It is meant

socially, as we can see from the paired concepts: well – sick, righteous – sinners, Pharisees – tax collectors. In the eyes of 'the scribes and Pharisees', 'sinners' are Jews who are not able or willing to keep the Torah and to follow the path of righteousness. 'Tax collectors' are Jews who have leased the customs from Gentiles and call in taxes for the Roman occupying power. They are forced to make their living by levying excessive taxes, or the power they possess tempts them to adopt corrupt practices. In the eyes of just and pure Jews, they were corrupt collaborators with the occupying power, infamous to the highest degree. By joining company with these 'sinners and tax collectors', Jesus was embarking on a social conflict which was religiously determined – the cleft between the just and the unjust, the good and the bad. This conflict is certainly provoked by injustice and lawlessness, but the rules are laid down by the good and the just, who claim God's justice for themselves, and enforce their own scale of values in the social context. The 'self-righteousness' of the Pharisees which Luke describes in parables (15; 18.9ff.) is not subjective vanity, but 'the possession of the good'.[61] Just as 'the possession of wealth' allows the poor to remain poor, so 'the possession of the good' produces the cleft between the good and the bad, and lets the bad remain bad.

If the distinction between good and evil were ended, the foundations of society would crumble. The system of values that distinguishes good from evil is the same for every member of society, but it is abstract. It takes no account of ability or non-ability. The Pharisees therefore despised 'the country people' (*àm ha'aretz*) because they did not keep the law. They were so poor that they were not in a position to do so. The righteous despised the prostitutes – women who saw no other possibility except to sell their own bodies – and called them 'sinners', because they could not keep the law. Similarly, the often relatively wealthy tax collectors were also despised because they did business with the Romans. No one asked why. The social cleft between rich and poor is in most cases the reason for the cleft between good and evil, the righteous and sinners.

In all societies there are the 'high fliers', who decide what is to count as good and what bad. And there are the people on the bottom rung of the ladder, whom the people further up have to use as a way of setting off their own excellence, because they embody everything that is bad. Where this dualization leads to the formation of different classes, a merciless struggle between 'good' and 'bad' begins, which

ends often enough with the extermination of 'the bad'. If this struggle
is linked politically with friend-enemy thinking, it leads to the final
apocalyptic struggle. Pharisees and tax collectors are 'fixated' on one
another, tied to each other in a vicious circle. We therefore have to
say with Leonhard Ragaz: 'The Pharisee is to blame for the tax
collector. The Pharisee thrust him into the religious and social
enslavement in which the law became for him a matter of indifference.'[62] In this sense 'the righteous' are to blame for 'the sinners', and
'decent people' for 'the whores'. They discriminate against them
publicly and overlook their real poverty.

By accepting 'sinners and tax collectors' and prostitutes, Jesus is
not justifying the sin, the corruption or the prostitution. But he is
breaking through the vicious circle of their discrimination in the
system of values set up by the righteous. In this way he is also
potentially rescuing 'the righteous' from the compulsion of self-
righteousness, and saving 'the good' from the possession of the good.
But in turning to those who are suffering from discrimination, his
commitment is one-sided and partisan. By turning to them in his own
person, he reveals to them and their oppressors the messianic
righteousness of God, which through the justice of grace *makes* the
unjust just, and the bad good, and the ugly beautiful. This is a
forceful attack on religious and civic morality. The reactions of 'the
good' and 'the just' are so aggressive just because they see 'everything
they hold most sacred' under attack, and feel that they themselves are
therefore called in question. Anyone who like Jesus and his disciples
gets into this kind of 'bad company' (A. Holl's phrase), suffers the
same fate as them. Anyone who seeks out 'the lost' is often lost
himself.

The story about the 'sinner' in the house of one of the Pharisees is
especially striking (Luke 7.36–50). Here we have the glaring contrast
between the rich and 'righteous' man and the enslaved woman, who
has to sell herself, and who in a moving scene wets Jesus' feet with her
tears, dries them with her hair, kisses them, and anoints them. Jesus
declares that her sins are forgiven – that is to say, whatever is cutting
her off from God; and he adds, as he does when he heals someone
who is sick: 'Your faith has saved you; go in peace' (7.50).

In the story about Zacchaeus (Luke 19.1–10), Jesus visits 'a
sinner's' house, much to the annoyance of the more select circles in
Jericho (19.7), and declares that through his visit 'Today salvation
has come to this house' (19.9). Through his presence and compan-

ionship, he himself brings into the house the salvation which makes the sick well, and the unjust just, and puts an end to discrimination, whether religious or civic. It is noticeable that Jesus forgives sins without any conditions – without confession and without any token of reparation. He does what according to Israelite ideas only the judge of the world can do at the Last Judgment: pardon the accused.

Jesus' eating with sinners and tax collectors acquires a special meaning in the context of his messianic message. Every shared meal in fact confers human fellowship. But the kingdom of God which Jesus proclaims and which he demonstrates through his dealings with the poor, the sick, sinners and tax collectors does not merely bring the lordship of God over his whole creation; it also brings the great and joyful banquet of the nations: 'And on this mountain the Lord of hosts will make for all peoples a feast of fat things, a feast of wine on the lees, of fat things full of marrow, of wine on the lees well refined: And he will take away on this mountain the veil with which all the nations are veiled, and the covering with which all the Gentiles are covered. And he will swallow up death for ever . . .' (Isa. 25.6–8). Jesus evidently expected the kingdom of God in the form of a great banquet; 'And they will come from east and west, and from north and south, and sit at table in the kingdom of God' (Luke 13.29).

The parable of the kingdom about the great marriage feast (Matt. 22.2–10) links this material expectation about the kingdom of God with the way Jesus himself took, when he sought out sinners and tax collectors: when the invited guests do not come to the king's supper, people from the streets are invited, 'both bad and good' (22.10); in Luke it is 'the poor and maimed and blind and lame' (14.21). It is in this context that we have to see Jesus' eating and drinking with sinners and tax collectors: together with these 'unrighteous persons' he is anticipating the meal of the righteous in the kingdom of God, and is demonstrating in his own person what acceptance by the merciful God and the forgiveness of sins means: it means being invited to the great festal supper in the kingdom of God. Forgiveness of sins, and eating and drinking in the kingdom of God are two sides of the same thing, as we also see from the homecoming and acceptance of the 'prodigal son' (Luke 15.22). Jesus celebrates the feast of the messianic time with those who are discriminated against in his own time. If he is the messianic Son of God, then in this celebration he is reflecting God's own way of doing things.

Jesus' meals with his disciples are celebrations of the kingdom in the same way. This is shown by the words of renunciation at the Last Supper (Mark 14.25 par.): 'For I say to you, I shall not drink again of the fruit of the vine until that day when I drink it new in the kingdom of God.' The special thing about the meal shared with the disciples is surely the fact that the disciples are drawn into Jesus' messianic mission 'to seek that which is lost', and participate actively in it. When Jesus sits at table with sinners and tax collectors, the disciples are there too. So although Jesus' supper with his disciples has a different meaning from his meals with sinners, it is none the less related to them.

Jesus last supper with his disciples has the unique significance which Jesus gives to the breaking of bread and to the cup of wine.[63] Here the kingdom of God which he has made present to the poor becomes wholly concentrated on his bodily person. He, the giver of the feast, is himself the gift of the feast. Here Jesus truly is 'the kingdom of God in person'. The breaking of the bread and the drinking of the wine make the kingdom of God present in the form of Christ's body given 'for us' and the blood shed 'for us'. We may say in retrospect that something of this ultimate theological meaning of Jesus' supper is also present everywhere where Jesus is present in person, and sits down at table with sinners and tax collectors. The one who brings to the poor the dignity of the kingdom of God, and reveals to sinners and tax collectors the righteousness of God which itself makes righteous, is also the messianic 'host', who invites the hungry to eat and drink in the kingdom of God, and demonstrates to them the fellowship which God shares with them at his table.

§7 THE MESSIANIC WAY OF LIFE

1. *Christian Ethics and the Ethical Knowledge of Christ*

Did Jesus teach a new ethic? Is there such a thing as a specifically Christian ethic today? Does Christian faith involve a new life style? Can one know Christ at all without following him? In asking these questions we are not merely touching the fundamental nerve of Christian ethics. We are coming face to face with an unsolved problem of christology itself.

A number of Christian moralists consider that it is impossible to arrive at a specifically *Christian* ethic today, because in modern society Christians bring no greater insight to the solution of burning social and political problems than other members of society; consequently all that is available to us is a common, natural or general human ethics, which Christians have to follow like other people. Is there any specifically 'Christian' solution in questions about taxation, or in genetic engineering? And even if there were, it could never be made generally binding in a pluralistic society. It could only apply to Christians in that society. So Christians should just act pragmatically and responsibly, as human beings like other human beings. Though of course in public life they will then be unrecognizable and anonymous.

It is in fact true that the familiar patterns of Christian ethics have almost ceased to rest on any christological foundation. The ethics of natural law, the secular ethics of the Lutheran doctrine of the two kingdoms, the ethics of 'orders' – whether it be the orders of creation, the orders of preservation, or the orders based on the covenant with Noah – are all conceived without a specific basis in any christology.[64] The christological substantiations are only indirect and hardly evident, if they exist at all. We seek in vain for anything that is uniquely and specifically Christian. As a result, in the modern societies in which these ethics have been developed, no specifically *Christian* ethic can be detected; and this is in fact just what is intended. But does this not presuppose that modern societies are considered to be Christian, or that Christianity is thought to have given them their hall-mark? Of course in a generally 'Christian' world, no special Christian ethic could be distinguished. But does this Christian world exist? Or is it an illusion under which the church has been labouring ever since Constantine?

If there is no specifically Christian ethic, then the acknowledgment of Christ is itself called in question; for then Jesus' message cannot have been ethically meant, in the sense of making a public ethical claim. It was then either purely religious, and hence non-political; or wholly apocalyptic, and hence without relevance for changes in the world itself; or confined to personal life, and hence without any relation to the public conditions in which personal life is lived. But can Jesus then still be called the messiah in a sense that is in any way relevant? In Israel's history of promise, to which all the gospels are related, the messiah is a public person. His proclamation of the messianic Torah in the messianic era is addressed to the whole people of God and, with this people, to all the peoples of the earth. If Jesus came forward without any messianic claim of this kind, why did the

Romans crucify him? Was the Roman inscription over the cross 'Jesus Nazarenus Rex Judaeorum' a regrettable misunderstanding? Or was it the truth? If it is called a 'misunderstanding', then the Christian faith in Jesus collapses. If it is taken seriously, then the confession of Jesus as the Christ also involves a practical discipleship that follows the messianic path his own life took; and that means an ethic which has to be made identifiably Christian. 'Indispensably linked with the messiah is a change in the social conditions of the world which has its specific place among the messiah's people. Indispensably linked with the messiah is the peace that he brings. If this peace does not come – and if it does not come in a tangible, social sense – then the messiah has not come.'[65]

So what today's dispute over the Christian nature of Christian ethics is really about is nothing less than the messiahship of Jesus. This is not a discussion about ethics, in the sense of questions of conscience or judgment. What is at stake is the acknowledgment of Christ. Christian ethics are not asked merely for good or better solutions to general problems. They are asked how far the way of Jesus is to be taken seriously.

Ever since the Reformation, this has been the critical question put by Anabaptists, Mennonites and Moravians to the Protestant churches. As long as these churches followed Article 16 of the Augsburg Confession in maintaining only the general responsibility of Christians for the world in the civil 'ordinances [which] are good works of God', the ethics of discipleship remained 'a Cinderella of the Reformation'.[66] But in a 'post-Christian' society, and especially in the deadly contradictions into which the modern social system has brought humanity and the earth, the special and identifiable Christian ethic of the discipleship of Jesus makes itself publicly evident. In this situation, faith in Christ can no longer be separated from ethics. The recognition that Christ alone is the Redeemer and Lord cannot be restricted to faith. It must take in the whole of life. It is the justifiable question which Mennonite theology puts to the Protestant doctrine of faith why 'Christ's perfect obedience' should for Protestantism be the yardstick only for saving faith, and not the yardstick for the obedience of faith as well.[67] The *solus Christus* of the Reformers cannot be normative merely for the doctrine of faith. It must be the rule for ethics too, for *solus Christus* also means *totus Christus* – the whole Christ for the whole of life, as the second thesis of the Barmen Theological Declaration of 1934 says.[68] But this means that christology and christopraxis become one, so that a total, holistic knowledge of Christ puts its stamp not only on the mind and the heart, but on the whole of life in the community of Christ; and it also means that Christ is *perceived and known* not only with mind and heart, but through the experience and practice of the whole of life. This too is an old Anabaptist truth which Hans Denk expressed at the time of the Reformation: 'No one is able verily to know Christ except he follow Him in life.'[69]

If praxis acquires this cognitive relevance in a holistic christology, then Christian ethics cannot be anything except ethical christology. But in this case Christian ethics are the ethics of Christians. Do they thereby lose their relevance for society as a whole? What is the importance of Christian existence for society generally? What does the universal horizon of the messianic way of Jesus Christ look like? If we call this horizon of Jesus' messianic gospel 'eschatological', then his gospel will be universal to the degree in which the eschatological horizon begins to shape the history of humanity, or the measure in which the history of humanity reaches this eschatological horizon of the end. But this eschatological horizon once again manifests that which gives creation at the beginning its impress, and fills it with life: the Spirit and Wisdom of God.

2. The Messianic Sabbath

If we look solely at Jesus' proclamation of the kingdom of God, this 'kingdom' often appears vague, and without any distinct content. It contains no social programme. With what kind of justice does God rule, and what laws obtain in his kingdom? The picture changes once we start specifically from Jesus' first proclamation in Nazareth, as this is recorded in Luke 4.18ff. What Mark and Matthew sum up as the proclamation of the imminent kingdom of God, and the conversion which is therefore required (Mark 1.15; Matt. 4.17), is developed in concrete terms by Luke, following Isaiah 61.1–2, as the proclamation of the Lord's 'Year of Jubilee' commanded in Leviticus 25.10ff.:[70] 'You shall hallow the fiftieth year, and proclaim a year of liberty throughout the land.' It is this which Jesus proclaims in the Spirit of God, and out of the Spirit, by whom he knows himself to be possessed.

If we take this literally, we can then comprehend Jesus' ministry and proclamation among the poor, which Luke 4.18 talks about, as well as Mark and Matthew. In history, the presence of God's kingdom takes the form of the year of liberty and its laws: (1) 'Each of you shall return to his property and to his family' (Lev. 25.10, 14–17). Debts are remitted, and enslavement because of debt is ended. The justice of God's covenant is restored among the people of the covenant. (2) You shall neither sow nor reap. . . . You shall eat what the field yields' (Lev. 25.11f., 19–23). The 'sabbath of the earth' guarantees that the people 'will dwell in the land securely' (Lev. 25.18). As Leviticus 25 and 26 show, the laws of the year of liberty contain a programme for a complete social reform, designed to do away with indebtedness and enslavement among the people, and to end the exploitation of the earth. If according to Isaiah 61.2 the promised messianic prophet is to proclaim 'the year of the Lord's favour', then this goes even beyond the Mosaic law given in Leviticus. The messianic year of liberty is the beginning of the messianic time; and the messianic time is time without end.[71]

The fundamental features of a messianic announcement and interpretation of the year of liberty laid down in Leviticus 25 can be discovered everywhere in Jesus' message and ministry. The call to have no worries (Luke 12.29ff.) corresponds exactly to the promise in Lev. 25.20–22. The remission of debts and the liberation of those who are enslaved because of debt, play a large part in Jesus' message. The 'forgiveness of debts as we forgive our debtors' in the Lord's Prayer, and the same teaching in the parables of 'the ungrateful servant' (Matt. 18.21ff.) and 'the unjust steward' (Luke 16.1ff.), are obviously laws for the year of release. The 'forgiveness of debts' corresponds literally to the 'remission of debts' according to Lev. 25.28, 54 in the Septuagint. In this respect the Lord's Prayer is 'a genuine Jubilee Year prayer'.[72] Hence the reciprocity of the 'forgive us our debts as we forgive our debtors', which sounds so un-Protestant. Jesus' 'sermon on the level place' according to Luke confers on the person who is encumbered with debt the liberation of the messianic Year of Jubilee, when one 'should lend expecting nothing in return' and 'forgive so that one will be forgiven' (Luke 6.34ff.). This breaks through the legal code of the credit business. In Israel, the remission of debts which was commanded every seven years according to the sabbath laws (Deut. 15.7–11) had led to the increasing freezing of credit, the closer the year of release approached. Rabbis such as Hillel and Shammai had evolved the so-called 'prosbul' solution: the claim for the repayment of a debt could be transferred to a judge, who could then call it in from the debtor: 'Transfer your loan to the court, which will recover it for you.'

In the face of this practice, the radical and final character of the year of release and liberty which Jesus proclaimed becomes clear. He did not merely proclaim *a* year of liberation. He evidently announced *the* messianic year of liberation. His radicalization of the Mosaic legislation shows his new messianic interpretation of the laws about the divine economy in God's kingdom. Unlike the Mosaic law, Jesus does not proclaim a year of liberty limited to a period of twelve months. What he announces is the messianic sabbath without end. If, as some historians believe, in the year 26 he actually proclaimed a Year of Jubilee to the impoverished, indebted and enslaved country people in Galilee,[73] then in the context of his proclamation of the kingdom this must be understood as a real foretoken of the imminent kingdom of God. At all events, it is clear that God's approaching kingdom in the history of Jesus takes the practical form of the messianic fulfilment of Israel's laws about the year of release and liberty. But if this is correct, then in Jesus' message the kingdom of God is bound up with a real programme of social reform, and moreover – although this is certainly not much developed – with a programme for ecological reform as well. The sabbath of the liberation of God's people, and the cancellation of their debts, is also the sabbath of the earth; for God's justice and righteousness brings shalom to both his people and his land.

Is Jesus' messianic interpretation of the laws of the year of liberation through the liberation of debtors, the enslaved, and the land itself, realistic and practicable?

If we see this interpretation in the light of the approaching kingdom of God, to act in this way is the only appropriate thing to do, and therefore the only reasonable thing. Once this creative expectation of the nearness of the kingdom is lost, it becomes more and more inappropriate and unreasonable to remit debts, free slaves, and respect the rights of the earth. The apocalyptic dimension of the approaching kingdom, and the end of the present world system which is bound up with it, are constitutive for the messianic interpretation of the laws of the year of liberation.

If we see this interpretation in the presence of God's Spirit and the Wisdom out of which Jesus speaks, then it is wise to act in this way, for it is accordant with the life of all created beings and the community of creation.

If we see this interpretation together with the person of Jesus Christ, God's messianic plenipotentiary, we see that in community with him people acquire the power and the right to live in the era of the messianic year of liberation without end, and to act accordingly. It is appropriate and reasonable that those who recognize him as the Christ of God should follow him in the praxis of remitting debts, liberating the oppressed, and ending the exploitation of the earth. If they were to act according to any other justice and any other law, they would be denying the messiahship of Jesus.

If we see this interpretation in the community of Jesus' brothers and sisters, its fulfilment becomes easy. The law for the year of liberation was given to the people of Israel, and was therefore a corporate justice; and in the same way the messianic interpretation of Jesus is related to the new corporate justice of God's messianic people. It is precisely and essentially not an individual ethic. But of course if a person 'keeps himself to himself' and is solitary, he is bound to feel that the demands made on him are too great.

Can this messianic activity in the remission of debts and the liberation of the oppressed be reconciled with this violent and therefore unredeemed world? That is certainly impossible. The community of Jesus which lives and acts messianically in the sense described, practises the great alternative to the world's present system. It is a 'contrast-society',[74] and through its existence it calls in question the systems of violence and injustice.

Not least, the messianic interpretations of God's year of liberation through Christ, and the alternative programme of the community of Christ, acquire increasing general plausibility the more our present-day political, social and economic systems destroy people and devastate the nature of the earth. Where the acts of men and women have in this way brought 'the end' so close for so many people and so many living things, it is reasonable and wise to look round for alternatives.

3. The Messianic Torah

There are evidently two possible ways of relating the gospel of Christ to Israel's Torah, theologically: (1) *antithesis*: the gospel is 'the end of the Law' (Rom. 10.4), and faith in the gospel frees people from the requirements of the Law; (2) *fulfilment*: the gospel of Christ is the messianic interpretation of Israel's Torah for all nations; and through love, the community of Christ fulfils the Torah in the dawn of the kingdom of God.

Protestant theology has always seen the relation between gospel and Torah in the light of the Reformers' antithesis between law and gospel. This viewpoint was one-sided. For one thing it did not do justice to Paul's differentiated view of gospel, law and promise (although it was to Paul that the Reformers appealed). For another, the Pauline identification of *nomos* and *torah* was not called in question.

There is rabbinic precedent for both possible forms of relation. 1. The thesis 'Christ is the end of the Law' goes back to the rabbinic hope that 'the Law will end when the messianic kingdom begins'.[75] 'In the school of Elijah [Rabbi Elijah ben Solomon, the Vilna Gaon] it is taught: the world will endure for 6,000 years: 2,000 years of chaos, 2,000 years of Torah, 2,000 years of the messianic era – but because of our many sins, some of these (years) have already lapsed.'[76] We can understand this periodization of God's history with the world to mean that the Torah will be abolished in the time of the messiah, and that an era without the Torah will then dawn. Probably what the saying really intends to say, however, is to be found in the final clause, about the delay of the messianic era 'because of our sins'. But sins are transgressions against the Law. In this case the messianic era cannot be a time without the Law, but must be understood as the time of the Law's perfect fulfilment – perfect because a matter of course. Rabbinic expectation looks for the complete understanding of the Torah and its matter-of-course observance in the messianic era. Paul belongs to this tradition, and in the light of its expectation will have perceived Jesus as the hoped-for messiah; so his thesis must be understood as meaning that Christ is the *goal* of the law (*telos*). The unconditional love which is possible through Christ and in the power of the Holy Spirit is the fulfilment of the Torah, and the form in which the Torah is carried over and translated into the messianic era.

2. But if Christ is the messianic fulfilment of Israel's Torah, how does this gospel come to the nations? In the first years of Christianity, did not Gentiles arrive at faith through the 'gospel free of the Law',[77] so that they did not have to become observant Jews first of all, in order to be Christians? Did not the Holy Spirit come directly upon Gentiles through the gospel, without awakening faith in Jews first of all? So the other possible way of relating the gospel of Christ to

Israel's Torah is evidently to see the gospel as *the messianic interpretation of the Torah* for the Gentile nations. This is the way Matthew presents Jesus' Sermon on the Mount: just as Moses brought the Torah from the mount of God to the people of Israel, so the messiah Jesus proclaims from the mountain the messianic Torah to 'his disciples and the whole people' (Matt. 5.1).[78] The author of the discourse is Israel's messiah, who is greater than Moses: 'But I say to you . . .' This turn of phrase expresses his authority, which surpasses the authority of Moses and all the prophets that succeeded him. In him we hear the voice of the end-time Wisdom of God, which from the beginning gives life to all created beings, and does not desire their death.

The proclamation is addressed first of all to *the people*. Matthew does not use the word *laos*, people of God, like Luke (7.1). He calls them *ochlos* – people who are poor, oppressed, lost. 'Seeing the people, he went up on the mountain and sat down; and his disciples came to him' (Matt. 5.1). At the end of the Sermon on the Mount we are told: 'And when Jesus finished these sayings, the people were astonished at his teaching, for he taught them as one who had authority, and not as the scribes' (Matt. 7.28f.). The double circle of disciples and people (*ochlos*) are important for the scene, because the messiah calls and teaches the people through his disciples, and with them. The Sermon on the Mount is popular preaching, not instruction for an élite. It is addressed to everyone, not to a chosen few. Its form is apocalyptic, but its content is Wisdom. Its intention is certainly the revival and gathering of the whole people of God, Israel – but the Israel of the messianic era. That is why this revival and gathering begins with the poor in Galilee, who cannot keep the Torah. It does not start in Jerusalem, the holy city. Probably *ochlos*, the word chosen for the people, was already unrestricted by any religious or national frontiers. It is so wide-open that all the weary and heavy laden on earth can find themselves in it – and have indeed done so throughout the centuries. But we must also remember that according to Isaiah 2, in 'the last days' of the messiah 'out of Zion shall go forth the law, and the word of the Lord from Jerusalem', and the nations will come to Zion in order to experience justice and rightousness; so in the messianic era Israel is to be in a unique way 'a light to lighten the Gentiles' which will be open to all the world.[79]

According to Matthew, the framework of the Sermon on the Mount points to *the people* and *the disciples*; so the beatitudes are also directed to the people and the disciples. The passive beatitudes can be distinguished from the active ones. The passive beatitudes probably go back to Jesus himself; the active ones to the experience of Christ in the community of Christians. If the poor, the sad and those who suffer are called blessed because the kingdom of God belongs to them, then the blessing is addressed to human beings in the state in which they passively find themselves. At the time of Jesus those meant were the poor, sad, suffering people (*ochlos*). If the merciful, the people who hunger for righteousness, those who are persecuted for righteousness' sake, the peacemakers and those with pure hearts are then called blessed, this means the men and women who follow Jesus in his messianic way of life and, like him, bring the kingdom of God to the poor. These two groups of beatitudes certainly reflect forms of the Christian community after Easter; but the distinction between them probably does actually go back to Jesus himself, who out of the people, with the people, and for the people, called those men and women who do the messianic will of his Father in heaven (Mark 3.32–35). Jesus' Sermon on the Mount is addressed to the people. In so far it is open to the world, and is universal in its trend and thrust. But men and women are called to follow Jesus, and to keep the messianic Torah. This is represented by the throng of men and women disciples. By way of the *antitheses*, 'the law of Christ' is related to Israel and to the law of Moses. By way of *the beatitudes* it is related to all human beings who hear it. The Sermon on the Mount therefore offers the ethic of a particular community, the messianic community of Christ. But this ethic is directed to the redemption of the whole people (*ochlos*), and claims universality.[80]

The ethics of discipleship is always *the ethics of community*. If it is the ethics of the community of Christ, it is bound to contrast with the ethics of the existing society, since the ethics of society as it exists are in contradiction to the liberation of the messianic sabbath, and the justice of the approaching kingdom of God. This, at least, is the way the contrast was felt, in the light of Jesus' life; and this was how it was experienced in the life of the early congregations: here service – there domination; here love – there violence (Mark 10.42–45). The messianic community rightly understands itself as a 'contrast society' (Gerhard Lohfink's phrase), which breaks through the fateful compulsion of violence which lies heavy on humanity, and offers a viable alternative to this deadly vicious circle. That is why this community is recognizable and identifiable. It is not anonymous.

It has a name. For it acts alternatively, not conformistically. Its righteousness is 'a better righteousness' (Matt. 5.20). What it does is 'the extraordinary thing' (περισσόν).[81] Because it attracts attention, its 'light shines before men' (Matt. 5.13–16). These statements about the messianic community of Christ would be inappropriate if the community were to withdraw into some kind of special social chimney corner, as an apocalyptic sect. Statements of this kind are only applicable if the community of Christ has its eyes turned to 'the people', as the ones to whom Jesus' Sermon on the Mount is addressed, and sees the people as the goal of its own mission. If it has this perspective, it will cling to the universal horizon of the Sermon on the Mount, and communicate its Wisdom of life to all who are threatened by death. It is only then that this community will offer a public alternative to the ethics of the world.[82] The Preacher on the Mount is not an apocalyptist who rejects the world. From him we hear the Wisdom of life.

If we wished to sum up the meaning and intention of Jesus' messianic interpretation of the Torah, we should have to put it like this: Taking the Sermon on the Mount seriously and following Christ go together. The discipleship of Christ, and brotherly and sisterly life in the community of Christ, go together. Life in the community of Christ, and the expectation of the universal kingdom of God among the people of the poor, the sad and the suffering, go together.[83] Hope for God's kingdom and the experience of poverty among the people; the community of brothers and sisters, and the discipleship of Christ – these things are a unity. And in this unity 'the law of Christ' is not an undue burden. It is a matter of course – 'the light burden' (Matt. 11.28–30) for all the weary and heavy-laden, who in it find rest. The Sermon on the Mount is the only 'wise thing', like 'the house that is built on rock', which cannot be swept away by the floods (Matt. 7.24–27). The Sermon on the Mount is not an ethic of particular views and sentiments. It says that everything depends on 'doing' (ποιεῖν). 'Everyone who hears my words and *does them* . . .' The flood that sweeps everything away that is without a foundation is the divine judgment which comes upon the world in the end-time of history. In that end-time, everything passes away that cannot stand before God. Anyone who in that end-time founds his life on what is future and eternal, which is the kingdom of God, is 'wise'. He does what is the only reasonable thing to do in the face of the world's situation. Anyone who does not think so far, experiences

Jesus' Sermon on the Mount as an unreasonable demand. But whoever thinks things through to the end perceives the wisdom of Christ's Sermon on the Mount, and acts accordingly. For the doing of it ensures continuance in the time of evanescence. So only the doing creates 'peace' of soul – that is, assurance.

Is the Sermon on the Mount capable of fulfilment? The answer cannot be discovered through an assessment of human possibilities. It has to be a theological answer: anyone who considers the Sermon on the Mount to be in principle impossible of fulfilment, mocks God; for God is the creator and lover of life, and he gives no commandments that cannot be fulfilled.[84] Anyone who considers that the Sermon on the Mount is fulfillable only in the sentiments of the heart, but not in public action, says that Jesus is wrong; for he preached the sermon precisely in order that it might be put into practice. Anyone who considers that it is fulfillable only for himself personally, but not in the context of his responsibility for other people, does not know God the Creator. Anyone, finally, who believes that only one person – Jesus himself – was able to fulfil the Sermon on the Mount, whereas everyone else is bound to fail in the attempt, thus to become a manifest sinner, is stifling the truth of the community of Christ, about which Paul says: 'Bear one another's burdens and so *fulfil* the law of Christ' (Gal. 6.2). In the community of Christ, which is a community of brothers and sisters, the messianic Torah, 'the law of Christ' is fulfilled. This community exists in the hearing of Jesus' word, and in the *doing* of it.[85]

4. The Messianic Peace

(a) Non-violent Action

Public discussions show that as far as public action is concerned, the centre of the Sermon on the Mount is the liberation from violence; enmity is to be surmounted through the creation of peace. The presupposition here is that humanity's real sin is the violence that leads to death; and that consequently humanity's salvation is to be found in the peace that serves our common life. Compared with Christian theology's traditional doctrine of sin and grace, this is an unusual position; and we are therefore stressing it particularly.

The primaeval history told in the Priestly Writing knows nothing of the story about the Garden of Eden and the Fall, which we find in Genesis 3. This story has dominated the doctrine of sin in the Western church ever since Augustine, although the terms 'sin' and 'guilt' do not in fact occur in the story at all. According to the Priestly Writing, the sin is the rampant growth of *violence* on earth, to which God responds with the annihilating Flood. Jewish exegesis does not interpret the story about the Garden of Eden through a doctrine of original sin either. Jewish interpreters see sin as beginning only with Cain's murder of his brother Abel.[86] According to Genesis 6.13, the earth was 'full of wickedness'. What does this wickedness consist of? Apparently the spread of violence and rape. Genesis 6 uses an ancient myth about the copulation of angels with women for the procreation of hybrid beings. According to 6.4, these are 'the mighty men' in the world, the 'tyrants'. So they are not mythical semi-gods, like the beings in the Gilgamesh epic – two-thirds god, one-third human being. They are the real rulers in Babylon and Egypt, who legitimated their rule of violence by having themselves worshipped as 'sons of God', and in the name of their gods subjugated the nations. Daniel 7 also talks about these chaotic world empires. Men who set up these kingdoms of violence no longer observe the divine Spirit of creation. They are 'flesh'. They live in protest against the Creator and their own creatureliness. They do not minister to life. They serve chaos. Human beings who adore and subject themselves to rules of violence like this are surrendering their own royal dignity as God's image. Only Noah 'led a godly life in his generation' (6.9) and lived in harmony with the righteousness of his own likeness to God. Genesis 6 says that the violence that rejects God and destroys life extended its grasp beyond the human world to 'all flesh in which is the breath of life'. That is, it even spread to the animal world, in the law of 'eat or be eaten'. That is why the annihilating Flood overwhelms 'all flesh'.

The counterpart to this depraved world of violence is then the covenant with Noah, in which the Creator of life himself becomes the revenger of deeds of violence (9.6). The covenant with Noah sets limits to human violence against animals too (9.4). It does not overcome the wickedness of acts of violence committed by one human being against another, and by human beings against animals, but it does restrict them, and imposes the death penalty for murder, so as to protect the perpetrators of violence from themselves, and in order to preserve the life of others.[87]

It is the Wisdom messiah who for the first time brings creation the peace that surmounts not only acts of violence, but also the violence used to restrict them. What is now ended is not only evil, but the law which repays evil by evil – not merely the act of violence, but also its restriction through violent resistance (Matt. 5.46). In the light of the messianic peace, it is not only the initial wicked act that is evil, but the pattern of retaliation too. The wickedness is not merely the first act of violence but the vicious circle of violence and counter-violence. Jesus demonstrates the messianic conquest of both in the rhetorical climaxes of the familiar passage:

> Do not resist one who is evil. But if any one strikes you on the right cheek, turn to him the other also; and if any one would sue you and take your coat, let him have your cloak as well; and if any one forces you to go one mile, go with him two miles. Give to him who begs from you, and do not refuse him who would borrow from you (Matt. 5.39–42).

This sequence looks like 'the renunciation of violence', and it has often been interpreted in that sense. But in actual fact its premise is a sovereign power over violence and counter-violence. The vicious circle of violence and counter-violence is broken. Non-resistance to evil shows up the absurdity of evil. Evil's strength is violence. Evil's weakness is its wrongness. Counter-violence supplies evil with its supposed justification, and often enough stabilizes it. It is only the non-violent reaction which robs evil of every legitimation and puts the perpetrator of violence in the wrong, 'heaping burning coals on his head' (Rom. 12.20). The rule of violence is built up on anxiety and terror. Where the rulers are unable to rouse either anxiety or terror, their violence loses its effect. This is the weakness of violence, and this is where the non-violent conquest of an act of violence starts. Gandhi understood the Sermon on the Mount correctly: talking about non-violent resistance, he said that counter-violence was better than resignation, but that non-violent action was better than counter-violence. This is also how Paul interpreted the Sermon on the Mount: 'Repay no one evil for evil. . . . Do not be overcome by evil but overcome evil with good' (Rom. 12.17, 21). To talk about 'not resisting' evil is merely a negative way of describing the positive response to evil through good. So even 'the renunciation of violence' is only a negative paraphrase of the conquest of violence through the non-violent creation of peace.

'Freedom from violence' does not mean de-politicization. Nor does it mean the renunciation of power; for our language distinguishes very clearly between violence and power. We give the name of power to the just use of force. Violence is the unjust use of force. All criticism of violence robs it of its legitimation, and emphasizes its character as 'naked violence' and pure brutality.[88] Christianity was not able to make Jesus' Sermon on the Mount the basis for abolishing 'the culture of violence' in the societies in which it spread. But it did require justification for every application of power – especially by the state. It broke with 'the innocence of power', which Nietzsche so extolled in the political 'brute beast', and it subjected the political exercise of power to a permanent compulsion to legitimate itself publicly to the people. The principle of non-violent action does not exclude the struggle for power, but it does oblige everyone to engage in a continuous struggle to make every exercise of power subject to law; for to subject the exercise of power to law is the first stage in the conquest of violence. The second stage in conquering the rule of violence is the solidarity of the people in rejecting that rule, and their refusal to co-operate with it in any form. The solidarity of other nations with a nation that is oppressed also contributes to the isolation of the ruler, and robs dictatorship of its stability. There are many examples of the way military dictatorships can be subdued by people in a bloodless, non-violent way – that is, through isolation.

The non-violent conquest of violence is not merely possible on the personal level. It is possible politically too. But the cost can be martyrdom. We need only think of Gandhi, Martin Luther King and Oscar Romero. But we also have to remember the Preacher on the Mount himself. And if we think of 'the sufferings of Christ' which Jesus and these others endured, we discover that it is not merely non-violent *action* that possesses liberating power, when it is successful. Liberating power is inherent in vicarious *suffering* too, and this suffering can in the long term be even more convincing in its results.

(b) Responsibility for our Enemies

Non-violent action is action that liberates from violence. This is what Jesus calls *loving one's enemies.*[89] Here we are translating it by *responsibility for one's enemies.*[90] According to the Sermon on the Mount, love of our enemies is the complete, divinely corresponding form of neighbourly love, and the way to lasting peace on earth. Whoever enters into a quarrel – whether personally or collectively – and engages in a conflict, is subjecting himself to the law of rejoinder and retaliation. Anyone who accepts this law in dealing with his enemy is drawn into a vicious circle of mutual hostility from which there is no escape. He has to become his enemy's enemy, and this fact puts its mark on him. If evil is repaid by evil, then one evil always makes itself dependent on another evil, because that is its way of justifying itself. And because it is hard to keep within the original bounds, there is always a surplus of evil, at least where the enemy is concerned. The inevitable consequence is an increasing spiral of mutual threat.

In our nuclear age, an arms race of just this kind is bringing the whole world to the edge of the abyss. We can only become free to live if we stop allowing the enemy's position to dictate ours, and if we end our obsession with the mutual threat, and let other criteria become more important. The criterion of the Sermon on the Mount is that we are the children of God, who lets his sun rise on the evil and on the good, and sends rain on the just and on the unjust, thus creating and sustaining life (Matt. 5.45). Here the ancient matriarchal symbols of the sun and the rain are used for God's love for everything he has created. In the messianic era, for us to take our bearings from the wisdom of the Creator of us all will break through our obsession with the enemy, and our insistence on paying back his hostility; for in the community of Christ, God as Father – Abba – has come as close to believers as his kingdom of peace.

Love of our enemies is not recompensing love, that returns what it has received. It is *creative* love. Anyone who repays evil with good has stopped just reacting. He is creating something new. Love of an enemy presupposes the sovereignty which springs from one's own liberation from enmity. Love of an enemy can never be subjection to the enemy, and the endorsement of his enmity which a surrender to him would imply. In the case of such a surrender, the sovereign agent of love of the enemy would no longer exist. What is in question is rather the intelligent conquest of the hostility. In loving one's enemies one no longer asks: how can I protect myself, and deter my enemies from attacking me? The question is then: how can I deprive my enemy of his hostility? Through love, we draw our enemies into our own sphere of responsibility, and extend our responsibility to them. Love of our enemies is therefore something very different from an ethic of particular views and opinions. It is a genuine ethic of responsibility.[91] It is superior to the ethic of self-assertion, which we find in friend-enemy thinking. Ultimately, therefore, it is the only reasonable thing, if we are to ensure lasting peace on earth. For it is impossible to secure this peace through the extermination of all potential enemies, or by threatening them with extermination. Politics in the modern age of nuclear threat demands thinking responsibly for the others concerned. This requires a large measure of sensitive understanding of the situation, and the fears and security requirements of others. But it is the only practical way to permanent peace.

The modern systems of deterrence and retaliation are logical enough in themselves, but their logic is the logic of universal death. On the other hand, if more and more Christian churches bind themselves to say 'no' to 'the spirit, the logic and the practice of the system of nuclear deterrent', then in the peril in which the world finds itself today they are acting in harmony with the logic of life, in accordance with the Sermon on the Mount. What counts as 'rational' in the general sense is always determined by the particular paradigm of feeling, thinking and acting in a given society. In this respect, 'rational' is not what is logical in itself, but what is 'a matter of course' at a particular time in a particular society – what seems plausible and convincing. Something that is excluded as irrational and impossible at one time, can at another very well count as rational and useful. At periods in which wars were a usual way of pursuing policies begun with other methods, conscientious objection and non-violent service for peace counted as 'unreasonable' and 'irresponsible'. In our own age, in which humanity cannot afford to engage in any major nuclear war, service for peace that renounces violence, and love of one's enemies, prove to be the only reasonable and wise behaviour. The demilitarization of public awareness and the democratization of dealings with those who are supposed to be 'enemies', are leading to a new sense that peace is a plausible objective.

5. 'Swords into Ploughshares'

Does the Sermon on the Mount count as valid? And is it something that has to be practised? This is going to decide whether in Western societies Christianity turns into a civil religion which (as J. B. Metz puts it) no longer demands anything and no longer consoles anyone; or whether we arrive at a community of Christians which confesses Christ, follows him alone, and follows him entirely. In an age when the nuclear annihilation of the world is possible at any time, the choice is going to be made through Christianity's witness for peace, and its public intervention on behalf of peace. The Old Testament's messianic promise of peace is expressed in almost identical words in Isaiah 2.1–5 and Micah 4.1–5, in both cases under the heading 'swords into ploughshares':

> It shall come to pass in the latter days that the mountain of the house of the Lord shall be established as the highest of the mountains . . . and all the nations shall flow to it, and many peoples shall come, and say: 'Come, let us go up to the mountain of the Lord . . . that he may teach us his ways. . . ' For out of Zion shall go forth the law, and the word of the Lord from Jerusalem. He shall judge between the nations and shall decide for many peoples; and they shall beat their swords into ploughshares, and their spears into pruning hooks; nation shall not lift up sword against nation, neither shall they learn war any more.

Micah 4.4f. adds:

> They shall sit every man under his vine and under his fig tree, and none shall make them afraid. . . . For all the peoples walk each in the name of its god, but we will walk in the name of the Lord our God for ever and ever.[92]

The time of universal peace is 'the latter days' – the final era. This is the time when the promises of God in history are fulfilled, the days of the messiah. The place of universal peace is Zion, the mountain of God, which will become the centre of the world when God with his glory finally takes up his dwelling there. Then 'the way of the Lord', the Torah, will be revealed and will convince not only Israel but all the Gentile nations too. Then the divine righteousness will dwell among all peoples, and because of it they will put an end to their godless wars and arrive at lasting peace. Through its justice and righteousness, the messianic Torah will bring final peace to all nations. The people of God, which already walks in the way of the Lord, counts as a model for all the other nations, who are still walking in the paths of their gods of war. That is why the vision of future peace ends in both Isaiah and Micah with the call to the people of the present: 'O house of Jacob, come, let us walk in the light of the Lord' (Isa. 2.5). 'All the peoples walk each in the name of its god, but we will walk in the name of the Lord our God for ever and ever' (Micah 4.5). According to the prophetic vision of peace, there is already a people which is turning swords into ploughshares, and which has ceased to wage war. In the promised days of the messiah, this peace through justice and righteousness is not merely proclaimed from Zion; it is actually practised by the messiah's people. This peace spreads through 'fascination', as Lohfink says, not through compulsion, not even through teaching. The light of peace-giving righteousness shines so brightly on Zion that the nations will come of themselves. But on the other hand the law 'goes *forth*' from Zion and then spreads to all nations. This, then, according to Isaiah, is a double movement of attraction and dissemination. Peace itself is pictured in earthly terms through the images of the vine and the fig tree, and justice for everyone. But it can be recognized by the abolition of war. It is future, but in its future existence it already determines the present of the people who walk in this way of the Lord.[93]

Before Constantine, the early Christian congregations related this prophetic promise of peace to themselves, for after Pentecost they lived in the awareness that they were experiencing those 'last days'. Consequently they tried to prove that this promise of peace had been fulfilled in their own community by turning away from all violence, and by a resolute, consistent service for peace. In the ancient world 'swords into ploughshares' was always and everywhere a recurring theme in the Christian church's picture of itself.[94]

> When the prophetic Spirit foretells the future it speaks thus: From Zion will go forth the law and the word of the Lord from Jerusalem. . . . They will forge their swords anew into ploughshares and their lances into pruning hooks. Never again will a nation raise its sword against another nation, and no longer will men teach the arts of war. That this has now come about, of that you may satisfy yourselves. For from Jerusalem men went into the world, twelve in number . . . all of them to teach the Word of God. And we who used once to slay one another now do not merely abstain from all enmity towards our antagonists: in very truth we even go . . . joyfully to death because of our confession of the Messiah (Justin, *Apology* 39).

There is overwhelming evidence that in the era before Constantine the church saw itself as the people of peace, called from the many hostile and warring nations. The apostles of Jesus the messiah bring the divine righteousness and peace from Jerusalem to all the nations; and out of all these nations the new people of God is gathered which, by creating this peace, teaches peace in justice and righteousness.

According to Origen, the church of the nations is the leader of that pilgrimage of the nations to Zion which the prophets promised.[95] The church is not the new people of God in Israel's stead. Nor is she herself 'the mountain of the Lord' and the instructor of the nations. But she is the first fruits of the hearing of the gospel of peace and the beginning of the conversion of people out of all nations, in all nations and for all nations. The church is 'the church of the nations', not only because of her mission but also because of her fascination: she is the vanguard of the nations who are coming to the peace of God.

It can hardly be said that the pre-Constantinian congregations were paralysed by the so-called 'delay of the parousia', so that they adapted themselves to the conditions which, things being as they are, are 'simply unalterable'. On the contrary, they lived in the consciousness that this was the messianic era, themselves practising the fulfilment of the prophetic promise of peace. It was evidently this that made these congregations so fascinating at that time, and which brought about the spread of Christianity. The Christian congregations evidently offered a real and livable alternative to the systems existing in the world of those days.

Did these congregations see their testimony to peace as a *demonstratio christologica*?[96] Does this mean that without the practical witness to peace of the community of his people, Jesus cannot be the messiah? This is Gerhard Lohfink's postulate, but it seems to me to go too far, binding Jesus' messiahship to the messianic works of his followers. But on the other hand, the holistic perception of Christ means that the messianic peace has to be grasped, not merely through the faith of the heart, but also through the deeds of the hands.

The testimony for peace of the Christian congregations was apparently so forcible that after the 'Constantinian revolution' the central Roman power moved against them, in the interests of the pacification of the empire. The *pax Christi* was now supposed to be realized through the *pax romana*.[97] The remembrance of 'the king of the Jews' crucified by the Romans under Pontius Pilate was overlaid by the myth of the victory of the Emperor Constantine in the sign of the cross – '*in hoc signo vinces*'. In the end, the conflict with the state was eliminated in the political theology of the Christian emperor by the providential birth of the Saviour at the time of Augustus, the emperor of peace.[98] Under the protection of the Roman legions the swords were certainly to be beaten into ploughshares – but of course not the swords of the legions themselves.

When the Christian Roman empire broke up under the onslaught of the Germanic tribes, and only the church stood fast, Augustine identified the *pax Christi* with the church's *pax eucharistica*, and emancipated it from its ties with the earthly *pax Romana*. But here on earth the eucharistic peace was to give no more than a sacramental foretaste. 'What we seek on earth is promised us [only] in heaven.'[99] But this postponed the 'doing' of the Sermon on the Mount to heaven; and a resigned adaptation to injustice and violence on earth was made theologically possible.

§8 JESUS – THE MESSIANIC PERSON IN HIS BECOMING

Up to now we have looked mainly at Jesus' ministry. We shall now enquire about his person, and shall make a first attempt to find our way from the conceptual angle into the stories about Jesus told by the synoptic gospels, so as to understand Jesus himself. Here we shall discover that Jesus' personhood does not exist in isolation, *per se*; nor is it determined and fixed from eternity. It acquires its form in living relationships and reciprocities, and becomes an open identity in the course of Jesus' history. In the traditional christologies, the *metaphysical concepts of nature* or essence are used to elucidate the constitution of the divine-human person of Christ. But these are not helpful, because they define divinity and humanity by way of mutual negations of the characteristics of the other: finite – infinite, mortal – immortal, passible – impassible, and so forth. The definitions are not drawn from the positive interplay of these attributes.[100] The *concepts of efficacy*, which are summed up in the Protestant doctrine of 'Christ's threefold office' as prophet, priest and king,[101] are also one-sided, because they do not take account of the living relationships and interactions in which Christ acts as prophet, as priest or as king. In this dogmatic doctrine, the picture of the solitary man and his unique work cuts Jesus off from reality and isolates him from the community of men and women. The more modern (and especially feminist) concepts about Jesus' being as *being-in-relationship* take us a step further.[102] But they do not yet enter into Jesus' being as a *being-in-history*, and the 'learning process' of his life and ministry, his experience and his suffering.

Here we shall try to take up the different christological concepts of person and integrate them, so as to arrive at a fuller, richer portrait of the person of Jesus Christ. We shall look at the divine person, the person in his messianic ministry, the public person commissioned by God, the person in the warp and weft of his relationships, and the person in the emergence and growth of his own life history.

1. The Messianic Person of Jesus

Whether Jesus himself believed that he was Israel's promised messiah and the expected Son of man sent by God is a historical question. The dogmatic question is: was he, and is he, 'the coming one' or not? We are starting here from the historical assumption that Jesus of Nazareth did in fact talk and act messianically; that he put himself in an identifying relationship to the messiah and the Son of man, who were figures of hope; and that the account of Jesus' messianic history is therefore not a projection by the Christian community after Easter on to a human life which in itself provided no grounds for this.[103] Historically speaking, it is inadmissible to assume that on the basis of its experience with the risen and present Christ the Christian community projected anything into the history of Jesus which was inconsistent with the remembrance of him as he was during his lifetime. Historically it is more plausible to assume that the experience of the present Christ and the remembrance of the Christ of the past corresponded, and complemented one another; for the fundamental assertions 'Jesus is the Christ' and 'Christ is Jesus' identify remembrance and experience, experience and remembrance.

In New Testament studies this problem is dealt with under the heading of 'Jesus' messianic secret'.[104] We shall adopt this heading and try to arrive at an interpretation of our own.

The synoptic gospels tell the life-history of Jesus in the light of the Easter experiences of the risen One, and for that very reason present Jesus' messiahship as a secret. They do not project a messianic identity on to a non-messianic life. But in the light of his resurrection the life of the earthly Jesus was bound to become the messianic secret. This is not merely in line with the character and behaviour of the earthly Jesus as he was remembered; it also corresponds to the openness for the future which people perceived in the light of his end. The key text here is Mark 8.27–31, and its centre is Jesus' question: 'Who do you say that I am?' When people judge what is new and strange, they work from analogy, taking as guideline what is already known and familiar, for 'like is known by like'. Consequently, people interpreted Jesus on the basis of analogy too, according to their remembrance of Israel's figures of hope: he was John the Baptist, risen from the dead, or he was the returning Elijah, or he was one of the prophets. Jesus is not asking the disciples for the answer to a riddle. It is a genuine question about the secret or mystery which Jesus himself is. He neither affirms nor denies the title of the Christ with which Peter acknowledges him. He suspends this answer, giving himself and the disciples an answer of his own: the announcement of his suffering. Who he truly is, is to be manifested in his death and resurrection. The disciples will perceive who he is when they follow him to the place where he is going, and when they take up their own cross. The announcement of suffering and the call to discipleship are Jesus' answers to the question about the Christ. The sequence is: suffering – great suffering – rejection – death at the hands of others; and this sequence shows step by step the total loss of self, the whole self-emptying, the loss of strength, the loss of dignity, the loss of human relationships, the loss of life. It is the road into a no-man's-land where there is no longer any sustaining tradition or human community – nothing but the God whom Jesus trusts.

Whether it is a post-Easter addition or not, the only path that leads out of this total death is the invisible hope for the resurrection from the dead. Whether Jesus himself went to his death in this hope we do not know, for the way of the messiah comes into being only under the feet of Jesus, who blazes the trail. A divine 'must' and the guidance of the Spirit of God draws him forward into death and the unknown future afterwards.

On the way which Jesus took, 'the messianic secret' is a secret even for him himself. According to that story in Mark 8.27–31, Jesus keeps his future open, and does not allow it to be conceived – or misconceived – in terms of analogies with anyone in Israel, either a historical figure or one hoped for. Whether their yardstick is Elijah or John the Baptist, the figure of the messiah or the Son of man, ideas of this kind, if they lead to preconceived judgments about what is to come, make the experience of what is new impossible or contradictory. Jesus does not reject the titles. He suspends them, and takes the path of suffering that leads to the cross. The titles, that is, are not the key signature for his history. His history is to provide the key to the titles. It is in the light of his road to the cross, and his experience of God on the cross, that the community of his people will determine what the title 'Christ' has to mean, when it is applied to

Jesus. Jesus' true 'messianic secret' is therefore *the secret of his suffering*. He did not 'claim' the messiahship; he suffered it. Through his suffering he 'learned obedience', says the Epistle to the Hebrews, and it is only in this 'obedience' that he will have experienced himself as Son of God and messiah.

'The messianic secret' should not be understood as the hiding of something that is already presently existent. We should see it as keeping a future open. The Christian community rightly understood the cross and resurrection as the revelation of that which Jesus truly is. In this light of what comes later, what is earlier appears as the way that leads there. The words and ministry of the earthly Jesus, and his fellowship with other people, are therefore presented in wholly messianic terms. But Jesus is as yet only *the messiah on the way* and *the messiah in his becoming*, led by God's Spirit and sustained by what he has experienced with other people through his energies and his words. That is why he responds to the question whether he is the one 'who is to come' by pointing to the 'signs and wonders' which take place in his presence (Matt. 11.5). Jesus does not *possess* the messiahship; he grows into it, as it were, since he is moulded by the events of the messianic time which he experiences. These events find their completion in him through the sufferings of the new Servant of God and the birth pangs of the new creation.

If, for these reasons, Jesus' relation to the messiah and the Son of man during his lifetime is seen as a relationship that is open and incomplete, this then does away with the old dispute as to whether Jesus came forward as a 'prophet' of his own future after Easter as the messiah-Son of man, or whether he already understood himself as this 'proleptically'.[105] Both notions fail to come to grips with the specific experience of Jesus' history of suffering and death. Instead, both start with his claim, and go on from the claim to deduce its 'endorsement'.

Did Jesus see himself as the messiah, or was he only declared messiah by the Christian community after Easter? The reason for the community's acknowledgment that Jesus was the Christ is undoubtedly the Easter event. By this we mean the appearances of Christ in the glory of God after his death, first of all to the women, and then also to the disciples, with the theological conclusion drawn by the people involved that God had raised him from the dead. But this confession of Christ on the basis of the Easter experiences is an acknowledgment of God first of all, and only after that an acknowledgment of Christ (Rom. 10.9). Because of their belief that God has raised him from the dead, believers confess Christ as Lord; and in confessing Christ as Lord, they believe that God has raised him from the dead. This confession says *what* Jesus is, on the basis of his resurrection; but it does not say *who* he is. Only the living remembrance of his life history and his message can say that. That is why the earthly Jesus had also to be brought into 'living memory' after Easter. *Easter* determines the *form* of belief in Jesus Christ, but not its content. The *content* is determined by *the history of Jesus' life*.

Does Easter permit anything to be said about Jesus which does not find support in the remembrance of him and the history of his life as it has been passed down? Can a life that was lived 'non-messianically' be declared a messianic one, in a process of hindsight, because of the Easter event? This is historically extremely improbable, and theologically wholly inadmissible. On the other hand, can anything new be known about Jesus after Easter, if everything is really already present and existent in him and with him? Does, in fact, the Easter event say nothing more than that 'the cause of Jesus goes on', as Willi Marxsen puts it? This too is historically improbable and theologically inadmissible.

In the patterns it traces, New Testament theology moves between these two extremes, while the extremes themselves become less and less convincing. What is manifested in the Easter confession of faith is in a certain way already implied and prepared for by Jesus himself; he placed himself 'indirectly' or 'cryptically' in an identifying relationship to the Son of man-Judge of the world. He acted messianically, while himself keeping the messianic secret. Consequently the earthly life and ministry of Jesus contains within itself what Conzelmann calls 'an implicit christology', which after Easter led to the explicit christologies of the Christian congregations. This view of the matter corresponds precisely to the stories about Jesus told in the gospels, for these present Jesus' life history as a history open to the future, because they look back from its end in his death and resurrection, and make him present in that light. They cannot present him as the completed and finished messiah, or as the Son of man in final form, because his suffering and resurrection are part of the history of his life. They therefore have to conceive of him as the messiah-Son of man 'in his becoming'. 'He is on the way to the one he will be', as Otto Weber says.

The implicit christology of the gospels is therefore theologically required. Is it also historically probable? If we judge the matter historically, unprejudiced by dogmatic or humanist postulates, we have to assume that there is a correspondence between the community's remembrance of Jesus, and their Easter experience of the One risen. Inconsistencies would have destroyed either the remembrance of Jesus or the experience of the risen One, and would in either case have broken down the identity involved in the acknowledgment 'Jesus – the Christ'.

Did Jesus see himself merely as the transcendent Son of man – Judge of the world, or did he also believe himself to be Israel's theo-political messiah? This is one of the 'tender spots' in New Testament theology, and not just today; it has been so ever since the early church. Here judgments were always unconsciously apologetic, and are so still. If Jesus indirectly identified himself only with the Son of man of the nations, but not with Israel's messiah, then Pontius Pilate made a mistake, and Jesus was the victim of a regrettable but isolated judicial error. The title written on the cross is wrong. The concern that is behind this way of thinking is obvious: in the Roman empire, so as not to be suspected of being adherents of someone justly executed as a terrorist and a subverter of the *pax romana* (which would have made them suspect themselves, and open to persecution), Christians from early on allowed Pilate to wash his hands in innocence. By suppressing the political side of Jesus' messiahship, they were able to lay the burden of Jesus' erroneous execution on the Jews instead.

The other concern behind the attempt to strip Jesus of his messiahship is to hand Jesus himself back to Judaism, so that on the basis of the kerygma of the death and resurrection of the Son of God, Christianity may be established as a world religion, detached from Judaism altogether.

The intentions behind both these trends are so obvious that they positively provoke the historical conclusion that Jesus must have come forward as Israel's messiah, that the title on the cross is correct, and that the Christian church is the community of the disciples of Israel's crucified messiah. But we must also see that, as his message shows, Jesus evidently had his own interpretation of his messiahship, which was wilfully individual compared with the Jewish history of hope; for his life, and the history of his impact, cannot be fitted into the long history of suffering of Israel's disappointed messianic claimants, from Bar Kochba to Shabbetai Zevi.

2. *Jesus – the Child of God*

In Israel's messianic promises the one who is anointed with God's Spirit is also called 'Son of God' (Ps. 2.7). Moreover Israel sees itself collectively as God's first-born son (πρωτότοκος). The special 'son of God' is the priestly king on Zion where, in the temple, God will allow his name to dwell. If Jesus of Nazareth is declared Son of God on the basis of his experience of the Spirit at his baptism, this initially means the messianic sonship. It does not yet signify a metaphysical identity of essence with God. Jesus is chosen by God, or 'adopted', to take the word used in modern so-called 'adoptionist' christology. But for Matthew and Luke this does not mean that Jesus was not from the very beginning born of the Spirit and filled with the Spirit. The fact that the Spirit 'descends' on him in baptism does not for them mean that the Spirit did not already act in him previously. In so far there is no alternative here between incarnation and adoptionist christology, as was claimed in the nineteenth century. But at the same time, Jesus' relationship to God as Son, like the sonship and daughterhood of later believers, is defined entirely and wholly pneumatologically (cf. Rom. 8.14, 16). Yahweh's *ruach*/God's Spirit creates the reciprocal relationship in which Jesus calls God 'Abba' and understands himself as 'child' of this Father.

The special characteristic of Jesus' relationship to God is made clear in the 'Abba' prayer.[106] In order to correct later misrepresentations, it is important to come back again and again to the intimacy of this prayer of Jesus'.[107] In Aramaic, 'Abba' is baby language. It is the word children use for their original person of reference. Whether it be mother or father, the important point is the sheltering, intimate closeness on which a child's basic trust depends. So when Jesus calls God 'Abba', he is not emphasizing the masculinity of a Father God, or the sovereignty of a Lord God. The stress lies on the unheard-of closeness in which he experiences the divine mystery. God is as close to him in space – as much 'at hand' – as the kingdom of God is now, through him, close, or 'at hand', in time. The kingdom is so close that God can be called 'Abba'; and when God can be called 'Abba', then his kingdom has already come. Jesus demonstrates this nearness of God by 'having mercy' and 'compassion' on the poor and suffering; and by doing so he substantiates God's 'feminine' attributes (Isa. 49.15; 66.13).

In his relationship to this Abba God, Jesus experiences himself as

God's 'child'. Again, stress is not on the masculinity of God's Son, but on his 'childlike' relationship. The reciprocal intimacy of the Abba and the child is lost the moment that this relationship is depicted as the relationship of God the Father to the Son of God.

The intimacy of this relationship also makes it impossible to see the persons as primary and the relationship as secondary. It is not a matter of 'God there' and 'Jesus here' first of all, and then the relationship between the two; it is much more that 'Abba' and 'the child' Jesus discover themselves mutually through one another. In his relationship to Jesus, God becomes 'Abba'; and in his relationship to his Abba God Jesus becomes 'the child'. This exclusive relationship of mutuality is brought out in the revelatory saying in Matt. 11.27. The Gospel of John uses the perichoresis idea: 'I am in the Father and the Father in me' (14.10, 11). The mutual relationship is a mutual indwelling, and is therefore constitutive for both. Because it stamps the personhood and name of both, it has to be viewed as equally primal. God's being as Abba and Jesus' being as child are in their mutual relationship roles, as it were, into which both grow together in their history from Jesus' baptism until his death on the cross. If this mutual relationship is constitutive for both persons and precedes the history they share, then it is not wrong to consider it to be – in the language of a later dogmatics – *pre-existent.*

The relationship to God described by the name Abba evidently influenced Jesus' understanding of himself quite essentially, for the results of this relationship to God are clearly evident in the scandalous behaviour passed down to us by tradition. He leaves 'his own people', his mother and his family, and goes to the poor among the people. Mark 3.31–35 par. reports his brusque rebuff to his mother Mary and his brothers:

> And a crowd was sitting about him; and they said to him, 'Your mother and your brothers are outside, asking for you.' And he replied, 'Who are my mother and my brothers?' And looking around on those who sat about him, he said, 'Here are my mother and my brothers! Whoever does the will of God is my brother, and sister, and mother.'

His family's opinion about him is like the judgment of the Pharisees: 'He is beside himself' (Mark 3.21). This is not merely a dismissal of his mother and his brothers. It is a formal secession from his family. As far as his mother was concerned, this was, and is, unheard of, for it is a Jewish mother that makes a person a Jew. Schalom Ben-Chorin quite rightly sees this as a deliberate breach of the fifth commandment.[108] And this will also have been the view taken by righteous Jews at the time of Jesus. If we follow up Ben-Chorin's point, we come upon Deut. 21.18–21: A 'stubborn and rebellious son' is to be given over to the elders to be stoned, as punishment. The parents are to say to the elders: 'This our son is stubborn and rebellious, he will not obey our voice; he is a glutton and a drunkard' (v. 20). The chapter ends with the comment: 'Accursed is the one who hangs on the tree.' The New Testament story of Jesus is full of echoes of this chapter in Deuteronomy on the fifth commandment.

What does Jesus put in place of the family bond and the ties with God's chosen covenant with the generations? He recognizes a new community among the people who do the will 'of my Father in heaven' (Matt. 12.50). The messianic community which is drawn into Jesus' Abba relationship is made up – in the transferred sense – not merely of 'brothers and sisters' but of 'mothers' as well. The people who follow him, both women and men, will again find in the messianic community everything they have left behind them in their natural families – brothers, sisters, mothers, children. But there are no longer any fathers! This is often screened out because it is so strange (Mark 10.29–30). But it means nothing less than that 'There must no longer be any partriarchal rule in the new family – only motherliness, brotherliness, and the relationship of the child to God the Father'.[109] Why no fathers? 'Call no man your father on earth, for you have one Father, who is in heaven' (Matt. 23.9). The Abba nearness of God apparently fills and permeates this new messianic community of Jesus to such an extent that the function and authority of earthly fathers disappear. In this respect the messianic community which Jesus gathers round himself really is at variance with the patriarchal society of that time. But it is not at variance with the mothers, fathers, sisters and brothers in person. Whoever does the will of the Father in heaven is a member of this new messianic community. That is why later on we find Jesus' mother and his brothers in the community of Christians – not as his mother, and not as his brothers, but as believers (Acts 1.14).

The divine 'Abba' secret breaks through Jesus' ties with his origins, aligning him totally towards the future of the messianic kingdom. Under the guidance of this Abba, Jesus enters into the social and religious no-man's-land of a still unknown future: the kingdom of God.

In Rom. 8.15 and Gal. 4.6 Paul cites Jesus' Aramaic address to God in prayer, 'Abba, dear Father', as the prayerful cry of the Christian congregation. It was probably the address used in prayer by the charismatics. Anyone who believes in Jesus the messiah is accepted into this intimate relationship with God: like Jesus and together with him, the believer talks to Abba, the beloved Father. The consequences are analogous. In community with 'the first born' among 'many brothers and sisters', believers see themselves as 'God's children'. Like Jesus and in his discipleship, they break with the archaic powers binding them to their origins in family, class and culture, and now live in the liberty of the Spirit, and out of the future of the messianic kingdom. That is why among the messianic people of God the cry 'Abba' becomes the supreme expression of liberty.

The later theological formula about 'the father of our Lord Jesus Christ' exactly preserves Jesus' way of speaking about 'my Father'; and that way of speaking, in its turn, preserves the 'Abba secret' which is the liberating centre of Jesus' messianic message. The praxis which this formula makes possible is not the formal address to God the Father, but the confident familiarity and intimacy of the Abba prayer.

To say this is certainly to run counter to the process of early Christian tradition. Matthew added to the 'Our Father' prayer the phrase 'who art in heaven', and by doing so he introduced a spatial distance into God's Abba nearness. Paul still knew that in Rome and Galatia the Christian congregations addressed God as Abba. But soon afterwards this prayerful address must have disappeared from Christian worship and have given way to more reserved salutations. The Hebrew words 'Amen' and 'Hallelujah' were taken over, and are still used today; but the early Christian 'maranatha' disappeared with the 'Abba'. This is not chance. It shows that the fatherly nearness of God signalized by 'Abba' goes together with the nearness of the kingdom to which Jesus' ministry belonged. With the delay of the parousia, people evidently became conscious of the spatial distance from heaven, and the temporal distance from the coming kingdom.

3. *Jesus - a Person in Social Relationships*

As we have seen, Jesus lived in mutual relationships with the poor and the sick, sinners, and the men and women who had been thrust

out of society. It was in these relationships that he spread his gospel.
It was in his reciprocal relationships with the faith of the people
concerned that the miracles of the messianic era came about. It was
in his reciprocal relationships with the men and women disciples
who followed him that Jesus discovered his messianic secret. We
have to look more closely at his life in the context of these social
relationships, for we can only understand the life-histories of men
and women in the light of their relations with other people, and the
communities to which they belong.

(a) Jesus and His Fellowship with Women and Men

We have already described how a community of people who
followed Jesus gathered together, so we shall here look only at the
reciprocal relationship between Jesus and the women in this community, and especially the group of women who are known to us.
They were the last witnesses of his death and the first witnesses of
his resurrection. But these women were close to him not only at the
end, but during his lifetime and ministry as well.[110] The woman
with the issue of blood (Mark 5.24ff.) exacts from Jesus the healing
she needs without his will. The Canaanite woman (Matt. 15.21ff.)
convinces Jesus of the generous magnanimity of his God, which
does not stop short at the borders of Israel. The poor prostitute
(Luke 7.36ff.) is not afraid to force her way into the Pharisee's
house, and anoints Jesus' feet. Martha, Lazarus' sister, induces
Jesus to raise her dead brother, and confesses him as the Christ of
God (John 11.19ff.). Finally, but not least, we must remember the
great unknown woman who in Bethany anoints Jesus' head as only
kings were else anointed (Mark 14.3ff.). For the synoptic gospels,
what these women do for Jesus is apparently just as important as
what Jesus does for them. At his crucifixion the group of women
stand there and see him die, 'perceive' his death (θεωρεῖν) – that is,
they share in his dying. They do not run away like the men
disciples. It is only when they are faced with the empty tomb that
'they are afraid'. They proclaim the Easter message to the disciples.
These women are close to the secret of Jesus' death and resurrection. Without them, the stories wish to say, there would be no
authentic witnesses of Jesus' death and resurrection. In Jesus'
voluntary 'service' (Mark 10.45), which is an alternative to political
domination and subjection, the women are again closest to him, for
this διακονεῖν is otherwise used only of them (Mark 15.41). In the

fellowship of mutual service without domination and without servility, they live out the liberty which Jesus brought into the world.

The closeness of the women to the service, death and resurrection of Jesus is important not only for the women but for Jesus himself too. Here the fact that Jesus was a man is irrelevant. The community of Jesus and the women manifests the truly human existence which the new creation of all things and all conditions sets free.

(b) Jesus and Israel

Jesus' life and the way he acted was related to community, and it was therefore always a receiving and an acting on behalf of other people, and in their stead. According to the gospels, it was just as much related to Israel as was the life and ministry of John the Baptist. For the early Jewish–Christian community, the unity between Jesus and Israel was especially important. Mark 3.14 tells us that 'he appointed twelve, to be with him, and to be sent out to preach . . .' According to this passage, Jesus called *twelve* to be special disciples out of the wider circle of those who followed him, passing on to them his own messianic mission (Matt. 10.5ff.). The number twelve represents the twelve tribes of the people of Israel, for the messianic hope was aligned towards the restoration of this people in the era of salvation. According to Ezekiel, this was also to be linked with the re-occupation of the land of Israel. Jesus' choice of twelve disciples is a messianic act: with them the end-time gathering of Israel, as the renewed people of God, is to begin.[111] Consequently, the twelve are also sent to 'the whole of Israel', but not to the Gentiles (Matt. 10.5). If the kingdom of God 'is near', the gathering of God's people for this kingdom must begin. Then Israel will become the messianic light of the Gentile nations, and the nations will come to Zion to receive God's righteousness and justice (Isa. 2.1–3). In this order of things, salvation comes 'first to the Jews and then to the Gentiles'.[112]

Although Jesus turns first of all to Israel, this is not meant exclusively, for in his concern for Israel God is concerned about the Gentile nations and the earth. The appointment of the twelve disciples for Israel's revival is not the same thing as the call to follow Jesus, or identical with the community of women and men who followed him. It has a symbolic meaning for Israel alone. In choosing the twelve, Jesus was not founding any church. He was thinking solely of Israel. Only one person was evidently 'co-opted' to this group later on: Matthias took the place of Judas. After that the group did not perpetuate itself. It probably broke up when Christianity spread beyond the bounds of what was open to it among the Jews. For that reason, to trace the church back historically and dogmatically to the calling of the twelve, and the special call to Peter, is untenable, and also pernicious, because it allows the church to push Israel out of salvation history. The church 'of Jews and Gentiles' only came into being after the resurrection, and through the experience of the Spirit, and with the rejection of the gospel by 'all Israel'.[113]

At the same time this early Jewish–Christian hope for the revival of the nation of the twelve tribes binds Jesus into a unity with his people which Gentile Christians must not destroy. The synoptics tell the life-history of Jesus in the pattern of the collective remembrance of the history of Israel. The future hope of the people is summed up in their expectation of the messiah. In the gospel to the Gentile nations, the presence of Jesus Christ makes Israel present also, just as, conversely, Gentile Christians through their faith participate in the remembrance, the hope and also the sufferings of Israel, the people of God.[114]

(c) Jesus and the People

According to the Gospel of Mark, there was originally a particularly close relationship between Jesus and the people (ὄχλος).[115] Mark 3.34 tells us that the people were his true 'family', although Matt. 12.46 replaces the people by 'the disciples'. Wherever Jesus goes in Galilee, the poor who have been reduced to misery gather round him. He teaches them. They bring him their sick. He heals them. They move about with him. The distress of the people awakens in him the divine compassion (Mark 6.34). His call to discipleship is directed to 'the multitude with his disciples' (Mark 8.34). The 'multitude' are the poor, the homeless, the 'non-persons'. They have no identity, no voice, no power and no representative. 'The multitude', 'the people', is the vocabulary of domination: the plebs, the riff-raff – this is the way the ruling classes define people in the mass, shutting them out into a social no-man's-land. 'The people' are also defined and shut out by cultural domination. They are the crowd without 'shepherds', without any religious or recognizable ethnic identity. Whereas the word λαός is used for the people of God and ἔθνη is used for the nation, these downtrodden masses are ὄχλος.

In Galilee 'the multitude' in this sense were *de facto* the poor Jewish country people. They were not so designated because they were Jewish, but because they were poor. So Jesus' solidarity with these people has a certain universalism which takes in all the poor who have been reduced to misery. Jesus takes as his family 'the damned of this earth', to use F. Fanon's expression, and discovers among them the dawning future of the kingdom and God's new creation. His 'compassion' is not charitable condescension. It is the form which the divine justice takes in an unjust world. These 'last' will be 'first'. Jesus does not merely *go to* the people in the name of God. He is actually their representative, just as the people represent him. He is one of theirs, and they are the least of his brothers and sisters (Matt. 25.40).

4. The Three-Dimensional Person of Jesus Christ

Let us sum up what we have discovered.

(*a*) To confess Jesus as the Christ of God means perceiving him in his *eschatological person*. In him are present Israel's messiah, the Son of man of the nations, and the coming Wisdom of creation itself. He is the kingdom of God in person, and the beginning of the new creation of all things. In this way he is the bearer of hope for the world. In him believers recognize *the messianic human being*.

(*b*) To confess Jesus as the Christ of God also means perceiving him in his *theological person*. He is the child of God, the God whom he calls Abba, dear Father. As the child of God, he lives wholly in God, and God wholly in him. He opens this unique relationship with God to all who believe him and who, as children of God, like him cry 'Abba'. They participate in Jesus' joy. In him believers recognize *the childlike human being*.

(*c*) To confess Jesus as the Christ of God further means perceiving him in his *social person*. He is the brother of the poor, the comrade of the people, the friend of the forsaken, the sympathizer with the sick. He heals through solidarity, and communicates his liberty and his healing power through his fellowship. In him men and women recognize *the brotherly and sisterly human being*.[116]

In each of these three dimensions Jesus as the Christ of God is a public person, not a private one. He is a person publicly commissioned by God, and he personifies the public concerns of the people.

Merely to take account of any single one of these dimensions in Jesus' person as the Christ leads to a one-sidedness that has fatal consequences. Traditional christology stressed only the *theological* person of the God-man Jesus Christ. Modern eschatological theology stressed the *eschatological* person of Jesus Christ. The most recent contextual christologies have disclosed the *social* person of Jesus Christ. These last two developments have again begun to take seriously the messianic and social mission of Christ, over against the christology of the Nicene and Apostles' creeds; for in these creeds there is either nothing at all, or really no more than a comma, between 'and was made man, he suffered' or 'born' and 'suffered . . .'. We cannot close this chapter on the messianic mission of Jesus Christ without offering a suggestion for an addition to these two ancient creeds of the church. The intention is not to alter the words of tradition; but one must know what has to be added in thought. After 'born of the Virgin Mary' or 'and was made man', we should add something along the following lines:

> Baptized by John the Baptist,
> filled with the Holy Spirit:
> to preach the kingdom of God to the poor,
> to heal the sick,
> to receive those who have been cast out,
> to revive Israel for the salvation of the nations, and
> to have mercy upon all people.

IV

The Apocalyptic Sufferings of Christ

§1 THE APOCALYPTIC HORIZON OF WORLD HISTORY

At the centre of Christian faith is the history of Christ. At the centre
of the history of Christ is his passion and his death on the cross. We
have to take the word 'passion' seriously in both its senses here, if we
are to understand the mystery of Christ. For the history of Christ is
the history of a great passion, a passionate surrender to God and
his kingdom. And at the same time and for that very reason it became
the history of an unprecedented suffering, a deadly agony. At the
centre of Christian faith is *the passion of the passionate Christ*. The
history of his life and the history of his suffering belong together.[1]
They show the active and the passive side of his passion.

In earlier times, the active passion of Christ which led him into
those sufferings was often overlooked. 'The Man of Sorrows'
became the prototype of dumb submission to an unhappy fate.
Today people prefer rather to overlook the suffering which is part of
every great passion. To be painlessly happy, and to conquer every
form of suffering, is part of the dream of modern society. But since
the dream is unattainable, people anaesthetize pain, and suppress
suffering, and by so doing rob themselves of the passion for life. But
life without passion is poverty-stricken. Life without the preparedness for suffering is superficial. The fear of passion has to be
surmounted just as much as the fear of suffering if life is to be really
lived and affirmed to the point of death.

Here we shall take the phrase 'the sufferings of Christ' as an
epitome of the theology of the cross we shall be developing. Like
passio in Latin and passion in English, πάθημα in Greek has the
double meaning of intense feeling or desire, and suffering. The

'sufferings', the 'affliction', the 'reproach' and the 'shame' of Christ are words used in the New Testament – and especially by Paul – to describe (1) the personal sufferings of Jesus from Gethsemane to Golgotha, (2) the sufferings of the apostle who proclaims the gospel of Christ, is therefore persecuted and has to suffer, (3) the sufferings of Israel, the prophets and John the Baptist, and (4) the sufferings of the whole groaning creation in this present time. So 'the sufferings of Christ' are not confined to Jesus. They have universal dimensions, because they belong within the apocalyptic setting of the time in which a term is set for all things. But the apocalyptic sufferings of 'this present time' are gathered up into 'the sufferings of Christ' on Golgotha. Jesus suffers them in solidarity with others, and vicariously for many, and proleptically for the whole suffering creation. We shall look at the exclusive aspect of Christ's sufferings and at their inclusive side, in order to develop a christology which is relevant in the sufferings of our own time.

In doing this I am choosing a new starting point compared with the theology of the cross I developed in 1972 in *The Crucified God* (ET 1974). In that book I was concerned with the question about God: what does the death of Christ mean for God himself? I tried to get over the ancient metaphysical apathy axiom in the doctrine of God, so as to be able to talk about God's 'essential' suffering, and to do so not merely metaphorically but quite directly. I saw the God-forsaken cry with which Christ dies on the cross as the criterion for all theology which claims to be Christian. For me the theology of the cross came to be seen in the context of the theodicy question, confuting not merely abstract atheism but abstract theism too.[2] I have no wish to retract anything I said there, and these earlier ideas are the presupposition for this apocalyptic theology of Christ's sufferings.

The doctrine of God which was developed in that book, then, grew out of the theology of the cross; and in 1980, in *The Trinity and the Kingdom of God* (ET 1981), I took this doctrine further, developing a doctrine of the Trinity founded on the essential love of God which can be discerned in the mutual relationships of the Father, the Son and the Spirit and which, in the perichoresis of the divine persons, becomes the archetype of the community of human beings and all creation.[3] In chapter III, 'The History of the Son', I went beyond cross and resurrection, integrating 'the sending of the Son' on the one hand and 'the future of the Son' on the other into trinitarian christology. Here too, in taking as my subject the apocalyptic horizon of Christ's sufferings, I am presupposing these earlier interpretations, and adding to them. I shall recapitulate where necessary, pointing out any modifications I have meanwhile come to make.

Jesus' life is already marked by suffering in the very light of his messianic message, not just at its end. His messianic passion brought with it the experience of apocalyptic suffering. That is why Jesus answers the disciples' question whether he is the messiah with the announcement of suffering, and with the call to follow him into suffering (Mark 8.27–35). It is not merely the ethical side of the Sermon on the Mount which brings us face to face with the kingdom of God, whose imminence Jesus proclaims and lives. This is equally true of the apocalyptic side, which has to do with the end of 'this world' (Mark 13; Matt. 24; Luke 21).[4] Understood apocalyptically, the kingdom of God brings the end of this world-time and the beginning of the new creation. That is to say, its coming brings the tribulations and assailments of the end-time. For 'this world', they mean the catastrophic end. But in fact they are the birth pangs of the new world. These 'worlds' are 'world eras', aeons, not heaven and earth themselves. Liberation from 'the godless ties of this world' frees people for 'grateful service' on behalf of 'all those whom God has created'.[5] Apocalyptic has nothing to do with Manichaeism. It is hope in the Creator of a new creation. Since this new world-time of God's kingdom comes into this world-time and to its power-centre Jerusalem in the form and message of the poor and defenceless Jesus from Galilee, the sufferings of the end-time manifest themselves in his conflicts and his sufferings. In the context of his message about the kingdom of God, his sufferings are not his own personal sufferings, which he suffers for himself. They are the apocalyptic sufferings which he suffers for the world. They are not fortuitous sufferings. They are necessary. They are not fruitless sufferings, through which something good is shattered. They are fruitful sufferings which, like labour pains, bring forth what is good: 'When a woman is in travail she has sorrow, because her hour has come; but when she is delivered of the child, she no longer remembers the anguish, for joy that a child is born into the world. So you have sorrow now, but I will see you again and your hearts will rejoice and no one will take your joy from you' (John 16.20–23).

Jesus' call to discipleship leads men and women to break their existing ties and the forces that dominate them, for the sake of the new creation. It may therefore lead to persecution by these forces, and to suffering. In the light of the new creation, the sufferings of those who follow Jesus are also sufferings belonging to the end-time (πειρασμός). Jesus' followers are sent 'like sheep among wolves'; and yet the future of the new creation belongs, not to the wolves, but to the Lamb of God (Matt. 10.34; Mark 13; Luke 12.51).

Jesus himself is bound into a community of tradition with suffering Israel and her persecuted prophets. John the Baptist was murdered by the powerful, like many other prophets before him (Luke 13.34; Matt. 23.37–39). Jesus' followers were not the first to undergo these end-time sufferings. His prophetic predecessors already had to endure them because of their message. The apocalyptic sufferings of Christ also show the characteristic features of the sufferings of Israel, God's people in this Godless world.

With his prophecy about the destruction of the temple and his announcement of the new temple of the messiah, Jesus apparently deliberately sets Zion in the context of the end-time he saw, thereby provoking the temple priests. This is the only way we can read the tradition about his encounter with Rome and Pontius Pilate, the imperial power of this world-time and its Jerusalem representative. This is the confrontation between the messiah of the new world and the violent men of the world that is passing away. Jesus apparently sought this confrontation, probably not in order to wring a judgment from God, as Schweitzer thought,[6] but doubtless in order to understand as part of the end-time his defeat in this confrontation, and so as to read in this context all that he suffered from his condemnation by the representatives of his people, and his death on the Roman cross. According to Mark 14.25, the Last Supper with the disciples links his death with the kingdom of God. According to Luke 22.18, Jesus will not drink wine again 'until the kingdom of God comes'.

It is in line with the link between messianism and apocalyptic when the synoptic gospels depict Christ's death on Golgotha with the accompaniment of apocalyptic phenomena: darkness descends on the earth, the veil in the temple is torn in two, the earth quakes, the rocks burst apart, the graves open, saints rise from the grave and appear . . . (Matt. 15.45–56 par.). In the light of his messianic message about the kingdom of God and the new world aeon, the opposition Jesus experienced and the suffering and death he endured is apocalyptically interpreted as summing up and anticipation of the end-time suffering in which 'this world' will reach its end and the 'new world' will be born.

An apocalyptic light is shed on 'the sufferings of Christ' not only by his messianic message about the Kingdom of God, but also by the Easter event. Since this crucified Jesus of Galilee has been 'raised from the dead' ahead of all others, he is now already living in the new world of eternal life. God has already done for this 'first fruits of those who have fallen asleep' what he will do for all human beings at the end. In Jesus he has already broken the power of death.

But if Jesus' resurrection is interpreted as the anticipation of the general resurrection of the dead, how is his death to be interpreted? His death is then the anticipation of the death that is universal and absolute. It is not merely his private, personal end. As an anticipation of universal death, Golgotha is the anticipation of the end of this world and the beginning of a world that is new. It is the anticipation of the divine judgment out of which the kingdom of righteousness and justice proceeds. What has already happened to Christ is representative of what will happen to everybody: it is a happening *pars pro toto*. Consequently he has suffered vicariously what threatens everyone. But if he has suffered vicariously what threatens everyone, then through his representation he liberates everyone from this threat, and throws open to them the future of the new creation. He did not suffer the sufferings of the end-time simply as a private person from Galilee, or merely as Israel's messiah, or solely as the Son of man of the nations. He also suffered as the head and Wisdom of the whole creation, and died for the new creation of all things. 'The suffering in this cosmos is universal because it is a suffering with the suffering of Christ, who has entered this cosmos and yet burst the cosmos apart when he rose from the dead.'[7]

In 'the sufferings of Christ' the end-time sufferings of the whole world are anticipated and vicariously experienced.

'The sufferings of Christ' are part of the history of suffering endured by Israel and God's prophets. So 'the sufferings of Christ' are open for 'fellowship' with them, the κοινωνία παθημάτων αὐτοῦ (Phil. 3.10). This 'fellowship of Christ's sufferings' is experienced by the apostles of the gospel, the martyrs of faith and resistance, the poor, and the whole sighing non-human creation. The παθήμ-ατα are in this way [i.e., through the phrase ὁ νυν καιρός, 'this present time', Rom. 8.18] designated as the sufferings which inevitably arise from the antithesis between the Christ event and the nature of this aeon. The παθήματα τοῦ νῦν καιροῦ ['the sufferings of this present time'] are therefore no other sufferings than the παθήματα or θλίψεις του Χριστοῦ ['the sufferings' or 'tribulation of Christ'].[8]

'The sufferings of Christ' are not just Christ's own sufferings. They are also sufferings which the apostles and martyrs endured for Christ's sake. 'Now I rejoice in my sufferings for your sake, and in my flesh I complete Christ's afflictions (AV: fill up that which is behind in Christ's afflictions) for the sake of his body, that is the church' (Col. 1.24). The apostle certainly does not consider Christ's sufferings to be insufficient, and in need of supplement. For he does not see himself as 'a second Christ' or as 'a prolongation of Christ'.[9] Nor is he seeking a 'mystical way' through suffering. But he is not suffering merely *for* Christ. His apostolic sufferings are sufferings *with* Christ. Christ suffers in him, for in the apostolic passion for the gospel and for the new creation of the community of Christ's people, Christ himself is present. Consequently the apostolic sufferings – persecution, imprisonment, poverty and hunger – are Christ's sufferings too, and as such they are the birth pangs of the new creation. Paul evidently understood his whole apostolic existence in this light: 'always carrying in our body the death of the Lord Jesus, so that the life of the Lord Jesus may also be manifested in our bodies' (II Cor. 4.10).[10] If he sees his sufferings as a manifestation of the sufferings of Christ, then he also sees them as participation in the apocalyptic sufferings in which this world passes away and God's new world is born. For him, the community of Christ is the true beginning of the new creation in the midst of this transitory world (II Cor. 5.17). So the apostle's sufferings are sufferings for the birth and life of the community in Christ.

'The fellowship of Christ's sufferings' (Phil. 3.10) reaches beyond the special sufferings of the apostle and embraces the whole community of Christ's people, where it witnesses to Christ and manifests the new creation in this world. It then takes up the confrontation with the powers of this world, injustice and violence, and makes the conflict between the two world eras its own. This gives the community of Christ the right and the duty to esteem its special martyrs, and to make their faith and their resistance an orientation point. To turn remembrance of the martyrs into a special cult of the saints can mean putting the martyrs at a safe religious distance. But for a church to forget and disregard its martyrs is certainly a sign that Christianity has turned into a civil religion; for the power of the resurrection is experienced in the fellowship of

Christ's sufferings in a very special way (Phil. 3.10). If the martyrs are disdained, then the power of faith in the resurrection disappears from a church at the same time.[11]

The fellowship of Christ's sufferings reaches beyond the community of Christ and its martyrs, for these sufferings are end-time sufferings, which take possession of *the whole creation*. But who are the first victims of 'the sufferings of this present time'? They are the weak, the poor and the sick. In the struggle for power which is the trademark of 'this world', the weak suffer most, the oppressed are sacrificed first of all, the children are the first to die. In the struggle for wealth people destroy the creatures that are weaker than themselves. Nature dies her dumb death first of all, and the death of the human race follows.

If this death is viewed against an apocalyptic horizon, and not as something normal or natural, then the great apocalyptic dying, the death of all things, has already begun. 'This world' is passing away. The human systems of injustice in the world-wide economy and the political hegemonies cost the lives of millions year for year, first and foremost the lives of children in the Third World. Scientific and technological exploitation systems are destroying the earth's biosphere, and are wiping out hundreds of animal and vegetable species every year. The system of nuclear deterrent is progressively destroying the humanity of the nations through fear and cynicism. In the face of this annihilation of the world caused and threatened by human beings, the victims of injustice and violence are today becoming the witnesses of God's indictment, and witnesses too to the necessity of conversion; for they are the least of the brothers and sisters of the Son of man who is the judge of the world (Matt. 25). But if these 'least' belong within the fellowship of Christ, their sufferings are also 'sufferings of Christ', for he is one of their own, and they are his people. The message of the human and non-human creation which is dying of injustice and violence is its collective martyrdom. 'Jesus will be in agony until the end of the world', wrote Pascal.[12] But the reverse is also true. In the agony of Christ this world finds its end.

To perceive the universal and apocalyptic dimension of Christ's sufferings means remembering these sufferings 'in the context of limited time',[13] or to be more precise: in the context of the end of time. The original Christian experience of time is characterized by expectation of the imminent end of days: 'The end of all things is at hand' (I Peter 4.7), 'the form of this world is passing away' (I Cor.

7.31), 'the night is far gone, the day is at hand' (Rom. 13.12). The sufferings of Christ acquired their significance for salvation in the framework of the impending end of this world era and the dawn of the new eternal creation which is already beginning.

Expectation that the end is near is not a calculation of limited periods of time according to the calendar; for here time is not understood as *chronos*. Nor is it an existential attitude, which expects eternity to arrive at any moment; for it does not view time as *kairos*. 'Imminent expectation' is the expectation of the end of this temporal aeon, which in its temporality is transient. That is to say, it is the expectation of the end of time in the dawn of the new aeon, which will endure eternally. The expectation of the imminent end of days is not a sense of catastrophe, although catastrophes in nature and history were often interpreted by Jewish and Christian apocalyptic as end-time portents of the approaching end of time. As the New Testament shows, expectation of the approaching end is directed, not towards the death of this world, but towards the birth of the world that is new. Because the kingdom of God is 'at hand', the end of this Godless world has also come into view. Imminent expectation has nothing to do with the metaphysical dialectic of time and eternity. It has to do with thinking in terms of aeons. Temporality is the nature of this aeon, not the coming one. That is why it is impossible to measure the end of time in the categories of time – neither chronologically as a date, nor kairologically as a set limit.

What will come afterwards can only be described in paraphrase as a 'time without time' and as a 'beginning without end'.[14] This is not the absolute eternity of God. It is the relative eternity or aeonic time of the transfigured new creation in which death, and therefore transitory time as well, will be no more.

If we perceive the unique character of this aeonic thinking, we see that it is an error to maintain, as Bultmann does, that the expectation of the imminent end is part of the Bible's 'mythical eschatology', and that it 'is untenable for the simple reason that the parousia of Christ never took place as the New Testament expected. History did not come to an end, and, as every sane person knows, it will continue to run its course'.[15] The notion of a world history which will go on and on for ever is nothing other than 'a time myth of the modern world', which has declared time to be vacant endlessly, free of all surprises, as Johann Baptist Metz has rightly pointed out, contrary to Bultmann.[16] Everything can happen in this vacant, end-less time –

everything except the moment 'through which the Messiah enters history', as Walter Benjamin put it.[17] The end of time becomes inconceivable, because endless time was actually made an image for eternity, although a poor image. But in this case the time myth of the modern world abolishes its true temporality, making the awareness of its limitation, its uniqueness and its finality impossible. This myth spreads the veil of an illusionary immortality over the modern world, so that its deadly perils are no longer perceived.

Today the expectation of the impending end is realistic, compared with this modern time myth. Hiroshima 1945 fundamentally changed the quality of human history. Our time has become time with a time-limit.[18] The era in which we exist is humanity's last era, for we are living in a time in which the end of humanity can be brought about at any time. The system of nuclear deterrent has a potential for annihilation which makes it possible to end human life in a few hours. The nuclear winter afterwards may well leave survivors no chance. The time of the possible end of humanity is 'end-time', not in a mythical sense, but in this nuclear one. For no one can expect this age to give way to another in which this threat to humanity will cease to exist. The human race has become mortal. Humanity is now engaged in the struggle for survival between the end-time and the end of time. Today no 'sane person' (Bultmann's phrase) is convinced that 'world history' will continue 'to run its course' just by itself. How can world history continue if there is no longer any world? The struggle for time between the end-time and the end of time is the struggle about the time-limit set for life. All coming generations will have to 'pass their time' in staving off the end of time by prolonging this end-time, and by making it as endless as possible.

Of course this nuclear apocalypse is not identical with biblical apocalyptic. It is the perception of the nuclear end-time without hope for a new world. Biblical apocalyptic is different. It awaits the end of time with passionate hope: 'Come, Lord Jesus, come soon' (Rev. 22.20). Just for that very reason we have to relate biblical apocalyptic to this modern apocalypse, in order to witness to the messianic hope in this situation of end-time hopelessness.[19] The apocalyptic horizon of 'the sufferings of Christ' also embraces the sufferings of this nuclear end-time. The cosmic sufferings of this ecological end-time also become 'sufferings of Christ'.

§2 THE HUMAN SUFFERINGS OF CHRIST:
WHAT DEATH DID JESUS DIE?

The answer to this question is of course: Jesus died his own death.[20]
But who was he in this death of his? Did he die the death of Israel's
messiah? Did he die the death of God's Son? Did he die the death of a
Jew? Did he die the death of a slave? Did he die the death of all the
living? The question how Jesus understood his own death is no more
than the historical side of the enquiry. The question what his death
means for us is the theological side. We have to distinguish between
the two, because the way Jesus himself may have interpreted his way
to death is an understanding formed before Easter; and it is only
because of Easter and since Easter that his death has a salvific
meaning for us. Taken by itself, Jesus' own interpretation of what he
was is not a theological source, and not a criterion for christological
statements.[21]

1. The Trial of Jesus

The trial of Jesus has been the subject of many modern investigations. Bultmann still sceptically maintained: 'Whether Jesus found
any meaning in it [i.e. his death], and how, we cannot know. The
possibility that he broke down is something we must not conceal
from ourselves.'[22] But since then confidence in the sources and the
complex instruments of historical research has apparently grown.[23]
Of course we are still dependent on presumptions, as we are in all
historical investigations. But a picture has none the less emerged
which allows us to answer the questions which we posed at the
beginning.

Why did Jesus and his friends leave Galilee for Jerusalem? It would
seem that he deliberately took this path in order to bring his
messianic message to the holy city. By moving to Jerusalem and the
temple, was he intending to call the leaders of his people to make the
decision of faith 'in the final hour'? Or did he 'seek the final decision'
in Jerusalem and the temple[24] – God's decision about his own
mission?

The people evidently greeted his entry into the city as a messianic
progress: 'Blessed is the kingdom of our father David that is coming!'
(Mark 11.10 par.). Without this popular excitement, his crucifixion
by the Romans as 'king of the Jews' would be incomprehensible.

Jesus was then arrested in the Garden of Gethsemane, presumably by the temple police, acting for the Jewish temple authorities. The disciples were allowed to escape. This does not suggest that the intention was a swift extirpation of the Jesus movement, for Roman soldiers could have achieved that quickly enough, and without creating any stir.[25] On the other hand, according to Mark (14.48), Jesus asked why they had arrested him in the night, as if he were the leader of a revolt ($\lambda\eta\sigma\tau\acute{\eta}\varsigma$), even though he had been quite openly in the temple every day. But to arrest rebels was a prerogative reserved for the Roman soldiers.

The reason why the priests had him arrested was probably Jesus' prophecy about the temple, and his symbolic act in cleansing the temple court (Mark 11.15–17; 13.1–2 par.). If the promise about building the temple goes back to the Nathan prophecy in II Sam. 7.13, then it is bound up with the coming of the messiah. 'The assumption that the saying about the building of the temple had a messianic significance because of the Nathan prophecy, is confirmed by the direct question which the high priest puts to Jesus about his messianic claim.'[26] According to II Sam. 7.14, the messiah is assured of the divine sonship: 'I will be his father, and he shall be my son.' In the cross-examination in the high priest's house, several people testified that Jesus said: 'I will destroy this temple that is made with hands, and in three days I will build another, not made with hands' (Mark 14.58). What is meant is the messianic people of God, among whom God will take up his dwelling through his Spirit. That is why the high priest follows this up with the direct question: 'Are you the Christ, the Son of the Blessed?' (14.61). According to Matt. 26.63 the high priest seemed to 'entreat' Jesus. Chaim H. Cohn concluded from this that during that night the priests tried to persuade Jesus to drop his claim to be Israel's messiah, so as to save him.[27] It was only when Jesus stood firm by his claim, and rejected this way out, that the high priest and the sanhedrin gave him up. Then all that was left to them was to hand him over to the Romans. According to this interpretation, Jesus' now direct and plainly spoken admission that he was the messiah was actually the decisive factor in his trial and his end: 'I am' (Mark 14.62).[28] The addition: 'And you will see the Son of man seated at the right hand of Power, and coming with the clouds of heaven' may have been an embellishment of early Christian tradition. It links the future of the Son of man with the immediate present of the messiah, in accordance with the ancient two-stage christology found in Rom. 1.3f.

Jesus' plain, unvarnished messianic acknowledgment before the high priest was viewed as blasphemy. The judges themselves were witnesses of the offence. Of course it cannot have been the blasphemy of a false prophet and seducer of the people in the more precise sense of Deut. 13, for no one reproached Jesus with having worshipped 'false gods'. But he was no doubt accused of putting himself messianically on the same level as almighty God himself, as John 10.33 says: '. . . because you, being a man, make yourself God'. If Jesus really was the expected messiah, his words about the temple and his acknowledgment of what he was could not be viewed as blasphemy. But if he was not, his claim was bound to be seen as a blaspheming of the God who had not in fact made him the messiah. A messianic pretender gives God the lie, and in this way blasphemes the Most High.

But how was the high priest so certain of this that he immediately rent his robe, thus symbolically pronouncing judgment? This simple question is difficult to answer. Did Jesus blaspheme God because, in spite of his helplessness, he wished to put himself on a level with God? This is Otto Betz's assumption.[29] Did the very fact of his arrest without resistance stand in 'blatant contradiction' to his messianic claim?[30] Was Jesus' messianic claim confuted in the end by the story of his own life? Is success or failure the proof of a true or false prophet? Is Israel's God too on the side of the biggest battalions? And if the Galilean's blasphemy is to be found in his powerlessness, why did the high priest not let him go, as a harmless figure? It emerged from the nocturnal cross-examination that Jesus really did consider himself to be the messiah, and was not prepared to renounce his claim in spite of everything that spoke against it. He was then presumably condemned as a blasphemous messianic pretender. Yet at the same time he was judged to be so dangerous politically that he was handed over to the Romans, on the grounds that he wanted to set himself up as 'king of the Jews'. The reason was no doubt the Sadducee policy of survival under Roman occupation: in the case of conflict, and if it was a question of saving the temple and securing the continued existence of God's people, an individual had to sacrifice himself, or be sacrificed: 'It is expedient . . . that one man should die for the people, and that the whole nation should not perish' (John 11.50). If this was indeed a policy of expediency, as Betz says, then the Sadducees were not so much afraid that the false messiah from Galilee would seduce the people from their God; what they were afraid of was Israel's downfall, in the wake of a 'utopian policy' towards the Romans.[31] If this is correct, then for all his apparent helplessness and the outward signs of his non-messianic status, Jesus with his messianic claim was quite evidently political dynamite.

The death sentence was pronounced on Jesus by the Roman procurator, Pilate, in the name of the *imperium Romanum*. The inscription on the cross names the political crime. 'King of the Jews' is the Roman formula for Israel's Jewish messiah. 'Jesus' messianic claim was an offence which touched the nerve of Rome's rule. It meant *seditio*, στάσις, and was bound to be condemned by the Roman court. It fell under the Lex Julia de majestate (Digesta 48, 4, 1; 48, 4.11). According to this, the claim to be king was considered to be a crime carrying the death penalty if it . . . led to rebellion.'[32] Before Pilate too, Jesus must have brought about the decision by his open messianic acknowledgment: 'You have said' (Mark 15.2). This was remembered by the Christian community: 'Christ Jesus . . . in his testimony before Pontius Pilate made the good confession' (I Tim. 6.13).

According to Roman law, execution through crucifixion was the punishment designed to deter rebels against the political order of the Roman empire, or the social order of the Roman slave-owning society. Jesus was publicly executed together with two Jewish insurgents, who had been arrested for revolt.

Pilate acted on Rome's authority and was certainly not implementing a Jewish sentence passed on Jesus, as some interpreters maintain, in order to exonerate him. The high priest judged only Jesus' messianic claim, on the basis of the traditions of Jewish law. The Sadducees probably handed him over to the Romans because they were afraid for the Jewish people. Jesus himself must have provoked his condemnation through his plain and direct acknowledgment of his messiahship before the council and Pilate. But this does not make him 'a victim of his claim to be the Son of man'.[33] He was a victim of Rome's despotic rule over Israel. He must have roused messianic expectation among the people of Jerusalem. Otherwise the anxiety of the priests and the swift action taken by the Romans is inexplicable. Even if Jesus did not call for a revolt against Rome, his messianic activity among the people must in any case have made him a public threat to the Romans, and therefore, in the

Sadducean view as well, a danger for the Jewish population of Jerusalem, who had to fear Roman retaliation. But the injustice was not on Jesus' side. It was the injustice of Roman despotism; for at the prospect of Roman cruelty to their people, the Jewish priests had good reason to tremble. The creed ought therefore to run: '. . . crucified *by* Pontius Pilate' (*Constitutio apostolorum* VII, 23, 2), not 'crucified *under* Pontius Pilate'.

2. The Death of the Messiah

Jesus died *the death of Israel's messiah* at the hands of the Romans. Jesus and Pilate were convinced of his messiahship, the sanhedrin was not, and the people wavered. In view of the traditions of Jewish messianic expectation, Jesus must have considered himself to be a messiah of a special kind, a *paradoxical messiah*. He did not redeem his people through powerful signs and wonders of liberation. He redeemed them, if at all, through suffering and through hope. He liberated and gathered God's people, not by driving out the Romans, but in a way hitherto unknown and unpredicted. When he went to Jerusalem, was his purpose to extort a divine judgment through the events of history? Did he wish to compel God to intervene publicly on his behalf, and on behalf of his cause? We can find no trace of this. Did he 'fail'? There is no such suggestion. Did he submit to the power of facts and the fact of godless power? We find no indication in the story of Jesus' passion of any such cult of *Realpolitik*. Did he see the path of suffering on which he entered through his messianic acknowledgment as an act of self-sacrifice? The Sadducees may have thought so, when they proposed to 'sacrifice' him to the Romans in place of the people; but we find no sign of it in Jesus. To whom is he supposed to have 'sacrificed' himself? To the Romans and their gods? For whom is he supposed to have sacrificed himself? For the people whom he endangered through his messianic acknowledgment, exposing them to the threat of Roman reprisals? And if he wanted to sacrifice himself to the God of Israel as 'a ransom for many', did this force him to draw on the assistance of Pilate and the Roman torturers?

It is neither possible to stylize Jesus into the messianic rebel against Rome – Bar Kochba's forerunner, as it were – nor can we reduce him to a purely inner-Jewish, purely religious messiah, victimized for the religious sins of his own people. But three points have to be established: (1) The message about the kingdom of God, with which Jesus went to Jerusalem; (2) his prophecy about the temple, uttered in Jerusalem for the first time, and his cleansing of the temple forecourts; and (3) his acknowledgment of his messiahship before the high priest of his people, and before the prefect of the Roman occupying power. What we have to notice about all these three points is the contradiction between Jesus' eschatological proclamation and his messianic claim on the one hand and, on the other, the obvious confutation of both proclamation and claim by the political power, and by the fact of his helplessness and his resulting suffering, to the point of death on the Roman cross. Jesus evidently endured the tension between these antitheses to the very end.

From where did he receive – and how did he retain – his certainty of the messiahship, in the face of this clash, this contention, this confutation through experience? The gospels make this problem plain, both at the beginning of his ministry, in the story of the temptations, and at its end, in the Gethsemane account – their conclusion being that Jesus *is* Israel's messiah according to the Nathan prophecy, but on the foundation of his *special* experience of God, and therefore in his own way. But there is no theological reason for resolving this antinomy in Jesus in the one direction or the other. The clash between his messianic acknowledgment and his death on the cross points to the transcendent solution: God's raising him from the dead, and his presence in the Spirit. This, at all events, was the early Christian answer to the contradiction in which Jesus ended. If we look at Jewish messianic expectation, Jesus is a paradoxical messiah – a messiah contrary to appearances, contrary to 'the judgment of history', and in defiance of the death sentence passed on him by the Roman despot Pilate. If we look at Roman fear of the messiah, and the history of his influence, Jesus is the only truly *revolutionary messiah*; for it was through Christianity that the Roman imperial power was fundamentally changed.

3. The Death of God's Child

Jesus died *the death of God's child* at the hand of men; for Israel's messiah is also 'God's son' (II Sam. 7.14), and in his 'Abba' prayer, Jesus experienced himself as 'child' of the divine Father. This contradiction between his experience of himself and his experience of death is so profound that it has to be understood as *the God-*

forsakenness of the Son of God.[34] Jesus evidently died after a few hours on the cross with a loud cry of torment. Mark (15.34) gives this with the opening words of Psalm 22: 'My God, why hast thou forsaken me?'[35] The idea that Jesus' last words to the God whom he had called upon as Abba, dear Father, could have been 'You have abandoned me', could surely never have taken root in Christian belief unless these terrible words had really been uttered, or unless they had at least been heard in Jesus' death cry. The much later Epistle to the Hebrews still retains this remembrance, that 'far from God – χωρὶς θεοῦ – he tasted death for us all' (2.9). The Gethsemane story (Mark 14.32–42) reflects the frightening eclipse of God in which Jesus died. Jesus began 'to shiver and quail', writes Mark. 'He began to be sorrowful and afraid', reports Matthew. 'My soul is exceeding sorrowful, even unto death', translates our 1611 Bible. Jesus begs his disciples to stay awake with him. On other occasions he had often withdrawn from them, in order to be joined with God in the prayer of his heart. Here for the first time he does not want to be alone with his God, and seeks the protection of his friends.

God does not hear his prayer that the cup of suffering might pass him by. Elsewhere we hear: 'I and the Father are one'. Here Jesus' fellowship with God seems to be shattered. That is why the disciples fall into the heavy sleep of grief. Forsaken by God and his disciples, Jesus falls to the ground. Only the ground supports him. It is only by denying himself that he can cling to the unity in the severence from his God: 'Not what I will, but what thou wilt' (Matt. 14.36). With the rejected prayer of Jesus in Gethsemane, the silence of God over his end begins: 'The hour has come when the Son of man is betrayed into the hands of the Godless' (Mark 14.41).

This death far from God is the agony of one who knew that he was God's child. Jesus' death cry on the cross is 'the open wound' of every Christian theology, for consciously or unconsciously every Christian theology is a reply to the 'Why?' with which Jesus dies, a reply that attempts to give theological meaning to his death. But when Christian theologians do not accept what Jesus suffered from God, they are like Job's friends, not like Job himself. The contradiction between the Sonship of God and forsakenness by God is a contradiction that cannot be resolved, either by reducing the divine Sonship or by failing to take the forsakenness seriously. Even the words of Psalm 22 on Jesus' lips do not solve the conflict, for the psalm ends with a prayer of thanksgiving for rescue from deadly peril. There was no such rescue on Golgotha; and with the psalm Jesus no longer speaks to God as his 'Father'; he addresses him as the God of Israel. Early manuscripts of Mark's Gospel intensify the cry into: 'Why have you exposed me to shame?' and 'Why have you cursed me?'

God-forsakenness is the final experience of God endured by the crucified Jesus on Golgotha, because to the very end he knew that he was God's Son. God's silence, the hiding of his face, the eclipse of God, the dark night of the soul, the death of God, hell: these are the metaphors for this inconceivable fact that have come down to us in the traditions of Christian experiences of God. They are attempts to describe an abyss, a sinking into nothingness; yet they are only approximations to Jesus' final experience of God on the cross, his Job-like experience. The uniqueness of what may have taken place between Jesus and his God on Golgotha is therefore something we do well to accept and respect as his secret, while we ourselves hold fast to the paradox that Jesus died the death of God's Son in God-forsakenness.

4. The Death of the Jew

Jesus also died *the death of a Jew* at the hand of the Romans. His cross on Golgotha stood between the crosses of two Jewish freedom fighters; and it stands also in the long series of persecuted, tortured and murdered Jews in history. That is why we have to recognize in the sufferings of Christ the sufferings of Israel too, and have to respect his fellowship in death with his people. Even if it is true that he was condemned as a blasphemer, even if he came into conflict with the leading religious forces of his people: Jesus died as a Jew. He experienced in his body what so many Jews before him and afterwards experienced at the hand of Gentiles – 'the heathen' – and at the hand of heathen Christians. Dying, Jesus entered into the fate of God's people. This too is brought out by the quotation from Psalm 22.

But the sufferings of Israel are always at the same time the sufferings of the God who chose Israel, who sanctifies his name through Israel, and who himself, in his Shekinah, lives in Israel and makes Israel's sufferings his own.[36] Israel's sufferings are not punitive sufferings which are a reflection of God's judgment. They are sufferings which God himself suffers. So in this context Christ's sufferings too are not sufferings far from God; they are sufferings close to him. In the messianic child, God himself suffers the sufferings of God-forsakenness. In the image of the Suffering Servant of God from Isaiah 53, the sufferings of Israel and the sufferings of Christ are united. That is why the gospels always describe Christ's passion with the features of the Suffering Servant and Isaiah 53. Hebrews 11–12.2 presents the chain of witnesses to faith from Abel to Jesus as the chain of martyrs who endured 'the reproach' of Christ (11.26). Here Christ's cross and 'shame' (12.2) are stamped through and through by Israelite and Jewish experience.

If Jesus died a Jew's death, then the sufferings of Christ are open for solidarity with 'the sufferings of Israel' – the Israel of that time, and the Israel of today. 'The suffering of despised Judaism is suffering in the orbit of Christ's suffering.'[37] If Jesus died the death of the righteous, then through his suffering he participates in the more comprehensive sufferings of God, to which the sufferings of Israel belong.[38] If the sufferings of Christ and the sufferings of Israel are linked, and belong within the framework of God's sufferings over the world and with the world, then it is not merely possible to see Golgotha and Auschwitz in a single perspective; it is actually necessary. This conclusion would be suggested even by the simple reflection that if Jesus had lived in the Third Reich, he would have been branded like other Jews, and would have died in the gas chambers of Auschwitz.

5. The Death of the Slave

Jesus died *the death of a poor man*. The Son of man from Galilee, without power, without rights and without a home suffered the fate of a slave in the Roman empire. When the Spartacus revolt was crushed, more than 7,000 slaves died on crosses set up on the Via Appia. Astonishingly, the pre-Pauline hymn about Christ in Phil. 2 says that the form of the Son of God, Jesus Christ, who humiliated himself, was 'the form of a slave'. If this is a reference to Jesus' humble origins among the humiliated people ($\H{o}\chi\lambda o\varsigma$) of Galilee, then in his suffering and death Jesus shared the fate of these enslaved people. Wretched and stripped of their rights as they were, it was their misery which Jesus experienced in his own body. Jesus is also the Lazarus Christ, and Lazarus is a 'figure' for Christ, his image (Luke 16). Jesus was one of these people, the poorest of the poor: a tortured, abused and crucified slave. In this sense 'the sufferings of Christ' are also the sufferings of the powerless masses of the poor in this world, who have no rights and no home; and in this sense their sufferings too are Christ's sufferings.[39]

6. The Death of the Living One

Finally, Jesus died *the death of all the living*, for he was mortal and would one day have died even if he had not been executed. Through his death struggle he participated in the fate of everything that lives – not merely the fate of human beings; for all living things desire to live and have to die. And yet in this sense the death of Christ was always a matter for dispute in Christian theology.[40]

Pauline and Augustinian dogma teaches that 'death is the wages of sin' – both the death of the soul and the death of the body. If we start from this assumption, then Jesus, 'the sinless' Son of God, cannot have died his own death. He was then immortal, both in his divinity and his humanity, and he died our death, the death of sinners, vicariously and only out of compassion. But in this case death can only mean human death, not the death of all living things.

If, on the other hand, with Schleiermacher, one disputes the causal connection between sin against God and the physical death of the human being, then the consequence of a sinful life, or a life that has gone astray, or one that has never been truly lived, is no doubt the fear of death, but not physical death itself.[41] In this case physical death is a 'natural death', as everyone can discover who believes in the forgiveness of sins and has no further need to fear death. Mortality belongs to creaturely finitude. Jesus could therefore die 'the accursed death of sin' vicariously for all sinners only because he was sinless and mortal at the same time. The death he died on the cross was hence not only a death for others, but his own natural death as well. If this is so, then Christ has certainly vanquished the death of the sinner, but not natural death. But how are we then supposed to conceive of the new creation in which 'death shall be no more' (Rev. 21.4)? What is 'eternal life', if natural death remains?

Jesus died the death of all living things. That is, he did not only die 'the death of the sinner' or merely his own 'natural death'. He died in solidarity with the whole sighing creation, human and non-human – the creation that 'sighs' because it is subject to transience. He died the death of everything that lives. The death of all the living can neither be called 'the consequence of sin', nor can it be termed 'natural'. It is a destiny to which everything living is subjected, and which hence spurs us on to yearn for cosmic deliverance. This death is the sign of a tragedy in creation; but because of the resurrection of the Christ who died, the sign is re-interpreted into a universal hope for a new creation in glory (Rom. 8.19ff.). Jesus therefore dies the death of everything that lives in solidarity with the whole sighing creation. The sufferings of Christ are therefore also 'the sufferings of this present time' (Rom. 8.18), which are endured by everything that lives. But we can also say, conversely, that created beings in their yearning for life suffer 'the sufferings of Christ'. The Wisdom of the whole creation, which is here subject to transience, suffers in Christ the death of everything that lives (I Cor. 1.24).

§3 THE DIVINE SUFFERINGS OF CHRIST: WHERE IS GOD?

We have considered the sufferings of Jesus in the light of his human, his Jewish, and his messianic life, and have stressed the contradiction between his claim and his experience of God on the cross. We shall now look in another direction, and shall consider his life and death in the light of his resurrection, and in the pre-reflection of his glory. We shall consider the unique nature and theological meaning of Christ's resurrection in more detail in chapter V. Here it will be sufficient to start from the fact that in the appearances of the risen One, it became clear to the women and the disciples concerned, *who* had died there on the cross on Golgotha, and who, in the truth of God, Jesus *is*.

All the titles with which the early Christian congregations expressed their faith in Jesus as the Christ have their theological foundation in the Easter event: if God has raised him from the dead, then Jesus is the 'Son of God' (Rom. 1.4), 'the Christ' who is to redeem Israel (Luke 24.21, 26), 'the Lord' of the universal divine rule (Rom. 10.9) and the saviour of the nations (Rom. 15.9). If the resurrection event is an eschatological one, then the risen One cannot be what he *is* only from the time of his resurrection. He must also have this same identity in his suffering and death on the cross, in his proclamation and ministry, in his whole life from the very beginning.

Raising from the dead is an eschatological act of God performed on Jesus, and in so far it is something new; but it also reveals the truth about the earthly Jesus. It endorses and fulfils his messianic claim. It endorses and fulfils his divine Sonship. The endorsement and the fulfilment of Jesus' claim are complementary. If we wished to confine ourselves to the endorsement, 'resurrection' would be no more than an interpretative theological category for his death; and all that would remain would be a theology of the cross.[42] If we were to concentrate solely on the fulfilment, the Easter Christ would replace and push out the crucified Jesus.[43] But if, as we have shown, the earthly Jesus is 'the messiah on the way', and the Son of God in the process of his learning, then Easter endorses *and* fulfils this life history of Jesus, which is open for the future. At the same time, however, resurrection, understood as an eschatological event in Jesus, is the beginning of the new creation of all things. For that reason this astonishing fulfilment of Jesus' messianic claim is stronger than the endorsement of his historical truth. 'How much more . . .' says Paul, when he compares Christ's death and his resurrection (Rom. 8.34; 5.10, 20).

Many people see the resurrection as resolving the contradiction with which, and from which, Jesus died, and as making good Christ's sufferings. But this is not the case. On the contrary: if Jesus had been executed by the Romans as a false messiah, there would be no riddle about his sufferings; for the same thing happened to many messianic claimants, before him and afterwards. If Jesus died as a prophet, or as one of the righteous men of his people, his death would be nothing special. If, finally, he had been killed as a poor, helpless human being, why should we remember this particular victim, in the long history of human cruelty? But if, for the sake of the God who raised him from the dead, people have to acknowledge that this Jesus of Nazareth, crucified by Pontius Pilate, was Israel's messiah, the Son of God and the Saviour of the nations, then this accentuates the contradiction with which, and from which, Jesus died. And the contradiction becomes a theological one: 'Why was it necessary for *the Christ* to suffer these things?' (Luke 24.26). Why was the true *Son of God* forsaken? Why did the risen *Lord*, the Wisdom of the new creation of all things, have to suffer and die in this way?

1. The Theodicy Trial on Golgotha

Far from resolving the contradiction of the cross of Jesus, the Easter faith actually deepens it into a divine mystery whose revelation has to be searched for. In the early Christian congregations, the fact and the meaning of Jesus' resurrection was so clear that there are no more than a few variant interpretations; yet this in itself made the death of Christ a tormenting mystery as well as a redeeming one, a mystery which continually evoked new interpretations. The question of the dying Christ: 'My God, why . . .?' elicited ever new theological answers, then as now. But it will only be adequately met and find its redeeming answer (or resolution) in the parousia of the risen One, and in his kingdom, in which God will finally 'wipe away every tear from their eyes' (Rev. 21.4). Yet because of Christ's resurrection and in the radiance cast ahead by the glory of his future, the sufferings of Christ are already manifested here and now as divine sufferings, and have to be understood as *the sufferings of God*.

2. *The Theology of the Surrender of Christ*

An early way of understanding the sufferings of Christ as divine sufferings may be found in the theology of surrender in the New Testament.[44] Because many systematic theologians today go back to this, in order to reduce to a common denominator the unique Christian idea of God, the theology of the cross and the doctrine of the Trinity (as I also tried to do in 1972 in *The Crucified God* [ET 1974)],[45] I will sum up this theology of the cross briefly here, in order to take a further step in the discussion with critics of this position.

The gospels present the death of Jesus in the light of his life and the gospel he preached; and in this presentation παραδιδόναι has an unambiguously negative significance. It means to deliver up, betray, hand over, cast off. We can see this from the way Judas 'the betrayer' is portrayed. When Jesus is forsaken by God on the cross, it means that he has been cast off by God. In Rom. 1.18ff. Paul also uses the expression 'give up' for the divine wrath and God's judgment on human sin. People who forsake the invisible God and worship created things are forsaken by God and 'delivered' or 'given up' to their own greedy desires.

Paul radically reverses the meaning of 'delivered up', however, when he views the God-forsakenness of Jesus, no longer in the light of his life, but in the light of his resurrection. The God who has raised Jesus from the dead is the same God who 'gave him up' to death on the cross.[46] In the forsakenness of the cross itself, out of which Jesus cries 'why?', Paul already sees the answer to that cry: 'He who did not spare his own Son but gave him up for us all, will he not also give us all things with him?' (Rom. 8.32). According to this, the Father has forsaken 'his own Son' (as Paul especially stresses here) and has given him up to death. Paul puts it even more forcibly: 'For our sake he made him to be sin' (II Cor. 5.21) and 'he became a curse for us' (Gal. 3.13). The Father forsakes the Son 'for us' – that is, he allows him to die so that he may become the God and Father of the forsaken. The Father 'gives up' the Son that through him he may become the Father of all those who are 'given up' (Rom. 1.18ff.). This transforms 'the almighty Father' too; for Christ was 'crucified in the weakness of God' (II Cor. 13.4). The Son is surrendered to this death in order to become the brother and saviour of all the men and women who are condemned and accursed.

Yet here we have to make a clear distinction: in the surrender of the Son the Father surrenders himself too – but not in the same way. The Son suffers his dying in this forsakenness. The Father suffers the death of the Son. He suffers it in the infinite pain of his love for the Son. The death of the Son therefore corresponds to the pain of the Father. And when in this descent into hell the Son loses sight of the Father, then in this judgment the Father also loses sight of the Son. Here what is at stake is the divine consistency, the inner life of the Trinity. Here the self-communicating love of the Father becomes infinite pain over the death of the Son. Here the responding love of the Son turns into infinite suffering over his forsakenness by the Father. What happens on Golgotha reaches into the very depths of the Godhead and therefore puts its impress on the trinitarian life of God in eternity. In Christian faith the cross is always at the centre of the Trinity, for the cross reveals the heart of the triune God, which beats for his whole creation.

But according to Gal. 2.20 the Son was not merely given up by the Father. He also *'gave himself* for me'. In the event of the surrender, Jesus is not merely the object; he is the subject too. His suffering and dying was a *passio activa*, a path of suffering deliberately chosen, a dying affirmed because of his passion for God. According to the hymn on Christ which Paul takes up in Phil. 2, the self-giving of the Son means that he empties himself of the divine form, and takes the form of a servant; his self-giving consists in his self-humiliation, and in his 'obedience unto death, even death on a cross'. For the Epistle to the Hebrews (5.8) 'he learnt obedience through what he suffered'. He suffered paradoxically from the prayer that was not heard, from his forsakenness by the Father. Through this, he on his side 'learnt' surrender. This is in line with the way the synoptic gospels tell the passion story.

Theologically this means an inward conformity between the will of the surrendered Son and the surrendering will of the Father. This is what the Gethsemane story is about too. Yet this profound community of will comes into being at the very point of widest separation of the Son from the Father, the Father from the Son, in 'the dark night' of this death. On the cross the Father and the Son are so widely separated that the direct relationship between them breaks off. Jesus died a 'Godless death'. And yet on the cross the Father and the Son are so much at one that they present a single surrendering movement. On Golgotha it is true in a special way that 'He who sees the Son sees the Father'. The Epistle to the Hebrews expresses this by saying that Christ sacrificed himself to God 'through the eternal Spirit' (διὰ πνεύματος αἰωνίου; 9.14). The surrender of the Father and the Son is made 'through the Spirit'. The Holy Spirit is the bond in the division, forging the link between the originally lived unity, and the division between the Father and the Son experienced on the cross. It was the Holy Spirit through whom Jesus proclaimed with authority, and performed signs and wonders; but the Spirit who was Jesus' active power now becomes his suffering power. The One who sent him in power to the poor, to bring them the kingdom of God, made him himself poor, in order that through his sufferings the poor might be made rich (II Cor. 8.9). The sufferings of Christ are also the sufferings of the Spirit, for the surrender of Christ also manifested the self-emptying of the Spirit. The Spirit is the divine subject of Jesus' life-history; and the Spirit is the divine subject of Jesus' passion history. This means we must even add that Jesus suffered death in 'the power of indestructible life' (Heb. 7.16), and through this power 'of the eternal Spirit' (9.14) in his death destroyed death. Consequently, through the slain Christ, indestructible life is opened up to all the dying.

Paul interpreted the event of God-forsakenness on the cross as the surrender of the Son, and the surrender of the Son as the love of God. What the love of God is, 'from which nothing can separate us' (Rom. 8.39), happened on the cross of Christ, and is experienced under the cross. The Father, who sends his Son into all the depths and hells of God-forsakenness, loneliness and annihilation, is in his Son everywhere among those who are his, so that he has become omnipresent. With the surrender of the Son he gives 'everything', and 'nothing' can separate us from him. This is the beginning of the language of the kingdom of God, where 'God will be all in all'. Anyone who has once perceived God's presence and love in the God-forsakenness of the crucified Brother, sees God everywhere and in everything (Ps. 139.8), just as a person who has been face to face with death senses the living quality of everything in a hitherto undreamed-of way.

The Gospel of John sums up the surrender in the key statement: 'God so loved the world that he gave his only Son, that whoever believes in him should not perish but have eternal life' (3.16). The word 'so' means 'in this way' – in the way of the forsakenness in death on the cross which was suffered with us and 'for us'. And the First Epistle of John (4.16) defines God by saying: 'God is love.' God does not love just as he might also be angry. He *is* love. His being and existence is love. In Christ he constitutes himself as love. This happened on the cross. The definition 'God is love' acquires its full weight only if we continually make ourselves aware of the path that leads to the definition: Jesus' forsakenness on the cross, the surrender of the Son, and the love of the Father, which does everything, gives everything and suffers everything for lost men and women. God is love: that means God is self-giving. It means God exists for us: on the cross.

Dorothee Sölle has protested vigorously against this theology of surrender. But her protest is unfortunately based on a misunderstanding, and this misunderstanding has perpetuated itself as legend in certain areas of feminist theology.

In *The Crucified God* (ET p. 241) I quoted the New Testament scholar Wiard Popkes: 'That God delivers up his Son is one of the most unheard-of statements in the New Testament. We must understand 'deliver up' in its full sense and not water it down to mean 'send' or 'give'. What happened here is what Abraham did not need to do to Isaac (cf. Rom. 8.32): Christ was quite deliberately abandoned by the Father to the fate of death: God subjected him to the power of corruption, whether this be called man or death. To express the idea in its most acute form, one might say in the words of the dogma of the early church: the first person of the Trinity casts out and annihilates the second. . . . A theology of the cross cannot be expressed more radically than it is here' (*Christus Traditus*, Göttingen 1967, 286f.). D. Sölle comments: 'The author is fascinated by his God's brutality' (*Leiden*, Stuttgart 1973, 38). Since her previous criticism was directed against me ('Moltmann tries to develop a *theologia crucis* starting

from the perpetrator, from the one who causes the suffering',
p. 37), every reader is bound to think that I am 'the author' she is
quoting. But this is not the case.[47] Apparently E. Sorge also
understood D. Sölle in this sense, for she cites me as the author of
this passage (which she has copied wrongly and quotes in
mutilated form): 'Moltmann thinks . . .' (*Religion und Frau.
Weiblich Spiritualität im Christentum*, Stuttgart 1985, 43).
D. Strahm then follows her (*Fama. Feministisch-theologische
Zeitschrift*, 1988, 1, 5); her formulation is certainly more cautious
('I read in Jürgen Moltmann . . .'), but she too gives the impression
that 'Moltmann' and 'Popkes' are interchangeable.

Yet underlying this misunderstanding is a serious question: 'Every
attempt to view suffering as caused indirectly or directly by God is in
danger of thinking about God sadistically', writes Dorothee Sölle.
'. . . God is not solely and not centrally understood as the Christ who
loves and suffers; at the same time he is forced to retain the position
of dominating, almighty Father.'[48] Is this the notion that is at the
root of the theology of surrender, and the trinitarian interpretation
of the event on the cross? If the 'surrender' of Jesus is interpreted to
mean that the Father is the active subject and the Son is the passive
object, then it would seem so. If the surrender of Jesus on the cross is
understood as a sacrifice made to appease the Father's wrath, this
would appear to be the case. If the surrender of Jesus is understood to
mean that God acted on Jesus through Judas, Caiaphas, Pilate and
his torturers, then this is true. But then the Father and the Son are not
one. They are divided. They are not present together. They are
opposed to one another. The church's later theology about the
expiatory sacrifice suggested notions of this kind. The hymn book
made these ideas common coin.[49] But in the New Testament the
Father of Jesus Christ is always on Jesus' side, never on the side of the
people who crucified him; for he is Israel's God, not Jupiter, the god
of the Romans. So the giving up of the Son reveals the giving up of the
Father. In the suffering of the Son, the pain of the Father finds a voice.
The self-emptying of the Son also expresses the self-emptying of the
Father. Christ is crucified 'in the weakness of God' (II Cor. 13.4). 'In
the forsakenness of the Son the Father also forsakes himself. In the
surrender of the Son the Father also surrenders himself. But not in the
same way. For Jesus suffers dying in forsakenness, but not death
itself; for it is impossible to "suffer" death, since suffering presup-

poses life. But the Father who abandons him and delivers him up suffers the death of the Son in the infinite grief of love.'[50] Here the Father is not in confrontation with Jesus as 'dominating, almighty Father', or as a God who, feeling no pain himself, causes pain. For where the Son goes, the Father goes too.

If we understand Golgotha as a theodicy trial, we ask: Jesus dies with the cry of abandonment – and where is God? Let us look at the answers that have been given:

1. *God hides his face* and *is silent*, and Jesus dies in the silence of God. That is not an answer. It merely lends extra rigour to the question 'why?'.

2. *God permits* Jesus' death in forsakenness *by abandoning him*, and Jesus dies this human death helplessly and without God. This is not an answer either, for it merely leads to the other question: how can God permit this?

3. *God wishes* Jesus to die in this way. God is the agent who is at work in everything, and he resolved that Jesus should die this death. Betrayer, judges and executioners are doing to Jesus what God charges them to do, so that he may die. This is not an answer at all. It is blasphemy, for a monster like this is not God.

4. *God himself was in Christ* (II Cor. 5.19). Jesus' weakness was God's weakness too; Jesus' suffering was God's suffering; Jesus' death also meant his death for God his Father: 'I am in the Father and the Father is in me', says the Johannine Christ. By virtue of this mutual indwelling (perichoresis) of the Father and the Son, Jesus' sufferings are divine sufferings, and God's love is love that is able to suffer and is prepared to suffer. The power of the divine Spirit *in* Jesus is transformed from an active power that works wonders to a suffering power that endures wounds.

5. Jesus was betrayed, condemned and murdered by human beings and *God protests* against Jesus' death by raising him from the dead. Through the resurrection, God confutes Jesus' betrayers, judges and executioners.

6. 'As for you, you meant evil against me; but God meant it for good' (cf. Gen. 50.20). After he had been sold into Egypt, Joseph became the saviour of the brothers who had sold him; and in the same way, through the resurrection of Christ God *turns* the cross on Golgotha *to good* for the betrayers, the judges and the executioners, Jews and Gentiles. Those who destroyed the living Christ by crucifixion are saved from their own final destruction by the cross of

the risen Christ. History confutes Jesus through crucifixion. The raising of Jesus confutes this history.

3. The Com-passion of God

The theology of surrender is misunderstood and perverted into its very opposite unless it is grasped as being *the theology of the pain of God*, which means the theology of *the divine co-suffering* or *compassion*. The Pauline and Johannine term 'delivered' or 'given up' certainly brings out only one side of this process. The other side is brought out by the words 'love' and 'mercy'. What the divine 'surrender' really means can be discerned best from the path Jesus Christ took in his passion. Without violence, Israel's messiah king goes his way to the Roman cross. The Son of God empties himself of his divinity and takes the way of a poor slave to the point of death on the cross. If we look at the divine power and sovereignty, this is a path of self-emptying. If we look at the solidarity with the helpless and poor which it manifests, it is the path of the divine love in its essential nature. If we abide by our conviction that Jesus *is* the messiah and the Son of God to the point of his death on the cross, then he brought the messianic hope and the fellowship of God to all those who have to live in the shadow of the cross, the men and women who suffer injustice, and the unjust. God's delivering up involves an *active suffering* (Acts 2.23: 'according to God's plan . . .'). But God does not cause Christ's suffering, nor is Christ the meek and helpless victim of suffering. Through his surrender God seeks out the lost beings he has created, and enters into their forsakenness, bringing them his fellowship, which can never be lost.

The vicarious quality of the surrender of Christ and his resurrection 'for us' and 'for many' should not be understood as an emergency measure made necessary by the predicament of human sin. Nor can it be viewed as a special case of the vicarious character underlying all human sociality. Many symbols and metaphors have been used to make that fundamental gospel phrase *'for us'* plausible. But whatever they may be, the inner secret of Christ's vicarious act 'for us' is the vicarious act and self-giving of God: 'If *God* is *for us*, who can be against us?' (Rom. 8.31f.).[51] The whole Trinity is caught up in the movement towards self-surrender, which in the passion of Christ reaches lost men and women and is revealed to them. It is pure lack of comprehension to maintain that 'one of the Trinity suffered, but the other caused the suffering.'[52] If this were so, it would be impossible to talk about 'the pain of God' which underlies 'the sufferings of Christ'.[53] But this is what all recent doctrines of the Trinity do, in considering the theology of the cross, because they have surmounted the metaphysical apathy axiom in the concept of God, and instead start from the love which is of its very essence capable of suffering, as the divine mercy.

> One of the first to take this approach was Origen: 'In his mercy God suffers with us (συμπάσχειν), for he is not heartless. . . . He (the Redeemer) descended to earth out of sympathy for the human race. . . . What is this passion which He suffered for us? It is the passion of love (*caritas est passio*). And the Father Himself, the God of the universe, 'slow to anger, and plenteous in mercy' (Ps. 103.8), does He not also suffer in a certain way? . . . Even the Father is not incapable of suffering (*ipse pater non est impassibilis*). When we call upon him, He is merciful and feels our pain with us. He suffers a suffering of love. . . .[54]

When Origen talks about God's suffering, he means the suffering accepted out of love, the sympathy inherent in all true mercy and pity. Anyone who 'has compassion' participates in the suffering of the other, takes another person's suffering on himself, suffers for others by entering into community with them and bearing their burdens. This suffering in solidarity, vicarious suffering which in its vicariousness saves, is the suffering of God. If we are to understand its full scope, we have to grasp it in trinitarian terms. It is the suffering of the Creator who preserves the world and endures its conflicts and contradictions, in order to sustain it in life. It is the special suffering of Christ, who in his community with us and his self-giving for us, suffers the pains of redemption. It is, finally, the suffering of God's Spirit in the birth-pangs of the new creation.

The idea of the com-passionate God, the God who suffers with us, is an ancient Jewish idea. The God who led Israel to freedom and made his covenant with her is a God with the passion and jealousy of love (Ex. 20.5). That is why the rabbis also discovered in their people's history of suffering the history of the sufferings of Israel's God. 'The Midrash tells that when the Holy One, blessed be He, comes to free the children of Israel from their banishment, they will say to him: Lord of the world, it was thou who first scattered us among the nations, driving us out of our home country; and is it again thou who now leads us back again? . . . And the Holy One, blessed be He, said to the children of Israel: When I saw that you had left my dwelling place, I left it also, in order that I might return there with you. God accompanies his children into banishment. This theme dominates the thought of the Midrash and the mysticism of the Jewish tradition.'[55]

We find this mystical response to the cry of the suffering for God among the Christian mystics too. Catharine of Sienna, we are told, once cried out: 'Where were you, my God and Lord, when my heart was full of darkness and filth?' And the answer she heard was: 'My daughter, did you not feel it? I was in your heart.' To discover in one's own pain the pain of God means finding fellowship with God in one's own suffering, and understanding one's own suffering as participation in 'the sufferings of Christ'.

This, then, is the answer of the theology of surrender to the God-cry of the God-forsaken Christ: 'My God, why hast thou forsaken me?' 'For a brief moment I forsook you, so that you might become the brother of forsaken human beings, and so that in fellowship with you nothing can separate anyone at all from our love. I did not forsake you eternally, but was beside you in your heart.' When the Gentile centurion acknowledges in the face of Jesus' divine cry on the cross, 'This is the Son of God' (Mark 15.39), his recognition points to this mystical answer. This is the consolation which in the long history of Christian experience has radiated from the persecuted, lonely, homeless, suffering and forsaken Christ:

> And when my heart must languish
> Amidst the final throe,
> Release me from mine anguish
> By thine own pain and woe.[56]

The Christ who in his dying was so totally given up to us and was forsaken for our sake is the brother and friend to whom we can confide everything, because he knows everything and has suffered everything that can happen to us, and more. That is why the Christian passion hymns are hymns of thanksgiving:

> Were the whole realm of nature mine,
> That were an offering far too small.

Let us sum up:
'The sufferings of Christ' are God's sufferings because through

them God shows his solidarity with human beings and his whole creation everywhere: *God is with us*.

'The sufferings of Christ' are God's sufferings because through them God intervenes vicariously on our behalf, saving us at the point where we are unable to stand but are forced to sink into nothingness: *God is for us*.

'The sufferings of Christ' are God's sufferings, finally, because out of them the new creation of all things is born: *we come from God*.

Solidarity, vicarious power and rebirth are the divine dimensions in the sufferings of Christ. Christ is with us, Christ is for us, and in Christ we are a new creation. In what sense is God love? God is the power of solidarity, the vicarious, the regenerating power.

§4 RIGHTEOUSNESS FROM THE SUFFERINGS OF CHRIST: WHY DID CHRIST DIE?

Now that we have looked at the human and the divine side of 'Christ's sufferings', we have to ask about their soteriological significance, trying to discover their liberating, redeeming and creative energies. We also have to ask about the meaning and purpose of 'Christ's sufferings'.

1. The Goal of the History of Christ

Reformation theology distinguished between the *historia Christi* and the *finis historiae Christ* – the event itself and its purpose or use (*usus*) – so as to discover in the history of Christ the revelation of the justifying righteousness of God, and in order to find the goal of this history in justifying faith. We shall take up this approach, but shall go beyond it.[57] We shall first of all ask quite simply: *why did Christ die? Why did Christ rise again? What future* is hidden in his death and his resurrection, and when will this hidden future be revealed? When we examine the answers which emerge from the experiences of Christian faith, we discover that the question 'why?' is a difficult one. It relativizes all the answers supplied by experience and perception, moving them into the eschatologically open dimension.[58] To think eschatologically means thinking something through to the end. But what is the end of the history of Christ's suffering and his resurrection? The answers offered are these:

1. *Christ 'was put to death for our trespasses and raised for our justification'* (Rom. 4.25). The meaning and purpose of his suffering is our liberation from the power of sin and the burden of our guilt. The meaning and purpose of his resurrection from the dead is our free life in the righteousness of God. Forgiveness of sins and new life in the righteousness of God: this is the experience of faith. And in this experience Christ is there 'for us'. But for what are people justified? What is the meaning of justifying faith?

We come to the next answer to the question about the meaning of the history of Christ.

2. *'Christ died and lived again, that he might be Lord both of the dead and of the living'* (Rom. 14.9). If justifying faith is the purpose of the history of Christ which is proclaimed and experienced first of all, then the meaning of justifying faith is the redeeming lordship of Christ over the dead and the living. In community with him, those who are separated by death again find their community with one another. The dead Christ became the brother of the dead. The risen Christ gathers the living and the dead into his community of love because this is community in a common hope. He is head of the new humanity, and the future of those who belong to the present *and* those who belong to the past.

3. *'For Christ must reign until he has put all his enemies under his feet. The last enemy to be destroyed is death . . . so that God may be all in all'* (I Cor. 15.25f., 28). The fellowship of Christ with the dead and the living is not a goal in itself. It is a fellowship on the way to the raising of all the dead to eternal life, and to the annihilation of death in the new creation of all things. Only then will 'all tears be wiped away' and perfect joy unite all created beings with God and with one another. So if the meaning of justifying faith is community with Christ, then the meaning of the community in Christ of the dead and the living is the new creation in which death will be no more.

4. *'Therefore God has highly exalted him and bestowed on him the name which is above every name . . . that every tongue should confess that Jesus Christ is Lord, to the glory of God the Father'* (Phil. 2.9, 11). Even the universal salvation of the new creation is not yet in itself the goal but serves the justification of God – that is, the glorifying of God, the Father of Jesus Christ. All created beings find their bliss in participation in his glory. But God only arrives at his rest in the sabbath of his new creation. Only then will the

theodicy trial – which is also a theodicy process – be finished. Only then will all created beings be able to say: 'True and just, Lord, are all thy judgments' (Rev. 16.7). The final goal of the history of Christ therefore lies in the healing of all created beings for the glory of God the Father. The goal is soteriological, yet it is at the same time doxological through and through. The bliss of the new creation finds expression in the eternal song of praise.

All these horizons of purpose and meaning emerge from the history of Christ. The first goal is justifying faith. The second goal is lordship over the dead and the living. The third goal is the conquest of death, and new creation. The fourth goal is the glorification of God through a redeemed world. The immediate goal is the justification of human beings, but the supervening goal is the justification of God, while the common goal is to be found in the reciprocal justification of God and human beings, and in their shared life in justice and righteousness. Righteousness creates lasting peace. Justification is not a unique event, pin-pointed to a certain moment in time. It is a process which begins in the individual heart through faith, and leads to the just new world. This process begins with the forgiveness of sins and ends with the wiping away of all tears. Here Luther's question about the gracious God is answered, and Job's question about God's justice is kept open until it finds its reply. With God's raising of the Christ murdered on the cross, a universal theodicy trial* begins which can only be completed eschatologically with the resurrection of all the dead and the annihilation of death's power – which is to say through the new creation of all things. Then the pain of the theodicy question will be transformed into the universal cosmic doxology. Because this is the ultimate goal, this doxology is already anticipated here and now in faith and in fellowship, in consolation and in hope. It is anticipated as a 'song of the Lord in a strange land'.

2. Justifying Faith

The true perception of Christ necessarily leads the perceiving person to justifying faith. It cannot remain purely theoretical knowledge (*notitia*), but leads on, beyond that, to existential involvement

*The German word *Prozess* means both trial (in the legal sense) and process, and this double aspect should be borne in mind. The theodicy *trial* is still open as an on-going *process*, and will be completed only when all the tears are wiped away: cf. pp. 211f. below [Trans.].

(*fiducia*). Only justifying faith corresponds to the Christ crucified 'for us', for it is only through justifying faith that the liberating power of Christ's resurrection is experienced. That is why christology and the doctrine of justification are inextricably bound up with one another theologically. This was the insight of the Reformers, and in arriving at it they were going back to Paul himself.[59]

Paul developed his christology in the conflict between the law of God and the gospel of Christ, with the help of the idea of dialectical conversion. Here he of course understood the law as the power in whose name he himself had persecuted the Christians. Christ died the accursed death on the cross, condemned in the name of God's law. If he has been raised by God and 'justified', then he redeems from the curse of the law those who are his (Gal. 3.13). If Christ met his earthly end through the law, then the law ends eschatologically through his resurrection. If the crucified Christ was counted among the sinners and 'made sin', then the risen Christ liberates from the power of sin. That is why the gospel in which the crucified Christ is present by virtue of his resurrection becomes the power of God for the salvation of everyone who believes. It brings the new justifying divine righteousness 'without the works of the law'. The gospel of Christ fulfils and surmounts in itself the divine Torah, ushering in the messianic era for Jews and Gentiles. 'The just shall live' was the promise of the Torah. But the law itself was the condition of this justice and righteousness. 'He who through faith is righteous shall live' (Rom. 1.17) is the assurance of the gospel of Christ. The power of the life-giving Spirit of God is now immanent in the gospel of Christ's resurrection. Consequently, this gospel now mediates the Spirit of the resurrection and of the new creation of all things, anticipating in believers the victory of life over death by liberating them from the power of sin. God is just because he makes the unjust just and creates justice for those who suffer under injustice.

Paul understood the righteousness of God as God's creative acts in and for those who are threatened by absolute death because they have come under 'the power of sin', which is contrary to God. We understand by 'sin' the condition in which a person closes himself off from the source of life, from God. A closing of the self like this comes about when the purposes for which human beings are by nature destined are not discovered or not fulfilled, because of hybris, or depression, or 'the God complex', or because of a refusal to accept what human existence is about. This leads to the self-destruction of the regenerating energies of life, and thus to death. The self-deification of human beings is the beginning of their self-destruction, and the destruction also of the world in which they live. This death has to be understood as absolute death, because it is not identical with the natural life process. 'Sin' in this sense means missing the mark of being, and has to be used in the singular. It is a happening in the created being as a whole, and it precedes morality, although it is the source of the acts and kinds of behaviour which in a moral sense can be recognized as infringing the laws of life – that is, sins in the plural. Because every created being belongs to a social context shared with other beings, 'sin' always destroys life in the social sense too. We talk about the trans-personal 'power of sin' because sin involves the inescapable structural processes of destruction over which Paul cries out when he acknowledges for himself personally: 'I do not do the good I want, but the evil I do not want is what I do' (Rom. 7.19). Today everyone can see these processes at work in the developments for which he shares responsibility and at the same time helplessly deplores. Ordered systems which once ministered to life are toppling over into their very opposite, so that they now work for death.

The gospel has its own time. Its kairos is 'this present time' in which 'the wrath of God', as Paul puts it, 'is revealed . . . against all ungodliness and wickedness of men' (Rom. 1.18). People are becoming beset by this end-time tribulation because universal death is descending on their godless injustice – since injustice has this death as its inescapable consequence. Time is running out. The end of time is approaching. Against the apocalyptic horizon where men and women sink into the nothingness which they are preparing for themselves and nature, the gospel of Christ brings the saving power of God into the world. It saves because it justifies. It is the power of rebirth from the life-giving Spirit and the beginning of the new creation. Here we may think too of the apocalyptic tribulation of all creation in 'the sufferings of this present time' (Rom. 8.18). Through *the forgiveness of sins* the gospel breaks through the compulsive acts of sinners which are the enemies of life, cutting sinners loose from sin, and creating the possibility of 'conversion', a turn to life. Through *the justification of sinners*, the gospel brings men and women who are closed in upon themselves into the open love of God. Through *rebirth from the Spirit*, it brings people who have been subject to death into touch with the eternal source of life, setting them in the closer framework of the rebirth of human community and against the wider horizon of the rebirth of the cosmos.

The universal meaning of the gospel of Christ for Jews and Gentiles is founded on the character of God's justifying righteousness, which is prevenient and has no preconditions. Because justification has no preconditions but is given only out of grace, there are no longer any privileges for the one, and no longer any disparagement of the other. The gospel of Christ saves and justifies 'sinners', and therefore turns to all human beings in what they are *not* and in what they do *not* have (Rom. 3.23), whatever differences there may be in the things they are and have.

The Lutheran theology of the Reformation period based justifying faith solely on the suffering and death of Christ 'for us'. But this was one-sided. They perceived the *pro nobis* in Christ's cross, but not in his resurrection. They therefore understood the justification of the sinner too narrowly as 'the forgiveness of sins', but not as new life in righteousness. The meaning of Christ's resurrection was reduced to this saving significance of his death on the cross.[60] But according to Paul, Christ was raised 'for our justification' (Rom. 4.25) and so that we might be saved (Rom. 5.10). Christ's resurrection has an added value and a surplus of promise over Christ's death: Christ 'died, yes, was raised from the dead . . .' (Rom. 8.34).[61] This surplus of Christ's resurrection over his death is manifested in the surplus of grace compared with the mere cancellation of sin: 'Where sin increased, grace *abounded all the more*' (Rom. 5.20). If while we were enemies we were 'reconciled' with God through his death, '*how much more* shall we be saved by his life' (Rom. 5.10). So justifying grace is not merely a making-present of the Christ crucified 'for us'; it is even more a making-present of the risen and coming Christ. Faith is Easter jubilation, and the forgiveness of all guilt springs from this joy, as the Orthodox liturgy proclaims: 'The day of resurrection! Let us be light on this feast. And let us embrace one another. Brethren, let us speak to those who hate us. For the resurrection's sake will we forgive one another everything, and so let us cry: Christ is risen from the dead . . .'[62]

What happened to the dead Christ in his resurrection to eternal life happens to us in a corresponding way in the justification of sinners: 'In illo resurrectio, ita in nobis vera justificatio.'[63] Because the raising of Christ shows this added value and surplus over against his death, the justification of sinners initiates a process of exuberant intensification: justification – sanctification – glorification (Rom. 8.30). Justifying faith is not yet the goal and end of Christ's history. For every individual believer it is no more than the beginning of a way that leads to the new creation of the world and to the justification of God. That is why those who are justified by faith are the people who 'hunger and thirst' for righteousness and justice (Matt. 5.6) and 'are persecuted for righteousness' sake' (Matt. 5.10). It is they who weep over this world which Albert Camus describes as the place 'where children suffer and die'. That is why they wait for the future in which 'all tears will be wiped away' (Isa. 25.8; Rev. 7.17; 21.4). The person whom God has justified protests against the injustice in this world. The person in whose heart God has put peace can no longer come to terms with the discord in the world, but will resist it and hope for 'peace on earth'. Injustice and suffering acquire a meaning only to the degree in which we refuse to accept them. Faith and hope for the righteousness and justice of God are the spur to keep us from surrendering to them, and to make us fight injustice and suffering wherever and however we can.[64]

Justification is more than reconciliation. Through Anselm in the middle ages, through Hegel in the nineteenth century, and through Karl Barth in our own time – even if in different ways – 'reconciliation' was made the quintessence of soteriology, and the framework for understanding christology as a whole. Christology was functionalized, and became reconciliation christology. But even a simple glance at a concordance to the New Testament shows that the words for reconcile, καταλλάσσειν and ἱλάσκεσθαι are relatively rare, and are neither central nor fundamental. The category of righteousness, on the other hand, is both central and fundamental.

Reconciliation is only emphasized to any considerable degree in the sphere of the epistles to the Ephesians and the Colossians. In the original Pauline letters, ideas about atonement and reconciliation are integrated into the event of the divine righteousness.[65]

Historically, the ideas about atonement and reconciliation evidently go back to the Jewish–Christian community. There, Jesus' death was already interpreted very early on as expiation, and the preaching of the cross echoed with the ideas about expiatory sacrifice found in Leviticus 16, and with reminiscences of the Suffering Servant in Isaiah 53. 'That Christ died for our sins according to the scriptures' (I Cor. 15.3b) is an ancient Jewish–Christian conception which Paul presupposed and accepted. With the help of this idea, the salvific meaning of Christ's death 'for us' could well be expressed in a limited framework: as expiatory sacrifice Christ takes our sins and

God's judgment on himself, and saves us from them and their consequences. But a 'scapegoat' like this, that 'takes away the sins of the world', and even a Suffering Servant of God on whom lies 'the chastisement that made us whole' are bound to disappear once the sin disappears. In either pattern of ideas, the return of this 'scapegoat' or 'Suffering Servant' by way of resurrection is inconceivable. Applied to Christ's death, the concepts about expiation say that the cause of our suffering is our sin, the cause of Christ's suffering is God's gracious will, the purpose of his suffering is the restoration on our behalf of the broken covenant. It is immediately evident that these ideas about salvation can be applied to Christ's death, but not to his resurrection, and that they cut Christ's death off from his resurrection, so as to relate that death to the restoration of a covenant with God which is the premise of the idea.

Re-conciliation is a backward-looking act. It presupposes an unscathed world which was destroyed by human sin, and which reconciliation restores. Reconciliation is the negation of the negative, its purpose being to put into effect once more the original, positive condition: *restitutio in integrum*. It is this old mythical pattern (primal condition—apostasy—return home) which Bultmann follows when he says: 'So what point has the divine righteousness, the forgiveness of sins? . . . It means that the original relationship of creation has been restored, that the complex of sin in which I am always involved—the complex of being-flesh, of being-world—is ended, and that the ancient revelation is made visible once again.'[66] Here the divine righteousness is reduced to 'the forgiveness of sins', and consequently its goal is supposed to be the restoration of creation as it originally was. But the statement says nothing about the totally new thing which the resurrection has brought into the world.

In Barth's theology, God's covenant with human beings is said to be 'the inner ground of creation'; but sin can then only be impairment of the community between human beings and God which existed under this original covenant. Consequently Jesus Christ came into the world, was humiliated and crucified, in order to bring about the divine work of reconciliation. Christ's resurrection is then reduced to 'the Father's judgment' and becomes the legitimation category for the cross of the Reconciler.[67]

But if, as we have said, the resurrection of Christ has an added value over and above the significance of his death, then it promises a 'new creation' which is more than 'the first creation' (Rev. 21.4: 'For the first . . has passed away'). Christ's resurrection does not say: *restitutio in integrum* through reconciliation. It says: reconciliation in order that the world may be transformed and newly created. It says: justification of sinners so that there may be a just world for all created beings. We may therefore say that the process of the justification of God and human beings has at least the following components:

1. Forgiveness of sin's guilt.
2. Liberation from sin's power.
3. The reconciliation of the God-less.
4. New life in the service of righteousness and justice.
5. The right to inherit the new creation.
6. Participation in God's new just world through passionate effort on its behalf.

3. The Community of the Living and the Dead

Justifying faith in Christ leads believers into the lordship of Christ over the dead and the living. They find themselves in a community in which the frontier of death has been breached. Through Christ's resurrection, God has thrown open the future to everyone, the living and the dead. The living maintain their community with the dead, for in the community of Christ the dead are not forgotten; they are present. The lordship of Christ therefore reaches far beyond the 'new obedience' and a life in sanctification. Because through his death and resurrection Christ has become Lord of the dead and the living, it is impossible to reduce his sovereign rule to ethics. But how can Christ be Lord over the dead? And how can he draw the dead into fellowship with him?

There is more to the death of Christ than merely the vicarious suffering of sin and absolute death which justifying faith discerns. Through his death, he also became the brother and deliverer of those who have died. It was this which the mythical images about Christ's descent into hell and 'the realm of death' wanted to express.[68] If God himself was 'in Christ', then God himself is also present in the dead Christ among the dead. According to I Peter 3.19f., Christ 'went and preached to the spirits in prison, who formerly did not obey, when God's patience waited in the days of Noah'. According to 4.6 'the gospel was preached even to the dead, that though judged in the flesh like men, they might live in the spirit of God'. Whatever we may think about the particular concepts underlying these images, the important point is that Christ is ascribed saving potentiality for the dead. So the dead are not lost. Like the living, they can draw hope from the gospel. That is to say, the dead too can arrive at faith, for Christ does not proclaim the gospel inefficaciously. Communications and energies of the divine Spirit belong to the fellowship of Christ even beyond death. No limits are set to the power of his sufferings, which are redemptive through their vicarious potency, because God was 'in him'. Consequently, the dead are included. Does this mean only Israel's dead, or all the dead? Certainly Israel's dead first of all, because 'the sufferings of Christ' also include Israel's sufferings. But, beyond that, all the dead are meant, as the hymnal conclusion of Phil. 2.9–11 explicitly declares.

Death can set no limits to the unconditional and hence universal love of God: this has to be said for God's sake. Otherwise God would not be God, and death would have to be called an anti-God. When we say that the dead are also reached by the gospel which is to be proclaimed to all nations, this statement is based anthropologically on the fact that humanity is created in a sequence of generations, and is therefore, in this temporal sense, a community between the living and the dead. Almost all peoples have celebrated this community in what is called (though wrongly) 'ancestor worship': the dead participate in their own way in the life of the community, and the living lead their lives in the presence of the dead, who are present among the living as their 'ancestors'. As social beings, men and women are also generation beings. So if Christ is experienced in faith as the brother and redeemer of the living, then this same faith sees him as the brother and redeemer of our 'ancestors'. Through his 'descent into the realm of death' Christ himself became the 'redeeming ancestor'.[69] Through his fellowship with the dead, he brings them God and the redeeming power of the Spirit, and liberates them from death's power.

It was therefore not wrong when in the seventeenth century Lutheran theologians saw Christ's 'descent into hell', not as the nadir of his sufferings, but as the beginning of his exaltation and his sovereign rule over the universe (contrary to the Reformed position, which here followed Luther himself).[70] Nor is it wrong when on the day of divine silence between Christ's death on Good Friday and his resurrection on Easter Sunday, Catholic 'Holy Saturday mysticism' remembers his hidden and inconceivably mysterious activity for the dead.[71] There is no real antithesis between Christ's 'descent into hell' and his 'descent into the realm of death': dying, Christ suffered on the cross the hell of forsakenness and absolute death; as someone dead, he became the brother of the dead and the redeeming ancestor, thus opening the world of the dead for the future of the resurrection and eternal life. It is a striking fact that the Easter icons of the Orthodox church picture the resurrection in the descent of Christ to the dead, the breaking down of the walls of their prison, and the leading out of the prisoners into the liberty of eternal life, Adam and Eve at the head.

However we may picture it, therefore, 'the descent of Christ into the world of the dead' brings with it the lordship of Christ over the dead: 'To this end Christ died and lived again, that he might be Lord both of the dead and the living' (Rom. 14.9). The dead are still the dead, and not yet raised, but by virtue of the fellowship of Christ they are already 'in Christ' and together with him are on the way into the future of the resurrection. When Christ 'appears' they will appear with him 'in glory' (Col. 3.4). Death cannot separate us from God's love (Rom. 8.38), but this love of God is not yet the glory of God through which death itself will be annihilated. The existence of the dead in the lordship of Christ is therefore not as yet 'resurrection' but only a *sheltering* for the resurrection. It is a 'Being with Christ', as Paul writes (Phil. 1.23), but not yet the redeemed Being in eternal life.[72]

The 'eschatological proviso' of the lordship of Christ also applies to the dead in that lordship: Christ is risen from the dead, but we are not yet risen. He has broken the power of sin, but the end of death's rule is still to come. His life-giving sovereignty will be completed only when he hands over 'the kingdom' to the Father, so that God is 'all in all' (I Cor. 15.28) and death disappears. In this 'intermediate state' of Christ's fellowship with the dead and the living, the dead are not separated from God, but they are not yet perfected in God either. They are 'in Christ' and with him on the way. Their fate depends on the future of Christ. They therefore exist in the same hope as the living, and consequently in the same peril. This is what Walter Benjamin meant with his dark and enigmatic saying: 'Even the dead will not be safe from the enemy if he conquers. And this enemy has never ceased to conquer.' For Benjamin, this 'enemy' is the Antichrist: 'For the Messiah does not come only as the Redeemer. He comes too as the vanquisher of the Antichrist.'[73] If the living are justifiably afraid that the future will bring the destruction of the world, this is also fear for the dead – fear that they will then have lived in vain, and that their death may have been meaningless. The dead also wait for justice; their trial is still on, as long as the world itself is still under trial.

The fellowship of the living and the dead is important for the life of the living, and for the life of coming generations.[74] If a society no longer lives in the coherent structure of succeeding generations, but is now only aware of the social cross-currents with contemporaries, brothers and sisters, comrades and friends, that society is breaking 'the generation contract' which is the only thing that guarantees the survival of humanity. That society represses the remembrance of the dead and represses too the unreconciled pains of the past and the sufferings of the dead which can never be made good. Who feels the dumb protest of the dead against the indifference of the living? Who senses that 'the dead cannot rest', as people used to say, unless justice is done to them? And if these dead have become the 'innocent victims' of the living, does forgetting them not lead to a repression of guilt? We see the result of these repressions in the growing collective indifference towards life.

After the war, it was experiences like these which in Germany led to a 'political theology', because we perceived the long shadows of Auschwitz that had fallen on our lives. Are the murderers to triumph once and for all over the victims, or is there any justice for the slaughtered victims of the Holocaust? The 'resurrection of the dead' and 'the judgment of God' are the ancient symbols for this justice, which binds together the living and the dead, and puts them in a common peril as well as a common hope. Anyone who forgets the rights of the dead will be indifferent to the rights of his children as well. Anyone who enjoys his present at the cost of the dead will also burden the future of those who come after him with a load of debt. Anyone who is cynical towards the dead will be cynical towards the living too. To acknowledge a hope for the common 'resurrection of the dead' means preserving our fellowship with the dead. Easter morning services in the graveyards where the dead are buried are an ancient Christian symbol of this community. Because every Sunday service can be lit by a spark from Christ's resurrection, every service is held in the presence of the dead.

4. *The Wiping Away of the Tears*

The fellowship of Christ with the dead and the living which is experienced in the present points beyond itself to the consummation of the lordship of Christ. This means that it turns suffering over this 'unredeemed world' into conscious pain. In the grief over the death of every beloved person and every abandoned child, we hear the eschatological cry: How long? 'Come Lord Jesus, come soon' (Rev. 22.20). The people who utter this cry are hungering and thirsting for the victory of God's righteousness through the raising of the dead and the annihilation of death itself. The people who weep over this unredeemed world and its victims love life, and are not prepared to come to terms with existing conditions. It is not unbelievers who are seized by this 'divine sadness', but believers. Nor is it merely men and women. In all created beings, the suffering Spirit of God himself cries out to God 'Come' (Rev. 22.17). It is only the person who has tasted something of the divine righteousness who is hungry for it. It is only the person who has tasted a drop of the water of life who is thirsty for it. Anyone who has experienced the love of God for a single instant thrusts forward to the manifestation of God's glory. Anyone who believes in the forgiveness of sins begins to weep over the injustice of this world, and waits for the wiping away of the tears which only this forgiveness of sins can and must complete. In other words, justifying faith places people in the still open, not yet answered theodicy question. For the consolation of faith does not blunt those who are consoled to suffering. It makes them sensitive to it, because it awakens hope for a new world in which suffering will find an end.

The fellowship with the dead preserved in the fellowship of Christ makes the hope which counters death both social and cosmic. For the individual does not believe and love, hope and weep for himself, but for other people. What he believes and hopes, he believes and hopes in solidarity and in representation for other human beings and other creatures.[75] Faith in justification and hope for the victory of Christ's righteousness mean that this world can be experienced as a world that is still profoundly 'unredeemed'.

Paul therefore conceived the great vision of the eschatological perfecting of the lordship of Christ (I Cor. 15.20–28). The Christ who through his resurrection from the dead and his exaltation has been installed as 'Lord' of the divine sovereignty 'must reign until he has put all his enemies under his feet' (v. 25), for otherwise God would not be God.[76] Christ completes his rule over the whole creation by abolishing every 'rule, authority and power' and by making life alive through his peace. 'The last enemy to be destroyed is death' (v. 26). Then the new creation will be perfected in which death will be no more (Rev. 21.4). Here the annihilation of death does not mean simply absolute death, the death of the sinner and human death. It means death as a cosmic power – the death of all the living. The annihilation of death is the cosmic side of the resurrection of the dead, just as the resurrection of the dead is the personal side of the cosmic annihilation of death. The two sides belong together. Otherwise the resurrection hope turns into a gnostic redemption myth. The completion of the justifying and life-giving rule of Christ is the eternal life of the future world. Paul calls the perfecting of the rule of Christ 'the kingdom' (v. 24), which is an expression he never uses anywhere else. As the Son, Christ will hand over 'the kingdom' to the Father, so that 'God may be all in all'. Here too, just as at the end of the hymn in Philippians (2.9–11), the goal of Christ's rule over the universe is the glorification of God through the new, redeemed creation. In the deutero-Pauline epistles to the Ephesians and Colossians, this eschatological vision of Paul's becomes the impressive picture of the cosmic Christ, through whose Wisdom everything was created, through whose blood everything has been reconciled, and through whose exaltation all things will be 'gathered together' (Eph. 1; Col. 1).

For a long time exegesis and theology viewed these dimensions of the redemption of the cosmos as mythological and speculative. But today, the more the ecological catastrophe of modern human civilization threatens to destroy all life on earth, the more relevant and existential these dimensions of 'Christ's sufferings' become for the whole creation – as well as the justice and righteousness which proceed from these sufferings. The sufferings of dying nature are 'Christ's sufferings' too, and where dying nature is concerned, 'Christ's sufferings' are surely to be discerned as birth pangs of a new earth on which righteousness will dwell. The modern reduction of the salvation which Christ has brought to the salvation of men and women, or merely to the salvation of their souls, led to the view that non-human creation is outside salvation, so that hope for its redemption was surrendered. A common hope for the new creation was replaced by cynical exploitation and extermination. Once this happened, the ecological end of time for the nature of our earth was pre-programmed. Today the rediscovery of cosmic christology will have to begin with an ecological christology if cosmic christology is to be of therapeutic relevance for the nature which is today suffering under the irrationality of human beings. We shall come back to this in chapter VI.

5. The Joy of God without End

Finally, the fellowship of Christ which Paul called his 'lordship' has from the very beginning the meaning of *glorifying God*. According to Rom. 15.7, 'Christ has accepted us for the glory of God'. According to Phil. 2.11, Christ will be Lord over the universe 'for the glorification of God the Father'. According to Rom. 6.10, the risen Christ 'lives for God'. According to Gal. 2.19, Paul 'through the law died to the law' so that he 'might live for God'. Again and again Paul describes this new 'life for God' as 'righteousness' (Rom. 4.25; II Cor. 5.21). The christocentricism of his theology conceals a theocentricism. 'The inner mystery of Christ's lordship' is the glorification of God.[77]

What does glorifying God mean here? In Paul, statements about God's righteousness and God's glory are parallel to one another, and often coincide. Christ is the revealer of the divine righteousness, and of God's glory too (II Cor. 4.4). The sinner has turned the truth into a lie, and transformed justice into injustice. He has lost his glory as God's image (Rom. 3.23). The gospel brings the justifying righteousness of God and is at the same time 'the gospel of the glory of Christ' (II Cor. 4.4). Righteousness and glory are one in the person of the raised Christ. His raising certainly means that God upholds the rights of the one who suffered the injustice of men. But it also means his transfiguration and transformation into God's glory (Phil. 3.21). Only then does Christ become the pattern 'image of God' and the all-embracing prototype of the new creation. Christ has this glory, not in himself, but only in his commitment to God the Father. By glorifying the Father he himself is glorified.

In the Luther Bible the word for 'glory' is often translated as 'Ehre', which is the German word usually rendered as 'honour'. Of course the term has something to do with respect and recognition, but the word 'honour' is much too weak. In Old Testament usage, 'glory' has something to do with the fullness of power and the display of pomp; but this interpretation merely stresses the weight which impresses, and oppresses, those who are weaker. 'Glory' is probably best understood as an aesthetic category. When glory is coupled with affection and love, we can talk about grace and beauty. This is what

Dostoievsky meant with his famous dictum 'Beauty will redeem the world'. It is the redeeming power of God's beauty which Orthodox worship and Orthodox icons seek to express. But the aesthetic category of beauty when it is applied to God's glory also holds within itself the shudder of the terrible. 'He who looks upon God must die', we are told, because a human being cannot endure the unmediated divine radiance. But anyone who 'looks upon God' and still lives has found grace in the eyes of the Eternal One and is called 'God's friend', like Abraham. Rilke comes close to the mystery of the divine glory when he writes:

> For beauty is only
> the dawn of the terrible, which we barely endure,
> and we revere it because it serenely disdains
> to destroy us.[77a]

Translated into positive terms, this 'disdaining to destroy us' is the *grace* in which the glory of God reaches us in the face of Jesus Christ. And this means, conversely, that the grace which reaches us is the present form of God's glory. That is why 'the kingdom of grace' is aligned towards 'the kingdom of glory', and the rule of Christ exists for the glorification of God. That is why the grace experienced finds expression only in the song of praise through which men and women adore and praise God. When does this happen? When the righteousness of God is victorious and human injustice and violence disappear from the earth. Through the justification of the unjust, and the creation of justice for those who know no justice, God glorifies himself on earth. Only when the theodicy trial is finished, the trial opened through the election of Israel and the surrender and raising of the messiah Jesus, will the accusing theodicy question turn into the eternal song of praise. But until then the tears and the dreams remain together. Until then the experience of the forgiveness of sins is entwined with the indictment of God because of the suffering in this world.

§5 THE FELLOWSHIP OF CHRIST'S SUFFERINGS: MARTYROLOGY TODAY

Ecclesia martyrum, church of the martyrs – that is an ancient and honourable title for the church of Jesus Christ. It describes the common destiny which the church shares with her Lord, the 'true' and 'faithful witness' (Rev. 3.14; 1.5). It points believers towards the martyrdom of Christ.

A church's martyrs link it in a special way with the testimony of Christ in his sufferings and death on the cross. It is therefore meet and right for us to honour the martyrs, to call them by their names, and to take our bearings from the story of their lives and their deaths. To turn remembrance of the martyrs into a special cult of the saints can be a sign that they are being put at a safe religious distance. But it is at all events a sign that Christianity has been politically assimilated when a church's martyrs are forgotten; for when they are forgotten, the Christ crucified by Pontius Pilate is disregarded too.

In our own century we are experiencing a wave of martyrdom such as has been seen in hardly any other century. We have to go back to Christianity's beginnings, and the organized persecutions by the Roman emperors, before we can find comparable situations and similar numbers. The ancient church knew her martyrs, and knew also how to interpret the martyrdom of the witnesses theologically. In our own time, many churches also know their martyrs, but without knowing how Christian martyrdom is to be understood theologically today; for nowadays the experience of the martyrs is different from what it was earlier. In hitherto unknown conflicts with the power of the state, and with violent groups, witnesses come forward whom the church does not quite know where to place, or whether they should be considered martyrs or not. This makes it all the more important to discover a theological concept for understanding martyrdom as it is experienced today.

In the early and patristic church, the concept of the martyr grew up out of the experiences of Christian persecution by pagan rulers.[78] Men and women were recognized and revered as martyrs when, like Christ himself, they freely and patiently accepted their violent deaths in faith and for his name's sake. They were brought before tribunals which demanded that they deny Christ. They publicly confessed their faith, and were publicly executed in order to deter other Christians and the people as a whole from adherence to the Christian faith. In this way they became 'public witnesses' to Christ. The martyrdom of the aged Bishop Polycarp of Smyrna, and the martyrdom of Bishop Ignatius of Antioch, became the model for many. In his letters to his congregations, Ignatius expounded the meaning of martyrdom by saying that here the believer does not die as a soldier dies, *for* his master. He dies *with* that master, and participates in Christ's sufferings. This gives him the certainty that like Christ he will rise again and will reign with him. If the martyrs in their own bodies 'complete what is lacking in Christ's afflictions' (Col. 1.24), then in his martyrs Christ himself suffers.

The mediaeval church expanded the concept of the martyr. Thomas Aquinas made this clear: 'Only faith in Christ grants the glory of martyrdom to those who suffer. . . . A Christian means one who belongs to Christ. Now a person is said to belong to Christ not simply because he believes in him, but also because he undertakes virtuous deeds in the Spirit of Christ.'[79] The martyr is accordingly someone who is persecuted and put to death because of his confession of faith – and also someone who is persecuted and put to death because of the obedience of faith. But in both cases death in the *odium fidei* must be accepted freely and deliberately.

This concept of martyrdom, then, was built up out of the experiences of the ancient church. If we compare it with the experiences of Christians who resist and are persecuted in our own day, the differences immediately spring to the eye:

1. Today martyrs are tortured to death and then 'disappear'. No one knows the place where they were murdered, no one finds their bodies, and no one knows their names. The public forum is deliberately denied today's martyrs.

2. In the age of 'religious freedom', persecution on the grounds of a person's confession of faith is diminishing. What has now come to the fore is persecution because of the uncompromising obedience of faith.

3. The persecution of Christians by pagan or atheist states is only one side of the coin. The persecution of Christians in states which call themselves Christian is growing. In the last ten years, more than 850 Catholic priests were murdered in Latin America, not to speak of unnumbered Christian laymen and lay women; and the people who murdered them consider themselves to be Christians.

4. Martyrdom in the ancient church was the personal and public martyrdom of individuals. Today martyrdom is generally anonymous, and is the martyrdom of whole groups, people, races, and so forth. Archbishop Romero was murdered in front of the altar. We know and reverence his name. At his funeral 40 people were murdered by the same opponents. But their names we do not know.

In order to develop a broad theological concept of martyrdom, I am going to start from the testimony of three people, in different situations. First I shall take Paul Schneider, 'the Buchenwald preacher', and then Dietrich Bonhoeffer, 'the theologian in resistance', both of whom are martyrs of the Confessing Church in Germany. Finally we shall look at the Catholic Archbishop Arnulfo Romero, 'the bishop of the persecuted people' of El Salvador.

First Example: Paul Schneider (1897–1939)

Paul Schneider was a Reformed pastor in the Protestant church of the Rhineland.[80] He was a man of prayer and a pastor in the true sense, and a strict upholder of Reformed discipline. 'Church discipline is the sinew of the church. If this sinew is severed, the whole body loses its strength', said Calvin. Paul Schneider followed him consistently and dispensed no sacrament without discipline. In 1934, a year after Hitler came to power, the first conflict with the state broke out in Schneider's new congregation, Dickenschied in the Hunsrück. A member of the Hitler youth had a fatal accident and was buried. At the end of Pastor Schneider's sermon, the local leader of the Hitler youth advanced to the grave and pronounced that the dead youth was now among 'Horst Wessel's heavenly storm troopers'. Paul Schneider rose and protested: 'This is a church service. There are no storm troopers in heaven.' In the years that followed, he tried to withstand the National Socialist 'German Christians' in his congregations with the help of the church discipline we have mentioned. This led to his expulsion from the Rhenish province on the grounds of 'political agitation against the National Socialist state'.

In spite of his expulsion, Paul Schneider and his wife returned to their congregation in the autumm of 1937 in order to hold the harvest festival service. Schneider was convinced that his call to preach the gospel to this congregation was a divine command which he had to obey, and which took precedence over an expulsion directive from the German state. He was arrested, was taken into Gestapo custody in Coblenz and, because of his steadfast refusal to recognize the expulsion decree, was sent to the concentration camp in Buchenwald. Here too he could have obtained his release at any time if he had recognized the expulsion decree. But to do this would have been for him a betrayal of God's charge, which was to be the pastor of his congregation.

In April 1938 the prisoners in Buchenwald were commanded to salute the swastika flag every morning. Paul Schneider refused, on the grounds that the salute was 'idolatry'. He was then cruelly tortured and put in the 'bunker', the camp's condemned cell. But from the window of his cell he continually proclaimed God's word to the prisoners who were drawn up in the square outside, giving them the courage to survive. And he arraigned the SS murderers by name before God. These addresses were always very short, because the prison warders fell on him and reduced him to silence. For thirteen months he suffered endless torments. Prisoners who survived that time in Buchenwald reported that at the end Schneider was no more than a piece of bleeding flesh. On 14 July 1939, he was murdered with a strophantin injection.

We can learn three things from the 'Buchenwald preacher' and his martyrdom.

1. Paul Schneider had a firm assurance of faith, and suffered martyrdom because of it. The grounds for this assurance were: prayer, God's call to preach the gospel, and the divine charge given to him to minister to the congregation in Dickenschied. He was prepared to die rather than to lose this assurance. And the assurance evidently grew in the face of his torments.

2. Church discipline brings God's commandments and God's promise into practical daily life. God must be obeyed more than any other powers. Without discipline there is no genuine Christian discipleship. And Paul Schneider learnt that church discipline is necessary not merely in the sphere of personal morality, but in the sphere of politics too.

3. Paul Schneider was not the passive victim of martyrdom. He took this path freely and patiently. He disregarded the state's expulsion edict. He refused to salute the swastika. Even in the condemned cell he refused to keep silent about political injustice, but proclaimed God's word. His martyrdom was *an active passion*.

Second Example: Dietrich Bonhoeffer (1906–1945)

Dietrich Bonhoeffer started off in the world of academic theology.[81] The ecumenical movement and the peace movement of the 1930s put an indelible mark on him. But what was really decisive was the struggle of the Confessing Church against the church's subordination to Hitler's totalitarian state.

Bonhoeffer belonged to the radical wing of the Confessing Church. For him it was 'the true church', and between the true church and the false he saw no mediation and no neutral 'middle of the road'. 'The person who cuts himself off from the Confessing Church is cutting himself off from salvation', he declared in 1935. He was appointed head of the Confessing Church's illegal theological seminary, or training college, in Finkenwalde.

In 1939 Bonhoeffer visited New York for the second time, returning to Germany just before war broke out. His friends warned him not to go, and wanted to keep him at Union Seminary. But Bonhoeffer knew that his place was in the conflicts which lay ahead in Germany. He continued to work for the Confessing Church, but at the same time joined a political resistance group round Admiral Canaris and Colonel Oster, which was active in the German Intelligence. Bonhoeffer became the group's courier. On 3 April 1943, he was arrested, and was murdered on 9 April 1945, in the concentration camp in Flossenbürg, together with Canaris and Oster.

We can learn three things from this 'theologian in resistance'.

1. He moved from *church* resistance against German dictatorship to *political* resistance. Why? Because the church must not begin to protest only when the state interferes in the church itself. It must already protest as soon as state power becomes lawless, unjust and inhumane. The church must protest when Jews are persecuted, Communists or democrats are murdered, or when a whole people is reduced to silence. Bonhoeffer did not die merely for the right to believe within the church. He also died for the right to obey the dictates of faith in political life. He deliberately participated in 'God's sufferings in the world'. His martyrdom was a political martyrdom for Christ's sake, whereas Paul Schneider's martyrdom was a martyrdom of faith for Christ's name.

2. Bonhoeffer himself called the source of his power to resist 'the arcane discipline'. By this secret discipline he meant the inward discipline of the spiritual life, prayer, meditation and immersion in the presence of the divine Spirit.

3. Bonhoeffer too was not overwhelmed passively by persecution, suffering and death. He returned voluntarily to Germany in 1939. He became involved in political resistance knowing exactly what he was doing; and it was a deliberate act of choice when he became a 'traitor' to a regime which had shown its contempt for human beings.

Third Example: Arnulfo Romero (1917–1979)

Arnulfo Romero, 'the people's bishop' in El Salvador, was conse-
crated priest in 1942 and bishop in 1970.[82] In 1977 he was appointed Archbishop of San Salvador. At that time presidential elections
were being held in El Salvador. The ruling military junta rigged the
results, and the other parties protested in a demonstration. They
were shot down by the National Guard. Two weeks later, on
12 March 1977, a priest was murdered for the first time in El Salvador, Father Rutilio Grande SJ, the parish priest of Aguilares. Romero
hurried to the place of his murder and spent the night of 12/13
March among the murdered man's parishioners. He said later that
on that night 'he was converted'.

Romero was 59. Up to then he had been a conservative church-
man. Now he recognized the connection between the persecution of
the church and the repression of the people by the ruling minority in
his country and their 'death squads'. He began to go among the
people and became 'their' bishop. 'What is really being persecuted is
the people, not the church,' he wrote, 'but the church is on the
people's side and the people are on the side of the church.' He
believed in 'the God of the poor', writes his biographer Jon Sobrino.
'For him, the crucified God became present in the crucified men and
women of history. . . . In the faces of the poor and oppressed of his
people, he saw the disfigured face of God.'[83] Romero learnt to hear
the gospel about the kingdom of the coming God in the sighs and the
protesting cry of the poor. The poor 'evangelized' him. The cathedral
in San Salvador became the place where the people gathered, a place
of liturgy and hunger strike, a hospital for the wounded, and a place
where leave was taken of many, many of the people's dead. Romero
also understood why and how the people were moving towards
becoming an 'organized people'. He supported the 'popular organizations' of the farm workers, the smallholders and the workers. For
him 'the people's project' was a solution to the problems of his
country. And this meant that he was drawn into the political conflict.
Archbishop Romero was shot during mass by a paid assassin in front
of the altar of his church.

In this martyrdom of Arnulfo Romero's, we can see a third
dimension of Christian martyrdom. It is a dimension that has
received little attention up to now, but today it is becoming more and
more important. *The first dimension* is suffering for faith's sake: Paul

Schneider. *The second dimension* is suffering through resistance against unjust and lawless power: Dietrich Bonhoeffer. *The third dimension* is participation in the sufferings of the oppressed people: Arnulfo Romero.

The Apocalyptic Side of Martyrdom

If we consider the martyrdom of these three people, we see that it is really only Pastor Paul Schneider who comes under the classic definition of martyrdom embraced expressly for Christ's sake and in his name, although he too deliberately disregarded a state order and was put to death as a result. With Dietrich Bonhoeffer we meet a martyrdom accepted as the consequence of 'virtuous political deeds in the Spirit of Christ'. Out of obedience to Christ, he engaged in active resistance. Admiral Canaris and Colonel Oster were executed with him. Were they martyrs for Christ's sake too? We do not know their religious motives. But seen objectively, they too, like Bonhoeffer, were martyrs for the cause of justice, which is God's cause. At this point the frontiers of Christian martyrdom become open transitions. The open frontier of martyrdom accepted out of a political obedience to Christ divulges a particular mystery: the martyrs are part of a wider community. They themselves have entered into this community with other witnesses to truth and justice, and they bring the church which reveres them as martyrs into fellowship with these other witnesses to truth and justice. Leonardo Boff calls these other witnesses the 'martyrs of God's kingdom and God's policy in history'.[84]

But Archbishop Romero goes even beyond this community of Christ's witnesses and the witnesses to justice and righteousness, for he points to the sufferings of the poor, helpless and oppressed people. In the struggle for power, the weakest suffer most, it is the poor who are sacrificed by the rulers, and the children die first of all. But that is why Jesus called them blessed, because the kingdom of God is theirs. Through them God's justice and righteousness comes into this violent and unjust world. The poor, oppressed, dying people is made the witness of justice and righteousness in this world. The message of the poor is to be found in their dumb, anonymous, collective martyrdom.[85]

The theological concept of martyrdom does not only have its familiar *christological* side, according to which the martyr is united to Christ in a special way. It also has the less familiar *apocalyptic* side.

This tells us that the martyrs anticipate in their own bodies the sufferings of the end-time, which come upon the whole creation; and dying, they witness to the creation which is new. Anyone who participates in 'Christ's sufferings' participates in the end-time sufferings of the world. The martyrs anticipate this end for their own time, and in so doing they become apocalyptic witnesses to the coming truth against the ruling lie, to coming justice and righteousness against the prevailing injustice, and to coming life against the tyranny of death.

§6 THE REMEMBRANCE OF CHRIST'S SUFFERINGS

A practice which corresponds to the christology of the crucified One cannot be merely ethical and political. It must be sacramental too, for it is the practice of Christ before it determines our lives. In discipleship, men and women try to become like Christ. But in his Supper, Christ is wholly there for human beings, so that through his self-surrender he may take them with him on his way into his future. The saving meaning of Christ's sufferings is to be found in the fact that Christ suffered and died vicariously, for our benefit – 'for us'. This saving meaning is 'practised' in the breaking of bread and the drinking of wine in the Lord's Supper. Theological interpretations of his death have to presuppose the eucharistic presence of his saving significance. Unless they do this they are abstract. The Lord's Supper is practised theology of the cross. If we understand the Supper in the wider framework of the eucharist, we can add: the eucharist is the practised doctrine of the Trinity, for in the cross the triune God reveals himself.

1. *The Remembrance of Christ and the Reminding of God*

We shall briefly sum up the essence and meaning of the Lord's Supper so that we can then go on to examine more deeply what it means when in this meal we remember Christ's sufferings. What is this dimension of *remembrance*?[86]

Jesus' Last Supper with his disciples has always had a constitutive meaning for the Christian feast. According to I Cor. 11, the community of Christians never celebrated this meal without the recollection of Jesus' Last Supper: 'In the night when he was betrayed . . .' The community of Christians is not imitating Jesus' Last Supper with this recollection. It is putting itself in the situation of Gethsemane and Golgotha, and experiencing Jesus' self-surrender in that eclipse of God and forsakenness by human beings. In the meals he had celebrated earlier with sinners and tax collectors, Jesus had anticipated messianically with these rejected people the eating and drinking in the kingdom of God. It was a sign; for if, as his proclamation says, the kingdom of God is 'near', then we must eat and drink together. If God's righteousness and justice comes in mercy to those who know no justice and to the unjust, we must 'accept' them, and eat and drink with them: 'This man receives sinners and eats with them' (Luke 15.2). But in his last meal Jesus links the breaking of the bread and the outpouring of the wine with the surrender of his life. And ever since, bread and wine make the kingdom of God present in Christ's person, and in his body broken 'for us' and his blood shed 'for us'.

Here the whole breadth of the kingdom of God which Jesus proclaimed is wholly and entirely concentrated in his person. He himself is 'the kingdom of God in person'. And in his person, the kingdom of God is wholly and entirely concentrated in his passion, indeed in the death of this person. In his death the kingdom of God has not merely 'come very close', as it does in his proclamation. It is actually 'there'. That is why his vicarious suffering and dying opens the kingdom of God to all who exist Godlessly and far from God. Through his death, the mercy of God which he presented and represented is realized in history. 'God was *in* Christ', as Paul says. Christ the giver of the feast is himself the gift of the feast. Because this feast binds men and women to him through his self-surrender, it brings them into the kingdom of God. In Jesus' last night the kingdom of God is present only in his person; but through his surrender of himself it is thrown open to every human being. In this way the feast of the kingdom becomes the memorial of Christ's suffering and dying, but the memorial of Christ's suffering and dying expands the horizon of the kingdom to embrace all abandoned creatures in this world.

It is helpful to make clear to ourselves the context of Jesus' Last Supper according to the synoptic gospels. Mark 14 tells us that first of all Jesus was anointed messianic king by an unknown woman.[87] What she did for him was supposed to be told wherever the gospel was preached 'in memory of her' (Mark 14.9). Then comes the last night. Jesus' supper with the disciples is encircled by Judas' 'betrayal', the disciples' 'flight', Peter's 'denial', the turning away of the people, and not least by the eclipse of God, which stretches from Gethsemane to Golgotha. 'The martyr messiah' dies alone. For him the experience of death becomes the experience of abandonment by God and human beings. It is indeed a 'dangerous remembering' when the meal of remembrance begins with the words: 'On the night when he was betrayed . . .' Many Christians sense this danger when they think about 'eating and drinking judgment upon oneself' (I Cor. 11.29).

Christian theology has liked to understand the Lord's Supper as a 'sacrament of time', because it joins together in a unique way past and future, remembrance and hope.[88] It is a *signum rememorativum* passionis et mortis Christi: 'Do this in remembrance of me . . .' It is at the same time, and inextricably one with that, a *signum prognosticum*, that is, a praenuntiativum futurae gloriae: 'As often as you eat this bread and drink this cup you proclaim the Lord's death until he comes.' In the coincidence, the simultaneity, of remembrance of Christ and expectation of him, the feast is a sign of the grace that liberates now, in the present, a *signum demonstrativum* gratiae.

We do, however, have to distinguish between the tenses or times here: what is made present is the history of Christ's suffering and his dying. It is made present in the Spirit of the resurrection. It therefore opens up for the suffering and the dying the expectation of his universal coming in glory. The remembering is historical but the expectation is apocalyptic. Christ's past suffering is made present – the coming of the resurrection and the new creation is expected. In the eucharistic experience of time, past and future do not lie on a single temporal line. These are two different world times: the passion history of death on the one hand – the resurrection history of life on the other. 'The future of Christ' does not lie on the line of future time (*futurum*). It belongs to the coming eternity which will end time (*adventus*).[88a] Otherwise it would be a future which would one day have to become past, just as everything which is *not yet* will one day become *no more*, when once it has come into being. With 'the coming of Christ', the annihilation of death and the new creation is expected in which 'all tears will be wiped away'. But this is the end of time. This can only be expected because the sufferings of Christ are recollected on the foundation of his resurrection from the dead, for his resurrection gives the suffering and the dying hope that their sufferings will be overcome. The remembrance of Christ's sufferings is direct and without any mediation. But the remembrance of Christ's resurrection takes place only indirectly, mediated through the remembrance of Christ's sufferings.[89] That is why we cannot really speak about a *memoria resurrectionis Christi*. But the Spirit of the resurrection hope is the impelling force for the continual remembrance of Christ's sufferings 'until he comes'.

Memory is more than the physical capacity to recollect something. As Gadamer said, it is an 'essential feature of the finite and historical nature of human beings'.[90] As long as human beings understand their existence 'historically', they are dependent for their orientation and decisions on remembrances and hopes. The remembrances mediate earlier experiences, and the experiences of earlier generations. They set people who are living in the present in the tradition to which earlier learning processes belong. Earlier experiences are told, so that people grow up in narrative communities. These traditions can break off, because they themselves are historical. They break off when they cease to offer any more help for the solution of present problems. If they all break off, the human being ceases to exist historically. But the remembered experiences of those who are past do not merely mediate the *wisdom* acquired from experience; they also mediate the unredeemed *sufferings* of those who belong to the past. Only pain that is still painful remains in the memory. These memories are the defeats, the omissions, the meaningless victims of history. These histories of suffering which have never been paid off (as Ernst Bloch put it) can certainly be repressed, both individually and collectively. But they cannot be undone or made as if they had never been. They do not acquire any meaning in history, not even through future history; they can only wait for their redemption.

Memory is a pre-eminent characteristic of the people of Israel, for ever since Abraham's exodus Israel has existed historically par excellence and paradigmatically.[91] Israel's religion is a historical religion. Consequently, Israel's faith is braced between the remembrance of the God of Abraham, Isaac and Jacob, and the hope for the coming of his kingdom. Israel's faith is remembered hope. By virtue of remembrance, people return to past events, in order to make sure of the promises for the future which were given there. The making-present of the exodus event in the Jewish passover supper is the direct model for the making-present of the Christ event in the Christian Lord's Supper. Because God must be remembered if we are to learn to trust him, his histories with his people must be told and passed on from generation to generation, and interpreted through personal experience. Israel's religion is wholly and entirely embedded in Israel's history.

But experienced history does not merely evoke this grateful remembrance of 'the great acts of God'. There is also the remembrance of Israel's suffering and her dead, which is both a lamentation and an impeachment. Hardly any other people has written down and kept account of its defeats and persecutions as have the Jews, most recently of all in the German annihilation camps in the Second World War. The struggle against death is always and before all else the struggle against forgetting by way of remembrance.

> Remembrance is the secret of redemption,
> forgetfulness leads to exile.

These words are written over Yad Vashem, the Jewish place of remembrance in Jerusalem. Remembrance is the secret which hastens redemption because it holds fast to the dead, and brings their names before God.

Finally, remembrance is not merely a human act of awareness bridging present and past. The psalms understand it as an act between human beings and God as well. Men and women remind themselves of what is past in thanksgiving and lamentation before God. Human beings remind God of his promises, when he hides himself, and they feel abandoned by him. There is a silent, unavowed correspondence between the people's memory and God's. The cry of the suffering is an appeal to God's memory: 'Remember, O Lord, what has befallen us; behold, and see our disgrace. . . . Why willst thou so wholly forget us and so wholly forsake us our life long?' (Lam. 5.1, 20).

For men and women, the remembrance in the Lord's Supper of Christ's sufferings means communicating the liberty which springs from his 'sufferings for us'. But it has another meaning too. It reminds God of these sufferings of Christ, in order through this reminding-remembrance to hasten the promised redemption for which this suffering world waits. The expectation of Christ's coming in which the *memoria passionis Christi* is embedded leads inevitably to the maranatha prayer – Come, Lord Jesus!

In the Christian traditions about the Lord's Supper, the remembrance of Christ's sufferings has an exclusive and an inclusive side. The exclusive side is the unique, human and divine suffering of the lonely Christ. This acquires its universal significance through the expression of its vicarious power: according to Mark 14.24 in his 'blood which is shed for many', according to I Cor. 11.24 in his 'body which was broken for you'. The inclusive side is the gathering together of human and divine sufferings in him, the messianic Jew, the brother of men and women, the Child of God, the first-born of creation.

The Christian tradition of the Lord's Supper has always expounded and stressed the first side: he suffered and died for us, so that we may be freed from our sins and in fellowship with him find God. In the sign of remembrance of Christ's death and in the sign of hope for his future, the grace of God which is efficacious in the present is experienced, and men and women are freed from the pattern of this world by being cut loose from the entanglements of sin. This 'liberation through the sufferings of Christ' was often interpreted by way of ideas about expiatory sacrifice, and was represented in the mass through sacrificial rituals. In a world full of acts of violence and their victims, interpretations of this kind have a certain limited value. They can be misused to justify a world in which there will always be victims. But they can also break through the sacrificial cults of a violent world (whether they be religious or secular and modern), presenting Christ as the sole and sufficient sacrifice, made once and for all; and in this way they can be a protest against the sacrificial cults. The discussion about the death penalty may serve as an example. For a long time Christ's death was given as a reason for accepting the death penalty. It is only in recent times that another argument has come to prevail: the argument that since Christ's death, there can no longer be any theological justification for the death penalty. Because he has 'atoned' for all injustice, there must no longer be any punitive law based on the notion of atonement.

The experience of *liberation through the remembrance of Christ's sufferings* becomes clearer if sin is understood as Godlessness and an act of violence. In this case Christ suffers under sin, and dies of it. If he suffers and dies in our place, then he takes us into his sufferings from sin and violence, and draws us on to his side. This is the idea implicit in the old negro spiritual:

> Were you there when they crucified my Lord?
> Were you there when they crucified my Lord?
> Oh, sometimes it causes me to tremble, tremble, tremble.
> Were you there when they crucified my Lord?[92]

But this means that we are set apart from the complex of sin and acts of violence. We become free of it through the contemplation of Christ's sufferings, and can begin with him to live out of God's new creation. Properly understood, the remembrance of Christ's sufferings evokes an event of mutual identification: Christ who died for us – we who are alive in Christ. A 'Christ for us' in the Lord's supper without the experience 'we in Christ' would lead to a forgiveness of sins without new life in righteousness. That is why the mutual identification belongs intrinsically to the remembrance of Christ itself. Anyone who is possessed by the sufferings of Christ becomes a stranger in the world of Pontius Pilate.

This in itself brings us to other aspects of Christ's sufferings, which are to be found in the collective solidarity of the apocalyptic Christ with the sufferings of Israel, with the sufferings of the people, with the sufferings of human beings as such, and with the sufferings of all living things. The forgiveness of sins and liberation from the Godless structures of violence are one side of the fruits of Christ's sufferings. The 'wiping away of the tears from every eye' is the other. Because 'the sufferings of Christ' are remembered in the Spirit of his resurrection and in hope for the new creation of all things, they bring the 'wiping away of the tears' very close. That is why in his divine, human and natural sufferings Christ gathers to himself the whole suffering history of the world. In the remembrance of his sufferings we also remember Israel's martyrs, who have borne 'the abuse of Christ' (Heb. 11.26). In the remembrance of his sufferings we remember the victims of sin and violence, the sufferings of the humiliated people, the sufferings of the sick and the dying, the sufferings of the whole sighing creation. In this sense the sufferings of Christ are universal and all-embracing, because through his resurrection from the dead they reach to the apocalyptic end of this world of death, and have themselves been made birth-pangs of the new world, in which all the tears will be wiped away, because death will be no more. 'The Christian memory of suffering is in its theological implications an anticipatory memory: it intends the anticipation of a particular future of man as a future for the suffering, the hopeless, the oppressed, the injured and the useless of this earth.'[93]

This means that it is neither religious poetry nor a disregard for the dignity of the individual and alien suffering of others when we see Golgotha and Auschwitz together, and say that Christ too was murdered in Auschwitz. The apocalyptic Christ suffers in the victims of sin and violence. The apocalyptic Christ suffers and sighs too in the tormented creation sighing under the violent acts of our modern human civilization. We therefore have to extend the remembrance of Christ's sufferings to all those in whose fellowship Christ suffers, and whom he draws into his fellowship through his sufferings. It is only when the remembering extends to their sufferings that hope will spread to the fields of the dead in history. But where forgetfulness is the order of the day, the dead are slain once more and the living become blind.

2. The Cry from the Depths

In the biblical traditions every experience of salvation begins with a *cry from the depths*: 'I have seen the affliction of my people who are in Egypt, and have heard their cry because of their taskmasters; I know their sufferings, and I have come down to deliver them'. It is with this divine saying (Ex. 3.7; similarly Deut. 29.7) that Israel's exodus from imprisonment into the promised land of freedom begins. Analogously, the raising from the dead to eternal life begins with Christ's tortured and terrified cry on the cross on Golgotha. That is why the eschatological hope of Jews and Christians begins with the cry from the depths of those who suffer injustice.[94]

Since this is so, we have to come back once more to the divine sufferings of Christ. The remembrance of Christ's sufferings does not merely make human beings mindful of these sufferings. It makes God mindful of them too. The meal of remembrance holds up Christ's sufferings to God, reminding him of the afflictions of his messiah and calling for his deliverance. Before we come to the epiklesis – the call for the Holy Spirit – we should listen to the cry for God with which the suffering Christ dies: 'My God, why hast thou forsaken me?' This cry of the dying Christ for God is certainly personally answered for him by *his* raising from the dead. But for all those in whose fellowship he died in such forsakenness, and for all those whom he draws into this fellowship through the remembrance of his sufferings, the cry is certainly answered *in him* but not yet for them personally, and not yet cosmically. Their tears have not yet been wiped away, and their theodicy question is still open.

In this inclusive and in this theological respect, we have to see the remembrance of Christ's sufferings as the continuation of that universal theodicy trial which culminates in Christ's death on the cross; for in Christ the trial was brought to the frontier of the resurrection and the new creation of all things. The charge given at the Lord's supper 'until he comes' does not simply set a date. It names the apocalyptic and hence universal goal of the remembrance of Christ's sufferings in the history of this world's suffering. As long as he has not come, the cry for God remains and so do the tears. The tidings of the resurrection of the crucified Christ and the experience of his presence in the Spirit brings the hope for a universal answer into this cry for God; and with that a hope is brought into the world that the tears are not the end. In this sense the feast of the remembrance of Christ is the feast of the co-sufferers, and the feast of all who hope for those who suffer in this world: it is a feast of expectation.

V

The Eschatological Resurrection of Christ

'If Christ has not been raised, then our preaching is in vain and your faith is in vain', declared Paul (I Cor. 15.14). For him and for earliest Christianity as we know it, God's raising of Christ was the foundation for faith in Christ, and thus the foundation of the church of Christ as well. And it is in fact true that the Christian faith stands or falls with Christ's resurrection. At this point faith in God and the acknowledgment of Christ coincide. Faith in the God 'who raised Christ from the dead' and the confession that 'Jesus Christ is the Lord' are mutually interpretative. In chapters III and IV we tried to discover what the confession of Christ means. We shall now turn to the faith in God which provides the foundation for that confession. We shall first of all ask the historical question: what does the original Christian belief in the resurrection say, and what does it not say? We shall go on to ask a theological question: how can belief in the resurrection be understood in the conditions and cognitive forms of modern times? And we shall finally put an ethical question, asking how faith in the resurrection can be convincingly maintained today: what are its consequences?

The event which is called 'raising' or 'resurrection' is an event that happened to the Christ who died on the cross on Golgotha. Where he himself is concerned, the cross and the resurrection are mutually related, and they have to be interpreted in such a way that the one event appears in the light of the other.[1] The cross of Christ is the cross of the Lord who was raised by God and exalted to God. It is only in this correlation that the cross acquires its special saving meaning. The raising by God was experienced by the Christ who 'was crucified, dead and buried'. It is only in this interrelation that the raising acquires its special saving meaning.

Christ's death and his resurrection are the two sides of the one single happening which is often termed 'the Christ event'. But we must notice here how questionable that innocuous 'and' is – the 'and' which adds together the two happenings which Christ experienced at the end. For these are not two happenings belonging to the same category, which can be listed one after another. On the contrary, here we have an antithesis which could not possibly be more radical. Christ's death on the cross is a historical fact – Christ's resurrection is an apocalyptic happening. Christ's death was brought about by human beings – his raising from the dead is an act on God's part. The cross of Christ stands in the time of this present world of violence and sin – the risen Christ lives in the time of the coming world of the new creation in justice and righteousness. If we look at the christological statements in the creed – 'suffered, crucified, dead' and 'on the third day he rose again from the dead' – what belongs between them is not an 'and' at all. It is a full stop and a pause. For what now begins is something which is qualitatively different: the eschatological statements about Christ.

Anyone who reduces all this to the same level, simply listing the facts of salvation one after another, destroys either the unique character of Christ's death on the cross or the unique character of his resurrection. Anyone who describes Christ's resurrection as 'historical', in just the same way as his death on the cross, is overlooking the new creation with which the resurrection begins, and is falling short of the eschatological hope. The cross and the resurrection stand in the same relation to one another as death and eternal life. Since death makes every life historical, death has to be seen as the power of history. Since resurrection brings the dead into eternal life and means the annihilation of death, it breaks the power of history and is itself the end of history. If we keep the two together, then the cross of Christ comes to stand at the apocalyptic end of world history, and the raising of the dead at the beginning of the new creation of the world. That is why we are talking about 'the eschatological resurrection of Christ'. History and eschatology cannot be added together, for if they are, either history is dissolved into eternity or eschatology is overtaken by history. The two can only be confronted with one another. It is this confrontation which we are talking about when we speak of 'the resurrection of the crucified Christ'. Paul expressed the incommensurability of Christ's death on the cross and his resurrection by using the phrase 'how much more' (Rom. 8.34).

In this way he was indicating the eschatological surplus of promise in Christ's resurrection. It is this which echoes through the overflowing Easter jubilation of early Christian and Orthodox worship.[2]

We shall begin with an analysis of the early Christian resurrection faith, so as to discover from the way it came into being what its essential content really is. We shall then turn to the modern question about *history and resurrection*, viewing the resurrection faith in the perspective of history and in the light of modern historical methods. After that we shall reverse the perspective and consider history as it is made and experienced by human beings, seeing it in the light of Christ's resurrection. Having looked critically at earlier theological outlines which reduced resurrection and history to a common denominator, we shall develop the resurrection of the crucified Christ as the foundation, goal and praxis of a history of liberation. History is undoubtedly the paradigm of modern European times, but it is not the final paradigm of humanity. The growing ecological awareness about the nature of the earth on which human history is played out is going to supersede the paradigm 'history'.[3] We shall take up this challenge, asking how Christ's resurrection can be seen *in the framework of nature*, and what this means; and we shall then reverse the question and ask about *the future of nature* in the framework of Christ's resurrection. The ancient church's doctrine of the two natures will have to be taken up once again in the framework of the post-modern, ecological paradigm, and will have to be newly interpreted. For this the problem of the bodily nature of the dead and raised Christ offers itself, a question which remained almost unnoticed in the discussion about 'history and resurrection'. A new understanding of the struggle of life against death will finally take us over to the praxis of the resurrection hope, which gives life to body and soul, to human being and fellow human being, humanity and nature.

§1 THE GENESIS AND UNIQUE CHARACTER OF THE CHRISTIAN FAITH IN THE RESURRECTION

Jesus was crucified publicly and died publicly. But it was only the women at his tomb in Jerusalem, and the disciples who had fled into Galilee who learnt of his 'resurrection'. These disciples thereupon returned to Jerusalem, where they openly proclaimed the crucified Jesus as the Lord whom God had raised from the dead.

These are the relatively well established historical findings.[4] And they are astonishing enough. At the same time, all that is historically provable in these findings is the assertion of the women that at his empty tomb they had heard an angelic message about his resurrection, and the assurance of the disciples that they had seen appearances of Christ in Galilee. After Jesus' death, there were evidently a great many manifestations to a whole number of his disciples, women and men both, manifestations in which Christ allowed himself to be seen as the One eternally alive in God. In the earliest testimony to the resurrection which we possess – the First Epistle to the Corinthians, written in AD 55 or 56 – Paul refers to testimonies that Christ had appeared to Cephas, to the twelve, and then to 5,000 brethren at once. At the end he adds himself, although he had never been one of Jesus' disciples but had actually persecuted the Christians. Paul's account is especially valuable because it is a personal record of his own experience of the way Christ had appeared to him. According to what he says himself, Paul *saw* Christ (I Cor. 9.1), apparently in the form of an inner experience: 'It pleased God through his grace to reveal his Son *in me*' (Gal. 1.15f.). He experienced this manifestation contrary to all expectation and against his will: 'I was seized by Christ', he says (Phil. 3.12). The manifestation changes him completely. He falls to the ground and is taken unconscious to Damascus, where he is later baptized and gets back his sight. Saul, the persecutor of the Christians, becomes Paul, the apostle of the Gentiles. Acts 9 relates this experience of Paul's in the form of a conversion story, on the model of the calling of the Old Testament prophets, with the vision of a blinding light from heaven and an audition: 'I am Jesus whom you are persecuting' (9.3, 5).

We ought probably to think of the experiences of the women at the tomb and the disciples in Galilee in terms not very different from these, if we can conceive of exceptional visionary experiences like this at all, and can enter into them imaginatively. The witnesses all agree in reporting that they saw the Jesus who had died as 'the living One'. They do not say that he had returned to this life. What they say is that he is alive in the glory of God and that it was in this glory that he 'appeared' to them in their earthly lives. They had visions of a supernatural light. But of course at this point the interpretations already begin. It is in any case impossible to discover the substance of these experiences in the form of naked facts without the subjective interpretations. The only result would be unhistorical abstractions.

Moreover, pure facts are inexpressible. In every perception, what is experienced is interpreted through the ideas which people bring with them. Of course these ideas do not remain what they were; in the process of perception they themselves change. And this is particularly true in the case of revolutionary experiences. Otherwise Saul could not have become Paul. If we perceive something 'wholly other', we ourselves are fundamentally changed. If we are not, we have not perceived the wholly other at all; we have merely assimilated it to what we already are and know, repressing its strangeness.

The experiences of Christ which are talked about here were evidently experiences which changed the very existence of the people involved. The disciples had flown from Jerusalem to Galilee out of disappointment and fear, in order to save their own lives. These same disciples are now turned into apostles who return to Jerusalem and risk their lives there in order to preach Christ 'boldly' (Acts 9.22, 28). But for the women who had 'looked upon' Jesus' execution and death on Golgotha (Mark 15.40f.), the appearances of the risen One were not quite so staggering. They were rather a transition from one kind of beholding to another, in the faithfulness of a reciprocal seeing, knowing and loving.[5]

According to the gospel accounts, the presupposition of the visionary phenomena was the disciples' flight into Galilee. This is probably described in such detail in order to exclude any kind of wishful thinking, or any notion of a 'projection' prompted by belief: the phenomena, that is, cannot be explained by the faith of the disciples. On the contrary, their faith has to be explained by the phenomena.[6] The disciples betray, deny and forsake their master. We are not told why. But their shameful flight is interpreted with the words of Zech. 13.7: 'I will strike the shepherd, and the sheep will be scattered' (Mark 14.27). John 16.32 explains: 'You will be scattered, every one to his own, and will leave me alone'. 'Every one to his own' can mean 'everyone looks to his own way' and follows his own interests. But it can also mean: 'Everyone will return to his Galilean home, his family and his occupation.' At all events, Jesus' disciples did return home, giving up their discipleship. But once there, contrary to all expectation, they are called back to Jerusalem by the visionary phenomena.

The localization of these phenomena is certainly a moot point. Mark and Matthew talk about Galilee, Luke and John about Jerusalem. John 21 puts the phenomena in Galilee in a coda.

Historically, it seems probable that the phenomena took place in Galilee, but that when the disciples returned to Jerusalem they were confronted with the experiences of the women at the tomb, so that the experiences of the two groups came together and confirmed one another. I would not myself suppose that the disciples needed months for this process, let alone years, as some scholars think. The question about 'the first vision' was important for matters of precedence as the early Christian community grew up; but it is not a question that can be decided historically. The fact that 'Peter and the twelve' are mentioned has merely symbolic importance for the Jewish–Christian community. Peter evidently had no practical function as leader in the first Christian community, at least not permanently.

The question as to how long the visionary phenomena continued in the early community is hard to answer. The 'forty days' which we are told elapsed between Easter and the ascension are symbolic, just like the testimony 'raised on the third day . . .' But what is certain is that the appearances of Christ came to an end, and that they were replaced by the proclamation of Christ through the gospel and the experience of Christ's presence in the Spirit. The 'seeing' of the risen Christ became faith.

The story of the ascension talks about Christ's absence; but we must not think of the transition from seeing to faith in terms of an unmediated breach. The visionary phenomena were evidently associated with ecstatic experiences of the Spirit, so they will also have passed into the pentecostal experiences of the young church and will have perpetuated themselves in these: from the presence of Christ in his appearances to the presence of Christ in the Spirit. The early Christian faith in the resurrection was not based solely on Christ's appearances. It was just as strongly motivated, at the very least, by the experience of God's Spirit. Paul therefore calls this Spirit 'the Spirit' or 'power' of the resurrection. Luke makes the end of the appearances with Christ's ascension be followed by the outpouring of the pentecostal Spirit. Believing in the risen Christ means being possessed by the Spirit of the resurrection. In the Spirit, the presence of the living Christ was experienced. Believing in Christ's resurrection therefore does not mean affirming a fact. It means being possessed by the life-giving Spirit and participating in the powers of the age to come (Heb. 6.5).

With the expressions 'Christ appeared' and 'Christ was seen'

(Mark 16.7; John 20.18; I Cor. 6.9; Luke 24.34; Acts 13.31; I Cor. 15.3–8) the theological interpretation of these phenomena already begins, for these are the words used in the Old Testament to describe the revelation of God and the light of the first day of creation. God 'appeared' to the patriarchs Abraham, Isaac, Jacob and Moses. At the beginning of the messianic era, according to Isa. 40.5, 'the glory of the Lord shall appear, and all flesh shall see it together'. The words 'appear' and 'see' are revelation formulas. They intend to say that God reveals himself in Christ and that Christ appears in the glory of God. The activity issues solely from the One who allows himself to be seen. The person affected is passive, and suffers this divine appearance. For that reason this kind of theophany is unrepeatable. Christ's appearances are not verifiable through repetition. Nor is there any standpoint outside the person or within from which he could be seen.

Paul links these christophany conceptions with the expression ἀποκάλυψις, and by doing so he gives them a special meaning: God unveils something ahead of time which is still hidden and inaccessible to the cognition of the present aeon, or world time. Under the present conditions of knowledge, the secrets of the end-time and God's future new world are still veiled and unknowable, for the present world of sin and violence cannot sustain the new world of God's righteousness and justice. That is why this righteousness of God's is going to create a new world, and will be manifested only at the end of the time of this world, and in the daybreak of the new creation. Only then will 'the glory of the Lord appear'. But even in the history of this world there are already revelations of the new world to come, revelations ahead of time. In the Old Testament, these revelations of God's future are linked with the callings of his prophets, and these calls are often founded on the vision of this coming divine glory (Isaiah 6). The people who experienced the christophanies became apostles, both women and men – Mary Magdalene and Paul and the rest. The anticipatory beholding of the glory of God in the face of Jesus Christ led directly to the call to the apostolate and to service in this transitory world for what is to come. The christophanies were not interpreted as mystical translations into a world beyond. They were viewed as radiance thrown ahead of itself, the radiance of God's coming glory on the first day of the new world's creation. And these christophanies are daylight visions, not phantasms of the night.

If we look at the way these christophanies and the Easter seeing of the men and women concerned were interpretatively perceived, we can discover three dimensions in their structure:

The first is *prospective*: they saw the crucified Christ as the living One in the splendour cast ahead by the coming glory of God.

The second is *retrospective*: they recognized him from the marks of the nails and in the breaking of bread: the One who will come is the One crucified on Golgotha.

The third is *reflexive*: in this seeing they perceived their own call to the apostolate: 'As the Father has sent me, even so I send you' (John 20.21).

It is this eschatological structure of the Easter seeing of Christ which explains the return of the disciples to Jerusalem after their flight, although as followers of the Galilean crucified by the Romans they were bound to expect persecution there, and their own execution. But they were compelled to return to Jerusalem, on the one hand because it was there that the one whom they had seen in divine glory had been crucified, and on the other because, according to prophecy, it was on Zion that they had to await the parousia of the messiah-Son of man (Rom. 11.26). This is a further indication that the christophanies were not mysterious private revelations, but were understood by the people concerned as the first, preliminary radiance of the imminent dawn of God's new creation. These christophanies awakened in those who experienced them an expectation which was highly tense and which embraced the whole world.

A number of ideas in Jewish tradition offered themselves as a way of interpreting the totally contradictory experiences of Jesus' death on the cross in shame and helplessness, and his appearances as the eternally living One in the presence of God. First, there was the pattern of the exaltation of the Servant of God who had been humiliated in suffering and death (Isa. 52.13ff.). Then there was the pattern of the just man carried up to God at the end of his life (Gen. 6.24; II Kings 2.1–18). And finally there was the pattern of the one raised from the dead (Isa. 26.19; Dan. 12.2). Whereas the first two patterns are bound up with the individual concerned, the third pattern has a universal scope and is in the strict sense an eschatological paradigm. As Christianity developed, it drew on the other conceptions too as a way of interpreting the christophanies: God has 'exalted' Jesus to his right hand (Acts 5.31); God has 'taken up'

Jesus into heaven (Acts 1.1–11). But the statements 'God has raised Jesus from the dead' and 'Jesus is risen' were evidently the original, primary interpretative categories for Christ's appearances.

The texts about the resurrection are the oldest Christian texts and the most widespread. If we ask why, we are compelled to come back to the premises on which the men and women concerned based their interpretation. They had gone with Jesus to Galilee and Jerusalem. They had believed his message about the imminent coming of the kingdom of God, and had seen the signs and wonders which testified to its nearness. In one way or another they had experienced his helplessness in Gethsemane and his forsakenness on Golgotha. And they had drawn their own conclusions from their experiences with Jesus. This was the immediate, personal framework for their interpretation. The further interpretative background – the prophetic and apocalyptic tradition of the Judaism of the time – comes only after that.[7] These men and women also lived and thought in the context of Jewish apocalyptic – the framework of its expectation and the world of its images. These became especially important when they tried to communicate their newly acquired faith in Christ to their fellow-countrymen and contemporaries by pointing out that Christ had been raised from the dead 'in accordance with the scriptures' (I Cor. 15.4). But it seems obvious that Christ's appearances, viewed as advance reflections of God's coming glory, should have been explained by his rising from the dead as 'the first fruits of those who have fallen asleep' (I Cor. 15.20), because the imminent eschatological expectation which this reflects so entirely corresponds to Jesus' proclamation of the imminent coming of the kingdom. If he has appeared as 'the first fruits of those who have fallen asleep' and as 'the leader of life', then 'the last days' before the end of this time have dawned. But this means that with Christ the general resurrection of the dead has already begun. The annihilation of death through the coming of eternal life is already in process. New creation is beginning in Christ in the very midst of this world of violence and death.

The eschatological symbol of the raising of the dead is an interpretative category well suited to comprehend the contradictory experiences of the men and women disciples with Jesus: crucified in weakness – living in glory. No more can be said about the verification in Jesus himself. What happened to him between his death on Golgotha and his appearances no one saw, and no one claims to have seen. Only Christian painters have given free rein to their imaginations in the darkness of this mystery, yet without making the darkness any less. When Christ was raised, there were no eye witnesses of the event. Only 'the empty tomb' gave ambiguous tidings of what had happened there. That Jesus' tomb was empty seems to be an extremely well attested fact, because both Jews and Christians knew of it. The message of the resurrection brought by the disciples on their return to Jerusalem could hardly have lasted a single hour in the city if it had been possible to show that Jesus' body was lying in the grave. But this does not prove who emptied the tomb – whether it was the disciples, as the Jews claimed, or God, as the apostles said. The proclamation that Jesus had been raised from the dead is not an interpretation of the empty tomb. The empty tomb was passed down by tradition only as an external sign of 'Jesus' resurrection'. The resurrection itself the interpretation of the experience of Christ's appearances. We may well suppose, however, that from early on there was a Christian cult at Jesus' tomb.

Is this eschatological symbol an appropriate way of describing the experiences with Jesus? Is it an arbitrary way of expressing them, or does it offer itself with an inward and inevitable cogency? It apparently grew up out of the apocalyptic structure of the 'seeing' of Christ. But does it also fit the experience of his death on the cross? The answer is 'yes', inasmuch as raising presupposes death, and the eschatological raising of the dead does not mean a revivification; nor does it mean a return to this life, which leads to death. The resurrection is not a revival, as in the case of Jairus's daughter, or Lazarus, whom Jesus brought back to this life but who later died once more. 'The raising of the dead' at the end of days means a qualitatively new life which no longer knows death and is not a continuation of this mortal life. Cosmically, the eschatological raising of the dead has been linked since time immemorial with the hope for the elimination of death from God's creation (Isa. 25.8; 26.19). The symbol of 'the raising of the dead' also excludes ideas about a 'life after death', the immortality of the soul, or the transmigration of souls; or that the cause of Jesus will continue in his spirit. All these notions can co-exist with death. They accept it by transcending it. But if 'the raising of the dead' means 'the annihilation of death', then the hope of resurrection is a hope against death, and a contradiction in the name of the living God of this most intransigent confutation of life. The expression 'resurrection from the dead' does not deny the deadliness of death or the totality of death. Jesus did not just seemingly die. He died truly, not merely physically but wholly, not merely for human beings but for God too. 'Raising from the dead' is the term for a new creative act of God's, an act with which the new creation of all mortal and transitory being begins. This eschatological symbol is appropriate for the contradictory experiences with Jesus because it denies neither the deadliness of his death nor his livingness in his appearances.

And yet to apply the eschatological symbol of the resurrection of the dead to the experiences with Jesus is to transform its very essence. The formula 'Christ was raised from the dead' says that he alone was raised, but not the other dead, and that he was raised ahead of all the other dead. According to prophetic ideas, God will raise the dead 'on his Day'. There was no mention of the earlier raising of an individual before time, not even if he was the messiah. All the same, we ought not to think merely of 'the Last Judgment'. The events of the end can also extend over a certain period of time, as talk about 'the last days' shows. The transformation of the universal eschatological symbol of 'the raising of the dead' into the christological symbol 'raising from the dead' is only justified as long as that universal expectation is still joined with the perception of the raising of Christ.[8] If the general 'raising of the dead' is left out, the testimony about 'the raising of Christ from the dead' becomes increasingly feeble, and finally loses its meaning. The Christian belief in the resurrection remains dependent on its verification through the eschatological raising of all the dead. As long as this has not been manifested, the belief is still only hope. But in this eschatological context the raising of Jesus speaks for itself. It speaks its own language of promise and well-founded hope, but it is not yet the language of accomplished fact. As long as the facts that determine this world are the facts of violence and suffering, the world is not able to furnish proof of the resurrection of life and the annihilation of death.[9] In this 'unredeemed world' the resurrection of Christ is still dependent on its eschatological verification through the new creation of the world.

Once this transformed symbol of the resurrection of the dead was applied to the crucified Jesus, the content of the old prophetic expectation changed. According to the Torah, the 'raising to eternal life' was promised only to the just, while the unjust had to expect 'resurrection to everlasting contempt' (Dan. 12.2). This makes it clear that in Israel the expectation of resurrection was not an anthropological symbol, nor was it a soteriological one. It was not aligned towards endless life, or towards celestial bliss. It was a theological symbol for faith in the victory of God's righteousness and justice at the end of history, through the glorification of the Torah in the just and the unjust. Righteousness has to triumph in the end because it is God's righteousness. Because even death can lay down no limits for God, the dead will be raised for God's final judgment. It is not the desire for eternal life that dominates the prophetic expectation of the resurrection of the dead; it is the thirst for righteousness.[10]

If this eschatological symbol is applied in its transformed Christian form to the condemned, forsaken and crucified Jesus, the question about God's justice and righteousness is the result. If God raised Jesus, he puts all those who condemned, abandoned and crucified him in the wrong. Then the raising of the One crucified is the divine justification of Jesus of Nazareth and his message, for which he was put to death (Acts 2.22ff.). With the raising of the condemned and executed Jesus, God himself re-opens the trial of Jesus, and in this theodicy trial of Jesus Christ the apostles are the witnesses. If in this context the raising of Jesus means the justification of Jesus as the Christ of God, then the resurrection endorses Jesus' proclamation of the compassionate justice of God, which sets everything to rights; and the double event of his surrender to death and his raising becomes the revelation of the messianic righteousness of God – which is to say his justifying righteousness.

This is how Paul saw it when he interpreted this double event as 'delivered up for our trespasses, raised for our justification' (Rom. 4.25). The God who calls into being the things that are not, who makes the dead live, is also the God who makes the Godless just. In the framework of eschatological symbolism this can only be interpreted to mean that in his death on the cross Christ has vicariously anticipated the final judgment of God for all the Godless and the unjust, so that as a result his raising from this death manifests to everyone the righteousness and justice of God which puts everything to rights and makes the unjust just. His own raising from the dead was not a raising for judgment, such as Daniel 12 envisages for all the dead; it was a raising into the glory of God and eternal life. And the Christian resurrection hope which is grounded on the remembrance of Christ's sufferings and resurrection is therefore an unequivocally 'joyful hope' for the resurrection and the life of the world to come. It is not a fearful expectation of a Last Judgment whose outcome for the human beings concerned is uncertain.

It is true that in the history of Christian theology and art the rapturous joy of Easter jubilation has continually been subdued, if not stifled, by fear of the final judgment; but wrongly so, and less in the Christian than in the apocalyptic sense. If at the Last Judgment the crucified One himself is the judge, the justice that will prevail is his merciful and justifying righteousness, and none other.

This impression becomes stronger still if we do not concentrate solely on the symbol 'raising from the dead' but also enter into the other symbol, 'risen from the dead'. The first phrase talks about God's own exclusive act in and for the dead Jesus. The second phrase designates 'an act of Christ performed in his own power'.[11] The first formula joins Jesus with the common fate of all the dead. The second stresses the special divine power in him. If God really was 'in Christ', as Paul says, then Christ was crucified in the weakness of God and rose in the power of God. God did not merely act on him from heaven; he also acted in him and out of him. Of course the two ideas dovetail, and are therefore not treated as alternatives. The one whom God wakens from sleep must rise himself; and the one who has to rise must first of all be wakened. In considering Christ's history with God his Father we have to draw on both ideas if we are to grasp the mutual relationship of the Father and the Son: the raised Son rose in the power of the life-giving Spirit.

For the first Christian community this idea about Christ's resurrection was also important as a way of describing the special position of the messiah in relation to the living and the dead. Just like all other human beings before him, Jesus 'died' and 'was buried'; but *the fulness and wholeness of his bodily nature* was preserved through his resurrection ahead of time 'on the third day'. He rose with *an uncorrupted body*. Peter's address in Acts 2.27 cites Psalm 16.10: 'Thou wilt not let thy Holy One see corruption.' God 'raised him up, having loosed the pangs of death, because it was not possible for him to be held by it' (Acts 2.24). We shall come back later to the theological meaning of this statement, which has received hardly any attention in the modern theological discussion about the resurrection.

Finally, we come to the astonishing transition from the 'seeing' of Christ in his appearances to 'faith' in Christ's gospel. Many hypotheses have been pressed into service to explain the early Christian christophanies. Proposals range from fraudulent deception to projection by the unconscious, and from the supposition of subjective visions to the assumption of objective ones. All these hypotheses are really superfluous, because there is nothing comparable which could provide the analogies on which to base an understanding. Wilhelm Herrmann rightly said that we cannot talk about these Easter experiences in the way that we talk about our own.[12] Nor did the early Christian apostles ever try to bring other people to similar visions of Christ. Paul did not proclaim his experience on the road to Damascus as a conversion experience that was open to everyone. Nor, probably, did he ever make it the subject of his preaching. The real problem is to be found in the transition from seeing to believing; for one day the christophanies came to an end. So why did the Christian community not come to an end too? Apparently this question was taken seriously and was answered by: 'blessed are those who have not seen and yet believe' (John 20.29). But then what is the relation of faith to sight? The people to whom Christ 'appeared' were so overwhelmed that they apparently had no choice. But among the people who had not seen, some believed the apostles and others did not. The transition from seeing to believing must have been made even in the Easter witnesses themselves. They did not remain in a 'seeing' relationship to the Lord; but when the seeing stopped, they believed. They testified to the Lord whom they had 'seen' through the proclamation of the gospel, and their preaching awakened faith without sight in other people. Whereas the seeing of Christ allowed those involved no freedom of choice, the word of the proclamation brings men and women face to face with the decision of faith. Faith of this kind – faith in response to the Word that a person has heard – is possible only when Christ's 'appearances' cease. It is only by returning to the hidden safe-keeping of God that Christ makes this faith possible. Yet because faith in the gospel of Christ came into being from the seeing of Christ in his appearances, this faith, in its turn, waits and hopes for the seeing of Christ 'face to face' (I Cor. 13.12), and in doing so it waits also for that 'coming again' of Christ in visible, universal glory which we call his parousia.

The history of the proclamation of faith goes back to its foundational beginnings in the seeing of Christ's appearances. It is therefore aligned towards Christ's parousia in visible glory. The *successio apostolica* is nothing other than the *successio evangelii* and is a true historical *processio* – a moving forward in expectation of the universal future of Christ at the end of history.

If the gospel takes the place of Christ's appearances, then it has to exhibit the same structures as these appearances: 1. The gospel is *retrospectively* 'the Word of the cross'. It makes the crucified Christ present. 2. The gospel is *prospectively* the anticipation in the Word of Christ's parousia, and therefore has itself a promissory character.[13] 3. The gospel which proclaims the one crucified as the one to come, the one humiliated as the one who is exalted, and the one dead as the one who is alive is *the present call* into the liberty of faith. Accordingly the Christian faith is a life lived out of Christ, a life lived with Christ and a life lived in expectation of Christ. And in being these things it is also a life of new creation in the midst of the shadows of the transient world.

§2 HISTORY AND THE RESURRECTION OF CHRIST: THE THEOLOGICAL PROBLEM

It is one thing to see Christ's resurrection in the perspective of history, where we are faced with the inescapable question: is the resurrection an event, or an interpretation of faith? It is another thing to see history in the perspective of Christ's resurrection. Then we are brought up against the eschatological question about the end of history and the new creation of the world.[14]

From the seventeenth century onwards, the comprehensive paradigm 'History' was developed in Europe, as a way of interpreting human beings and nature, God and the world. In this paradigm time ceased to be conceived of in terms of the cycle of the recurring seasons; it was now thought of as the line of human goals and purposes. In the human project 'scientific and technological civilization', correspondences with nature and harmonizations with the cosmos were replaced by the new blueprint of progress from an ageing past into the new era of the future. The further the lordship of the Europeans over the other nations spread, and the more the domination of human beings over nature proceeded, the more the rich multiplicity of cultural histories gave way to the notion of the unity of mankind: the great singular concept 'history' came into being, together with those other singulars 'the past' and 'the future'.

This modern paradigm 'history' provided the framework for *the modern science of history*, with its historical criticism of the legends of rule in church and state, and with its historical sense, which dissolved the presence of what was past into memory, and tradition into temporal detachment, in order to historicize what was past and free the present from past decisions and past judgments. 'The true criticism of dogma is its history', wrote David Friedrich Strauss,[15] and made the historian the ideological critic of religious and political dogmas. In the awareness of history, events of the past are transformed into past events. They lose their relevance for the present and turn into facts which have had their day. If, taking our stance in the modern paradigm 'history', we look at the tradition about Christ's resurrection with the categories of the modern historical mind, the resurrection appears to be either a product of fantasy or an irrelevant miracle. As a past event which moves further and further away from us as time progresses, it can neither determine the present nor can it have any relevance for the future. Whether the historical evidence speaks in favour of the resurrection or against it, it arouses neither faith nor disbelief. We may accept an event which lies so far in the past, or we may doubt it; in either case it changes nothing in our present lives. The modern historical category has already made the event a past event, because 'historical' means whatever takes place and passes away. All that remains in the transience of time is the past itself.

The modern intellectual and theological problems about faith in the resurrection are posed by the scientific interpretation of the world, and by the technological shaping of the world, but above all by the historical sciences in their correspondingly positivist form. They have cut the historical ground from under the feet of the Christian resurrection faith and have forced Christian theology (which is supposed to present the underlying reasoning) into the apologetic defensive. Theologians who allowed themselves to be drawn into this position looked for different categories as a way of proving that the Christian faith was well founded and meaningful. They left the field of history to 'the historical mind' and the historical sciences without calling these in question. It is only in recent years that the apologetic defensive has given way to a critical and productive offensive.

It is true that even for the historians Troeltsch no longer has the last word, but in the 1920s his treatise on 'Historical and Dogmatic Methods in Theology' (1898)[16] enjoyed authoritative status for the theology of the resurrection. Troeltsch carried over scientific methods into historical scholarship and laid down three axioms for the critical historical method, as a way of arriving at soundly based knowledge. We shall put the resurrection of Christ to the question by subjecting it to these three axioms.

1. Historical research can never arrive at absolute knowledge – only at judgments based on probability. Can theology base the assurance of faith on judgments of historical probability?

2. All the phenomena of historical life influence one another mutually. These reciprocal effects provide the ontological foundation for the cohesion of cause and effect, which is universally applicable. Is the resurrection of Christ an exception, and a breach of the natural laws to which all life is subject?

3. Since it is a general rule that historical events affect one another, we have to assume that historical events are in principle identical in kind. Analogy is the necessary guideline for historical understanding. 'The almighty power of analogy' is based on the homogeneity of all historical happening. Can an event without analogy such as 'Christ's resurrection from the dead' be understood in historical terms?

The objective study of history, then, is subject to the principles of probability, correlation and analogy. It presupposes human beings as the subject of history. Troeltsch did not specifically stress this in his treatise. But he assumes that history is made by human beings, not by obscure powers, gods and demons, and that it can therefore also be known by human beings. For after all, the historical elucidation of the past is positively designed to make human beings the responsible subjects of their history. How can we talk in a historical sense about the acts of a transcendent God in history generally and about the raising of Christ by God in particular?

If these principles are considered to be valid both for history as past events and for history as the record of those events, then Christian theology is brought up against the fundamental question: in what category can it talk about God and resurrection at all? Troeltsch already complained about the schizophrenia of Christians in the modern world, for whom, he maintained, there was a 'Sunday causality', in which God was the determining subject of history, and a 'weekday causality', in which all events have their own immanent causes. Can this mental split be overcome by a new 'public' theology, or must theology detach itself from the view of truth publicly held in modern society, in order to maintain its own truth? Does Christian theology enter into the public dispute about the truth, or is it becoming a sectarian ideology on the fringe of society? Is it going to be a critical potential in the common future of humanity, or is it losing itself in the religious pluralism of modern society?

1. *The Category of Divine History*

For Karl Barth, even in the earlier, 'dialectical' phase of his theology, the horizontal question about the connections between the events of the past which are accessible by way of historical investigation was unimportant compared with the vertical question about the reality of God, whose eternity confronts all the times of history simultaneously. In his interpretation of I Corinthians 15, *The Resurrection of the Dead* (1924), Barth therefore interprets that Pauline history of the end in the sense of the eternal and primal history, and by doing so – as Bultmann already remarked in his 1926 review – fundamentally demythologized Paul's apocalyptic.[17] 'For there is no doubt at all', Barth writes, 'that the word "resurrection from the dead" is for him [i.e., Paul] nothing other than a paraphrase of the word "God".'[18] The phrase 'nothing other than' is a typical reduction formula in Feuerbach style. By using it Barth is reducing the end-time reality of 'the raising of the dead' to the eternal present of the wholly-other God. In this way he transposes the apocalyptic language about 'the end of time' into the metaphysical language about 'the finitude of time'.[19] 'What else could the Easter message be but the message that God is the Lord – a message that has now assumed a wholly concrete form?'[20] As 'the Lord', God is the eternal boundary of time, at once its beginning and its end.

With this Barth determines the theological category. Whatever else resurrection may be, in space and time, causally or in purpose, historically and in human terms, Barth thinks of it for the sake of the God whose reality cuts through all human reality and is vertical to the horizontal of time. 'Resurrection' is an act of God's *with* the world, not an act *in* the world, and it belongs to the vertical category of God's history, not to the horizontal character of the history of the world. Even in the *Church Dogmatics* (IV/1 §59) Barth adheres to the conviction that in the Easter stories there is no disagreement among the witnesses about the fact that 'in the story which they recount we have to do with an "act of God", the act of God in which it was revealed to the disciples that the happening of the cross was the redemptive happening promised to them, on which therefore the community and its message were founded'.[21] What he is saying is that the raising of Christ is solely the act of God, performed in the interests of the divine revelation which takes places in this happening. Compared with the cross it is a 'new' act of God. It is not a symbol for the conviction of the salvific meaning of Christ's cross in the minds of the disciples; it is 'the great verdict of God, the fulfilment and proclamation of God's decision concerning the event of the cross'.[22] But it does not create anything new, and does not complete the reconciliation of the world with God already 'accomplished' in Christ's death. It merely brings this truth to light. It reveals 'the Father's verdict'. So Christ's cross and resurrection are 'two acts of God' which 'with and after one another are the two basic events of the one history of God with a sinful and corrupt world'.[23]

For Barth, Troeltsch's axioms about history and the knowledge of history have no meaning for the theology of the resurrection. If Christ's resurrection is a divine act *sui generis*, then the theology that corresponds to it is a thinking *sui generis* also. But if the resurrection of Christ is viewed only in the category of God's history with the world, then all that emerges from it is the idea of God's revelation of himself. This reduction of Christ's resurrection to God's sovereignty does not merely demythologize the resurrection; it de-historicizes it as well. The way Jesus took from Galilee to Jerusalem to his cross and resurrection, and the way of the risen Lord to his parousia and the new creation lose their importance. When Barth sees in the raising of Jesus only 'the verdict of the Father' about the reconciliation accomplished in the death of the Son as divine revelation, this is then no longer an eschatological happening. It is simply and solely the transcendent endorsement of the redemptive significance of the cross of Christ. The raising of Christ from the dead then has no saving meaning of its own. Nor does it mean a 'how much more' compared with Christ's death. It simply reveals the truth of this redemptive fact.

With this Barth has excised the historically irritating and objectionable element from the message of the resurrection. What really happened in human history is only Christ's death. The message about his resurrection sets this historical event in the light of God's eternity, and in that light pronounces the divine verdict on the already accomplished reconciliation with the world.

This theology can provide no starting point for a criticism of the world view underlying historicism. Misunderstood in a 'neo-orthodox' sense, a 'Sunday causality' like this can co-exist quite happily with the 'weekday causality' generally adopted. It is only if we trace back Barth's *Church Dogmatics* to his early 'dialectical theology' that the hidden germ of a criticism emerges: the transcendence of God's history over against the closed 'cause and effect' system of the world does not mean a total lack of relation; what it means is total criticism. Underlying Troeltsch's axioms is a pantheistic world view: 'everything is at heart related', so 'nothing new under the sun can ever happen'. God understood as the Wholly Other does not interfere with this at all. But God experienced as 'the fact that changes everything' breaks open the closed system of the world. Is the resurrection of Christ and the annihilation of death in him not the one 'fact' which changes all that history means here?

2. The Category of Existential History

In Bultmann too a reduction statement à la Feuerbach is at the centre of his new interpretation of the resurrection faith: 'If the event of Easter Day is in any sense an historical event additional to the event of the cross, it is nothing else than the rise of faith in the risen Lord, since it was this faith which led to the apostolic preaching.'[24] For Bultmann as for Barth, the meaning of the resurrection is to be found in the revelation of the redemptive meaning of Christ's cross for the reconciliation of the world. But unlike Barth, Bultmann does not see Christ's 'resurrection' as an act of God in the category of divine history. He sees it as an experience of faith in the category of existential history. He takes over the premise of Troeltsch's axioms, which is that history means human history and that human beings are its determining subject. For him, 'Easter' is therefore not an act of God in and for the dead Jesus, but an existential happening to the disciples from which their faith emerged.

Bultmann grappled with historicism very early on, in order to find a foundation for a 'theological exegesis of the New Testament'.[25] He supplemented and superseded what Troeltsch had to say about the historical method by his own view about the existential method: text-interpretation and self-interpretation are the two sides of every exposition which strives to arrive at understanding. In the process of arriving at understanding, the two sides deepen one another mutually: the self-interpretation of the person as a historical person can come about only in the interpretation of history and its testimonies; and this interpretation, in its turn, can take place only by way of the self-interpretation of the person who tries to understand it. The 'closed cohesion of cause and effect' with which historical science works according to Troeltsch can certainly show the connections between events in the past, but it does not affect our own historical existence, for this is not objectifiable; and in the same way the god about whom faith speaks is not objectifiable either. In this way Bultmann established the theological category in the non-objectifiable subjectivity of faith, in detachment from the cohesion of historical cause and effect.

For the interpretation of the Christian faith in the resurrection, this means that the 'resurrection of Christ' is a mythological expression for the birth of the disciples' faith in the redemptive meaning of the cross of Christ. It is 'simply an attempt to convey the meaning of the cross'.[26] Historically, no salvific meaning can be discerned in the cross on Golgotha. It also becomes a 'saving event' only as the 'permanent historical fact originating in the past historical event which is the crucifixion of Jesus'.[27] The cross of Christ becomes historically significant when it touches a person's historical existence, is grasped as an expression of the judgment of God because a person has become a prey to the world, and is absorbed into his own existence as an experience that liberates him from the fetters binding him to this present world. 'Believing' in the cross of Christ means 'to undergo crucifixion with him',[28] and that means understanding oneself in the light of the transcendent God, no longer in the light of the world as it now exists. This significance of Christ's cross is made a present reality in the proclamation of the Word of the cross. Faith frees people for authentic being from God, liberating them from the idols of power and possession.

Like Barth's idea about the gracious self-interpretation of God, Bultmann's fundamental idea about the believing self-interpretation of the human being results not only in the demythologization of the message of the resurrection but in its dehistoricization and de-eschatologization as well. What does 'the cross of Christ' as 'the always present' liberating judgment of God on the 'worldliness' of human beings have to do with the cross of Jesus of Nazareth on Golgotha? The stress on the presentative existential significance of the statements about the cross of Jesus means that the real historical significance of the statements – their importance for historical reality – becomes unimportant. In the process of entering existentially into Christ's crucifixion, the saving meaning of his death *for us*, 'while we were still enemies' (Rom. 5.10) gets lost. All that remains is the 'Christ in us' of Christian mysticism. Once the existential categories of human historicity are elevated into theological categories, theological statements can quite well co-exist with historical ones. The 'closed cohesion of cause and effect' which determines the underlying world view is in no way infringed.

§3 THE RESURRECTION OF CHRIST AND HISTORY: THE HISTORICAL PROBLEM

Whereas in his research the historian has to work analytically and inductively, he also has the task of writing history. He then has to gather together the details analysed into their wider contexts. He has to present the phenomena against the background of their time and put what has been transmitted into the context of his own present. He has to grasp the future for which the phenomena have a meaning. As far as historical facts are concerned, he may come to definite conclusions; but history itself, it has been rightly said, must be continually re-written. And this means that in the writing of history particular ideas about history as a whole have to be presupposed, however related to the present and to the particular stance of the writer these may be. Every encyclopaedia and every 'history of the world' shows this. In this respect written history also takes over the task of developing a theory of reality as a whole, in so far as this is part of history, and of apprehending and clothing the times in ideas.

From the end of the eighteenth century onwards, universal history became a blueprint for finding one's way in time. History, not metaphysics, was now the universal science.[29] But because human beings exist in history, not in the next world, 'we should first have to await the end of history in order to possess the complete material which would permit their meaning [i.e., the meaning of the individual parts] to be defined'.[30] 'Universal history' is therefore only possible in the perspective of the expected 'end of history'. This is also confirmed by the life history of every individual: 'Every design for living is the expression of a particular understanding of the meaning of life.' To exist 'in anticipation of the future' is the unique character of all historical being.[31] It is true that people in history do not know the end of history, but this end is nevertheless at stake in every historical present. The modern survey of the times in the form of universal history was determined either messianically as 'the new time' or apocalyptically as 'the end-time'.

1. The Category of Universal History

It is in the framework of general reflections like these that Wolfhart Pannenberg has developed his 'theology of universal history',[32] drawing first conclusions for a theology of history from the resurrection faith. Here we shall confine our attention to the problem of the resurrection and history.

Jesus' proclamation of the imminent kingdom of God was a proleptically eschatological proclamation, and was as such aligned towards future endorsement. What the disciples proclaimed as his 'resurrection from the dead' embodied the eschatological endorsement of his anticipation of the kingdom of God, because the resurrection of the dead was the symbol under which the end of history was imagined. But since initially only Jesus was raised, not all the other dead as well, his resurrection must for its part be understood as a proleptically eschatological event, which remains dependent on its eschatological verification. Yet in Jesus' resurrection 'the end of history' is nevertheless present in the midst of history. Consequently, it is not merely possible to grasp the concept of universal history; this is even required by the Christian viewpoint. The verdict of the disciples about Jesus' resurrection is not a reflective verdict of their faith. It is a reality judgment about Jesus' fate: he has in very truth been raised. This judgment is certainly not verifiable in terms of positivist historical reconstruction, but it can be authenticated from the viewpoint of universal history, in the perspective of the end of history. So in the framework of an anthropology based on the openness to the future of human existence, in the framework of a historical ontology, and in the framework of a concept of anticipatory reason, the proleptically eschatological resurrection faith is intelligible and by no means alien. Christian faith in the resurrection must lay claim to being the true philosophy of world history.

There are two sides to this attempt to bring back faith in the resurrection into the historical viewpoint with the help of the changes in historical reasoning we have considered. On the one hand, Christian theology enters the field of history and reason once more, in order to join issue with other views of reality about the truth of history and the meaning of its future. But on the other hand, it can easily become the confirmation of what takes place in history and human reason anyway. 'The raising of Christ' could then become the historical and symbolic endorsement of the proleptic structures of being, and would then offer nothing new.

2. The Horizon of Historical Expectation and the Sphere of Historical Experience

Historical studies do not merely have history as their subject. They themselves are embedded in history and are part of it. We therefore have to fit historical methods and categories into the meta-historical concepts and categories on which they are based. Heidegger tried to make the historicity of human existence the foundation of history, but this was too subjective. History is interaction and process between human beings, groups, classes and societies, and not least between human beings and nature. We therefore have to formulate the unique character of historical experience more broadly and also more flexibly if we are to do justice to the experience of history. Historical studies can only exist as long as reality is experienced as history. Reality is only experienced as history as long as there is a perception of time. Time is only perceived as long as the difference between past and future exists. The difference between past and future is determined in the present of both – the present of the past in experiences and remembrances, the present of the future in expectations and hopes. It is the difference between 'the sphere of experience' and 'the horizon of expectation' that determines the historical perception of historical time.[33] If there are no longer any expectations of future experiences, the remembrance of experiences in the past disappears too. If there are no longer any remembered experiences, the expectations also slip away and cease. Remembrance and hope are the conditions for possible experiences of history. That is why they are also the metahistorical conditions for the concern about history and the knowledge of history. In 'post-histoire' there are neither remembrances nor expectations.

The experience of reality as history presupposes hope for its future. Hope for the future is based on remembrance. This, as has been shown, is the disclosure of reality as history, which came about through the Jewish and Christian faiths.[34] We shall therefore look at the fundamental difference between expectation and experience in order to unfold the nature of history in the perspective of the resurrection of Christ. To talk about Christ's resurrection is meaningful only in the framework of the history which the resurrection itself opens up – the history of the redemption of human beings and nature from the power of death. In the framework of a history determined in any other way it has no meaning. Anyone who talks about Christ's resurrection from the dead and who believes in the power of God to raise the dead is talking in a single breath about the foundation, the future and the praxis of the liberation of human beings and the redemption of the world. This means that what *we can know* historically about Christ's resurrection must not be abstracted from the questions: what *can we hope* from it? and what *must we do* in its name? The resurrection of Christ is *historically* understood in the full sense only in the unity of knowing, hoping and doing.

Israel's experience of 'history' was disclosed through her *faith in the promise*. The theologically disclosed experience of reality as history really already begins with Abraham's exodus from his home country. Abraham followed the call of the promise and came to perceive reality as history in the course of his wanderings. For God's promise is like a horizon which moves with us and into which we move.[35] Promise has fulfilment ahead of it. That is why the hoping person begins to seek for the fulfilment of his hope, finding rest only in the reality of fulfilled promise. What was imagined in individual terms with Abraham was Israel's collective experience in the exodus from Egypt, an experience which was told from generation to generation. Exodus means leaving an old reality which was endured as an imprisonment and seeking the land of promise. If we transfer this to the experience of time, exodus means leaving what is behind and reaching out to what lies ahead (Phil. 3.13). Past and future become distinguishable in the transition of the present. The three Abrahamitic religions – Judaism, Chrsitianity and Islam – are religions of history, aligned towards the future. This is made plain in every encounter with the Asiatic religions of external and internal equilibrium – equilibrium in nature, as in Taoism, equilibrium in society, as in Confucianism, and equilibrium in one's own soul, as in Buddhism.

In the 'historical' religions, reality is understood as history to the extent in which reality is disclosed by God's promise. Of course there are also promises in these religions which history has superseded, and which have therefore been forgotten. But what is really promised in all the specific promises is the presence of the promising God himself. And the result is the continual rebirth of hope, either out of disappointment, or out of fulfilment. All the individual promises – descendents 'as the dust of the earth', promised land, blessing for the nations and whatever they may be – point beyond themselves to the coming presence of God himself – to the kingdom of his glory – to the full and perfect theophany – to the new creation: 'The whole earth is full of his glory' (Isa. 6).

This horizon of expectation makes events in the human world and the world of nature temporal, and events are then experienced in their time, historically. They are not finished processes, and are not in this sense 'facts'. They are moments in a process and point beyond themselves. They do not yet have their meaning in themselves, but only in relation to the goal of the history of promise. It is not only the already pronounced *words of promise* which are called to mind through narrative and remembrance, in order to awaken hope; the *events* experienced in the past have not passed away either, but point to what is future, so that they too must be told and made a present reality. 'According to the Jewish and Christian view of history, the past is a promise of the future. Consequently, the interpretation of the past is backward-looking prophecy', wrote Karl Löwith,[36] although his formulation is somewhat biased by his belief in progress; for in the biblical stories the reverse is also true: because the future is also a promise for what is past, the past must be retained in the memory and must not be forgotten. In the historical religions, the precedence of the horizon of expectation over the sphere of historical experience is based on the surplus of promise, which exceeds the historical fulfilments of promise. This surplus for its part is founded on the inexhaustibility of the creative God, who 'arrives at his rest' only when heaven and earth are in complete correspondence with him.

In the community of the historical religions we have named, the special thing about Christianity is the central importance of Christ, and above all the importance of Christ in his death and resurrection. Only the Christian faith is essentially a resurrection faith. Does this faith in the resurrection of Christ and the resurrection of the dead at the end of days project faith in the historical promise into the next world, in order to make immanence, as the sphere of the transient, acceptable? Has Christianity 'misappropriated' (Rilke's word) its future hopes by transferring them to heaven, as a way of reconciling itself to the earth as it is? Has the end of the world which has never come robbed Christianity of the historical dynamic which transforms the world? Faith in the resurrection has often been interpreted as a transcendent fulfilment of God's promises, so that people surrender all their hopes in this world. But a resurrection faith of this kind is not Christian. It is merely apocalyptic. It literally shows 'no spirit', because between the accomplished fact of the raising of Christ, and the raising of the dead expected in the transcendence, it is unaware of the presence of the risen Christ in the life-giving Spirit of the resurrection.

If we apply the fundamental metahistorical concepts of experience and expectation to the Christian faith in the resurrection, we see that 'the resurrection of the dead Christ' talks about the future of this past, and that the hope which it establishes for the raising of all the dead also ascribes a corresponding future to those who have gone. This is a totally unique interlocking of future and past. The resurrection of the dead does not say merely that the past is open to the future, and that it is pregnant with future. It also talks about a future for those who belong to the past, and in so doing it reverses time's direction. We might say that God's future will unroll the whole scroll of the past once more, from the last hour to the first. The symbol of the resurrection of the dead expresses a *historical hope for the future* – hence the dating 'in the last days' or, as German says, *am Jüngsten Tag* – 'on the Final Day', or the Last Judgment. But the resurrection symbol links this with an eschatological hope: at the end of time all the dead will be raised together and suddenly 'in a moment, in the twinkling of an eye, at the last trumpet', as Paul puts it (I Cor. 15.52) – and that means *diachronically*. The 'final day' which is awaited at the end of history is also 'the Lord's day', and as such eternal and simultaneous with all past times. 'The raising of the dead' links *the end of the time* of this history of death with the beginning of the *eternity* of the new creation in which death will be no more.

This means that it is possible by remembering the dead to fan the spark of hope for those who belong to the past. It means that it is necessary to hold fast to the dead and to work against innocent forgetting as well as against the guilty repression of the dead. It is not death which has the last word in history. It is God's righteousness: 'Behold I make *all* things new' (Rev. 21.5).

If this is true eschatologically, then nothing is lost historically either. Everything 'will be restored'.[37] In this horizon of expectation, 'history as remembrance' already leads to a kind of 'rediscovery of the dead'.[38] The whole past stands in the light of the future in which the dead will be awakened. The person who looks back, the person who remembers the dead, hears behind him as it were the sound of the last trump. 'Universal history' would fail in its object if it were concerned only to extend the present as far as possible into the times of the past; for its true impulse is the eschatological hope for the dead.

From this eschatological horizon of expectation a corresponding but narrower and more specific horizon of expectation emerges. Here we no longer ask about the future for the dead, but about the future in the lives lived by those who belong to the past. Every past was once present, and existed in its own projects for the future. Every present has come into being out of the fulfilled and thwarted, dawning and dying hopes for the future cherished by those who are gone. The historian is failing to grasp the past if he merely asks what it was really like, and does not succeed in uncovering and absorbing past possibility as well as past reality, and past horizons of expectation together with past experience. The present representation of the prospective reality of things that are past must be a part of history too. In the historical retrospective the past prospective must be perceived and made present. It is only then that the maimed, neglected or suppressed hopes of those who are past can be brought into relationship with the hopes of those who are living in the present, and can be absorbed into the present project of the future. Historical research that does full justice to its subject asks about the future in the past.[39] The positivist, materialist reduction of history to the level of past facts and times that have gone suppresses the future in the past. This kind of historicism was in its trend and effect anti-historical. Rather than the experience of history, it meant a farewell to history. What we call 'historical' past is past future. What we call 'historical' present is present future. According to this interpretation, 'history' is *the history of the future*, whether it be the future of a person, a society, a nation, humanity as a whole – or the future of the relation between human civilization and the nature of the earth.

3. The Historical Process of Resurrection

Seeing history in the perspective of resurrection means participating through the Spirit in *the process of resurrection*. Belief in resurrection is not summed up by assent to a dogma and the registering of a historical fact. It means participating in this creative act of God. A faith of this kind is the beginning of freedom. If God reveals himself in the raising of the Christ crucified in helplessness, then God is not the quintessence of power, such as the Roman Caesars represented. Nor is he the quintessence of law, such as the Greek cosmos reflects. God is then the power that quickens into life, that makes the poor rich, that lifts up the humble and raises the dead. Faith in the resurrection is itself a living force which raises people up and frees them from the deadly illusions of power and possession, because their eyes are now turned towards the future of life. The proclamation of the resurrection of Christ is a meaningful statement against the horizon, or in the context, of the history which the resurrection itself begins – the history of the freeing of human beings and the whole sighing creation from the forces of annihilation and death. Understood as an event that discloses the future and opens history, the resurrection of Christ is the foundation and promise of life in the midst of the history of death.

Paul brought out the connection here very clearly: 'If the Spirit of him who has raised Jesus from the dead dwells in you, he who has raised Christ Jesus from the dead will give life to your mortal bodies also through his Spirit which dwells in you' (Rom. 8.11). He links the *perfect* tense of the raising of Christ with the *present* tense of the indwelling of the Spirit, and the present tense of the Spirit with the *future* tense of the resurrection of the dead. The perfect tense of the raising of Christ therefore designates, not a past event but an event in the past which in the Spirit determines the present, because it opens up the future of life. Without this history which it throws open in the Spirit and in hope, the resurrection is incomprehensible. The present liberating experience of the Spirit is grounded in the perfect of Christ's resurrection. That is why the risen Christ is known in the present energies of the Spirit and is perceived through them. The future of the 'giving life to mortal bodies' (as Paul calls the resurrection of the dead in this passage) is ontically based on the resurrection of Christ and is noetically grasped through the experience of 'the life-giving Spirit'. In talking about Christ's resurrection we have therefore to talk about a *process of resurrection*. This process has its foundation in Christ, its dynamic in the Spirit, and its future in the bodily new creation of all things. Resurrection means not a *factum* but a *fieri* – not what was once done, but what is in the making: the transition from death to life.

The formula about 'giving life to mortal bodies' indicates that the hope of resurrection is not related to a different life. It is this mortal life that is going to be different. Resurrection is not a deferred consolation – 'the opium of the next world'. It is the power which enables this life to be reborn. The hope is directed, not towards a different world but towards the redemption of this one. In the Spirit, resurrection is not merely expected; it is already experienced. Resurrection happens every day. In love we experience many deaths and many resurrections. We experience resurrection by being born again to a living hope through love, in which we already, here and now, wake from death to life, and through liberation: 'Where the Spirit of the Lord is, there is freedom' (II Cor. 3.17).

If we see resurrection as this process, it is then possible to integrate the fundamental ideas of Barth, Bultmann and Pannenberg, and to correct their one-sidedness. As the beginning of the annihilation of death and the appearance of eternal life, the raising of Christ from the dead is 'the fact that changes everything' and is therefore in itself the revelation of God. As the Wholly Other, God is the radical criticism of this world. As 'the One who changes everything', God is the creator of the world that is new. Faith in the resurrection is itself a rising up in the power of life. The 'liberating judgment' pronounced over the bondage of existence to the world of sin, power and possession is the beginning of the rising to true life. The raising of Christ from the dead must not be viewed merely as a retrospective act which affirms Christ's death to be a redemptive event, whether this affirmation be the verdict of God's revelation or the human verdict of faith. The resurrection must be seen 'much more' as an anticipation of eternal life for mortal beings. The resurrection of Christ designates the history of the world to be the history of the end, and places the spheres of historical experience in the context and against the horizon of expectation of the new creation. In order to grasp the process of resurrection, we ought to make it a rule in theology never to separate Kant's three questions: the theoretical 'What can I know?', the practical 'What ought I to do?' and the eschatological 'What may I hope for?' These questions have to be answered in relation to one another and therefore together. Only then can we understand the event, the Spirit and the future of the resurrection in their integrated whole.[40]

Finally, let us look again at Troeltsch's historical axioms, which we must now call in question.

1. Faith in the resurrection is based on the present 'proof of the Spirit and of power' (Lessing's phrase), not on historical judgments based on probability. Historical research and historical judgments are made possible by 'history as remembrance' and are necessary in their own sphere. In the remembrance of the resurrection faith the effects of Christ's appearances on the women at the tomb and the disciples in Galilee, and finally on Paul, are historically ascertainable. The empty tomb also belongs to the sphere of what is historically ascertainable. But what is not historically ascertainable is the event of Christ's resurrection from the tomb, because there are no witnesses of it. Faith in the resurrection takes the historically ascertainable testimonies about those first appearances of Christ as remembrances – which are also reminders – of its hope for the seeing of Christ face to face. The horizon of expectation of the resurrection of the dead is wider than the sphere of remembrance of the origin of the Christian faith in the resurrection. And the sphere of remembrance of the first Christian testimonies of the resurrection is again wider than the sphere of historical research and historical judgments. Judgments of faith cannot be founded on historical judgments based on probability, but in the historical religions judgments of faith for their part make historical judgments necessary, while at the same time holding them in the balance in which judgments based on probability exist.

2. There is an interplay between the phenomena of historical life. But the nexus of causality is no more than one process in the many-sided network which goes to make up the living person. Death cuts life short, and with it the interplay of the living person. The eschatological resurrection of Christ means that what has been cut short is gathered up into the eternal life of the new creation. This is not an exception within the nexus of causality, which has its limited validity. It is the beginning of the gathering up of the mortality of all historical life into the immortal interplay of the eternal presence of God. This horizon makes it possible to discern, not only the interplay of historical life, but also the deficits and truncations of historical death. History is not merely the production process of inexhaustible life. It is also the destruction process of insatiable death. A historical view of the world without a perception of the power of death is an illusion. History in the perspective of resurrection leads to a perception of the history of death because it communicates hope contrary to death. It is therefore moved by the eschatological

question about future for the dead. It does not ask about the identity of kind of all happening. It asks about justice for the living and the dead.

3. Historical understanding is achieved with the guideline of analogy. But analogy is at most a result of historical understanding, not its beginning. The beginning is the encounter with what is strange and *the discovery of the other*. Anyone who begins instead with the correspondence always finds in everything that is strange and different only himself. He projects himself and his own unique character into what is alien and different, whether it be other cultures or other times. But this is blind cultural imperialism.[41]

'Like is known only by like' is the ancient Greek principle of perception. But why should like know like? There is no profit to be had here. Anaxagoras's ironical comment is therefore quite true: 'What is not different is to the other who is no different a matter of indifference.' What Troeltsch describes as 'the almighty power of analogy' makes all happening 'indifferent' and destroys all true interest in history. Under its sway all historical curiosity is lost. Profitable knowledge comes only from a readiness to perceive what is strange, and from openness to the other. 'An entity is revealed only in its opposite, and it is beings that are unlike which perceive one another.'[42] This is not an 'epistemological breach'.[43] It is the first principle of epistemology. Empedocles maintained: 'For with the earth we see earth, with water water, with air the divine air, with fire fire, with love love . . .'[44] But Anaxagoras countered: 'We come to know the cold by the hot, the sweet by the sour, what is light through what is dark. All sense perception is fraught with pain, for the unlike when brought into contact with our sensory organs always brings distress.'[45]

If we apply this insight to historical knowledge, we see that its beginning is the discovery of others, the pain which their difference causes, and our own preparedness to let ourselves be changed through this encounter. Our knowledge of ourselves develops in our understanding emptying of ourselves in confrontation with the other.[46] If this were not so, self-knowledge would be nothing but self-endorsement. It is only through knowledge of others in their otherness that we learn to know ourselves. With the one-sided principle of analogy, which is transfigured into an 'almighty power', we perceive nothing at all historically. We merely subject things belonging to the past to the cultural absolutism of the present. In the encounter with other civilizations, the incapacity and unwillingness to recognize and accept them has led to the destruction of cultures that are different, and to the dissemination of the homogeneous and monotonous civilization of the West. The perception of the dead Christ in the eternal livingness of God has to be understood as the most profound and most primal form of knowledge of the other – namely 'the Wholly Other'; for there is no greater antithesis than that between absolute death and eternal life. The knowledge of God in the perception of the crucified Christ must be grasped as a painful knowledge which transforms one's own existence from its very foundations. Here knowing God begins with suffering God. Anyone who perceives God in the crucified One dies and is born again to new life from the Spirit of the resurrection, as we see in the symbol of baptism. Only then are the healing analogies to God perceived in the life-giving Spirit. All knowledge of God begins with the terrible perception of the Wholly Other and with the experience of fundamental change in the self. All knowing of God ends in the richness of analogy of the eternal song of praise of the new creation. The pain of suffering God and pain from God lead to joy in God.

Finally, we must consider the question whether *the human being is the subject of history*. If history does not consist merely of human experience and decision, but is also a matter of interaction and interplay, then history always has more than merely one subject. It was only the modern claim to domination that elevated the human being into the subject of history. Human history always comes into being out of its interplay with the history of nature. In this warp and weft of humanity and nature, we cannot proceed from a centre, as do both modern anthropocentricism and the cosmocentricism which claims to be post-modern. If we wish to understand the history of the interplay between civilization and nature, we have to give up the notion of centricism altogether. If history is interaction and interplay, then we no longer have to ask: are human beings the subject of history, or is God? This alternative no longer arises. History is what takes place between God and human beings, human beings and God. History, we might say, putting it generally, is the community of human beings and nature, and the community between that humanity-and-nature relationship and God. It is a community in contradictions and correspondences, in expectations and in disappointments.

§4 NATURE AND THE RESURRECTION OF CHRIST: THE THEOLOGICAL PROBLEM

From the beginning of modern times, the historicity of Christ's resurrection was made the central problem of Christian theology, because 'history' had become the great paradigm of the modern world. But history meant only human history, as distinct from nature. Consequently, from the middle of the nineteenth century, university studies were divided into 'the natural sciences' on the one hand, and 'the humanities' on the other. In Germany the humanities were also given the name of *Geisteswissenschaften* – the sciences of the mind or spirit. Like history and nature, mind and nature were also defined over against one another: history is the field of freedom, nature the field of necessity. The mind is something quite separate from nature, because it can know and dominate nature; and nature is separate from mind because it can be subjected by the mind. Only medicine wavered between these two categories, and it was only from the middle of the nineteenth century that it came to be numbered among the natural sciences. But because human beings are themselves a unity of mind and body, the fundamental distinction between history and nature could not be completely carried through in human beings themselves. This is a sign that the paradigm 'history' did not provide an all-accommodating model for the perception of reality as a whole, and consequently the science of history could not become the universal science either.

The paradigm 'history' involves the human claim to sovereignty over nature, which was said to have no history, and over the body, which was considered to be something separate from mind and spirit. Lordship and subjugation are certainly a one-sided pattern of relationship, but even this creates community. If this relationship is to lead to the survival of both sides, however, and not to the death of the side subjected, then it has to be liberated from its one-sidedness and freed for reciprocity. History and nature must not be defined over against one another. They must be seen in the light of one another, in their reciprocal dependence, just as mind and body cannot be defined over against one another in an individual life, but must be seen as going hand in hand, if the person is not to be destroyed. And just as a human being's mind or spirit is embedded in his bodily nature and is wholly dependent on it, human history is wholly embedded in the natural conditions which provide its framework, and is dependent on these. It is not human history that is all-comprehensive. The ecological conditions of the nature of the earth are much more so, because they make the evolution of the human race possible, so that every radical change here can mean the end of the human race and its history.

This means that Christian theology is not going far enough if – as in the last one hundred and fifty years – it discusses belief in the resurrection only in the framework of the paradigm 'history' and in critical acceptance of the corresponding historical sciences. Theology must go deeper than this, and look beyond the world of history to the ecological conditions of history in nature. But when we are considering the natural conditions of history, it is not so much the eschatological 'act in history' of the God who raises from the dead which is important; it is rather the bodily character of the Christ who died and rose again. The bodily character of his dying and his resurrection raises the critical question about the resurrection in the perspective of nature, and the constructive question about nature in the perspective of the resurrection. Earlier, in the era preceding modern times, christology took these perspectives into account by way of the doctrine of the two natures. This was superseded in the historical christology of modern times. But today modern historical christology must be, not abolished, but gathered up into an ecological christology – and at the very points where the paradigm 'history' has proved to be insufficient and destructive.

Essays in this direction have certainly been made in the christ-ologies of 'the cosmic Christ', and we shall look at these in the next chapter. But no attempts have yet been made to move from the historical-eschatological theology of the resurrection to a historical-ecological theology of rebirth. We shall venture some steps in this direction, beginning with the biblical symbolism.

1. *The Rebirth of Christ from the Spirit*

1. The apocalyptic symbol is God's '*raising Jesus from the dead*'. Here God alone is active; Jesus is passive. The theological pattern of thinking is theistic, the christology adoptionist.

2. The theological symbol of God's raising from the dead is logically balanced by its anthropological correspondence which is *the resurrection of the dead*. The person who is wakened has to get up. Unless he does, the waking is ineffective. The reaction from

below has to meet the action from above. In the symbol 'raising', the dynamic comes from above. In the symbol 'resurrection', the dynamic comes from below. Here the theological pattern of thinking is christological.

3. If we put the two symbols together systematically, then the event meant has to be thought of as *a reciprocal relationship* of raising and resurrection. On the one side God is the one who 'has raised Christ from the dead'. On the other side God was himself 'in Christ', who has risen from the dead. Here the theological pattern of thinking is theological-christological.

4. 'Raising' and 'resurrection' are symbols for God's activity and Christ's own act. But when Christ dies and lives again, these acts also take place 'in the Holy Spirit'. Christ offered himself up through the eternal Spirit (Heb. 9.14) and he lives 'in the life-giving Spirit' (I Cor. 15.45). In the divine Spirit he endured the pains of dying, and out of the divine Spirit he was born again to eternal life, just as Ezekiel 37 sees the living breath of God blowing over the wide valley of dry bones: 'Then the *ruach* came into them, and they lived, and stood upon their feet' (37.10). What is understandable in the paradigm 'history' as the eschatological *act of God the Father* in and for the Son – the act which raises the dead – must in the wider ecological paradigm 'nature' be understood as *the rebirth of Christ* from God's life-giving Spirit. Here the theological pattern of thought is pneumatological-trinitarian. In the pneumatological context, metaphors from nature are used for Christ's dying and his rebirth, not metaphors from history.

Paul explains the resurrection of the dead to his readers with the image of the grain of wheat: 'What you sow does not come to life unless it dies' (I Cor. 15.36). 'What is sown is perishable, what is raised is imperishable. It is sown in dishonour, it is raised in glory. It is sown in weakness, it is raised in power. It is sown a physical body, it is raised a spiritual body' (vv. 42–44). Here the echoes are clearly christological. In John 12.24 the same image is used for 'the transfiguration of the Son of man' – that is for Christ's death: 'Unless a grain of wheat falls into the earth and dies, it remains alone; but if it dies, it bears much fruit.' But in actual fact the grain of wheat only undergoes a transformation: out of the seed comes the plant, and out of the plant the fruit. One form decays so that another may come into being. In the metaphor of the grain of wheat, death and life are not contrasted as radically as they are in the metaphor of death and raising. Here we are shown a *transition*, not a total breach and a new beginning.[47] That is why Christ is called 'the first fruits' of the dead (I Cor. 15.20).

The other image for Christ's death and life is a woman's labour pains and her joy over the newly born child (John 16.20–22). This is the picture with which John interprets the grief of the disciples at the hour of Christ's death and their joy when he comes again: 'When a woman is in travail she has sorrow, because her hour has come; but when she is delivered of the child, she no longer remembers the anguish, for joy that a child is born into the world' (v. 21). This image too talks about a transition to a new life, not a breach and a new beginning. According to this analogy, Christ's death pangs are themselves already the birth pangs of his new life. Apocalyptic used the same image in order to interpret the terrors of the end-time as the labour pains of the new creation. The image of rebirth was itself an apocalyptic metaphor for the becoming-new of the cosmos in the coming of the Son of man (Matt. 19.28).

Instead of 'raising' and 'resurrection', Paul also talks about Christ's 'becoming alive', even about his 'becoming alive again' (Rom. 14.9; I Cor. 15.45; II Cor. 13.4; and frequently). This happens 'in the power of God' and in God's 'life-giving Spirit'. The nature metaphors describe the activity of the divine Spirit who gives birth to Christ once more for eternal life, through and beyond his death. In Christ's rebirth out of his death, it is the Holy Spirit who is active. That is why the living Christ is present in this Spirit, and the experience of the Spirit's presence gives life. Christ is 'the first-born from the dead' (Col. 1.18; Rev. 1.5). Christ was born in Bethlehem and born again from the dead. His birth in a cave as Orthodox icons depict it points to his rebirth from the tomb. His incarnation is consequently completed by his resurrection, not in his death on the cross.

According to Phil. 3.21, Paul expects that the parousia of Christ in glory will bring with it *a complete change of form* (μετασχηματίζειν) in 'our lowly body' so that it may be made like in form (σύμμορφος) to Christ's 'glorious body'. He therefore understands the raising of Christ and his coming to life as his bodily transmutation – as his *transformation* out of lowliness and his *transfiguration* in the glory of God; and he expects that in the general raising of the dead human beings will come to life in an analogous way. Here again these images present death and life, not as a breaking off and a new beginning, but as a *transition*. Mortal bodies come alive, lowly bodies are transfigured, violated bodies are glorified. Dying and coming to life are two elements in the transformation process of the new creation of all things.

2. Nature's Openness for Analogy

If we look at 'the resurrection of Christ' from the perspective of nature, we first of all find ourselves asking critical questions. If the resurrection of Christ is supposed to be a 'natural event', then it must have been a breach of the natural laws which otherwise apply, and therefore a meaningless miracle. For the other dead are dead and will never return. But 'the resurrection of Christ' cannot mean a cytological phenomenon. Resurrection is not a return to mortal life by way of natural reanimation. It is therefore not a fact of nature which could be reconstructed on the basis of objective proofs. It finds no place among the natural facts of life. As we have shown, this is an eschatologically determined happening – the raising of a dead person into the eternal life of the new creation, and the transformation of his natural, mortal body into the body of God's glory, interpenetrated by the Spirit. This does not interrupt the natural laws of mortal life. It is rather that the whole quality of mortal life is changed – and with it, of course, the laws of its mortality too.

Yet 'eternal life' is also life, 'resurrection' is also an awakening, and 'rebirth' is also a birth. That is to say, even if this eschatologically determined event in Christ means the transformation of the quality of mortal life itself, yet this same mortal life is open for analogy with the wholly other, eternal life. This openness for analogy is already evident in the metaphors used: waking from sleep, getting up, being born again, and transformation. From time immemorial the Christian congregations have celebrated the feasts of Christ's resurrection and the experience of the Spirit in the rhythms of nature and this mortal life, finding the natural analogies for these feasts in the dawning of the day, the spring of the year, and the fertility of life. This is made clear by the link between the feast of the resurrection and 'Easter' – the spring festival whose goddess was the goddess of the sunrise. And in the Easter hymns natural joy over the return of the sun is taken as a parable for the joy of all creation over Christ's resurrection. The link between the feast of the experience of the Spirit and the month of May in which it is celebrated also draws on the analogy between nature, as it bursts forth into leaf and flower, and the eternal enlivening of the whole creation in the breath of God's Spirit.[48]

The liturgy of the Orthodox Church especially emphasizes this cosmic dimension of Christ's resurrection, which strips death of its power:

> Now all is filled with light
> – heaven and earth and the realm of the dead.
> The whole creation magnifies Christ's resurrection,
> the veritable ground of all its being.[49]

In speaking of nature's joy over Christ's resurrection these hymns talk about the redemption of enslaved creation from the fate of transience, and about its final healing. The transfiguration of Christ's dead body is the beginning of the transfiguration of all mortal life.

In the same way the Pentecostal hymns about the experience of the Holy Spirit in the community of Christ's people gather all longing and waiting creatures into the hope for the greening and blossoming of the new creation, pointing as sign to the fertility of the springtime.

> The Holy Spirit is the giver of life,
> the Universal Mover and the root of all creation,
> refiner of the world from its dross,
> brings forgiveness of debts and oil for our wounds,
> is radiance of life, most worthy of worship,
> waking and rewaking both earth and heaven.
> (Hildegard of Bingen)[50]

The rhythms of creation – night to day, winter to spring, barrenness to fertility – are interpreted as foreshadowings and ciphers for the final rebirth of creation from suffering and dying, a rebirth which has begun with the first-born from the dead. Yet it is only in the light of Christ's rebirth that these regeneration processes in nature become parables of the new creation. Although every morning is followed by evening, every spring by winter, and every birth by death, in the light of Christ's final resurrection it is only in these natural *beginnings* of life that pointers to eternal life are seen, so that they are lifted out of the cycle of the eternal return of the same to which they otherwise belong.

Analogies always work in both directions. On the one side these natural events become a parable of eternal life. On the other side eternal life is already prefigured in these natural events. Through this they acquire a new, eschatologically determined quality. In this there is already a certain symbolic 'transfiguration' of nature, which is not merely capable of being *used* as an analogy but is also itself in need of analogy. Not only history but nature too is symbolized, becoming God's mode of appearance and the advance radiance of his kingdom.

The natural process of dying-and-becoming is embodied in many myths and metaphors of what are called 'nature' and 'animist' religions. It is not syncretism when the Christian theology of the resurrection takes them up and uses them in 'Easter theology', as a way of grasping the cosmic significance of Christ. After seedtime and harvest, the most important process in the regeneration of life is the process of birth. It is symbolized in the myth about the death of the woman who dies in giving life. The pains of birth and the natural blood shed, bring new life into the world. In many myths the birth of life is imagined with the death of the mother, or as the rebirth of the mother in the child, out of her death throes.[51] It is only against this feminine background of deity that the dying and reborn gods emerge as cultic figures.

§5 THE RESURRECTION OF CHRIST AND NATURE: THE NATURAL PROBLEM

1. *The Cosmic Dimension*

If we look at nature from the perspective of Christ's resurrection, then the sphere in which nature is experienced moves into the horizon of expectation of its new creation. The experiences of life's transience and the unceasing suffering of all living things no longer end only in grief, but also already lead to hope. Creation is 'subjected' but 'in hope' (Rom. 8.20). Luther translates 'auf Hoffnung hin' – 'for hope's sake'. This eschatological reinterpretation of transience has to be concentrated on a single point: death; for death is the end of all the living. But in the eschatological vision of the new creation, 'death will be no more'. New creation is new from the root up only if it issues from the cosmic annihilation of the death of created being. That is why according to the Christian understanding the new creation begins with Christ's resurrection:

> Christ is risen from the dead.
> He has conquered death through death
> and has given life
> to those who are in the grave.
> (Orthodox Easter liturgy)

If 'the whole creation is to rejoice' in the resurrection, then Christ cannot have died a 'natural' death, but must have died the 'unnatural' death of all the living. For although the death of all the living is a destiny to which all life is subject, it is not an intrinsic part of life. All life is intended to live and not to die. That is why all life longs to live and endures death with pain. Christ did not die 'a natural death'. He died by violence. He was murdered, and died the death of all the men and women who suffer violence, and in solidarity with them. But he also died in solidarity with all living things, which have to die although they want to live. He did not merely die the violent death which belongs to human history. He also died the tragic death of nature. If his resurrection is the death of death, then it is also the beginning of the annihilation of death in history, and the beginning of the annihilation of death in nature. It is therefore the beginning of the raising of the dead *and* the beginning of the transfiguration of the mortal life of the first creation in the creation that is new and eternal. Christ is then in person not merely 'the first born' of the dead who are reborn through the eternal Spirit of life. He is also 'the first born' of the whole reborn creation (Col. 1.15). In raising him, God brought not merely eternal life for the dead but also the first anticipatory radiance of immortal being for mortal creation.

Nature is the term and concept which sums up the experience of creation in its present condition. 'The time of nature' is a kind of winter of creation. Nature is frozen, petrified creation. It is God's creation, alienated from the source of its life and in the imprisonment of the Spirit that animates it. In this context the conquest of death's power through Christ's rebirth and the outpouring of the divine Spirit 'on all flesh' have to be seen as the great sign of 'the springtime of creation',[52] 'the resurrection of nature'[53] and 'the deification of the cosmos'.[54] The Spirit of the resurrection who acts in Christ, and through him in human beings, is also the Spirit who brings all living creatures into the springtime of eternal life. The divine energy which the experience of believers calls the Holy Spirit is the Spirit of creation and the Spirit of the new creation of nature – 'the beginning of glory', as it is called in the New Testament. Nature is not aligned towards human history, as the anthropocentric thinking of modern times complacently assumed. It is much more the case that human history is consummated in 'the resurrection of nature', because only in and through that is a 'deliverance' of human life conceivable.

The cosmic bond between Christ's resurrection and new creation was described by Gregory of Nyssa in a splendid interpretation of Holy Saturday:

> Behold the blessed sabbath of the first creation. Know through that sabbath this one, the day of rest which God has blessed for all other days. For on this day the only begotten God did verily rest from all his works, granting his body a time of repose, because of the redemptive order of his death; and since through the resurrection he returned to what he was, he let everything that with him lay in the dust now rise with him as life and resurrection and sunrise and daybreak and the light of day for those who sit in darkness and the shadow of death.[55]

If the day of Christ's resurrection is the first day of the new creation, then it also brings the creation of new light, a light which lights up not merely the senses but the mind and spirit too, and shines over the whole new creation. 'Christ's appearances' and the Easter 'seeing' must have been grasped in these cosmic dimensions from the very beginning. Paul makes this clear in II Cor. 4.6, when he traces back 'the glory of God in the face of Jesus Christ' to the Creator who on the first day of creation 'let light shine out of darkness'. So from very early on, Christians called 'the day of the resurrection' 'the eighth day', because it was 'the first day' of the new creation.

Human history is stamped by the violence which the strong commit against the weak, the rich against the poor, men against women. The relation of human civilization to nature is determined by the structural violence with which human beings subject nature and press it into service for their own purposes. The rule of violence grows out of self-isolation and leads deeper and deeper into self-isolation, until it ends in death. The rule of violence destroys the interplay of life and the equilibrium of nature because it spreads injustice. The rule of violence threatens annihilation and leads first of all to the death of what is subjugated and then to the death of the subjugators too. Human history will only minister to life when acts of violence disappear from it and peace rules. But there can only be peace on the foundation of justice. Justice creates peace. This is also true of the relationship between human civilization and nature. Only if there is an end to structural violence in the relationship to nature and other natural living things, and only if just equilibriums are established, will there be a peace which will allow human beings and nature to survive. If this is to happen, human beings will have to recognize the values and rights of other living things, and must cease to judge them merely according to their utility value for human beings.

In the Epistle to the Colossians a vision of cosmic peace is developed which is grounded on *a cosmic christology*. Through Christ everything will be reconciled 'whether on earth or in heaven, making peace by the blood of his cross, through himself' (1.20). According to what is said here, Christ did not only die vicariously the death of suffering men and women, and 'the death of the sinner', so as to bring peace into the world of human beings. He also died 'the death of all the living' so as to reconcile everything in heaven and on earth, which means the angels and the beasts too, and to bring peace to the whole creation. Through the power of his resurrection he became 'the first-born from the dead', and was therefore revealed as 'the first-born of all creation' (1.15, 18).

What is said in the Old Testament about the Wisdom of God, which is the life of creation, is said in the Epistle to the Colossians about the cosmic Christ. Reconciled through his death and gathered up into his rebirth, all created being is drawn into the peace of the new community of creation. There the self-isolation of individual creatures ends. There all acts of violence end. There ends injustice. There ends the power of death. Mutual destruction is replaced by a community of peace in which all created beings are there for one another, with one another and in one another, and through the interchange of their energies keep one another in life, for one another and together. Christ is called 'the head' of this new community of creation because 'in him the whole fulness of the Godhead dwells bodily' (Col. 2.9), and through him this Shekinah overflows into the new fellowship of creation, so that with Orthodox theology we can truly talk about a 'deification' of the cosmos.

If we were to confine the meaning of the resurrection within narrower boundaries than this, whether existentially in the faith of the individual, or historically in the hope of humanity, christology would remain bogged down in the unreconciled nature of this world, and would itself become a factor of enmity. It is only a cosmic christology which completes and perfects the existential and the historical christology. It is only the peaceful vision of the reconciliation of the cosmos which opens up the horizon of expectation in which the nature wounded by human violence can be healed through a human history of peace. If Christ has died not merely for the reconciliation of human beings, but for the reconciliation of all other creatures too, then every created being enjoys infinite value in God's sight, and has its own right to live; this is not true of human beings alone. If according to the Christian view the uninfringeable dignity of human beings is based on the fact that 'Christ died for them', then this must also be said of the dignity of all other living things. And it is this that provides the foundation for an all-embracing reverence for life.

2. *'Christ's Transition' to the New Creation*

In the embodiment of a human being his nature and his history coincide, and the two together form the configuration or Gestalt of his life. Personhood is nature structured by the reflection of the mind and spirit, and by history. Every individual person is a hypostasis of nature. There are no human persons without nature, and there is no human nature without personhood. To be a person is more than to be a subject of understanding and will. A person is a living body.

In his embodiment Christ suffered both the 'historical' and the 'natural' torments of death: he was crucified and he died. But in what embodiment did he rise and appear to the women and the disciples? In what embodiment does he live now, and how will he one day universally appear in his parousia? These questions may sound speculative, because we apparently experience nothing comparable in the mortality of our existence. But the questions are justifiable ones because they touch the very essence of the resurrection faith itself.

The apocalyptic symbol of the resurrection of the dead always means the whole dead individual in his or her personhood, body and soul. This person cannot be spiritualized without being destroyed: raising means being raised bodily, or it is not raising at all. The early Christian faith in the risen Christ means the whole Christ in person, body and soul: Christ's resurrection is bodily resurrection, or it is not a resurrection at all. The Christian faith cannot be spiritualized either, without its being destroyed. Christ's resurrection means that the whole bodily Christ 'lives'. It is not merely his spirit which continues to be efficacious and his cause which goes on. For it is only in the presence of 'the living' Christ that his spirit is efficacious and that his cause goes on. Christ's 'appearances' were bodily appearances. If they were not, no one could have identified him from the marks of the nails, and he could not have broken bread with his friends. He would have appeared to the women and the disciples only as a ghost. Finally, Christians expect that at the universal parousia of Christ their mortal bodies will be made 'alive for evermore'. The expectation of the parousia is a bodily, earthly, 'natural' or material expectation. Unless it is this it can provide no foundation for the hope of the new creation. But how are we supposed to think of Christ's bodily resurrection?

Let us gather together once more the terms that are used – raising, resurrection, making alive, transfiguration, transformation – seeing them as words describing a *transition*, a passage.[56] They all point analogically to a progression, a way: from sleep to waking, from defeat to walking with the head held high, from death to life, from shame to honour, and so forth. When they are applied to the experience with the dead Christ and to Christ's 'appearances', the terms are talking about *Christ's transition* from human violation to divine glory, from mortal existence to immortal divine being. This did not make him a god. But his mortal human body was transformed so that he now 'lives' in the body of glory which is wholly and entirely permeated by the life-giving divine Spirit, and it is in this transfiguration that he 'appeared' and will appear. What men and women fragmentarily experience here and how, even before their deaths, in rebirths to true life in the energies and powers of love, happens in perfected form and right into mortal flesh itself in the resurrection of the dead. The person who is wholly and entirely seized and pervaded by the living power of the divine Spirit becomes immortal, because death loses its power over him.

The Christ who is bodily risen is the beginning of the new creation of mortal life in this world. In his body the bodily risen Christ leads human nature into the kingdom of God.[57] Just as Moses led the people of Israel out of Pharaoh's slavery into the liberty of the promised land, so Christ leads humanity out of the slavery of death into the liberty of the new creation. The first exodus led out of a historical tyranny into a historical freedom. Christ's exodus leads out of the tyranny of history into the freedom of the new creation.

The transition of Christ has more than merely historical significance. It has cosmic meaning too. Through this transition resurrection has become the universal 'law' of creation, not merely for human beings, but for animals, plants, stones and all cosmic life systems as well.[58]

The raised body of Christ therefore acts as an embodied promise for the whole creation. It is the prototype of the glorified body. Consequently, a transfiguring efficacy emanates from it. It is wholly and entirely permeated by the life-giving Spirit. It therefore radiates the Spirit which already gives life here and now. It stands in the light of God's perfection, so 'from the raised body of the Lord streams a boundless ocean of light'.[59] It is the perfected body, so it provides the hope for 'the resurrection of the body'. It partakes of God's omnipresence, so its bodily presence is freed of its spatial limitations. It partakes of God's eternity, so its presence is no longer temporally restricted. It lives in the heaven of God's creative potencies and reigns with them, and is no longer tied to the limited potentialities of earthly reality. So in this body and through it the powers of the new creation act upon and penetrate the world.

On the level of theological reflection, Christ's passage from death to new creation is the point where we can again take up and re-interpret the ancient doctrine of the two natures, seeing it in the context of a 'physical' doctrine of redemption, which is what is required today. On the cross Christ died the violent death of human beings. But he was mortal, and died the death of vulnerable human nature too. Through his resurrection, not only was the violent death of human beings conquered; the mortality of vulnerable human nature was also overcome. But if through his resurrection the mortality of human nature was overcome, this also meant the conquest of 'the death of all the living', under which enslaved creation here 'sighs'. But if he has overcome this death too, then his resurrection is indeed the beginning of the new creation of that world in which death will be no more. With the raising of Christ, the vulnerable and mortal human nature we experience here is raised and transformed into the eternally living, immortal human nature of the new creation; and with vulnerable human nature the non-human nature of the earth is transformed as well. This transformation is its eternal healing. But if this mortal human nature was accepted, raised and transfigured like this, then Christ's resurrection also raised and gathered up the original good creation which is the ground of human nature, perfecting it in its own new creation. In Christ's resurrection human nature in its primordial form triumphs over its unnatural imprisonment in transience.

The mystery of Christ's transition is unveiled in several different strata:

1. *The raising of the crucified Jesus* has the direct historical relevance signified by the historical Roman cross.

2. *Giving life to the Jesus who died* has the present natural relevance which is determined by the mortality of human nature.

3. *The glorification of this human being* in God has the created natural relevance which is determined by the human character of the human race.

4. *Christ's exaltation* to be the head of the new creation brings into the light of the eternal peace heaven and earth and all created being.

3. The Resurrection of the Dead – the Resurrection of the Body – the Resurrection of Nature

The special thing about Christian eschatology is its surmounting of the enmity between soul and body, spirit and matter, and its full affirmation of the body and the matter of which earthly things are composed. This can be seen from the article about the resurrection of the body in the Apostles' creed (where the German version talks even more bluntly about 'the resurrection of the flesh'). Eternal life can only be bodily life; if it is not that it is not life at all. The corresponding statement in the Nicene creed says the same thing, but does not stress the material embodiment so strongly: 'I look for the resurrection of the dead and the life of the world to come.' The modernized ecumenical version of the Apostles' creed has replaced the resurrection of the body by 'the resurrection of the dead' – a modernization which tries to banish from Christian eschatology its offensive fleshliness, and by doing so makes its hope a cloudy one. The idea is to surrender hope for the carnal, sensuous nature of human beings in favour of the personhood of the dead. But this is pointless, because human beings *are* 'flesh' and participate in the energies as well as the infirmities of the flesh of all the living. If there is no material 'resurrection of the body' there is no personal 'resurrection of the dead' either. If there is a personal 'resurrection of the dead', there is a material 'resurrection of the body' too.

These forms of hope are not speculative fantasies. They are knowledge which founds and sustains existence. They have a direct relevance for the way human beings act towards themselves and one another. If there is eternal hope only for the soul in the immortality of heaven, the result is the soul's hostility towards the weak and mortal body to which it is tied from birth, and the soul's yearning for the death of the body, from which it longs to be finally released. This hostility of the soul towards the body leads to the body's subjugation under the domination of the soul, to the suppression of the body's drives and needs, and their sublimation.[60] The longing to be free of this unloved companion through its death turns into the death instinct towards everything that flesh means in one's own life and in the life of other people, and the death instinct too towards the material nature of the environment. The passion for life (libido) is pushed away into particular organs and localized there. The total eroticism of the lived life turns into a desire for the satisfaction of objectified, purely sexual needs.

But if eternal life can only be bodily life, the consequence is the abolition of the soul's repression of the body and the unreserved *ensouling of the body*.[60a] The consequence is the gathering up of the body regimented through self-control into the spontaneous body of love. The consequence is the liberation of one's own isolated body for union with others in sensuous mutuality and community. The consequence is, not least, the readiness to die which affirms the body that has come alive in love. If through fear of death the life of the body is restricted or avoided, the passion of love is denied as well. If the passion of love is affirmed, then the body is ensouled and alive, but it also becomes conscious of its vulnerability and its mortality. The body of love integrates dying into the affirmation of life, and does not suppress death. In the life of love, dying is experienced daily and a resurrection every morning. Every act of love is experienced by the man as 'a little death' and every birth is experienced by the woman as a surrender of life. So loving and dying are not antitheses. They are correspondences. For loving and dying are simply the immanent sides of the resurrection and eternal life. Dying and death can be integrated into the loving affirmation of life if there is hope for 'the resurrection of the body'. It is only this hope which makes a person prepared to live and love in the body, here and now, wholly and without reserve, and in love to die, and through loving affirmation here and now, to reconcile and to transfigure, to sanctify and to glorify the natural body.

Life is energy, and the energies flow from the body. Are they not the energies of the creative Spirit of God? Do they not illuminate body and soul with the eternal light? The praxis which is dialectically bound up with the hope for 'the resurrection of the body' is to be found in *the mysticism of the body*, which first makes possible the true mysticism of the soul. It confutes the self-isolation of the soul which denies the world and is hostile to the body, and it replaces the techniques for repressing and sublimating the 'drives' by the spontaneous passion of love, in which body and soul, unconscious desires and conscious will are attuned in a single harmonious configuration.

The resurrection of the body is the 'nature' side of the 'person-hood' conception about the resurrection of the dead. This conception for its part is based on the eschatological raising through which God will create all things anew, and perfect them. If the foundational link between these two aspects is clear in the context of this eschatological conception, then it must also be possible to interpret the connection in the converse sense: those whom God 'raises' at the end of time must 'rise' themselves. Their power from below corresponds to the power from above. Is there an immanent power of this kind in 'the flesh' too, which will raise it on that Day of God's? Is there anything in this vulnerable and mortal 'flesh' which is immortal and can provide the energy for the regeneration of the flesh? From the image of the grain of wheat which dies and rises into the plant, the fathers of the church, following I Cor. 15.38, concluded that there is a principle of this kind in the body which is not depraved by sin and out of which the body will rise.[61] This principle is to be found in the enduring *somatic identity* in death, without which a 'raising of the dead' would be inconceivable. The dead must still be indentifiable for God even if they decay. God remembers them. He knows their names. Death does not destroy this relationship to God. It is the divine presupposition for the raising of the dead in their personhood. And on the human side this principle is the immanent power for resurrection: what endures in the transitions from life to death, and from death to resurrection, is *the* identity of the person in the mutual relationship with God. Is this a *somatic identity* as well? Because personal identity is found in a person's life history, it is inconceivable without somatic identity too. So what endures is the whole person, body and soul, in the Gestalt that has come into being through the history of his lived life, and in which God sees him.

What is changed? The vulnerability of this personal configuration, its mortality, its sins, its suffering and its grief will be overcome: '*This* perishable nature must put on the imperishable, and *this* mortal nature must put on immortality' (I Cor. 15.53). Historical identity and eschatological transformation do not exclude one another, but are two sides of the one, single transition to eternal life.

When the sinfulness and the mortality are overcome, will other characteristics of the bodily existence in which men and women are created be set aside too? Will human needs and human dependence on food, air, climate and so forth be abolished? If we had to assume this,[62] it would also mean an end to the earthly community of creation in which human beings live bodily and practically. Will human sexuality be abolished as well, so that there will no longer be 'male or female' (Gal. 3.28), but all human beings will be 'like the angels' (Luke 20.35)?[63] If we have to assume this, then it is not this creation which is going to be created anew, for in place of the human being who is created male and female there will be a different being altogether, and 'the second creation' will displace the first. But the eschatological new creation of this creation must surely presuppose *this whole* creation. For something new will not *take the place* of the old; it is *this same 'old' itself* which is going to be created anew (I Cor. 15.39–42). The transformation into glory of this whole real creation takes place diachronically, from the last day to the first, on the day of the Lord. It is not something that happens *after* this world, but something that happens *with* this world. The lived life of created beings in the succession of the generations and times will *as such* be redeemed from guilt and grief and transformed into eternal joy. And from this neither human dependence on nature nor human sexuality can be excluded. The ideas which we have called in question above would seem to be gnostic rather than Christian. They do not fit into the horizon of expectation of 'the resurrection of the body'.

Is there a power of resurrection immanent in the flesh? In the image of the grain of wheat, this power is the power of surrender, the power to become seed in the earth. It is only out of this power that the plant grows. Put without metaphors, this means: the love which makes bodily life here live is also the power which here ensouls bodily life. Life ensouled by the power of love becomes vulnerable and dies painfully. The hope for the resurrection of the flesh which lives and is ensouled through love sustains love through the wounds and the dying, and does not let it give up. The love which is the power of the 'sowing' here and the resurrection which is the power of the 'harvest' there are two sides of the same thing. What is there called the resurrection of the body is here called the love that ensouls the flesh. Love which here spends itself and surrenders itself in love, there rises up to glory. Love is therefore the immanent power of resurrection in the flesh. The resurrection is the transcendent perfecting of love.

So with what body will the dead rise? With the body of love. Not the unlived, might-have-been or wasted life, but the life lived in love will rise and be transfigured.[64]

§6 BECOMING ALIVE IN THE SPIRIT OF THE RESURRECTION: THE UNITING OF WHAT HAS BEEN SEPARATED

What praxis is bound up with hope for 'the resurrection of the dead and the life of the world to come'? The ideas which hope takes always both open up and limit the way and the experience of any life. The horizon of expectation makes the sphere of experience accessible. These forms given to hope are not imaginary wish-fulfilments, although of course we in fact find that they are sometimes misused in this way. But essentially speaking these are expectations and hopes which release energies in all those who cherish them and make experiences possible because they 'set people on the move'. If we ask about the praxis of the resurrection hope, we are asking about the way of life and the experience of life of the people who are animated – 'ensouled' – by this hope. The expected 'resurrection of the body' is already present in 'the Spirit of the resurrection' and is effective here and now. Life in the Spirit of God is consequently a life in the power of the resurrection. Traditionally it was understood as rebirth through the Spirit, and was symbolically sealed in baptism. Taken literally, it means 'being born again to a living hope through the raising of Christ from the dead' (I Peter 1.3). This spiritual rebirth of a human being is nothing less than the anticipated rebirth of the whole cosmos. It is a personal happening with cosmic relevance. The people who are 'born again' through the Spirit of the resurrection are not redeemed from 'this wicked world'. They are called to the liberation of suffering creation and are made alive for that purpose. The living hope to which we are reborn is an inclusive hope by virtue of its very origin – that is, it is a vicarious, a representative hope for all sad created beings, but never an exclusive hope in which believers assure themselves complacently of their own salvation and let the rest of the world go to hell.

At the end of our reflections about resurrection and history we discussed the principles of a practical theory of liberation.[65] At this point we shall concentrate on the experiences of the body and bodily nature in the context of the resurrection hope, and shall look at the practical consequences that correspond to them.

Christian faith starts from the assumption that it is impossible to reconcile life and death without the future of God. Should we accept death as a natural part of life? Then we must renounce love, which desires the life of the beloved and not his death. Should we renounce the body because it is mortal? Then we must renounce love altogether. If we accept death and if we repress death we cannot love life. Consciously or unconsciously, the knowledge of death destroys love's ability to affirm life. Whether we accept death as unavoidable, or whether we repress it, the result is that the natural life drive is perverted into an unnatural death instinct. The liberation of the life drive from the death instinct is the authentic effect of hope for 'the resurrection of the body'. Surprising though it may sound, it is hope for the resurrection of the body which is the foundation and motivation for what Bonhoeffer called 'Christianity's profound this-worldliness'. It is precisely this hope which – contrary to what Nietzsche said – moves men and women to 'remain true to the earth', even in the face of individual, collective and universal death.[66]

The Spirit of the resurrection is 'the life-giving Spirit'. The Spirit is experienced wherever life here is quickened and its living energies awake. This happens wherever this mortal life is unreservedly affirmed. It is affirmed where its self-isolation is overcome through communication with other life. For life is communion in communication.[67] Death acts on this life and in it as the power of division and isolation. But the resurrection actively penetrates life too, by virtue of hope, and cancels the results of death's power.

We shall try to illustrate this from the unity of body and soul in personhood, the unity of the person in the sequence of the forms personhood takes in time, the unity of persons in community, the unity in the succession of human generations, and finally the unity of human civilization and nature. Death is the power of disintegration in these relationships, which make and keep life alive. Hope for the resurrection of the body wakens the energies for living, and through reconciliation and healing brings human beings on to the path of eternal life. Death divides – the Spirit unites.

1. The Unity of Body and Soul

The original unity of body and soul in a human person is broken once the self-consciousness awakens. The child's spontaneity in receiving and reacting is replaced by mental reflection and the deliberate act of will. The human being is no longer at one with himself. He has gone out of himself and confronts himself. He takes up 'an excentric position' towards himself.[68] In his self-consciousness he is subject and object at the same time. He experiences his body in the double mode of being and having. I am there in the body and I possess a body.

In the cultural history of the West the distance between the soul and the conscious self on the one hand and the body on the other has been increasingly extended by religion and upbringing; and the original unity of body and soul has been increasingly divided. It is only the human soul which is related to the divine, not the body. It is only through control of the body that the self-conscious ego becomes like its God, the controller and ruler of the world. What is truly human was seen in the cognition and will of the determining human subject, not in the unconscious needs and drives of the human body, which had been degraded into an objective possession. For the degraded body this was deadly, for the distinction between the soul and the body was understood as the spiritual anticipation of the separation of the soul from the body at death. Self-awareness is the anticipatory awareness of death. If the body is given over to mortality, the soul which dissociates itself from the body can be certain of its immortality. If the body is turned into an object, perceived and controlled in the same way as natural matter, the cognitive ego can become aware of its transcendent subjectivity. The original unity of body and soul is broken by a self-awareness which anticipates the death of the body, and practises it through the body's subjugation, as the Jesuitical saying about *Kadavergehorsam* – corpse-like submission – illustrates in such drastic form.

The Spirit of 'the resurrection of the body' throws open the horizon of the divine which spans soul *and* body. The body is not inferior to the soul, and is not subordinated to it. It is given the same dignity. The likeness in which God created human beings means their whole bodily existence; for he created them 'male and female'. The image of the resurrection in which they will be redeemed embraces the whole bodily existence. Neither in creation nor redemption is there any primacy of soul and inferiority of body.

But this means that in the Spirit of the resurrection soul and body find the way to their wholeness even *before* death. It means that their life-hating divisions and their necrophilic conflicts can be ended and healed. If the suppressions of the body are ended, soul and body again interpenetrate one another, together forming the person's living configuration or Gestalt. The body which had been objectified to a possession is now integrated into the human life as a whole. The soul that had dissociated itself from the body returns to it and ensouls it. The spontaneity that had been lost returns on a new level. In that image of hope which we call the resurrection of the body, life and death can be brought into harmony because death needs neither to be accepted nor repressed. The configuration of the whole human person, body and soul, wins from that hope a new direction for living which ends its inner dichotomies. 'Wholeness is the Spirit as the total thrust of the human being.'[69]

If this is already true of human existence as it is now, then it is true even more of the whole 'set' and alignment of the human being towards God's future in the resurrection. In the hope for the final victory of life over death, mortal life here can be fully loved and human beings can fully die. When the fear of death disappears the fear of life disappears too. The new wholeness of body and soul in the resurrection hope is not a reversion from the conscious life to childish spontaneity. It is a transition to the new spontaneity of faith, which ends the dichotomies caused by reflection and control. In faith the child returns – but as the child of God: not as nature but as grace. The new wholeness is a unity which absorbs into itself the differentiations and disunions, and heals them.

Knowledge of their mortality makes human beings sick, body and soul. The therapeutic meaning of the Spirit of the resurrection is the becoming-whole of the human being who is split into two by death. If there is hope for the universal elimination of the germs of

corruption and death, then 'my flesh also shall rest in hope', the hope
of experiencing the livingness of God.

2. *The Unity of the Person in Time*

Being human is not merely a differentiated unity of body and soul. It
is also personhood in a history. The human person goes through a
whole series of temporal configurations or Gestalts which can be
distinguished from one another, but in which the person's identity
must be preserved. The human being begins as a fertilized ovum,
becomes an embryo, a foetus, a child, an adolescent, an adult, an
ageing man or woman, a sick and then a dying person. Personhood is
really nothing other than the continuity of the human being in the
transmutations of his temporal Gestalt and the different phases of his
development. As long as a person can identify himself with himself in
the transmutations of the times of his life, and as long as he is
prepared to do so, he is a person. If he begins to deny himself or
forget himself, he destroys his personhood and no longer knows who
he is. He then loses his reliability and authenticity for other people
too. No one knows who he is any longer.

Many discussions about the concept of person unconsciously
presuppose adults who are in full possession of their powers, and see
them merely synchronically in the time of the present, but not
diachronically in the transmutations of their temporal Gestalts. A
concept of person like this cannot of course be applied to someone
who is old or handicapped, and even less to an unborn life or an
embryo. The breach of continuity with their own earlier temporal
Gestalts makes it hard for many people to recognize themselves in a
fertilized ovum, a foetus or an embryo, and to concede ovum, foetus
and embryo full human dignity and full human rights, even though
all human beings were once in that state, and although as soon as the
ovum is fertilized the human person is genetically already perfect.
People then say that the foetus or embryo is human but not a person
– human material but not yet a human being. Is this not inflicting
death on other people and oneself? Hope for the resurrection of the
body is not merely a hope for the hour of death; it is a hope for all the
hours of life from the first to the last. It is directed, not towards a life
'after' death, but towards the raising of this life. If the whole human
being is going to rise, he will rise with his whole life history, and be
simultaneous in all his temporal Gestalts, and recognize himself in

them. What is spread out and split up into its component parts in a person's lifetime comes together and coincides in eternity, and becomes one. If what is mortal puts on immortality, its mortality is ended and everything past becomes present.

Because the hope of resurrection embraces the human being's whole life history, this person will remember his past temporal configurations, and will be able and willing to identify himself with them. He will not view any one of them as a mere preliminary stage to what he is at present. Each temporal Gestalt has the same dignity in God's sight, and hence the same rights before human beings. Every devaluation of the foetus, the embryo and the fertilized ovum compared with life that is already born and adult is the beginning of a rejection and a dehumanization of human beings. Hope for the resurrection of the body does not permit any such death sentence to be passed on life. Fundamentally speaking, human beings mutilate themselves when embryos are devalued into mere 'human material', for every human being was once just such an embryo in need of protection.

3. The Unity between Person and Community

All self-isolation leads to violence. Every act of violence leads to suffering and ultimately to death. In the unity of body and soul every human person is dependent on human community, and participates in life together with other people. The bodily existence of human beings always means a *social existence* among other things, for its sensuous quality is also its capacity for communication. The horizon of 'the resurrection of the body' spans not merely the bodiliness of the individual person but sociality too. It is the community between human beings that will be raised and transfigured in the light of God, not the isolated and private individual soul. Significantly enough, when Paul is talking about community he uses the image of 'the body' with 'its many members' – an image which affirms embodiment (I Cor. 12).

But because of the religious and ethical primacy given to the individual soul, modern society has engendered the individualism in which every human being wants his own freedom and no one pays too much attention to anyone else. The principle of competition means that the capable and the effective are rewarded, and the weak are looked down on. If opportunities for living are scarce – and all the more if the scarcity is artificially created – the struggle of every man for himself begins, because 'there is not enough for everybody'. This scarcity ideology makes people lonely, robs them of their relationship to other people, isolates them, and forces many of them into social death. The individualism of modern society undoubtedly has narcissistic features, because every individual is bound to be in love with himself if he wants to 'make the grade' and 'get on'. Yet the Narcissus myth itself tells us that narcissism is deadly. The isolated individual is the perversion of what a person is. If people are to be able to live as persons, body and soul, they must discover the divine dignity of community and look for the future of community. It is only in sociality that personhood can be developed, if it is not to be perverted into egoistical individualism. But sociality can be built up only by persons if it is not to be debased into collectivism. Once they are isolated into individuals, people can be dominated, as we see from the ancient Roman principle of subjection, 'divide and rule'. But in solidarity with one another, people become strong. The humane community is the best shield for personhood against the threat of social death. On the other hand a human community is creative only to the degree in which the individual persons belonging to it are creative. Communities themselves tend towards conservatism. Only single persons are creative. So human communities are renewed in the persons who constitute them.

4. The Unity of the Human Race in the Generation Contract

We have become accustomed to seeing human life in horizontal cross-sections: all human beings living at a single time. But a mere glance at the Old Testament and at civilizations existing before modern times shows us that human life also has to be perceived in the longitudinal section of the times: all human beings in the sequence of the generations. Human beings are not merely personal and social beings. They are *generation* beings too. They are created as generations and live with one another and for one another in generations. That is why human life is alive when an unwritten generation contract is kept, and dies when that contract is irreparably broken by any given generation. In its simplest form, the generation contract says that parents look after their children when they are small and in need of help, and that children look after their parents when these are old and in need of care. But in the reality of social life, it is not only families that are bound to this contract. It applies to all the human beings who live together in the generations that make up a society. Since everyone lives in the sequence of generations and owes his life to it, everyone is also in duty bound to care for the older and the younger generations. Co-humanity is lived in the solidarity of old and young, as well as in social partnership.

As well as the personal egoism which we call individualism, there is also the egoism of the present generation towards the generations to come. Human community preserves and promotes human life if it is concerned about a just distribution of the opportunities for living between the present and the coming generations. But if the present generation uses up the greater part of the non-replenishable sources of energy on earth (oil, natural gas, coal, uranium and so on) it is destroying the life of future generations. If in its national and local government budgets this generation piles up horrific mountains of debt, it is destroying the life of future generations. If this generation utilizes economic resources and shuffles off the cost on to coming generations, it is spreading the death of humanity. The children are the weakest link in the chain of the generations, and the coming generations have no voice at all. They are therefore the first victims of the acts of violence increasingly inflicted by present generations on humanity as a whole.

Hope for the resurrection of the dead challenges and resists the self-isolation of the individual from the community of persons, and challenges and resists the self-isolation of the present generation from humanity's generation sequence and generation contract; for this hope challenges and resists the power of death in the midst of life.

5. The Unity between Human Civilization and Nature

Hope for the resurrection of the dead has to do with *human persons*. Hope for the resurrection of the body has to do with *human nature*. Both aspects belong to the reality of human existence as it is lived, for to be human is to be a unity of person and nature. Of course human beings can confront nature and make it the object of their cognition and their will. But they themselves are still nature for all that. Every individual is nature in the form – the hypostasis – of a person. Human beings are not persons without nature, although the subjectivism of the modern world inclines to this extreme. But neither are they nature without personhood, although many a prophet of the New Age movement sees the salvation of the world in just such a naturalization of human beings.[70] To be human is to exist in the equilibrium of the two extremes. Human beings *are* nature and they *have* nature. They have to find their viable Gestalt in the balance between being and having. In the modern hypertrophy of the 'have' category, movements which lead to authentic being are helpful. But they are only attempts to right the balance. If they wanted to put 'being' in place of 'having', they would merely be indulging in childishly regressive dreams and flights from the responsibility which is given to human beings with their power over nature.

The humanization of nature is the great project of modern scientific and technological civilization. People are increasingly becoming the masters of natural processes. Nuclear physics and genetic engineering are penetrating the secrets of nature's own architectural blueprints. But we have discovered that this technical humanization of nature by no means leads to a humanization of human beings. Human beings have certainly acquired power over nature, but they have not as yet found any power over their own power. They have succeeded in integrating part of nature into the human world, but the political controls and the ethical responsibility for this power have not yet been acquired. The more human beings put themselves above nature the less they know who they really are. The modern crises of identity and humanity are an inescapable result of the self-isolation of human beings from nature. A pure despot becomes a riddle to everyone and to himself most of all – 'a man without qualities'.

The counter-movement is the naturalization of human beings. This would like to integrate the human world once more into the wider framework of the cosmos, so that people can again live their lives 'in harmony with nature', as Diogenes Laertes put it long ago – their own nature and the nature which forms their environment. Only harmony with nature can heal the sicknesses which spring up out of the self-isolation of human beings. Only a solicitous reverence for life can limit, and perhaps one day heal, the damage which modern civilization has inflicted on the nature of the earth. Modern anthropocentrism judges all other living things only according to their utility value for human beings. It pays no attention to their value for themselves. The alternative counter-movement (which is as old as modern civilization itself) wants to replace this by

cosmocentricism. In religious experience human beings must feel
their unity with the cosmos, and in their praxis they must integrate
themselves into its eternal laws. But this cosmocentricism runs
aground on two facts which people like to overlook. (1) The nature
of the earth is itself involved in a history which manifests itself partly
as evolution and partly as a series of catastrophes. Consequently,
nature itself cannot be called divine. Anyone who becomes 'one with
the universe' senses the sadness which suffering imposes on nature.
In its present condition nature can certainly become the partner of
human beings on the path they share, but it cannot yet be the divine
homeland. (2) Men and women cannot shake off the responsibility
imposed on them through their acquisition of power over nature.
Modern cosmocentricism has the fatal tendency to push this
responsibility on to nature itself, and to naturalize human beings in
irresponsible childishness. This helps neither human beings nor
nature.

Human beings and nature can be drawn into the mutual movement of naturalization and humanization once we relinquish the
notion of a unified centre. Human history and the history of nature
can be attuned to one another so that they come together in
harmonies and correspondences. Just as soul and body interpenetrate one another, so human beings and nature find one another in
mutual perichoresis. Civilization can be brought into a relationship
which promotes the life of both by way of a *covenant*. But as long as
it is death that reigns in nature and the world of human beings, there
can be no permanent condition of peace. The human world and
nature can therefore not be brought into an equilibrium without that
future of God which is conceived of as 'resurrection'. Human beings
cannot redeem nature, and nature cannot redeem human beings. The
divine redemption must reach them both. It is only the redemption of
nature which will again make her God's creation and the home
country for human beings. It is only the redemption of human beings
which will make them once more God's image and a blessing for
nature. And since this is so, we must enlarge the image of hope for
this divine future. '*The resurrection of the dead*' means human
persons. '*The resurrection of the body*' means human nature. Only
'*the resurrection of nature*'[71] will complete the horizon of expectation that belongs to this hope. Without the resurrection of nature
there is no 'life of the world to come'. This cosmic horizon of
expectation opens up spheres of experience in nature in which it is

neither subjected to human beings, as mere material, nor turned into their god. Instead a brotherly and sisterly relationship to fellow-creatures will spring up, the relationship expressed in the mystical hymns of Francis of Assisi. All creatures on this earth find their way to one another in the community of a common way, a common suffering and a common hope.

The solidarity of this community of creation in the all-embracing compassion of God was beautifully expressed by Isaac the Syrian: 'What is a loving heart? It is a heart that burns with love for all creatures – men and women, demons, all created things. . . . Immeasurable pity wrings the heart. . . . It can no longer endure even the slightest pain inflicted on a created being. . . . It prays even for the snakes, moved by the infinite compassion which is awakened in the hearts of those who are becoming like God.'[72]

VI

The Cosmic Christic

§1 'THE GREATER CHRIST'

1. The Recent Ecumenical Discussion

The interpretation of Christ's death and resurrection took us beyond the bounds of christology in the framework of history and led us to christology in the framework of nature. Unless nature is healed and saved, human beings cannot ultimately be healed and saved either, for human beings are natural beings. Concern about the things of Christ therefore requires us to go beyond the christology developed in modern times, which was christology in the framework of history, and compels us to develop *a christology of nature*. Like the patristic church's doctrine of the two natures, the cosmic christology of the epistles to the Ephesians and Colossians was dismissed by modern Western European theology as mythology and speculation. Anthropological christology fitted the modern paradigm 'history', and itself unintentionally became one factor in the modern destruction of nature; for the modern reduction of salvation to the salvation of the soul, or to authentic human existence, unconsciously abandoned nature to its disastrous exploitation by human beings. Only a growing awareness of the deadly ecological catastrophes in the world of nature leads to a recognition of the limitations of the modern paradigm 'history' and makes us enquire again into the wisdom of ancient cosmic christology and its physical doctrine of redemption.[1]

In the ancient world, cosmic christology confronted Christ the redeemer with a world of powers, spirits and gods. The proclamation of 'universal reconciliation' liberated believers from their fear of the world and their terror of demons. Today a cosmic christology has to confront Christ the redeemer with a nature which human beings have plunged into chaos, infected with poisonous waste and condemned to universal death; for it is only this Christ who can save men and women from their despair and preserve nature from annihilation. At that earlier time the theme was 'Christ and the cosmos'. Today it is 'Christ and chaos'. The realistic subject of discussion is no longer 'Christ and the forces of the stars' but Christ and the nature which has been reduced to a human rubbish heap. The modern age has given birth to the age of ecological catastrophes. A *new* cosmic christology must end the historical christology of modern times, not abolishing it but gathering it into something more which will overcome its limitations and preserve its truth. This is required of us if faith is to discover the therapeutic powers of Christ in the world's present situation, and allow them to be experienced.

In the context of the ecological crisis of modern civilization, this is not merely a matter of extending Christian ethics. It is first and foremost a conversion of Christian faith itself. The decisive question is often posed in the following form: is Christianity an anthropocentric or a cosmocentric religion? This question is thrown back at the Christian faith today by Christian missions and the dialogue with other religions. Unlike the Asiatic religions, which were called nature religions, the Christian faith was proclaimed as 'a personal religion', and then interpreted as 'a religion of history', because the personal and the historical dimensions fitted in best with the inner premises of the Western civilization which Christian missions helped to spread. It is therefore all too understandable that people in Europe and America who became alive to the ecological catastrophes should turn to the Asiatic nature religions in order to seek healing there for their wounded souls, and for their sick world as well.[2]

Yet in its original, biblical form Christianity was by no means personal, anthropocentric and historical in the modern Western sense. It was much more *a way* and a moving forward, in the discovery of 'the always greater Christ'. Christ is the first-born among many brethren – Christ is the first-born of the new humanity – Christ is the first-born of the whole creation: Jesus is Israel's messiah – Jesus is the Son of man of the nations – Jesus is the head of the reconciled cosmos: the body of Christ is the crucified and raised body of Jesus – the body of Christ is the church – the body of Christ is the whole cosmos. Christ existent as Jesus of Nazareth – Christ existent as 'the community of his people' – Christ existent as cosmos: *Christus semper maior*, Christ, always more and more.

Just because it is a call to personal faith in Christ, Christianity is not anthropocentric: it is really christocentric. Just because it exists as the community of Christians, Christianity is not ecclesiocentric; it is theocentric. Christocentricism and theocentricism include the cosmos; they do not exclude it. For in personal faith a rebirth is experienced which will one day extend to heaven and earth; and the church prefigures and foreshadows the temple of the Holy Spirit which the whole cosmos is destined to become. It is only the cosmic dimension which gives the human, historical experiences of Christ their all-embracing meaning. We can only think of Christ *inclusively*. Anyone who thinks of Christ *exclusively*, not for other people but against them, has not understood the Reconciler of the world. And yet a narrow, personally-centred and church-centred Christianity does exist, with its tragic incapacity to discover Christ in the cosmos – an incapacity which has made it guilty of destroying nature through its refusal to give help where help was needed.

The modern discussion about cosmic christology began long before there was any general awareness of the ecological crisis. It was initiated in 1961 in a splendid and moving address by the Lutheran theologian Joseph Sittler at the General Assembly of the World Council of Churches in New Delhi.[3]

Sittler was supposed to talk about 'the unity of the church', but instead he talked about the unity of the world, basing what he said on the cosmic Christ hymn in Col. 1.15–20. Christ is the foundation of all things (τὰ πάντα), so all things have access to his cosmic redemption. 'Why does Paul in this letter, and in the Epistle to the Ephesians too, expand his vocabulary so radically beyond its usual terminology?', he asked. 'Why are the concepts of guilt, sin, law, and the whole Jewish catalogue of demonic powers suddenly translated here into a general vocabulary, cosmic in its scope, so endlessly rich in cross-threads that it fills the furthest ends of metaphysical speculation with the energy and substance of Christ?' He answered his own question historically by saying that it was the error of the Colossians to assume that apart from Christ there were also 'thrones, principalities and powers' which had to be respected and reverenced. Against this dualistic division of the world into a good world and an evil one, Paul preached that 'everything is claimed for God and everything is related to Christ'. A doctrine of redemption only has any point if it moves within the wider sphere of a doctrine of creation.

From this, Sittler drew the self-critical conclusion that the dualism in the Western church between nature and grace (which he traced back to Augustine) does not do justice to the cosmic vision of Christ in the Colossians hymn. He wanted with Orthodox theology to go back to Irenaeus, in order to unite nature and grace in the vision of an all-comprehensive *recapitulatio mundi*. For according to Sittler, the Western church's distinction between nature and grace led to the contempt for nature which has resulted in her subjugation in modern times and her destruction today: 'The man of the Enlightenment could penetrate the realm of nature, and to all intents and purposes take it as his sphere of sovereignty, because grace had either ignored this sector or rejected it. And with every new conquest of nature a piece of God died; the sphere of grace diminished to the degree in which structures and processes in nature were claimed by the now autonomous human being.'[4] 'Men strut blasphemously about this wounded and threatened world as if it were their own property.' We are therefore living in a kairos in which Christ and chaos meet, and we must confront 'the threat to nature' with a 'christology of nature' in which the power of redemption does not stop short at the hearts of men and women and their morality, but extends to the whole of nature. Nature is 'the scene of grace and the sphere of redemption' just as much as history. A christology which is expanded to its cosmic dimensions will kindle 'a passion for the threatened earth'. 'Concern for the earth, for the sphere of nature as the scene of grace, the order of practical, material processes which bring people bread and peace – or deprive them of these things: all this is first and foremost an element of a christological attitude of obedience – and then a practical necessity.' Sittler closed with the moving image: 'This radioactive earth, so fruitful and so fragile, is his creation, our sister, and the true, embodied place where we can meet our brother in the light of Christ.'[5]

Sittler's lecture triggered off a lively discussion even at the assembly itself. Indian theologians such as Paul Devanandan and D. T. Niles picked up the conception of 'the cosmic Christ' but understood it to mean that Christ also testifies to himself in and through other religions, and was therefore always 'already ahead' of Christian missions.[6] Missions must consequently take up the dialogue with the people of other religions 'in the awareness that

Christ encounters us in them'. In the interests of the ancient church's
doctrine of the redemption of nature, Orthodox theologians welcomed and supported Sittler's turn from Augustine to Irenaeus and
his 'cosmic christology'. German criticism was confined to some
objections prompted by Lutheran dogmatics: 1. that sin was no
longer taken seriously; 2. that creation was unduly stressed compared with redemption; 3. that the eschatological testimony to the
coming kingdom of God was missing; 4. that 'the cosmic view of
being' allowed no room for an understanding of the justification of
the sinner; and 5. that Sittler had fallen victim to India's own self-
contained cosmology.[7]

To re-read Sittler's lecture after this is to be struck by the fact that
he does not touch on the problem of other religions at all. In turning
to cosmic christology his sole concern was nature, which is
threatened by human violence. He did not set cosmic christology
over against 'historical christology' but saw it as the universal
horizon against which history is experienced. The five Lutheran
objections I have listed miss the mark altogether in their criticism.
On the contrary, the personal and historical experiences of sin and
grace are themselves left in the air without the context of the mortally
threatened cosmos reconciled in Christ. Finally, talk about 'the
cosmic Christ' cannot mean that Christ has to be fitted into the laws
and rhythms of the cosmos as it is. It can only mean the very
contrary: the subordination of these cosmic powers and laws to
Christ's reconciling sovereignty. Christ is not integrated into the era
of this world, as some New Age thinkers would like to have it,
following C. G. Jung. 'In the fulness of time' the ages of this world
will be gathered into his eternity. Cosmic christology cannot identify
the lordship of Christ with the one supposedly existing 'harmony of
the world', for its starting point is the reconciliation of all things
through Christ; and the premise of this reconciliation is a state of
disrupted harmony in the world, world powers which are at enmity
with one another, and threatening chaos. Cosmic christology talks
about a reconciled, Christ-pervaded cosmos and in this way differs
from every other cosmic mysticism, old and new, whether Indian or
'post-modern'.

Christology can only arrive at its completion at all in a cosmic
christology. All other christologies fall short and do not provide an
adequate content for the experiences of the Easter witnesses with the
risen Christ. If Christ is the first-born from the dead, then he cannot

be merely 'the new Adam' of a new humanity. He must also be understood as the first-born of the whole creation. All things are created in the vista that stretches forward to the messiah, for the messiah will redeem all things for their own truth, and will gather them for the kingdom of God, thus completing and perfecting creation. But this means that the risen Christ is not present only in the Spirit of faith and in the Spirit that animates the community of his people. Nor is he present merely in hidden form in world history. He is also immanently efficacious in 'the heart of creation', as Teilhard de Chardin put it. He is present not only in the human victims of world history but in victimized nature too.

Karl Barth cautiously considered this possibility but did not pursue it. Talking about the hymn in Colossians, he asked 'whether we do not have to take into account a third form of [Christ's] existence', in addition to his being with God and his being with the community of his people: 'Does He not already exist and act and achieve and work also as the *Pantocrator*, as the $\varkappa\varepsilon\phi\alpha\lambda\grave{\eta}\ \acute{\upsilon}\pi\grave{\varepsilon}\varrho\ \pi\acute{\alpha}\nu\tau\alpha$, as the One who alone has first and final power in the cosmos? Concealed though He may be in the cosmos and not yet recognized by it as by His community, does He not already exist in it with supreme reality, with no less reality than He does at the right hand of God the Father or in His community?'[8] Barth was thinking here of Calvin's doctrine of the Holy Spirit as 'the principle of life which rules . . . in the whole created cosmos', and he concluded that Christ's parousia, his 'coming forth . . . from the hiddenness of God' must also be expected as 'His coming forth from His hiddenness in world-occurrence'. If Barth had followed up these ideas about a cosmic christology, his distinction between creation and covenant, nature and grace, body and soul, would probably not have ended up in so rigorous and one-sided an emphasis on covenant, grace and the soul.

Let us take up Barth's passing reflection and develop it. If the risen Christ is already the pantocrator now, in a hidden sense, because he has overcome hostility in the whole creation and brings reconciliation into all its different spheres, is he not then to be identified with 'the hidden subject of nature', about which Ernst Bloch talked?[9] 'The Lord' is a designation for a determining subject. Christ's lordship consists in his conquest of enmity and violence and in the spread of reconciliation and harmonious, happily lived life. Reconciliation binds together what is separated and confers peace. It quickens what has been dead and petrified. Christ's sphere of sovereignty is the whole creation, visible and invisible – all the spheres, therefore, by which humanity is surrounded and in which human beings partici-pate – even the spheres which are remote from human beings because they are inaccessible to them, such as the heavens, the worlds of divine potencies.

Christ's parousia in glory cannot be thought of and expected in merely historical terms, as the end of this world time. It must also be conceived of and awaited as the final coming forth of the Pantocrator hidden in the cosmos, and as the finally accomplished manifestation of the hidden subject nature in a reconciled, redeemed and hence newly created cosmos. To put it simply: the coming of Christ in glory is accompanied by a transformation of the whole of nature into its eternal discernible identity as God's creation. Not only the heavens but the earth too will provide the evident signs. This eschatological transformation of nature was prefigured in Christian tradition, not merely in the sacraments but also in the parable of the earthly spring:

> Lay out your leavés lustily,
> From death take life now at the least
> In worship of that Prince worthy
> *Qui nobis puer natus est.*[10]

In the final 'greening of the earth' the cosmic Wisdom-Christ will come forth from the heart of creation, setting that creation in the light of God's glory.

2. Early Christian Tradition

In Paul's own epistles we already find statements about the cosmic Christ, when he is talking about Christ's mediation in creation. In I Cor. 8.6 he says: 'For us there is only one God, the Father, *from whom* are all things and *for whom* we exist, and one Lord, Jesus Christ, *through whom* are all things and *through whom* we exist.' If all things are 'from God' the creator, and 'through' Christ the Lord, then Christ is interpreted as 'the creator-mediator' and identified with the Wisdom who was beside God *before* the creation of this world and *through* whom God made all things (Prov. 8). The knowledge that Christ was the mediator in creation gave Christians the freedom to live everywhere in the lordship of Christ, and no longer to pay any attention to the idols of this world (I Cor. 8.1–13).

For Paul, the lordship of the risen Christ who is present in the life-giving Spirit is for God's sake universal in its trend, and knows no other gods or lords beside. The pre-Pauline hymn in the Epistle to the Philippians already praises the universal lordship of the exalted Christ (Phil. 2.9–11). The missionary preaching in the Acts of the Apostles, especially Paul's Areopagus address, proclaims Christ in universal, cosmic dimensions. Unlike the preaching addressed to the Jews, early Christian preaching to the Gentiles is universalist in what it says about creation and the resurrection of the dead.[11] Here Christ is hardly presented as Israel's messiah any more. He is rather humanity's 'new Adam'. And God is not so much the God of Israel's patriarchs as the creator of the universe 'in whom we live and move and have our being' (Acts 17.27).

The *epistemological foundation* for the cosmic Christ 'through whom are all things' is in my view the Easter experience of the risen One. What was 'seen' there goes beyond all historical remembrances and experiences, and touches the innermost constitution of creation itself. According to Rom. 4.17, resurrection and creation are closely linked. The God who raises the dead is the same God who as creator calls into being the things that are not; and the One who called the world into existence out of nothing is the God who raises the dead. Beginning and end, creation and resurrection, belong together and must not be separated from one another; for the glorification of creation through the raising of the dead is the perfecting of creation, and creation is aligned towards the resurrection of the dead. The statements about creation do not 'serve' redemption,[12] and redemption is not merely 'the restoration' of creation, whose original order has become deranged.[13]

The light of the resurrection appearances, then, was already identified very early on with the light of the first day of the new creation; and if this is so, then the One who 'appeared' in this light as the first in the resurrection of the dead is also 'the first-born of all creation' (Col. 1.15). 'First' does not mean the created being who is first in the numerical sense; it means 'the image of the invisible God' who 'is before all creation, and in whom all things hold together' (Col. 1.15,17). According to Heb. 1.3, this 'first-born' is 'the brightness of his glory and the express image of his person, upholding the universe by his word of power' (Heb. 1.3). The same is said about the divine Logos in John 1.1–3. This is a reference to the Wisdom messiah[14] *through* whom and *for* whom God has created all things. According to Prov. 8, 'Wisdom' is God's 'comrade in creation'.[15] She is not yet called 'first-born', but she is 'before all things, from eternity' (Ecclus. 1.4). All things owe their existence to her, for they have come into being through her mediation. The Creator 'makes fast' the universe through the immanent presence of his Wisdom in all things. The Christ who annihilates death in his resurrection from the dead reveals himself in the dimensions of this creation Wisdom, and was already understood in this sense very early on.

The later Nicene formula 'begotten not made' is not yet found in this terminological form in the New Testament. But in substance it is completely congruent with this creation Wisdom which 'appears' in the risen Christ. The Wisdom of creation is pre-existent in all things, because all things are created through her. She is the inexhaustible creative ground of cosmic history. But she is not merely creation's mediatrix. She is also its sustainer.[16] All things exist not merely *through* Wisdom but *in* her. She is therefore also *inexistant*, or inherent, in all things. This second aspect is often overlooked in the doctrines of creation. God creates the world and he 'makes it fast' and secures it, because it is in constant danger of disintegrating into its separate parts. This making-fast of heaven and earth can be understood as God's covenant with his creation. Wisdom gives all things their cohesion and the harmony which lends them their abiding quality. These ideas have a long pre-history in Platonism and Stoicism, and in Philo. The idea that the cosmos is a great universal organism, a world-body with a world-soul, also derives from pre-Christian hellenistic Judaism. In this conceptual world, 'Wisdom' is the secret bond of creation. She suffers the enmity of created things, their lack of order and their mortality. In her patience she holds together everything that is, quickening it 'new every morning'. Logos christology is originally Wisdom christology, and is as such cosmic christology.

The *ontological foundation* for cosmic christology is Christ's death. In the light of the cosmic dimensions of his resurrection, his death on the cross takes on universal significance. According to the Epistle to the Ephesians, through his death on the cross Christ has 'slain enmity' and 'reconciled' Jews and Gentiles with God (2.16). According to the Epistle to the Colossians, 'all things' in heaven and on earth are reconciled with God through him, since he has 'made peace through the blood of his cross' (1.20). Christ did not die for the reconciliation of men and women. He died for the reconciliation of the cosmos (II Cor. 5.19). There is nothing poetical about the concept of reconciliation. It is a legal term and means the restoration of a legally established association which has been infringed. In this respect the difference between Paul's own letters and the epistles to the Ephesians and Colossians is not very great.[17] There are probably two trains of thought leading from the knowledge of personal reconciliation with God in faith to the perception of the reconciliation of the world:

On the one hand, the logical outcome of God's raising of Christ and Christ's installation as Lord is his sovereignty over the universe; for God would not be the creator of all things if he did not desire the redemption of them all: 'For Christ must reign until he has put all his enemies under his feet.' It is this divine *must* which brings Paul to the eschatological horizon of Christ the pantocrator (I Cor. 15.28). It is the bodily 'fulness of the Godhead' (Col. 2.9) which burst all the barriers and 'must' lay hold of all things and redeem them.

On the other hand, there is no personal redemption without the redemption of nature – both human nature, and the nature of the earth with which human beings are indivisibly bound up because they live together with nature. The connecting link between the redemption personally experienced in faith and the redemption of the whole creation is the *embodiment* of human beings. Together with the whole sighing creation, we wait 'for the redemption of our bodies' (Rom. 8.23) – the redemption, that is, from the fate of death. The vision of cosmic redemption through Christ is therefore not a speculation. It emerges logically from the christology and the anthropology. Without these wider horizons, the God of Jesus Christ would not be the creator of the world, and redemption would become a gnostic myth hostile to the body and the world.

But the idea of cosmic reconciliation and cosmic peace presupposes cosmic conflicts, cosmic unrest and a universal deadly threat to the cosmos through chaos; if this were not so, it would be impossible to talk about a reconciliation 'of all things'. If reconciliation comes about through God the creator, we even have to talk about the 'sin' of the whole creation, which has isolated itself from the foundation of its existence and the wellspring of its life, and has fallen victim to universal death. But hardly anything is said in any detail about this sombre background to the reconciliation of the world through Christ.[18] Later theological notions about 'the fallen world', 'creation in chains' or 'the princes of this world' who are anti-God are not very specific, but they do say that the world as it exists at present is no longer God's good creation, and is not yet the kingdom of God either. It is in need of redemption. Because the worship of cosmic forces was a part of their environment, the Christian congregations in Ephesus and Colossae had apparently found themselves faced with the question about the scope of Christ's lordship. The Christian answer was that since Christ is the mediator in the creation of these powers, he is also their redeemer, and therefore their true Lord (Eph. 1.21; Col. 2.10). This meant that in the worship of Christ as reconciler of the world, these cosmic powers lose their threatening and fascinating power and become spirits that can be put at the service of Christ's universal peace. The practical result was that in those multi-religious cities of the ancient world the Christian community no longer came forward as yet one more religion, devoted to a hitherto unknown deity. Instead it acted as the peace-giving and unifying community of the Creator and Reconciler of all things. Its missionary task was not to enter into a competitive religious struggle. The purpose was integration into the reconciliation and peace which was the eschatological horizon of the cosmos. The Christ proclaimed to the people of other religions – 'the heathen' – is 'the Christ *in us*, the hope of glory' (Col. 1.27), and according to the Letters to the Ephesians and Colossians, this hope is the expectation of the cosmic Christ through whom heaven and earth and all things will find peace.

According to Paul, 'reconciliation' is the beginning of the new creation, not its final goal. 'For if we were reconciled to God by the death of his Son, *how much more*, now that we are reconciled, shall we be saved by his life' (Rom. 5.10). This logic of the 'how much more'[19] has to be carried over into the idea of the reconciliation of the world. The reconciliation 'of all things' through his blood on the cross is not the goal, but the beginning of the gathering together of 'all things' under Christ who is 'the head'; and hence the beginning of the new creation of all things through the annihilation of death itself. Elsewhere Paul applies the image of 'the head' to the relationship between Christ and the community of his people. Here it is used for the gathering together of all things through the Wisdom out of which they were first created. All things came into being out of this Creator Wisdom, and through it all things will be redeemed for the eternal peace of creation.

When the image of 'head and body' is transferred from the church to the cosmos, this cannot be understood to mean that one day, through the growth and spread of the church, the whole cosmos will turn into the church. On the contrary: the church must be seen as the beginning of the reconciled cosmos which has arrived at peace.[20] It is the historical microcosm for the macrocosm which has become God's temple. It is the cosmic dimensions of the church that are meant, not the 'churchifying' of the world. As 'the body of Christ', the church is always already *the church of the whole creation* here and now. It points away from itself to the glory of God which fills heaven and earth: 'The Most High does not dwell in houses made with hands; as the prophet says, "Heaven is my throne, and earth is my footstool. What house will you build for me, says the Lord, or what is the place of my rest? Did not my hand make all these things?"' (Acts 7.48f.; Isa. 66.1f.). God is to be adored and worshipped in the temple of his creation: that is the meaning of every church and every cathedral built by human hands. It is only as the church of the whole creation that the Christian community is anything more than a sect or a religious society. If God is not worshipped in creation, he is not properly known in the church either. The true church of Christ is the healing beginning of the healed creation in the midst of a sick world.

Yet at this point it is important to notice the difference between Paul and the writers of Ephesians and Colossians. What for Paul still stands under 'the eschatological proviso' (in Ernst Käsemann's phrase) and is reserved for Christ's eschatological future, is for these hymns in Ephesians and Colossians a present reality, an already implemented fact. According to Eph. 1.22, God 'has put all things under his feet and has made him the head of the church over all things'. According to I Cor. 15.28 this is the end that still has to be awaited: 'When all things *shall be* subjected to him . . .' Consequently, while Eph. 1.21 says that the exalted Christ already 'rules' over them all – principalities, dominion, power and authority – not only in this world but in the future world too, I Cor. 15.24, 26 states that Christ will *at the end abolish* 'every rule and every authority and power. The last enemy to be destroyed is death.' Where Paul talks about the powers of death which are hostile to God and to life, the writer to the Ephesians evidently has in mind powers of creation that are good, which will be put right in Christ's rule of peace.

It is not possible to harmonize the two viewpoints and there is no point in trying to do so. But one thing must be noted: the powers of death which are hostile to God and life are not going to be reconciled and will not be integrated even into Christ's rule of peace. His rule means that they will be eliminated from creation. Otherwise cosmic christology would do away with the foundation of all christology, which is Christ's resurrection from the dead and his conquest of the power of death; and its result would be to induce resignation in the face of these forces of transience. But in God's creation the risen Christ cannot co-exist with death. One of the two must give way. We shall therefore interpret what is said about 'the gathering together of all things in Christ' (ἀνακεφαλαίωσις τῶν πάντων) in the light of the resurrection of the body.

Cosmic christology adds to the historical titles for Christ – Son of God and Son of man – the other titles Logos, Wisdom, *the life of the world*: 'All things were made through him, and without him was not anything made that was made. In him was life' (John 1.3, 4a).

3. An Outline for a Differentiated Cosmic Christology

Previous cosmic christology has shared the one-sidedness of the traditional doctrine of creation. That is to say, it understands by creation only creation-in-the-beginning (*creatio originalis*) but not continuous creation (*creatio continua*) or the consummated new creation of all things (*nova creatio*). Creation and redemption then cleave apart and become two separate things. Creation is 'down-graded' into being a preparation for redemption, or redemption is reduced to the restoration of creation-in-the-beginning. In order to acquire a comprehensive concept of creation, we have talked about a unified creation process, which begins with creation-in-the-beginning, continues in the history of creation, and is perfected in the new creation of all things.[21] In a similar way we shall interpret Christ's mediation in creation in three separate strands or movements: 1. Christ as the ground of the creation of all things (*creatio originalis*); 2. Christ as the moving power in the evolution of creation (*creatio continua*); and 3. Christ as the redeemer of the whole creation process (*creatio nova*). By proceeding in this way we are really taking up the old Protestant doctrine of Christ's threefold office (*officium regium Christi*), developing it in the context of today's recognitions: Christ rules in the kingdom of nature (*regnum naturae*), in the kingdom of grace (*regnum gratiae*) and in the kingdom of glory (*regnum gloriae*).[22]

This integral viewpoint makes it possible to avoid the one-sided stresses which have hitherto hampered cosmic christology. If Christ is described only as the ground of creation, this world, which is often so chaotic, is enhanced in an illusory way, and transfigured into a harmony and a home. If Christ is described solely as the 'evolutor' (Teilhard de Chardin's term), the evolutionary process itself takes on redemptive meaning for the initial creation; but the myriads of faulty developments and the victims of this process fall hopelessly by the wayside. If, finally, we look simply at the coming Christ who is to redeem the world, we see only this world in its need of redemption, and nothing of the goodness of the Creator and the traces of his beauty in all things.

§2 CHRIST – THE GROUND OF CREATION

According to the conceptions of cosmic christology and the doctrine of the messianic Wisdom, all things have been created through the Wisdom messiah and in him acquire their continuance. This Christ is the divine foundation of creation and therefore its inexhaustibly creative ground; and he is this in a threefold sense: 1. All things from God are created 'through him' and through him find their forms and the community that binds them together; 2. All things from God are made fast 'in him', their lives and existence being sustained against the threat of chaos by his presence in them; 3. All things are 'for him' – that is to say all things are created for his sake, and for him all things are waiting.

From Johann Gerhard onwards, the old Protestant, or Lutheran, doctrine of the *officium regnum Christi* said that Christ exercises his lordship already, in the sustaining and ruling of the world. Because everything is created through him, he preserves everything and rules it so that it draws towards his goal. In the *regnum potentiae* his activities are *conservatio* and *gubernatio*, preserving and governing.[23] The Reformed theologians added that Christ exercised his function over the world (*munus regium*) in the *regnum essentiale, naturale seu universale*, as the eternal Son together with the Father and the Holy Spirit. Here, it was maintained, Christ rules through 'power', not through 'grace', in order that all creatures in heaven and on earth, and even his enemies, may be made to serve the welfare of his kingdom.[24]

1. *Creation through the Spirit and the Word*

If all things (τὰ πάντα) are created by a God, then *a transcendent unity* precedes their diversity and their historicity. It is not a matter of many worlds belonging to many gods or powers. This is *the one* creation of *the one* God. If all things are created by the one God *through* his Wisdom/Logos and are held together in that, then underlying their diversity in space and time is an *immanent unity* in which they all exist together. Their unity does not come into being in a subsequent process, emerging from their relationships and the warp and weft into which they are bound. All things have their genesis in a fundamental underlying unity, which is called God's Wisdom, Spirit or Word. The fellowship of all created beings goes ahead of their differentiations and the specific forms given to them, and is therefore the foundation underlying their diversity. If God withdraws this foundation, all things disintegrate and become a nothingness. If God lends it fresh force, their forms are renewed (Ps. 104.29f.). The Jewish and Christian doctrines about Wisdom or the Logos as mediator in creation are in direct contradiction to the atomism of Democritus. The beginning was not the particles. The beginning was 'the symmetry', the concord. 'The elementary particles embody the symmetries. They are its simplest representations, but they are merely a result of the symmetries.'[25] Jewish and Christian doctrines of creation have therefore always maintained the idea of 'the unity of nature'.

If we look back at the creation story told in the Priestly Writing, we find the immanent *unity of creation* expressed in two formulas: 1. In the formula of *creation through the divine Word*: 'God said, "Let there be light"; and there was light' (Gen. 1.3). 2. In the presupposition for creation through the Word, a presupposition which has received too little notice: *the vibration of the present Spirit of God*: 'The Spirit of God hovered over the face of the waters' (Gen. 1.2). The Hebrew word *ruach* is better translated as 'wind' or 'breath' than Spirit. The Hebrew word *rahaph* is generally translated 'hover' or 'brood'. But according to Deut. 32.11 and Jer. 23.9 it has rather the meaning of vibrating, quivering, moving and exciting. If this is correct, then we should not think only of the image of a fluttering or brooding dove. We should think of the fundamental resonances of music out of which sounds and rhythms emerge.[26] In thinking about 'creation through the Word', we should not therefore think primarily in metaphors of command and obedience. A better image is *the song of creation*. The word names, differentiates and appraises. But the breath is the same in all the words, and binds the words together. So the Creator differentiates his creatures through his creative Word and joins them through his Spirit, who is the sustainer of all his words. In the quickening breath and through the form-giving word, the Creator sings out his creatures in the sounds and rhythms in which he has his joy and his good pleasure. That is why there is something like *a cosmic liturgy* and *music of the spheres*.

> Sleeps a song in every thing
> That is dreaming still unheard.
> And the world begins to sing
> If you find the magic word.[26a]

The ancient Pythagorean symbol of the music of the spheres and the harmony of the universe already pictures the unity between music and the cosmos. In considering how the unity of creation is to be understood, the Priestly Writer suggests that the creative and distinguishing word of God is preceded by the presence of the pulsating breath of God which translates the divine energies into vibrations. Cosmic vibration is the origin and ground of all forms of energy and matter in the cosmos. The vibrating breath of God is, as it were, the note to which the creation of the world is tuned. We therefore have to say that God creates all things through his defining and differentiating Word in the primordial vibrancies of his Spirit. If the Spirit of God is understood as the quickening breath of God, then no Word goes out from God other than in the vibrancies and the keynote of his Spirit. In the unity of created things, Word and Spirit complement one another. The Word specifies and differentiates through its efficacy; the Spirit binds and creates symmetries, harmonies and concord through its presence. God is 'He who breathes through all creation', says one of our hymns. Through the Spirit and the Word, God communicates himself to his creation and enters into it. His Spirit, immanent in the world, is the pulse of the universe. In the later Wisdom literature, Word and Spirit are used interchangeably.[27] The New Testament writings do not make any systematic distinction either, between Word and Spirit in creation. The two together circumscribe the mystery of God in the world and stress Christ's mediatorship in creation, out of which all things receive both the fellowship that binds them and their own unique character.

These two aspects also make it clear that the creation is not merely a 'work' of 'God's hands', but that through his vibrant, quickening Spirit, God already dwells in it; for through his ceaselessly uttering and creating Word he is the foundation and continuance of all things. God is the innermost life of the world. The creation psalms tell us that creation-in-the-beginning was already understood as 'God's temple'. Heaven and earth are his home, the home in which he desires to dwell and arrive at his rest. And in designating the cause and basis of creation, this also names its purpose and end: God's endless sabbath. In the apocalyptic writings this is described as the new creation in whose midst 'the heavenly Jerusalem' stands, as the cosmic temple which is able to receive the unveiled glory of God, so that the Creator can dwell in his creation and can arrive at his rest in it, and so that all created beings may find their happiness in his infinite abundance.

2. *The Securing of Creation*

The second aspect of mediation in creation is its *securing* and preservation.[28] This idea leads over from creation-in-the-beginning to continuing creation. *Conservatio mundi* can be understood to mean that God sustains what he has created and watches over his once created world in order to preserve it from the chaos that unremittingly threatens it. But *conservatio mundi* can also be understood as *creatio continua*: in every instant the creative God reiterates his primal 'yes' to his creation. But both conceptions are related to creation-in-the-beginning, and are therefore one-sided. They do not permit us to think forward to the consummation of creation. Neither idea about the preservation of creation expresses a positive relationship to the redemption of all things. The *regnum gratiae* is cut off from the *regnum naturae* or *potentiae* and unrelated to it. But this obscures the grace which is already shown in the preserving and sustaining of creation, human sin and cosmic disorder notwithstanding. God preserves his creation from corruption because, and inasmuch as, he has patience with what he has created. His patience creates time for his creatures. His longsuffering leaves them space. His patience, which is prepared to suffer, and his waiting forbearance are the virtues of his hope for the turning back and homecoming of his creatures to the kingdom of his glory. The God who preserves the world endures the self-isolation of his creatures and puts up with their contradictions, keeping their future open for them through his suffering and his silence, and conceding them the opportunities for conversion which they neglect. *Conservatio mundi* does not belong only to the kingdom of nature. It is already part of the kingdom of grace. In the preservation of the world, nature and grace are so closely interwoven that it is impossible to talk about the one without talking about the other.

3. The Renewal of Creation

If we think about the aspect of the preservation of the world which is orientated towards the future, then *creatio continua* is not merely the securing of the original creation because God holds it fast. It is at the same time already *the anticipation of the new creation* of all things. Continuous creation is creation's ongoing history. In this historical creation God 'renews the face of the earth' (Ps. 104.30), looking towards the final new creation of all things. He creates justice for those who have never known justice. He raises up the humble and obscure. He fulfils his promises in historical experiences.

The divine creative and redeeming activity experienced in this way in the human world has its hidden correspondences in the world of nature. What we see in the world of nature is not merely God's activity as preserver, but his activity as innovator too. The history of nature displays not merely the preservation of species but also their evolution. Continuous and contingent happening mark the historical process not merely of the human world but of the natural world as well. This means that it is possible to discover even in the history of nature parables and true symbols for the future of creation in its completion and perfecting. In nature's preservation and development, God already prepares the consummation of his creation, for his grace thrusts forward to the revelation of his glory. Paul sees this in imprisoned nature's 'sighing' and 'longing' for liberty in God's glory. The men and women who in faith experience 'the first fruits of Spirit', recognize the same longing of the Spirit as the driving force and torment in everything. The mediators of creation – the Spirit and the Word – wait and strive in all things for the liberation of them all. So 'creation in chains' is not merely in need of redemption. It is also consumed by hunger and thirst for the righteousness of God.

§3 CHRIST – EVOLUTION'S DRIVING FORCE OR ITS VICTIM?

It was Teilhard de Chardin especially who interpreted the continuation and completion of creation through Christ with ideas taken from the theory of evolution. In fact to a considerable degree he identified the two processes. For him, the cosmic Christ is 'the Christ of evolution'.[29] Faith in God and faith in the world coincide in faith in the universal Christ, who drives and beckons the world forward to its perfecting. Karl Rahner adopted this viewpoint in his famous essay 'Christology within an Evolutionary View of the World',[30] in which he elevated the concept of 'self-transcendence' into being the fundamental universal concept for ongoing creation, for the unique character of human beings, and for the nature of Christ. My purpose here is neither to give a detailed account nor to enter into a detailed discussion of these evolution christologies. Our concern is simply the limited question of how the elements of truth they contain can be absorbed into a differentiated cosmic christology.

1. Teilhard de Chardin: Christus Evolutor

Teilhard took up the vision of the cosmic Christ from the Epistle to the Colossians, wishing to expand the church's one-sided presentation of *Christus redemptor* through that universal completer of creation whom he called *Christus evolutor*.[31] If the Christian doctrine of redemption is related only to original sin, it offers no perspectives for the completion of creation through a gathering together of all things under the head, Christ, and through their entry into that fulness of God which will one day be 'all in all'. But Teilhard discovered 'the creative side of redemption',[32] and saw this discovery as the step forward to a new theology. The completion of creation in the divine unification is higher than the redemption of the world from its sins, and is redemption's goal. 'Christ-the-Redeemer being fulfilled, without this in any way detracting from his suffering aspect, in the dynamic plenitude of a CHRIST-THE-EVOLVER.'[33]

In the interests of this view, Teilhard transferred salvation history as it was understood by Christian faith to the history of life and the cosmos, understanding this history of nature as evolution from the simple to the manifold, from what is individual to what is shared, from the lifeless to the living, and to ever more complex forms of living awareness. For him, salvation history and the evolution of life coincided. He saw the appearance of human beings in the framework of the evolution of life in general. Human beings are the organic continuation of that development which in the realm of the living – the biosphere – has proceeded ever since the beginning of life, and which appears in the very organization of matter. With human beings a new phase of life begins, for human beings are reflective, conscious beings. 'We are carried along by an advancing wave of consciousness.'[34] What comes into being is what the language of evolutionary theory calls the noosphere.

But where, then, is the development of the human awareness leading? Teilhard used Nietzsche's words about the 'superman' and the development of a 'super-consciousness', and said that, in analogy to the forms of organization found at the other stages of evolution, the compression of the many leads to an evolutionary leap into a new quality. A new form of organization is evolving which will lift humanity into the sphere of 'the ultrahuman': 'The ultra-human perfection which neo-humanism envisages for Evolution will coincide in concrete terms with the crowning of the Incarnation awaited by all Christians.'[35] The completion of evolution in this transcendent sphere corresponds to 'the completion of God' in the visible world. For the 'divinization' of the world is simply the reverse side of God's incarnation, and vice versa. United, self-transcending humanity ends in God, while at the same time God 'incarnates himself' in the process of this development.

By incarnation Teilhard understood a process which is not exhausted in the one, unique historical person of Jesus of Nazareth, but which strives towards the 'Christification' of the whole cosmos.[36] Because he understood the reality of the world as evolution, he saw this processual incarnation of God 'as coming from what is in front of us'. It is not God in heaven who saves his fallen earth; it is 'le dieu en avant' – the God ahead – who lends the cosmos the impulse towards completion, because he desires to draw everything to himself and into his own fulness. The incarnation of God in Christ is to be understood as the beginning of a new phase of humanity, and hence as a new phase in the evolution of life in general. Christ is the beginning of the divinization of humanity, which will also bring with it the deification of the cosmos; for in this cosmic Christ the becoming-human of the universe and the becoming-human of God converge. If the process of the humanization of the earth and the humanization of humanity is thought through to the end, then we discover at the peak of the anthropogenesis that final goal and focus of the consciousness which he calls the Omega Point. He asks if this is not now the ideal place from which the Christ whom we worship can radiate, and answers: 'Evolution preserves Christ (by making him possible), and at the same time Christ preserves evolution (by making it specific and desirable).'[37]

In the face of this bold speculation, which goes far beyond the bounds of any personal experience, we must remember that for Teilhard the practical point of departure for the theological outlook on the secular process of evolution is the eucharistic 'transubstantiation' of the natural elements of the material bread and wine into the body and blood of Christ. It is the experience of the church's eucharist which is the source of his vision of cosmic 'eucharistization' – the transformation of the cosmos into Christ's body.[38] Ultimately his christology of evolution is nothing less than the vision of the cosmic eucharist through which God becomes part of the world and the world is deified.

Theological criticism of Teilhard was directed not so much at his cosmic christology as at his largely uncritical absorption of evolutionary theory into a theology of salvation history. Some people reproached him for overlooking the power of evil in human history in his cosmic optimism. In this form the objection will hardly stand up.[39] But in his firm faith in progress Teilhard does seem to have overlooked the ambiguity of evolution itself, and therefore to have paid no attention to evolution's victims. Evolution always means *selection*. Many living things are sacrificed in order that 'the fittest' – which means the most effective and the most adaptable – may survive. In this way higher and increasingly complex life systems, which can react to changed environments, undoubtedly develop. But in the same process milliards of living things fall by the wayside and disappear into evolution's rubbish bin. Evolution is not merely a constructive affair on nature's part. It is a cruel one too. It is a kind of biological execution of the Last Judgment on the weak, the sick and 'the unfit'. If men and women adopt the same way of doing things, what we very soon have is 'euthanasia' – 'the killing of valueless life'. Teilhard can therefore never have taught 'universal reconciliation' in whatever form, for this contradicts the whole idea of evolution.[40]

Teilhard did not merely consider that natural catastrophes have a point in the interests of the greater evolution. With the help of the evolutionary idea, he continually also tried to wring a meaning out of the experience of human catastrophes. In the letters he wrote during the First World War to friends shattered by the senselessness of the massacre, he tried to convert them to a positive view of the war, as a noble contribution to natural evolution.[41] When the first atomic bomb was dropped on Hiroshima on 6 August 1945, Teilhard was filled with enthusiastic admiration for the scientific and technological advance which this achievement of a scientific super-brain acting in teamwork had brought humanity. He believed that the control of atomic power would promote the evolution of humanity and the human consciousness in a hitherto unheard-of way. Here Teilhard gave no thought to Hiroshima's hundred thousand dead and the people who are still dying today from radiation damage. He also took a purely positive view of the hydrogen bomb tests on Bikini: 'For all their military trappings, the recent explosions at Bikini herald the birth into the world of Mankind both inwardly and outwardly pacified. They proclaim the coming of the *Spirit of the Earth*.'[42] Trusting in 'life's planetary instinct for survival', he brushed aside the possibility that humanity could ever suffer a nuclear catastrophe: 'The earth is more likely to stop turning than is Mankind, as a whole, likely to stop *organizing and unifying* itself.'[43] He was incapable of recognizing the possibility of an atomic apocalypse, about which Günter Anders, Albert Schweitzer and Karl Jaspers were talking even in 1958, because his confidence in the world made him incapable of considering humanity as a whole to be mortal.

For Teilhard, the perspectives of evolution were evidently so vast that while he was no doubt able to join together the remotest points of their beginning and their goal, he found it difficult to perceive what was close and closest. 'We still have several million years in front of us,' he wrote from Peking in 1941, thinking of the stage of evolution next to be reached in the socialization and totalization of humanity. He did not see that time is running out, because the ecological catastrophes which this very socialization and humanization are producing could very well put an abrupt end to any further evolution on humanity's part.

The cosmic perspectives and the sights set on evolution's remotest goals also mean that the ever-'greater Christ' also departs further and further from Jesus of Nazareth; while the point in time in the cosmic development which Teilhard calls Omega Point allows the recollections of salvation history to fade away and be forgotten – both

Jewish remembrances of the God of Abraham, Isaac and Jacob, and
Christian remembrances of the Father of Jesus Christ. But if this is a
trend in Teilhard's thinking, the outcome is really a cosmic
gnosticism which makes historical faith antiquated.

The real theological problem, however, is to be found in the
content of his christology. It is true that with his idea about the
Christus evolutor he wished merely to augment the Christian
doctrine about *Christus redemptor*, so as to bring out the creative
side of redemption, which had been overlooked for so long. But
would he not then also have had to describe the redemptive side of
creation's completion? A *Christus evolutor* without *Christus redemptor* is nothing other than a cruel, unfeeling *Christus selector*, a
historical world-judge without compassion for the weak, and a
breeder of life uninterested in the victims. There is certainly a history
of ongoing creation; there are evolutions to richer and more complex
forms of life; there are socialization processes in atoms, molecules,
cells and organisms, in animals and human beings; all this is
undeniable. Here the creative energy of the ground of the whole
cosmos can also be theologically perceived. The process of creation is
not yet finished. As long as the time of creation lasts, something new
is continually being created, and always will be. But in this history of
creation there is also dying, violent death, mass extermination and
the extinction of whole species through natural catastrophes and
epidemics. In our special human history there are undeniably
elements of progress; but they are equivocal. The history of every
form of progress has its other side in the history of its victims. The
history of the victors, the survivors and the well-adapted 'fittest' has
its price in the suppression of those who are called 'the unfit'. The
various processes of evolution in nature and humanity can only be
brought into a positive relationship to Christ, the perfecter of
creation, if Christ is perceived as a victim among evolution's other
victims. The crucified One was present in the Spirit, not among the
inventors and constructors of the atomic bomb, or those responsible
for it. He was present in the Spirit among the dead of Hiroshima.
There is no conceivable human evolution in the near or remote future
which could give any meaning to the mass deaths of the fallen and the
murdered in the two world wars of this century. Nor can a peace
secured by way of a universal nuclear deterrent provide any justification for the victims of the dropping of the atomic bomb. Not even
the best of all possible stages of evolution justifies acquiescence in

evolution's victims, as the unavoidable fertilizers of that future – not even the Omega Point, with its divine fulness.

There is therefore no meaningful hope for the future of creation unless 'the tears are wiped from every eye'. But they can only be wiped away when the dead are raised, and when the victims of evolution experience justice through the resurrection of nature. Evolution in its ambiguity has no such redemptive efficacy and therefore no salvific significance either. If Christ is to be thought of in conjunction with evolution, he must become evolution's redeemer.

2. *Karl Rahner: Self-Transcendence*

In the essay to which we have referred, Karl Rahner was not concerned with evolutionary theory as such, and not even with christology as such. What interested him was the limited question of whether christology fitted into – or could be fitted into – the evolutionary world view which he presupposed as a given fact.[44] He asked about a possible 'inward affinity, a kind of identity of style', and about the relation to one another of christology and evolution. Since he worked out this relation as a Thomist theologian and philosopher, not as a scientist, he neither felt dependent on Teilhard nor bound to his views. At the end of his outline he himself raised a few critical theological questions, and also perhaps questions expected of the magisterium, in order to forestall the objections he anticipated would come from Rome.

With the concept of self-transcendence, Rahner found a term open for analogy – a term which can be applied to all levels of being, as a way of understanding the transitions to stages which are higher and more elaborately organized, and hence more complex. Self-transcendence is the effect of the Spirit, which already dwells in matter, and which has to be understood as divine Spirit because it strives towards the 'infinite mystery' called God. But if this Spirit is God's Spirit, then, even seen from God's point of view, this self-transcendence always already involves God's own *communication of himself*: 'God does not merely create something other than himself – he gives himself to this other. The world receives God, the Infinite and ineffable mystery, to such an extent that he himself is its innermost life.'[45]

If this Spirit is already efficacious in the self-transcendence of matter, then the relationship between matter and Spirit has to be viewed as history, and that means also as a *becoming* and as an *evolution* to ever higher forms. The history of nature transcends itself in the direction of human history. In the human being and his free and conscious self-transcendence, the Spirit arrives at itself, as it were. Self-transcendence is 'a surpassing of self or active filling up of the empty.'[46] But if this is not to make what is empty, itself the wellspring of the abundance (as Ernst Bloch did with his phrase about 'transcending without transcendence') then self-transcendence can only be understood as the being-moved, and the active self-movement, of finite being towards infinite being. It does not mean self-development on the same level. It means 'the leap to higher being'. If this were to be excluded we should end up with a faulty concept of infinity as endlessness. Since what transcends itself continues to exist in the particular goal of its self-transcendence (because the higher order always embraces and preserves the lower one) the converse may also be said: that what is lower 'precedes' or 'preludes' in itself the higher order of being in each given case.[47] Where nature and humanity are concerned, this means that 'man is the self-transcendence of living matter',[48] and nature and the history of the Spirit form an inward unity.

In the free history of the Spirit, the history of nature arrives at its goal. This goal is certainly to be seen in the direction in which human self-transcendence itself points: the infinite fulness of God, which is inaccessible to human beings themselves and remains hidden from them. Just as God's creative self-communication already makes itself known in the self-transcendence of matter, so at the peak of human development human self-transcendence and divine self-communication coincide in 'the Saviour'. In him, human nature transcends itself into the divine mystery. In the Logos which became world and matter, God communicates himself utterly. To put it theologically, human self-transcendence and divine self-communication coincide in the hypostatic union of the incarnate God-human being, forming the culmination and the summit of the world's development. But that means seeing the incarnation not merely as the descent of the divine Logos, but as at the same time 'an absolutely individual and new rung in the hierarchy of world-realities'. All earlier stages are inherent in it through the force of self-transcendence. In it the absolute future of the divine mystery is present through grace by virtue of self-communication.

There is no need to enter here into the details of this christology. The concept of self-transcendence is used today by many evolutionary theorists, though without the lustre of christological dignification. According to Rahner, the view that the incarnation was God's first intention, and is hence the climax and summit of the divine plan of creation, is Scotist in origin. The magisterium never took exception to it. The connection between this christology of creation's completion and the grace which blots out sin and guilt is provided by the postulate that this self-communicaton of God in the fully realized self-transcendence of the God-human being is made in grace and without merit. But according to the ontology of self-transcendence, as well as according to the logic of evolutionary theory, the completion of creation through the appearance of the God-human being presupposes a preparation by way of human history. Otherwise it would be impossible to say that with his appearance world history reached, if not yet its absolute completion, at least its 'final and highest phase'. In Christianity's early days, the coming of Christ was rather seen in apocalyptic terms, and people talked about 'the end of the world' and Christ's imminent second coming. But the patristic church was already familiar with the idea that the incarnation and the victory of Christ meant the dawn of a new epoch of world history – the 'divinization of the world' which begins with Christ.[49]

Rahner himself thinks that today the number of human beings who have lived 'since Christ' is greater than the number that lived 'before him', and he concludes from this that Christ should be understood as the beginning of a new history rather than as the end of the world: 'If we look at Western history from Christ onwards (which therefore includes modern times and the planetary future now beginning, which will be sustained by a higher social organization and will continue to dominate nature), seeing it as something which . . . is beginning to be the epoch towards which the whole of human life has hitherto tended . . . then incarnation [stands] at the beginning of this epoch, which is really human for the very first time.' It is an epoch in which the world has been turned into 'a material which man himself can manipulate technologically' and 'cosmocentricity has been turned into anthropocentricity'.[50]

The misgivings which this outline of an evolutionary christology suggest are to some degree similar to the objections raised against Teilhard. It is true that the concept of self-transcendence does not involve a selection procedure like the concept of evolution; but it too fails to draw attention to the victims which the process actually costs.

It suggests nothing of the breaches in the world process which have in fact occurred. It passes smoothly from the history of nature to human history and – as the last quotations show – moves with unbroken continuity from the history of human civilization to the technological civilization of modern times, and from the modern European era to the future planetary age. If modern 'anthropocentricism' really means that the world is turned into material for human beings, then it no longer preserves ancient, pre-modern 'cosmocentricism' within itself, nor does it permanently embrace the lower orders of nature. On the contrary, these are surrendered to destruction: nature becomes material. The final sentences (which no one could echo today, in the face of our obvious ecological crisis) describe besides the atomic peril the only planetary thing which modern times have achieved; and in these sentences we see the fatal result of the fact that Rahner merely presupposes the 'evolutive world view' as a given datum, without adopting it in a critical way.

Once again, the real theological question is to be found in the christology. This christology, fitted as it is into the evolutive world view, sees Christ as the summit of development, but not as the redeemer of that development from its ambiguities. Here the God-human being is emphasized as 'the true human being' by virtue of his self-transcendence, and as 'the true God' by virtue of his self-communication; and his mystery is apprehended in the concept of incarnation. It is noticeable that the passion and Christ's death by violence on the cross play hardly any part. The fully realized humanity of Christ is at the centre, not the humanity put to death on the cross. Christ stands on the summit of successful self-transcendencies in the history of nature and human beings, opening up the vista of the new, the divine history. He does not stand beside the self- transcendencies which have miscarried and been thwarted. It is hard to see what redemption this Christ can bring to the graveyards of nature and human history. What would happen to the picture of Christ, and his relationship to the history of nature and human beings – how would the picture change – if his self-transcendence through his active obedience (*potentia oboedientialis*) were replaced by his rising from the dead? And if this commenced completion of the evolution of nature were instead to be his 'restoration of all things' through the raising of nature? The theodicy problem with which the evolutive view of the world confronts us is not merely the question of moral evil– the human guilt which can be blotted out by grace. The problem is also physical evil; and this can be overcome only through an eternal new creation of all temporal things.

§4 CHRIST – THE REDEEMER OF EVOLUTION

Creation is not a work once performed and then finished and done with. It is a process, extended over time and open to the future. God continually creates something new, and develops what he has already created. From the inexhaustibly-creating creative ground of all things, continually new forms of life emerge. In this creative process God is not only a maker. He communicates himself in a certain way to what he has made, for through Spirit and Word the Creator enters into his creation and drives it forward. Has this creative process a goal? Is it possible to detect a divine creative plan which gives meaning to all things and all circumstances in this process?

It is certainly possible to detect certain evolutionary series in the history of nature. Matter is built up stage by stage into ever more complex forms. But we can also see catastrophic breakdowns in evolutionary series. Consequently it is difficult to extrapolate a holistic goal for the universe out of the trends that are discernible in the history of nature, without falling victim to irrelevant speculations. In human history too, evolutions of cultures, populations and human phenotypes can be discerned. But is it possible to discover any objective plan for humanity with a universal historical goal? 'The God of history' is a very hidden God, whose plans and ways may after all only be manifest and comprehensible in the seeing face to face.

Theological cosmology has always seen the goal of creation together with creation's beginning: all things are *from* God, so all things are *for* God and move in his direction. Aquinas says that the origin of the world and its goal are like two semi-circles which encompass the universe in time.[51] In Rahner's cosmic christology, the self-communication of God the Creator to the world and in it, effects the world's self-transcendence towards him and into him.[52] Teilhard too sees the goal of the evolution of life, with its increasing richness and elaboration, in the pleroma, or plenitude, of God himself. And in the same way classic theology always defined the

purpose of creation as the glorification of God (*gloria Dei*) and, in
that glorification, the salvation of the world (*salus mundi*).

The biblical traditions share this viewpoint, but without the
finalistic metaphysics through which later theologians formulated
it. In these biblical traditions the goal of creation is not God in
himself – God in his essential being; it is the God who is present
to all the beings he has created in his *sabbath rest*. Rahner likes to
call God 'the absolute mystery'; but biblically we should think,
not of 'God in heaven', but of the earthly presence of God in the
sabbath stillness, which we perceive only when everything in us
falls silent.

Jewish apocalyptic already carried over the order of the original
creation (Gen. 1) into world history, with the result that the history
of the world finds its goal and its consummation in *God's eschatological sabbath*.[53] God desires to come to his rest. That is the goal of
all things he has created. So in their history God is restless and keeps
all things in a state of suspense – he holds his breath, as it were; but in
this breath all things are also held, for it is the breath of his Spirit. The
Creator will arrive at his rest when the whole creation becomes his
temple, into which his glory can enter and dwell. This is the
eschatological image in the Revelation of John too (Rev. 21). So
creation does not return home to God in order to be absorbed into
the divine eternity from which it has come. On the contrary, God
enters the world, making it the dwelling place which corresponds
utterly to him. All things then take an unhindered share in the
indwelling glory of his inexhaustibly-creating creative life. We can
call this 'the deification of the cosmos' if we see its ground in *the
cosmic incarnation* of God.

The Counter-Movement

Is it conceivable that this future of creation will be *teleologically*
achieved by way of evolution or self-transcendence? No. It is not
conceivable, because the process of creation takes place in time, and
'becoming' inevitably involves transience. There is no evolution
without selection. It is true that we can say that all the lower forms of
life are still inherent in life's higher forms. But this is true only of the
form itself, not of its individual examples, and does not lead to their
immortality. Even the individual contribution to the evolution of the
whole brings the individual no eternity. Teleologically, a perfect

being at the end of evolution is certainly conceivable, but not the perfecting of all created things.

The perfecting of the whole creation, extended over time in the creation process, is only conceivable *eschatologically*. The teleology of creation is not its eschatology. What is eschatological is the new creation of all things which were and are and will be. What is eschatological is the bringing back of all things out of their past, and the gathering of them into the kingdom of glory. What is eschatological is the raising of the body and the whole of nature. What is eschatological is that eternity of the new creation which all things in time will experience simultaneously when times ends. To put it simply: God forgets nothing that he has created. Nothing is lost to him. He will restore it all.

What has to be called eschatological is the movement of *redemption*, which runs counter to evolution. If we want to put it in temporal terms: this is a movement which runs from the future to the past, not from the past to the future. It is the divine tempest of the new creation, which sweeps out of God's future over history's fields of the dead, waking and gathering every last created being. The raising of the dead, the gathering of the victims and the seeking of the lost bring a redemption of the world which no evolution can ever achieve. This redemption therefore comprehends the redemption of evolution itself, with all its ambiguities. In this redemption, evolution turns and becomes re-volution, in the original sense of the word. The linear time of evolution will be carried into a unique and then final eschatological cycle: into the return of all the pasts in the eternal aeon of the new creation of all things. Eschatological future is to be understood *diachronically*: it is simultaneous to all the times, and in being so it represents eternity for all things.

The *Christus evolutor* is the *Christ in his becoming*. But the *Christus redemptor* is the *Christ in his coming*. Walter Benjamin discerned the difference between the two categories with particular sensitivity: 'It is only the Messiah himself who will fulfil all historical happening, and he will do so in the sense that it is only he himself who will redeem, complete and create its relation to the messianic perspective. That is why nothing that is historical can ever of its own volition strive to relate itself to what is messianic. That is why the kingdom of God is not the *telos* of the historical dynamic; it cannot be made the goal. For historically it is not a goal; it is the end.'[54] Yet Benjamin detected a dialectical relationship between the purposeful 'dynamic of the profane' and that other direction, 'messianic intensity': 'The profane is therefore certainly not a category of the kingdom, but it is a category, and the most appropriate category, of its stealthiest approach.'[55] The forces of messianic intensity act in a counter-movement to the dynamic of the profane, and the profane order acts in a counter-movement to the coming of the messianic kingdom. In this way they enforce one another mutually.

For cosmic christology this means that it is only the reconciliation of all things, whether on earth or in heaven (Col. 1.20), and their redemption from the fetters of the transience of the times which leads to the gathering together of all things in the messiah, and therefore to the completion of creation. The evolutionary series in the history of nature and in human history are the outcome of *continuous creation*. The redemption and the new creation of all created things can be expected only from *the coming of Christ* in glory. The *recapitulatio mundi* presupposes the *resurrectio mortuorum*, for the cosmic Christ will not only become the Lord who fills all spaces of creation with 'the messianic intensity' of the divine peace (shalom). He will also become the Lord who fills all the times of creation with the messianic extensity of redemption. In the Epistle to the Colossians, the spatial picture of the cosmic Christ is dominant, in Paul the temporal picture of the eschatological Christ (I Cor. 15). The two images must complement one another if they are to comprehend the risen and exalted Christ in his spatial and temporal dimensions: his messianic intensity pervades the spaces of creation to their depths; his messianic extensity pervades the times of creation to their furthest origins.

This universal eschatology of redemption provides the foundation which then makes it justifiable to discern and acknowledge tendencies in the evolution of nature and in human history as being also parables and hints, anticipations and preparations for the coming of the messianic new creation. The active self-transcendence which is at work in these processes really does point beyond the historical present and beyond history itself to a future which fills it and brings it to rest. But the hunger for this future is not in itself this future's realization. The 'absolute self-communication of God' about which Rahner speaks is heralded in the radical self-transcendence, but no more than that; it is not itself already the other, divine side of this human self-movement. Only as a whole (τὰ πάντα) will creation be reconciled, redeemed and recreated. Without the redemption of nature and the raising of the dead, even successfully realized human self-transcendence into the divine life remains a fragment, and is at best a glimmer of hope for this unredeemed world.

§5 THE COMMUNITY OF CREATION IS A COMMUNITY BASED ON LAW

In many sectors of science and technology today, evolutionary theory provides the intellectual basis for an aggressive ethical attitude towards nature. Nature becomes the material for human beings which can be 'technologically manipulated', especially by way of modern genetic engineering.[56] What ethical conclusions must be drawn from the cosmic christology we have developed here?

It was through Paul's answers to ethical questions that cosmic christology emerged for the first time. If 'all things' are 'through Christ' and 'we through him' (I Cor. 8.6), then Christians live everywhere in the liberty of Christ, and no longer have to pay any attention to the powers of this world and the idols of human beings. For Christians there are 'no sectors of our life in which we belong not to Jesus Christ but to other masters, no sectors in which we do not require justification and sanctification through him', as the condemnatory clause in Thesis II of the 1934 Barmen Declaration of the Confessing Church says. Through Christ, says the Thesis itself, 'we experience glad liberation from the godless ties of this world, and are freed for free, grateful service for his (God's) creation'.[57] Paul proclaimed the liberty of Christ in a religious world in which natural forces were divinized and demons were feared. Today we are asking about the love of Christ in a technological civilization in which nature has been turned into material for human beings and degraded into a dumping ground for human refuse. Over-population, profligate industrial society and the injustices of the world-wide economic system have plunged nature into chaos. The gases that are rising into the ozone layer and the poisons that are seeping into the groundwater are no longer retrievable. The costs of the evolution of this modern society are in fact greater than its utility. But they are shuffled off on to nature and future generations, in order that the present generation in 'developed' societies may enjoy the profits. In an age when nature is being progressively destroyed, what Sittler said is proving to be true: 'With every new conquest of nature a piece of God dies.' Today's cosmic christology must confront Christ with this modern chaos. It is not at the supreme points of evolution that Christ is present. He is present in nature's weakest creatures, who are the first victims of developed human societies. Without the healing of wounded nature, human evolution cannot be saved.

1. *The Reconciliation of Human Beings and Nature*

For Christian faith, it is cosmic christology itself that provides the spiritual foundations for the conversion of men and women from their ruthless exploitation of nature to a caring reconciliation with nature. Cosmic christology does not abolish personal faith in Christ, and does not replace it by a religious *Weltanschauung*; what it does do is to set personal faith in the wide horizon of the lordship of Christ.

1. *The peace of Christ* is personally experienced through faith in the depths of the individual heart. Inner peace of soul with God is important because it overcomes the insatiable greed which stifles the profound anxieties of the godless heart. But if this peace of soul is Christ's peace, then it points every soul it touches beyond its own confines to the community of all created being in the cosmos; for through his death on the cross Christ has 'slain enmity' – the enmity of human beings towards themselves and one another, the enmity of human beings towards nature, and the enmity between the forces of nature itself. The peace of Christ is universal and pervades the whole cosmos. Otherwise Christ is not the Christ of God.

2. *Reconciliation with God* is experienced by men and women in Christ through faith, personally and together. If God himself is present in Christ, then in him the desires of men and women are stilled, the desires which are the expression of an unquenchable longing for God.[58] Then men and women can simply *be*, and no longer need to *have* so much. If these desires are stilled, then there is enough for everyone, as was said in the first Christian congregation in Jerusalem (Acts 4.34). What human beings experience from God as *reconciliation* in themselves and with one another, takes them beyond themselves and even beyond their human world into the wide expanses of the cosmos: 'Through him all things are reconciled, whether on earth or in heaven' (Col. 1.20). Unless *the whole* cosmos is reconciled, Christ cannot be the Christ of God and cannot be the foundation of all things. But if he is this foundation, then Christians

cannot encounter other creatures in any way other than the way they encounter human beings: every creature is a being for whom Christ died on the cross in order to gather it into the reconciliation of the world. But the *reconciliation* of the cosmos is the restoration of the *righteousness* and *justice* of the cosmos. None of these other creatures has been destined to be 'technologically manipulated' material for human beings. In the reconciled community of creation, human beings experience nature no longer as an object and a vis-à-vis, but as a continuum: they themselves are nature, and nature is in them.

The aggressive ethic of the modern world reflects the mentality of unreconciled human beings and their nihilistic dreams of almighty power. An ethic of reconciliation serves the common life of all created beings. It is bound to assume a defensive character, solicitous of life, over against the aggressive ethic of the modern era. Today the Christian acknowledgment of creation is an act of resistance against 'modern man's' destruction of nature and himself. But a defensive preservation of life and a productive furtherance of life are not mutually exclusive; they belong together. An ethic which aims to reconcile the requirements of human civilization with the conditions and regenerative powers of nature has as its objective not merely a just balance, but productive co-operation, in the interests of common survival.

What is needed if there is to be collaboration based on life together is the recognition of the particular and the common dignity of all God's creatures. This dignity is conferred on them by God's love *towards* them, Christ's giving of himself *for* them, and the indwelling of the Holy Spirit *in* them. A recognition of this dignity leads to the perception of the *rights* of every individual creature in the all-comprehensive community of creation, a community which is based on law.

2. A Community of Human Beings, Animals and Plants Based on Law

Reconciliation through Christ is the foundation for a community based on law, in the cosmos as well as among God's people. Just as human dignity is the source of all human rights, so the dignity of creation is the source of all the rights of animals, plants and the earth. Human dignity is simply the human form of general creaturely dignity. Unless the community of creation is codified as a community based on law in the covenant of God's creation, and unless this is enforced, all ecological endeavours will be nothing more than poetry and ideology.

The modern aggressive ethical attitude towards nature is a product of the European Renaissance and of European imperialist expansion in America, Africa and Asia. It was the Renaissance which for the first time stripped nature of its rights and declared it to be 'unclaimed property' which belonged to whoever took forceful possession of it. It was the same aggressive spirit of conquest which took possession by armed force of inhabited America, Africa and Asia, turning them into European 'colonies'.[59] Earlier, land, water, the forests and the air counted as God's property, which had been given over to human beings for their common use. Today this is still just about true of the air, which everyone has to breathe, although the increasing atmospheric pollution in many cities already shows the outcome of this aggressive and a-social ethic of the modern world. If the community of creation is a community based on law, then before all else human beings must recognize that the earth system and all animal and plant species have their own rights, and that these must be observed. And there must be a recognized codification of 'the rights of the earth', animals and plants, corresponding to the General Declaration of Human Rights of 1948.

A Universal Declaration on Animal Rights of this kind has existed ever since 1978.[60] An animal is not a thing and not a product. It is a living being with its own rights. To respect this fact means ending factory farming for the purpose of 'animal production' and introducing a way of keeping animals which will be in accord with the requirements of their species. Industrial hormone-controlled 'animal production' is not only brutality towards the animals themselves. It is also in the highest degree detrimental to human health. And do the practical results gained from the countless experiments on animals really outweigh the moral costs incurred by our society? Christ's relation to animals is no more than touched on in muted form at the end of the story of the temptations (Mark 1.13): 'And he was with the beasts, and the angels ministered to him.' But this is an allusion to the messianic peace of creation, which is part of Israel's hope according to Isaiah 11. Because human beings are embodied and natural beings, it is in any case impossible to implement human rights without at the same time observing the rights of animals, plants and the earth. Without the formulation of their ecological rights and duties, the rights of human beings in their own lives remain unrealistic. Rights for non-human creatures could be maintained and enforced if guardians and trustees for them were to be appointed by human courts.

The community of creation is a community based on law: this idea is especially well developed in the laws about the sabbath in the Old Testament. The weekly sabbath is not a day of rest for human beings alone. It is also a day of rest for the animals who belong to the family community (Ex. 20.10). This is the day on which human beings are supposed not to intervene in nature, either through work or harvest, but are meant to perceive nature as God's creation, and respect it accordingly.

Israel was commanded to celebrate every seventh year in the land that was God's as a sabbath year, in which the earth was to be left uncultivated, so that 'the land shall keep its great sabbath for the Lord' (Lev. 25.1–7). The sabbath year is a sign that the earth belongs to God, not to human beings, and that it has its own rights in its relationship to God. When Israel enters the promised land, this injunction is given her on her way as a charter of possession: 'When you come into the land which I give you, the land shall keep its sabbath to the Lord . . . in which you shall not sow your field or prune your vineyard.' 'Do my statutes, and keep my ordinances and perform them; so you will dwell in the land securely' (Lev. 25.2–4, 18). According to Lev. 26.1ff., this sabbath commandment takes the place of the heathen fertility gods who were otherwise invoked for the blessing of the earth: 'You shall make for yourselves no idols . . . keep my sabbaths and reverence my sanctuary.' The person who keeps the sabbath year commandment will enjoy the harvest and live in peace. Whoever disregards 'the sabbath of the earth' will be visited by drought and will be forced to leave his land: 'And I will devastate the land. . . . And I will scatter you among the nations . . . and your land shall be a desolation and your cities shall be a waste. Then the land shall enjoy its sabbaths as long as it lies desolate, while you are in your enemies' land; then the land shall rest, and enjoy its sabbaths' (v. 34). According to II Chron. 36.19–21, God delivered Israel up to the Babylonians and sent her into captivity because she had disregarded the sabbath year of God's earth. And Israel remained in Babylonian captivity 'until the land had enjoyed its sabbaths', that is, until the land had recovered from its exploitation by human beings.

According to these ideas, God's people and his land belong within a common order of law. The land is not only given to *God's people*; the people is also given to *God's land*. The sabbath year is the ecological secret of life in the promised land. If it is disregarded, the ground dies and the people must be deported until the land has recovered. If it is observed, the people will live long in the land which the Lord gave them. 'The sabbath of the earth' is the sign of God's covenant with the earth, just as the sabbath is the sign of God's covenant with his people.

In agrarian societies, people have always known that to disregard fallowing exhausts the ground, causes erosion, diminishes the yield and leads to famine. Investigations into the link between agriculture and civilization show that great civilizations in Mesopotamia, the Ganges valley, North Africa and Mexico crumbled because the land was ruthlessly exploited and its fertility was permanently destroyed in the process. Generally speaking, it was the great empires which exploited and laid waste their fruitful provinces in order to feed their capital cities and their armies.

The modern change-over from farming to agricultural industry has pushed out the ancient, natural principle of fallowing, replacing it by chemical fertilizers. Fertilizers force the earth into permanent fertility, monocultures have replaced the old rotation of crops. Herbicides, insecticides and pesticides promise ever more abundant harvests, but in the long run they destroy the ground and poison the ground-water. It is short-sighted to destroy the long-term foundations of one's own life for the sake of quick profits. It is just as short-sighted in the interests of one's own profits to push off the costs on to coming generations, who will have to make the damage good if they want to live. In the long-term, this way of dominating nature is also the principle of humanity's self-destruction.

The wisdom of the sabbath year has rightly been called God's 'ecological wisdom'.[61] Ancient Israel's hopeful, tragic history on God's earth is a warning to the whole of humanity: the earth will survive — but perhaps not human beings.

The community of creation is a community based on law. In Israel's Old Testament period and in mediaeval Europe animals were put on trial. But it was always only animals who had attacked, injured or killed human beings that were punished, never also the human beings who had assaulted animals, except in the case of sodomy. (According to Lev. 20.15, in the case of sodomy the human being and the animal had both to be put to death, the animal being strangled. Article 116 of the Carolina, Charles V's penal code of 1532, says the same thing.) Apparently swine were particularly often put on trial in the middle ages, because swine were still undomesticated and occasionally attacked children. There must have been a whole number of cases where swine were publicly executed, not only in front of human beings but in front of herds of swine as well.[62] This curiosity is worth mentioning only because it shows that in the middle ages the legal order was evidently not confined to human society. In the trials of those days the rights of human beings were safeguarded against aggressive animals. Nowadays the important thing would surely be to safeguard the rights of animals against aggressive human beings.

The Christian faith, like the Jewish one, has specific ideas about God's justice. If God is the creator of heaven and earth, then heaven and earth are his property and must as such be considered holy, and respected. Anyone who calls nature 'God's creation' will respect God's right to his earth and will resist the human destruction of nature, which proceeds from the fiction that nature is 'unclaimed property', which belongs to whoever first lays hands on it for himself.

If God is the owner of his creation, then disposal over that creation belongs to him alone. Human beings and animals are allowed only a right of use, so that they can feed themselves and live, and can do so in the framework of creation's general purpose: God wants all those he has created to live in peace with one another 'each according to its kind'. It is not yet fully clear what it means to withdraw from human beings the right of disposal over the creatures which they are in a position to dominate. But it quite certainly includes the protection of species, for God created animals and plants 'according to their kinds' (Gen. 1.11, 21, 24). The extermination of whole plant and animal species must therefore be viewed as sacrilege, and punished.

Human ownership of God's creation can only be seen as just if it is used in solidarity. This use in considerate solidarity has a specific reference to our present human society. According to the Basic Law, the written constitution of the German Federal Republic, property involves *social obligation* and must not be enjoyed at the expense of other people, but only for their benefit. Property also involves *an obligation to those to come* and must not be enjoyed at the expense of future generations, but only for their benefit. Finally, property involves *a duty to the environment* and must be used only in such a way that the requirements of the environment are met – in accord with the natural world, not at its expense.[63]

Whenever and wherever men and women testify to the reconciliation of the world through God, whether in personal life, in the wider community or in the cosmos, the righteousness of God is restored and manifested. The people of Israel had become unjust and impure. Its reconciliation on the great Day of Atonement (Lev. 16) was for the purpose of Israel's justification and aimed at the implementation of God's righteousness and justice, which alone secures life and peace. The reconciliation of the whole cosmos through Christ (Col. 1.20) is for the justification of all created beings who have been injured and have lost their rights, and aims at the implementation of God's righteousness and justice, which alone secures the life and peace of creation. The reconciliation of human beings with God, their reconciliation with one another, and their reconciliation with themselves must therefore include reconciliation with nature, quite directly and immediately, so that a community with nature based on law and capable of survival may be created.

VII

The Parousia of Christ

§1 A LITTLE APOLOGIA FOR THE EXPECTATION OF THE PAROUSIA

For modern theology the early Christian expectation of the parousia is an embarrassment which it thinks it can get rid of with the help of demythologization. In recent theological christologies the subject is hardly mentioned at all.[1] Although all the recognized Christian creeds talk about the One 'who will come again in glory to judge both the quick and the dead, whose kingdom shall have no end' (Nicene creed), theology has expended very little thought on 'the coming Christ'. And this neglect left the way clear for the wildly proliferating fantasies surrounding the expectation of the parousia which we come across in many Christian sects.

But was it not also a sign that Christianity was becoming a civil religion when the expectation of the parousia lost its force and ceased to have anything to say to the enlightened world? Renunciation of hope for the messiah was the price the Jews paid for emancipation in modern society; and similarly, very early on, renunciation of hope for the parousia was the price paid for Christianity's integration into the Roman empire. In their worship and their persecutions, the first Christian congregations prayed passionately: 'Maranatha, come Lord Jesus, come soon' (I Cor. 16.22; Rev. 22.20). But the Constantinian imperial church began to pray *pro mora finis* – that the end might be delayed – hoping thereby to recommend itself as a religion that supported the state and preserved the world. People who are trying to fit into the world and to gain its recognition are bound to dispense with hope for the messianic kingdom which will change and renew everything. They

have to do without the vision of an alternative future in the kingdom
of Christ. But for people who embark on a true conversion which
takes them out of what they are, present hope for the coming of
Christ and his kingdom is important. They need this sustaining staff
of hope, in order to free themselves from the present and to confront
it freely (I Cor. 7.31). They no longer love 'the nature of this world',
which is injustice and violence, but begin to 'love the appearance of
the Lord'. They suffer together with all other created beings from the
power of death; and together with the divine Spirit who sighs in and
with the suffering, they cry: 'May your kingdom come and this world
pass away.' In resistance to the godless powers of repression, in
persecution and in suffering, men and women experience the power
given by the expectation of the parousia.

In the history of the church and Christian communities and sects,
the most varied motives have coalesced in the expectation of what is
wrongly called 'Christ's second coming'. A critical examination of
the parousia hope must uncover these motives and clear them of their
dross. The expectation of the coming Christ must not become the
dream of revenge for people who 'have had a poor deal' here. Nor
must it be turned into a dream of almighty power for people who are
at present powerless. Finally, it has nothing to do with religious
compensation for people who have been disappointed on earth. It is
only the hope that was born of Christ's resurrection and is alive in the
power of his Spirit which finds its completion in the expectation of
Christ and the prayer for his coming. The parousia of Christ is first
and foremost the completion of the way of Jesus: 'the Christ on the
way' arrives at his goal. His saving work is completed. In his
eschatological person he is perfected and is universally manifested in
the glory of God. This means that the crucified Christ is the criterion
for the expectation of the parousia, just as he was already the
criterion for his Easter appearance. Only christological concentration can prevent the fantasies surrounding the expectation of the
parousia from running riot. Only faith in Christ can purify the
apocalyptic motifs in the parousia hope.

The histories of Christian theology and Christian art (especially
mediaeval art) show that the expectation of Christ's 'coming again'
was linked in so one-sided a way with the Last Judgment of 'the
quick and the dead' that hope for 'the kingdom that shall have no
end' received very little attention, or was forgotten altogether. The
way the Apostles' creed is formulated was a contributory factor –

and this is the customary creed in the West. The images of the great Judgment in mediaeval churches plunged the common people into apprehension and terror, rather than filling them with joyful expectation. Christ the Judge of the world aroused no yearning expectation for his imminent coming – on the contrary.

The one-sided way in which Christ's 'second coming' was linked with the Last Judgment obscured the meaning of this judgment, which is solely the victory of the divine righteousness that is to become the foundation of the new creation of all things. Of course judgment must be expected too, together with the consummation of Christ in the glory of God, for the perfecting of the kingdom includes the ending of injustice. There is no need to leave out the expectation of judgment, or to demythologize it as an antiquated apocalyptic concept. But neither is there any reason for giving way to fear and panic at the thought of it, and for visualizing 'the Last Judgment' in the horrible visions of hell. The judgment of the living and the dead is one more reason to hope for Christ's coming; it is not a subject for fear. The Judge who is expected is the One who gave himself up for sinners and who suffered the pains and sicknesses of men and women.[2] The crucified One will judge according to his gospel of the saving righteousness of God, and according to no other law. He will not judge in order to punish the wicked and reward the good, but so as to make the saving righteousness of God prevail among them all. He will 'judge' in order to raise up and to put things right. The expectation of the Last Judgment must be integrated into the expectation of Christ, not vice versa. It must not become the projection of suppressed guilty fears, as a way of satisfying a masochistic lust for self-punishment. Nor, of course, must it become a projection for the notorious self-excuses of men and women. It is based on the remembrance and the present experience of Christ, and is directed towards his future. The crucified One will be the judge, and he will judge according to his gospel. His saving righteousness will renew the world. Only when the apocalyptic expectation of judgment is completely Christianized does it lose its terror and become a liberating hope, in which we go to meet the future with heads held high. Only when judgment is viewed as the precondition for the coming of the eternal kingdom and is therefore understood in its provisional character, can we pray that it may come soon. Then the fear of judgment will no longer hinder and paralyse the expectation of the parousia.

It is only more recent, eschatologically orientated theology which has brought back the expectation of the parousia into christology, historically and theologically.[3] Christ's parousia is not a dispensable appendage to the history of Christ. It is the goal of that history, for it is its completion. As the New Testament sees it, it is not something mythically determined and historically conditioned – a garment which theology could lay aside in passing over to a different age. It is the keystone supporting the whole of christology, and this also makes it the key to the understanding of the history of Christ. Christ's messianic mission, his apocalyptic suffering and his eschatological resurrection from the dead would remain incomprehensible fragments if we were not to take into account the future 'Day of the Messiah', the future of the Son of man, the coming 'Day of the Lord' – which is to say Jesus' parousia in the universal glory of God. The expectation of the messiah belongs indissolubly together with the essential christological 'titles of sovereignty' – messiah, Son of man and Lord. In the expectation of the parousia all the threads of christology are drawn together, as it were. In his coming in glory, Jesus is expected as the Lord of the church, as the messiah of Israel, as the Son of man of the nations, as the creative Wisdom from which all things will be born anew. That is why the parousia of Christ is a subject that belongs to christology, not to eschatology alone. Because the eschatological 'person' of Christ is always defined in the light of the parousia, the parousia also belongs to the doctrine about Christ's person, not merely to the doctrine about his work. The fundamental christological assertions 'crucified – raised' are left in the air unless they are related on the one hand to the messianic mission of the earthly Jesus and on the other to his eschatological coming.

The Christian expectation of the parousia has been brought into disrepute through talk about the so-called *delay* of the parousia. The expectation of the imminent coming held by Jesus and the first congregations is said to have been overtaken by history, which 'continued to run its course'. With this argument of Schweitzer's, the school of consistent eschatology pursued the consistent abolition of eschatology.[4] But their premise was *a temporalized parousia expectation*, for they identified Christ's parousia with the temporal future. In this way Christ's parousia was allotted a place in the general 'flow of time', and expected sooner or later, according to wants and needs. But if Christ's parousia takes place in time, then it is transient, like every other temporal future; it cannot be thought together with 'the end of time'. Nor can this be the expectation of a coming kingdom that 'shall have no end'.

At this point we must distinguish between *advent* and *future*. Translated literally, the word παρουσία means 'coming', or 'presence'. Latin renders it *adventus*, German *Zukunft*. Both words mean *what is coming towards* the present – what English is expressing when it talks about 'a coming' event. The word *futurum*, on the other hand, means 'what brings forth' or 'what is becoming': *futurum* is what *will be*. But in actual fact the three grammatical tenses, or modes of time, do not talk about the *future* of being at all. They talk about its becoming and its passing away: they speak of that which was, and that which is, and that which will be. But everything that *will be*, will one day be no more. What will be, passes away, and being-that-is-not-yet will one day become being-that-is-no-longer.[5] This means that it is impossible to talk about an enduring future by way of the future tense. We can talk only about future transience. But 'that which is coming', although it is certainly close ontologically to what is not yet but can be, is not totally congruent with that, and absorbed by it. What *will come* according to the Christian expectation of the parousia brings the end of time and the beginning of eternal creation. It is therefore related, not merely to the future of being, but to its present and its past as well. As the end of time, the parousia comes to all times simultaneously in a single instant. For the future of Christ also brings the end of becoming and the end of passing away.

On the other hand, Christian expectation of the parousia was also stifled by the theologians who declared that the so-called delay of the parousia was a fictitious problem which had nothing to do with true faith, since faith experiences and expects God's grace every moment.[6] Over against the temporalized expectation of the parousia they set an eternalized expectation: every time is 'the final time'. Every moment is 'an atom of eternity'. 'Every epoch stands in a direct relation to God.' 'Incomparable, the eternal moment confronts all moments, just because it is the transcendental meaning of all moments.'[7] Consequently, the parousia of Christ is not something that happens in time. It is supra-temporal and identical with eternity.[8] Christ's parousia is therefore a *futurum aeternum*. In the face of the eternity of God which breaks in with the parousia, all the divisions of time disappear. Time itself is abolished, or gathered up, in eternity. But if Christ's parousia is equated with God's eternity, then there is no moment at which it can enter time. There is then no future end of time – nothing but the limitation of all the times of human history through God's eternal moment. But this puts an end to all the real and futurist expectation of the parousia which echoes in the early Christian 'maranatha – come soon!', and transforms eschatology into mysticism. 'I myself am eternity when I forsake time and gather myself together in God and He in me', wrote Angelus Silesius.

The enumeration of several parousias of Christ, which was continually reiterated from Justin to Karl Barth, is also misleading. If we say 'Christ came in the flesh – Christ comes in the Spirit – Christ will come in glory'[9] we are simply adapting Christ's eternity to the three modes of time: past – present – future. And in this process the eschatological orientation of the Christian faith is lost; for why should believers have Christ's future more at heart than his past and his present? What is more, talk about 'the threefold parousia of Christ' is unbiblical, for in early Christianity 'hope of an imminent coming of the exalted Lord in Messianic glory is . . . so much to the fore that . . . παρουσία is never used for the coming of Christ in the flesh and παρουσία never has the sense of return.'[10]

Neither the temporalization nor the eternalization of the parousia expectation meets the eschatological orientation of early Christian faith adequately. And the result for theology is the problem of how to think this 'eschatological moment' which ends time in time in such a way that Christ's parousia and his kingdom can be thought of simultaneously as the end of time and the beginning of eternity.

It is not least the modern stress on the presentative experience of salvation which has robbed the expectation of the parousia of its content. If the whole salvation of the world has 'already been accomplished' in Christ's death on the cross, as Barth maintained, then the New Testament's futurist assertions about salvation are meaningless. The future tense of Christ's parousia can do no more than disclose the perfect tense of salvation. Christ's parousia adds nothing new to salvation's perfecting: 'It has all taken place; the only thing wanting is that the covering be removed and all may see it. He has already accomplished it and He has power to make it manifest.' 'What is the future bringing? Not, once more, a turning point in history, but the revelation of that which is. It is the future, but the future of that which the Church remembers, of that which has already taken place once and for all. The Alpha and the Omega are the same thing.'[11]

To see the foundation for the expectation of the parousia in the remembrance of Christ, as Barth does here, is correct, but what follows is not this one-sided stress on the perfect tense of salvation, over against its perfecting still to come. If the raising of Christ and his parousia were to be related solely to the saving event of Christ's vicarious death on the cross, then salvation itself would be reduced in a way which would fail to bring out the full scope and reference of the New Testament gospel. Christ's resurrection and Christ's parousia are saving 'events' too, since through them the process of healing this world in its deadly sickness is completed. What happened through Christ's death on the cross is what Paul calls the justification of sinners and the reconciliation of enemies through the revelation of *God's love*, which is unconditional and runs to meet us. This event, perceived in faith, is the reason and occasion for hope for the redemption of the body and the whole sighing creation from death, and the reason also for the hope for the new creation of all things through the revelation of *God's glory*.

Paul does not talk about an end of history that has already happened. He talks about an End-time process, which the resurrection of the crucified One has irrevocably set going. Just because for him Christ's cross and resurrection are at the centre, his theology is directed in a wholly eschatological way towards Christ's parousia. For Paul, it is not the soteriology of the reconciliation of the world that is in the foreground; it is the eschatology of the glorification of God. Christ reconciles and Christ rules 'until' he can hand over the completed kingdom to God the Father 'so that God may be all in all' (I Cor. 15.25–28). That is why the history of Christ is subject to what Ernst Käsemann calls 'the eschatological proviso' and is engraved with the hallmark of eschatological anticipation.

Christ's parousia therefore does not merely 'unveil' the salvific meaning of Christ's death. It also, and much more, brings the *fulfilment* of the whole history of Christ, with all that it promises; for it is only with Christ's parousia that 'the kingdom that shall have no end' begins. It is only in Christ's parousia that 'all the tears will be wiped away'. It is only in the parousia that Israel will be redeemed, and this 'unredeemed world' created anew. That is why this future of Christ does not bring the turn of history 'once more'; it brings it 'once and for all'. Presentative faith in salvation and hope for the coming parousia do not belong on the same level, in a way that would make it possible to waver to and fro theologically with one's emphases, depriving either Christ's cross or Christ's future of their content. The resurrection of the crucified One is the anticipation of his parousia in glory, and his parousia is the fulfilment of his resurrection. The reconciliation of the world is the promise of the new creation of all things, and the new creation is the fulfilment of the reconciliation of the world. The remembrance of Christ and the expectation of Christ deepen one another mutually. They do not detract from one another.

But what can be said about something that is coming but which has not yet come? Are not all statements about what is to come speculative? And surely what does come is always different from what we expect? Anyone who wished to narrate the course of the End-time events at Christ's parousia in advance would be turning this future, this coming event into the past, for it is only what is past that can be narrated. We can only *await* what is to come, anticipating it in fear or hope, in order to adapt ourselves to it now, in advance. 'What is coming' is present in the mode of promise, not in the mode of *logos*, which is based on experience. So how is it possible and legitimate to talk about Christ's parousia?

The statements about Christ's future are proved necessary by the dynamic of the provisional in the experience of Christ's history. The messianic mission of Jesus, his apocalyptic sufferings and his eschatological resurrection point beyond themselves to his eternal kingdom. The history of Christ manifests the *trend* which points to his future. So there are no special apocalyptic revelations and numerical mysteries in the Book of Revelation to give the allegedly initiated information about Christ's parousia. The information is given by the clear and simple gospel of Christ, for this is the *promise* of his coming and the *heralding* of his arrival. The future of Christ is expected in the hope which is kindled by the remembrance of him. Everything thrusts forward to his future. The *faith* which trusts the word of promise presses forward to the seeing face to face. The *love* which takes upon itself the sufferings of this present time cries out for God's righteousness and justice. *Hope*, finally, is in love with its own fulfilment, and desires to become the experience of joy. The legitimate statements about Christ's parousia do not rest on cloudy surmises about the end of the world, or on the visions of special prophets. They are founded on the historical revelation of God, which points beyond itself.

The community of Christ's people expects that his parousia will bring the fulfilment of the history of salvation and the termination of the history of affliction and disaster, the fulfilment of liberation and the end of suffering. That is why the parousia of Christ and the end of this world-time belong together. They do not belong together in the sense that we could talk about a 'coming of Christ at the end of the times',[12] as if this end were fixed once and for all. The relation between the parousia and the end is the very reverse of that: we have to talk about the end of time in the coming of Christ. It is not 'the end of the world' that will bring with it Christ's parousia. It is the parousia of Christ which will bring the wretchedness of 'this world time' to its end in the glory of his eternal kingdom.

Without anticipating the detailed eschatology planned for the next volume, we shall now try to discover the christological significance of the parousia expectation. We shall ask: Who is coming? When is he coming? Where is he coming from? How is he coming? We shall look first of all at the images of 'the One who will come', shall then consider the problem of time and eternity (which is bound up with 'the day of the Lord'), shall go on to the question of the spaces of heaven and earth, and shall come last of all to the question about the transformation of the transitory world into the eternal kingdom.

§2 'THE COMING ONE'

1. In the Old Testament 'the coming One' is initially a cipher for *God himself.* If we remember the difference between *adventus* and *futurum* discussed above, we cannot really talk about Yahweh as 'a God with "*future* as his essential nature"';[13] rather faith in this God of history is from the beginning bound up with hope for his *coming* in glory which will fill the world. When Abraham and Moses, Elijah and Isaiah 'see' God's glory, this exceptional event establishes this universal expectation. Prophets and psalms promise 'the coming of Yahweh', or continually pray for it (Isa. 35.4; 40.3–5; 60.1ff.; Ps. 96.13; 98.9; and frequently elsewhere).[14] The God of hope is also the coming God. It is in these contexts that the prophets talk about 'the day of the Lord' (Joel 2.1; 2.11; 2.31; Amos 5.18) and about 'the year of redemption' (Isa. 63.4). We may assume that these Old Testament expectations of God influenced New Testament usage, especially in Paul.

We have therefore first of all to do with the idea of a *divine parousia*: on his day God will come forth from his hiddenness in history. He will lead those who are his to victory and will pronounce judgment on his enemies. He will judge Israel too, as Amos stresses. But at the end of it all he will fill the world with the radiance of his glory, so that all will see him as he is, extol him, and become righteous in the praise of God (Isa. 35.10; 40.5). When the living God comes, he will swallow up death for ever (Isa. 25.8). All things and every living being will be liberated for his kingdom of glory, and created anew.

So in the framework of the expectation of God, 'the coming one' is also a cipher for the bearers of hope who mediate his coming and prepare the people for his coming – for the *kyrios*, for the messiah of Israel, for the Son of man of the nations, and for the Wisdom through whom the cosmos will be born anew. They too have their day and their kingdom, and without the expectation of the parousia these figures cannot be employed. It is noticeable here that Paul quite directly, and as if it were a matter of course, identifies 'the day of Christ' with 'the day of the Lord' (I Cor. 1.8; 5.5; II Cor. 1.14; Phil. 1.6; 2.16; I Thess. 5.2), therefore equating Jesus with Yahweh, apparently because he believes that the exalted Jesus is now the Lord of God's kingdom.

2. As *the Lord*, Christ is expected by those who are his. On 'the day of Christ' he will appear in glory. So the day of the Lord is a day of salvation, not a day of doom. This distinguishes the New Testament expectation from the apocalyptic one.[15] It evokes confidence, not fear, even if it should be 'a judgment according to what each has done' (II Cor. 5.10). Because the parousia is unforeseeable, to expect the unexpected is part of the unique nature of its expectation. Even if this day comes unforeseeably 'like a thief in the night' (I Thess. 5.2), believers will meet it 'pure and blameless' (I Cor. 1.8: Phil. 1.6, 10), and on that day sinners will experience their salvation (I Cor. 5.5). For the now suffering and persecuted apostle, it will be the day of his 'pride' (II Cor. 1.14; Phil. 2.16). It will be a day when what is now true only in hiddenness will be manifested, and the salvation which is now experienced only in its beginnings will be completed (Phil. 1.6). What is now believed will then be seen. In the seeing of Christ's glory the lowly body will be transformed (Phil. 3.21), which means that the bodily and earthly world will be redeemed from the power of death.

It can be pointed out that in Paul the apocalyptic and cosmic pictures of that day of the Lord are missing – pictures of the kind we find conjured up in II Peter 3.10, with the crashing down of the vault of heaven and the raging storm of fire. But vision is not lacking in Paul for all that. He himself became an apostle through a visual revelation of Christ, and one day Christ will come forth from his hiddenness, revealing himself universally in the same way. We already saw that the Easter appearances of the risen Christ provide the foundation for the history of believers, making Christ's parousia their lodestone, in hope. The parousia of the End-time is the universal Easter appearance of Christ, just as the Easter appearances are the historical anticipations of the coming 'day of the Lord'.

Finally, it should be noted that on his day Christ is expected, not as a private person but as a collective one. His future is also the future of those who are already 'in Christ' here and now. They also 'will appear with him in glory' (Col. 3.3–4). In their sufferings and weaknesses, those who are 'in Christ' participate here in his shame, and hope with him there to be glorified and with him to reign. This can be thought of as 'the first resurrection' (I Cor. 15.23: '. . . then at his coming those who belong to Christ'). But it may also be understood as the 'becoming manifest' of the eternal life of believers, which is now hid with Christ in God (Col. 3.4).

3. As *Israel's messiah*, Jesus is to appear on 'the day of the messiah' and redeem God's people.[16] Paul evidently expected that Christ's parousia as Lord of the church would also be his parousia as the messiah of Israel (Rom. 9–11): when Christ has completed his way through the world of the nations and 'the full number of the Gentiles have come in' to salvation, then 'all Israel will be saved'; for 'the Deliverer will come from Zion, he will banish ungodliness from Jacob' (Rom. 11.26). Even if 'all Israel' cannot believe in the gospel of Christ, God remains true to his covenant and his promise, and he will arrive at his goal, which is the redemption of Israel, in spite of Israel's resistance. Paul imagines Israel's End-time redemption as 'raising from the dead': 'What will their acceptance mean but life from the dead?' (Rom. 11.15). But this means that it is not only those Israelites who are alive and see Christ on his day who will be redeemed, but all Israel, from the first Israelite to the last. 'Life from the dead' will be experienced diachronically by them all, 'the quick and the dead' together. Such an event of resurrection on 'the day of

the messiah' will not evoke faith, but will be experienced as eternal life. It therefore belongs to the eschatological category of 'seeing'. From denying Christ, Paul was converted into being his apostle, because Christ revealed himself to him (Gal. 1.16); and he will not have imagined the redemption of all Israel in any other terms.

If we sum up the two expectations of the parousia – the parousia of Christ for the church, and the parousia of the messiah to all Israel – what emerges is the astonishing image of an End-time redemption of Christians and Jews for the eternal kingdom of their common Lord.

4. As *the Son of man*, Jesus is to appear on 'the day of the Son of man', when he will judge the living and the dead, in order to make of them the new humanity of his kingdom.[17] The expectation of the parousia was a firm component in the Son of man concept from the very beginning, and the one idea cannot be taken over without the other. It is 'the Son of man' who 'comes in the glory of his Father with the holy angels' (Mark 8.38), who 'comes with clouds with great power and glory' (Mark 13.25–27). It was with him that Jesus identified himself before his judges: they will 'see the Son of man seated at the right hand of Power, and coming with the clouds of heaven' (Mark 14.62). Elements of the Son of man concept also put their stamp on the Christian creed. The notion of the great universal judgment especially, goes back to the prophetic and apocalyptic expectation of the Son of man. According to 'the image of the monarchies' in Daniel 7, it is a theopolitical hope. To the Son of man who comes from heaven will be given 'dominion and glory and kingdom, that all people, nations, and languages should serve him; his dominion is an everlasting dominion, which shall not pass away, and his kingdom one that shall not be destroyed' (Dan. 7.14). The horizon of the expectation of the Son of man is universal and spans the whole of mankind: the humanity of all human beings will be fully implemented and arrive at its truth in his kingdom. At the same time the Son of man displays Israelite features.[18] According to the vision of Yahweh's throne in Ezekiel 1.26, God himself bears 'the likeness of a human form'. The 'one like a son of man' in Daniel 7.13 is certainly distinguished from the 'ancient of days' in Daniel 7.9. But we may assume that he is a divine figure. This is also suggested by the references to his 'everlasting dominion' and his 'kingdom that shall never be destroyed', which in Daniel 6.27 are applied to 'the God of Daniel'. According to Daniel 7, the Son of man is the representative

of Israel's God and in this sense Israel herself is present in him, being described in Daniel 7.18 as 'the saints of the Most High'.

We may conclude from this that in 'the Son of Man' the God of Israel will make his righteousness prevail against unjust ruling powers on earth and that he will bring the nations to the peace of humanity. That is why judgment of the living and the dead is in the hands of the Son of man, and that is why his kingdom will have no end.

As most of the texts show, Jesus identified himself indirectly and in an anticipatory way with the Son of man of the End-time. But through this identification he also drew the future of the Son of man into his suffering (Mark 8.31), so that 'the presence of Jesus is the hidden anticipation of the functions and acts of the future Son of man'.[19] This makes it understandable that the future of Christ should also have been thought about in the image of the coming Son of man, and that the day of the Lord was also imagined as the 'Last Day' – the Son of man's universal judgment. It is not merely the Lord of the church who is to come, and not only Israel's messiah. It is also the universal Son of man, who through his judgment will make the righteousness of God prevail, and will establish his kingdom of peace which will have no end.

The Lord – the messiah – the Son of man are representatives of God's rule. As figures they are transparent, not impermeably fixed, as it were; for through them the coming God himself can be seen. Consequently, they do not detract from one another. The expectation of the parousia does not have to be tied down to only a single form. The many different strata of the configurations of hope serve to highlight in a realistic way the various different groups to which this expectation is related – Christians, Jews, the peoples of the world.

5. Finally, remembering the new creation of all things for the kingdom of glory, it will also be permissible to expect the parousia of the Mediator of creation, *the Spirit and the Word*. If at the end the Creator says 'Behold, I make all things new' (Rev. 21.5), then the Word of creation must also be present in the Spirit of creation. Christian language talks about the raising of Christ 'from the dead' and calls Christ 'the first born' from the dead; and this implies the parousia of the general resurrection of the dead for the kingdom of eternal life. From this we may conclude that Jesus will appear as

Wisdom at the centre of the new creation of all things. The day of the Lord will become 'the first day' of the new creation. It is therefore full of light and can be imagined as the sunrise over a world that is 'in darkness and in the shadow of death.'

§3 'THE DAY OF THE LORD'

As we have seen, ideas about God as well as the ideas about the messiah and the Son of man are *essentially* bound up with the expectations of the parousia. The connection is not merely fortuitous. Phrases about the day of the Lord, the day of the messiah and the day of the Son of man are a way of expressing this. Notions waver about *when* and *how* this 'Day of his coming' will happen. On the one hand the day will come unexpectedly, 'like a thief in the night', 'suddenly' and 'abruptly', like the onset of labour pains (I Thess. 5.2–4; Matt. 13.35–36). On the other hand this day of his coming will be heralded by 'the trumpet of God' (I Thess. 4.16; I Cor. 15.52; Matt. 24.31), so that the dead may rise and the living can prepare themselves. Finally, there is also the idea of a continuous transition from the first streaks of dawn to the full light of day: 'The night is far gone, the day is at hand . . .' (Rom. 13.12). Here, certainly, Paul is not talking about 'the day of Christ', but he is speaking about 'the day of salvation' which is so close that the hour has already come to 'get up' from sleep.

What do these forms of expectation mean for practical life? Whereas the 'suddenly' expected dawn of the day of the Lord merely makes believers ready to expect him at any time and to be prepared every moment, the idea of the sound of the trumpet which will wake the dead makes us think of the entry of that day by stages, and the preparation of the dead and the living for his coming. What is being thought of here is a kind of liturgical entry procession. But if this day has already come as 'close' as the kingdom of God which Jesus proclaimed, then its effects must already be noticeable everywhere, like the first rays of the morning sun. The new world's 'weapons of light' are already at hand, 'the power of the resurrection' is already experienced.

As the expectation of the parousia shifts from an unforeseeable day to a day that has been announced, and then to the day which is already dawning here and now, we can see how apocalyptic tradition has been permeated by Christian thought. The centre of gravity moves from the apocalyptic future of the Lord still to come, to the future of salvation that is already dawning with Christ. The first two assertions are to be found in Jewish apocalyptic too. The third is possible only in a Christian context.

What is meant by 'the day of the coming' of the Lord, the messiah and the Son of man? It is remarkable that this is a day, not 'the night'. This transitory time does not end in the night of the eclipse of God. There is no 'end of the world' in which the world will go down into nothingness. What is to come is a 'day' without any evening, the eternal light, the day of the new creation. The time that was created in the alternation between the evening and the morning will come to an end, and will be consummated in the morning glory of eternity and in the eternal spring of the new creation. The sabbath of the world described in Gen. 2.1–4 differed from all the days of creation, for we are never told that it had an evening. And this sabbath points beyond itself to that new eternal creation in which 'the glory of God is its light, and its lamp is the Lamb' (Rev. 21.23). So in Rev. 10.6 the mighty angel swears that 'time shall be no more' – χρόνος οὐκέτι ἔσται.

1. 'The Last of Days' – the Day of Days

'The day of his coming' is supposed to be a day like all other days. It is to take place in time. So in Christian tradition it has often been called 'the last day'. But the day is determined by what happens in it, by the coming of the Lord in his eternal glory. This breaks off the time of transience and ends time in time. If this last of days is also the dawn of the eternity of the new creation, then it is more than a day in the calendar. Since it is the day of God's coming, it is rightly called 'the day of days';[20] for the eternity which appears on this day is simultaneous to all days, and lights up all the nights of world history. That is why the living are to experience this day together with the dead: the living will experience it as 'transformation', the dead as 'raising'; and for both the living and the dead it will mean a 'transfiguration' in the radiance of the divine glory. As the day of the Lord it is not the 'last day' in the sequence of the days and the times. It lies athwart all the days and times. It will come not merely 'from ahead', as it were, but also 'from above'. It will happen not only *in* time but also *to* time.

If the last day is also 'the day of days', and if 'the day of days' is at the same time 'the last day', then we are faced with the theoretical problem of how we should think of time and eternity at this point. If the last day belongs *within time*, then it cannot bring the end of time. If the day of the Lord falls in the *eternity* which is simultaneous to all times, then it cannot happen at a particular time, nor can it end time. So how are we to think of 'the eschatological moment' which ends time in time?

2. The Primordial and the Eschatological Moment

We can first of all go back to the discussion about 'the beginning' of creation which Augustine initiated.[21] Does 'the beginning' (Gen. 1.1) in which God created the world belong to time or eternity? If it belongs to time, then creation presupposes time, and there was a time before creation. If it belongs to eternity, then God is the eternal Creator and his creation is as eternal as he himself. Augustine offered the helpful suggestion that God created the world not *in tempore* but *con tempore* – that is, time was created *together with* creation. And this will be correct as far as the created time of the evening and the morning is concerned; but it does not answer the question whether 'the beginning' of creation – and therefore the beginning of created time – is to be understood in terms of time or in terms of eternity. Augustine was inclined to see the beginning in the eternity of the divine creative resolve, and to understand God as 'the eternal Creator of all times'.[22] If we transfer these conceptual possibilities to 'the end of the world', we can then say that the world does not end *in time* (so that there continues to be time afterwards) but that it ends *together with* time, time ending with the world. But in this case the end-point cannot be in time; it must be simultaneous to all the times. And from this it would then follow that God himself is 'the eternal end of all the times'.

In thinking about *the eschatological moment* we therefore come up against the same dilemma that faces us when we try to grasp the primordial moment. There is a genuine, factual reason for this, because the moment in which time enters eternity is the mirror-image of the moment when time issued from eternity. In both cases it would seem helpful to differentiate between the *primordial moment* and the *moment of inception*, and also between the *last* and the *eschatological* moment.

Isaac Luria developed the idea of *zimzum* as a way of understand-

ing the primordial moment. Schelling took this up philosophically
later on. By *zimzum* Luria meant the self-limitation of God which
precedes his creation. God makes room for his creation by with-
drawing his omnipresence. God gives his creation time by restricting
his eternity: 'Only where God withdraws "himself to himself" can he
call forth anything which is not itself divine essence and divine
being.'[23] In this self-determination God acts on himself first, before
he calls his creation to life. He creates heaven and earth in 'the space
of creation' which he has previously conceded to it,[24] and in 'the time
of creation' which he has previously conferred.[25] In this divine self-
determination we find the transition from eternity to time which we
are seeking. This is the primordial moment for the time of creation.
In that moment all the potentialities are gathered together and
prepared which God then unfurls in the time of creation. At this
point Orthodox theology talks about 'the inceptive aeon' because
out of God's primordial moment creation's moment of inception
proceeds. The primordial moment contains within itself eternity's
readiness for time, while in the moment of inception time issues from
eternity and, in the wake of the creation process, fans out as created
time into before and after, future, present and past.

The *eschatological* moment corresponds to the *primordial*
moment. It is to be found in God's own ending of his self-restriction.
God de-restricts himself and manifests his glory so that in the
transfigured creation he may be 'all in all'. Created time ends and 'the
time of creation' passes away. The created spaces will be dissolved
and 'the space of creation' passes away. Heaven and earth find their
final, transfigured form in God's unrestricted omnipresence itself.
The original divine self-limitation which made the time and space of
creation possible gives way to God's all-embracing, all-pervading
derestriction of himself. What now comes into being is the new
creation of all things in which, as Dante says, 'His glory, in whose
being all things move, pervades creation'. Then the time of creation
will become the eternal aeon of creation, and the space of creation
will become the cosmic temple for God's indwelling. Created beings
emerge out of time into the aeon of the divine glory through the
raising of the dead and the cosmic annihilation of the power of death.
Then all things will be brought back again from time, and will be
gathered together.

The eschatological moment, then, has these two sides: God
derestricts his glory, and creation enters into the kingdom of glory.

At the end of time God receives in the kingdom of his glory those he has created. So in this way the final moment passes into the eschatological moment. 'The last day' leads over to the eternal day of the new creation. No night follows this last day. It is followed by the eternity which is a beginning that knows no end.

> Can there be any day but this, though many suns to shine
> endeavour?
> We count three hundred, but we miss: there is but one,
> and that one ever.[26]

3. Aeon – the Relative Eternity of Created Being

Which eternity is meant here? Not *the absolute eternity* of God but *the relative eternity* of the new creation. This is not an *eternity of essence*; it is a *communicated eternity*, which consists in participation in God's essential eternity. The modern discussion about the parousia, which wavered between its temporalization and its eternalization, suffered from the fact that time and eternity were defined over against one another by way of reciprocal negations, and the word eternity was always used to mean the absolute eternity of God. We can escape from this false alternative if we again take up the patristic church's term 'aeon'.[27] 'Aeon' is not the absolute eternity of God. It is the relative eternity of those he has created who partake of his eternal being, first of all the angels in heaven. Aeonic time is therefore the time of the angels. Aeonic is the sphere of the invisible creation, which is called heaven and stands over the visible world, which is called earth, where time is experienced in the alternation between day and night. Aeonic too will be the new creation in the time of eternal life. If we use this aeon concept, then the transition from the time of creation into the eternity of the new creation can be conceived without difficulty. The world does not 'end', either in nothingness or even in God, but will be changed from time into the aeon.

One essential difference between time and aeon is to be found in the movement of the two. It is part of the nature of created time to be experienced by way of irreversible changes. In the 'before' and the 'after', future and past become distinguishable. Experiences of this kind make it possible to talk about linear courses of time, and enable us to project lines of time teleologically. But the movement from which aeonic time, or relative eternity, is perceived is different: this movement is circular. From time immemorial, the circle and the cycle were viewed in many cultures as an image of eternity. It is Dionysius the Areopagite (pseudo-Dionysius) to whom we owe the most detailed (even though highly speculative) doctrine of angels, and he thought that in their hymns of praise the angels 'circle round' God's throne in heaven, in spiral movements. They are transformed from one radiance to another, without growth or decrease. We could say correspondingly that created time, which is aligned towards the future, will be transformed into the circular movements of the aeonic time of the new creation. In the presence of God's absolute eternity, created time becomes the relative eternity of the new creation that corresponds to him. Cyclical and full of repetition are the hymns and dances in which created beings express their wondering love of God and their joy in their own existence. Cyclical too are the regeneration processes of everything that lives. What we call eternal life is determined by both. Time makes things old. Only eternity remains young, the eternity of which desire and joy can already give a foretaste here and now. Eternity is one of life's dimensions: it is life in depth. It means the intensity of the lived life, not its endless extension.

§4 'FROM THENCE HE SHALL COME . . .': THE CATEGORY OF HEAVEN

According to the biblical traditions and the Christian creeds, the spatial premise for Christ's parousia is 'heaven'. Christ's ascension permits the expectation that he will come from heaven. The modern historicization of reality has made creation's ancient duality 'heaven and earth' obsolete.[28] If the single, whole reality of the world is apprehended in terms of history, then only a single, universal eschatology can be thought – one which no longer differentiates spatially. This is no doubt another reason why the expectation of the parousia was either temporalized or eternalized. But without the spatial category of heaven the expectation of the parousia is inconceivable. We saw that aeon, the concept of relative eternity, mediates temporally between the absolute eternity of God and the time of the earthly world; and in the same way the concept of heaven provides the spatial mediation between the eternal being of God and his coming to earth.

We shall again look first of all at the biblical imagery. Like the expectation of Christ's coming at the end of time, the idea of heaven as the 'place' from which he comes is derived from Son of man theology. According to Daniel 7, the godless and violent rulers of the kingdoms of the world rise up from the sea of chaos (7.3). Their empires are therefore not merely godless and inhumane in themselves; they also spread a chaos of injustice and violence. But 'the Son of man', to whom God has given all power and glory and strength, comes 'in the clouds of heaven' – that is to say from above, from God the Creator himself. That is why he will bring peace to creation and drive out the forces of chaos. When we are told that the Son of man will come from heaven and in the clouds of heaven, what this is saying first of all is that he will come 'in the glory of his Father' (Mark 8.38) and therefore with the 'great power and glory' (Mark 13.26) of the Creator and Judge of all things. This presupposes that beforehand he sat 'at the right hand of Power' (Mark 14.62). He already participates in God's universal rule and can therefore eschatologically complete it. He comes from there – from the centre of divine power – and represents that power through his coming.

If, then, Christ comes 'from heaven' to set up the eternal kingdom, this is not simply a cipher for his coming 'from God'. It also designates the sphere of creation which is to be understood as 'the invisible world', over against the visible one. That is why he comes 'with the holy angels' (Mark 8.38; 13.27), whom he will send out to gather the elect from all the four corners of the earth. 'Heaven' means the upper side of the creation which according to Old Testament ideas consists of the duality 'heaven and earth'; heaven is the side beyond, the side which is indisposable and invisible. It is not the visible astral heaven that is meant, but the sphere of God's creative potentialities and powers – that is, the sphere of creation that is open to God, the sphere which the eternal God already 'indwells' and which therefore already partakes of his eternity. When we are told that the Son of man comes on the clouds of heaven, we will hardly be supposed to think of the earthly cloudy sky. We should probably think of the veiling of God's glory (Ex. 16.10) and the sign of his presence (Ex. 13.21; Rev. 10.1). God is never imagined in the transcendent 'nowhere' beyond creation. He is always thought of as the present 'God in creation', as 'the Father in heaven'. This is pictorially depicted with the idea of the heavenly throne. Heaven is the sphere of creation which already totally corresponds to God because it is totally pervaded by his glory.

The relation between heaven and earth, the invisible and the visible world, is a relation of correspondence: heaven is *the relative transcendence of the earth*, earth is *the relative immanence of heaven.*[29] In this reciprocal relationship, heaven and earth show that the world is not a self-sufficient, closed universe. It is a creation open to God. To say that Christ comes 'from heaven', is to say that he comes from the side of creation which totally accords with God and glorifies God, and that he brings the righteousness of God and his glory to earth, so that earth, like heaven, may become God's dwelling. God will reign 'on earth as in heaven'. What the Son of man brings to earth therefore has its archetype and beginning in heaven. The heaven that corresponds to God is the forecourt for the whole creation pervaded by God.

If Christ comes from heaven to earth, then he will also finally reconcile these two spheres of creation again with one another, so that there can be a fruitful exchange of heavenly and earthly energies. Isaiah 45.8 expresses this exchange symbolically when it talks about 'the skies raining down righteousness' and salvation 'sprouting forth' from the earth.

The time of heaven is different from the earthly time of transience, since it is the cyclical time of the aeon. This relative temporal eternity which mirrors God's primordial eternity stands over against the transitory time of earth. When the heaven opens itself for the earth, this relative eternity will be simultaneous to all the times of earth, and transitory time will be replaced on earth by aeonic time. The kingdom which Christ sets up is therefore 'the kingdom without end'. As we have seen, in the eschatological moment on 'the day of the Lord' this kingdom will be simultaneous to all times, embracing at once both the living and the dead and transfiguring both.

Human beings are obviously finite and mortal. It is said of the heavenly beings, the angels, that they are finite but immortal. As finite beings they participate in God's absolute eternity through their self-forgetting, unceasing contemplation of his glory, and by virtue of this participation are themselves eternal. The same may be said of the mode of existence of the dead who are raised and rise on the day of the Lord: they are created – even if newly created – beings, and yet live in eternity (Luke 20.36). Eternal life is creaturely life which becomes immortal in its inextinguishable participation in the divine wellspring of life. The God who indwells his whole creation in heaven and on earth gives all his creatures a share in his inexhaustible livingness, and expels the deadly powers of chaos.

§5 '. . . . TO JUDGE BOTH THE QUICK AND THE DEAD'

Injustice cries out to high heaven. The victims of injustice never hold their peace. The perpetrators of injustice find no rest. That is why the thirst for righteousness and justice can never be repressed. It keeps alive the remembrances of suffering, and makes people wait for a tribunal which will make right prevail. For many people, the longing for God is alive in this thirst for righteousness and justice.[30] The murderers must not be allowed to triumph over their victims for ever. The innocent victims must not be forgotten. The expectation of the great Last Judgment in which the divine justice will triumph was originally a hope cherished by the victims of world history. It was only later that Judgment was understood as punishment imposed on evil-doers. The divine universal judge was originally the God who 'creates justice for those who suffer wrong'. It was only later that he was made the penal judge of humanity, before whom all human beings have to tremble.

1. The Righteousness of God which Creates Justice

Ideas about a judgment after death were already developed in the Egyptian and Iranian religions. Whether and to what extent Jewish apocalyptic was influenced by these may be left on one side in our present discussion. We shall start here from the assumption that the Old Testament's ideas about judgment developed out of the historical experience of the righteousness and justice of the God of Israel in his covenant; and we shall therefore pay particular attention to this complex.

Yahweh judges the nations: his universal judgment will take place on 'the Day of Yahweh'.[31] It will not come about in another world beyond death, but will happen 'in the latter – or last – days' (Isa. 2.2; Micah. 4.1). Then the nations will stream up to Zion, the mountain of the Lord, and will receive justice and righteousness from him. The God of Israel will 'judge' the nations and will administer justice to all human beings. The result will be the great kingdom of peace in which all the nations will turn their swords into ploughshares and their spears into pruning hooks (Isa. 2; Micah 4; Isa. 9; 11). God's righteousness and justice creates peace. That is the meaning of the divine judgment. God will become the great arbitrator of the nations (Pss. 94; 96–99).

Yahweh will judge Israel too: 'You have I chosen before all the families of the earth. Therefore I will punish you for all your iniquities' (Amos 3.2). Judgment begins at the house of God. The great prophets of judgment preached this before all else. But Yahweh will also judge between Israel and the nations. He will bring about justice for Israel when she is powerless and oppressed, and will convict of injustice the enemies who are now triumphing over her. It was Israel's hope for justice in her oppression which gave birth to the ideas which we find expressed in the so-called 'psalms of revenge'. But these are not really visions of revenge. What they are about is how the injustice which Israel is suffering in God's name will be made good. And since this suffering is in God's name, it is not Israel's suffering only; it is God's too. God puts himself in the right when he puts Israel in the right, punishing the wickedness of the godless (Ps. 94).

What is quite generally true about the judgment which is to take place on the day of God, is particularly related to Israel in her messianic hope. The messiah king will 'establish and uphold Israel with justice and righteousness' and will create the kingdom of freedom without end (Isa. 9.7). For 'with righteousness he shall judge the poor, and decide with equity for the meek of the earth' (Isa. 11.4). He will bring righteousness and peace to the animal world as well, so that the wolves will live with the lambs (11.6). It is quite clear that the divine righteousness which is under discussion here has nothing to do with rewards and punishments. It is a righteousness that creates justice and puts people right, so it is a redemptive righteousness (Isa. 1.27). 'The day of the messiah', like the day of Yahweh, is ultimately not a *dies irae*, a day of wrath. It is the day on which peace begins. By passing judgment on injustice and enmity, the messiah creates the preconditions for the universal kingdom of peace.

2. The Apocalyptic Law of Retaliation

Jewish apocalyptic linked the idea of the universal judgment with the coming of the Son of man. The Day of Judgment was also called 'the last day' because it brings to an end not only a historical epoch but a world-time as well (II [4] Es. 7.73). The Son of man will judge, and that means he will judge everyone individually, each according to his works: 'recompense shall follow, and the reward shall be manifested; righteous deeds shall awake, and unrighteous deeds shall not sleep' (II [4] Es. 7.35). The conflict between the good and the godless, true believers and idolators, the children of light and the children of darkness, will be finally decided at the Last Judgment through 'the sword of God'. The one group will receive eternal bliss, the other eternal damnation.

In these apocalyptic pictures of the universal judgment, the idea of the divine righteousness which *creates* justice recedes in favour of the righteousness which merely *establishes facts* and reacts accordingly. The universal judgment turns into a criminal court in which the law of retaliation is applied, good being requited with good, and evil with evil. The new aeon of righteousness and eternal life is now only for the people who already count as righteous here on earth. Here we can detect the influence of the Iranian dualism of good and evil. And Jewish apocalyptic intensifies it into the notion of a final struggle between the devout and the godless, which will be decided through the intervention of the divine Judge.[32]

3. The Christian Dilemma

In taking over the title Son of man, the early Christian congregations also took over the apocalyptic expectation of judgment. The crucified One will appear at the end of days as the Son of man-Judge of the world: 'God has fixed a day on which he will judge the world in righteousness by a man whom he has appointed. and of this he has given assurance to all men by raising him from the dead' (Acts 17.31).

This is not the place for an interpretation of all the statements about judgment in the New Testament.[33] Here we shall consider only one theological problem:

The Gospel of Matthew presents the judgment in apocalyptic terms, the most detailed account being Matt. 25.31–46.[34] It is impossible to overlook the contradiction between the divine righteousness which Jesus proclaims to the poor and to sinners according to Matthew's Gospel itself, and the punitive law of retaliation which the universal Judge apocalyptically enforces. In the Gospel of John the apocalyptic judgment is present in the mission and gospel of Christ, so that it can be said on the one hand that God 'sent the Son into the world, not to condemn the world, but that the world might be saved through him' (3.17), and on the other that 'he who does not believe in him is condemned already' (3.18). In Paul too there is still tension between the Christ who pleads for those who are his, as their representative, so that there is no charge that can be brought against those who are in Christ (Rom. 8.33f.), and Christ the Judge in the final judgment, before whose judgment seat everything will be revealed, 'so that each one may receive good or evil, according to what he has done in the body' (II Cor. 5.10). The one conception is the justification of the sinner, which runs ahead; the other is the judgment according to works, which follows after.[35]

The theological problem is not the relationship between the future and the present of judgment. The problem is the difference between the righteousness of Christ in the different passages. All the New Testament writing agree in saying that in his gospel Jesus proclaimed the justice of the divine mercy to those who have received no justice, and the justice of divine forgiveness to the unjust. That was the difference between his proclamation of the kingdom and John the Baptist's. The divine righteousness which Paul makes the subject of his apostolic gospel is the creative righteousness which creates justice and justifies; it is not the penal law of retaliation

The love of God which Jesus proclaimed and embodied is not love in mutuality; it is prevenient and unconditional love. Its most perfect form is the love of one's enemies. The reconciliation in whose light the Epistle to the Colossians sees the whole cosmos, took place through Christ's self-surrender on the cross. Through his sufferings Christ has 'slain enmity', says the Epistle to the Ephesians (2.16). Through the prevenient love of enemies and by overcoming enmity, the messiah Jesus creates his kingdom of peace. That is what the gospel of peace is about.

Is it conceivable that in the final judgment the coming Christ will act in contradiction to Jesus and his gospel, and will judge according to the penal law of retaliation? He would then put Jesus himself in the wrong, and would be appearing as someone different, someone Christians do not know, and therefore a universal judge whom they would have to fear. Any such clash between the Christian faith and the Christian hope would be unendurable. It would destroy the consistency of the Christian message.

Unfortunately this tension has never been resolved in Christian tradition. On the one hand we have apocalyptic Christianity, which subordinates the saving gospel of Jesus – viewed as God's last offer in history – to the ultimate law of retaliation in the Last Judgment. On the other hand we have Christian eschatology, which sees *Jesus* in the figure of the universal judge and expects that he will finally bring justice to those who have never received justice, and will make the unjust just; which expects that he will 'slay' enmity for ever – enmity, but not his enemies, whom he will transform through the power of his love, so as finally to set up his kingdom of peace without end. The purpose of Jesus' judgment is not retaliation in all directions. Its aim is to set up the kingdom of peace, founded on the righteousness and justice which overcomes all enmity. The law which this judge applies, we might say, is a law whose purpose is rehabilitation.

The final judgment is at all events no more than the beginning of the new creation of all things, and must be viewed in this provisional character. It is not an end but a beginning. If it is seen like this, then it of course raises the question about universal reconciliation and the redemption of the devil. But this does not have to be affirmed in order to spread confidence about the judgment, any more than a double outcome of the judgment for believers and the godless has to be affirmed in order to emphasize the seriousness of the human situation. Whatever the outcome of Christ's judgment of the living and the dead – whether all will be saved or only a few – this is *Jesus'* judgment, and Christians can wait for it only in the light of the gospel of Jesus Christ which they know and believe. But this Jesus does not come to judge. He comes to raise up.[36] That is the messianic interpretation of the expectation of Christ's judgment.

§6 EXPECTANT CREATIVITY: THE EXPECTATION OF THE PAROUSIA AND AFFIRMED EMBODIMENT

When it is talking about Christ's parousia, the New Testament hardly talks about it in speculative terms at all. The context is always eucharistic and parenetic. The practical testimony to the eschatological expectation of Christ is the celebration of the eucharistic feast through which 'the Lord's death is proclaimed till he comes' (I Cor. 11.26). In act and in the Word of promise, the shared meal calls to remembrance Christ's death and anticipates his coming in glory. The feast itself is celebrated in expectation of the parousia. That is why the cry 'maranatha' probably has its origin in the celebration of the Lord's Supper. The congregation begs the Christ who is present in the Spirit of God for the coming of his kingdom. The fellowship of the eucharistic feast is therefore understood as a gift given in advance, and as an anticipatory presentation of the great banquet of the nations at which all human beings will be satisfied.

On the one hand the Christian ethic expressed in the New Testament paranesis on the one hand takes its impress from the eucharist: those who have shared the supper of the Lord should live in the fellowship of Christ and lead their whole life in his Spirit. But on the other hand its orientation is eschatological. The expectation of Christ's parousia directs all the senses towards his future, and makes them receptive here and now for the experience of history.

Where the expectation of the parousia is strongly apocalyptic in character, the paranesis stresses the need to 'endure' in faith until the end: 'Be patient. Strengthen your hearts, for the coming of the Lord is at hand' (James 5.8). 'He who endures to the end will be saved' (Matt. 10.22; 24.13). Experience of life here is always determined by assailments and hostilities. The danger of falling away from faith is obvious. But the person who hopes for Christ's impending parousia will stand fast and will not run away. The people who stand fast are the true believers, for at his coming Christ will find them to be the men and women who have hoped for him. The people who run away show that they are unbelievers, because they have not had this hope. So *perseverantia usque ad finem* – endurance to the end – always counted as the sign and testimony of true faith, and as the effect in personal life of the hope for the parousia. 'The patience of hope' (I Thess. 3) is part of the fundamental structure of new life in the community of Christ. Faith is not a matter of continually new decision. It means faithfulness to the decision which God made for men and women in Christ. Those who believe in Christ will become 'sharers in the tribulation and the kingdom and the patient endurance of Christ' (Rev. 1.9).[37]

Where expectation of the parousia is more strongly marked by awareness of the presence of Christ, it calls men and women to reshape their lives in the community of Christ. The 'day' is at hand, so believers can already 'rise' now, in this life: 'Awake, O sleeper, and arise from the dead, and Christ shall give you light' (Eph. 5.24; Rom. 13.11). Believers are 'children of light' (Eph. 5.8f.) and as children of light they should give their lives the appropriate form, casting away 'the works of darkness' and laying hold of 'the weapons of light' (Rom. 13.12). It is in this light symbolism that the kingdom of Christ and the new creation are described. Although in this world-time of violence and injustice it is still dark, believers can anticipate the light of the new creation and can already live here and now from the future of Christ.

In the parousia parenesis *the body* of human beings evidently acquires a special importance: 'Put on the Lord Jesus Christ and keep your bodies in such a way that no desires arise' (Rom. 13.14). Here, in my view, Paul is talking about destructive dependencies and obsessions which are the enemy of life; the idea is not that lust should give way to a general listlessness. In I Cor. 6 too all attention is devoted to the body. 'The body belongs to the Lord and the Lord to the body', says I Cor. 6.13, stressing the reciprocity between the body and the Lord in an astounding way. The reason is the resurrection: 'God raised the Lord and will also raise us up by his power' (v. 14); the experience is an experience in the Spirit, for: 'Your body is a temple of the Holy Spirit' (v. 19); and the conclusion is: 'Glorify God in your body' (v.20). So the Holy Spirit is experienced in the body, for the body is already pervaded by the life-giving powers of the future world. Because Christ came for the sake of the bodily resurrection, and on his day will complete the redemption of the body from the destructive power of death, God is not experienced merely in the soul. Paul stresses that he is experienced in the body too, and is therefore praised in the body. This, finally, is what Paul's hope for the parousia also has to say: 'From there we await a Saviour, the Lord Jesus Christ, who will change our lowly body to be like his glorious body' (Phil. 3.20, 21). The expected real transfiguration of the body there, corresponds to the bodily quickening in the Spirit here. The hope for the parousia is not a flight from the world. Nor does it provide any foundation for hostility towards the body. On the contrary, it makes people prepared to remain true to the earth, and to honour the body.

Life in hope for the parousia is not a matter of mere 'waiting', guarding oneself, and holding fast to the faith. It goes far beyond that, reaching out to the active shaping of life. It is *life in anticipation* of the coming One, life in 'expectant creativity'.[38] People do not live merely from traditions. They live from expectations too. In their fears and hopes they anticipate their still unknown future and adapt their present to it, shaping their lives accordingly. The expectation of the future of Christ sets the present in the light of the One who will come, and makes bodily life in the power of the resurrection experienceable. In this power it becomes life lived 'with raised heads' (Luke 21.28) and with what Ernst Bloch called 'an upright walk'. It becomes a life which is committed to working for the kingdom of God through its commitment to justice and peace in this world.

It was to this life in anticipation that the World Council of Churches called at its assembly in Uppsala in 1968.[39] The message of Uppsala brings out the creative hope for the parousia and is more relevant today than ever:

'We ask you, trusting in God's renewing power, to join in the anticipation of God's Kingdom, showing now something of the newness which Christ will complete on his day.'

NOTES

I The Messianic Perspective

1. P. Althaus, *Die letzten Dinge. Lehrbuch der Eschatologie*, Gütersloh 1957, 309.

2. K. Barth, *CD* II/2, 288f., seems to have thought in this direction. Cf. B. Klappert, *Israel und die Kirche. Erwägungen zur Israellehre Karl Barths*, Munich 1980, esp. 47ff.

3. P. von der Osten-Sacken rightly protests against this suggestion; cf. *Christian–Jewish Dialogue. Theological Foundations*, trans. Margaret Kohl, Philadelphia 1986, 83 with n. 88. It would lead only to E. Hirsch's anti-Judaism. E. Hirsch, *Jesus Christus der Herr*, Göttingen 1926, 27f.: 'It is not for nothing that we Christians find "messianism" the most alien feature of Jewish religion as it remains to the present day – as the real Jewish calamity. . . . The satanic tempter whom Jesus rejected in the story of the temptations is the Jewish messianic idea.' Because he found 'Jewish messianism' alien, Hirsch himself became the uncritical victim of the political messianism of the Führer and the Third Reich.

4. M. Buber, *Der Jude und sein Judentum*, Cologne 1963, 41.

5. G. Scholem, 'Zum Verständnis der messianischen Idee', *Judaica* I, Frankfurt 1963, 73.

6. M. Buber, *Werke* II, Munich 1964, 388; R. R. Geis, *Vom unbekannten Judentum*, Freiburg 1961, 158f.

7. J. Moltmann, *Theology of Hope*, trans. J. W. Leitch, London and New York 1967, ch. II, 141.

8. Here I am in agreement with H.-J. Kraus, *Systematische Theologie im Kontext biblischer Geschichte und Eschatologie*, Neukirchen 1983, 331ff., 347ff.

9. J. Moltmann, *The Crucified God*, trans. R. A. Wilson and John Bowden, London and New York 1974, ch. III, 82ff.

10. H. Vogel, *Christologie* I, Munich 1949, 21. Similarly earlier H.-J. Iwand, *Die Gegenwart des Kommenden*, Siegen 1955, 37: 'For Jesus Christ is the coming One. He encounters everyone whom he truly encounters from the perspective of the future, as the coming life, as the Lord of the coming world.' This christology also runs right through his *Predigtmeditationen*, Göttingen 1963. Cf. also C. Duquoc, *Messianisme de Jésus et discrétion de Dieu*, Geneva 1984.

11. J. Seim, 'Messianismus in christlicher Sicht', *EvErz* 34, 1982, 125–141, has emphatically drawn attention to this.

12. Of the extensive literature, attention must be drawn especially to M. Buber, *Das Kommende. Untersuchungen zur Entstehungsgeschichte des messianischen Glauben*, I: *Das Königtum Gottes*, Berlin 1936; II: *Der Gesalbte* in *Werke* II, 727–845. For a discussion of Buber's theory about a pre-monarchical, direct theocracy in Israel, cf. W. Dieterich, 'Gott als König. Zur Frage nach der theologischen und politischen Legitimität religiöser Begriffsbildung', *ZThK* 77, 1980, 251–268; S. Mowinckel, *He that Cometh*, trans. G. W. Anderson, Oxford 1956; G. von Rad, *Old Testament Theology* II, trans. D. M. G. Stalker, Edinburgh and London 1965, 169ff. (ET from 1960 ed., but changes made by von Rad in 4th [revised] edition are inconsiderable here); H. Gese, 'Der Messias' in *Zur biblischen Theologie*, Munich 1977, 128–151; H. Ringgren, *The Messiah in the Old Testament*, London 1956; J. Klausner, *The Messianic Idea in Israel*, trans. from Hebrew by W. F. Stinespring, London 1956; S. Herrmann, *Die prophetischen Heilserwartungen im Alten Testament. Ursprung und Gestaltwandel*, Stuttgart 1965; J. A. Soggin, *Das Königtum in Israel. Ursprünge, Spannungen, Entwicklung*, Berlin 1967; J. Becker, *Messianic Expectation in the Old Testament*, trans. D. E. Green, Philadelphia and Edinburgh 1980. Cf. also N. Füglister's summing up under the aspect of biblical theology, 'Alttestamentliche Grundlagen der neutestamentlichen Christologie' in *Mysterium Salutis*, ed. J. Feiner and M. Löhrer, 3/1, Einsiedeln 1970, 107–226.

13. H. Gese, op. cit., 130, whom I am following in this section.

14. M. Buber, op. cit., II, 913.

15. H. Gese, op. cit., 133.

16. Contrary to M. Buber, *Der Jude und sein Judentum*, 98: 'When they are forced to despair of fulfilment in the present, they project the image of the fulfilment's truth into the absolute future; the form taken by messianism is the creative expression of this despair.'

17. S. Mowinckel, *He that Cometh*, 153.

18. M. Buber, *Werke* II, 384.

19. H. Gese, op. cit., 134.

20. M. Buber, op. cit., II, 399.

21. H.-J. Kraus, op. cit., 329.

22. G. von Rad, op. cit., II, 112ff.

23. According to H. Gese, op. cit., 137, the fact that the messiah himself has to pass through the judgment makes him the martyr messiah, as Zech. 13.7 also says: 'I will strike the shepherd that the sheep may be scattered.' Mark 14.27 and Matt. 26.31 quote this passage in order to interpret Jesus' experience in Gethsemane.

24. Cf. H.W. Wolff, 'Schwerter zu Pflugscharen, Missbrauch eines Prophetenwortes?', *EvTh* 44, 1984, 280–92.

25. M. Buber, op. cit., II, 388.

26. Ibid., 389.

27. Ibid., 386.

28. M. Buber, *Der Jude und sein Judentum*, 41.

29. K. Rahner took over the term 'the absolute future' from Buber, also meaning by it eternity, not a historical dimension of time. Cf. 'Marxist Utopia and the Christian Future of Man' in *Theological Investigations* VI, London and Baltimore 1969, pp. 59–68.

30. M. Buber, *Werke* III, 756.

31. W. Benjamin saw this particularly clearly: cf. 'Geschichtsphilosophische Thesen VII' in *Illuminationen. Ausgewählte Schriften*, Frankfurt 1961, 271f.

32. G. von Rad, op. cit., II, 303.

33. K. Koch, 'Spätisraelitisches Geschichtsdenken am Beispiel des Buches Daniel', *HZ* 193, 1961, 1–32, 30.

34. Cf. here O. Plöger, *Das Buch Daniel*, Stuttgart 1965, 101ff.; also his *Theokratie und Eschatologie*, Neukirchen 1959 (ET *Theocracy and Eschatology*, Oxford 1968).

35. K. Koch, op. cit., 24.

36. M. Noth, *Gesammelte Studien zum Alten Testament*, Munich 1957, 274ff. (*The Laws in the Pentateuch and other Studies*, trans. D. R. Ap-Thomas, Edinburgh and London 1966). For a different view, cf. G. von Rad, op. cit., II, 313.

37. H. Gese, op. cit., 138.

38. G. von Rad, op. cit., II, 313.

39. H. Gese, op. cit., 144.

40. Ibid.

41. G. Scholem, 'Verständnis', 38.

42. Here I am following N. Füglister, 'Alttestamentliche Grundlagen', although he himself sets the Old Testament material under the dogmatic aspects of Christ's threefold office.

43. H. Gese, op. cit., 134.

43a. Cf. S. Mowinckel, *He that Cometh*, 187ff.; J. Smart, *History and Theology in Second Isaiah*, London 1967. For the history of research during the last hundred years. cf. H. Haag, 'Der Gottesknecht bei Deuterojesaja', *Erträge der Forschung* 233, Darmstadt 1985.

44. Cf. H. Schweizer, 'Prädikationen und Leerstellen im 1. Gottesknechtslied (Jes. 42, 1–4)', *BZ* NF 26, 1982, 251–258.

45. Thus also S. Mowinckel, op. cit., 213.

46. Ibid., 255.

47. Ernst Bloch originally wished to set up a 'system of theoretical messianism', but what actually came into being was 'the spirit of utopia' (*Der Geist der Utopie* [1918], 1923).

48. Cf. J. Moltmann, *God in Creation*, trans. Margaret Kohl, London and New York 1985, 118ff. G. Scholem made a similar distinction, op. cit., 21.

49. G. Scholem, op. cit., 20; W. Benjamin, op. cit., 227f., 280.

50. G. von Rad, op. cit., 113.

51. W. Benjamin, op. cit., 270.

52. Ibid., 269.

53. Quoted in G. Scholem, op. cit., 26.

54. J. Moltmann, 'Die nukleare Katastrophe: wo bleibt Gott?', *EvTh* 47, 1987, 50ff.

55. M. Buber, *Werke* IV, 756.

56. E. Fackenheim, *To Mend the World. Foundations of Future Jewish Thought*, New York 1982, esp. 250ff.

57. Schalom Ben-Chorin, *Die Antwort des Jona. Zum Gestaltwandel Israels*, Hamburg 1956, 113.

58. W. Benjamin, op. cit., 279.

59. G. Scholem, op. cit., 34.

60. Ibid., 73f.

61. This is what the black slaves said in the southern states of America: 'Bent down so low 'till down don't bother you no more.'

62. F. Rosenzweig, *Der Stern der Erlösung*, 3rd ed., Heidelberg 1954, III, 67 (*The Star of Redemption*, trans. W. W. Hallo, London 1971); J. Seim, 'Messianismus', 140f. Cf. also J. Moltmann, *God in Creation*, ch. XI, 'The Sabbath: the Feast of Creation', 276ff.

63. Berakoth 57b.

64. Cf., here J. Petuchowski and J. Moltmann, 'The Messianic Hope', *Christians and Jews*, *Concilium* 98, 10/1974, 56–67.

65. R. Ruether, *Faith and Fratricide. The Theological Roots of Antisemitism*, New York 1974, has put this question with all the necessary sharpness.

66. M. Buber, *Der Jude und sein Judentum*, 562. Cf. also G. Sauter, 'Jesus der Christus. Die Messianität Jesu als Frage an die gegenwärtige Christenheit', *EvTh* 42, 1982, 324–349. I am not able to follow his interpretation because he seems to replace the concept of redemption in Christian terms through the concept of reconciliation, and so pushes it out.

67. Schalom Ben-Chorin, *Die Antwort des Jona*, 99, with reference to his writing *Die Christusfrage an die Juden*, Jerusalem 1941, 25.

68. G. Scholem, op. cit., 7–8.

69. I have gone into this in more detail in P. Lapide and J. Moltmann, *Israel und Kirche: ein gemeinsamer Weg?*, Munich 1980. Cf. also however A. Dempf, *Sacrum Imperium. Geschichts- und Staats- philosophie des Mittelalters und der politischen Renaissance*, Munich 1982.

70. Cf. W. Elert's remarks, 'Das Problem des politischen Christus' in *Der Ausgang der altkirchlichen Christologie*, Berlin 1957, 26ff.

71. Cf. also R. Ruether, 'In what sense can we say that Jesus was "The Christ"?', *The Ecumenist*, 10, 1972, 22, for whom Jesus will only be the Christ in the fullest sense of the word at the end of time. Jesus is the Christ now in the sense that he has anticipated the divine victory at the end. Because she has taken the basic ideas of an eschatological theology from the *Theology of Hope*, I agree with her, contrary to her critics. Cf. also F. Mussner, *Tractate on the Jews*, ET Philadelphia 1984, ch. VI, 'Dialogue with R. Ruether'; C. Thoma, *A Christian Theology of Judaism*, trans.

H. Croner, New York 1980; P. von der Osten-Sacken, *Christian–Jewish Dialogue. Theological Foundations*, trans. Margaret Kohl, Philadelphia 1986. Also H.-J. Kraus, 'Aspekte der Christologie im Kontext alttestament-lich-jüdischer Tradition' in E. Brocke and J. Seim (eds), *Gottes Augapfel, Beiträge zur Erneuerung des Verhältnisses von Christen und Juden*, Neukirchen 1986, A: *Christologie*, 1–23. J. Seim, 'Methodische Anmerkungen zur Christologie im Kontext des christlich-jüdischen Gesprächs' in *'Wer Tora vermehrt – mehrt Leben.' Festschrift für H. Kremers*, Neukirchen 1986, 25–31.

72. Cf. J. Moltmann, *Theology of Hope*, 87: 'Jesus reveals and identifies himself as the Lord on the way to his coming lordship, and to that extent in differentiation from the one he will be' (ET slightly altered).

73. P. van Buren has rightly made these ideas the foundation of his new theological outline; cf. *Discerning the Way. A Theology of the Jewish – Christian Reality*, New York 1980.

74. For a more detailed exposition cf. J. Moltmann, *The Church in the Power of the Spirit*, trans. Margaret Kohl, London and New York 1977, IV §2: 'The Church and Israel', 136ff.; B. Klappert, *Israel und die Kirche*, Munich 1980.

75. I am here initially following O. Hofius, 'Das Evangelium und Israel. Erwägungen zu Römer 9–11', *ZThK* 83, 1986, 297–324.

76. The reason for the mission to the nations was not the Jewish 'no' but the coming of the Spirit of God upon Gentiles who believed in Christ. The Jewish 'no' is merely a historical presupposition for the mission, not its cause. This is often overlooked in modern over-interpretations of the Jewish 'no'.

77. F.-W. Marquardt, 'Feinde um unsretwillen. Das jüdische Nein und die christliche Theologie' (1977) in his *Verwegenheiten. Theologische Stücke aus Berlin*, Munich 1981, 311.

78. Contrary to E. Grässer, 'Zwei Heilswege? Zum theologischen Verhältnis von Israel und Kirche' in *Festschrift für F. Mussner, Kontinuität und Einheit*, Freiburg 1981; G. Klein, '"Christlicher Antijudaismus" – Bemerkungen zu einem semantischen Einschüchterungsversuch', *ZThK* 79, 1982, 411–450; for earlier church declarations cf. H.-J. Kraus and D. Goldschmidt (eds), *Die ungekündigte Bund*, Stuttgart 1962; on the 1980 resolution passed by the Rhenish Synod, which began a new chapter, cf. B. Klappert and H. Stark (eds), *Umkehr und Erneuerung*, Neukirchen 1980.

79. O. Hofius, op. cit., 319, rightly says: '"All Israel" does *not* attain salvation through the *preaching* of the gospel.' But he believes that 'The Israel who encounters the returning Christ will therefore believe in *him*.' But the glory of the coming Christ awakens the dead and is perceived in the seeing that is face to face, no longer 'as in a mirror, darkly'. To use the word 'believe' here, makes belief in the gospel the equivalent of the 'seeing' in the epiphany of Christ.

80. Cf. J. Klausner, *Jesus von Nazareth. Seine Zeit, sein Leben und seine Lehre*, 2nd ed., Jerusalem 1952 (*Jesus of Nazareth, his Life, Times and Teaching*, trans. from Hebrew by J. Danby, London and New York 1925),

572: 'From a general human point of view he is certainly "a light to the Gentiles". His disciples carried Israel's teaching to the Gentiles in all parts of the world, even if in mutilated and incomplete form. In this sense, no Jew can deny the importance of Jesus and his teaching for the history of the world. And in fact neither Maimonides nor Jehuda Halevi failed to recognize this aspect' (trans. from the German text). Schalom Ben-Chorin goes a step further; cf. 'Did God Make Anything Happen in Christianity? An Attempt at a Jewish Theology of Christianity', *Christian Identity*, *Concilium* 196, 2/1988, 61–70. He seeks for a reunion of the divided people of God through a world-wide fellowship which will embrace 'the children of Abraham – Jews, Christians and Moslems'. In order to make this possible the church must recognize God's 'unrevoked covenant' with Israel, and Israel must recognize that in Christianity the God of Israel has revealed himself.

II   *Trends and Transmutations in Christology*

1. I am thereby extending the hermeneutical principles from which I started in *The Crucified God*; cf. J. Moltmann, *The Crucified God*, trans. R. A. Wilson and John Bowden, London and New York 1974, ch. I.

2. W. Kasper, *Jesus der Christus*, 3rd ed., Mainz 1975; ET *Jesus the Christ*, trans. V. Green, London 1976, 41ff. has rightly localized 'the religious question about Jesus Christ' today in 'the quest for salvation in an historicized world' (52ff.). B. Forte, *Gesù di Nazaret, storia di Dio, dio della storia* (German trans., *Jesus von Nazareth: Geschichte Gottes – Gott der Geschichte*, Mainz 1984, 16ff.) goes a step further, taking up the cry for freedom from 'the systems of oppression' (German trans. 22ff.) and 'the riddle of suffering' (ibid., 27ff.) in 'a historicized world'. I am going even further, in talking about what has become an 'end-time' world, meaning by that the situation in which the end can come at any moment through a nuclear catastrophe and is possible in the future through an ecological collapse of the earth.

3. I have called this principle 'thinking in relationships and communities' and termed it 'ecological' thinking. Cf. J. Moltmann, *The Trinity and the Kingdom of God*, trans. Margaret Kohl, London 1981 (= *The Trinity and the Kingdom*, New York 1981), 19. Modern feminist theology has declared 'being in relationship' to be its principle. Cf. Carter Heyward, *The Redemption of God. A Theology of Mutual Relation*, Washington 1980; D. Sölle, *Lieben und Arbeiten. Eine Theologie der Schöpfung*, Stuttgart 1985, 44ff.; E. Moltmann-Wendel, *A Land Flowing with Milk and Honey*, trans. John Bowden, London and New York 1986, 137ff.

4. This is the error in the approach of modern English liberalism, as represented in John Hick (ed.), *The Myth of God Incarnate*, London 1977. Cf. here I. Dalferth's critical and suggestive essay 'Der Mythos vom inkarnierten Gott und das Thema der Christologie', *ZThK* 84, 1987, 320–344.

5. W. Kasper, *Jesus the Christ*, 35 has already stressed this approach.

6. Latin American liberation theology has the dialectical unity of orthodoxy and orthopraxis as its premise. Cf. G. Gutiérrez, *A Theology of Liberation*, trans. C. Inda and J. Eagleson, Maryknoll, New York, 1973, London 1974; reprint 1985, 5ff.; C. Boff, *Theology and Praxis*, Maryknoll, New York, 1987, especially Part III: 'Dialectic of Theory and Praxis', 159ff. We are taking up this idea and developing it further. The same approach has been taken by F. Herzog, *God-Walk. Liberation Shaping Dogmatics*, New York 1988. He is thereby trying out an alternative to neo-orthodox theology (K. Barth) on the one hand and to liberal theology (Schleiermacher) on the other. His stress on 'theo-praxis' is directed against the restriction of theology to 'God-talk', the title which J. Macquarrie gave his dogmatics in 1967; and Macquarrie had many followers.

7. Cf. here J. H. Yoder's Mennonite christology, *The Politics of Jesus; vicit Agnus noster*, Grand Rapids 1972, and his *Nachfolge Christi als Gestalt politischer Verantwortung*, Basle 1964.

8. See here C. Blumhardt, *Werke*, Göttingen 1968–, III, 340.

9. J. Moltmann, *The Crucified God*, 65ff.

9a. Cf. here W. Schrage, 'Heil und Heilung im Neuen Testament', *EvTh* 46, 1986, 197–214, esp. 203ff.

10. Thus rightly W. Pannenberg, *Jesus – God and Man*, trans. L. C. Wilkins and D. A. Priebe, London and Philadelphia 1968, 38ff.

11. For a more detailed exposition here cf. J. Moltmann, *Theology Today*, trans. John Bowden, London 1988 and Philadelphia 1989, ch. 2, 'Mediating Theology Today', 53ff.

12. This connection is made clear by The United Methodist Council of Bishops, *In Defense of Creation. The Nuclear Crisis and a Just Peace*, Nashville 1986, esp. 59ff., where the document talks about 'a deep-seated fear of "futurelessness"'.

13. M. Gorbachev, *For the Sake of Preserving Human Civilization*, Moscow 1987.

14. Cf. Here D. Staniloae, *Orthodoxe Dogmatik*, Einsiedeln and Gütersloh 1985, 45. Pages 291ff.: 'The world, as the work of God's love, is destined to be deified.'

15. Athanasius, *De incarnatione*, cap. 54. Cf. here A. Gilg, *Weg und Bedeutung der altkirchlichen Christologie*, Munich 1955.

16. Quoted in A. Gilg, op. cit., 83f.

17. Cf. also J. Meyendorff, *Christ in Eastern Christian Thought*, New York 1975, who describes the post-Chalcedonian history.

18. Aristotle, *Nic. Ethics*, III, 5, III2b.

19. H. Schmid, *Die Dogmatik der Ev.-luth. Kirche, dargestellt und aus den Quellen belegt*, 7th ed., Gütersloh 1983, §32: 'Unitio-unio personalis', 211ff.; H. Heppe and E. Bizer, *Die Dogmatik der Ev.-ref. Kirche, dargestellt und aus den Quellen belegt*, Neukirchen 1958, Loc XVII: '*De mediatore*', 323ff.

20. Even in Irenaeus and Tertullian, Jesus' likeness with us is still stressed,

with Rom. 8.3 as evidence. The anti-Arian approach to the problem, however, meant that from Basil onwards (ep 261, 3 PG 32, 972) it was stressed that the Logos did not assume the flesh of sin but an unscathed and hence immortal nature. Cf. finally Augustine, *De Genesi ad litteram* 10, 18 (CSEL 28/1, 320) and the doctrine about the sinless (virgin) birth of Jesus, which therefore became necessary (Ench. 41, PL 40, 252 and *de Gen. ad litt.* 10.18 CSEL 28/1, 320) Originally, therefore, the idea was that Jesus was *in actual fact* sinless, and that he thereby won back immortality for human flesh. But as early as Origen, the stress certainly shifts: the eternal Son is now so joined to the Father that there is no way in which he can turn away from his will. Jesus was sinless *by nature*, not because of a life lived out of grace (*de princ.* II, 6, 5, GCS 5, 145).

21. W. Pannenberg, op. cit., ch. 8: 'The Impasse of the Doctrine of the Two Natures', 283ff.

22. Cf. G. Gutiérrez, *The Power of the Poor in History*, Maryknoll, New York, and London 1983, and *We Drink from Our Own Wells: the spiritual journey of a people*, trans. M. J. O'Connell, Maryknoll, New York, and London 1984.

23. Is this what K. Rahner means with his double thesis that 'anthropology is deficient christology' and 'christology is self-transcending anthropology' (*Theological Investigations* I, trans. C. Ernst, Baltimore and London 1961, p. 164 n. 1)?

24. Thus K. Barth, *CD* IV/1 and IV/2 passim.

25. Cf. W. Pannenberg, 'The Appropriation of the Philosophical Concept of God as a Dogmatic Problem of Early Christian Theology' in his *Basic Questions in Theology*, II, trans. G. H. Kehm and R. A. Wilson, London 1971, 119ff.; J. Moltmann, *Theology of Hope*, trans. J. W. Leitch, London and New York 1967, 143f.; *The Crucified God*, 267ff.

26. K. Barth, *CD* IV, 1 passim; W. Pannenberg, *Jesus*, 324ff.

27. Cf. here W. Elert, *Der Ausgang der altkirchlichen Christologie*, Berlin 1957, 26ff.: 'Das Problem des politischen Christus'; F. G. Maier (ed.), *Byzanz*, Fischer Weltgeschichte 13, Frankfurt 1973, 21ff., 33ff.; A. Schmemann, 'The Problem of the Church's Presence in the World in Orthodox Consciousness' in S. C. Agouridès (ed.), *Deuxième Congrès de Théologie Orthodoxe*, Athens 1978, 236–249. The idea that the relation between church and society is like the relation between soul and body also dominates the religious ideology of the United States. Cf. S. E. Mead, *The Nation with the Soul of a Church*, New York 1975; E. L. Tuveson, *Redeemer Nation. The Idea of America's Millenial Role*, Chicago 1968.

28. R. L. Heilbroner, *Die Zukunft der Menschheit*, Frankfurt 1976.

29. G. W. F. Hegel, *Werke*, 1, 1, 140.

30. J. G. Herder, *Werke*, ed. B. Suphan, Berlin 1877–99, 13, 290.

31. E. Günther, *Die Entwicklung der Lehre von der Person Christi im 19. Jahrhundert*, Tübingen 1911; R. Slenczka, *Geschichtlichkeit und Personsein Jesu Christi. Studien zur christologischen Problematik der historischen Jesusfrage*, Göttingen 1967; C. Brown, *Jesus in European Protestant*

Thought 1778–1860, Durham, N.C., 1985; M. Baumotte (ed.), *Die Frage nach dem historischen Jesus. Texte aus drei Jahrhunderten*, Gütersloh 1984.

32. E.g. the Heidelberg Catechism of 1563, question 45.

33. P. Melanchthon, *Loci Communes* 1521, *Werke*, ed. R. Stupperich, Gütersloh 1952, II, 7.

34. I. Kant, *Der Streit der Fakultäten*, A 50ff.

35. I. Kant, *Religion within the Limits of Reason Alone*, A 67, 70.

36. F. Schleiermacher, *Glaubenslehre*, 1821/2; 2nd revised ed. 1830; ET of 2nd ed. by H. R. Mackintosh and J. S. Stewart, *The Christian Faith*, Edinburgh 1928, Philadelphia 1976, §11.

37. Ibid., §94.

38. Ibid., §93.4.

39. Ibid., §93.2.

40. Ibid., §99.1.

41. Ibid., §104.

42. C. Ullmann, *Die Sündlosigkeit Jesu. Eine apologetische Betrachtung* (1828), 7th ed., Gotha 1863, 52: 'Jesu is the one who is completely independent, the one who is from his inmost being unconditionally free and the master of himself.' (Cf. *The Sinlessness of Jesus*, trans. from 7th ed. by S. Taylor, Edinburgh 1870. The quotations here and in the text have been translated directly from the German.)

43. K. Rahner, 'Current Problems in Christology', *Theological Investigations*, I, trans. C. Ernst, London and Baltimore 1961, 149ff.; 'On the Theology of the Incarnation', *Investigations* IV, trans. K. Smith, 1966, 105ff.; 'Anonymous Christians', *Investigations* VI, trans. K.-H. and B. Kruger, 1969, 390ff.; 'Two Basic Types of Christology', *Investigations* XIII (= Pt. III of German X), trans. D. Bourke, 1975, 213ff. Cf. also K. Rahner and W. Thüsing, *Christologie – systematisch und exegetisch*, QD 55, Freiburg 1972. In recent Spanish theology also the question about Jesus and his message has forcibly changed traditional christology. Cf. O. Gonzalez, *Jesús de Nazaret, Aproximación a la christología*, 6th ed., Madrid 1975: J. I. Gonzalez Faus, *La Humanidad Nueva. Ensayo de christología*, 6th ed., Madrid 1983; R. Aguirre and P. Loidi, *Jesús el profeta de Galilea*, Bilbao 1980; J. A. Pagola, *Jesús de Nazaret. El hombre y su mensaje*, San Sebastián 1981; R. Blasquez, *Jesús, el Evangelio de Dios*, Madrid 1985.

44. K. Rahner, op. cit., VI, 393.

45. K. Rahner, op. cit., IV, 109.

46. K. Rahner and W. Thüsing, op. cit., 60.

47. K. Rahner, op. cit., VI, 394.

48. Ibid.

49. K. Rahner, 'Christology within an Evolutionary View of the World', *Investigations*, V, trans. K.-H. Kruger, 1966, 157ff.

50. On the discussion about Rahner's christology, cf. W. Kasper, 'Christologie von unten? Kritik und Neuansatz gegenwärtiger Christologie' in L. Scheffczyk, *Grundfragen der Christologie heute*, QD 72, Freiburg

1975, 141–169; J. Moltmann, 'Christsein, Menschsein und das Reich Gottes', *Stimmen der Zeit*, 1985, 619–631.

51. Thus, following Rahner, H. Vorgrimler, *Jesus – Gottes und des Menschen Sohn*, Freiburg 1984.

52. J. B. Metz, *The Emergent Church: the future of Christianity in a postbourgeois world*, trans. P. Mann, New York and London 1981; J. Moltmann, *Politische Theologie – politische Ethik*, Munich and Mainz 1984.

53. G. Gutiérrez, *The Power of the Poor in History*.

54. Cf. also J. B. Metz, 'Unterwegs zu einer nachidealistischen Theologie' in J. B. Bauer (ed.), *Entwürfe der Theologie*, Graz 1985, 209–234.

55. Cf. here J. Roth, *Armut in der Bundesrepublik*, Hamburg 1981; *Faith in the City. A Call for Action by Church and Nation*. The Report of the Archbishop of Canterbury's Commission on Urban Priority Areas, London 1985; *Economic Justice for All. Pastoral Letter on Catholic Social Teaching and the U.S. Economy*, Washington 1986.

56. M. D. Meeks, 'Political Theology and Political Economy' in M. Welker *et al.* (eds), *Gottes Zukunft – Zukunft der Welt. Festschrift für J. Moltmann*, Munich 1986, 446–456.

57. G. Anders, *Die atomare Drohung*, Munich 1983, 11ff. Cf. also *EvTh* 47, 1, 1987, on the subject 'peace', and *Concilium* 195, 1/1988, on the subject 'A Council for Peace'.

58. Ibid. Cf. also D. Henrich, 'Nuklearer Frieden' in *Konzepte*, Frankfurt 1987, 104ff.: 'It [i.e., the nuclear threat] has threatened us and all following generations with achieving their final condition, not in the eschatology of the process of reason but in the apocalypse of self-elimination. . . . From now on the possibility of the apocalyptic turn of events is one of the fundamental facts of humanity.'

59. J. Moltmann, 'Peace the Fruit of Justice' in *Concilium* 195, 1/1988, 109–120.

60. C. Chapman, *Facing the Nuclear Heresy*, Elgin (Ill.) 1987.

61. This question has been put in urgent form by H. Falcke, 'Theologie des Friedens in der einen geteilten Welt' in J. Moltmann (ed.), *Friedenstheologie – Befreiungstheologie*, Munich 1988, 17–66.

62. For more detail here cf. J. Moltmann, *God in Creation*, trans. Margaret Kohl, London and New York 1985, ch. II, §1 'The Crisis of Domination', 23ff.

63. W. Müller-Römhild (ed.) *Bericht aus Vancouver 1983*, Frankfurt 1983.

64. Cf. K. Barth, 'Die dogmatische Prinzipienlehre bei Wilhelm Herrmann' in *Die Theologie und die Kirche*, Munich 1928, 340ff.; W. Pannenberg, *Basic Questions*, 33ff. For critical comment on both, J. Moltmann, *The Crucified God*, 87ff. Pannenberg's self-correction is to be found in 'Christologie und Theologie', *KuD* 3, 1975, 159–175. Cf. also C. E. Gunton, *Yesterday and Today. A Study of Continuities in Christology*, London and Grand Rapids 1983.

III   The Messianic Mission of Christ

1. Cf. H.-J. Kraus, *Systematische Theologie im Kontext biblischer Geschichte und Eschatologie*, Neukirchen 1983 §146: 'In accordance with the Old Testament Spirit-Messiah promise, the secret of Jesus of Nazareth's messiahship is a pneumatological one. All the Gospels answer the question who Jesus is by pointing to the chrism of the Spirit of God.'

2. F. Christ, *Jesus Sophia. Die Sophia-Christologie bei den Synoptikern*, Zürich 1970: E. Schüssler-Fiorenza, *In Memory of Her. A Feminist Reconstruction of Christian Origins*, New York and London 1983, 130ff.; G. Schimanowski, *Weisheit und Messias. Die jüdischen Voraussetzungen der urchristlichen Präexistenztheologie*, Tübingen 1985.

3. G. W. H. Lampe, *God as Spirit* (the Bampton Lectures 1976), Oxford 1977, develops an interesting new pneumatological incarnation theology. Cf. also H. Berkhof, *Theologie des Heiligen Geistes*, Neukirchen 1968; Y. Congar, *I Believe in the Holy Spirit*, trans. D. Smith, London and New York 1983, and J. Dunn, *Christology in the Making. An Enquiry into the Origins of the Doctrine of Incarnation*, London and Philadelphia 1980; revised edition London 1989.

4. J. Moltmann, 'The Trinitarian History of God' in *The Future of Creation*, trans. Margaret Kohl, London and Philadelphia 1979, 80–96.

5. It is a valuable tendency in Orthodox theology to stress this dimension of christology. Cf. N. Nissiotis, *Die Theologie der Ostkirche im ökumenischen Dialog*, Stuttgart 1968, 67f., 72ff.; L. Vischer (ed.), *Geist Gottes – Geist Christi. Ökumenische Überlegungen zur Filioque-Kontroverse*, Frankfurt 1981, 13ff., 159ff.

6. E. Käsemann, *Essays on New Testament Themes*, trans. W. J. Montague, London 1964, 15ff.: 'The Problem of the Historical Jesus', esp. 27: 'The Evangelist's eschatology has determined the shape he has given to the life story of Jesus.' And 'the whole life history of Jesus as Matthew presents it is not only seen from the standpoint of eschatology, but basically shaped by it.'

7. E. Schillebeeckx, *Jesus. Die Geschichte von einem Lebenden*, Freiburg 1975 (ET *Jesus: An Experiment in Christology*, 1979).

8. Cf. Ch. V §1, and Ch. VII §3.

9. This is an objection to W. Pannenberg, *Jesus – God and Man*, trans. L. C. Wilkins and D. A. Priebe, London and Philadelphia 1968, 53ff.

10. O. Weber, *Grundlagen der Dogmatik* II, Neukirchen 1962, 75; similarly, E. Käsemann, 'On the Subject of Primitive Christian Apocalyptic' in *New Testament Questions of Today*, trans. W. J. Montague, London 1969, 108–137.

11. U. Luz, *Das Evangelium nach Matthäus*, EKK I/1, Zürich, Einsiedeln, Cologne, Neukirchen-Vluyn 1985, 108ff.; H. Gese 'Natus ex virgine' in his *Von Sinai zum Zion*, Munich 1974, 130–146; I. Broer, 'Die Bedeutung der "Jungfrauengeburt" im Matthäusevangelium', *BiLe* 12, 1971, 248–260; J. H. Raatschen, 'Empfangen durch den Heiligen Geist. Überlegungen zu Mt 1, 18–25', thbeitr 11, 1980, 52–72; A. M. Durable, 'La conception virginale

et la citation d'Is Vii, 14 dans L'Evangile de Matthieu', *Revue Biblique* 85, 1978, 362–380: L. Cantwell, 'The Parentage of Jesus: Mt 1:18–21', *NT* 24, 1982, 304–315; W. Barnes Tatum, '"The Origin of Jesus Messiah" (Matth. 1:18a). Matthew's Use of the Infancy Traditions', *JBL* 96, 1977, 523–535; H. Schürmann, *Das Lukasevangelium*, HThK III, 1, 2nd ed., Freiburg, Basle and Vienna 1982; R. E. Brown (ed.), *Mary in the New Testament: a collaborative assessment by Protestant and Roman Catholic scholars*, London and Philadelphia 1978.

12. H. F. von Campenhausen, 'Jungfrauengeburt in der Theologie der Alten Kirche' in his *Urchristliches und Altkirchliches*, Tübingen 1979, 63ff. (*The Virgin Birth in the Theology of the Ancient Church*, trans. F. Clarke, London 1964); M. Luther, *Large Catechism* in *The Book of Concord*, ed. T. G. Tappert, Philadelphia 1959; H. Zwingli, *Fidei Ratio*, BSRK 80; F. D. E. Schleiermacher, *The Christian Faith*, trans. of 2nd revised ed. by H. R. Mackintosh and J. S. Stewart, Edinburgh 1928, §97.2; B. Bauer, *Kritik der evangelischen Geschichte der Synoptiker* I (1841), Hildesheim and New York 1974, 90f.; K. Barth, *CD* I/1, 138ff. esp. 172–202; P. Althaus, *Die christliche Wahrheit* II, Gütersloh 1948, 217; H.-J. Kraus, *Reich Gottes: Reich der Freiheit*, Neukirchen-Vluyn 1975, 261, 269; H. Koch, *Virgo Eva – Virgo Maria*, Arbeiten zur Kirchengeschichte 25, Berlin 1937; K. Rahner, 'Mary's Virginity' in *Theological Investigations* XIX, trans. E. Quinn, London 1984, 218–31; K. Riesenhuber, *Maria im theologischen Verständnis von K. Barth and K. Rahner*, QD 60, Freiburg 1973.

13. Cf. e.g., M. Schmaus, *Katholische Dogmatik*, V: *Mariologie*; §3: 'Maria die Mutter des menschgewordenen Gottes'; §4: 'Maria die jungfräuliche Mutter Jesu Christi', Munich 1955; also *Mysterium Salutis* III, 1, Einsiedeln, Zürich and Cologne 1970, 64ff.: 'Das Christusereignis als Tat des Vaters: Die Urheberschaft Gottes des Vaters beim wunderbaren Eintritt des Gottmenschen und Erlösers Jesus Christus in die Geschichte.'

14. This is what S. Ben-Chorin supposes in *Mirjam – Mutter Jesu*, Munich 1971.

15. Cf. E. Brunner, *Dogmatik* II, Zürich 1950, 377f. (Cf. *Dogmatics*, trans. Olive Wyon, 3 vols., London 1949–62); P. Althaus, *Die christliche Wahrheit* II, 212ff.; W. Pannenberg, *Jesus – God and Man*, 141ff.; also *The Apostles' Creed in the Light of Today's Questions*, trans. Margaret Kohl, London 1972, 71ff.; cf. also G. Lohfink, 'Gehört die Jungfrauengeburt zur biblischen Heilsbotschaft?', *ThQ* 159, 1979, 304–306. W. Kasper, *Jesus the Christ*, trans. V. Green, London 1976, is a Catholic christology without mariology. On the other hand there was and is in the Koran a recognition of Jesus' virgin birth without belief in his divine sonship. Cf. H. Räisänen. *Das koranische Jesusbild. Ein Beitrag zur Theologie des Koran*, Helsinki 1971, 92.

16. Cf. H. Küng and J. Moltmann (eds), *Mary in the Churches*, *Concilium* 168, 8/1983.

17. U. Luz, *Matthäus*, 105.

18. W. Pannenberg, *Apostles' Creed*, 74f.; Luz, op. cit., 109.

19. W. Pannenberg, ibid., 73f.

20. K. Barth, *CD* I/2, 138ff.

21. O. Weber, *Grundlagen der Dogmatik* II, Neukirchen 1962, 121: 'It is, in the language of "the age of magic", a kerygmatic statement about Jesus' origin, not about his family tree. "Eschatological history" applied to the origin of Jesus!' U. Luz, op. cit., 109: 'Christ is *creatura* of the Spirit.' This should be compared with Schleiermacher's criticism of old; cf. *Christian Faith*, §97.2.

22. U. Luz, op. cit., 104, however, does not wish to think of the Spirit as 'Mary's sexual partner', but rather of 'the creative intervention of God through the Spirit'. But with this he is replacing the generative metaphor by a creative one. This would make Christ God's created being, but not his Son. And since this idea has to do with the Fatherhood of God, the generative metaphor has to be preserved.

23. M. Meyer, 'Das "Mutter-Amt" des Hl. Geistes in der Theologie Zinzendorfs', *EvTh* 43, 1983, 415–430.

24. Thus M. Scheeben calls the Holy Spirit the 'virgin-bridal-motherly person in the Trinity'; cf. *Die Mysterien des Christentums* (1865), Freiburg 1941, 155ff.

25. E. Hennecke and W. Schneemelcher (eds), *Neutestamentliche Apokryphen* I, 4th ed., Tübingen 1968, 199ff. (ET of 1st edition, *New Testament Apocrypha*, I, trans. A. J. B. Higgins, G. Ogg, R. E. Taylor and R. McL. Wilson, London 1963); E. Pagels, *The Gnostic Gospels*, London 1980, New York 1981, 62f.

26. E. Brunner rightly asks, op. cit., 417f., 'whether it is permissible to interpret it [i.e., the parthenogenesis] in such a way that generation can be, not creation in time, but *assumptio carnis?*' (Cf. ET *Dogmatics*).

27. For this reason Brunner, ibid., 421, wished to believe in the divinity of Jesus in the sense of his eternal divine sonship not *because of* but '*in spite of* the doctrine of the virgin birth'.

28. W. Pannenberg, *Apostles' Creed*, 72.

29. E. Moltmann-Wendel, H. Küng and J. Moltmann (eds), *Was geht uns Maria an?*, Gütersloh 1988.

30. Cf. J. Moltmann, *The Church in the Power of the Spirit*, trans. Margaret Kohl, London and New York 1977, Ch. V. 3: 'Baptism', esp. 232ff.; *The Trinity and the Kingdom of God*, trans. Margaret Kohl, London 1981 (= *The Trinity and the Kingdom*, New York 1981), Ch. III, 2.1: 'Jesus' Baptism and Call', 65ff. Cf. also F. Lieb, 'Der Heilige Geist als Geist Jesu Christi', *EvTh* 23, 1963, 283ff.

31. P. Vielhauer, 'Johannes der Täufer', *RGG*[3] III, col. 805.

32. J. M. Robinson, 'Jesus as Sophas and Sophia: "Wisdom, Tradition and the Gospels"' in R. Wilken (ed.), *Aspects of Wisdom in Judaism and Early Christianity*, Notre Dame 1975, 1–16.

33. Cf. H. Gese, 'Der Messias' in his *Zur biblischen Theologie*, Munich 1977, 128–151; H.-J. Kraus, *Systematische Theologie*, op. cit., 372. The son of God idea is used in all sacral monarchies as legitimation for the royal

authority. H. Gese sees the Davidic form of this idea in Yahweh's indwelling on Zion, which comes about when the Ark is brought there (130f.). The idea of the son also implies the fatherhood of God, e.g., Ps. 89.26f.: 'He shall cry to me, "Thou art my Father, my God, and the Rock of my salvation". And I will make him the first-born.' II Sam. 7.14 may also be cited here: 'I will be his father (i.e., of the Davidic king), and he shall be my son.' Because the idea of the son of God and the idea of the first-born are also applied to Israel as a whole (Ex. 4.22; Deut. 1.31; 32.6, 18; Isa. 63.16; and frequently), king and people stand in a relationship of mutual identity.

34. J. Jeremias, *New Testament Theology* I, trans. John Bowden, London 1971, 62.

35. J. Calvin, *Institutio* II, 15.2–3.

36. Thus V. Lossky, *In the Image and Likeness of God*, London 1974, 92.

37. J. Calvin, *Inst.* II, 15.2.

38. Cf. here J. Moltmann, *The Church in the Power of the Spirit*, Ch. III. 2: 'The Messianic Mission of Jesus', 76ff.

39. J. Schniewind, *Ursprung und erste Gestalt des Begriffs Evangelium*, I Gütersloh 1927, II Gütersloh 1931; P. Stuhlmacher, *Das Evangelium und die Evangelien*, WUNT 28, Tübingen 1983, 1–26.

40. G. Friedrich, 'εὐαγγελίζομαι', *TDNT* II, 707–737.

41. This was rightly stressed by H. Schlier, *Wort Gottes. Eine neutestamentliche Besinnung*, 2nd ed., Würzburg 1962.

42. Cf. J. Moltmann, *The Church in the Power of the Spirit*, Ch. IV.5: 'The Kingdom of God in the Future and the Present', 189ff.

43. Thus rightly L. Schottroff and W. Stegemann, *Jesus von Nazareth – Hoffnung der Armen*, Stuttgart 1978, on whose research I am drawing here. Cf. also W. Schottroff and W. Stegemann (eds), *Der Gott der kleinen Leute*, I and II, Munich 1979.

44. A. Kuschke, 'Arm und Reich im Alten Testament', *ZAW* 16, 1931, 3ff.; G. Gutiérrez, *The Power of the Poor in History*, trans. R. R. Barr, Maryknoll, New York and London 1983.

45. Contrary to K. Barth, *CD* IV/2, 188: 'The beatitudes denote and describe the situation of these men, and its significance and promise for them, as grounded in the presence of Jesus. They are blessed because Jesus is there, and in relation to what He brings them. That is why they are put into the mouth of Jesus. . . . The Gospel beatitudes are not analytical but synthetic statements.'

46. G. Theissen, *The First Followers of Jesus: a sociological analysis of the earliest Christianity*, trans. John Bowden, London 1978 (= *Sociology of Early Palestinian Christianity*, Philadelphia 1978); also *The Shadow of the Galilean*, trans. John Bowden, London and Philadelphia 1987.

47. Cf. D. Sölle, 'Die Zukunft der Armen' in *Gottes Zukunft – Zukunft der Welt. Festschrift für J. Moltmann*, Munich 1986, 404–413.

48. W. Stegemann, *Das Evangelium und die Armen. Über den Ursprung der Theologie der Armen in Neuen Testament*, Munich 1981, 24.

49. W. Lohfink, *Wem gilt die Bergpredigt? Beiträge zu einer christlichen Ethik*, Freiburg 1988, 99ff.

50. I am here taking the direction which E. Käsemann struck out almost on his own, and am accentuating it. Cf. E. Käsemann, 'Wunder im NT', *RGG*³, VI, col. 1835–1837. Following his life-long researches on the idea of the body of Christ, Käsemann termed it his final insight to have discovered 'the relevance of salvation as healing and de-demonization': *Kirchliche Konflikte* I, Göttingen 1982, 33. His teacher E. Peterson was admittedly already on the same track; cf. *Was ist der Mensch* (1948) in *Theologische Traktate*, Munich 1951, 227–238, esp. 228. For an account of the exegetical situation, cf. W. Schrage, 'Heil und Heilung im Neuen Testament', *EvTh* 46, 1986, 197–214.

51. Schrage, ibid., 210.

52. Ibid., 200.

53. Cf. H. Seesemann, 'ὅλος', *TDNT* V, 174–5.

54. The World Missionary Conference in Bangkok in 1973 expressed this in Section II as follows: 'The salvation which Christ brought and in which we share offers us holistic life in this divided world. We understand salvation as the renewal of life – as the development of true humanity in "the fulness of the Godhead" (Col. 2.9). It is the salvation of the soul and the body, of the individual *and* the community, mankind *and* the whole sighing creation (Rom. 8.19). . . . This work of liberation will be complete only when "death is swallowed up in victory" (I Cor. 15.55). . . . In the comprehensive concept of salvation we recognize four social dimensions of the work of healing: 1. Salvation acts in the struggle for economic justice against the exploitation of human beings by other human beings 2. Salvation acts in the struggle for human dignity against the political oppression of human beings by other human beings. 3. Salvation acts in the struggle for solidarity against the cultural alienation of human beings by other human beings. 4. Salvation acts in the struggle for hope against despair in the life of the individual.' Cf. also M. Lehmann-Habeck (ed.), *Dein Reich komme. Weltmissionskonferenz in Melbourne 1980*, Frankfurt, 1980, 127ff.

55. Cf. D. Bonhoeffer, *Letters and Papers from Prison*, ed. E. Bethge, trans. R. H. Fuller, [4th] enlarged ed. London and New York 1971, 361 (letter of 16.7.44): 'Only the suffering God can help.'

56. K. Barth, *CD* IV/2, 238ff., distinguishes between 'the way from faith to miracle' and 'the way from miracle to faith'.

57. G. Ebeling worked this out with particular care; cf. 'Jesus und Glaube' in *Wort und Glaube*, Tübingen 1960, 203–254 (cf. *Word and Faith*, trans. J. W. Leitch, London 1963).

58. Cf. Carter Heyward, *The Redemption of God. A Theology of Mutual Relation*, Washington 1982; E. Moltmann-Wendel, *A Land Flowing with Milk and Honey*, trans. John Bowden, London and New York 1986, 121ff., to whom I am indebted for the pointer to the following stories about women, and the interpretation of these stories.

59. This is rightly stressed by Ebeling, op. cit., 235.

60. J. Jeremias 'Zöllner und Sünder', ZNW 30, 1931, 293–300.

61. Thus L. Ragaz, *Die Gleichnisse Jesus. Seine soziale Botschaft* (1943), Hamburg 1971, 109.

62. Ibid., 112.

63. For more detail here cf. J. Moltmann, *The Church in the Power of the Spirit*, ch. V. 4: 'The Lord's Supper', 242–260.

64. J. Moltmann, *Politische Theologie – politische Ethik*, Munich 1984, 124ff.

65. G. Lohfink, '"Schwerter zu Pflugscharen"', *ThQ* 166, 1986, 184–209, esp. 206.

66. E. Wolf, 'Schöpferische Nachfolge' in *Peregrinatio II. Studien zur reformatorischen Theologie, zum Kirchenrecht und zur Sozialethik*, Munich 1965, 231. Only D. Bonhoeffer took up this theme in contemporary German theology in *The Cost of Discipleship*, trans. R. H. Fuller, London 1959.

67. J. Yoder, 'Der prophetische Dissenz der Täufer' in G. F. Hershberger (ed.), *Das Täufertum*, Stuttgart 1963, 95: 'The recognition that Christ alone is Redeemer and Lord was certainly the most valuable recognition of the Reformation; but it was confined by the Reformation itself to a single sphere of application. In *the doctrine of salvation* as in church order, the thesis about the uniqueness of Christ contributed to a polemic against the mass, the veneration of saints and the hierarchy. Yet the authority of Christ remained curiously limited. He could not count *as normative for ethics*. The perfect *obedience of Christ* is for orthodox Protestantism not a yardstick for *the obedience of faith*; it is merely the premise for Christ's innocent and hence vicarious death.'

68. Cf. the second thesis in the Barmen Declaration: 'Jesus Christ is God's promise of the forgiveness of *all* our sins; equally and with equal seriousness, he is also God's powerful claim to our *whole* life . . .' (my italics).

69. Quoted in J. Yoder, op. cit., 95. Cf. also J. Fast, *Beiträge zu einer Friedenstheologie. Eine Stimme aus den historischen Friedenskirchen*, Maxdorf 1982, 15; cf. for a Quaker account of George Fox's christology cf. L. Benson, 'George Fox's Teaching about Christ', *Quaker Religious Thought* 39/40, winter 1974–75 (volume title *Christ as Prophet*), 20–45. Cf. also N. Blough, *Christologie Anabaptiste. Pilgram Marpeck et l'humanité du Christ*, Geneva 1984.

70. We are here taking up the unjustly forgotten thesis of A. Trocmé, *Jésus Christ et la revolution non-violente*, Geneva 1961, which J. H. Yoder pursued further in *The Politics of Jesus: vicit Agnus noster*, Grand Rapids 1972, 64ff. For the Old Testament concept, cf. W. Zimmerli, 'Das "Gnadenjahr des Herrn"' in *Studien zur alttestamentlichen Theologie und Prophetie*, Munich 1974, 222–234. Cf. also now S. H. Ringe, *Jesus, Liberation and the Biblical Jubilee*, Philadelphia 1985, which takes account of the latest exegetical findings.

71. C. Westermann, *Isaiah 40–66*, trans. D. M. G. Stalker, London and Philadelphia 1969, 364ff.

72. J. H. Yoder, *Politics of Jesus*, 67.

73. Ibid., 68. Cf. also L. Schottroff and W. Stegemann, *Jesus von Nazareth – Hoffnung der Armen*, 1978.

74. G. Lohfink, *Wie hat Jesus Gemeinde gewollt?*, 7th ed., Freiburg 1987, (ET of 1982 edition, *Jesus and Community: The Social Dimensions of Christian Faith*, trans. John P. Galvin, Philadelphia and London 1985).

75. A. Schweitzer, *The Mysticism of Paul the Apostle*, trans. W. Montgomery, London 1931, 189.

76. P. Schäfer, 'Die Tora der messianischen Zeit', *ZNW* 65, 1974, 27–42, esp. 36. I am following Schäfer here.

77. E. Käsemann, *An die Römer*, Handbuch zum Neuen Testament 8a, 4th ed., Tübingen 1980, 85ff. (*Commentary on Romans*, trans. G. W. Bromiley, Grand Rapids and London 1980).

78. U. Luz, *Das Evangelium nach Matthäus*, 197ff.

79. For the interpretation of the Sermon on the Mount cf. the following: H. D. Betz, *Studien zur Bergpredigt*, Tübingen 1985; H. Büchele, 'Bergpredigt und Gewaltfreiheit', *StZ* 106, 1981, 632–640; C. Dietzfelbinger, 'Die Anthithesen der Bergpredigt im Verständnis des Matthäus', *ZNW* 70, 1979, 1–15; G. Eichholz, *Auslegung der Bergpredigt*, 3rd ed., Neukirchen-Vluyn 1975; H. Gollwitzer, 'Bergpredigt und Zwei-Reiche-Lehre' in J. Moltmann (ed.), *Nachfolge und Bergpredigt*, Kaiser Traktate 65, 2nd ed., Munich 1982, 89–120; P. Hoffmann, 'Auslegung der Bergpredigt I–V', *BiLe* 10, 1969, 57–65, 111–122, 175–189, 264–275; *BiLe* 11, 1970, 89–104; K.-S. Krieger, 'Das Publikum der Bergpredigt (Mt 4, 23–35). Ein Beitrag zu der Frage: Wem gilt die Bergpredigt?', *Kairos* 28, 1986, 98–119; J. Lambrecht, *Ich aber sage euch. Die Bergpredigt als programmatische Rede Jesus (Mt 5–7, Lk 6.20–49)*, Stuttgart 1984; W. Lienemann, *Gewalt und Gewaltverzicht. Studien zur abendländischen Vorgeschichte der gegenwärtigen Wahrnehmung von Gewalt*, Munich 1982; G. Lohfink, 'Wem gilt die Bergpredigt? Eine redaktionskritische Untersuchung von Mt 4,23–5,2 und 7,28f., *ThQ* 163, 1983, 264–284; U. Luz, 'Die Erfüllung des Gesetzes bei Matthäus (Mt 5,17–20), *ZThK* 75, 1978, 398–435; H. Merklein, *Die Gottesherrschaft als Handlungsprinzip. Untersuchung zur Ethik Jesu*, 3rd ed., Würzburg 1984; P. Schäfer, 'Die Torah der messianischen Zeit', *ZNW* 65, 1974, 27–42; L. Schottroff, 'Gewaltverzicht und Feindesliebe in der urchristlichen Jesus tradition. Mt 5, 38–48; Lk 6,27–36' in G. Strecker (ed.), *Jesus Christus in Historie und Theologie. Festschrift für Hans Conzelmann*, Tübingen 1975, 197–221; W. Schrage, *Ethics of the New Testament*, trans. David E. Green, Edinburgh 1988; G. Strecker, *Der Weg der Gerechtigkeit. Untersuchung zur Theologie des Matthäus*, FRLANT 82, 2nd ed., Göttingen 1966; P. Stuhlmacher, 'Jesus vollkommenes Gesetz der Freiheit. Zum Verständnis der Bergpredigt', *ZThK* 79, 1982, 283–322; G. Theissen, 'Gewaltverzicht und Feindesliebe (Mt 5, 38–48; Lk 6, 27–38) und deren sozialgeschichtlicher Hintergrund' in his *Studien zur Soziologie des Urchristentums*, WUNT 19, Tübingen 1979, 160–197.

80. Cf. the dispute between K.-S. Krieger, 'Das Publikum der Berg-

predigt', and G. Lohfink, *Wem gilt die Bergpredigt?*, Freiburg 1988, 199–209.

81. D. Bonhoeffer, *The Cost of Discipleship*, 104, 109. Also here J. Moltmann (ed.), *Nachfolge und Bergpredigt*, with contributions by H. Gollwitzer, R. Heinrich, U. Luz and W. H. Schmidt.

82. P. Hoffmann, 'Tradition und Situation' in K. Kertelge (ed.), *Ethik im Neuen Testament*, QD ·102, Freiburg 1984, 108f.: 'But if Jesus' precept belongs in the context of the dawning *basileia* of God, which has as its goal God's saving acts for *the world*, and in so far – going beyond Israel – means God's commitment to *every* human being, then the interpretation of the commandment must also pursue this universal dimension. It aims in the specific historical situation first of all at the conversion of Israel, but by virtue of its message is directed beyond Israel – to the world as a whole, in which God is to be recognized as Lord and his lordship is to be perceived and implemented as the lordship of the good.' In the eschatological dimension of the messiah, the pre-existent Wisdom of God evidently returns. The identification of the divine Wisdom with Jesus himself is part of Matthew's messianology. Cf. G. Schiamanowski, op. cit., 313f.; E. Schüssler-Fiorenza, op. cit., 130ff. From the perspective of the Wisdom of creation, the universal dimension of the Sermon on the Mount emerges of itself.

83. Thus especially E. Arnold, *Salz und Licht. Über die Bergpredigt*, Moers 1982. E. Arnold was the founder of the 'Bruderhof' in the Rhön mountains in 1920, and after expulsion by the Gestapo in 1937 joined the Hutterian Brethren in the United States.

84. Thus E. Käsemann, 'Bergpredigt – eine Privatsache?' in Aktion Sühnezeichen/Friedensdienste (ed.), *Christen im Streit um den Frieden. Beiträge zu einer neuen Friedensethik*, Freiburg 1982, 74–83; contrary to M. Hengel, 'Die Bergpredigt in der aktuellen Diskussion' in the same volume, 60–73.

85. D. Bonhoeffer, *The Cost of Discipleship*, 104, 175f.; G. Lohfink, *Wie hat Jesus Gemeinde gewollt?*, 78.

86. M. Buber, *Bilder von Gut und Böse*, 2nd ed., Cologne-Olten 1953, 29, 32ff.

87. C. Westermann, *Genesis 1–11. A Commentary*, trans. J. J. Scullion, Minneapolis and London 1984, 363ff., does not bring out the political reference of the story as clearly as this.

88. W. Benjamin, 'Zur Kritik der Gewalt', *Gesammelte Schriften* II/1, Frankfurt 1980, 179. Cf. also R. Girard, *Des choses cachees depuis la fondation du monde*, Paris 1978, and *La violence et le sacré*, Paris 1972; R. Herzog, 'Gewalt', *EStL*, 2nd ed., 1975, 852–854; H. Siemers, 'Gewalt', *ESL*, 1980, 520–573; K.-G. Faber, 'Macht' III–IV, 1, *GGB* 3, 1982, 837. L. Ragaz. *Die Bergpredigt Jesu*, Gütersloh 1979, 19: 'Violence divides from God and from human beings. . . . Anyone who comes to God can no longer be a person of violence. . . . Anyone who reverences God, reverences also the sacred rights of the other, the other human being, the other nation, the other race, the other religion.'

89. P. Hoffmann, op. cit., 50–118; W. Klassen, *Love of Enemies. The Way to Peace*, Philadelphia 1984; J. Becker, 'Feindesliebe – Nächstenliebe – Bruderliebe. Exegetische Beobachtungen als Anfrage an ein ethisches Problemfeld', *ZEE* 25, 1981, 5–18; D. Lührmann, 'Liebet eure Feinde (Lk 6, 27–36/Mt 5, 39–48)', *ZThK* 69, 1972, 412–438; L. Schottroff, 'Gewaltverzicht und Feindesliebe in der urchristlichen Jesustradition. Mt 5, 38–48; Lk 6, 27–36' in G. Strecker (ed.), *Jesus Christus in Historie und Theologie. Festschrift für H. Conzelmann*, Tübingen 1975, 197–221; G. Theissen, 'Gewaltverzicht und Feindesliebe (Mt 5, 38–48; Lk 6, 27–38) und deren sozialgeschichtlicher Hintergrund' in his *Soziologie des Urchristentums*, Tübingen 1979, 160–197.

90. See H. Falcke, 'Theologie des Friedens in der einen geteilten Welt' in J. Moltmann (ed.), *Friedenstheologie – Befreiungstheologie*, Munich 1988, 17–66.

91. Ibid., 45.

92. G. Lohfink, 'Schwerter zu Pflugscharen', 184–209, which I am following in this section. Cf. also H. W. Wolff, 'Schwerter zu Pflugscharen – Missbrauch eines Prophetenwortes?' *EvTh* 44, 1984, 280–292, and W. Pannenberg's 'Diskussionsbeitrag', ibid., 293–297.

93. Thus H. W. Wolff, op. cit., 289; G. Lohfink, op. cit., 190.

94. Cf. K. Wengst, *Pax Romana, and the Peace of Jesus*, trans. John Bowden, London and Philadelphia 1987.

95. Origen, *Contra Celsum*, trans. and ed. H. Chadwick, Cambridge 1953, V.33: ' "All nations" are coming to it [the house of the Lord], and "many nations" go, and we exhort one another to the worship of God through Jesus Christ which has shone out in the last days, saying: "Come, and let us go up to the mountain of the Lord and to the house of the God of Jacob, and he will proclaim to us his way and we will walk in it."

96. G. Lohfink, op. cit., 195.

97. E. Peterson, 'Monotheismus als politisches Problem' (1935) in *Theologische Traktate*, Munich 1951, 45–147: G. Lohfink, op. cit., 195ff.

98. Eusebius, *Praeparatio evangelica* I, 4–5: 'But when the Messiah of God appeared, about whom it had once been said through the prophets: ... They will reforge their swords into ploughshares and their lances to pruning hooks . . . the fulfilment followed in complete correspondence to the prophecy. For with *the Romans all rule by the many was immediately abolished* – since at the very time when our Redeemer appeared Augustus assumed sole rule. . . . But with the teaching of our Redeemer, which was so well pleasing to God and so incomparably peaceable, the purification from the error of the worship of many gods was achieved, and with the purification from the worship of many gods, *rivalry among the nations* ceased, the ancient evils being thereby immediately abolished.'

99. Quoted by Lohfink in *Wem gilt die Bergpredigt?*, 183.

100. Cf. Ch. II, §2.

101. J. Calvin, *Institutio Religionis Christianae* II, 15; K. Blaser, *Calvins Lehre von den drei Ämtern Christi*, ThSt 105, Zürich 1970. Cf. also earlier:

A. Krauss, *Das Mittlerwerk nach dem Schema des munus triplex*, JDTh 17, 4, Gotha 1872; E. F. K. Müller, 'Jesu Christi dreifaches Amt', *RE*³, 1900, col. 733–741.

102. Cf. Carter Heyward, *The Redemption of God. A Theology of Mutual Relation*; E. Moltmann-Wendel, *A Land Flowing with Milk and Honey*, 121ff.; I am indebted to her for the pointers to Jesus' relationships.

103. Cf. here now P. Stuhlmacher, *Jesus von Nazareth – Christus des Glaubens*, Stuttgart 1988, 27ff.

104. W. Wrede, *Das Messiasgeheimnis in den Evangelien* (1901), 3rd ed., Göttingen 1963 (ET, *The Messianic Secret*, trans. J. C. G. Greig, London and Cambridge 1971). R. Bultmann, *Theology of the New Testament*, trans. K. Grobel, London 1952, I, 27, assumed that 'Jesus' life and work . . . was not messianic'. Consequently for him Jesus' proclamation counted as a presupposition for the theology of the New Testament, but was not part of it.

105. Cf. R. Bultmann, op. cit., 29: 'It must be admitted that in them he speaks of the Son of Man in the third person without identifying himself with him.' W. Pannenberg, *Jesus – God and Man*, 58: 'Jesus' claim means an anticipation of a confirmation that is to be expected only from the future.'

106. J. Jeremias, *Abba. Studien zur neutestamentlichen Theologie und Zeitgeschichte*, Göttingen 1966, 1–80 (The Prayers of Jesus [selections], trans. John Bowden, London, Naperville Ill., 1967); J. Sobrino, *Christology at the Crossroads*, London 1978, 146–178: 'The Prayer of Jesus'.

107. J. Moltmann, 'Ich glaube an Gott den Vater. Patriarchalische und nichtpatriarchalische Rede von Gott?', *EvTh* 43, 1983, 397–415.

108. S. Ben-Chorin, *Mutter Mirjam*, 99ff.

109. G. Lohfink, *Wie hat Jesus Gemeinde gewollt?*, 62. It is however incomprehensible why according to Lohfink there should indeed be no 'patriarchal rule' in the new family of Christ, but no 'sisterliness' either – only 'brotherliness'.

110. I am here taking up the results of the researches of E. Moltmann-Wendel in *A Land Flowing with Milk and Honey*, 117ff.; for further details see there.

111. G. Lohfink, *Gemeinde*, 21: 'With the constitution of the twelve and with their proclamation of the kingdom of God, the existence of the Israel of the end-time already begins.'

112. E. Käsemann, 'On the Subject of Primitive Christian Apocalyptic', in *New Testament Questions of Today*, 119.

113. This was stressed with particular clarity by E. Peterson, 'Die Kirche aus Juden und Heiden', *Theologische Traktate*, 239–292.

114. See Ch. I, §4.

115. Cf. here Ahn Byung-Mu, 'Jesus und das Minjung im Markusevangelium' in J. Moltmann (ed.), *Minjung-Theologie des Volkes Gottes in Süd-Korea*, Neukirchen 1984, 110–132, and the new Korean Minjung theology, which renders *ochlos* by the Korean word 'Minjung', which is not identical with the word 'people' or the German word *Volk*. Cf. here J. B. Metz,

'Kirche und Volk' in *Glaube in Geschichte und Gesellschaft*, Mainz 1977, ET, 'Church and People'. *Faith in History and Society*, trans. D. Smith, London, 1980, 136–153; J. Moltmann, 'Solidarität des Volkes' in *Neuer Lebensstil. Schritte zur Gemeinde*, 2nd ed., Munich 1977, 114–136 (cf. 'Hope in the Struggle of the People' in *The Passion for Life: A Messianic Lifestyle*, free trans. by M. D. Meeks, Philadelphia 1978 = *The Open Church. Invitation to a Messianic Lifestyle*, London 1978).

116. I do not understand the earthly Jesus as 'the royal man' like K. Barth, *CD* IV/2 § 64.3, 154ff., because I assume that 'the royal rule' of Jesus begins only with his exaltation and will be completed only in his parousia. According to my own view, its projection back on to the earthly Jesus leads merely to a *christologia gloriae*, which makes it possible to ignore the poverty and human weaknesses of the earthly Jesus.

IV The Apocalyptic Sufferings of Christ

1. The gospels are more than merely 'passion narratives with extended introductions', as Martin Kähler 'somewhat provocatively' maintained in *Der sogenannte historische Jesus und der geschichtliche biblische Christus*, 2nd ed., Leipzig 1896, 80; ET *The So-Called Historical Jesus and the Historic Biblical Christ*, trans. C. E. Braaten, Philadelphia 1964, reprinted 1988.

2. Cf. M. Welker (ed.), *Diskussion über 'Der gekreuzigte Gott'*, Munich 1979; P. F. Momose, *Kreuzestheologie. Eine Auseinandersetzung mit J. Moltmann*, Freiburg 1978; W. McWilliams, *The Passion of God. Divine Suffering in Contemporary Protestant Theology*, Macon, Georgia, 1985; J.-P. Thévenaz, 'Passion de Dieu, passions humaines et sympathie des choses', *Revue de Théologie et de Philosophie* 119, 1987, 303–321; P. S. Fiddes, *The Creative Suffering of God*, Oxford 1988.

3. Cf. here W. Breuning (ed.), *Trinität. Aktuelle Perspektiven der Theologie*, QD 101, Freiburg 1984.

4. Contrary to Albrecht Ritschl's ethical view of the kingdom of God, Johannes Weiss proved its apocalyptic character; cf. *Die Predigt Jesu vom Reiche Gottes*, 1892, 2nd ed., 1900; ET *Jesus' Proclamation of the Kingdom of God*, trans. R. H. Hiers and D. L. Holland, London 1971.

5. Cf. the formulation of Thesis II of the Barmen Theological Declaration (see also Ch. III, n. 68).

6. A. Schweitzer, *Geschichte der Leben-Jesu-Forschung*, 1913, 6th ed., Tübingen 1951, XXI: 'Die Lösung der konsequenten Eschatologie', 390ff. (*The Quest of the Historical Jesus*, trans. W. Montgomery, London 1910 = ET of 1st German ed., 1906, published under the title *Vom Reimarus zu Wrede*).

7. E. Peterson, 'Zeuge der Wahrheit' in *Theologische Traktate*, Munich 1951, 187f. But here we are reversing his idea: the sufferings of Christ are universal because they are a suffering with the cosmos. Cf. here J. Moltmann, *The Crucified God*, trans. R. A. Wilson and John Bowden, London and New York 1974, 57ff.

8. 'πάθημα', *TDNT* V, 933. Thus also P. Stuhlmacher, *Gerechtigkeit Gottes bei Paulus*, Göttingen 1965, 232: 'The suffering which anonymously enslaves the world is transparent for Christians (and through them!) as the Creator's struggle with the powers of the world for his right to his creation – a struggle initiated by Christ.'

9. This is how Pius XII viewed the church in the encyclical *Mystici corporis* (1943).

10. W. Schrage, 'Leid, Kreuz und Eschaton. Die Peristasenkataloge als Merkmale paulinischer theologia crucis und Eschatologie', *EvTh* 34, 1974, 141–175.

11. J. Moltmann, 'Die Leiden dieser Zeit. Die Kirche und ihre Märtyrer', *EK* 18, 1985, 440–444.

12. Blaise Pascal, *Pensées*, No. 553: 'Jésus sera en agonie jusqu'à la fin du monde.'

13. I am here taking up an idea which J. B. Metz expressed in *Faith in History and Society*, trans. D. Smith, London 1980, ch. 10, 'Hope as an imminent expectation or the struggle for forgotten time. Non-contemporaneous theses on the apocalyptic view', 169ff. Metz has frequently made the same point since.

14. Cf. Ch. VII §3.

15. R. Bultmann, 'New Testament and Mythology' in H. W. Bartsch (ed.), *Kerygma and Myth*, trans. R. H. Fuller, London 1953, 5 (altered).

16. J. B. Metz, op. cit., 173.

17. Quoted by J. B. Metz, op. cit., 175.

18. Cf. G. Anders, *Endzeit und Zeitende. Gedanken über die atomare Situation*, Munich 1972; G. M. Martin, *Weltuntergang. Gefahr und Sinn apokalyptischer Visionen*, Stuttgart 1984; U. H. J. Körtner, *Weltangst und Weltende. Eine theologische Interpretation der Apokalyptik*, Göttingen 1988.

19. J. Moltmann, 'Die atomare Katastrophe: wo bleibt Gott?', *EvTh* 47, 1987, 50–60.

20. H. Schürmann put this question about the *ipsissima mors* of Jesus in *Jesu ureigener Tod. Exegetische Besinnungen und Ausblick*. Freiburg 1974.

21. P. Stuhlmacher would seem to accept this; cf. *Jesus von Nazareth – Christus des Glaubens*, Stuttgart 1988.

22. R. Bultmann, *Das Verhältnis der urchristlichen Christusbotschaft zum historischen Jesus*, Sitzungsberichte der Heidelberger Akademie der Wissenschaften, Heidelberg 1960, 12.

23. J. Blinzler, *Der Prozess Jesu*, 2nd ed., Regensburg 1955; A. Strobel, *Die Stunde der Wahrheit*, Tübingen 1980; O. Betz, 'Probleme des Prozesses Jesu' in H. Temporini and W. Haase (eds), *Aufstieg und Niedergang der römischen Welt* II, Berlin 1982, 565–647; P. Lapide, *Wer war schuld an Jesu Tod?*, Gütersloh 1987.

24. H. Conzelmann, 'Jesus Christus', *RGG³* III, 647, and G. Bornkamm, *Jesus of Nazareth*, trans. I. and F. McLuskey, with J. M. Robinson, London 1960, 153ff.

25. O. Betz, op. cit., 594.

26. Ibid., 628.

27. C. H. Cohn, *Reflections on the Trial and Death of Jesus*, Jerusalem 1967, quoted in O. Betz, op. cit., 626.

28. This is also Betz's view; op. cit., 640.

29. Ibid., 636.

30. Ibid., 633. Betz thinks that in Gethsemane at the latest Jesus' eyes must have been opened, and his hopes for an enthronement in Jerusalem destroyed.

31. Ibid., 600. Betz evidently views the policy of the Sadducees as *Realpolitik* in the German sense, and approves it.

32. Ibid., 642f.

33. Thus Betz, ibid., 645.

34. For more detail cf. J. Moltmann, *The Crucified God*, 145–159; G. O'Collins, *The Calvary Christ*, London 1977, 40ff.; J. Sobrino, *Christology at the Crossroads. A Latin American Approach*, London 1978, Ch. 6: 'The Death of Jesus and Liberation in History', 179ff.

35. Cf. here J. Moltmann, *The Trinity and the Kingdom of God*, trans. Margaret Kohl, London 1981 (= The Trinity and the Kingdom, New York 1981), 75–79: cf. Also B. Pascal, *Pensées*, No. 553: 'Jésus souffre dans sa passion les tourments que lui font les hommes; mais dans l'agonie il souffre les tourments qu'il se donne à lui-même; *turbare semetipsum*; c'est un supplice d'une main non humaine, mais toute-puissante, car il faut être tous-puissant pour le soutenir'. ['In the passion Jesus suffers the torments which men imposed on him; but in the agony he suffers the torments which he lays upon himself; *turbare semetipsum*. This is the suffering not from human hand but from the hand that is almighty, for he has to be almighty in order to endure it.'] On Jesus' cry from the cross cf. L. Caza, 'Le relief que Marc a donnéau cri de la croix', *Science et Esprit* XXXIX 12, 1987, 171–191; R. Feldmeier, *Die Krise des Gottessohnes. Die markinische Gethsemane-perikope als Schlüssel des Markuspassion*, diss. Tübingen 1986.

36. P. Kuhn, *Gottes Selbsterniedrigung in der Theologie der Rabbinen*, Munich 1968.

37. Thus rightly B. Klappert, 'Weg und Wende Dietrich Bonhoeffers in der Israelfrage' in W. Huber and H. E. Tödt, *Ethik im Ernstfall*, Munich 1982, 122. Klappert draws attention to Bonhoeffer's poem, written during the Jewish persecution: 'Menschen gehn zu Gott in seiner Not,/finden ihn arm, geschmäht, ohne Obdach und Brot,/sehn ihn verschlungen von Sünde, Schwachheit und Tod,/Christen stehn bei Gott in seinem Leiden' (1944).

38. B. Klappert, *Die Eschatologie des Hebräerbriefes*, ThEx NF 156, Munich 1979.

39. Cf. here also G. Gutiérrez, *The Power of the Poor in History*, trans. R. R. Barr, Maryknoll, New York, and London 1983, 12ff., 50ff.

40. For more detail cf. J. Moltmann, 'Schöpfung, Bund und Herrlichkeit, Zur Diskussion über Karl Barths Schöpfungslehre', *EvTh* 48, 1988, 122ff.

41. F. Schleiermacher, *The Christian Faith*, trans. By H. R. Mackintosh

and J. S. Stewart from 2nd, rev. ed. of *Glaubenslehre*, §77; K. Barth, *CD* III/2, § 47, 5, 587ff.

42. R. Bultmann, 'New Testament and Mythology' in *Kerygma and Myth*, 38: 'Can the resurrection narratives and every other mention of the resurrection in the New Testament be understood in any other way than as an attempt to convey the meaning of the cross?' (altered)

43. W. Pannenberg, *Jesus – God and Man*, trans. L. C. Wilkins and D. A. Priebe, London and Philadelphia 1968, 53, with the postulate: 'Jesus' unity with God was not yet established by the claim implied in his pre-Easter appearance, but only by his resurrection from the dead'.

44. For the exegetical findings, cf. W. Popkes, *Christus traditus. Eine Untersuchung zum Begriff der Dahingabe im Neuen Testament*, Göttingen 1967; W. H. Vanstone, *The Stature of Waiting*, London 1983, esp. 2: 'The Handing Over of Jesus', 17–33. For the systematic theology: H. Mühlen, *Die Veränderlichkeit Gottes als Horizont einer zukünftigen Christologie*, Aschaffenburg 1969; H. U. von Balthasar, 'Mysterium Paschale' in *Mysterium Salutis* III/2, Einsiedeln, Zürich and Cologne 1969, 133–326; E. Jüngel, *God as Mystery of the World*, trans. D. L. Guder, Grand Rapids, Mich., and Edinburgh 1983; W. Kasper, *The God of Jesus Christ*, trans. M. J. O'Donnell, New York and London 1984; L. Boff, *Der dreieinige Gott*, Düsseldorf 1987.

45. J. Moltmann, *The Crucified God*; M. Welker (ed.), *Diskussion über 'Der gekreuzigte Gott'*, (cf. n. 2); J. Moltmann, *The Trinity and the Kingdom of God*, Ch. II, 'The Passion of God', 21ff.

46. K. Barth, *CD* II/2, 488f.: 'God has acted as Judas acted.' Cf. here H. Gollwitzer, *Krummes Holz – aufrechter Gang. Zur Frage nach dem Sinn des Lebens*, Munich 1970, Ch. VIII: 'Gute Nachricht für Judas Ischarioth', 271ff. I do not consider this indentification of surrender and betrayal to be correct, for the self-emptying is one thing, and the humiliating of another is something very different.

47. A. E. Carr, *Transforming Grace. Christian Tradition and Woman's Experience*, San Francisco 1988, 152ff., shows that there is also a sound feminist theology of the cross.

48. D. Sölle, *Leiden*, Stuttgart 1973, 37 (*Suffering*, trans. E. R. Kalin, Philadelphia 1975).

49. Isaac Watts' 'Not all the blood of beasts' will hardly be much sung today. But W. Bright's 'And now, O Father, mindful of the love' also draws on the idea of Christ's expiatory sacrifice:

'We here present, we here spread forth to thee
That only offering perfect in thine eyes,
The one true, pure, immortal sacrifice.'

50. J. Moltmann, *The Crucified God*, 243 (slightly altered).

51. Thus rightly H. Gollwitzer, *Von der Stellvertretung Gottes*, Munich 1967, contrary to D. Sölle, *Christ the Representative*, trans. D. Lewis, London 1967, and W. Pannenberg, *Jesus – God and Man*, 274ff.

52. W. Popkes, op. cit., 286f.; D. Sölle, *Leiden*, 37 (*Suffering*).

53. Thus now also D. Sölle, 'Gottes Schmerz teilen', *Publik-Forum*, 1988/4, Feb. 26, 33–34.

54. Origen, *Selecta in Ezechielem* (c. 16; PG 13, 812A) and *Homilia VI in Ezechielem* (PG 13, 714f.). For more detail here cf. J. Moltmann, *The Trinity and the Kingdom of God*, 24f.

55. E. Wiesel, 'Der Mitleidende' in R. Walter (ed.), *Die hundert Namen Gottes*, Freiburg 1985, 70; cf. here H. Jonas, 'Der Gottesbegriff nach Auschwitz. Eine jüdische Stimme' in F. Stern and H. Jonas, *Reflexionen finsterer Zeit*, Tübingen 1984, 65–86. E. Jüngel replies to him in 'Gottes ursprüngliches Anfangen als schöpferische Selbstbegrenzung' in *Gottes Zukunft – Zukunft der Welt. Festschrift für J. Moltmann*, Munich 1986, 265–275. Jewish and Christian thinking over God 'after Auschwitz' tends in the direction of the irrelinquishable suffering from God in the form of the cry out of the depths and the call for the coming of his righteousness and justice.

56. J. Moltmann, *Experiences of God*, trans. Margaret Kohl, London and Philadelphia 1980, 42: 'The Anxiety of Christ'.

57. J. Moltmann, 'Justification and New Creation' in *The Future of Creation*, trans. Margaret Kohl, London and Philadelphia 1979, 149–171.

58. E. Stuaffer also makes this clear in his article 'ἵνα', *TDNT* III, 323ff.

59. E. Wolf, 'Die Rechtfertigungslehre als Mitte und Grenze reformatorischer Theologie' in *Peregrinatio* II, Munich 1965, 11ff.; H. J. Iwand, *Glaubensgerechtigkeit nach Luthers Lehre*, Munich 1941; E. Käsemann, '"The Righteousness of God" in Paul' in *New Testament Questions of Today*, trans. W. J. Montague etc., London 1969, 168ff.

60. This was A. Schlatter's critical comment in connection with the Reformation jubilee in 1917; cf. his book *Luthers Deutung des Römerbriefes*, Gütersloh 1917.

61. P. Ricoeur, 'La Liberté selon l'espérance' in *Le Conflit des interprétations*, Paris 1969, 393ff. (ET *The Conflict of Interpretations*, Evanston 1974).

62. N. Nissiotis, 'Die österliche Freude als doxologischer Ausdruck des Glaubens' in *Gottes Zukunft – Zukunft der Welt*, 78–88.

63. Augustine, *Enchiridion*, cap. 48.

64. Cf. the South African Kairos document: *Challenge to the Church. A Theological Comment on the Political Crisis in South Africa*, 1985, in which the theology of reconciliation is criticized as 'church theology' and a 'prophetic theology' of justice and righteousness is demanded.

65. I consider E. Käsemann's critical 'Erwägungen zum Stichwort "Versöhnungslehre im Neuen Testament"' in *Zeit und Geschichte, Festschrift für R. Bultmann*, Tübingen 1964, 47–59, to be exegetically unconfuted and systematically not yet assimilated. I am following his exegetical insights here.

66. R. Bultmann, 'Der Begriff der Offenbarung im Neuen Testament', *Glauben und Verstehen* III, Tübingen 1960, 26; cf. also 29.

67. K. Barth, *CD* IV/2, §64.2: 'The Home coming of the Son of Man',

p. 141: 'The resurrection and ascension of Jesus Christ are the revelation which corresponds to this completion of his work.' Thus also K. Rahner, 'Dogmatic Questions on Easter', *Theological Investigations* IV, trans. K. Smith, London 1966, 128: 'The resurrection of Christ is not another event *after* his passion and death . . . the resurrection is the manifestation of what happened in the death of Christ'.

68. Cf. earlier W. Bieder, *Die Vorstellung von der Höllenfahrt Christi*, Zürich 1949. Also W. Maas's comprehensive study *Gott und die Hölle. Studien zum descensus Christi*, Einsiedeln 1979. I may also point to the excursus on Christ's descent into Hell in W. Pannenberg, *Jesus – God and Man*, 269–74.

'Descended into the realm of death' is the phrase which in the modern German ecumenical version of the Apostles' creed replaces the older 'descended into hell'.

69. My attention was first drawn to this dimension through African theology; cf. C. Nyamiti, *Christ as our Ancestor*, Gweru, Simbabwe, 1984. At a time when modern societies are threatening to break the unwritten 'generation contract', recognition that human beings are 'generation' beings, and the rediscovery of the wisdom hidden in the cult of ancestors, are of vital importance.

70. W. Pannenberg, *Jesus – God and Man*, 273.

71. H. U. von Balthasar, *Mysterium Paschale*, section 4: 'Der Gang zu den Toten (Karsamstag)' in *Mysterium Salutis* III/2, op. cit., 225ff.

72. Cf. here P. Hoffmann, *Die Toten in Christus. Eine religionsgeschichtliche und exegetische Untersuchung zur paulinischen Eschatologie*, 3rd ed., Münster 1969; also my essay 'Entwurf einer personalen Eschatologie: Liebe – Tod – ewiges Leben' in H. Becker, B. Einig and P. O. Ullrich (eds), *Im Angesicht des Todes. Ein interdisziplinäres Kompendium* II, St Ottilien 1987, 837–854.

73. W. Benjamin, *Illuminationen. Ausgewählte Schriften*, Frankfurt 1961, 270f.

74. I am here taking up ideas which were expressed in the 'Beschluss der Gemeinsamen Synode der Bistümer in der Bundesrepublik Deutschland: Unsere Hoffnung', 1975. The resolution was drawn up by J.-B. Metz.

75. Thus E. Käsemann, 'The Cry for Liberty in the Worship of the Church' in *Perspectives on Paul*, trans. Margaret Kohl, London and Philadelphia 1969, 122–137.

76. E. Käsemann, 'On the Subject of Primitive Christian Apocalyptic' in *New Testament Questions of Today*, 108–137.

77. W. Thüsing, *Per Christum in Deum. Studien zum Verhältnis von Christozentrik und Theozentrik in den paulinischen Hauptbriefen*, 2nd ed., Münster 1969, 78.

77a. R. M. Rilke, *Duineser Elegien* I:

Denn das Schöne ist nichts
al des Schrecklichen Anfang, den wir noch gerade ertragen,

und wir bewundern es so, weil es gelassen verschmäht,
uns zu zerstören.

78. E. Peterson, 'Zeuge der Wahrheit' in *Theologische Traktate*, Munich 1951, 165–224.
79. Thomas Aquinas, *STh* IIa IIae q 124, a 5, Blackfriars ed., vol. 42, 55, 57, London 1966. Cf. here L. Boff, 'Martyrdom: An Attempt at Systematic Reflection', *Concilium* 163, 3/1983, pp. 12ff.
80. M. Schneider, *Der Prediger von Buchenwald. Das Martyrium Paul Schneiders*, Stuttgart 1981.
81. E. Bethge, *Dietrich Bonhoeffer: Theologian, Christian, Contemporary*, trans. E. Mosbacher *et al.*, London 1970.
82. O. A. Romero, *Die notwendige Revolution*, Mainz and Munich 1982, and the comments by J. Sobrino, 'Political Holiness: A Profile', *Concilium* 163, 3/1983, 18–23.
83. J. Sobrino, preface to O. A. Romero, op. cit., 17.
84. L. Boff, 'Martyrdom', 15: 'They are not martyrs of the Christian faith, not heroes of the Church; they are *martyrs of the kingdom of God*, martyrs to the cause that was the cause of the Son of God when he was in our midst. They help to carry out God's policy in history.'
85. M. Lange and R. Iblacker (eds), *Christenverfolgung in Lateinamerika. Zeugen der Hoffnung*, Freiburg 1980. Cf. here K. Rahner, 'Dimensions of Martyrdom: A Plea for the Broadening of a Classical Concept, *Concilium* 163, 3/1983, 9–11. L. Kaufman and N. Klein, 'Ökumene der Märtyrer' in E. Schillebeeckx (ed.), *Mystik und Politik, Festschrift für J. B. Metz*, Mainz 1988, 383–393.
86. I have expounded a theology of the Lord's Supper in detail in *The Church in the Power of the Spirit*, trans. Margaret Kohl, London and New York 1977, Ch. V: 'The Church in the Presence of the Holy Spirit', §4 'The Lord's Supper', 242–260.
87. E. Schüssler-Fiorenza, *In Memory of Her. A Feminist Reconstruction of Christian Origins*, New York and London 1983, has worked out the theological importance of this woman, whose memory was repressed.
88. O. Weber, *Grundlagen der Dogmatik* II, 5th ed., Neukirchen 1977, 708: 'Every spatial interpretation of what happens in the meal is a sign of one-sidedness. For the problem is *primarily* the problem of *time*.' I am here taking up the sacramental terminology of Thomas Aquinas in *STh* III q. 60, a. 3.
88a. Cf. *God in Creation*, Ch. V, 132ff.
89. Thus rightly J. B. Metz, *Faith in History and Society*, ch. 6: 'The future in the memory of suffering. The dialectics of progress', 100ff., esp. 113f.
90. H.-G. Gadamer, *Wahrheit und Methode* Tübingen 1960, 13 (*Truth and Method*, trans. W. Glen-Doepel, London 1975).
91. Y. H. Yerushalmi, *Zahor: Erinnere Dich! Jüdische Geschichte und jüdisches Gedächtnis* Berlin 1988; A. Friedländer, 'Zachor – Gedenke!', *EvTh* 48, 1988, 378–387; E. Fackenheim, *God's Presence in History. Jewish Affirmation and Philosophical Reflection*, New York 1970; cf. also

W. Schottroff, *'Gedenken' im alten Orient und im alten Testament*, Neukirchen 1964; B. S. Childs, *Memory and Tradition in Israel*, London 1962.

92. Or, in the German tradition, we may remember Paul Gerhardt's passion hymn 'O Welt, sieh hier dein Leben', which contains the lines:

> Wer hat dich so geschlagen . . . so übel zugericht'? . . .
> Ich, ich und meine Sünden . . . die haben dir erreget
> das Elend, das dich schlägt.

93. J. B. Metz, op. cit., 117.

94. Cf. J. S. Croatto, *Exodus, a Hermeneutics of Freedom*, New York 1981.

V   The Eschatological Resurrection of Christ

1. This is especially stressed by B. Klappert in *Diskussion um Kreuz und Auferstehung*, Wuppertal 1967; cf. also his *Die Auferweckung des Gekreuzigten. Der Ansatz der Christologie Karl Barths im Zusammenhang der Christologie der Gegenwart*, 2nd ed., Neukirchen 1974.

2. N. Nissiotis, *Die Theologie der Ostkirche im ökumenischen Dialog. Kirche und Welt in orthodoxer Sicht*, Stuttgart 1968; D. Stanliloae, *Orthodoxe Dogmatik*, Gütersloh 1984. It is worth a reminder at this point that the Western and Eastern churches will have to agree on a date for Easter if they mean to take the ecumenical age seriously. In my view, closeness to the Jewish passover should be the determining factor.

3. Cf. H. Küng and D. Tracy (eds), *Paradigm Change in Theology*, German contributions trans. Margaret Kohl, Edinburgh and New York 1989, esp. Section IV: The Role of History in the New Paradigm, 307–351.

4. Cf. the historical accounts by G. Lohfink, 'Der Ablauf der Osterereignisse und die Anfänge der Urgemeinde', *ThQ* 160, 1980, 162–176, and K. H. Schelkle, *Theologie des Neuen Testaments* II, Düsseldorf 1973, 128ff.; also Schelkle, 'Auferstehung Jesu. Geschichte und Deutung' in *Kirche und Bible. Festschrift für Bischof E. Schick*, Paderborn 1979, 389–408. See also G. Kegel, *Auferstehung Jesus – Auferstehung der Toten. Eine traditions-geschichtliche Untersuchung zum Neuen Testament*, Gütersloh 1970; G. O'Collins, *The Easter Jesus*, London 1973; K. Lehmann, 'Die Erscheinungen des Herrn. Thesen zur hermeneutisch-theologischen Struktur der Ostererzählungen' in *Festschrift für K. H. Schelkle*, Düsseldorf 1973, 361–377; R. Pesch, 'Die Entstehung des Auferstehungsglaubens', *ThQ* 153, 1973, Heft 3, with a discussion of his theses; H. Küng, 'Zur Entstehung des Auferstehungsglaubens', *ThQ* 154, 1974, 102–117; D. Müller, *Geisterfahrung und Totenauferweckung*, Kiel 1981. An excellent summing-up is to be found in P. Hoffmann, *Zur neutestamentlichen Überlieferung von der Auferstehung Jesu*, Wege der Forschung 522, Darmstadt 1988. The new study by P. Carnley, *The Structure of Resurrection Belief*, Oxford 1987, is quite excellent. For the general reader cf.

J. Kremer's little book *Das Evangelium von Jesu Tod und Auferstehung*, Stuttgart 1985.

5. Cf. G. O'Collins and D. Kendall, 'Mary Magdalene as Major Witness to Jesus' Resurrection', *Theological Studies* 48, 1987, 631–646. Leo the Great called Mary Magdalene 'persona Ecclesiae gerens'. Gregory the Great called her 'the new Eve', who proclaimed life not death. Hippolytus of Rome elevated her to be the 'apostola apostolorum'. It is disastrous to exclude this feminine apostolate from the present discussion about the ordination of women. It is wrong to maintain that Jesus only called male disciples and apostles, and to make this a reason for rejecting the ordination of women, as John Paul II does in his encyclical *Dignitas mulieris* of 1988.

6. K. H. Schelkle, 'Auferstehung Jesu', 395.

7. Thus also W. Kasper, *Jesus the Christ*, trans. V. Green, London 1976, 124ff., contrary to W. Pannenberg, *Jesus – God and Man*, trans. L. C. Wilkins and D. A. Priebe, London 1968 53ff., who goes back directly to the apocalyptic horizon of understanding of contemporary Judaism. Cf. also L. Scheffczyk, *Auferstehung. Prinzip des christlichen Glaubens*, Einsiedeln 1976.

8. Cf. W. Pannenberg (ed.), *Offenbarung als Geschichte*, Göttingen 1961 (ET *Revelation as History*, trans. D. Granskou and E. Quinn, London and New York 1969), who has rightly made the prolepsis of the resurrection of the dead in Jesus the foundation of his theology of history. Cf. also E. Schillebeeckx, *Die Auferstehung Jesu als Grund der Erlösung*, Freiburg 1979, 144ff.

9. J. Moltmann, *The Crucified God*, trans. R. A. Wilson and John Bowden, London and New York 1974, 172f., in contrast to W. Pannenberg, *Offenbarung als Geschichte*, 112.

10. Thus rightly Ernst Bloch, *Das Prinzip Hoffnung*, Frankfurt 1959, 1324 (ET *The Principle of Hope*, Oxford 1986).

11. K. H. Schelkle, 'Auferstehung Jesus', 391.

12. W. Herrmann, *Dogmatik*, Gotha 1925, 82ff.

13. Cf. H. Schlier, *Wort Gottes. Eine neutestamentliche Besinnung*, 2nd ed., Würzburg 1962, 18ff.; P. Stuhlmacher, *Das paulinische Evangelium* I, Göttingen 1968, 287f.

14. Thus, with reference to my *Theology of Hope*, R. Garaudy, *Die Alternative*, Vienna 1972, 115ff.; also his *Menschenwort. Ein autobiographischer Bericht*, Vienna 1975, 202ff. For the last twenty years or so the theological discussion about Christ's resurrection and history has stood still, and almost nothing has appeared to take the discussion a stage further. I must therefore pick up the highly stimulating discussions of the 1960s. I have no intention of repeating myself, but neither can I supersede what I said then. I am presupposing here what I said in 1964 in *The Theology of Hope* (ET 1967) and in 1972 in *The Crucified God* (ET 1974).

15. D. F. Strauss, *Die christliche Glaubenslehre* I, Tübingen and Stuttgart 1840, 71.

16. E. Troeltsch, 'Über historische und dogmatische Methode in der Theologie' (1898) in *Gesammelte Schriften* II, Tübingen 1913, 729–753.

17. R. Bultmann, 'Karl Barth, *"The Resurrection of the Dead"*' (1926) in *Faith and Understanding*, trans. Louise P. Smith, London 1966, 66–94.

18. K. Barth, *Die Auferstehung der Toten*, 4th ed., Zürich 1953, 115 (*The Resurrection of the Dead*, trans. H. J. Stenning, London 1933).

19. Ibid., 59.

20. Ibid., 115.

21. *CD* IV/1, 338.

22. Ibid., 309.

23. Ibid., 310.

24. R. Bultmann, 'New Testament and Mythology' in *Kerygma and Myth*, ed. H.-W. Bartsch, trans. R. H. Fuller, London 1953, 42.

25. R. Bultmann, 'Das Problem einer theologischen Exegese des Neuen Testaments' in J. Moltmann (ed.), *Anfänge der dialektischen Theologie*, Munich 1962–, 47ff.

26. R. Bultmann, 'New Testament and Mythology', 38.

27. Ibid., 37.

28. Ibid., 36.

29. Thus Karl Marx, following Hegel; cf. K. Marx, 'Die Deutsche Ideologie' (1845/46) in *Frühschriften*, ed. S. Landshut, Stuttgart 1953, 346: 'We know only a single science, the science of history.'

30. W. Dilthey, *Gesammelte Schriften* VII, Leipzig and Berlin 1927, 233.

31. W. Pannenberg, *Basic Questions in Theology*, trans. G. H. Kehm and R. A. Wilson, London 1970, pp. 170–71 (altered).

32. W. Pannenburg, *Revelation as History*, with my discussion in *Theology of Hope*, trans. J. W. Leitch, London and New York 1967, 76ff.; also Pannenberg, *Jesus – God and Man*; R. R. Niebuhr, *Resurrection and Historical Reason; a Study of Theological Method*, New York 1957.

33. Thus R. Kosellek, *Vergangene Zukunft. Zur Semantik geschichtlicher Zeiten*, Frankfurt 1979, 349ff. P. Ricoeur defines historical present similarly in the intersection of expectation and experience; cf. *Temps et Récit* III, Paris 1985, 332ff. Cf. here also M. Raden, *Das relative Absolute. Die theologische Hermeneutik P. Ricoeurs*, Frankfurt 1988. Cf. also J. Moltmann, *Theology of Hope*, Ch. II, §3: 'The Experience of History', 106ff.

34. Thus K. Löwith, *Weltgeschichte und Heilsgeschehen*, 2nd ed., Stuttgart 1952; G. Picht, *Die Erfahrung der Geschichte*, Frankfurt 1958; R. Kosellek, *Vergangene Zukunft*, 353: 'Irrespective of the Christian origin of this viewpoint . . .'

35. Cf. *Theology of Hope*, 106ff.: 'The Experience of History.'

36. K. Löwith, *Weltgeschichte*, 15.

37. Cf. Paul Gerhardt's Christmas hymn 'Fröhlich soll mein Herze springen': 'Lasset fahr'n, O liebe Brüder,/ was euch quält,/ was euch fehlt:/ Ich bring alles wieder.' The hymn is familiar to English readers in Catherine Winkworth's version 'All my heart this night rejoices'. But her lines

You are freed, all you need
I will surely give you

do not bring out Paul Gerhardt's idea, which is not the giving of what is required but the restoration of what has been lost. Cf. also D. Bonhoeffer's comment on these lines in his letter to E. Bethge of 19.12.43 in *Letters and Papers from Prison*, trans. R. H. Fuller, enlarged ed., London and New York 1971.

38. O. Weber, *Grundlagen der Dogmatik* II, Neukirchen 1962, 108.

39. For more detail cf. J. Moltmann, *God in Creation*, trans. Margaret Kohl, London and New York 1985, Ch. V, §5, 'The Interlaced Times of History', 124ff. See also J. Ebach, *Ursprung und Ziel. Erinnerte Zukunft und erhoffte Vergangenheit. Biblische Exegesen, Reflexionen, Geschichten*, Neukirchen 1986.

40. I have presented this in more detail in 'The Hope of Resurrection and the Practice of Liberation' in *The Future of Creation*, trans. Margaret Kohl, London and Philadelphia 1979, 97–114.

41. This is impressively shown by T. Tordorov in *Die Eroberung Amerikas. Das Problem des Anderen*, Frankfurt 1985, in which he draws on the accounts of Columbus, Cortez, Las Casas and Durán.

42. This was my epistemological thesis in *The Crucified God*, 25ff. It gave rise to considerable discussion. Cf. M. Welker (ed.), *Diskussion über 'Der gekreuzigte Gott'*, Munich 1979, 188ff.

43. Thus J. Sobrino, 'Theologisches Erkennen in der europäischen und der lateinamerikanischen Theologie' in K. Rahner (ed.), *Befreiende Theologie*, Stuttgart 1977, 136ff.

44. W. Capelle, *Die Vorsokratiker*, Berlin 1958, 77f., Fragment 99 and 100.

45. Cf. the quotations in G. M. Stratton, *Theophrastus and the Greek Physiological Psychology before Aristotle*, New York and London 1917, 90ff.

46. This is impressively emphasized by E. Lévinas, *L'humanisme de l'autre homme*, Montpellier 1972.

47. Cf. H. Riesenfeld, 'Paul's "Grain of Wheat" Analogy and the Argument of I Cor. 15' in *The Gospel Tradition*, Philadelphia 1970, 171–186.

48. Ambrose: 'In springtime is Easter, when I was redeemed; in summer is Pentecost, when we laud the glory of the resurrection as the reflection of what will be', *Expositio evangelii sec. Lucam*, quoted in R. Cantalamessa, *Ostern in der alten Kirche*, Berne 1981, 157.

49. German version in E.-M. Bachmann, *Machet herrlich sein Lob*, Neukirchen 1988, 55.

50. Hildegard von Bingen, *Lieder*, Salzburg 1969, 229.

51. M. Kassel, 'Tod und Auferstehung' in M. Kassel (ed.), *Feministische Theologie*, Stuttgart 1988, 212.

52. Hildegard von Bingen, *Lieder*, Salzburg 1979, 229, 233, 245, 315. Hildegard called the divine power of life *viriditas*, the power of greening. 'In

the beginning all creation greened.' Through Christ, the Spirit as 'greening power of spring' comes upon all things. Cf. M. Fox, *Illuminations of Hildegard of Bingen*, Santa Fe 1985, 30ff.

53. K. Marx, *Nationalökonomie und Philosophie* (1844) in *Frühschriften*, 237. Marx wrongly sees 'the true resurrection of nature' already in 'the implemented naturalism of the human being and the implemented humanism of nature'.

54. D. Staniloae, *Orthodoxe Dogmatik*, 291ff.

55. Gregory of Nyssa, *De tridua inter mortem et resurrectionem Domini nostri Jesus Christi spatio, Opera* 9, ed. E. Gebhardt, *Sermones* 1, Leiden 1967, 274. Cf. also V. Kesich, *The First Day of the New Creation*, New York 1982.

56. Like the Alexandrine Fathers, Augustine did not relate 'passover' to Christ's 'passion' but to his *transitus*: 'Per passionem enim transit Dominus a morte ad vitam; et fecit nobis viam credentibus in resurrectionem eius, ut transeamus et nos de morte ad vitam', *Ennarationes in Psalmos*, 120, 6. Cf. *De Civ. Dei*, 16, 43. But by understanding the passion as the beginning of the transition itself, he integrates the ancient passover-passion tradition with the Alexandrine *transitus* tradition. See also *Chronicon Paschale*: 'The Church of God therefore necessarily called not merely the Lord's passion but also his resurrection passover. For through the Lord's passion and his resurrection, human nature won the transition, exodus and passover from that which had the power of death, from death itself, from Hades and from perdition. For if Christ's death gives us all this, how much more is this conferred on us by his resurrection, when he rose from the dead, as the first fruits among those who sleep, in order no longer to turn back to destruction. For according to the doctrine of the holy apostle, death has no longer any power' (quoted in R. Cantalamessa, op. cit., 85).

57. V. Lossky, *Orthodox Theology. An Introduction*, New York 1978, 116. Cf. also G. Florovsky, *Creation and Redemption* II, Belmont, Mass. 1976.

58. V. Lossky, op. cit., 118.

59. Ibid.,

60. Thus N. O. Brown, *Life against Death. The Psychoanalytical Meaning of History*, New York 1959, ch. 16: 'The Resurrection of the Body', 307ff.; also his *Love's Body*, New York 1968, 191ff. Cf. also R. Alves's fine meditations *Ich glaube an die Auferstehung des Leibes*, Düsseldorf 1983.

60a. Cf. R. W. Emerson, 'Love', *Essays*, 1841–44, : 'The soul is wholly embodied and the body is wholly ensouled.'

61. Chrysostom, Homily 41 in *Nicene and Post-Nicene Fathers of the Christian Church*, vol. XII: Saint Chrysostom, *Homilies on the Epistles of Paul to the Corinthians*, ed. P. Schaff, Grand Rapids 1979, 249ff. Cf. also V. Kesich, *The First Day of Creation*, 147.

62. Thus Cyril of Jerusalem, cited in Kesich, op. cit., 148. But how are we supposed to eat and drink in the kingdom of God if there are no longer to be any bodily needs?

63. Gal. 3.28 is probably drawing on a rabbinic tradition according to which 'Adam' was the original human being before sexual differentiation (Gen. 2.21–23). But then God must have sinned in the sexual differentiation of the original human being, or in the new creation he would have to revise part of his own creation. Both conceptions are theologically impossible.

64. Cf. J. Moltmann, *God in Creation*, Ch. X, §2: 'Soul and Body', 255ff.

65. Cf. §3 of this chapter. I already expressed my views on this earlier: 'Gott und Auferstehung. Auferstehung im Forum der Theodizeefrage' (1968) in *Perspektiven der Theologie*, Munich and Mainz 1968, 36–56 (*Hope and Planning*, selections trans. Margaret Clarkson, London and New York 1971); 'The Hope of Resurrection and the Practice of Liberation' (1972) in *The Future of Creation*, 97–114.

66. Thus D. Bonhoeffer, *Dein Reich komme* (1932), Hamburg 1958.

67. Cf. J. Moltmann, *God in Creation*, 3.

68. H. Plessner, *Lachen und Weinen*, 3rd ed., Berne and Munich 1961, 48 (*Laughing and Crying: A study of the limits of human behaviour*, trans. J. S. Churchill and M. Greene, Evanston 1970).

69. C. A. van Peursen, *Leib, Seele, Geist*, Gütersloh 1959, 66.

70. F. Capra, *Uncommon Wisdom*, London 1988.

71. K. Marx, cf. n. 53 above. E. Bloch, *Das Prinzip Hoffnung*, 802ff. (ET, *The Principle of Hope*).

72. Quoted in P. Evdokimov, 'Die Natur', *KuD* 11, 1965, 12.

VI   The Cosmic Christ

1. Cf. here H. Küng and D. Tracy (eds), *Paradigm Change in Theology*, German contributions trans. Margaret Kohl, Edinburgh and New York 1989.

2. F. Capra, *The Turning Point*, Toronto and New York 1982, speaks for many people.

3. In F. Lüpsen (ed.), *Neu Delhi Dokumente. Berichte und Reden auf der Weltkirchkonferenz in Neu Delhi 1961*, Witten 1962, 300–311. Sittler was only expanding the ideas which A. D. Galloway had already put forward in *The Cosmic Christ*, London 1951, but Galloway's ideas went unnoticed at the time. The discussion which followed Sittler's paper are collected in T. Ahrens, *Die ökumenische Diskussion der kosmischen Christologie seit 1961. Darstellung und Kritik*, Lübeck 1969. A systematic evaluation is given by H. Bürkle, 'Die Frage nach dem "kosmischen Christus" als Beispiel einer ökumenisch orientierten Theologie', *KuD* 11, 1965, 103–115. Cf. also J. Winterhager, 'Ökumenischer Vorspruch' in O.-A. Dilschneider, *Christus Pantokrator. Vom Kolosserbrief zur Ökumene*, Berlin 1962. It is noticeable that neither W. Pannenberg in *Jesus – God and Man*, trans. L. C. Wilkins and D. A. Priebe, London 1968, nor W. Kasper, *Jesus the Christ*, trans. V. Green, London 1976, enter into this discussion.

4. J. Sittler in F. Lüpsen, *Neu Delhi Dokumente*, 305.

5. Ibid., 311.

6. See P. D. Devanandan, *The Gospel and Renascent Hinduism*, London 1959, and the quotation from D. T. Niles in Devanandan's lecture at the New Delhi conference; cf. F. Lüpsen op. cit., 496. Also the comment in H. Bürkle, op. cit., 110f.

7. Thus G. Rosenkranz, 'Die Rede vom kosmischen Christus angesichts der indischen Geisteswelt', *Evangelische Missionszeitschrift*, Stuttgart 1963, 159f.

8. K. Barth, *CD* IV/3, 756.

9. E. Bloch, *Das Prinzip Hoffnung*, Frankfurt 1959, 729ff. (ET, *The Principle of Hope*, Oxford 1986).

10. William Dunbar (c. 1460–c. 1520), 'Et nobis Puer natus est'. In the old mystical German Advent hymn 'O Heiland reiss die Himmel auf' the earth is exhorted to put forth leaves, and herself to bring forth the Saviour: 'O Erd, schlag aus, schlag aus, O Erd,/dass Berg und Tal *grün alles werd!*/ O Erd, herfür dies Blümlein bring,/ O Heiland aus der Erden spring.' In connection with this verse Barth asks: 'Do we not have here something true and important which ought to be seen and sung?', *CD* IV/3, 756. The ideas in the hymn probably go back to Hildegard von Bingen.

11. B. Gärtner, *The Areopagus Speech and Natural Revelation*, Uppsala 1955, rightly stresses these dimensions. Cf. here also A. Vögtle, *Das Neue Testament und die Zukunft des Kosmos*, Düsseldorf 1970; K. H. Schelkle, *Vollendung von Schöpfung und Erlösung*, Düsseldorf 1974.

12. As W. Kasper maintains in *Jesus the Christ*, 186.

13. Thus R. Bultmann, *Glauben und Verstehen* III, Tübingen 1960, 26.

14. Cf. here G. Schimanowski's extensive study *Weisheit und Messias. Die jüdischen Voraussetzungen der urchristliche Präexistenzchristologie*, Tübingen 1985. Evidence for this was already presented by W. L. Knox in *St Paul and the Church of the Gentiles*, Cambridge 1939, 55ff.

15. I have taken over this formulation from J. Gnilka, *Der Kolosserbrief*, HThK X/1, Freiburg 1980, 60.

16. Ibid., 66.

17. E. Schweizer, *The Letter to the Colossians*, trans. Andrew Chester, London and Minneapolis 1982, 84ff., would like to allow the universalism of the reconciliation of the world to apply only in the form of hymnal doxology, but not as a 'doctrine', a distinction which seems somewhat artificial in view of the doxological character of all theological doctrine. Cf. here also J. Gnilka's critical comment, op. cit., 87.

18. R. Schnackenburg, *Der Brief an die Epheser*, EKK X, Neukirchen 1982, 59: 'The epistle to the Ephesians (also Col.) deviates from this Greek view of the world because it presupposes a disruption of the cosmic order, a crumbling of the unity, so that a "reconciliation" (Col.) or a gathering together (Eph.) will be necessary.' However, to maintain that the whole creation is 'fallen' because of human sin sounds like human hybris in reverse: if human beings cannot be like God the Creator, then they want at least to be the reason for creation's ruin. There are demonstrable disruptions and destructions enough caused by human acts of violence in the earthly

world and perhaps even – who knows – in the heavenly world of powers and potencies as well. But human beings do not enjoy sole responsibility, either in the positive or in the negative sense.

19. Cf. Ch. IV, §3.

20. This is rightly stressed by G. Strachan in *Christ and the Cosmos*, Dunbar 1985. He adduces as evidence the cosmological measurements of Solomon's temple and 'the heavenly Jerusalem' in Revelation ch. 21. The Romanesque churches built in the middle ages show similar cosmological correspondences.

21. Cf. J. Moltmann, *God in Creation*, trans. Margaret Kohl, London and New York 1985, esp. Ch. VIII, 'The Evolution of Creation', 185ff.

22. Cf. the quotations collected in H. Schmid, *Die Dogmatik der Evangelisch-Lutherischen Kirche*, 7th ed., Gütersloh 1893, 266ff., and H. Heppe and E. Bizer, *Die Dogmatik der Evangelisch-Reformierten Kirche*, Neukirchen 1958, 361ff.

23. Cf. H. Schmid, op. cit., 267.

24. Cf. H. Heppe and E. Bizer, op. cit., 361.

25. W. Heisenberg, *Der Teil und das Ganze*, Munich 1969, 324f. (ET *Physics and Beyond*, trans. A. J. Pomerans, London and New York 1971).

26. Thus G. Strachan, op. cit., 70ff. For the exegesis see G. von Rad, *Genesis*, ATD 2/4, 10th ed. Göttingen 1976, 30 (ET based on 9th edition, London and Philadelphia 1972); C. Westermann, *Genesis: A Commentary*, trans. J. J. Scullion, Minneapolis and London 1984, translates 'Der Gottessturm bewegt sich . . .' (ET 'God's wind was moving to and fro . . .'), and also ascribes to the verb the meaning of vibrating (107).

26a. Joseph von Eichendorff, translated Frederick Herzog. The German text is as follows: Schläft ein Lied in allen Dingen,/die da träumen fort und fort,/und die Welt fängt an zu singen,/triffst du nor das Zauberwort.

27. G. Schimanowski, op. cit., 306. Calvin sees the immanent efficacy of the transcendent Spirit of God analogously; *Inst. Rel. Christ.* I, 13, 14: 'Ille enim est qui ubique diffusus omnia sustinet, vegetat et vivificat in coelo et in terra. Iam hoc ipso creaturarum numero eximitur, quod nullis circumscribitur finibus.'

28. Cf. *God in Creation*, Ch. VIII, §4, 'Continuous Creation', 206ff.

29. Cf. Teilhard de Chardin, 'Christology and Evolution' in *Christianity and Evolution*, trans. René Hague, London 1971, 76–95. Cf. here S. M. Daecke, *Teilhard de Chardin und die evangelische Theologie. Die Weltlichkeit Gottes und die Weltlichkeit der Welt*, Göttingen 1967, and W. Beinert, *Christus und der Kosmos. Perspektiven zu einer Theologie der Schöpfung*, Freiburg 1974.

30. *Theological Investigations* V, trans. K.-H. Kruger, London and Baltimore 1966, 157ff.

31. 'Christ the Evolver' in *Christianity and Evolution*, 138–50.

32. Ibid., 144, 'The Creative Aspect of Redemption'.

33. Ibid., 147.

34. *Letters from a Traveller*, (8 September 1935) London 1967, 161.

35. *The Future of Man*, trans. N. Denny, London and New York 1964, 268. Cf. 304: 'The incarnation is a renewal and a restoration of all the forces and powers of the universe; Christ is the instrument, the centre, the goal of all animated and material creation.'

36. *The Future of Man*, 305; 'The mystical Christ has not yet attained his full growth . . . Christ is the fulfilment even of the natural evolution of being.'

37. *Christianity and Evolution*, 155f.

38. E. Benz saw this quite correctly; cf. his *Schöpfungsglaube und Endzeiterwartung*, Munich 1965, 243ff.

39. This was H. de Lubac's quite correct judgment in *The Religion of Teilhard de Chardin*, trans. René Hague, London 1967, New York 1968.

40. Contrary to E. Benz, op. cit., 248.

41. *Genèse d'une pensée. Lettres, 1914–19*, Paris 1962.

42. *The Future of Man*, 147.

43. Ibid., 152.

44. K. Rahner, *Theological Investigations* V, 157ff., 'Christology within an Evolutionary View of the World'.

45. Ibid., 171f., cf. also 160.

46. Ibid., 164.

47. Ibid., 167.

48. Ibid., 168.

49. Rahner adopts this view, op. cit., 160: The incarnation is 'something which must happen once, and once only, at the point where the world begins to enter into its final phase in which it is to realize its final concentration, its final climax, and its radical nearness to the absolute mystery called God. Seen from this view-point, the Incarnation appears as the necessary and permanent beginning of the divinization of the world as a whole.' Cf. also G. Altner, *Die Überlebenskrise in der Gegenwart – Ansätze zum Dialog mit der Nature in Naturswissenschaft und Theologie*, Darmstadt 1988, 130ff.; also G. Altner (ed.), *Die Welt als offenes System – Eine Kontroverse um das Werk von Ilya Prigogine*, Frankfurt 1986, 161ff.

50. K. Rahner, op. cit., 190 (retranslated). Cf. here J. B. Metz's critical comments on thinking in terms of evolution: 'Against wrong choices in Christian eschatology' in *Faith in History and Society*, trans. D. Smith, London 1980.

51. Thomas Aquinas, *STh* I, q 90, a 3 2: 'Praetera, finis rerum respondet principio: Deus enim est principium et finis rerum. Ergo et exitus rerum a principio respondet reductioni rerum in finem.' Cf. here M. Seckler, *Das Heil in der Geschichte. Geschichtstheologisches Denken bei Thomas von Aquin*, Munich 1964.

52. K. Rahner, op. cit., 182.

53. Cf. J. Moltmann, *God in Creation*, Ch. XI, 'The Sabbath: the Feast of Creation', 276ff.

54. W. Benjamin, 'Theologisch-politisches Fragment' in *Illuminationen. Ausgewählte Schriften*, Frankfurt 1961, 280f.

55. Ibid.

56. Cf. G. Altner, *Leben auf Bestellung? Das gefährliche Dilemma der Gentechnologie*, Freiburg 1988.

57. A. Burgsmüller and R. Weth, *Die Barmer Theologische Erklärung. Einführung und Dokumentation*, Neukirchen 1983, 35f.

58. E. Cardenal, *Love*, trans. Dinah Livingstone, London 1974, offers a contemporary interpretation of Augustine's 'cor inquietum donec requiescat in te' ('the heart is restless until it rests in thee'). A secular version is to be found in E. Fromm, *To Have or to Be*, New York 1976, and H. E. Richter, *Der Gotteskomplex. Die Geburt und die Krise des Glaubens an die Allmacht des Menschen*, Hamburg 1979.

59. Cf. E. Galeano, *Die offenen Adern Lateinamerikas. Die Geschichte eines Kontinents von der Entdeckung bis zur Gegenwart*, Wuppertal 1972.

60. Cf. also P. Singer, *Animal Liberation; a new ethic for our treatment of animals*, New York 1975; G. M. Teutsch, *Mensch und Tier. Lexikon der Tierschutzethik*, Göttingen 1987.

61. Thus G. and E. Strachan, *Survival and the Sabbatical Year. The Ecological Crisis in Relation to the Biblical Principle of Fallowing*, Edinburgh 1980.

62. J. Friedrich, 'Das Schwein vor dem Strafrichter. Tierprozesse im Mittelalter' in *Freibeuter. Vierteljahrsschrift für Kultur und Politik*, Berlin 1988, 36, 8–16.

63. From the wealth of relevant literature the following may be mentioned: G. Liedke, *Im Bauch des Fisches. Ökologische Theologie*, Stuttgart 1979; U. Duchrow and G. Liedke, *Schalom – der Schöpfung Befreiung, den Menschen Gerechtigkeit, den Völkern Frieden. Eine biblische Arbeitshilfe für den konziliaren Prozess*, Stuttgart 1987; G. Altner, *Schöpfung am Abgrund – die Theologie vor der Umweltfrage*, Neukirchen 1974; also his *Leidenschaft für das Ganze – zwischen Weltflucht und Machbarkeitswahn*, Stuttgart 1980; also his *Die Überlebenskrise der Gegenwart*, Darmstadt 1987; K.-M. Meyer-Abich, *Wege zum Frieden mit der Nature. Praktische Naturphilosophie für die Umweltpolitik*, Munich 1984; A. Auer, *Umweltethik. Ein theologischer Beitrag zur ökologische Diskussion*, Düsseldorf 1984; J. Moltmann, *God in Creation*, trans. Margaret Kohl, London and New York 1985.

VII   The Parousia of Christ

1. See W. Pannenberg, *Jesus – God and Man*, trans. L. C. Wilkins and D. A. Priebe, London 1970; W. Kasper, *Jesus the Christ*, trans. V. Green, London 1976; E. Schillebeeckx, *Jesus, an Experiment in Christology*, trans. J. Hoskins, London and New York 1979.

2. Cf. the Heidelberg Catechism, Question 52: 'How doth the coming again of Christ to judge the quick and the dead console thee?' 'That in all tribulation and persecution I with uplifted head expect from heaven that same

Judge who before presented himself for me before the Judgment Seat of God and hath taken from me all condemnation . . .' But when it goes on '. . . that he may cast all his and my enemies into eternal damnation . . .' this does not in my view correspond to the christology of the judged Christ as judge.

3. Of fundamental and pioneer importance in New Testament studies were E. Käsemann's essays 'The Beginnings of Christian Theology' (1960) and 'On the Subject of Primitive Christian Apocalyptic' (1962), both in *New Testament Questions of Today*, trans. W. J. Montague etc., London 1969, 82ff., 108ff. They profoundly influenced my *Theology of Hope* (1964, ET 1967). P. Schütz, *Parusia: Hoffnung und Prophetie*, Heidelberg 1960, was a solitary forerunner.

4. A. Schweitzer, *Von Reimarus zu Wrede. Eine Geschichte der Leben-Jesu-Forschung*, (1913), 6th ed., Tübingen 1951, 437f. (*The Quest of the Historical Jesus*, trans. W. Montgomery, 3rd ed., London 1954). For comment cf. F. Holström, *Das eschatologische Denken der Gegenwart*, Gütersloh 1936.

5. Cf. E. Brunner, *Das Ewige als Zukunft und Gegenwart*, Munich 1965, 25 (*Eternal Hope*, trans. H. Knight, London 1954); G. Sauter, *Zukunft und Verheissung*, Zürich 1965, 154; J. Moltmann, 'Antwort auf die Kritik der Theologie der Hoffnung' in W. D. Marsch (ed.), *Diskussion über die 'Theologie der Hoffnung'*, Munich 1967, 210ff.; also *God in Creation*, trans. Margaret Kohl, London and New York 1985, 124ff.

6. Thus P. Althaus, *Die letzten Dinge. Entwurf einer christlichen Eschatologie*, Gütersloh 1922; K. Barth, *Der Römerbrief*, 2nd ed., Munich 1922 (*The Epistle to the Romans*, trans. from 6th ed. by E. C. Hoskyns, London 1933); also *Die Auferstehung der Toten*, Munich 1924 (*The Resurrection of the Dead*, trans. J. J. Stenning, London 1933); R. Bultmann, *Jesus*, Tübingen 1926 (*Jesus and the Word*, trans. from 2nd ed. by L. P. Smith and E. H. Lautero, London 1934); cf. *Jesus and the Word*, 51: 'The future Kingdom of God, then, is not something which is to come in the course of time. . . . The Kingdom of God is a power which, although it is entirely future, completely determines the present'. K. Rahner's judgment is not essentially different in 'The Church and the Parousia of Christ' in *Theological Investigations* VI, London and Baltimore 1974, 295ff. Cf. also R. Bultmann, *Geschichte und Eschatologie*, Tübingen 1958, 48 (*History and Eschatology*, the Gifford Lectures for 1955, Edinburgh 1957). For C. H. Dodd's concept of 'realized eschatology' see his *The Apostolic Preaching and its Development* (1936).

7. K. Barth *Der Römerbrief*, 482.

8. P. Althaus, *Die letzten Dinge*, 98.

9. K. Barth, *Dogmatics in Outline*, trans. G. T. Thomson, London 1949, reprint 1972, 128ff.; Ignatius, *Philadel.* 9.2; Justin Martyr, *Dialogue* 14.8; *Apology* 48.2; 52.3.

10. A. Oepke, 'παρουσία' in *TDNT* V, 865. The expression 'second coming' is also misleading inasmuch as it presupposes Christ's absence and suppresses his presence in the Spirit. Cf. here also P. Minear, *Christian Hope*

and the Second Coming, Philadelphia 1953, 202ff. I am therefore translating parousia by the word 'future', as Luther and Paul Gerhardt also did, and am speaking of 'the future of Christ'. Cf. my *Theology of Hope*, trans. J. W. Leitch, London and New York 1967, 202ff. I am unable to understand how M. Barth can say in *Das Mahl des Herrn. Gemeinschaft mit Israel, mit Christus und unter den Gästen*, Neukirchen 1987, 97: 'It is true that today many people talk about a theology of hope, but not even Jürgen Moltmann seems to be willing to bring out the central importance of Christ's Second Coming (sic!).'

11. K. Barth, *Dogmatics in Outline*, 133, 135.

12. Thus H. Wenz, *Die Ankunft unseres Herrn am Ende der Welt*, Stuttgart 1965, a formulation which K. H. Schelkle makes his own in the formula 'the coming of Christ at the end of the times', because he quotes Wenz incorrectly; see Schelkle, *Theologie des Neuen Testaments* IV/1: *Vollendung von Schöpfung und Erlösung*, Düsselfort 1974, § 5 'Parusie, 61ff.

13. Cf. *Theology of Hope*, 16, following Ernst Bloch.

14. Cf. G. von Rad, 'The Origin of the Concept of the Day of Yahweh', *JSSt* 4, 1959, 97–108; also his *Theologie des Alten Testaments* II, 5th ed., Munich 1968, 129–133 (*Old Testament Theology* II, trans. D. M. G. Stalker, Edinburgh and London 1965); A. J. Everson, 'The Days of Yahweh', *JBL* 93, 1974, 329–337; Y. Hoffmann, 'The Day of the Lord as a Concept and a Term in the Prophetic Literature', *ZAW* 93, 1981, 37–50.

15. W. Radl, *Ankunft des Herrn. Zur Bedeutung und Funktion der Parusieaussagen bei Paulus*, Frankfurt 1981, 177ff.

16. Cf. above Ch. I, §2.

17. Cf. above Ch. I, §2.

18. This is rightly pointed out by B. Klappert, 'Perspektiven einer von Juden und Christen anzustrebenden gerechten Weltgesellschaft', *Freiburger Rundbrief. Beiträge zur christlich-jüdischen Begegnung*, XXX, 1978, 67–82.

19. Ibid., 70.

20. This is the original German title of G. Gloege's book: *Aller Tage Tag*, Stuttgart 1960; in English *The Day of his Coming*, trans. S. Rudman, London 1963.

21. For more detail cf. J. Moltmann, *God in Creation*, Ch. V, §3: 'The Time of Creation', 112ff.

22. Augustine, *Confessions*, XI, 10: 'Quod si exortum est aliquid in dei substantia, quod prius non erat, non veraciter dicitur aeterna illa substantia; si autem dei voluntas sempiterna erat, ut esset creatura, cur non sempiterna et creatura?' ['If something began to be in God's Substance, something which had not existed beforehand, we could not rightly say that his substance was eternal. But if God's will that there should be a creation was there from all eternity, why is it that what he has created is not also eternal?' (*Confessions*, trans. R. S. Pine-Coffin, Harmondsworth 1961)]

23. G. Scholem, 'Schöpfung aus Nichts und Selbstverschränkung

Gottes', *Eranos* 1956, vol. XXV, 87–119, esp. 116.

24. Cf. *God in Creation*, Ch. VI: 'The Space of Creation', 140ff.
25. Ibid., Ch. V: 'The Time of Creation', 104ff.
26. George Herbert (1593–1633). Cf. also the hymn by Johann Walter (1496–1570), which looks forward to 'the last judgment' as the dawn of the new creation in all its glory:

> Herzlich tut mich erfreuen die liebe Sommerzeit,*
> wann Gott wird schön erneuen alles zur Ewigkeit.
> Den Himmel und die Erden wird Gott neu schaffen gar,
> all Kreatur soll werden ganz herrlich schön und klar.
>
> Kein Zung kann je erreichen die ewig Schönheit gross:
> man kanns mit nichts vergleichen, die Wort sind viel zu bloss.
> Drum müssen wir solchs sparen bis an den Jüngsten Tag;
> dann wollen wir erfahren, was Gott ist und vermag.

*the summer of eternity

27. D. Staniloae, *Orthodoxe Dogmatik, Ökumenische Theologie* XII, Zürich and Gütersloh 1985, 303ff. Cf. also H. Sasse 'αἰών, αἰώνιος', *TDNT* I, 197–209. Sasse believes that underlying the Jewish and Christian apocalyptic of the present and future aeon, is the eternity doctrine of oriental astrology, with its idea about the eternal return of the same; he cites for this the idea of 'the rebirth of the cosmos' and the principle 'τὰ ἔσχατα ὡς τὰ πρῶτα' – the end like the beginning (Barn. 6.13). The idea of the return of the same thing in the succession of world eras dominates the mind of the preacher Solomon: 'Is there a thing of which it is said, "See, this is new"? It has been already in the ages (aeons) before us' (1.10); but apocalyptic broke through that doctrine of the aeons with the ideas of uniqueness and finality: this world time is the transitory aeon of pain and is therefore determined by time (χρόνος). The future aeon is the new creation and will be determined by the resurrection of the dead. Its 'time' is relative eternity, 'world without end'. In Christian thought apocalyptic ideas about the two aeons are broken through once more because of the resurrection of Christ '*from* the dead' and the experience in the Spirit of 'the powers of the age to come' (Heb. 6.5). In Christ and in the Spirit the new, eternal creation is already present in this transitory world time (II Cor. 5.17). If apocalyptic thinking is once again taken back to the astrological thinking of the eternal return of the world-age, e.g., the Pythagorean year, then the Christian experience of faith loses its meaningful horizon. Christ's death and resurrection then decline into the symbol for the eternal return of the same thing, and bring nothing new under the sun. That is the danger of C. G. Jung's interpretation: *Aion*, Princeton 1959. He is followed by G. Strachan, *Christ and the Cosmos*, Dunbar 1985, and a whole series of other 'New Age' thinkers. But 'New Age' has nothing to do with the Christian hope for the future new creation of all things, for the 'new age' will in principle bring 'nothing new under the sun'; it will merely cyclically renew the old.

28. For the following passage cf. my detailed discussion in *God in Creation*, Ch. VII: 'Heaven and Earth', 158ff.

29. Ibid., 180f.

30. M. Horkheimer, *Die Sehnsucht nach dem ganz Anderen*, Hamburg 1970, 51f.

31. Cf. the material presented by K. H. Schelkle, *Theologie des Neuen Testamentes*, IV/1, 92ff.

32. This dualistic apocalyptic has led today to an Armageddon theology, which in place of the mission of the gospel seeks an apocalyptic 'final struggle' with the religions of the world, and would like to turn the nuclear war that will annihilate the world into the 'final struggle' of the good with 'the kingdom of evil'. Cf. H. Lindsey, *The Late Great Planet Earth*, New York 1970; also his *The 1980's. Countdown to Armageddon*, Pennsylvania, 1980.

33. This will be the subject of full discussion in the fourth volume of these contributions, which will be devoted to eschatology.

34. What actually happens to 'the least of the brethren' of the Son of man-Judge of the world at the Last Judgment? They are not mentioned there at all. They belong neither to 'the sheep' nor 'the goats', and yet the whole mighty image has to do with them.

35. Cf. here L. Mattern, *Das Verständnis des Gerichtes bei Paulus*, Zürich 1966.

36. Cf. here C. Blumhardt's 'confessions of hope' in *Ansprachen, Predigten, Reden, Briefe 1865–1917*, ed. J. Harder, Neukirchen 1978, vol. II, 131: 'The end has to be: Behold, everything is God's! Jesus comes as the one who has borne the sins of the world. Jesus can judge, but not condemn. My desire is to have preached this to the lowest circles of hell, and I will never let myself be confounded.'

37. For more detail cf. J. Moltmann, *Prädestination und Perseveranz. Geschichte und Bedeutung der reformierten Lehre 'de perseverantia sanctorum'*, Neukirchen 1961. H. E. Richter discusses the psychological and social side of the problem in *Flüchten oder Standhalten*, Hamburg 1976.

38. Cf. V. J. Genovesi, *Expectant Creativity: The Action of Hope in Christian Ethics*, Philadelphia 1982, who pursues the line of my theology of hope in the field of ethics.

39. N. Goodall (ed.), *The Uppsala Report, 1968*, World Council of Churches, Geneva 1968.

INDEX OF NAMES

INDEX OF CONFESSIONS, CREEDS AND OTHER DOCUMENTS

W9-AQD-343

WOMAN'S CREATION

WOMAN'S
CREATION

Sexual Evolution and
the Shaping of Society

Elizabeth Fisher

JUL 2 3 1979

ANCHOR PRESS/DOUBLEDAY
GARDEN CITY, NEW YORK
1979

301.412
F533w

ELMHURST COLLEGE LIBRARY

An earlier abbreviated version of "Mother and Child: The First Couple" was published in *APHRA*, Spring-Summer 1976, Vol. VI, Nos. 3 and 4, under the title "In the Beginning Was the Dyad."

Grateful acknowledgment is made for the following quotations: "Because I Know So Little" by Jane Mayhall, © 1972 by The New York Times Company, reprinted by permission of the author and the *New York Times*; *The Mountain Gorilla* by George B. Schaller, pp. 283–84, The University of Chicago Press, 1963, © 1963 by George B. Schaller, permission granted by the publisher; *The Masks of God: Occidental Mythology* by Joseph Campbell, pp. 82–83, Viking Compass Edition, © 1963 by Joseph Campbell, reprinted by permission of the publisher, Viking Penguin Inc.

Library of Congress Cataloging in Publication Data

Fisher, Elizabeth.
    Woman's creation.

    Bibliography
    Includes index.
    1. Sex role.   2. Social evolution.   I. Title.
GN479.65.F57   301.41′2
ISBN: 0-385-00551-2
Library of Congress Catalog Card Number 77-77650

Copyright © 1979 by Elizabeth Fisher
ALL RIGHTS RESERVED
PRINTED IN THE UNITED STATES OF AMERICA
FIRST EDITION

Because I Know So Little

Because I know so little, I grope for more.
If I knew as much as you, I'd be afraid to
try my luck. I'd be stuck on the sticks of
reason, information that comes to naught.
You, who tell me life is useless rubbish,
and you can prove it with a twirl of diagrams,
heavy numbers. I can't concentrate on that,
I search through my dumb old feelings. And
trust and plough into what I'd like to be
true, mysteries, dark, unending, and all the
black night of search and dreaming, always
open, unanswered, shining through.

Jane Mayhall

To my parents and to *APHRA*

Acknowledgments

There were many who helped me along the way. This book would not have been possible without the revival of feminism, in the Women's Liberation Movement beginning about 1967, and the innumerable women whose thinking contributed to my own ideas.

I want to thank all those who wrote for and edited APHRA; it was in our discussions about the magazine and the movement that my ideas took form. In the early years particularly, from 1969 to 1973, method and feeling were united and the creative process of the group endeavor—the very real lift of women helping women—was carried over into the initial stages of this work also. There were fruitful interchanges with Ellen Harold, Margaret Lamb, Vivien Leone, and Leah Zahler, all of whom contributed ideas, intellectual stimulus, and research leads.

In the academic world many new acquaintances gave time and critical thought. Sally Binford read an early draft of Part I; Ruby Rohrlich-Leavitt read a draft of Parts I to III; while Eleanor Leacock read the next to last draft of Parts I to IV. They were generous with comment, corrections, and reference sources.

Two three-month fellowships at the MacDowell Colony and one three-month stay at the Virginia Center for the Creative Arts supported me in parlous times. Libraries became my dearest haunts; the several libraries of New York University provided the major sources from which I worked. There were also the University of Virginia Library with its open stacks, the State Library of New Hampshire through the patience of the Peterborough Town Library, the library of the Wenner-Gren

Foundation, and a fruitful month at the Frederick Lewis Allen Room of the New York Public Library. To all of them I owe thanks and apologies, for books borrowed and kept overlong.

Alix Shulman encouraged and advised. Gloria Dialectic read and criticized and discussed. My agent Ellen Levine maintained belief in the book during the long waiting.

After I had already handed in a draft of the book, Rosemary Poulos suggested a missing piece of the puzzle, in conversation, enabling me to revise Part IV so as to make a more cohesive theory.

Mary Nelson and Lillian Shelton helped with typing and research for the earlier versions. Evelyn Patterson typed the final draft, fitting my needs into her very limited time, deciphering my chicken tracks to produce accurate typescript, and enjoying the work besides. Nina Masonson helped track down recalcitrant sources and read and corrected notes and bibliography. Candace Watt proofread galleys.

Dolores Walker provided counsel over the years. Vera Schneider helped me to clarify and organize the book into its present form and prepared the bibliography. At a crucial moment she restored my confidence in myself and in the work, enabling me to bring it to a conclusion. Savelli stayed with me in a rocky period and helped me by advice and example. During the seven years it took me to write this book, I could always count on my long-time friend and sister Gerry Sachs for encouragement and support. In a world where even one friend is a miracle, I found I had several.

Contents

Introduction

This book began to write itself in 1971. It grew out of an essay I wrote that spring for Volume 2, Number 2, of *APHRA*, which we called The Whore Issue, for it was devoted to prostitution. Partly by default, partly by desire, I was elected to write an article that would tie together the magazine's contents. With ten days before deadline, I found myself in the Reference Room of the New York Public Library on Fifth Avenue and Forty-second Street, looking at two drawers of cards listing their material on prostitution. The enormity of the subject and the small amount of time available made it clear that research was impossible at the moment so I sat down and did a speculation about the meaning of prostitution in a patriarchal society, titling it "Hustlers All."

Afterward, dissatisfied and provoked, I had a halcyon week of intense cerebration in which the plan and themes of the book were born. After one visionary night, I said to myself, "I've just rewritten Engels' *Origin of the Family, Private Property, and the State*," which was patently untrue since at that moment I had written nothing, though later on it would be true and untrue. I had no concept of how far afield the research would take me, of how many byways I would traverse or disciplines enter upon, of what an extraordinary self-education would be involved.

There was one time around 1973 and 1974 when, dissatisfied with the extant translations of Sumerian and Akkadian, I contemplated applying for a grant to learn cuneiform—the wedge-shaped signs on clay that are believed to have been the first written language. I slogged on instead, comparing one transla-

tion with another and trusting also to my judgment as a translator—though I had worked only from Italian and French—and
as a researcher. In the process of digging one finds information
to prove many points. In the long run one scholar's version is
chosen over another's on the basis of past experience and past
reading and of what seems logical and valid; obviously emotional response plays a critical role in the decision.

Once embarked upon the project I realized that the book
had been many years, most of my adult life, in the shaping,
though the immediate impetus came from the thinking engendered by those early years of the Women's Liberation Movement. It did not begin as a women's liberation book per se. I
had been struggling over these problems from my first introduction to political ideas in early adolescence. It was, however,
an attempt to look with a female perspective at what till now
had been seen largely through the male eye. The stimulus and
excitement born of the movement, of shared ideas and of
women talking and writing to and for each other, gave me
courage to see my disadvantages as assets and to dare such an
ambitious undertaking. In the idealism of those first years, we
had had a vision that the whole sickness of civilization could be
seen in miniature in the power nexus between the sexes and
that in attacking the latter we could also come out with a
kinder, more just, and loving world. Things have not turned
out to be that simple, but it should be remembered that the
movement's origins were political and idealistic, a search for
understanding which would change thinking and doing.

In my years of editing APHRA I saw much of the work that
came out of the movement: the underground newspapers, the
manifestoes, the pamphlets, the articles, the books. Within the
mass were brilliantly provocative ideas and facts, and much,
much testimony. Ideas fed on each other, going back and forth;
new intellectual possibilities arose. For thousands of years,
men's experiences had been considered objective reality,
women's labeled narcissism. We realized we must develop a
new methodology. Carol Hanisch formulated the statement,
the personal is political, a concept not new to art or artists, and
we decided that our thinking could and should be shaped by

our own and other women's personal experiences. At the same time we had to go back and to re-examine everything we had been taught, testing it in the light of our new awareness about the upper-class male framework in which history had been written as well as the sexual bias inherent in the English language. Later I was to hear academic women complain that perhaps the worst crime perpetrated on women was the internalization of male thinking. Whatever the defects of my education, I was spared much of that approach. I had not had to write for the grades and approval of a male-oriented academic establishment, permitting me fresh insights and an unconventional approach.

In a recent television interview Simone de Beauvoir said that all her intellectual influences were male. Though I was introduced early on to certain beacons—Marx-Engels, Wilhelm Reich, Kropotkin, in that order and widely separated in time— many of my influences were female. As it happened, women, not men, encouraged me to write, and read and discussed my work. When I began to write seriously, women writers treated me as a colleague and provided intellectual stimulus. In the late nineteen fifties and early sixties I met several women whose dedication to art and ideas provided examples I could follow.

Two feminist classics taught me to question received authority. I came across Virginia Woolf's A Room of One's Own one summer when I was seventeen and never saw the world—and male dignity—in the same light again. A few years later Ruth Herschberger's Adam's Rib confirmed for me what I was learning in life about the slanted vision and particularity of the experts. At the time I was earning my living with skills centered around writing and editing. From finding mistakes in the Encyclopaedia Britannica to watching the process of arbitrary judgment and borrowing involved in producing a new dictionary, lessons in skepticism were not wanting.

As the work progressed, many of my hunches would be verified by material published after I had formulated my own ideas so that I could go back and rewrite with more confidence. I had already questioned the received tenets of ethology in the first section of the book when David Pilbeam's article attacking

naked apery came my way. And I had written the first version
of the Sumerian chapters before Thorkild Jacobsen published
The Treasures of Darkness, confirming and adding substance
to my vision of Sumerian religion as a political expression of
support for hierarchical authority.

In our time the myth of neutrality, impartial intellectual objectivity, has finally been demolished. There is no intelligence
without feeling. In order to think you need to care. One may
feel in negative, destructive ways, but hostile or positive, you
cannot think without wanting to think, and that's desire.

Numbers are not without association, as in the probably
apocryphal tale about the now-extinct Tasmanians' counting
system—one, two, plenty—or our own special feelings about the
holy three and cabbalistic magic in numbers. Words are all the
more replete with associations and with their specific historical
uses in each language.

Observers bring their own experiences with them: women
and men have a different reality. Several articles and books
have been written to point up how the limitations of English,
where the male form is the prototype and the female the variation, force a certain amount of sexism on the most recalcitrant
writer, womanfully though we struggle against it.

The usage of the generic term *man* and of male pronouns to
cover both sexes effectively excludes women from conscious
thought much of the time. With one word to cover two meanings—the abstract generic for humanity, humans, or humankind that in Latin is *homo,* and the specific gendered individual of the male sex known as *vir* in Latin—writers switch back
and forth between both meanings or use them interchangeably
with resultant confusion. For this reason, I avoid the male pro-
noun unless I am specifically referring to male individuals, and
I use *man* or *men* in the limited sense only, choosing deriva-
tives of *homo* for the generic usage. In quotations from other
writers, I italicize *man* or *he* when it is used in the general
sense, not for sarcasm or irony, but to point up what I consider
intellectually questionable usage, a confusion which serves to
misdirect thinking and keep women invisible. Similarly, unless
otherwise indicated, italicized emphasis in quotations is mine,

not the authors', to call attention to the cultural bias we have inherited from the past.

A related decision concerned the use of dates. In the first four parts of the book, the archaeologists' term B.P. (before the present), refers to actual years past rather than the supposed beginning of the Christian or Common Era. In Part V, when I take up the beginnings of historical civilization with the invention of writing, I have adopted the dates used in most sources, so as not to place an extra burden on reader and author. From Chapter 29 to the end of the book, I use B.C.E. and C.E. Thus first millennium refers to the thousand years between the presumed birth of Jesus Christ and 1000 B.C.E., second millennium to the previous thousand years, and so forth.

In the Hebrew calendar, by coincidence, I would find myself with a dating scheme rather closer to the initiation of writing since it begins 5,738 years before this current year of 1978; in the Chinese I would be using the date 4738. Though custom forces a Western, white, European date scheme on one who is writing within our time and context, we can, and we must, remind ourselves of the limitations and artificial conventions within which we are constricted even as we strive after closer approximations to understanding.

Finally, in the words of Herodotus, I will not apologize for my digressions: digression is part of the plan.

New York City
June 1978

Part I

―――――――――

MOTHER
AND CHILD:
THE FIRST COUPLE

Men have had every advantage of us in telling their
own story. Education has been theirs in so much
higher degree, the pen has been in their hands. I
will not allow books to prove anything.
                              —Jane Austen, *Persuasion*

1

Science Imitates Society

How did woman come to be the prototype possession? Almost universally, she has been treated as property to be traded, sold, or otherwise disposed of. In Western culture it is the father who gives the bride away, in the Trobriand Islands the mother's brother, among the African Hadza it is the mother who receives strings of beads as bride price for her daughter, but the girl herself is still being bestowed on a man.

In some societies women are measured in cattle—so many head to acquire a bride; in others the groom and his kinsmen baldly describe marriage, "We pay for her genitals."[1]

Long before Descartes shaped his proof of existence by way of the mind, the first principle of man's dawning consciousness would seem to have been "I own, therefore I am." And shaped by human preconceptions, behavioral scientists—psychologists and ethologists—have looked at animals and tried to interpret their actions by the same theorem. They have seen possession as the first aim of man and animal, and interpreted nature as a scheme of conquest and arrogation, with sex as the first battleground, the female the first conquered territory.

Moreover, since maleness has been associated with aggression for so long, the scientists have tended toward certain value judgments and confusions. There has been a basic assumption that male sexual activity and positions are admirable, the female's humiliating, and a second assumption that, maleness and aggression being almost synonymous, aggression is more to be admired than peacefulness, which latter is humiliating as well as female.

How did civilized man come to be dominant over woman? How did it get to be the way it is between the sexes?

The traditional answer is that it is a fact of nature, the result of the male animal's superior strength. Our whole civilization has taken it for granted, and language and culture are shot through with particulars sustaining and re-enforcing this position. Pyramidal hierarchy is seen as the basic order of nature, of all organic and often inorganic phenomena. Philosophy, science, and religion have based their premises on the female's natural inferiority to the male; in recent years ethologists, behavioral scientists who study animals, have charted animal life in terms of dominance-submission relationships with the female seen as universally submissive to the male. Aristotle, Hobbes, Rousseau, Darwin, Freud . . . most of the world's great thinkers have accepted women's inferiority as a first principle or an unexamined substratum when they presented their contributions to human understanding. Men and women, we have been exposed to it all our lives in almost every form of human intellectual or artistic striving and we are all, often unconsciously, deeply indoctrinated with this belief.

A more recent theory has it that in its origins the human species was socially organized as a matriarchy before the present patriarchal system was instituted. Nineteenth-century thinkers saw matriarchy as a lower order. Women, the reproducers, are closer to nature. In due time this lower social order gave way to the higher order of patriarchy, for intelligence is possessed in greater degree by the male; some thinkers saw it as a male attribute. And the patriarchy under which we now live was a necessary development for progress and civilization, though the more tolerant thinkers looked forward to a future when it would give way to a less cruel society. Forms of this theory were presented by the nineteenth-century scholar Bachofen and sustained by Marx and Engels. Discredited by late nineteenth- and early twentieth-century science, it was taken up by students of the human psyche and by artists.[2] In recent years some women have also seen in primitive matriarchy a partial redemption from the overwhelming blackness of the picture presented by the world of actuality and imagination as we know it. They have shaped the theory to say that matriarchy was not only the first but also the better order of human life and have traced our troubles—the actual position of women and the general ills of civilization—to the aggressiveness and misguided intelligence of the male dominators.[3]

A third theory, which has only very slowly gained ground among scientists, both ethologists and physical and social anthropologists, has it that humanity, being based on co-operation, has its origins in primitive egalitarianism and that this egalitarianism may even apply to the sexes, that the earliest humans shared tasks and that dominance is inherent neither in the animal world nor in humanity. That, in the last analysis, we have been misled by comparatively recent patterns of human history into misinterpreting what we see around us in nature and what we dig up to interpret the past.

One problem in studying our origins and the world around us is that language itself assumes that all life is constructed on the principles of the human patriarchy of Western civilization.

Biology as a science is very new—Darwin's *Origin of Species* was published in 1859, *The Descent of Man* in 1871. In the even newer sciences of psychology, anthropology, and ethology, historical preconceptions of the female's role have shaped the formulation and presentation of information. Scientists projected Western customs—where woman is treated as man's possession and the father gives his daughter to a son-in-law of his choice—onto unrelated fields and treated us to a view of animal and human behavior with the female as the universal possession. Thus ethologists tell of a male monkey "taking" or "possessing" a female, though their own descriptions make it clear that it was the female monkey who took the initiative, choosing time, place, and partner. They discuss sexual relations and "presenting"—an animal's act of offering or showing its hindquarters to another animal. Though this might be considered a sexual gesture with a connotation of genital pleasure, it has been made into an indication of both female behavior and submission. As Wolfgang Wickler says, "In the social context, male sexual actions imply dominance and female sexual actions submissiveness. . . . if a male rhesus monkey mounts another male, it is the more dominant individual that plays the masculine role."[4]

According to many ethologists, the subordinate male presents to the dominant male as a conciliation-humiliation technique, and he is described as "cringing," "crouching," etc., words also frequently used to refer to the female animal. If it were viewed as distraction behavior—some animals don't feel like fighting, as some humans don't feel like fighting—we would have less emotional response. And the fact of the matter is that it is not a clear-cut distinction, except in the minds of the observers and the possibly artificial categories invented by the ethologists. Sometimes it is the "subordinate" who mounts, rather than presenting, and sometimes the "dominant male" presents his rear. Infant langur monkeys have a syndrome at about age two of "mounting": they jump up on adult males and hug them around the waist. Clearly the words are far from adequate to describe what really goes on.[5]

As long as the masculine role is aggrandized and the female role derogated, as long, that is, as nature is seen from a male-supremacist view, human sexual encounters will be tainted. We are imprisoned in a conquest vocabulary which places females in the "submissive position." Convention equates the female's role in sex with surrender rather than admitting that, animal or human, surrender-aggression is involved for each sex, a reciprocal relationship in which sometimes the female approaches the male and the male refuses or accepts and vice versa; reciprocity exists among animals as among people, though on different and more shallow levels, and both sexes participate. Among mammals, rape does not exist, and it is the female who calls the tune, whereas among humans, with the invention of sexual coercion, it is more often the male who leads.

Anthropologists' reports on human groups which took shape outside the enslaving and colonizing traditions of the West are also distorted by subjectivity. Claude Lévi-Strauss based a whole theory of human relatedness on the premise that in human society a man must obtain a woman from another man, who gives him a daughter or a sister.[6] In *The Elementary Structures of Kinship* he described all human relations in terms of men, with women as the medium of exchange connecting them. He used Radcliffe-Brown's reports on Australian Aborigines, gathering and hunting peoples who had never developed agriculture, to formulate universal rules about marriage and kinship systems, whereby marriage and family were forms of communication for men, based on reciprocal exchanges of women. It was a typical male cosmology; how or whether women communicated or what existence they had beyond serving the purpose of their male relatives was none of his concern.

Fortunately for human knowledge, some other anthropologists did field work among these bands and discovered that the elegant symmetry of Lévi-Strauss's theory had no relation to the Australians' reality. The complicated exchanges across group subdivisions described by Radcliffe-Brown were not those the Aborigines themselves observed. However, though the later anthropologists negated the Lévi-Strauss concept, they themselves decided that women were still being exchanged by men, not as communication, but because they belonged to different clans with gathering and hunting rights on specific land areas. Accordingly men enlarged their economic possibilities by marrying women of different clans, thus gaining hunting rights over additional pieces of land. Women were still being seen as the primordial possession, whether used for economic advantage or for communication.[7]

The truth of the matter is that none of these anthropologists really told us how the Australians themselves regarded women, for they interpreted the Aborigines' actions in light of their own assumptions. The tribes under discussion did not recognize paternity. For them a woman was a being who produced children regularly thoughout the period between puberty and menopause. In the Aborigines' eyes the man with whom she was living had no connection with these biological facts. Although it was recognized that biological paternity did not exist for these Australians, man-woman relationships were still described in a projection from Western mores: "A woman passes through the possession of quite a number of different men in her lifetime."[8] It was as though a man possessed a woman just by the act of going to bed with her, when the simple fact was that a woman could expect to have several husbands during her life.

Actually the relationship of the Australian Aborigine woman and man is a reciprocal economic one: she gathers and does some hunting, supplying 70 to 80 per cent of the food, he hunts for the remaining 30 or 20. She cooks the food she has found, and he prepares that which he has obtained. Marriages are arranged by older men and women, but after adolescence the participants usually manage to assert their own desires. This information has become available only in the past decade or so, partly because of the increased participation of women anthropologists and the revival of hitherto buried material, partly through the application of new ecological perspectives.[9]

Modern science developed out of a civilization based on war and slavery, and it has produced the threat of planetary destruction, along with numerous benefits. In consequence, there is a new respect for those long-surviving peoples who used to be called primitive, ignorant, and incompetent, as well as interest in other forms of life that can enlighten us about the destructive elements now threatening our own society.

2

The Idea of Dominance

Civilization is stratified, and in consequence when scientists looked at nature they tended to see it in terms of pyramidal hierarchy rather than interlocking vectors. The twentieth-century science of ethology was no exception. It was founded on principles of dominance-submission and the charting of animal hierarchies. Like Lévi-Strauss's kinship theory, these would seem to be elegant constructs bearing a limited relation to reality. Dominance is, after all, a laboratory concept. It simply means that when a piece of food is thrown before two animals, one of them often defers to the other, seeming to acknowledge the other's prior right rather than risk a fight. It was first noted in relation to chickens, and it does not extend in ramifications to the liege-lord fealty value human psychologists have assigned it. Once accepted, it was used in laboratory experiments to prove all kinds of things: that males dominate females, elders youngers, largers smallers, but mostly on the basis of projections already in the minds of the experimenters. Small wonder that it was ill-fitting and uncomfortable when applied to observations in the wild. And small wonder also that male and female observers often came up with different results, with males being more likely to discern sharp dominance-submission relations than females.

Phyllis Jay's studies of langur monkeys in India found them unaggressive and unhierarchical, the females strongly oriented to maternal behavior. She noted that when a langur was born, it was often passed around from female to female and touched and caressed.[1] When a team of Japanese and Indian men studied langurs, their description of langur troop organization and aggressive behavior was significantly different from Jay's. One of the most startling discrepancies was that where she had only seen baby langurs passed from monkey to monkey and returned to their mothers, they also saw infants "kidnaped" by females from other troops and observed that "when a newborn infant was taken by a female from a neighboring troop, it was usually difficult for the mother to get her infant back."[2]*

Another example of what might well be a subjective view is the description by Kinji Imanishi of male dominants monopolizing female Japanese macaques at Takasakiyama: "It is observed that some estrous females *escape* from the central part and make a *secret* consort relation with one of the males in the peripheral part."[3]

In recent years, both the concept of dominance and the related hypothesis that the highest-ranking males produce the most offspring have been questioned by female and male investigators. It was found that the various measures of dominance were not consistent one with another: a monkey who ranked high on the dominance scale by one criterion—say, mounting—did not necessarily achieve a high rank if measured by aggressive encounters. Thelma Rowell studied forest baboons in Uganda, and it is her opinion that dominance hierarchies are often a product of artificial laboratory situations. Observers make monkeys compete for a reward and then chart the ranks they themselves have produced.[4]

Within the diversity of nature isolated examples to prove almost any thesis can often be located, not to mention that a

* In partial explanation, the langurs studied by Jay lived in forested sections of India, while some of those studied by the Indian and Japanese observers lived in closer proximity to humans and to each other, factors believed to encourage aggressive and aberrant behavior. In recent years Sarah Blaffer Hrdy has studied langurs in southern India and observed infants kidnaped and murdered by males who were not initially troop members but who then joined the troops to which the murdered infants had belonged.

lively imagination can twist the supposed evidence of observation into proof of a subjective preconception. The notion of the
female as passive and the male as active is a time-honored one,
and many scientists of the last century took it for granted in
their work. However, it is not so in nature, and the evidence
has been as close as any country cat or dog.

Darwin's chivalrous notion of sexual selection—that the
males fight for the possession of the female, who stands by and
then accepts the winner ("the female, though comparatively
passive, generally exerts some choice and *accepts* one male in
preference to the others"), thereby ensuring the amelioration
of the species—was a projection of Arthurian legends, the
knight jousting for the favors of the fair lady.[5] In fact, Konrad
Lorenz gives the latter as an example of sexual selection in
humans, though surely medieval knights represented an in-
finitesimally tiny proportion of the human population at the
time, the age of chivalry being more a literary phenomenon
than an actual one.[6]

In any case, the notion that the male animal possesses a passive female is hogwash. No one possesses anyone. Animals
meet, mate, and part, sometimes immediately, sometimes after
the rearing of the young, even, as is presumed in the case of
gibbons, wolves, and Canada geese, after a lifetime. There is no
notion of possession in the limited mind of a male animal. Possession is a figment of human imagination. Perhaps it is human
bravado in front of the universe, a way of asserting oneself
against its immeasurable force. Still, the puny man who thinks
he possesses land, or almost any commodity, is clearly illuding
himself. Sometimes possessions possess us, but we are all possessed by time's sweep: even when we consume our possessions,
it is only temporary; we are ourselves eventually consumed.

Mice are impervious to the labels attached to their behavior
by human observers as well as to the philosophical implications
out of which our language has grown. The female wild mouse
is about as passive as Mae West. She marks her burrow with
her own brand of perfume—her urine—a sign which says, in
effect, "Hey, fellows, come up and see me. I want you." Or possibly "it," because what she wants is sex—or, in the language

of the biologists, "relief of genital tension." She certainly
doesn't want impregnation, though that is probably what will
occur as the result of her actions. Male mice are attracted by
the odor of the estrous female's urine. They mark the area with
their own urine in response, rolling on her marking. If two
males happen on her trademark at the same time, they may
fight, but not if she's around. If she's there she begins sex relations, though whether she takes her choice or the one closest to
her is not a question human observers can yet answer, Darwin's
theory of sexual selection to the contrary. The female mouse
copulates with numerous males in succession. Once copulation
has begun, males do not fight or interfere.[7] The other mice
wait patiently until the female is ready for them: they also
service who only stand and wait. This is what occurs also
among humankind's closest animal relatives, the chimpanzees,
and there is certainly a long tradition of promiscuity or free sex
in human life, whether in the recent custom of sexual swinging
or in various sanctioned and unsanctioned forms throughout
our existence.

Animal behaviorists often attempt to explain the order in
which females copulate with males in terms of hierarchy, but
actual observations are inconsistent with rigid theories about
brute strength and bullying power being the directive behind
sexual relations—at least where animals are concerned.[8]

The vocabulary of humankind gives us many semantical ab-
surdities as it is applied to animals. Among the simians, for instance, in species where there is no sexual swelling—a visible in-
dicator to mark the female primate's sexual desire—it is the
female monkey who initiates sex. Thus, in one description of
howler monkeys, "When a howler female's endocrines make
her *receptive*, she *approaches* the male."[9] Primate observers
constantly talk of the male or series of males "possessing" the
female, though how anyone can know who possesses whom is
beyond me. True, it is the male who is perched behind and over
the female, but he cannot copulate without her aid and co-
operation. Harry Harlow, famous psychologist at the University
of Wisconsin, demonstrated this fact on rhesus monkeys, by
rearing them in isolation so that they had no chance to learn

about sexual behavior. (Afterward, being left with a batch of virgin monkeys, civilized humans introduced rape into the monkey cosmos. In order to breed the unco-operative females, the psychologists invented "a restraining device to hold the female in proper position . . . we call it the rape rack."[10])

"Mounting" is the male-oriented but not always accurate term of biology. The male chimpanzee sometimes stands behind the female, clasping her round the waist; other times he squats, with his buttocks barely clearing the ground. Gorillas have been observed to sit with the female before them, a position which George Schaller describes as seated in his lap, though to a woman observer the female gorilla might well appear to be on top, with her partner underneath.

When the male primate approaches the female with sex in mind, zoologists usually describe him in some admiring term of force or activity; when the female does likewise she is "soliciting" him—the same word used to describe a human prostitute. If a male ape or monkey looks at a female for purposes of sexual invitation it is a glare; if the female looks fixedly at the male for the same reason it is only a look or at best a stare. Lionel Tiger and Robin Fox speak of the female's estrous period as "a kind of sexual mania," though she is only doing what comes naturally and there is nothing maniacal about it for her, while K. R. L. Hall describes the female patas monkey's sexual approach as "a *cringing* half-run with short quick steps toward the adult male."[11] One wonders what adjective a male approach would have elicited.

Jane Goodall's articles on chimpanzees written for the academic communities use the conventional zoologists' phrase "period of sexual receptivity" to describe a chimpanzee in heat, but when she writes for the general public she speaks of sexual attractiveness. In *My Friends the Wild Chimpanzees* she describes ugly old Flo, the most aged female of the fifty-odd animals she had come to know individually during the years of her study: "Despite her decrepit appearance, she had more suitors than any other female," and she adds that while the female chimpanzee is normally attractive for ten days or so, one time Flo's period of sexual attractiveness lasted almost five weeks.[12]

The prospect does indeed rouse admiration in humans, taught that sexual attractiveness is chiefly a property of youth and beauty. Still, why not call it Flo's "period of sexual desire"? According to Goodall, she was followed constantly by a crowd of eager chimpanzees, so it must have been she who decided when, though whether copulations were indiscriminate or chosen does not come out in the report—only that there were seven in succession one time, twenty another. Nor was there any fighting or restiveness on the part of the waiting males, any particular dominance order observable.

Desire and sexual satisfaction as related to the female have been hard for the biologists to swallow. People thought that a scream emitted by female cats during the sex act was a scream of pain because the male cat's member is spiny. Still, we do not know what goes on in the mind of an animal when it screams, and animals are not the only creatures who have been known to scream with pleasure. An experiment with a smooth glass rod used in place of the male cat produced exactly the same sort of scream from the female cat—and the scientists were forced to admit that perhaps females, at least among the felines, do it because they want to, not because they are overpowered by a masterful male.[13]

In *The Naked Ape* Desmond Morris acknowledges satisfaction and orgasm in the human female but explains the woman's orgasm as "a borrowed male pattern" stemming from our upright posture. By his reasoning it is useful for the woman to lie still after sex, giving the sperm enough time to reach the egg. He claims there is no equivalent among the nonhuman primates. "The female monkey shows little sign of emotional upheaval and usually wanders off as if nothing had happened."[14] Recent researches contradict him. Animals are difficult to observe in the wild, and there are no primatologist equivalents of Masters and Johnson wiring apes and monkeys to meters and sensors in an effort to penetrate their physical and emotional responses. In 1971 Suzanne Chevalier-Skolnikoff conducted a year-long study at the Primates Laboratory of the Department of Psychiatry, Stanford University School of Medicine. She chose to observe stump-tail macaques, monkeys whose sexual behavior has several characteristics that make them easier to observe than other monkeys. She produced incontrovertible evidence of orgasms in the females—"the first observations of orgasms in any nonhuman female mammal." She recorded both heterosexual and homosexual behavior among her subjects, reporting that homosexuality occurred in the rather high proportion of one to every four heterosexual encounters. Female homosexual behavior was observed more frequently than male homosexual activity—twenty-three female-female encounters, several of which led to orgasm, as opposed to thirteen male-male ones. "All normal animals probably have the capacity for both male and female sex roles throughout their lives," she concluded. Primatologists now acknowledge that female primates are capable of taking active roles in coitus and their capacity for orgasm is more similar to that of males than was previously thought.[15]

In Goodall's field observations the female chimps "remained still, moved away calmly, or rushed off screaming." Active participation by female as well as male is indicated by field studies, with varied reactions by each at the conclusion of each copulation. If anything, observations of the female primate's sexual activity corroborate Masters and Johnson's findings that women were capable of multiple orgasms, though one should be cautious in drawing analogies between animal and human behavior. On a purely physiological basis, female primates demonstrate, at certain given moments, a more intense sex drive and greater capacity for coitus than the male—behavior human males tend to characterize as "insatiable" or the afore-cited "sexual mania."

As far back as 1948, Ruth Herschberger had looked with a critical eye at the pronouncements of the supposedly objective scientists. In *Adam's Rib* she questioned the findings of the Yerkes Laboratory, where studies of chimpanzees were supposed to shed new light on the behavior of humans. She questioned the assumptions of experiments which purported to demonstrate that males were "naturally dominant" over females and to reveal a "biological basis of prostitution . . . the mature and sexually experienced female trades upon her ability to satisfy the sexual urge of the male." She pointed out that

Yerkes had manipulated his material. He had thrown out all observations "for Lia and Patti (two females) because they are highly dominant."[16] In other words, when females show dominance over males, their actions are disregarded in the statistical analysis because they might disprove the thesis already in the mind of the scientist.

In 1971, Naomi Weisstein commented on the limitations of psychology as a science. She describes the self-fulfilling prophecy built into experiments—how subjects perform to bear out the expectations of the experimenters: "If one group of experimenters has one hypothesis about what they expect to find, and another group of experimenters has the opposite hypothesis, both groups will obtain results in accord with their hypothesis. The results obtained are not due to mishandling of data by biased experimenters; rather the bias of the experimenter somehow creates a changed environment in which subjects act differently . . . students become intelligent because their teachers expect them to be intelligent, and rats run mazes better because experimenters are told rats are brighter [than the students thought they were]."[17]

In other words, experiments generate their own answers according to what is in the experimenters' minds. Possibly the experimenters choose a form which prefigures results consistent with their prejudices or preconceptions.

One doesn't know how much effect the earlier book of Herschberger or the later paper of Weisstein has had. Yerkes is still revered as the father of a whole new area of science, and from its modest beginnings his laboratory has grown into a network of primate laboratories across the United States, while the study of apes and monkeys has mushroomed and spread all over the world. Laboratory science has been useful in medical research, testing drugs, discovering the pathology of cells, even for rough observation, say, on the growth cycle of animals. But when it comes to describing the behavior of animals, let alone predicting that of humans, its validity is questionable.

3

Our Primate Relatives

Still humans are primates—if we are going to speculate on the road to humanity, a look at the other members of our order should be useful. So it had seemed to the scientists, though they started with a strong anthropomorphic bias. Yet, they, too, began to feel that captive conditions and a human environment might well have considerable distorting effect on the behavior of animals. If one looks at domesticated cats and dogs and sees how they take on the characteristics of the people with whom they live, or at prison populations, it seems fairly obvious that we cannot learn much about the "natural" behavior of animals without seeing them in their usual environment.

In 1931 Clarence Carpenter was a psychologist at Pennsylvania State University who had been influenced by *Mutual Aid*, the book in which the anarchist Peter Kropotkin took exception to the extremes of Darwin's followers. Where they argue that evolution and survival of the fittest meant constant aggression, exemplified by a competitive pyramid, Kropotkin theorized that animal and human societies were based on sharing and co-operation, one individual helping another. Carpenter was the first scientist to go out and spend a lengthy period of time observing primates in their natural habitat—fifteen months in the jungle blinds watching howler monkeys on Barro Colorado Island in Central America—and to report in detail on what he found. The results supported Kropotkin rather than the social Darwinists. Howler monkeys live in troops: they are not aggressive, they do not have sharp dominance hierarchies, and they do not compete for females; each female mates with many males—in general they are a co-operative society which operates for the defense and protection of all its members.

Since then, but above all in the sixties and seventies, more than fifteen species have been studied in the wild. Not only were laboratory studies incorrect, but later field studies often contradict the generalizations drawn from earlier ones. Every variety of behavior has been found and every combination of sexual grouping: monogamy (among gibbons); mixed male-female groups, all-male groups, all-female-and-young groups, one male and several females (under hardship conditions); aggressive females among the patas monkeys, aggressive males among the baboons, aggressive males and females among the macaques, pacific males and females among the langurs; fairly rigid hierarchies and loose open groups; small groups and large ones. The only consistent relationship is the one between mother and child.

Jane Goodall's study of chimpanzees on the Gombe Stream Reserve in Tanzania, which began in 1960 when she was twenty-six years old and is to be continued at least until 1980, did the most to revolutionize scientists' thinking about primate and early-human societies.[1] A young woman with a passion for animals and no formal training, she had worked as secretary to the physical anthropologist Louis Leakey. He encouraged and enabled Goodall to go out alone and watch chimpanzees. He was interested in comparing them with the earliest humans, and the fact that she had no academic background, not even an undergraduate degree, was in her favor: he felt she would have a freer mind in consequence. It was in the early years that she made her great discoveries about tool use, meat eating, open groups, and free sex among chimpanzees. She found that, although highly social, chimpanzees were little interested in dominance and aggression per se and that they had no stable groupings at all, let alone the male-dominated families or harems postulated by earlier scientists. They moved in small temporary groups, which might consist of any combination of age/sex classes. Lone males and, occasionally, lone females were also encountered. The only group that was stable over a period of months was a mother with her infant and older offspring. During those first years also she found few dominance interactions.[2]

A year-long study of chimpanzees in the Budongo Forest, in Uganda, by a husband-wife team, Vernon and Frances Reynolds, confirmed Goodall's report. They concluded that dominance interactions formed a minute fraction of observed chimpanzee behavior. No evidence of a linear hierarchy of dominance among males or females was found, nor were any permanent leaders of groups discernible.[3] Both study projects reported that in the wild the apes mate most frequently during moments of social excitement—on arrival at a particularly rich feeding place or at a meeting of two large groups—and that, as mentioned before, they are sexual swingers, though it is in the nature of the primate physiology that the female gets to swing more than the male.

Evolutionary theory used to be based on the fact that humans were thought to be the only primates who ate meat as well as vegetables. The hunting syndrome was used to explain the human condition. War, aggression, divergence of sex roles, and male dominance were the results of group hunting activities in which males alone participated to provide the principal sustenance for our prehuman forebears. Goodall's work with chimpanzees was the first of many studies which resulted in the overturn of such simplistic ideas about human evolution. To begin with, we are not the only omnivorous primate; the amiable, noncompetitive, nonhierarchical chimpanzees of the Gombe Stream Reserve were discovered to eat meat in addition to vegetables. Baboons and vervets had previously been observed to eat insects, small rodents, and birds' eggs; Goodall saw the forest-savanna chimpanzees catch and eat baby monkeys, bushbuck, and bush pig. She also watched as they shared their prey with other chimpanzees who held out a hand to beg for meat—the only primate besides humankind known to share food. Moreover, the chimpanzees engaged in what looked like the beginnings of group hunts: they deployed themselves at the base of several trees so as to trap an animal within a given area.

Today, aggression is being discarded as a prime mover. It makes little evolutionary sense to consider that it is the function of maleness to be overbearingly aggressive, to fight constantly, and to be dominant.[4] A 1975 newspaper article headed "Study Links Aggression in Rats to Prenatal Zinc Deficiency" indicates the current direction: aggression viewed as aberrational rather than normal behavior.[5]

Prepared or manufactured tools were long considered a human invention and were associated with the killing of animals. Goodall discovered that chimpanzees also used prepared tools, though not for hunting. A chimp will pick up a blade of coarse savanna grass and trim off the edges to taper it, or take a twig and strip it of its leaves, then carry the tool until she or he finds a termite hill, often as far as a hundred feet, once for almost half a mile. They use these instruments as probes and, when the insects bite, draw them out covered with termites, which they then eat.

This is a technique chimpanzee infants learn by observing their mothers and are able to perform at the age of about three. Before Goodall's report, a standard definition of humankind had been "the toolmaker." After it, she pointed out that social scientists must accept chimps as man, by definition; they must redefine man; or they must redefine tools.[6]

Till recently, archaeologists have based their accounts of the development of humankind on stones and bones, on tools and fossils. Tools of the kind Goodall's chimpanzees use would not, of course, survive in the archaeological record, nor, it has been observed from recent ethnographic work in Africa, would vegetable debris; hence the great overvaluing of hunting as the significant behavior pattern of prehistoric humans, rather than one complex of behavior among many others.

Goodall found among chimpanzees many syndromes and gestures shared by humans. Most of the primates are both highly social and highly tactile. Among the lower monkeys, grooming—a kind of picking over of the skin and finger-combing of the fur—takes up hours of each day's time. Chimpanzees not only groom each other; they communicate by calls and gestures and touch. They greet or reassure by touching; they embrace, they pat, they kiss, they reach out a hand to beg. She theorizes that either these gestures in humans and chimps have evolved along parallel lines or they have a common origin in a remote ancestor of both species.[7] Today's encounter groups, "please touch" therapies, etc., testify to the felt need when this kind of nonverbal emotional communication dwindled among humans.

Vernon Reynolds goes even further in finding parallels between humans and chimpanzees. He sees a paradigm for the flexibility and growth of human societies in the open, shifting groups of the chimps—as opposed to the tight bands and rigid hierarchies of, say, the baboons and the rhesus monkeys.[8]

Another exception to the male-aggression competitive-pyramid theory of existence came from George Schaller, who spent a year in 1959–60 studying the mountain gorilla of Africa. Schaller's gorillas were remarkably pacific, a far cry from the would-be rapist and murderer depicted in the original *King Kong*. His description of gorilla relations between the sexes contradicts the projection of unwilling females pursued by ravening males. Engels, for instance, assumed that monogamy was an advance desired by the females so that they would be spared the necessity of "surrendering" to many males.[9] And as late as 1927 anthropologist Robert Briffault could write:

> The congress of the sexes is assimilated by the impulse to hurt, to shed blood, to kill, to the encounter of a beast of prey and its victims, and all distinction between the two is not infrequently lost. It would be more accurate to speak of the sexual impulse as pervading nature with a yell of cruelty than a hymn of love. The circumspection which is exhibited by animal females in yielding to the male, the haste which is shown by most to separate as soon as impregnation has taken place would appear to be due in a large measure to the danger attending such relation rather than to "coyness."[10]

Compare this sadistic fantasy with Schaller's observations:

> The group rests scattered over a steep hillside. A peripheral male stands looking down the slope. A female appears behind him, clasps him around the waist and mounts him, thrusting about 20 times. The male at first pays no attention, but after about 10 seconds turns his head and looks at her. Suddenly he swivels around and sits. With his right hand he reaches over, grabs the female by the hip and pulls her to him. She sits in his lap, facing away from him, her body supported by stiff arms propped on the ground, as the male thrusts about 10 times.

> The dominant male, who has been resting 15 feet away, slowly rises and walks toward the pair. The copulating male immediately desists and ambles 10 feet uphill. The dominant male sits behind the female one minute, then moves and rests 15 feet away. The other male reoccupies his former spot, and the female approaches him. He reaches out with both hands, swivels her around and again pulls her into his lap. He thrusts rapidly, about two times per second. After about seventy thrusts he begins the copulatory sound —the rapid o-o-o noted in the previous copulation. The female waves her head slowly back and forth, and, at about the hundredth thrust, suddenly twists sideways and sits beside the male, who then rolls over and rests on his abdomen for 10 minutes. . . .

> After a prolonged rest, the female rises and stands by the rump of the male. He glances up and they stare at each other. The process of pulling her into a sitting position and thrusting is repeated. At about 75 thrusts he begins his copulatory sound. His eyes are closed, and the thrusts rock her back and forth, a motion not only aided with his hands on her hips but also by her body. His lips are pursed and the sounds grow more rapid, become slurred; her lips are also pursed and her mouth slightly parted. At about 120

thrusts the male suddenly opens his mouth with a loud sighing "ahh," and the female opens her mouth at the same time. He relaxes but she rises and leaves.[11]

Schaller's gorillas sound almost tender in their "love-making," though it is still a fairly rudimentary business. In Goodall's reports, chimpanzees come somewhat closer to certain human stereotypes: females sometimes approach the males, but more often the male initiates activity, sometimes with persistent, almost bullying displays of branch shaking and foot stamping. In other observations, of free-ranging chimpanzees not fed by humans, as often as not a female or male would quietly approach the other, and females were more likely than males to initiate mating.[12]

Rape is nonexistent among chimpanzees. If the female persists in ignoring a male chimpanzee's courtship displays, he eventually wanders off. But chimpanzee females have a bright pink sexual swelling which advertises their readiness to engage in sexual activity during estrus; Goodall describes it as looking, from a far distance, like a pink flower among the trees. Neither gorilla nor human females have a visible indication of their sexual desire; hence, among gorillas it is the female who approaches the male. Since the upright posture would preclude a visible indication of desire among early hominid females, during our earliest evolution it must also have been the human female who approached the human male. The implications of this will be far-reaching when we come to look at later myths and restrictions—the ambivalence of human male attitudes toward the human female's sexual role.

There are no gorilla families, in the human sense, no more-or-less permanent mating relations, though they move in fairly stable groups. Dian Fossey spent several years in the late sixties and early seventies studying gorillas. She has found more flexible groupings than the one silver-backed (mature) male, several young males, and several females composing the groups Schaller charted. In the wild, groupings comprised of gorilla females and their young are common, while adult male gorillas are frequently solitary.[13]

The original theories of dominance and male possession of the female as the rule among apes and monkeys were based on Solly Zuckerman's observations of a colony of hamadryas baboons in the London zoo. "Every ape or monkey enjoys a position within a social group that is determined by the interrelation of its own dominant characteristics and those of its fellows. The degree of its dominance determines how far its bodily appetites will be satisfied. *Dominance determines the number of females that a male may possess*, and except on occasions where there is a superfluity of food, it also determines the amount a monkey eats," he wrote.[14]

Till ethologists went out into the wild and disproved Zuckerman's theses, the so-called "harem organization"—groups consisting of one adult male, several females, and their young—was believed to be the characteristic primate family. Dian Fossey demonstrated that this is not necessarily the case among gorillas. Like chimpanzees, male gorillas have a fierce-appearing threat display, but it is just that, noise and motion unaccompanied by actual fighting. Schaller's final conclusion was that gorillas are unaggressive and undersexed, presumably by human standards.

Still there was always the baboon to fall back on. This ill-tempered and ugly monkey was a favorite point of departure for the neo-Darwinists. Those who used the baboon as a model for human evolution saw our earliest groupings as fascist states. Wherever the baboon analogy was cited, one could expect a denigratory view of women coupled with talk of man's innate aggressiveness—as though human males were composed of electric circuits with little aggression condensers wired in forever. The popularizers Konrad Lorenz, Robert Ardrey, Desmond Morris, Robin Fox and Lionel Tiger, and even some of the academics who had studied baboons in the field—K. R. L. Hall, Hans Kummer, Sherwood Washburn, and Irven DeVore—were very fond of basing their speculations about prehistoric and present-day humankind on these creatures. It was argued that baboons, like early hominids, lived on the ground, in a savanna environment, and that both baboons and hominids evolved with strict controls, in large troops organized for aggressive-defensive tactics against predatory animals. Baboon organization was thus taken as a model for early human organization.

The analogy between baboons and humans, popular as it was, is extraordinarily far-fetched. Baboons are four-footed monkeys with tails; they belong to the catarrhine family—the Old World monkeys—which parted company with us some thirty to forty million years ago. Gorillas and chimpanzees are much closer to us physiologically and phylogenetically; they belong to the same family, the hominoids, though they are pongids and we are hominids; they stayed in our line for some twenty to thirty-six million more years. Recent blood analyses indicate that the pongids may have branched off from our line as recently as five million years ago. Chimpanzees and gorillas approach erect posture; in fact, it is probable that their knuckle walking and brachiation developed after humans diverged from the anthropoid apes. They have no tails, and they have larger brains than other monkeys, though smaller ones than humans, and, as noted before, many more gestures and syndromes in common with humans than do the lower monkeys.

Baboons further differ from us in that they have a considerable degree of sharp physical differentiation between the sexes. The male baboon is twice the size of the female baboon and has built-in weapons, large protruding teeth, which are lacking in the female. Human males, on the other hand, are only slightly larger, on the average, than females, a difference roughly proportionate to that between male and female chimpanzees, and their teeth are not specialized for aggression. Almost the only point of comparison between baboons and early humans is the fact that both are largely ground-living, though four out of five baboon species sleep in trees at night.

The first troops of baboons to be studied, in the nineteen fifties, consisted of groups of forty to eighty or more baboons, depending on the locality, who lived in moderate harmony among themselves, and even with neighboring troops, despite a great show of bullying and threats. They were also relatively promiscuous: female baboons copulated with the younger and less dominant baboons during the beginning of their period of sexual desire; toward the middle or the end of the estrous pe-

riod, when "they were most fertile," they formed "consort relationships"—"a spatial relationship lasting for *an hour*, a day, or
several days" with the most dominant male of the group, thus
facilitating impregnation by a stronger male, and, *q.e.d.*, sexual
selection.[15] However, not taking into consideration the difficulties of observation, it was also found that one could not always
chart the linear gradations of dominance, for a lower-ranking
male would sometimes combine with the most dominant male
of the group—or even the second in the hierarchy—and ar-
rogate rights to which he was not entitled, according to the
human theories about rank which then prevailed.[16]

In the field it developed that, unlike all other species of baboons, the hamadryas do have the harem family organization
observed by Zuckerman in the London zoo. Hamadryas baboons live in deserts, and, wherever researchers studied monkey
species in hardship conditions, they found it not unusual for
the ecological problem of survival to be facilitated by several females clustered around one male. The first formulation was
that where the male is twice as large as the female, as among
the hamadryas, one male consumes twice as much food as two
females, hence it is economical to cut down on the number of
males. This is the common teleological fallacy. As varying species turn up with the same organization, the scientists finally
acknowledged the obvious: one male can impregnate a number
of females, and before the species disappears, the emergency
pattern concentrates on reproduction—something like flowers
going to seed in a drought. Eventually, when conditions are too
severe, as has been observed in specific instances among vervets
and baboons, the animals do not copulate or reproduce themselves at all.

Humans have never had any hesitation about adopting this
hardship principle with regard to domestic animals. Except for
one or two males kept as studs, male animals are slaughtered
for food while females are kept for breeding. The zoologists'
reluctance to admit the secondary, though essential, nature of
the role in reproduction played by males points up one source
of male hostility to women and the need to derogate female

functions: the overcompensation which stems from the fear of superfluity so deeply ingrained in male consciousness.

The macaque is another largely ground-living, social, and highly aggressive monkey who has been much studied and who seemed to fit the dominance-hierarchy approach fairly well. However, in order to study troops of macaques, humans have often instituted artificial feeding stations. When the monkeys gather at an artificial source of food, there is a plethora of aggressive incidents, as well as ample opportunity to chart the dominance pyramid.

In a colony of Japanese macaques at a primate research center in Oregon, the animals are already crowded into artificial conditions—230 animals in two acres—so that ethologists can observe "dominance hierarchies." When the monkeys were jammed into a fifty-foot-square pen, "group attacks greatly increased in frequency." This research is funded by the National Institutes of Health—i.e., taxpayers' money.[17]

In the same way, Goodall installed banana feeding stations so as to study the chimpanzees at close range. With an almost unlimited source of bananas in one place, instead of food scattered through the trees, she found an increase of "dominance interactions" and aggressive behavior among the chimpanzees, the males in particular. There are fewer such incidents when the chimpanzees feed on their own or even when they catch wild animals. Dominant males do not force the possessor of a dead animal to drop his prey; they are more likely to wait and beg for a share, though there were instances where one animal distracted another one so as to grab a choice morsel.

What, then, is "natural behavior"? In recent years the Gombe Stream Research Center has been supported by Stanford University. Though Goodall had begun as an independent researcher, it was only through accreditation in the male-dominated academic world that she could continue her investigations and avail herself of the facilities—money and people—necessary to extend them. She took her doctorate under Robert Hinde at Cambridge University and is presently working with David Hamburg of Stanford University, who helped her to obtain generous grants for her center. Students from all over the

world pursue their studies there. With a population of research
students almost as large as the indigenous population of chimpanzees wandering through the forest, both human and ape
species enter on a new form of coexistence, in which the chimpanzee is in neither a wild state nor a domesticated one. Humans introduce alien elements, e.g., the current dominant male
is described as having acquired his position by clattering some
large gasoline tins downhill in a noisy display. Studies increasingly emphasize male aggression and dominance hierarchies,
since those are the questions with which ethology concerns itself
in large part.

Moreover, almost at the same time the students recorded vicious behavior among chimps—males attacking males—they
themselves were under threat from outside political elements
in Tanzania. The first chimpanzee attack was recorded in 1974.
In 1975 a student was kidnaped by local terrorists and the center was subsequently closed for two and a half years. Nonethe-
less, in 1978 Goodall announced that she had evidence of war
among the Gombe Stream chimpanzees, citing five attacks and
six male deaths. Some animal behaviorists applaud the finds as
evidence of innate aggression and beastliness among the chimps.
Others feel that intruding humans changed the ecology and introduced alien and life-threatening elements into the original
habitat, thus provoking the chimpanzees to behave like civilized
humans.[18]

As to the baboon-human analogists, they had long rejected
the comparison of chimpanzees or gorillas with humans on the
grounds that the first two are "unsuccessful species"—there are
few of them left—while baboons and humans are numerous
and have adapted to a wide variety of environments. On this
reasoning, the brown rat and the German cockroach would be
the most successful of all—like humans they are spread
throughout all the continents, rather than the single continent
where baboons are found.

But "success" is one of those subjective words whose meaning constantly changes. Humans, who in Darwinian terms are
successful because they leave the most progeny, have found
that the leaving of children reaches a point of no return. The

old Darwinian concepts, revolutionary in their day, are only a partial explanation of the complexities existing between life and environment, hence the twentieth-century emphasis on ecology. And once the human brain entered the picture, physical development was only one factor. Kropotkin pointed out back in 1891 that "thousands of weak-bodied and infirm poets, scientists, inventors and reformers, together with other thousands of so-called 'fools and weak-minded enthusiasts,' have been the most precious weapons produced by humanity."[19]

The baboon explanation for *Homo sapiens* was that once humans left the trees, they were more vulnerable to predators, hence the development of aggression, hunting, and weapons, as well as physical and role differences between the sexes. Still, baboons do not use tools, and they have not been notably effective in advancing themselves culturally over the forty million or so years they have been evolving. Chimpanzees do use sophisticated tools—and their tool use is more efficient than their weapon use. Though they pick up stones and branches to throw, it is unaimed throwing, for display rather than directed aggression. They play with objects, as humans do, and some groups live in a more or less savanna environment.

One feels that an antidemocratic attitude is implicit in the claim that humans are like baboons. The statement made by Irven DeVore on a CBS television program that "each individual has its own rank and knows its own place . . . only in this way could baboons and man have beaten the odds" is a typical example of this need to exalt aggression, rigid closed societies, and dominance far above their true position in the constellation of human characteristics.[20] It is a position which can be used to justify the military-corporate state, unequal opportunity, and current forms of world dominance, just as Darwinism was often used to support exploitative capitalism and imperialism in the nineteenth century.

Moreover, even baboons are not like baboons—at least not like those cited in the baboon-human analogy. The popularizers had drawn their examples from abnormal groups. The initial studies were of animals who live in game parks—open country where predators, especially humans, are abundantly present—and the animals are under considerable tension. When the same species is studied in different environments, in open country and in forest, away from human contact, the results are quite different.

Forest baboon groups are fluid; they are not tightly closed but change composition regularly. The core of the stable group is formed by adult females and their offspring. Food and cover are scattered, and there is little fighting over the one or the other. Aggression is infrequent, and it is difficult if not impossible to discern dominance hierarchies. Intertroop meetings are rare, and when they occur they are friendly. If the troop is frightened, it flees. The males do not form a rear guard; on the contrary, since they are the biggest and strongest, they are often the first up the trees, leaving the females, encumbered as they are with infants, to fend for themselves. The adult females determine when the troop will move, and where, and adult males are not always found in protective positions, in front and at the rear.[21]

The argument for evolution based on male aggression among ground-living primates was also thrown off when K. R. L. Hall did a study of an even more terrestrial monkey than the baboon. The patas monkey is faced with problems not unlike those of the baboon and incipient humans, but the adaptation was a very different one. The patas live in a plains environment even more treeless than that of most baboon species. And they have evolved with marked sexual dimorphism—the male patas is twice as large as the female, just as the male baboon is twice as large as the female baboon. However, the solution to survival in a hostile environment was to develop silence, caution, and speed—patas monkeys can sustain a fifty-mile-an-hour pace over long distances and look somewhat like greyhounds. They rarely fight—the male acts as a watchman and decoy while the females flee. Although quite unaggressive, within this context, it is the female who displays fighting behavior more than the male. They are organized in small groups, like those of the hamadryas baboons, with one male to several females, as well as their young, but the male displays none of the dominance observed among the game-park baboons, and, as has been noted before, it is the female who initiates sex, though her approach is not the usual presenting of the hindquarters; she runs toward the male to signify desire.[22]

Other land-living monkeys who are neither aggressive nor hierarchical are the vervets, also known as the thicket or savanna monkey. Since they are relatively unspecialized in their physical development, and since they represent a transition between arboreal and terrestrial existence, they, too, are being studied for analogies with early human evolution.[23]

The most salient observation to come out of primate studies is the fact of varying adaptations within individual species. Every kind of "family" organization can be found. As noted earlier the only consistent relationship in all the primate groupings is the one between mother and child. Just as human groups have developed diversely, the result not only of differing environments but also of the quirks of isolation and genetic drift, so animal populations vary according to their ambiance. To a certain degree, this variation depends on how the observer interprets what is seen.

Is there anything positive we can take from ethology for our speculation on the origins of human sexual behavior? Even allowing for observer bias and special interest, the evidence for change and individuality among nonhuman primates stands and will certainly apply in even greater measure to humans. We can suppose that there is no one way in which we evolved and no one position for the human female, save when certain societies became so strong that they tried to impose their ways on other societies, as happened in the past four hundred years with the expansion of Western European culture.

4

Aggression and Maleness

Another question to consider is the equation of aggression with the male hormone testosterone, resulting in the generalization that males are more aggressive than females.

In animals, this is often but not always true. Ethologists have not found male wolves to be more aggressive than female wolves, though the females are probably shyer of observation, as are, for example, the Gombe Stream chimpanzees. Elephant females dominate the elephant herd, chasing out males as they grow up; female lions and tigers are reported to be more aggressive than the males; while among the simians not only patas but also gibbon females are described as more aggressive than the males. A corollary to this is that when primatologists find a species with aggressive females we are normally informed that the male is "undersexed." But in studying aggression among female animals, while they may be normally unaggressive, presumably because they are occupied with pursuits other than dominance, per se, when it is a threat that concerns them, as to their young, it is a byword that the female fights like hell. Male rats rarely attack female rats, but if an unknown male enters the nesting area where a female is nursing she attacks and always succeeds in driving him away. While female rats are seen to fight less often than males, when they do, they attack viciously, without the preliminary threat postures and aggressive grooming displayed by male rats.[1]

Among zebras, the stallion protects his group from hyena attackers, who follow in a semicircle behind. If one zebra is in poorer condition than the others or is slowed down by hyena bites and falls back, the whole pack immediately surrounds it. At that point the stallion does not try to defend the individual, though a mother will defend her foal.[2]

In terms of being less aggressive than the male, primate females carry their infants with them, so that much of the time they are held down, literally, by an infant clinging to their stomachs, cradled temporarily in one limb, or riding on their backs. Carnivore females leave their infants in the den while they go out to hunt, which gives them considerably more mobility than primate, including early hominid, females.

In nature—a nonexistent abstraction invented by humans to describe everything that is—there are no value judgments. What works, even if somewhat inefficiently, survives; what doesn't, disappears. Females, who are more necessary over the long run for the survival of the species, must also be more shy and cautious—which is not to be equated with lack of aggression. Males are expendable, and among many species, including the social primates, they are often described as serving as shock troops or advance guard; even isolates, who are commonly male, may have some scouting function: the ultimate existence of the species rests on a less exposed position for females and infants. In the wild, primatologists have reported an almost universal inhibition of aggression against infants; they enjoy tolerance from both males and females within their own species. This is an attitude common among humans, too, though far from universal, as witness Mylai, Dachau and Auschwitz, etc. The atypical behavior of zoo and captive animals is also worth noting in this context: they may unpredictably attack and kill their own or strange infants.

The linkage of male sexuality to aggression, almost axiomatic in our history, has led to hideous brutality among humans, not least of which is the justification of rape. Scientists have had a tendency to project recent human history onto physiology in their conclusion that testosterone is a cause of aggression. The study of hormones—a word which dates back only to 1904—is still in its infancy. What is clear is that sex is energizing, be it testosterone or estrogen. When that energy finds no outlet, it gets displaced into irritability and, on occasion and in some species, into fighting behavior. Yet the relationship is not at all clear-cut, and there are hints that, operating on the basis of human preconceptions, scientists have jumped to conclusions. The castrated animal loses its spirit—but this applies also to females when they are spayed. We are told that injecting testosterone makes a female more aggressive; we are not usually told that injecting estrogen is also likely to make her more aggressive. Estrogen increases mounting and fighting behavior in female and male rats. And large doses of testosterone injected into animals of both sexes make them so passive that they neither feed nor fight.[3]

Environmental and social factors influence the secretion of hormones, so that behavior is a two-way street. Perhaps a simpler statement with regard to humans is that behavior often originates in the head, and the body follows the brain: e.g., people who "fall in love" secrete more sex hormones. The question of hormones is far more complex than was first realized; new hormones and hormone relationships are still being discovered. David E. Davis wrote in 1962 about the finding that LH, a hormone produced by the pituitary gland, also increased aggression: "At the moment we cannot say whether LH, testosterone, or some other hormone was the first to be associated with aggressive behavior. A speculation may be made, and perhaps it will be tested some day. Since one function of LH is to stimulate production of testosterone through the Leydig cells of the testis, it would seem that LH is more basic and the connection of testosterone with aggression is secondary."[4]

Studies of rhesus monkeys at the Yerkes Primate Center in Atlanta, Georgia, probed for proof of a relationship between dominance rank, as measured by aggressive behavior, and the quantity of offspring given males produced. Biochemical tests revealed no correlation between high rank and reproductive success; in fact, low-ranking and even adolescent males fathered as many infants as did the highest-ranking males.[5]

In the Japanese-macaque colony in Oregon where aggressive

behavior patterns were produced by confined conditions and provisioning, no correlation was observed between dominance position and testosterone level. High-ranking males did not mate more frequently than low-ranking males, and the mating appeared to be random on the part of the females, who were making the choices. The researchers concluded that testosterone was less important than social stimuli in eliciting masculine patterns of aggressive behavior. They also concluded that rank was not highly correlated with aggressiveness; the dominant males were not at the top of the hierarchy because of fighting ability or physical characteristics such as size. These data, published in 1976, contradict many earlier reports.[6]

Male bias in the early part of the twentieth century led researchers into many false assumptions—semantic and cultural—about aggression and active sexuality. They were believed to be dictated by hormones possessed chiefly or solely by males. As of 1978 hormone research indicates that current terminology is incomplete and inadequate. Testosterone is an androgen, a family of hormones produced in large part by the testes but also found in the adrenal glands of both sexes and in the ovaries. Estrogens are a family of sex hormones produced in largest quantities by the ovaries, but also found in the testes and adrenal glands. Moreover, androgens are normally converted by cells in many parts of the body, including the brain, into estrogen, in both sexes![7]

5

Maternal Sexuality

In order to probe the origins of the myth of male supremacy and the reality of male power over women, we must consider the nature of human sexuality. One of Freud's great contributions to human understanding was his delineation of infant sexuality—gratification from the oral pleasures of nursing. However, he paid little attention to the physical responses of the other half of the couple—the mother's sensual joy. I believe that female primates, including humans, have two kinds of sexuality, maternal and genital. Because of our history, this area—the sexual pleasure that comes after childbearing—has been largely ignored. Many male scientists and male doctors—and there are very few women in these fields as yet—think in terms of the "race of man" and see the female as existing for male use and male gratification, so nursing, like motherhood, is a noble and giving function. The female is the font of life, but it is rarely acknowledged, at least in modern Western society, that she might just nurse because she enjoys it.

According to Niles and Michael Newton, long before the concept of "duty" evolved, the survival of the human race depended on the satisfactions gained from the two voluntary acts of reproduction—breast feeding and coitus. They had to be pleasurable enough to ensure that they would occur frequently.[1] One has only to look at the beatific expression on the face of a Nambikwara woman photographed by Lévi-Strauss as

she lay on the ground nursing her baby to see an exemplifica-
tion of these pleasures. Why do primitive women go on having
and rearing babies? Many of them have access to forms of birth
control—from abstinence to abortion to plant potions to infanticide—which are used when need dictates. There are nonliterate societies where moral strictures like those of the
Judeo-Christian religion are lacking, where there is no great
idealization of the mother, and where children are welcomed
and fed equally by the whole group.

In such a situation, mothers enjoy having babies not because
they are sacrificing and noble, not necessarily for the prestige,
but because it is a pleasurable experience. Even parturition may
not always be painful, as is usual among us; Niles Newton argues that in societies where sexual attitudes are not puritanical,
it is less arduous, and she finds parallels between uterine contractions of orgasm and those of childbirth. But whether one
accepts this theory or not, and it would certainly be difficult of
investigation, there is no doubt that the sensual contact between mother and child after birth is relatively undiscussed and
unexplored, except from the point of view of its utility for the
physical and emotional development of the child.

In peasant and primitive societies babies are nursed not for
the six months usual with us, but for periods of from two to
four years. This is done not only as a birth-control measure but
also because it is a sensually pleasing experience for mother and
child, else there would surely have been a rising of women long
before this century.

A contemporary of mine who had nursed her two babies was
mildly shocked when I asked her about nursing as sexual pleasure. "Not sexual," she said, "but irresistibly moving. I felt it
deep inside, in my belly, in my womb." She spoke of the intense, almost indescribable sensation when the baby begins to
suck and the milk flows—milk letdown—and of the need to caress the baby, to touch her or his head, arm, or foot, making
clear that it is a reciprocal and active happening "but not sexual, oh, no."

"Do you know," I asked her, "that in many societies it is
normal for the mother to caress her baby's genitals during nurs-

ing?" Alice Rossi writes of non-Western societies which show
an easy natural pattern of maternalism and finds them characterized by an indulgence and acceptance of the sexual component of maternalism that is denied by Western societies. Even
a slight exposure to ethnographic literature points up the contrast with Western mother-child relations, where sexuality is
culturally repressed. We can hardly imagine an American
mother engaging in labial, clitoral, or penis stimulation of her
infant without guilt or social condemnation, yet this is an accepted and expected pattern in many societies where mothering and sexuality are closely linked.[2]

As Western taboos have begun to loosen, more and more
women acknowledge the eroticism of the mother-infant relationship. The sensation of nursing is another kind of orgasm.[3]
In their discussions of the sensual gratification for the mother
in nursing, both Rossi and the Newtons tend to talk in terms
of its usefulness—how it will stimulate milk flow, provide better
nutrition and psychological health for the child, etc. Well, useful it may be, as coitus is useful; but both are pleasurable, and
looking at mammals, I would think that for the female—cat,
monkey, ape, or human—there are two areas of sexual pleasure,
the one being coitus, the other lactation.

In our culture, where civilization and brain have begun to
control physical and purely emotional responses and where the
patriarchy has ruled these thousands of years, there is rejection
and fear of maternal sexuality. Psychoanalysis is afraid that the
baby may be swallowed by the mother's sensual needs. Rossi
discusses Western analysts' argument that the woman's need to
mother is often greater than the optimum required by the infant. In many primitive societies women satisfy both sexual and
caretaking desires by nursing their young. The male-dominant
family and political systems of the West, in combination with
Christian theology, make a sharp distinction between motherhood and female sexuality. Maternity is culturally defined and
differentiated from sexuality, so that women are asked to deny
the evidence of their senses by repressing the sexual component
of infant care. She suspects that the more male dominance
characterizes a Western society, the greater the separation be-

tween sexuality and maternalism. It is to men's advantage to restrict women's sexual gratification to adult heterosexual intercourse, though women and children may pay the price of a less
rewarding relationship, physically and psychologically.[4] Until
very recently our culture insisted that the breast could be displayed publicly only in a sexual connotation, but not when
nursing, with the result that women refused to try nursing their
babies or stopped when they discovered that it involved a
psychological blend of the sexual and the maternal.[5]

But of course, while maternal sexuality may have been repressed, it has also been transmuted and transformed and translated into the heterosexual experience. The breast is an erotic
area, and the whole elaboration of sexual enjoyment between
humans, in which foreplay—kissing and caressing, nibbling,
nuzzling, and sucking, including stimulation of the breast—
produces vaginal lubrication and clitoral sensation, just as
nursing does, shows that it has been brought over into the
meeting between men and women. Masters and Johnson spoke
of women who could achieve orgasm through stimulation of
the nipple. And Goodall suggests that some forms of kissing
may come from the sucking response—as chimpanzee infants
reach for or hold their mothers' nipples in their mouths when
they are frightened or hurt.[6] Like so many parts of our animal
nature, the sexuality is there if unacknowledged. And looking
at maternal sexuality, one realizes that this, too, is what the female has brought to the human sexual experience—not only
prolongation, but enrichment and elaboration.

If humans are the only animals who make love face to face,
the personalizing of the act comes not from the genital meeting alone but from the ornamentation and affection around it,
a personalizing which does not exist among the animals nor often enough among humans. In the emphasis on genital orgasm
of, say, Wilhelm Reich, we detect a curious anti-female and
anti-art component, a denial of the aesthetic variations, the
enormous extension and adornment of sex which can occur
among humans at their best.

Having absorbed certain facets of the mother-infant sexual
relationship into the meeting between woman and man, male

thought then rejected the sensual side of childbearing. Characteristic of male resentment of the female body is the etherealiz-
ing of motherhood. We like to think of virgin birth, of motherhood as the one selfless, pure act, and today, in the final
exaggeration, mothers are attacked for being anything less than
all-giving and undemanding. Since so much depends on them,
they are always being judged. They are supposed to give birth,
give food and tender care and let go without asking for anything in return and with little help from society. But there has
always been interaction—among animals and among early and
later societies.

Robert Briffault's three-volume *The Mothers* is on the surface a great glorification of women, in actuality a not-so-subtle
put-down. He speaks of sex as a nasty business made beautiful
by the tenderness and love transferred from the maternal relationship, and "maternal love is sacrifice."[7] From this premise
comes the sadomasochistic foundation of male-dominated sex:
one person is the tender, sacrificing giver, another the receiver;
one the instrument, the other the player, and so forth. To see it
as a linked, reciprocally enjoyable experience takes enormous
cultural reconditioning. Tenderness and love, yes, but also sensual exploration that incorporates the physical side of motherhood as a fructification of the sexual act. It is common among
male writers to denigrate woman by calling the clitoris an imitation of the penis, her orgasm an imitation of a male syndrome. One is much more likely to hear psychoanalysts discussing the breast as penis symbol than the penis as breast symbol,
but fellatio, in which the penis becomes the breast, is an imitation of nursing. Extensions, inversions, and variations of the
theme of our sexual patterns are usually imitations of maternal
functions. And it is through love-making only that the mature
male can return to earlier sensations or, on a now-different
level, partake of a universality of experience so that in the most
playful and fanciful way, man becomes woman and woman becomes man, exchanging and recapturing roles, in the caressing,
say, of his nipples, vestigial organs which are biologically useless
but not sensually so.

Since sexuality was defined in the narrow Western patriarchal sense, when the ethologists looked at the primate world some of them marveled at how small a part sex played in the female monkey's life: "During most of life a female is not involved in sexual activity. Most of the time, she is either juvenile, out of estrous, pregnant, or lactating."[8] Clearly they were under a misapprehension. Copulation may be infrequent, but sex in the broad sense ("the whole sphere of behavior related even indirectly to the sexual functions and embracing all affectionate and pleasure-seeking conduct"—Webster's New International Dictionary) is more present in her life than in that of the male. As a baby she participates in the mother-infant relationship, she copulates, then she gives birth and participates again in the nursing relationship. For the male, on the contrary, sex is represented by the months or years of infancy, after which he is limited to the brief acts of coitus permitted by diverse estral females. The frequency of these matings is not dependent on dominance hierarchies or male aggression as had been postulated by the ethologists, but on the female's choice.[9] Among one troop of forest baboons, it was an old male with broken canines who most frequently completed successful matings, even though he was less aggressive than and frequently lost fights with younger and more vigorous adult males.[10]

As far back as 1926 it was suggested that, among humans, the sexual gratification inherent in childbirth and nursing might well account for a difference in focus between the sexes.[11] The male looks for gratification only in the sex act, whereas the woman has prolonged periods of sexual pleasure available with each childbirth. With this deprivation, male animals crowd around a female in estrus, waiting and at the ready. Can we infer from this the later emphasis in human males on any possible sexual encounter? Yes, from our general animal inheritance; no, for our specifically human endowment. For both women and men, the biological inheritance of our status as mammals—the breast-feeding animal—is at variance with our human capacities. This is what humanity and its concomitant social elaborations have meant, that we spend our energies not so much on primary gratifications of the senses as on the

more complex and controlled pleasures and satisfactions which
have grown out of these elemental needs. But the substitution
of quantity for quality is culturally imposed, the result of a perversion of sexual expression into the comparatively recent
human invention of winning and losing, not to say counting,
with the male as the winner, the female the loser, and the keeping score thereof.

Now that humans have translated maternal sexuality into
adult sex, most modern women are willing to forgo the basic
pleasures of mother-child sensuality for the greater part of their
adult lives. Men, too, have begun to realize the price of vertical
relationship. As Jean Baker Miller points out, "Civilizations developed inequalities enforced by power and made most people
spend their lives doing work without pleasure, at the same
time evolving all manner of ways to separate and isolate people
from pleasurable interaction with one another."[12] As women
have fewer children and patriarchal pressures relax, people are
beginning to insist on the affective sensory satisfactions that
have so often been missing from bare-boned heterosexual relationships. On one level there is struggle to unloose women and
men from the distortions imposed by sex as conquest, puritanical contempt for sex, and male emotional rigidity, which are
the heritage of the past. On another there is wide experimentation with formerly forbidden unions—woman-woman,
man-man—as well as a search for variations in the one-to-one
bonds of traditional monogamy.

In the past, homosexuality, particularly between males, has
often caricatured the more ugly aspects of heterosexual relationships defined as male dominant, female submissive. Today
women and men may refuse imposed standards, as in the past a
few individuals undoubtedly have rejected descriptive labels
imposed by society and acted intuitionally. There have been
sexual meetings on an equal basis, despite the heavy socializing
to which we are and have been subjected by our dichotomizing
tradition. More and more women and men seek relationships
combining passive and active roles. Homosexuality is also more
open and more tolerantly viewed by society and is probably on
the increase. Lesbianism would seem to make more sense than

male homosexuality, however, given the female's broad range of sexual possibility, our animal inheritance, combined with the human brain which elaborates on this heritage. We all loved our mothers first.

The theory of evolution by aggression grew out of our cultural ideas comprising possessive monogamy, the warlike nature of man, though not woman, and the view of nature as a constant state of hostilities, an unending battle in progress. Though Darwin's theory of survival of the fittest was its implicit base, for the social Darwinists, if not for Darwin himself, these are concepts which go back before Tennyson's "nature red in tooth and claw" of the nineteenth century, to Thomas Hobbes, with his "warre, as if every manne against every manne," and to earlier philosophical formulations. Today as more women participate actively in scientific research, new understandings and new information enable us to achieve a more holistic view of human origins.

Part II

WOMAN EVOLVING

Eons long, those low-browed creatures
Lived without the help of teachers.
—Nineteen-thirties summer-camp song

6

From Man the Hunter to Woman the Gatherer

Just as the study of animal sexual behavior was colored by cultural projections, so were early researches into human origins. One school presented a dogma of human evolution shaped by tools and killing because our forerunners on the dry savannas of Africa took to meat eating. It stressed the role of headmen and their access to more women than ordinary mortals, with the result that they left more progeny, on the model of the now disproven animal-behavior thesis that dominant males are more successful in reproducing themselves than low-ranking ones. It successfully mingled the two meanings òf the word *man:* generic, to refer both to women and to men, and specific, to refer to males only, further contributing to the invisibility of women. A somewhat more sophisticated phrasing explains the rise and spread of humanity and our conversion to civilization thus: "Hunting is the master behavioral pattern for the human species. It is the organizing activity which integrated the morphological, physiological, genetic and intellectual aspects of the individual human organism. . . . Man evolved as a hunter; he spent over 99 percent of his species' history as a hunter; and he spread over the entire habitable area of the world as a hunter."[1] There is little room for women in this theory, which is based on the education of male children for hunting and on the belief that man made tools in order to hunt.*

On the basis of artifacts dating back several million years and on the progression of fossil bones, particularly the ever-enlarging skulls found by the paleontologists, textbooks were wont to ascribe the use of tools to the fact that prehumans stood on two legs and had their upper limbs free to manipulate objects. They developed brains because they used the tools to take meat. They had begun to eat meat because they lived in a savanna where game was plentiful and fruit sparser than it had been in the forests where their ancestors lived. They developed the nuclear family because human infants were slower in developing than those of other animals, and women therefore took care of children while men became food suppliers and protectors—a particularly pat and inaccurate oversimplification.

In recent years it has been pointed out that too much attention was focused on hunting and too little on gathering and on the mother's role in child raising. Women anthropologists have outlined our development in terms of Woman the Gatherer rather than Man the Hunter, based on the fact that in climates of the sort in which prehumans first emerged from the ancestral ape population, among the gatherer-hunters who are the sole remaining representatives of the way of life practiced by our ancestors for more than 99.5 per cent of human existence, women supply most of the food, often as much as 80 per cent, with men bringing in the minor portion.[2]

Human development was not a question of first standing up, second developing tools, third evolving group hunting, even food sharing, and fourth developing brain and humanity. All the processes were occurring simultaneously. We stood up at

* The new and quickly popular school of sociobiology is the most recent expression of this kind of blatant sexism in the treatment of evolution. The approach and the name were originated by Edward O. Wilson of Harvard University. A glance at the chapter on sexuality in his book *On Human Nature* (Harvard University Press, 1978) reveals his bias and his reluctance to acquaint himself with the recent labors of physical anthropologists, archaeologists, primatologists, physiologists, and others outside his chosen field of laboratory entomology.

the same time our brains were in process of becoming human, though we do not yet know just how and when this took place.[3] The first prehumans must have had the beginnings of self-awareness and human responsiveness buried within their flattened skulls. Along with human relatedness there were the beginnings of human—that is, reasoning and malicious rather than thoughtless and passing—aggressiveness.

To use hunting as an explanation for humanity, including human aggression, begs the whole question of evolution. By itself, hunting explains neither its own development nor the other components of human behavior.

It was the work of Raymond Dart, a professor of anatomy at the University of Witwatersrand in South Africa, which presented the initial evidence for the step-by-step male-aggressive theory of evolution, whereby *man* first stood up, leaving his arms free to manipulate tools, then developed a "striding walk" to cover great distances on the desiccated savanna, made tools, and became a hunter. It focuses on "the violent nature of man"—not humanity—and sees sex as part of his "innately violent instinct," with woman surfacing only occasionally as prey, victim, tool, or masochist. The theory was first given wide circulation in the books of Robert Ardrey, amiably but firmly amplified by Konrad Lorenz, and has since been widely disseminated in film and fiction.

In 1925 Dart discovered the first skeletal remains of a creature presented as the precursor of humankind. Ever since Darwin's theory of evolution was accepted by the scientific community, paleontologists and physical anthropologists have been searching for the "missing link," a fossil that would provide the connection between humans and the animal world, the ape from which our species had ascended. Dart's find, a child's skull at first dated to some half a million years ago, provided a solution which was accepted by many theoreticians. After that first fossil, which Dart named the Taung baby, other skeletal remains were dug up in South Africa, by Dart himself and by a colleague, Robert Broom. Their dates were pushed back to about a million years before our time. Dart and Broom did not find stone tools in the immediate vicinity, but there were ani-

mal bones with or near the disparate portions of hominid skeletons. Though it was not clear whether the prehumans were the
eaters or the eaten, Dart thought he could distinguish signs of
wear on some of the million-year-old bones. He concluded that
the earliest tools and weapons used by our ancestors had been
shaped from the bones of their kill, and he extrapolated this
lurid hypothesis:

> The blood-bespattered, slaughter-gutted archives of
> human history from the earliest Egyptian and Su-
> merian record to the most recent atrocities of the Sec-
> ond World War accord with early human universal
> cannibalism, with animal and human sacrificial prac-
> tices or their substitutes in formalized religions and
> with the world-wide scalping, head-hunting, body-
> mutilating and necrophiliac practices of *mankind* in
> proclaiming this common bloodlust differentiator, this
> predaceous habit, the mark of Cain that separates
> *man* dietetically from *his* anthropoidal relatives and
> allies *him* rather with the deadliest of carnivora.[4]

Popularizers like Robert Ardrey went even further, calling
the animal bones weapons pure and simple, claiming that
"*man* is a predator whose natural instinct is to kill with a
weapon" and that when archaeologists discuss "tools" they really mean weapons. He described our predecessors as killer
apes and gave a more extreme version of the aggression
theory of evolution. His ideas are graphically enacted in the
Clarke-Kubrick film 2001: A *Space Odyssey*, which opens on an
arid desert with piles of bones here and there and several hairy
creatures crouch-hopping about. Suddenly one of the apelike
individuals picks up a bone hesitantly, swings it idly, and, in a
flash of genius, brings it down on a fellow creature's head.
From this first scene of unmotivated violence, the film leaps to
others depicting group hunts and skirmishes against neighboring bands. In four scenes with a total of twenty-odd males, only
one female appears: a nighttime shot shows a group huddled
on the ground sleeping as one member holds a baby to her
breast.

Theories of evolution in which only men evolve are still widely circulated and widely taught in both popular and semi-scientific media, though they relate much more to the ethos of historical civilizations than to that of primitive peoples or to the animal world.[5]

In the past, creation myths commonly attacked, blamed, or punished women for the human condition. The almost total disappearance of woman in 2001 typified the high misogyny which characterized the nineteen fifties and sixties. If the ratio of females to males presented above—the section in the film titled "Dawn of *Man* Four Million B.C."—had actually obtained, there would have been no proliferation, no evolutionary success, and no human race. Taken to its extremes, the devaluing of women, highly illogical but not at all uncommon in many cultures, accomplishes just this—witness the example of the King William Island Netsilik Eskimos, who were described by Rasmussen in 1931 as a tribe on the way to extinction because of their high rate of female infanticide.[6]

Physical-anthropology textbooks used to focus on hunting as the chief occupation of our ancestors:

> Let us consider an early human hominid hunting group as it rests after the day's activities. The males are planning the next day's hunt. They ask for the support of supernatural entities; they decide which animals to hunt and how to divide the carcasses among the hunters and their families; and they conclude the planning session by talking about the females *who are not present. Of course we dare not speculate about what the females were doing.* After this human condition was achieved, nothing could stop the evolutionary success and progress of this fortunate primate except *man* himself.[7]

Thus Buettner-Janusch in 1966.

Much was made of the males' superior strength and intelligence and it was assumed that one of their functions was to defend females and children against predators in the open savanna. In 1970 David Pilbeam described our hominid forebears more evenhandedly, speculating that the females would have provided most of the food by foraging for plant food and small game, but he still saw the males as responsible for planning and protection, a position he later abjured.[8]

Recently, voices have been raised to point out that there is little substantiation for the view that there are more predators on the savanna than in the forest. Louis Leakey decided in 1972 that predators were not that much of a danger to our first ancestors,[9] while Clifford Jolly feels that there is little evidence for the "catastrophic desiccation" depicted in the desert scene from 2001 as well as in other male-aggression evolution theories.

Jolly is one of the younger anthropologists who would set aside "the current obsession with hunting and carnivorousness" and look for a different kind of behavior in early hominids associated with open-country grassland alternating with patches of woodland and forest edges. His paper "The Seed-Eaters" offers an interpretation of human evolution based on an analogy with gelada baboons and would have had us sitting on our haunches chewing grass and weed seed for some ten million years while we were becoming prehumans. During this time, he feels, we developed fatty buttock pads and such sexual differentiations as beards and breasts. It's a somewhat deterministic theory which claims that our grinding molars and the manipulative tongues that were later so useful in speech developed out of a diet of hard, round pellets. He sees a fairly early division of sex roles in which males, who had been used as scouts against danger, became mammal hunters, while females and young, in continuing to gather vegetable produce, invented cultural devices, such as bags and digging sticks, enabling them to bring back enough for the males to eat. Jolly's theory would have had one species of hominid continuing to be chiefly vegetarian and coexisting with an omnivorous line that developed into humanity.[10]

It is a projection of Western civilization's imperialist values to perceive hunting as conquest, as an extension of aggression, and to admire or dislike it as such. The reports of anthropologists who have studied extant gatherer-hunters—African

Pygmies, the Hadzas, the Kalahari San (the people who used to be known as Bushmen), and Australian Aborigines—provide some sharp contrasts between the stereotype of hunting as aggressive male adventure and actuality. Colin Turnbull's studies of African Pygmies overturned many of our preconceptions about size, dominance, and subject-master relations. In the two Pygmy groups he studied he found very little aggression, emotional or physical, citing as proof the absence of warfare, feuding, witchcraft, and sorcery. Moreover, their hunting was not in itself an aggressive activity. Knowing that they were depleting natural resources, there was regret at destroying life, even an element of compassion for the animals killed. His belief that the Pygmies were very gentle people is an opinion shared by many others who have worked with hunters.[11]

Since the nineteen twenties and thirties, when Dart and Broom were making their discoveries, other very early prehuman skeletal parts have been unearthed, in Kenya, Tanzania, and Ethiopia, often in association with crude stones that have been shaped by other than natural agencies and can be identified as tools. Many of these predate the remains discussed by Dart and Broom, carrying the story of human evolution back four or five million years, and most scientists no longer believe that the first implements our ancestors used were the bones from their kill. In the caves in the Transvaal where Dart and Broom had worked, all the bones—of hyenas, baboons, and prehumans among others—were in varying states of preservation. It could not really be demonstrated that the wear on those claimed as tools had not been caused by time, weather, and accidents of displacement, similar to the elements affecting the remains of the presumed tool users.[12] It was not clear which were the eaters and which the eaten.

Moreover, few anthropologists today give credence to the killer-ape theory, and some previous exponents of the baboon-human analogy have recanted in favor of the chimpanzee. At the moment, a rare species of pygmy chimpanzee, *Pan paniscus*, which lives in the forest regions of Zaire, is under scrutiny as our closest animal relative.

That the notion of instinct aggression still lingers on in the popular mythology is not surprising. If, over millions of years, male humans hunted and developed tools primarily as weapons and butchery instruments, then there is little hope for change since these "behavior patterns" are biologically inherent, genes for aggression having been selected for successful evolution over the eons. Books and films that glorify male violence and possession take the onus of moral responsibility and change off the public. Kubrick and Lorenz reciting their "new litany of 'innate depravity'" are only the latest version of the Calvinist notion of original sin, and Ardrey's claim for a territorial imperative is a reworking of the earlier argument for property rights versus human rights, which grew out of the nineteenth century's "instinct of property," used as a justification for capitalism and imperialist expansion.[13] Both arguments have had a wide popularity through the ages; they have always been useful for defending the status quo against demands for more equitable treatment by the underclasses, and they save the bother of thinking. Even a thinker as great as Freud in certain areas fudged the social implications of carrying his thoughts to their logical conclusions by accepting ideas already exploded in his own time with regard to instinct, evolution, and anthropology.

The vision of man as an angry beast with an instinct for destruction does not apply to the beasts themselves. It is human brain power, with its capacity for cruelty and kindness, which projected the former onto the beasts. An animal who hunts is not aggressive, she or he is hungry, while the cat playing with a mouse is unaware of the mouse's suffering (a suffering which is certainly made less acute than a human's would be by the relative simplicity of the mouse's brain and nervous system).

On the basis of the animal studies discussed in Chapter 1, as well as newly discovered fossils and new approaches to social anthropology, evolutionists are changing their minds. They are coming to realize that co-operation, mutual aid, and kindness have been more conducive to survival than the nineteenth-century battle mentality projected onto nature.

The male bias in anthropology led to systematic undervaluation of the role of women. The price of having a civilization largely recorded by men has been the glorification of what men are, do, or have, the denigration of women's occupations, faculties, and physiology. Only child care, which involved the upbringing of males, was spared, to a certain extent.

Today the androcentric nature of science has come under scrutiny, and the theories of Dart, Broom, and their popularizers are seen as a reflection of our recent culture rather than that of our past, theories which arose in a society that glorifies competitiveness, out of a civilization distinguished by the brutality with which it has attacked less fortunate people.[14]

7

The Carrier Bag Theory of Evolution

Since hunting is of less importance than was earlier
thought . . . it might then be equally profitable to
consider *Man* the Gatherer or *Man* the Potter.
　　　　　　—D. W. Deetz, *Man the Hunter*

Without trying to grasp all of the fortuitous combination of accidents and purposes which created a larger brain and human
evolution, something which may be beyond the scope of the
most sophisticated minds and computers, let us take a glance at
our past in the light of new discoveries and with a feminist consciousness. The previous explanation for human evolution gave
hunting as the master behavior pattern for the human species,
claiming this activity provided a school of learning wherein children—boys, of course—were informed about animal behavior
and anatomy, men learned to co-operate, and thus the human
nervous system developed.[1] Perhaps there is an alternative: I
submit woman's invention of the carrier bag as the take-off point
for the quantum advance which created the multiplier effect
that led to humanity.

Humans developed from hominids who lived in tropical and
semitropical zones, in Africa it is now believed. For the first several million years our history was made in frost-free zones.
There is good reason to believe that during this time we were

eating mostly vegetable food and that it was women who supplied the major portion of what we ate.

Present-day anthropologists look at opposite ends of the spectrum when they seek to divine the nature of our predecessors four to five million years ago. In the older part of the spectrum, they make analogies with close animal relatives like the chimpanzee, as we saw in Part I. At the same time, however, they study extant Stone Age foragers for subsistence clues, always realizing that there must be an enormous gap between the first prehumans and any present-day humans, no matter how limited their technology. In the second area, and with tools several million years more advanced than those of our ancestors, the scientists were astonished to discover that among the few remaining people in the world who do not (or did not in the near past) practice agriculture but live (or lived) in a way reminiscent of our Stone-Age origins, food gathered by women supplied the bulk of the daily diet. In temperate and tropical zones, plant and vegetable food, sometimes shellfish, supplied 65 to 80 per cent of the diet, and women did the gathering, though men might satisfy their own individual needs by gathering food when out alone. According to Richard B. Lee, hunting is the dominant mode of subsistence only in the highest latitudes (60 or more degrees from the equator). In cool to cold temperate latitudes, 40 to 59 degrees from the equator, fishing dominates. In warm temperate, subtropical, and tropical latitudes, gathering is by far the most important means of subsistence.[2] Only among the tiny segment of Central Arctic Eskimos does hunting (including seal hunting and fishing) provide the entire food supply. And Eskimos, who until quite recently lived farther south than they now do, prove nothing except the extreme hardship conditions to which the human species is able to adapt, though probably only temporarily since Eskimos as Eskimos in a primitive habitat were a dying people ten years ago; today there are probably more anthropologists studying them than extant tribespeople.

While humans are and always have been omnivorous, during the major part of our evolution, as in most parts of the earth even today, vegetables provided most of our sustenance, a fact

which is reflected in our eight-yard-long gut, the shape and surface of our teeth, possibly in the fact that animal fats seem to
contribute to hardening of the arteries and that most of the
known long-lived peoples—the Hunzas, the Abkhasians, and
the Ecuadorians—eat very little meat.

Our early ancestors did more rather than less gathering, for
they did not have weapons like those of recent Stone Age peoples, let alone the ones present-day humans use.[3] The savanna
mosaic with its varied terrain was rich in fruits, nuts, seeds, and
other plant foods. Judging by recent fossil finds, the earliest
prehuman groups lived near water sources with forest cover adjacent; later they moved out into the patchy savanna with its
many different kinds of vegetation: high grass, bushes, and
trees along river courses.[4]

Plant food leaves little trace in the archaeological record,
while animal bones remain. Laboratory analysis of human coprolites—fossilized feces—can provide more exact information
on what our ancestors ate. Developed only in the last ten years,
few studies have been completed. The results are often ambiguous, but they tend to confirm the proposition that vegetables
were predominant and that in most places protein sources were
infrequently supplied by big-game hunting. We have no studies
going back to our African antecedents, but coprolites from a
seaside camp at Terra Amata on the French Riviera dated to
about two hundred thousand years ago—a time when most
textbooks claim big-game hunting was the predominant human
activity—have been analyzed. They showed flecks of charcoal,
indicating the use of fire, and portions of undigested seafood in
the form of mollusk shell. The seaside campers may have been
enjoying roast oysters. Twelve-thousand-year-old coprolites
from Mexico indicated a diet based largely on millet seed,
while comparatively recent remains, from archaic Indians in
Southwest Texas about 3000 B.P., showed a diet consisting of
plant food—flowers, grasses, seeds, and fruit—with grasshoppers
as the major source of animal protein and lizards, rodents, and
fish as minor sources.[5]

Essential to the procuring of all these foods is the container.
The first cultural device was probably a recipient. Jane Goodall

commented that when she provided an unlimited source of bananas at her camp, the chimpanzees were particularly frustrated at being unable to take away more fruit than they could hold in their arms. Though chimpanzees share some food, mothers in particular sharing with infants, one distinction that scientists make between animals and humans is that the latter universally share food, given the delayed development of the human child, born with a large head and brain and a weak, small body.

Chimpanzees catch small animals without weapons, and several scientists have demonstrated that early hominids could have captured small animals like rabbits and baby gazelles by hand and scavenged the uneaten portions of cheetah and lion kills. Where male evolutionists used to believe that *men* first stood up in order to use tools for hunting, today women scientists suggest that women and men stood up in order to have their hands free for gathering and carrying.[6]

Meat, which would have been a rare and welcome treat, can be dragged back to camp in one piece; small animals, taken by the hand, can be torn up and shared out at the spot, but gathered food needs something to hold it. The first container could have been adapted from nature—a large leaf for folding, a piece of bark, a broken ostrich egg, like those still used for carrying water by the Kalahari Desert San. If the early hominids made nests for sleeping, as chimpanzees and gorillas do, they could have applied their knowledge of nest making for contriving a basketlike device, or adapted a netlike sling or an animal skin, similar to those used for carrying babies.

Many theorizers feel that the earliest cultural inventions must have been a container to hold gathered products and some kind of sling or net carrier.[7] The baby carrier was particularly important, given the increasing immaturity of infants, as demonstrated by the ages of tooth eruption on fossil jaws.[8] Moreover, five million years ago our ancestors had already evolved the flat foot for standing upright, running, and walking much as we do, in contrast to the grasping foot which characterizes chimpanzees, gorillas, and other primates less close to us, and the evolutionary process which resulted in the comparative hairlessness of humans must also have been in course; so infants could not cling with their feet and had less and less to which to cling. As a result of the long period during which offspring had to be carried, females had to develop a method of portage for their infants. Plenty of material was available—vines, hides, human hair. In Sally Slocum's theory, the technique was extended from carrying babies to carrying food and was followed by other cultural inventions—choppers and grinders for food preparation, and eventually weapons.

Women, then, would have been the first to devise containers: they themselves were containers of children, and they were used to carrying small children on their backs or their hips, or in their arms. Much later, they are associated with the earliest traditions of basketry and pottery, and even now they frequently serve as bearers or porters in non-Western societies.

Human mothers did not stay home with babies until very recently. The earliest evidence for settled living shows up in the archaeological record only some twelve thousand years ago. Most humans on earth were nomadic long after that, staying in one spot for only brief periods, in some places for a short season. People on the move carry their babies with them. Both baby carrier and food carrier are universal among gatherers and hunters, even those with the sparest range of material equipment.

The invention of the container can be seen as fundamental in the evolution of a large-brained, two-legged human being. It freed the hands for gathering and provided temporary storage for food such as nuts and fruits. Moreover, the concept of the container was essential in the development of an infant sling. In the civilized West, this last disappeared for centuries, not to say millennia. In the nineteenth century c.e., it was replaced, for the affluent, by the expensive and cumbersome baby carriage, which had to be wheeled with two hands. Most women had to carry their babies in their arms or in a shawl, to stay indoors with them, or to find someone else to stay with them.

The infant carrier bag was not reinvented until after World War II, when the first canvas sling seats were introduced. I remember being stared at on the subway when I carried my six-months-old daughter on my hip so that I could make my way down from exile in the Bronx to my former home in Greenwich Village. Now many forms are on the market—back packs similar to those in which Indian papooses were carried, shoulder slings, and hip carriers—but they are still not all that common. The baby carrier enables a woman to get around and to have her arms free—for gathering fruit or for digging into her purse for change. But our Western image is of an immobile woman, seated indoors, holding a babe in arms or rocking a stationary cradle.

Is it devolution in Western civilization that we lost this cultural device after the invention of village life and agriculture, though peoples like the American Indian kept it all the time?

8

Woman the Potter: Household Equipment as the Key

When the Indian potter collects clay, she asks the consent of the riverbed and sings its praises for having made something as beautiful as clay. When she fashions the clay into a form, she does so by evoking the shapes of sacred things in which the power moves and the life dwells. When she fires her pottery, to this day, she still offers prayers so the fire will not discolor or burst her wares. And, finally, when she paints her pottery, she imprints it with the images which give it life and power—because for an Indian, pottery is something significant, not just a utility but a "being" for which there is as much of a natural order as there is for persons or foxes or trees.

—Jamake Highwater[1]

The carrier bag and women's gathering activities could have been the master pattern in human evolution. An extension of this idea involves the invention of many kinds of household equipment, from containers to baskets and pottery, from digging sticks to stone pounding tools and scrapers and cutters, all used primarily by women in the recent past.

The use of the carrier bag facilitated the accumulation of botanical information. Hominid females would communicate the whereabouts of a rich stand of fruiting bushes, when seeds or nuts could be picked from grass or trees and where they grew, so that a whole store of knowledge of different kinds of plants enlarged the human brain, which in turn enabled the developing hominids to classify and investigate the natural world about them, in the classic model of the feedback mechanisms that shaped the evolution of humanity.* Experimentation with the materials necessary for containers and carriers led to the exploration of the raw materials in the world around so that the developing hominids came to penetrate the resources of their environment and to develop technology.

Food was shared first with infants but also with older siblings and with compatible females who went out to gather, thus increasing both socializing and planning capacities of the new species. Divining different uses for materials exercised the brain, which in turn allowed the hominids to improve their inventive utilization of natural resources in the immediate vicinity. Most of these resources—both containers and foods—would not survive in the fossil record, of course.

We can imagine the great discovery when a mother was able to carry water back to a sick child in a temporary camp or resting place, by using a natural container—an empty ostrich shell or a hollowed-out gourd, perhaps the bole of a tree, or even an animal-hide pouch or natural sponge. Chimpanzees use leaves as sponges to sop up water from the hollow of a tree trunk, say, an example of animal tool use, but they have never reached the evolutionary level which would permit them to give their infants or other chimpanzees water.

Materials which do show up in the archaeological record are stone tools. The earliest remaining tools—natural stones, called manuports by the archaeologists, and very simple flaked stones —are two to five million years old. As recently as ten years ago, their use was credited to men, and they were interpreted as

* "There is of course a constant feedback so that tool use contributes to the patterning of the brain, thus becoming both subject and object in both a neurological and philosophical sense."—William S. Laughlin[2]

weapons or implements for big-game hunting. Today they are being re-examined in the light of the greater importance now assigned to women, as well as to plants, in human evolution, and they look more like household equipment. Tools which used to be called choppers were probably used for pointing digging sticks (today used chiefly by the women of foraging as well as of horticultural peoples), and for cutting by means of a sawing action. Others of heavier stone were used for hammering and bashing, for example, breaking open nuts and preparing parts of plants inedible in their natural state but palatable and digestible after pounding. They would also have served for breaking open animal bones and for dealing with tough parts of animal hide, eaten even today by foraging peoples.[3]

The digging stick was probably the second hominid invention, after the container. This universal tool of present-day women foragers and horticulturalists could have been developed by combining two techniques, known to be used by chimpanzees, in a conception imagined several million years ago by the larger and more complex brain of our forebears. Jane Goodall has described (see Chapter 3) the process by which young chimpanzees learned from their mothers how to prepare leafy branches as probes with which they extracted juicy white grubs from termite hills. In laboratory studies, chimpanzees have been observed to use sticks as levers to open doors as well as to draw fruit within their reach. With more brain and manual dexterity, our ancestors would have been more inventive, combining the principle of the lever and the probe to produce the digging stick.

These tools would have been used for collecting plants and eggs and for extracting honey, termites and other insects, and small burrowing animals. Implements included sticks for digging and knocking down, rocks to crack open nuts or fruits with tough outer coverings, and several kinds of containers. Sharp-edged rocks may also have been used for cutting some of the savanna roots and tubers in the hominids' new environment, foods that were tough and fibrous but large enough to be divided.[4]

The temporary windbreak or shelter made from branches

was another invention that would grow almost naturally out of the primate's nest-making ability. Even today it is women who are responsible for building windbreaks or branch huts among such foraging groups as the Mbuti Pygmies and the Kalahari San, as well as among many groups, both foraging and horticultural, with much more advanced techniques.

With the passage of time, tool use and manufacturing ability improved. Roughly round stones of about a million years ago, formerly described as missiles, proved on close examination to have been shaped by battering and bashing. Under the old aggression-evolution theories they had been viewed as leather-thonged bolas like those used by South American tribes for throwing. Now it is believed that they were used primarily for pounding vegetable food and for breaking and splitting open animal bones to reach the marrow within. Large cutting tools of the same period—one million years ago—also evidence growing technical command. They appear to be only incidentally associated with meat eating and were probably connected with the collection of vegetable foods more than with animal-food preparation.[5] Although archaeologists used to claim that all the stone tools of these early periods were used for killing animals and cutting meat, it is now thought that only the light-duty tools of a million years ago—flake knives, small scrapers, and chopping tools—may have had some connection with butchery practices.[6] Scrapers are used in connection with the tanning of hides, a technique performed only by women among such northerly peoples as the Eskimos, the Montagnais Naskapi, and the Cree, and both women and men among, for example, the Kalahari San.

By this time the pounding stones may have been used not only for tenderizing roots and tubers to make them more palatable and more digestible but for making meal out of seeds, and for removing the husks of nuts, fruits, and seeds.

A few million years after the invention of the container, the digging stick, the pounding stone, and cutting and chopping or pointing tools, women may have come upon a discovery which was to revolutionize the world for the species we now know as humanity. This was fire, which is presently thought to have come into use about a million years ago.

Most of us have read Charles Lamb's story of roast pig, in which the accidental burning of their house produced the world's first gourmet dish for the male protagonist and his son. Archaeology tells us that fire was invented long before both the keeping of animals and the building of permanent houses. Despite Lamb's own tenderhearted care of and collaboration with his sister Mary, it is unsurprising in the context of the times that he saw only men involved with the first use of fire. In my own fantasy I can picture an accidental discovery of fire. After millions of years of hominid existence in Africa, a severe electrical storm ignited a dry stretch of savanna grassland. The fire blazed, destroying miles of terrain, forest and plain. The sparse inhabitants of the valley—scattered bands of ten or more people—fled as did the animals, those which were not caught and consumed by flames. Many perished. It was weeks before one band ventured back to their old round, the fields and clumps of bushes where they were wont to pick fruits and dig tubers. One woman idly probed the scorched ground with her digging stick and a blackened tuber came to light. She picked it up and her daughter began to play with it. Charred on one side, baked dark on the other, it still retained some of the fire's heat, and as the child held it, tossing it from one hand to the other, the vegetable broke open. Experimentally, she put it to her mouth, then excitedly offered the roast yam to her mother. It was delicious—mealy, tender, and fluffy—and tasted far better than the raw or even pounded product they were accustomed to eat.

More realistically, did the process of chipping away at a piece of wood with a particularly hard stone or flint while sharpening a digging stick produce a spark which ignited the wood? Or possibly, in making a stone tool, using one implement as shaper, the other as shaped, a woman produced a spark which ignited her grass basket of seeds or roots, and the same fortunate experimental probing led to further developments. Whatever the sequence of events which produced the fire and the brain power to use it—whether brilliant flash or long-term experiment—women's connection with vegetable and animal food must be placed at the pivot of the plot; they were early and initially involved in the utilization of fire.

Fire proved to be one of the most effective instruments known to humans. Historically it has been used by women and men, on individual and group scales. It seems to me more likely that from its use in cooking came its other uses, not proof but evidence for its invention by women. Fire made available foods which in their raw state were poisonous or barely edible. It tenderized meat, making meat protein more accessible; it made starches more digestible. It also enhanced aesthetic appreciation by improving flavors and offering opportunities for creative combinations of foods. It enabled humans to store meat and fish through smoking and, eventually, made possible a wide variety of prepared dishes. It offered the possibility of cleanliness, another aesthetic improvement and an aid to health, through the heating of water, in containers or by placing hot stones in natural rock basins.

In hunting it serves, in small, to smoke out animals from their burrows, a technique currently used by the South-West African G'wi women as well as by the women of the Pitjandjara and other Australian Aborigine peoples. In large, fire drives which forced herd animals into prepared traps—over precipices, into pits or runways—required the co-operation of groups of women and men. Before farming, fire was used to change the ecology of the landscape, to produce desired plants, to increase grass cover, and to attract grazing animals for easier hunting. One example is given where burns were set primarily to encourage certain much-prized plants; as a secondary result, fleeing animals were intercepted by lines of hunters.[7] Once people began to farm, clearing by fire was the most energy-saving method of cultivation known to preindustrial humans, as it still is.[8]

Women are still the keepers of the flame among nomadic foragers; they cherish a lighted coal in their carriers as they go from camping ground to camping ground; they nurse the fire and they may also start one with the most primitive of fire-producing devices.

Later in history they will be associated with the hearth as goddess of warmth and fire. Sculptured female figures found buried by or in the hearth in paleolithic mammoth-hunting cultures have present-day counterparts in the goddess who appears under various names in Siberian and Aleut tribal folklore.[9] The Cherokee Indian town of Chota was supposed to be the home of the "mother fire" and was therefore considered the leader and most important of the seven Cherokee towns. There is a double association, with maternal warmth, the mother's body heat, and the maternal nursing function, which was extended to the preparation of food.

After the initial use of fire for cooking and nighttime warmth in the species' African homeland, it was, of course, used for heat, in fact made possible our perdurance in the chillier climates to which we spread. The knowledge of fire enabled us to sojourn in cooler places and in Europe, to survive the ice ages, which came so much later in the unfolding story.

The container invented by woman had increased in complexity—a varied range of forms and materials would have been in use—by the time fire was utilized. The baked clay pot was far in the future, but the first cooking utensil could have been an animal-hide sack into which hot stones were dropped to make broth, mush, or cooked fruits and vegetables, with or without meat and fish ingredients. Tubers, roots, and meats could be roasted in the coals; the techniques involved were rudimentary and immediately available to the less imaginative. Building a fire utilizes principles of convection and heat radiation; it is a process of energy conversion whose principles were only later articulated in the science of physics. Cooking is chemistry. The initial experiments for the production of fire and kitchen equipment and an inductive range of food production and cooking methods involved considerable imaginative projection and ingenuity. By the time they occurred, woman's large brain was ready for the challenge that the material and the ingredients presented. In the recent past, women did the scraping and tanning of hides in many foraging societies. In her field work among the Montagnais Naskapi Indians, Eleanor Leacock observed a Montagnais woman who was busy tanning an animal hide while her husband sat beside her rocking their sick baby. Either of them could comfort the ailing child but only the woman knew how to tan leather.[10] A half million years ago we can see women using their stone scrapers to produce the first cooking pot.

The experiments in science and technology that produced cooking also, much later, produced the first pottery, initially made of unbaked clay, later fire-hardened. Leather bags and pottery for carrying water made it possible to sleep for a few days away from a water source. Women carrying water are universal images, whether in Africa and Australia, or in the biblical tale of Rebecca bringing the water jar from the well.

Women, then, would have been the primary inventors and users of a whole complex of devices and techniques around which group activities and subsistence were organized, leading to the creation of culture and, eventually, civilization.

9

Woman the Hunter

There was probably little differentiation by sex, both in size and in occupation, among human ancestors of some millions of years ago.[1] Even today, in societies where men hunt animals and women gather plants, as among the African San, the division of labor is not hard and fast: men will stop to gather vegetable food for themselves; if—as often happens—the hunting is unproductive they may bring back gathered food rather than return empty-handed; in season, they help the women collect a particularly plentiful resource, such as mongongo nuts.[2] The division of labor that exists is related to mobility: women with infants to protect and carry cannot move fast enough and far enough to hunt efficiently.[3]

In group hunting, particularly in net hunting and fire drives, women have always participated, whether among the fairly egalitarian African Pygmies or the horse-riding, male-dominant North American Sioux. Prairie tribes like the Shoshone, the Paiute, and the Ute organize community rabbit hunts in which young and old take part.

Women frequently scout and set nets. Australian Aborigine women are trackers and they hunt small game; on occasion they also bring down a kangaroo with their trained dingoes, while in certain tribes women supply the major portion of animal and fish food, as well as the preponderant plant food. Foods hunted by Tiwi women in northern Australia include opossums, iguanas, bandicoots, several kinds of snakes and lizards and rats, as well as shellfish and vegetables. They provide most of the protein and all of the plant food, with equipment consisting of a trained dog, an ax, fire, and a bark container.[4]

There are many other specific examples of women participating in hunting despite the fairly general sex differentiation which prevailed in the recent historical past. Occupational differences between women and men are quite sharp among the Ojibwa and Greenland Eskimos, yet both are such individualistic societies that women have often hunted with weapons, taught by their fathers or by necessity when no man was available, or even because they wanted to.[5]

Women have been the bearers and nurturers; they have also worked alongside men and made major innovations, something observers of the human scene could easily have verified. Everywhere one looks, except for a few technologically advanced cultures, women turn out to be the base on which first life, then society are built.

Three to five million years ago the activity which supplied the modest proportion of meat eaten by our hominid forebears was probably closer to scavenging than to hunting in the modern sense. Small animals and vulnerable young would have been captured by hand or brought down with a stick or a stone, and large animals that were ill or caught off guard would also have been captured. Even in the recent past, San and Hadza were not above following vultures to the lair of a sick or wounded animal, or otherwise competing with animal scavengers.

Males could have been more far-ranging than females, since the latter would have carried their infants with them, on the hip or the shoulders, and would often have been accompanied by half-grown children while they collected plant food. But not always. Though most of the females would have been occupied looking after infants and young children, foraging for plant food not too far from the base, females without offspring and males would have engaged in hunting and carrying back the food obtained from the chase.[6] Female chimpanzees have recently been observed to participate in the hunt. In a year-long

study project Geza Teleki recorded ten kills by male chimpanzees and two by females.[7]

Nancy Tanner and Adrienne Zihlman point out that early
hominids hunted by day, as primates—baboons and chimpanzees—do now, thus avoiding competition with and danger from
the larger animal predators, who hunt at night and sleep during
the day. They suggest that the females used their digging sticks
to unearth burrowing animals—hares, porcupines, gophers,
moles, etc.—and that in the process of exchanging information
about animal holes, as earlier about plant locations, they
stretched their brain power and communicating ability, thus
furthering human development. If defense against predators
was needed the hominid females and males would jump up and
down and wave their arms and make noises to frighten away
the larger animals, methods still used by present-day gatherer-
hunters.[8]

That the idea of women hunters was not unknown to later
authors is clear from Classical accounts and Greek vase paintings. The tradition of women participating in these activities
lingered on long after the actuality seems to have disappeared.
It must have been based on some memories of the past. Indo-
European women hunting on horse and on foot are frequently
depicted and evidence of their activities will be discussed in a
later chapter. Though the late stages of pregnancy and the
nursing of infants would interfere with the pursuit, young
women and nonmothers evidently joined the young men in the
hunt, as Cherokee and Iroquois Indian women often did.[9] The
concept of the woman hunter is known to Greek mythology
and must have been based on some experience. The goddesses
of the hunt prove that exceptional women did hunt, as exceptional women have done everything males do.

There are two reasons why we have had so many fulsome descriptions of Man the Hunter. As noted earlier, Western men
have seen hunting as conquest activity and chosen to focus on
it. They wrote extensively about the glories of the chase and
paid little attention to women's food-gathering activities. One
much quoted description of the Australian Aborigines devoted
five times more space to the former than to the latter, though

the women provided the bulk of the tribes' daily diet, about 70 per cent by weight.[10]

Moreover, we think in terms of man the hunter, instead of women and men the hunters, because men had time to invent the myth. Among modern hunter-gatherers, where both women and men have more leisure time than people in technologically advanced societies, women put in time regularly for gathering—every day or several days a week—else the people would not eat. While men may, infrequently, go out on a hunt which lasts for long hours, overnight, even days, they also rest for days, weeks, or sometimes months after the fatigues of hunting. The kind of hunting which developed in our species' maturity was a young person's game, requiring magnificent eyesight, co-ordination, and endurance. The G'wi, the Hadza (who spent more time gambling their arrows than shooting them), the Ainu, all tended to retire from long-distance spear or arrow hunting—both of which developed long after the earliest hominid period—by their middle or late thirties, though they continued to participate in the kind of hunting done by women with children.[11] In after years there was plenty of time to sit around and tell of past exploits, to create a mythology, as, in the past five thousand years, surviving older men talked and wrote about the exciting battles in which so many younger men had lost their lives.

If one factor could be offered to explain why man has played a greater part than woman in taking credit for civilization, if not in creating it, the concept Man the Idler is illuminating. E. H. Gombrich tells of an isolated tribe in Africa, close to the center of the Sudan, where the young men spend most of their time decorating their own and each other's bodies with colored earth, modifying or repainting the elaborate designs as soon as they become smeared. He comments that here, as elsewhere, it is the women who do most of the work.[12] Back in 1623, when the Englishman Richard Jobson anchored in the mouth of the Gambia, he noted that among the Mandingo the women did most of the work and that the men were occupied for only two months of the year. His observations were substantiated in a book published a hundred years later, *Travels into the Inland*

Parts of Africa by Francis Moore. The men worked without respite at seed time and harvest, but for the rest of the year they lay on the *bentang* in the shade, smoking, gossiping, and playing a game which resembled chess. Although game abounded in the forest and the river swarmed with fish, they hardly even bothered to hunt or fish.[13]

After all, is it not idle speculation which is at the bottom of so much human knowledge and art? Humans are the only animals that ask why, and men have been freer than women both to seek the answers and to take credit for answers found by women and men.

10

The First Teachers

There was nothing resembling the nineteenth- or twentieth-century family among early hominids. They would have had even longer and closer mother-child relations than have been described for chimpanzee and gorilla groups. Social groupings would have been the rule, but there may have been occasional male solitaries, as there are among great apes, and in line with the recently documented cases of two World War II Japanese soldiers who managed alone for decades in the South Pacific. Human behavior has always been subject to flexibility and change, and it is likely that even the very earliest societies took different forms in different environments.[1]

With the understanding gained from studying our primate relatives we can see the flexible human group (or band) as an advance over other primate groupings. Let us not be fooled by the seeming anarchy of forest chimpanzees and baboons at one end of the evolutionary scale or of foraging humans at the other. A flexible structure is still a structure. Randomness does not prevail; in fact it is a more complex organizational form than the comparatively inflexible ordering of, say, a game-park baboon troop.[2] Evolutionists note that the most permanent tie among chimpanzees is that between mothers, infants, and half-grown young—the human family without a father. Adult male chimpanzees are attracted to the group by the mother-child relationship and not for sexual reasons. In the same wise it is speculated that early hominid bands would have consisted of two or three compatible families of mothers and offspring, to which three or four adult males might attach themselves.[3] The basic human organization centers also around the mother, and in times of crisis society breaks down to this form. Elaborations on this unit are the product of our social evolution.

On the surface rigidity looks easier and more efficient than an open structure, but it doesn't advance the group. Authoritarianism is a specious efficiency: you have one leader and when that leader goes the group falls apart, not having learned to share or to devise peaceful transitional ways of adapting to change. In the long run, authoritarianism and rigidity are counterproductive. Flexibility is the only way we've survived, for conditions are always changing and living organisms must change, too. This is even more true in the case of humans who change their environment and then have to adapt to the new environment. The more radically they change the environment, the more radical the necessary adaptations.

Since promiscuity has remained a constant in human society throughout history, despite the strongest societal controls at times, and since it is a relatively universal characteristic among the primates, it would have been more rather than less prevalent in our remote past. Out of the family of mother and infant and older children would develop close relations between brothers and sisters—words that evoke the strongest connotations of loyalty for most human groups. We shall not look for a father as father until millions of years later—perhaps nine or eight thousand years ago. This does not mean that a male was not associated with an adult female for a period of time or that he would not have taken a playful, tolerant, and protective interest in her children or in all the children of the group.

In the savanna-fringe life of early hominids, mothers were —as they still are—the first teachers. They showed their children how and where to gather food. They taught, by example and precept, the principle of food sharing. Chimpanzees do not teach their children directly; females are accompanied by their offspring, who learn by watching their mothers termite.

With the larger hominid brain and some means of communication, hominid mothers would have instructed their infants directly, a basic difference between animal and human capacities. Early lessons would have been in the use of a digging stick to locate tubers, roots, and burrowing animals.[4]

The food-sharing adaptation was necessitated by the delayed development of the human child. Till the last decades, an artificial relationship was postulated, based on the modern Western industrial family, which assumed that women stayed in the home, or at the home base, taking care of babies while men brought home the bacon, going out to hunt and providing food and protection.

Any observation of non-Western societies would have disproved this projection immediately. Before industrialization, women usually had their babies with them, whether they went out to work or gathered close to shelter. Sometimes, as among the San and the Mbuti Pygmies today, women went away to gather or hunt, and young children or elderly adults were left in charge of infants, a practice also common among agricultural peoples. Male protection of females is not characteristic of foraging societies; it is a phenomenon that seems to have grown with the conquest syndrome, myth and reality, and with the invention of war, which will not be seen in human society until millions of years later—about 5000 B.P.

Sometimes women's contributions to subsistence were used as evidence of the brutalization of our non-Western fellows, but certain obvious deductions were not drawn. The fact is that, with mothers supplying most of the food for small children, increased co-operation was taught on all levels. Mothers gathering together, with and for children, increased communicating abilities, enlarging the brain, and further facilitating human intercourse and sociability. The institution of meat sharing was also affected by the set toward group activities encompassing plant and animal food.

Within the last ten or twenty years studies at both ends of the evolutionary time scale have controverted the past teachings about males going out to hunt while females stayed at the home bases. At the beginning of the time scale males would seem to have played a peripheral role. At our end, when we speak of contemporary gatherer-hunters, we must remember that *Homo sapiens* is another species, albeit related to our ancestors who lived some four million years ago. Moreover, even though present-day foragers may seem to be using technologies as primitive as those used by members of our own species as recently as ten to twenty thousand years ago they—we—have been evolving constantly in the relatively brief period during which our own species has existed, let alone the several million years that separate us from our antenators.

Two elements of distortion creep into reports on foragers written by members of our own Western culture. One is the already mentioned projection of our society's values and preconceptions. The other is the often unrecognized fact of Western influence: there is no society on earth today that has not been touched to a greater or lesser degree by the dominant West. Sometimes this influence has been at work for centuries; in other instances it is more recent; in either case, present-day communications make it omnipresent.

Comparisons with hominids of four million B.P. have bearing, then, not so much in terms of brain and consciousness as on the basis of ecological circumstances; they are always a rough approximation.

Hominids' language abilities would have been inferior to those of the later human species though superior to chimpanzee and gorilla capacities for communication. In the field, chimpanzees are known to employ more than twenty-three different calls or vocalizations, each with its own specific message, and they also use a number of gestures, facial expressions, and body postures to signal information. At a minimum, toolmaking hominids would have had a much larger range of sounds and gestures on tap.[5] However, the early hominid brain would hardly have encompassed the abstract idea of possession, which comes much later in evolution, nor would any hominid male conceive of copulation as meaning male possession of females.

The development of humanity centers around the first couple, mother and child. The children remain close to their mother. Other males are brought in as her temporary or long-term mate, but daughters, sons, even grandchildren, remain in close association with the mother figure over a period of years, stretching out into decades. The mother is the first teacher and out of her teaching came the communicative and socializing abilities which characterize human beings. For the spark that set off the chain of events leading to the later development of our species, in trying to pinpoint the place where a difference in degree becomes a difference in kind, it is necessary to look at the fossils which document human development and change.

11

---··--··--··--··--··--··--··---

Early Stages of Evolution

Archaeology and paleontology developed in an age of expanding technology, and the initial explorations of our past tended to focus on tools more than on people, particularly since the former were more commonly unearthed than the latter. In line with the thinking that had defined our species as *man* the toolmaker, the stages of human evolution were originally classified not so much by the physical or human attributes of the changing fossils as by the European place names where different kinds of tools made by our ancestors had first been found.

But the material culture remaining is only the tip of the iceberg. Some years ago Lewis Mumford complained that it wasn't the tools, or the bricks, or the labor which created the Pyramids, it was the human imagination. In that instance human imagination took shape in an exploitative and power-oriented conspicuous display. The songs and stories of the workers, male and female, have not come down to us, though they, too, were products of the human imagination. When it comes to our earliest ancestors, we do not know what degree of imagination they possessed, just where in time the phenomenon we think of as human consciousness began to take form.

Today, the more we learn from scientific advances, the more we are able to face the limitations of our knowledge till now. The resultant enlargement of thought allows us to contemplate, emotionally if not intellectually, the concatenation of forces, understood and undreamed of, which must have been responsible for the world and people of today. New methods and new disciplines are being utilized and old disciplines are adapted to new uses: radiocarbon dating for periods as far back as fifty or sixty thousand years ago; potassium argon dating for long-range calculations, from the millions to several hundred thousand years ago; geology; geography; climatology; paleobotany to analyze pollens; demography; statistics; chemistry and physics; ethnography and social anthropology; to name just a few. Specialists in all these fields have joined hands with the diggers and explorers—the archaeologists and paleontologists—though unfortunately investigations based on technology all too often overvalue the mechanical at the cost of the creative.

Parallel systems of classification of tools and fossils have been devised and are used in combination in attempts to fathom our beginnings. The fossils were originally named after the places where they had been found, and a family tree of human origins was constructed, synchronizing with the millions of years which had been labeled in terms of the kinds of tools our ancestors made. Eventually Louis Leakey coined a name for the creature he considered to be our first forebear: *Homo habilis*, translated by him as able or handy *man*, representing a group of fossils he defined as toolmaking hominids. Other physical anthropologists preferred to see these fossils as a subgroup of one species of advanced ape they had previously classified as *Australopithecus*, the southern ape.

Because one has to start somewhere, let us begin, more or less arbitrarily, with this creature, the ape person so inaccurately depicted by Ardrey, Kubrick, Dart, Broom, etc. An earlier ape, *Ramapithecus*, dated to some fourteen million years ago and known only from jaws and teeth, may or may not have been on the direct line of humanity and may or may not have made stone tools, depending on which paleontologist's theory one accepts.

Until the last few years, however, few scientists questioned both the toolmaking abilities and the close relationship to humanity of the fossils classified under the names *Australopithecus africanus* and *Homo habilis*. No stone tools had been found near the remains described by Broom and Dart, so that the two primate species identified by them as *Paranthropus* were only dubiously assigned to the hominid line. In 1959, however, at Olduvai Gorge, a Tanzanian section of East Africa's Great Rift Valley, where Mary and Louis Leakey had been excavating for twenty-five years and had already found numbers of stone tools and other signs of hominid activity, Mary Leakey came upon a 1.75-million-year-old skull which has been equated with the line of *Paranthropus*, or, as it was eventually denominated, *Australopithecus robustus*.

On the basis of Broom and Dart's South African findings, it had been thought that *Australopithecus* dated back less than a million years. After Mary Leakey's discovery, several more fossil remains were found at Olduvai, giving a fairly complete chronology going back some two million years.

Since 1959 more and more specimens and more varied parts of prehuman lines have been located. To the onlooker it seems as if the story is revised every time the paleontologists find a new fossil—heel, jaw, tooth, or skull as the case may be. Fortunately the slowness of academic publication and scientific caution, debate, and study provide some braking action.

The few stone and bone relics of the remote past which do remain are preserved only under very special conditions of climate and geology: limestone caves, volcanic ash, and dryness.

What is found is not, of course, a true random selection; it is governed by the limiting conditions which permit fossilization, particularly when we go back into the millions of years. Africa's Rift Valley is a lode which has produced a long and fairly consecutive record; in the rain forests not too far away all indications of human habitation would be destroyed by forest rot and humidity. Excavation proceeds apace, and all too often the odd bits and pieces which do emerge are put together and looked at as a linear record of the past, with modifications each time a new piece of "hard evidence" is found. Serious scholars realize that at the moment we have only discrete pages, not a complete book.

Richard Leakey made a spectacular announcement of a new discovery in 1972; in the six years since then, the story of human evolution has once again been rewritten, on the evidence of subsequent discoveries, and it is in constant process.

Two species of *Australopithecus* are presently traced. The first specimen found by Mary Leakey would have belonged to a physically larger line which is thought to have died out because it used natural tools (manuports) but did not manufacture them. Other specimens with a more delicate skeleton were found in coexistence with the larger *robustus* line, but they occurred also at earlier strata. They were initially classified as *Australopithecus,* though some of them were later dubbed *Homo habilis* by Louis Leakey. It is from this species that most paleontologists considered the human race to have descended—or perhaps ascended would be more accurate.

In early books on the subject Mary Leakey was not mentioned. We were told that Louis Leakey discovered that famous first specimen in East Africa, though his wife had actually discovered the skull in situ. Some accounts say that Louis Leakey was indisposed that day and that when Mary sent word he came rushing from his tent to examine the prize of twenty-five years' searching. Louis, however, spoke at the scientific conference where he announced the discovery and presented the skull, strikingly displayed in a black-velvet-lined case.

It is part of the general invisibility of women that husbands have long taken credit for the combined work of husband-and-wife teams, often with more or less generous acknowledgments to their wives. Evidently, Mary Leakey, who recently published a two-volume report on her diggings at Olduvai Gorge, is the diligent and painstaking worker while Louis was the organizer and administrator, as well as the showman. It was he who met the press and the public, who rounded up grant money for support and handled all the other components which are so essential in our present society to back up and make possible scientific research. He was the one who originally staked out the Rift Valley as a place to dig because of its geological components and would seem to have had great enthusiasm and organizing ability.*

The Leakeys' son Richard continues the tradition of his parents. Fossil discoveries in South and East Africa have pushed hominid ages back as far as three to five million years. Digging at one of the sites where australopithecine and habiline fossils had been located, Lake Turkana (formerly Lake Rudolf) in the Omo Basin, Leakey produced, in 1972, a skull of far larger capacity than had been thought possible for the 2.6-million-year-old stratum in which it was located. "The skull had been crushed to hundreds of fragments that were found, eroding on a slope, *and have been pieced together by Dr. Meave Leakey, Richard Leakey's wife*," the *New York Times* reported.[1] If the discovery holds up, it means that the next accepted date of human evolutionary change—the species nominated *Homo erectus*—would have to be pushed backward from one million years ago to almost three million, contemporaneous with *Australopithecus* and *habilis*.

Perhaps the most amusing case of the wife's work being absorbed by and credited to the husband occurred in 1961 when, according to François Bordes, "M. Yves Coppens discovered in Chad, 600 kilometers northeast of Fort-Lamy, a cranium and facial bone fragments of a being similar both to the *Australopithecus* and to *Pithecanthropus*, which was provisionally christened *Tchadanthropus uxoris* ('the Tchad man of the wife,' for it was in fact discovered by Madame Coppens)."[2]

One is reminded of the debate about whether Edmund Hillary or Tenzing Norgay should be called the conqueror of Everest. The need to credit one individual with conquest or discovery is part of our Western individualist way of thinking, the aggressive, hierarchical, and pyramidal context and language in which we shape and express our ideas. We talk about low man on a totem pole, but there can be no high man without the low man, just as, in the circus pyramid, the man or woman who stands on top of other shoulders is certainly not more impor-

---

* As noted in Chapter 3, he also played a role in primate research, steering several young women into the neighboring aspect of human evolution constituted by animal behavior studies.

tant than those who form the base of the pyramid. Most discoveries are co-operative feats which could not take place
without the combining of several intelligences: ideas belong to
everybody, and new ideas and discoveries come from the synthesis of those of the past.

As recognition for women began to penetrate the popular
consciousness, Mary Leakey was introduced into the texts more
often, though Louis still held the main spotlight. At the time
of his death, in 1972, they were separated, and since then she
has emerged from the shadows. Three years later, she took a
leaf from his book and held a press conference in Washington
to announce a spectacular new discovery, thus reaching the
front pages of the *New York Times*.

She had located 3.75-million-year-old jaws and teeth "from at
least eleven specimens," leading her to the conclusion that
"true *man* had evolved and lived in East Africa" at the same
time the physical anthropologists were claiming the human pre-
cursors—*Australopithecus* and *habilis*—existed in Tanzania, in
Kenya, and in Ethiopia.[3] In the light, then, of recent finds, the
debate over *Australopithecus* may be beside the point: both
delicate and robust forms may have become extinct, and we
would be descended from a separate line represented by the recent, independent finds of Mary Leakey and her son Richard.

The latter has now augmented the controversial skull fragments announced in 1972 and labeled East Rudolf Skull 1470
with other finds. There are similar large-brained skulls as well
as two thighbones "of remarkably human proportions."[4] Skull
1470 had a cranial capacity of 800 cubic centimeters, within the
parameters of the species known as *Homo erectus* and one
third larger than the 1.9-million-year-old skull that Louis Leakey found at Olduvai Gorge in 1963, together with a variety of
stone tools, and that provided the basis for his *Homo habilis*
classification. Moreover, C. Donald Johanson, working with a
team in Ethiopia, has dug up three-million-year-old teeth and
bones that he places in the same species as Richard Leakey's
specimens. Johanson and young Leakey hold out for a chronology pushing the origins of the human line back at least three

million years, while Mary Leakey would extend the story by another three quarters of a million years.[5]

This would mean that humans must have diverged from other apes at least five or six million years ago, probably earlier. The British anatomist C. E. Oxnard suggests that the two species of *Australopithecus* are species unrelated to humans, closer to orangutans, and that they became extinct about a million years ago.[6]

Going along with the Leakeys' theory of human origins, what do we know about how our ancestors, *habilis* or *erectus* as the case may be, lived? They probably walked upright, judging from the shape of their hip- and thighbones and the position of the foramen magnum, the hole in the skull through which the spinal cord joins the brain. Richard Leakey claims, on the basis of the thighbones and an anklebone from Lake Turkana, that his *erectus* discovery had a slouching walk more erect than that of the australopithecine specimens. Both had small humanlike teeth, not the large tearing canines of, say, the male baboon or the relatively large canines of both female and male chimpanzees.

The assumption that both must have had a more complex organization of the brain, prefiguring the brains of later prehumans and eventually humans, has been given substantiation by studies of extant fossil skulls. Close comparison with the skulls of gorillas and chimpanzees shows that there was more space and height within the *habilis* skull for forward and middle lobes of the brain, where thought and speech are supposed to originate, somewhat less for visual areas. Moreover, the cerebellar lobes—the areas controlling balance, motion, and manipulation—were located under the cerebrum (the roof brain), as in humans, rather than behind it, as in great apes, giving the skull a more humanlike shape.[7]

Habilis brains were about the size of the present-day gorilla's, one third larger than that of today's chimpanzee; if Richard Leakey's *erectus* discoveries hold up, an even larger brain is indicated. Since the habilines were considerably smaller than both chimpanzees and gorillas, the hominid's brain-size ratio indicates far more intellectual capacity than is possessed by our ape cousins.

The *Homo erectus* stage in human evolution was formerly dated to a million years ago in Africa, perhaps 600,000 years ago in China, to which it was believed the new species had spread in the intervening 400,000 years. The African estimate may be pushed back two million or more years by the findings of the Leakeys, mother and son, in Tanzania and Kenya respectively, and by C. Donald Johanson's Ethiopian discoveries, while Chinese reports now place their *erectus* species (formerly known as *Homo pekinensis*—Peking *man*) as far back as a million years ago. *Homo erectus* is the least studied stage in our prehistory. Brains were larger and more human, skeletons taller and more erect, though one must still imagine a creature far removed from our present condition, both in physique and in brain power. Since the original discovery in Choukoutien in 1927, fragments of *erectus* skeletons and artifactual evidence of their occupations have been discovered in wide-ranging areas—Africa, Spain, Hungary, and Indonesia. In some areas *erectus* made handaxes, in others they did not, but the tools found in conjunction with their living sites are identified as the Acheulian tool culture and span a range of almost a million years. They are more complex and better worked than previous tools, and an increasing number of large animal bones are found nearby, while charcoal fragments indicating the use of fire also appear for the first time.

Formerly these stones and bones were taken to mean that hunting shaped humanity, but with our more sophisticated knowledge, as well as the evidence from studies of recently existing foraging groups like the African San and the Australian Aborigines, who leave similar quantities of preservable debris at their campsites though plants are their major food source, we can take these surviving relics as indicating increasing acculturation in all areas. There is, however, no evidence of artifacts of adornment until, possibly, about 300,000 years ago, nor of art or religious ceremony, not even ritual burials, one of the earliest signs of awareness of mortality—i.e., human consciousness—among our forebears.

With *erectus*, however, hunting becomes a more organized,

less fortuitous activity. Wooden spears may have been in use toward the end of this period: a fifteen-inch tip found in Clacton, England, is dated to about 250,000 years ago, and fragments of what may have been wooden spears are found in Germany and Spain for about the same date. At Torralba, Spain, stone and bone tools and the remains of large mammals were found together; at Ambrona, Spain, the bones of some twenty elephants, along with butchery tools. These animals could hardly have been killed by individuals or with the weapons then available. Group hunts in which both sexes participated, using fire drives, could have enabled hominids to trap large animals in swamps or pits.

Tools of this period are more varied and require more complex abilities than those of the previous epochs. Though what many of them were used for is not exactly known, we have seen that their functions are presently being reinterpreted. They would have been used by males and females, though males would have been freer to participate in group and individual hunts and, possibly, to develop skill with wooden spears.

It seems likely, however, that the hunting activities of *Homo erectus* have been overrated. The first unquestionable wooden spears are dated to about a hundred thousand years ago. In excavations outside Europe, in Southeast Asia, in Syria, in the Near East, and in East Africa, animal bones are scarce or absent, so scientists hypothesize that these early humans lived largely on plants, insects, and small animals. Moreover, the wear on stone tools found in England and dated to several hundred thousand years ago shows that they were used for woodworking, for scraping hides, for cutting plant material, and for boring wood or bone, as well as for cutting meat.

Though fruits and vegetables must have been the major source of nourishment for almost all hominids, the first evidence of plant food is found in the most northerly area to which *erectus* has been traced. These were hackberry seeds from Choukoutien, in China, a dig now placed at one half to a million years before our time. In that cold-temperate climate one can imagine that the berries would have provided a welcome sweet taste sensation in the comparatively short season during which they fruited. Evidence of gathering does not usually survive. From the tool kit, with its broader variety of better-worked tools, we surmise that an augmented range of foods was used and that knowledge and methods had increased in sophistication. Some plant products—roots, nuts, pith, etc.—need preparation like soaking and cooking to make them edible or palatable; from the evidence, women would have invented cooking by this time (see Chapter 3).

While we can only speculate on *erectus'* sexual and cognitive life, we must imagine an increased capacity for both cruelty and kindness. The discovery of bashed-in brain cases at Choukoutien led earlier writers to accuse *Homo erectus* of beastly crimes like murder and cannibalism. The actual beasts do not normally kill and eat other members of their own species. It is humans who invented the purposeful killing of their own kind. However, the Choukoutien evidence is ambiguous.

Charcoal remains in the North China caves show that fire was used by their inhabitants, permitting Robert Ardrey to describe *erectus* as dining on "roast brother," instead of marveling at the female experiments in physics and chemistry which produced heat and cooked food for early humans.

On the other hand, myth-oriented writers like Joseph Campbell presume that the open brain cases were evidence of sympathetic magic practices. He compares *erectus* customs with present-day human beliefs whereby eating the brain, heart, liver, body, or blood (symbolically in the form of the Catholic host) of one human gives another human some of the attributes of the person consumed. In certain cultures it is a mark of love and respect to eat parts of one's dead in a mourning ceremony. In New Guinea among the Fore, the brains of relatives recently dead were consumed at ritual feasts, while in parts of northern South America mothers customarily ate their dead children at funeral observances, in token of deepest affection.[8]

Bone marrow and brain from whatever sources seem to be cherished delicacies among our animal cousins and our forebears. Observers have described the care with which chimpanzees open the skulls of their kill—baby baboons and small monkeys—and scoop out the brain with the aid of leaf sponges and fingers. The elephant skulls at Torralba were opened at the base for extraction of the brain by *erectus*. One can imagine brain and marrow as rare natural sources of rich, tender fatty food.

Cannibalism as a last resort against starvation is—and has been—engaged in many times in human existence. The Eskimos, the Ojibwa, many Siberian tribes and other far northern peoples have often been forced to eat their fellows. They do it reluctantly—the Ojibwa have developed cultural defenses like the Windigo syndrome with which to handle their repugnance. Sumerian and Egyptian writings document the bitter times of war and famine "when the mother ate her child," while, in the year 1973, a young woman and man in the Canadian Arctic and a group of South American athletes in the high Andes all survived plane crashes by eating their fellow victims.

The stimulus to our human storytelling propensities is there; the actualities are still unknown.

12

Sex and Consciousness

When I'm playing the piano, I make love. It's the
same thing.

— Arthur Rubinstein

What were the sexual meetings of the first prehumans like?
Did the females have numerous quickies, like chimpanzees, or
slow, ponderous encounters like the gorilla? Judging by the
brain cases, one can assume a wider range—more possibilities,
more individual variations, more factors to be combined resulting in more diversity and more choices. Here the studies of
Jane Goodall and her comments on the differing personalities,
sexual and otherwise, of her chimpanzee subjects come to
mind. Anyone who has kept pets knows how much animal personalities differ, as gardeners know that each plant, even each
rose, is unique, but it is hard to keep that tremendous scale in
mind, from the minimal to the major variations. Three million
years ago our forebears probably had long, dreamy and short,
intense encounters, and more besides.

   Did the females have estral cycles like every other primate
but the human one? That is, did they have periods of up to ten
days every month (except during nursing and pregnancy) when
they mated with every male available? And if they were loosely
promiscuous, like the majority of primates, when did estrus,
with its intense sexual activity followed by a period of disin-
terest on the part of the female, disappear and the human con-

dition, in which sexual desire occurs at any time, make itself felt?

There are those who say that estrus never did disappear in the human female, that it is merely masked by culture. Lionel Tiger and Robin Fox make this claim in *The Imperial Animal*, and Mary Jane Sherfey, a psychoanalyst, also has a long discussion about cornification, the second half of the menstrual cycle in the human female, in which she makes a fairly ambiguous implication for the same claim.[1] She cites Kinsey's report on sexuality in the human female as supportive evidence. This report consisted of circumstantial and uncontrolled subjective evidence from a relatively small group of women, but it was the only evidence we had had, up to that time, on many of the subjects Kinsey asked about. I have heard it used to make a case for the opposite, i.e., that women had more sexual desire just previous to and around the time of menstruation, which was put forward as a natural form of birth control.[2] Tiger and Fox's evidence for estrus in the human female is similarly scant and unconvincing. I myself have never met any female who felt that she became more passionate at ovulation time: if they know when it is, they are likely to become dispassionate—for obvious reasons.

It used to be assumed that sex was the glue which kept primate societies together, a premise known as Zuckerman's theory of sociology in primates, after its originator, the English primatologist who had based so many theories of human and monkey social organization on his London zoo studies of the hamadryas baboon. Of course, in the nineteen thirties when this theory was elucidated, when scientists said "sex" they meant male activity and female receptivity. Artists never had any doubt about the active status of female sexual desire, from the anonymous author who wrote about Potiphar's wife through Aristophanes in *Lysistrata*, Chaucer's Wife of Bath, Racine's Phèdre, and so on.

But knowledge of female physiology is still in its infancy. In the last two or three decades, science has emerged from its Victorian fairy-tale world and acknowledged that female animals, including primates and humans, have assertive sexual drives, though the underlying attitude still considers active sexuality a male characteristic. There is a hangover of the old terms. "What does it matter whether you call it receptivity or desire?" said a leading physical anthropologist. "It's all behavior." Which is like saying, What does it matter whether you call it murder or self-defense, it's all behavior. This kind of semantic confusion exerts considerable influence on human thought. We often think what we say instead of saying what we think. The peculiar scientific illogic which nominates admired qualities as male so that when a female has them she is described as having male components, is still all too prevalent. Freud's outdated explanation of libido as a male attribute[3] is echoed by endocrinologist John Money's description of androgen as the hormone causing sexual desire in males and females.[4] Since androgen is produced in large amounts in the male testes, and in smaller amounts in the female adrenals, this would seem to be a new version of the Freudian statement making desire a male characteristic which is present in females to a minimal degree, so that an active female can be derogated as a "masculine" woman. Mary Jane Sherfey's *The Nature and Evolution of Female Sexuality* is a peculiarly contradictory effort to reconcile Freudian theory with newer biomedical information. Discussing the effects of estrogen and androgen on women's and men's desire and performance, she notes that new discoveries about hormones necessitate a complete revision of currently held opinions with regard to their control of sexual activity.[5] (The inadequacy of earlier assumptions about male and female hormones was discussed in Chapter 4, and reference was made to the enormous new body of knowledge about the complexities of hormone interaction that has been and is still being accumulated.)

In both sexes orgasms are caused by muscular contractions against the body chambers which fill with blood to produce erection. Male and female orgasms are biologically identical. The body chambers which produce erection in the male are located externally in the penis; in the female they are in the vestibular bulbs within the surface tissue alongside the opening of the vagina. On the basis of Sherfey's review of Masters and

Johnson's anatomical and physiological findings, with clarification from other sources, there is today no doubt about the human female's activity in sex.

There has been a tendency to attribute passivity to the female because the male organ must be inserted into the vagina. However, the act of penetrating is only one part of a much more complex sexual sequence. The female genital is extremely active in the sex act; it is not just a passive receptacle for sperm. The clitoris has a greater concentration of sensitive nerve endings than the penis or any other organ in the body. The clitoris is like a submerged iceberg; its functioning cannot be understood if it is seen merely as a small penis. The clitoral shaft extends to the mouth of the vagina and is connected to the vestibular bulbs, which encircle the vaginal opening. Circumvaginal muscles connect both structures so that the movement of one pulls on and is felt by the other. Wider areas of sensitivity are encompassed in erotic stimulation in the female than in the male, and she has a more extensive network of blood vessels which become engorged with blood—the process of vasomotor congestion that causes the penile erection and produces enlargement of the clitoris and swelling within the female genital.[6]

After Zuckerman voiced his theory that primate societies are glued together by continuous male sexual activity with diverse periodically receptive females, the field primatologists came back with incontrovertible evidence that females initiate sexual activity, but they also discovered something else. The famous year-round male sexual activity seemed to be limited in the wild. Monkeys, too, had mating seasons, like many of the lower mammals, as witness the fact that babies were born at given periods of the year. Among the monkeys which have birth seasons are langurs, macaques, savanna, hamadryas, and gelada baboons. Rhesus monkeys who breed all year round in laboratory and zoo conditions also have breeding seasons in the wild, alternating with periods of several months when the females do not come into estrus.[7]

So, to balance the acknowledgment of female sexual desire, the scientists happily pronounced that while a she-baboon or rhesus was definitely active in estrus, she was fortunately not in estrus much of the time. According to Phyllis Jay, "The majority of a female monkey's time is spent either pregnant or lactating, she is able to engage in sexual activities only for a small portion of her life, and yet the troops still stay together."[8]

One feels that the day was saved for male sexuality since the troops stayed together in spite of rather than because of aggressive female sex. In fact, one ethologist, Wolfgang Wickler, registered a grand protest against his confreres' happy conclusion that it was not sex—in the female—which kept the troops together. Yes, he said, it is true that the females are not engaged in sexual activity with the males during the major part of the year, but this does not mean that the males are not sexually potent—a fine distinction, since if they are not copulating, how can one tell about the state of their desires? But Wickler insisted that spermatogenesis went on all year round, though how he knew this and what kind of desire it indicated I cannot say, nor did he bring forth evidence of male masturbation or homosexuality in the wild to support his claim. (Alison Jolly contradicts his assertion about year-round spermatogenesis, at least where the squirrel monkey is concerned. In this New World species, the males grow fat around the shoulders during breeding season in connection with seasonal spermatogenesis.[9]) If male monkeys of other species do have year-round potency, one wonders whether they, unlike human males, are able to control themselves, since rape, homosexuality, and masturbation to orgasm are not seen in the wild. In nature it is the male who is "responsive" to the female's active desire for intercourse.

When we take maternal sexuality into account, the fact that nursing females are also gratifying a broad sexual drive, so that female sexual opportunity is more constant than males', the whole brouhaha may tell us more about the human male ego and how it is tied up with the notion of "continual potency" than it tells us about the state of a male monkey's putative potency when he is not utilizing it.

It is a male assumption—and an extremely harmful myth—that human males are "sexually potent" at all times. This is far from the case, just as it is not true that human females are "sexually receptive" all the time. (The possibility may exist, but in fact sexual desire in both sexes is controlled by many conscious and unconscious factors—liking, deprivation, habit, social expectation, fatigue, to name a few.) This great oversimplification, which is still common usage in the literature, just about eliminates from consideration everything that makes us human: art, beauty, choice, affection, imagination, etc. Still, it has been a myth of long standing and is behind the use of rape as a reward for soldiers and the hideous entanglement of sex and conquest which is so basic to our social ills.

In animal sex we do not know the extent to which choice enters. Hierarchy had been postulated as the controlling element in primate sexual encounters, in demonstration of Darwin's principle of sexual selection and evolutionary logic. As was pointed out, recent field studies have cast doubt on the cardinal tenets of animal behaviorists, and dominance theory is falling into disrepute among scientists today. Where charted in the wild, dominance hierarchies were unstable and contradictory.[10] Results were largely anthropomorphic projections, except where caused by stress conditions, many of which could be related to human contact. Sexual encounters never did fit neatly into the predictions of human observers, despite considerable rationalization and bending of evidence. All that could be said was that, to the extent to which choice entered, it was the female who made the decision, though not with Darwinian logic.[11]

The way in which sexual selection applies to human relations is clear: "Let's face it, the man with the most money and the biggest Cadillac still gets the prettiest chicks," said a film star on television. The dominance factor with us is not size or strength or intelligence but money, which might well be quite deleterious from an evolutionary point of view, *vide* Tommy Manville, the much-married playboy of the nineteen thirties and forties.

For our ancestors in a prematerialist world in which it is ecology rather than economics which describes their life-support system, the choice made by the female would have been determined by the male's attractive qualities. Tanner and Zihlman have postulated sociability as the determining factor.[12] They feel that hominid females chose the more amiable males as mates, thus encouraging our evolution toward cooperation and food sharing.

With the acknowledgment that female primates exercised an active role in sex relations and frequently became more aggressive in estrus, primatologists (and other writers on human evolution) often explain human females' loss of estrus in terms of the dangers of aggression—in the female. As Wolfgang Wickler tells it:

> In general females in heat appear to become more aggressive. . . . In the rhesus monkey, oestrous females often cross group boundaries, according to Carpenter: "Estrus only makes it possible for the female to penetrate and to be tolerated within a foreign group." Washburn and DeVore (1962) state that oestrous in baboons disrupts all other social relations; the female leaves her preference group and child (if present).
>
> Most authors agree that the rank of the female is altered for the heat period . . . *The female in oestrus even takes food morsels from the hands of the male.*
>
> That females in oestrus leave their preference group and follow the highest-ranking male is an *indication that they are very "self-confident" during this phase.* In some cases, this has been more closely investigated: rhesus monkey females in oestrus are particularly aggressive (Carpenter, 1942); they become aggressive toward other females and at the same time begin to approach males (Rowell, 1963), *they even threaten their prospective male consorts* (Chance, 1956). The same applies to the chimpanzee (Reynolds and Reynolds, 1965). *Receptive female chimpanzees present without any sign of fear;* at other times they present in a timid manner, and this at least indicates that fear is compensated when the female is in heat.[13]

Clearly such behavior in a human female would never do; estrus had to go. What there is in the world scheme which pronounces male aggression useful and female aggression harmful, this writer cannot say, but so it would appear to many of the primatologists. Phyllis Jay finds that "there are apt to be striking changes in a female's behavior during estrous periods. She is more active and aggressive, and seeks the attentions of adult males, often including the ones she may have avoided when she was not sexually active. Not only are some social relationships at least temporarily altered by the stresses of increased activity, but when many adult females in a group are receptive at the same time, there may also be substantial changes in the behavior of the group as a whole."[14] For John Pfeiffer, it goes beyond primate activity. "The typical pattern among mammals involves regular bursts of *sexual frenzy* which take precedence over all other activities. At every ovulation or immediately after, all nonhuman females including occasional nursing females come into estrus, or 'heat.' Sexual activity is so concentrated during such periods that it tends to interrupt the care of the young and all other forms of behavior. . . . If all the females in a primate troop were subject to three days of *sexual mania* every month or so, it would probably be to the detriment of their slow-maturing infants.[15]

The general consensus in the academic community, then, is that estrus disappeared among human females because it was useful for developing a monogamous family life, the usual teleological fallacy.

In fact, Jane Goodall, in a burst of human self-congratulation, compassionates her chimpanzee friends: "It is obviously fruitless to speculate as to the sorts of heterosexual relationships that might develop if chimpanzee physiology were different: if, for example, *Flo had been able to offer Rodolf continuing sexual satisfaction,* if the female reproductive cycle of the chimp were the same as the human cycle."[16]

On the other hand, the aforementioned claim by Mary Jane Sherfey, a practicing psychoanalyst, not a prehistorian or an ethologist, that estrus—"the ungovernable sexual drive of women"—never did disappear was advanced to justify the *status quo ante.* "The forcible suppression of women's inordinate sexual demands was a prerequisite to the dawn of every modern civilization and almost every living culture. Primitive woman's sexual drive was too strong, too susceptible to the fluctuating extremes of an impelling aggressive erotism to withstand the disciplined demands of a settled family life." Sherfey's work was presented first to her Freudian colleagues, just as the women ethologists had to be accredited by their male superiors in the academic hierarchy. So female sexual desire—"the intense insatiable erotism in women," she terms it—calls down upon itself the fiercest of reprisals; once again the victim is blamed for the crime.[17]

Having been forced to acknowledge the existence of active female sexuality some millennia after the artists, the scientific mind still finds it a threatening concept. Therefore, periodic active sexual desire, in animals, is countered by a formulation which declares that human females have permanent sexual receptivity—passive—else we could not have had, first, humanity and, second, civilization. While most historic civilizations have involved forcible sexual repression of the female, this is not necessarily the case in nonliterate cultures. We have paid a high price for female sexual repression: the thinking which says because it happened that way, that was the way it had to happen, ignores the lesson of science. There are and there can be myriad forms in nature and myriad solutions to given situations: one can get to Mars by a planet collision as well as with a space ship, though neither event may happen in our lifetime.

My own thinking on the disappearance of estrus and birth seasons involves looking not at why it happened but at how it happened. To look for a cause and tell us that estrus disappeared because it would interfere with the human family is circular reasoning which tells us nothing. It sees the human family—an extremely varied and far from immutable phenomenon—as a given and sees it usually in the current nuclear form, despite the many contradictions from ethnography and history.

The problem is that most of the discussants talk about sex and reproduction as discrete entities, as though the higher centers of the brain were not involved. The physiology of the present-day human brain—described as the most intricate piece of matter in the known universe—has still not been thoroughly studied and is most imperfectly understood. The workings of imagination, cognition, creativity, as well as the involvement of the brain in sex, are mysterious but not unconnected. The deeper nerve centers, where emotion is commonly located, are also involved in every action, be it intellectual or physical. "There is no behavior without emotion," was the way Piaget put it. Emotions drive our intellect. The mind controls the body; the emotions control the mind; sometimes the emotions bypass the mind.

Common sense, art, and certain deductions from the effects of lobotomy and from the functioning of brain-damaged people tell us that the creative and imaginative faculties are linked with sexual energies; they are the wellspring. Creative artists often comment on the similarity between the sex act at its best and the creative act—the passion, the sweating, the sense of being outside oneself, of communion with the universe, the exhaustion and, usually, pleasant draining that ensue. Both involve a successful mingling of conscious and unconscious control not often or easily achieved, though sex can be and usually is practiced on partial and rudimentary levels that come nowhere near its larger possibilities. The reconciliations of tenderness and force, thought and spontaneity, the infinite variations and balances possible in human sex are, of course, nonexistent among animals.

Much has been learned about the brain and the body in the last two decades. Molecular biology has discovered the secret of life, but human consciousness is almost as much of a mystery as ever. We have no equations to explain imagination. There are hints of how the process takes place: evidence of electric activity along with indications that it is the deeper emotion centers which set the level of activity involved in memory fixation. According to C. U. M. Smith, a constant rearrangement, reordering, and turning around of the representations of the perceptual world seem to occur.[18] But the brain works as a whole, which is why damage to any one part affects the personality, a gestalt of all the individual parts and functionings that constitute a human essence.

One cannot localize areas of the brain by experimental means, as has been attempted, and say this area controls speech, this area controls vision, this area controls sexuality. Motivation, drive, is said to be located in the hypothalamus, with the emotions; memory is placed in the amygdala; but it is not known whether these are ultimate locations or only way stations on the road to the cerebrum. Cerebration, logic, is by definition a function of the higher centers, the cerebrum, yet this ascription was made before biophysicists and biochemists began their examinations of molecular psychobiology, the latest approach to brain physiology. The ascription is not wrong; it is incomplete. The large cortex of the human cerebrum, with its many uncommitted areas, is seen not only as the differentiation between humans and all other animals but also as a source, roughly, of our human thinking, reasoning, feeling, conscious powers. An intricate network of associative connections throughout the brain is activated whenever we exercise these powers. There is far more evidence that the "buck" stops in the cerebral cortex than that it starts in the hypothalamus.[19]

Sex takes place in the head. Negative evidence from the use, or perhaps one should say the misuse, of lobotomy confirms that the brain works as a whole, as well as that there is a relationship between sexual energies and creativity. The excision of the frontal lobes, by cutting connections with the thalamus, is a butchery technique which invariably results in personality deterioration. Any psychosurgery—of necessity a relatively blind amputation—mutilates the brain and destroys or injures personality.[20] Lobotomized patients can perform routine work, but, lacking neural connection with the centers for creativity and imagination, they cannot perform executive or inventive work. Lobotomy has been more frequently performed on female than on male patients: in Canada it was recommended as a technique enabling hospitalized housewives to return home and fulfill their household tasks; partial lobotomy has also been used to "cure" female patients diagnosed as suffering from "nymphomania"—uncontrollable eroticism as the doctors called it. It was recently used on youths to subvert homosexuality. The basic effect of lobotomy is to eliminate or cut down on fantasy and imagination, thereby damping down sexual expression.[21]

The hypothalamus was usually given as the controlling factor in sexual behavior when discussion was not limited to androgen and estrogen. Sometimes we were told that estrogen or androgen, released, operates on the neural pathways to the hypothalamus. But recent studies by John Money and Anke Ehrhardt indicate that cultural and social training are far more influential than hormone action in shaping the sexual orientation and behavior of boys and girls after birth. Interpreted, this means that the higher centers of the brain are the ultimate factors in sexual, as in other conscious, and self-conscious, human behavior. Emotional elements, from the deeper centers, are also called into play, while the endocrines are probably the most malleable elements—in contradistinction to animals. In this connection, common scientific parlance, which equates feminine, passive, and neuter, is responsible for much confusion. For example, patients are given cortisone to counteract masculine behavior and secondary sex characteristics ascribed to androgen. This is called feminizing them, though what is actually accomplished is neuterizing, since cortisone has a negative effect on sexual expression of any kind, male or female.

In modern Western society, a sexually incomplete person of either sex is directed toward femaleness, since the long tradition of equating femininity with passiveness makes it more socially acceptable to be a partial female human being. A tragic example was the instance of a male baby accidentally injured and castrated as the result of a circumcision operation. According to the *New York Times*,[22] specialists advised changing the baby's sex to female. While operations can be performed to approximate a vagina, neither clitoral nerves, ovaries, nor uterus can be inserted in this unfortunate individual, whose sexuality has been irreparably damaged and who will never be able to produce a child.

In early hominid society there were no sophisticated medical techniques to implement such artificial "advanced concepts." Fortunately for us, the ecology of survival demanded that all its members be actively and integrally related to nature. And survive and thrive it did, or we would not be here to project ourselves backward attempting to describe it.

The role of sex as a source of energy and creative imagination has been given much more weight by artists, theologians, and psychoanalysts than by the scientific community. Sex is, after all, not only the source of love poetry but an indirect force in all religion and art. The meshing of sexual drive with emotion and with the higher centers, in all its complexity and pervasiveness, may be little understood but it is not in doubt. Whether the sexual energy is tapped by sublimation, as Freud felt, or by direct involvement, on the model of Wilhelm Reich, is far from clear. I would guess that they are both right in part; that it can work either way and both ways. According to Reich, the relation between sexual gratification and sublimation is not mechanical, i.e., the more suppression of sex, the more achievement in other areas; it is functional. Sexual energy can be sublimated to some degree, but if the diversion goes too far, sublimation changes into the opposite, an interference with the capacity to work.

Hormone information has been much misused. Laboratory researchers report that testosterone injected in female mice will make them mount and otherwise display male behavior, yet there are women who cannot enjoy sex unless they are on top of the male instead of in the more usual supine position. Surely this is not testosterone but cultural consciousness, an association of the inferiority assigned to women in our culture along with the internalization of male values. Being on top is identified with the whole hierarchical structure which assigns superiority to the superior position. It is therefore a refusal to be trapped or victimized by social values, rather than a physiological response. In the same wise one could cite women of the past who rejected sex because of the inferiority assigned to the woman's role in our culture. Virginia Woolf and Harriet Taylor Mill, wife of John Stuart Mill, both seem to have suffered from sexual inhibition not as a lack of hormone secretion but from an abundance of mental ability which made them reject the patriarchal tradition, where sexuality is defined in terms of submission-domination, with femininity and submission used interchangeably. In such a society, free sexual expression with the person you love might well be a threat to an intelligent woman. As long as sex is defined as man possessing woman,

woman will be threatened, though the actualities of the situation would seem to be the opposite: man enters woman and woman possesses man, at least that part of his body which is inside her. Perhaps the emphasis on male possession of females stems from the male fear of being twice possessed by woman—once inside her womb and a second time, partially, inside her vagina. Since he is the more vulnerable one, it is he who has felt the necessity to assert and enforce the opposite: that she is weak, vulnerable, and possessed by him.

We apprehend our senses through our brain. Therefore, the growth of the brain gave us a more acute awareness of sensation, and the consequent feedback encouraged the development of sensual areas. We cannot know what *Homo habilis* and *Homo erectus* looked like—whether they had all-over hair or how their fleshy features were shaped. Desmond Morris has described humans as "the sexy ape," citing the male's large penis, the female's enlarged breasts, the increased tactility of human skin, our many erogenous zones, and the year-round potential for sexual intercourse, none of which can be deduced from fossil evidence.[23] These human features cannot be unrelated to the growth of the brain, i.e. the degree of conscious control over sexuality and the greater range of bodily and mental possibility for elaboration, as against the capabilities of animals. In addition there is the continuance of sexual drive after reproductive powers wane, not only in the female after menopause, but also in the male despite a falling off of sperm production. We can look at this human sexuality not in terms of its function for the human family, since the extremely varied human family has as often required sexual inhibition as it has sexual expression, but as a result of brain enlargement and complication. It is human range which distinguishes us from animals, the multiplying of input factors which go to make up our behavior, the enormous enlargement of possibilities and possible combinations.

All of this rich sexuality with its embroidery and complications is adaptive not so much in the sense of its limited, defined-after-the-fact practical usefulness as in the added possibilities it gave us as humans. The richness and ornamentation of life are made possible by the human brain with its power of naming and visualizing, the mysterious imagination. What I take to be the magic mingling of body and mind, sexual and emotional drive with the capacity for memory and combining that begin to add up to creativity bring pleasure and enjoyment, which certainly need no excuse in nature. The orchid's beauty may, to some extent, be a functional adaptation, but the human's is a development of self-awareness. The orchid's beauty exists in the human's eye, but the orchid does not know whether it is beautiful or ugly nor does the chimpanzee—though the latter may just begin to have glimmers of aesthetic appreciation for a bright color or an interesting object. As long as aesthetic quality doesn't interfere with survival, it will endure, and to the extent to which it facilitates survival by adding pleasure, it will be encouraged to increase.

The increase and refinement of sexuality is an increase in humanity; it accompanies and cannot be dissociated from all our other human qualities, nor from human culture. Humanity's self-awareness added a premium to brain and consciousness and sexual elaboration. The more they are enjoyed, the more they are facilitated and encouraged by the feedback relationship which is a tenet of Darwinian natural selection. Thus we may owe culture to the fact, also, that we have more sexual energy and more diffusion of sexual energy into other pursuits. This is a more positive view than the negative Freudian claim that repression and sublimation were necessary for humanity; not so much repression as diversion and diversity were the human qualities.

The loss of estrus is vaguely recognized by both ethologists and physical anthropologists as a crucial marker on the road to humanity. It is significant particularly to those attached to the idea of the "pair-bond" and to the notion of a male-female-child grouping as an inherent characteristic of humanity. They see it as useful for maintaining the nuclear family, for attaching a father to the basic mother-child pattern of the primate world. So, in their descriptions, all too often, the loss of estrus seems to be tantamount to a loss of active sexuality in the female, making possible her "permanent receptivity" to one male, as opposed to the promiscuity of, say, the female chimpanzee "swinger."

The rare primates whose groups consist of male-female-infant are often described as undersexed.[24] The teleological explanation of the loss of estrus in human females would make her undersexed also. We know that this is far from the case, despite valiant efforts throughout patriarchal history to impose or support this concept. To me the loss of estrus relates to the human development of consciousness and conscious control of and participation in the basic acts of life, reproduction being the primary one, with nourishment and survival to reproductive age as corollaries. We lost estrus because we were human, as a concomitant of humanity: we didn't become human by losing estrus.

The more brain the more sex; primates have more than other animals, and humans have more than primates. And because human sex is so much more than mere brief copulation, there is an enlarged component of sex in other behaviors. Sex is vitalizing and pervasive. Thus the loss of estrus was not a loss but a gain.

For a clue as to how it might have happened, a sentence in Jane Goodall's article on chimpanzee communication stirs the imagination: "In the field I once observed a slight swelling in the sex skin of an anoestrous female in response to prolonged inspection by a male."[25] What we have here is a phenomenon related to human responsiveness, a personal relation rather than a glandular one. This is the process that would have been taking place in our own evolution. The popularized version of science says the brain enlarged in order to facilitate culture. I say as it enlarged it was more efficient, but also just more in every sense.

Hominid females lost estrus because people—even hominid people—liked making choices. And there was, as I have said, no visual estral signal among hominid females once they stood upright. There may never have been a visual signal, as there is not among certain monkeys. In the same way, we do not know human canine teeth were reduced, either because weapons were used or because hominids ate seeds some fourteen million years ago: maybe there never were large canines among our lemur ancestors. Judging by the wide range of human behaviors to be found today, and judging also by the individuality displayed among such animals as the chimpanzee, among early hominids sexual behavior would already have been quite varied. It is likely, however, that sex and affection need not yet have been related, as they are not in many human cultures—from classical Greece to Victorian England to the Mae Enga of New Guinea.

In the upright position there was no possibility of a visual genital indication of estrus in the female, though the male's erection was more visible than that of his chimpanzee or gorilla cousin's. To the extent to which verbal relating was unestablished, it would have been the female who selected the male for mating, rather than vice versa, as is conventionally felt to happen among humans. The enlarging brain was the human specialization. Since sex in humans is regulated by the brain more than by the glands, there was no pressure to develop a specialization like the female chimpanzee's unwieldly genital swelling. The invisibility of the female organ might have contributed to the loss of estrus, the visibility of the male's erection to human male vulnerability and the imposition of forcible male dominance in later human history.

Choice was another human specialization resulting from the enlarging human brain. Males and females who have been deprived of sexual outlet for a considerable length of time may be excited by any member of the opposite sex of reasonable appearance by culturally imposed standards of aesthetics. Normally, however, the sexual approach is selective, rather than generalized as in the case of apes and monkeys. What motivates the choice is enormously variable and at times quite mysterious, recognized in such popular phrases as "love at first sight," "a chemical attraction," etc.

If we think of the female hominid approaching the male, we can see the periods of sexual license which have existed in many human cultures as atavistic relics of prehuman society. Dionysian festivals of Greece, medieval weddings in Germany and Sweden, the *katayausa* of the Trobriand Islanders described by Malinowski, various celebrations among the Australian Aborigines and the Ojibwa permitted and encouraged public mating with the woman making the advances, or general promiscuity. And if we think of *habilis* and *erectus* as being on

the way to human status, though with few of the material possessive complexities of our own times, we might envision a
rather more amiable choice and coming together, by mutual
agreement, of male and female—with more coming together,
relatively less choice.

However, the idea that a male would have much voice in
choosing a female or would have maintained any kind of individual long-term control over her or her offspring is a modern
invention; there would have been no place for such a phenomenon in the lives of early hominids.[26]

Sexuality among human males and females is not seasonal
but it is also far from constant. In the female both pregnancy
and nursing probably interfere, psychologically and physically.
But males, too, have other interests, and their cyclicity is on a
much smaller time scale—in terms of hours, days, weeks. Constant sexual expression is not possible for them either, as many
a frustrated woman has been forced to accept under monogamous conditions. The myth of the ever-ready human male is a
cultural stereotype which oppresses the male no less than the
female.

Much is often made of the fact that humans are supposedly
the only animals to copulate face to face and its relation to the
upright position and to the forward placing of female and male
sexual organs. Many scientists think in terms of the missionary
position. Actually, human postures in coitus are extremely
varied, *vide* the *Kama Sutra*, Greek vase paintings, and other
artistic and ethnographic sources.

But standing up did make us more vulnerable, in intercourse as in other pursuits. Some primates perform their sexual acts in the middle of the group, often with youngsters running up to peer curiously, to touch or otherwise harass the
linked couple. For us sex implies surrender, hence the usual
desire for some privacy. Human positions, whether seated face
to face, as among the Trobriand Islanders, lying flat or on one's
side, kneeling on all fours, face to face or face to back, to mention only a few possibilities, all involve coming together in an
unordinary posture. Sex on the fly is not feasible; standing positions are not comfortable or easily achieved. Female animals on
all fours can escape more readily, though the male might have

somewhat more difficulty in disengaging himself. In this respect we are more like the ponderous and shy gorillas, who were thought to avoid being seen in intercourse by the ethologists. In zoos, gorillas have been observed copulating face to face.

Actually, the whole growth of humanity makes it impossible to separate normal copulation from other aspects of consciousness. As the human brain enlarged, so were sexual acts beginning to be elaborated. We can only speculate on the degree to which the plasticity of human behavior, in sex as in social organization, would have been in effect some millions of years ago. In our present state of evolution, the brain is so adaptable that societies can train both women and men to the most contradictory and seemingly unnatural sexualities, passive or active, abstaining or indulging. *Habilis* and *erectus* would have been rather closer to the animals than the angels.

Clifford Jolly and Ralph Holloway, along with Wolfgang Wickler and Desmond Morris, talk of the growth of human female breasts as a sexual signal to males, since the upright posture precluded visual genitals in the female. It is hard to believe that *habilis* and *erectus* males were so dim-sighted they couldn't tell the difference between the male and female pubic area. Moreover, the breast is not an erotic stimulus save in certain cultures. Among the Mangaians, Donald Marshall reports their surprise at Western male fixation on the breast, for "they consider this organ of interest only to the hungry baby."[27] Different societies have found the female ankle, collarbone, buttocks, hair, hips, eyelashes, whatever, sexually arousing. We have fewer reports on what it is that stimulates the human female's sexual desire. The fact that the human male's penis is both larger and better equipped sensually than the organ of any other primate is related to the increased capacity for pleasure made possible by the human brain. The relative hairlessness of humans makes our entire bodies into erogenous zones. And the development of the human female's breast, in all its variety—small and round as among the Balinese, or long and pointed as described in the *Arabian Nights*—is a part of the growth of maternal sexuality, along with the growth of other forms of sexuality which accompanied the enlarging human brain.

The search for purpose in these features is misleading, while the claim that females became more sexually interesting and interested—Holloway says that there was "an increase in epigamic features of such secondary sexual characteristics as permanent breasts, fat distribution and other possible changes toward facilitating more permanent sexual receptivity of the female"[28]—so as to facilitate male-female bonding is a ridiculous and false analogy. Humans don't bond, they relate, and not necessarily permanently or predictably. There are societies like the Nayar in India where there is no way of telling who is the father of the child, for individual women are, in effect, married to a group of men; there are societies where women live with their children in separate houses while men live together in a men's house. Many versions of the extended family in which children are communally raised exist. Sometimes all women of a certain relationship are called "mother," all men "father," though the child usually knows who is its real mother, if not necessarily its father.

For early hominids there were other complications and dangers, besides sexual vulnerability, as a result of our newly assumed upright position. It's hard to hold a brief for the efficiency of natural selection when we look at our bodies, and women may have even more reason to cavil at those who have misinterpreted the theory so as to project purpose outward. Human childbirth is a good example of the looseness with which natural selection functions. When we stood upright, the position, shape, and size of the pelvic girdle changed so as to facilitate balance and walking on two legs. In the process childbirth became more difficult, since at the same time the bony skull was enlarging and the period of gestation increasing. Neoteny, the process by which human children are born undeveloped—though not as undeveloped as, say, the kangaroo infant which continues to develop within its mother's pouch—was one result, with a consequent longer period of infant dependency. In humans, the process became circular, demanding more responsibility and interaction from mothers and more cooperation from the group, as a result of which further brain enlargement occurred.

13

The Brain Is the Human Adaptation

Struggling with the origin of consciousness, which is what I would take as the index of humanity, one notes that the growth of the human brain brought us discomforting polarities. If human nature is social in its simian origins, human consciousness is solitary. I am I, alone, separate—and the realization must have been frightening, indeed, still is, often enough. This is the cosmic loneliness which propelled humanity to project purpose outward: the conviction that there is a divinity which shapes our ends seems to embody a universal human yearning, and it is hard to shake, hence the tendency to project purpose onto nature and natural phenomena, leading to the widespread teleological fallacies.

Neither natural selection nor even the catch-all "cultural evolution" explains the poems of Sappho or Shakespeare, the novels of Tolstoy or Emily Brontë. What utilitarian function is served by lovemaking, Lucullan feasts, or so many other delightful components of human life and society? Necessity may be the mother of invention, but she can hardly be credited with art, ornaments, and most of the pleasures to which the poet invited us.

Asking the question of how the human brain evolved, Noam

Chomsky suggests that natural selection is the answer only if we realize it is no answer: "The processes by which the human mind achieved its present state of complexity and its particular form of innate organization are a total mystery. . . . It is perfectly safe to attribute this development to 'natural selection,' so long as we realize that there is no substance to this assertion, that it amounts to nothing more than a belief that there is some naturalistic explanation for these phenomena."[1] Chomsky seeks some understanding of the human mind through the study of language. He says of this uniquely human phenomenon that it is wrong to think of it solely as informative. Human language can be used to inform or to misinform, to clarify one's own thinking or to display one's cleverness, or just for fun in play. This concept seems to me to be applicable in a larger sense to humanity itself. We are both purposive and purposeless.

To the extent to which natural selection does exist, it is looser and allows for more inefficiency than was envisioned by Darwin. Genetics did not exist as a science when he was writing, and the experiments of Mendel were unknown to him, so he hypothesized about inheritance without knowing the details. Mendel's work substantiated some of Darwin's hypotheses, but it made others, like sexual selection, less tenable. Genes are not inherited along sexual lines; a male offspring receives genes from both mother and father, though some genes, like the one for hemophilia, are sex-linked, i.e., carried by the mother and transmitted to the son. Intelligence is not one of these, though theorists as diverse as Darwin, Freud, and Erich Neumann have often written on the assumption that it is.

We saw how untenable are the theses of man the toolmaker and man the hunter as explanations for the growth and development of humanity, and why women and men would have had similar manual dexterity and intelligence. Both used their heads and hands, and they collaborated and worked together, though men may have been able to do the more showy things when women took care of the necessities.

About the possibilities for malignity, motivated and motiveless, which began with humanity, and that linking of aggression and sexuality which is a human expression, not an animal one, and, in my view, a recent one, we must hypothesize and dig for connections. We can only speculate on the sexuality of early hominids and humans, through *erectus*, and on the development of conscious control over sexuality which led to the disappearance of estrus and to human groupings, in whatever forms they took in the long beginning of our species' existence. In Chapter 12, however, we saw that it was the enlarging human brain which brought about the loss of estrus, or rather the gain of increasing responsiveness, both emotional and physical, in female and male.

From the sparse evidence, we cannot know when societal controls on sexual encounters began, though conscious control and elaboration of sexual encounters and family and friendly relations are incipient in the incipient human brain.

There is considerable debate about the degree of humanity possessed by early hominids. Many physical anthropologists see them as closer to animals like the gorillas and the chimpanzees than to any humans living today or in the recent past. The difficulties of postulating theories about human origins on the actual brain organization of our presumed fossil ancestors, with only a few limestone impregnated skulls—most of them bashed, shattered, and otherwise altered by the passage of millions of years—as evidence, would seem to be astronomical. It is, however, a characteristic of the present-day human brain that it is not only undaunted but actually provoked and stimulated by intellectual and objective problems.

There is one branch of physical anthropology called paleoneurology which is attempting to do just that—to add to our knowledge of human evolution by studying casts of fossil skulls of *Australopithecus*, *Homo habilis*, and *Homo erectus*. The paleoneurologist Ralph Holloway quarrels with earlier interpretations of human development as stemming from hunting and looks to the skulls for evidence of brain power shaping behavior, rather than vice versa. He also disagrees with other physical anthropologists about the subhuman characteristics of the earliest hominids.

He argues that the early hominid skulls—*Australopithecus*,

habilis, and the presumed *erectus* skull E.R. 1470 pieced together by Meave Leakey—differ from chimpanzee and gorilla skulls not only because they have more space for brains (the usual measurement is in terms of cubic contents: the habiline brain is described as averaging 600 cc. as compared to the 400 cc. average for chimpanzee brains) but also because they have another shape. He reminds us that actual brain size has long been recognized as a very crude index of intelligence and cognition: Anatole France's brain at 1,000 cc. is said to be one of the smallest human brains on record (smaller than the brains of one-million-year-old *erectus* skulls estimated at 1,200 cc.), despite his indubitable intellectual achievements. Holloway gives an example of two Bantu brothers suffering from pathologically small brains (microcephaly), with brain measurements roughly the size of most australopithecine skull capacities, about 500 cc., who yet learned to talk and perform most other human acts.

Holloway feels that the position of the parietal and temporal lobes on the skulls he analyzed, from cleft marks showing that the cerebrum was above the cerebellum rather than behind it as in apes, is evidence of an enlarged cerebral cortex in habiline and erectine skulls. He would allow them more cerebration, i.e., more facility for communication and problem-solving ability, than other physical anthropologists admit. He also feels that Broca's area, the place in the frontal lobe most sharply associated with speech though not necessarily the only one nor even the source of origin for our language capacities, is farther forward, making language possible, if not proven, several million years ago. For Holloway the specifically human brain organization was already in force, and he agreed early on with the Leakey classification of *habilis* as a human not an ape, as presently with the newer Richard Leakey claim that *erectus* existed in Kenya as far back as 2.6 million years ago and was the precursor of modern humans.[2]

In 1969 Holloway had already claimed evidence for the humanity of australopithecine and habiline brain cases, distinguishing a capacity for speech not only in their shape and spaciousness but because their possessors had produced tools to pattern. In a lump of stone they could imagine the finished implement, he said, enabling them to create stone tools, a process which required more conceptual ability than merely trimming the leaves off a stick, as chimpanzees do. On this basis he concluded that they had the beginnings of human imagination and conceptualization.[3]

Analyses of later *erectus* skulls convinced him that human language and human cognition were already operant during the million or more years when bands of *erectus* roamed through Africa and into Asia and Europe.[4] Other students of the period disagree with him, though all acknowledge that the beginnings of speech and thought must have existed.[5]

At the present time the scientific community acknowledges only that the chief distinction between humanity and other animals is food sharing, a social co-operative process believed to have begun some four or five million years ago. The straightline simplistic thinking of the human brain shaped and enlarged by the syndromes of hunting is all too prevalent. Popularizers still write about "the hunting hypothesis."[6] In 1972 John Pfeiffer insisted that "the increasing emphasis on big game which started perhaps 2 million years before had an enormous effect on *man*, nearly doubling the size of *his* brain and transforming an advanced form of Australopithecus into Homo erectus."[7]

Despite recent research to the contrary academics also find it difficult to surrender their cherished notions about the formative role of hunting in evolution. In 1967, Sherwood Washburn stated flatly that "our intellect, interests, emotions, and basic social life—all are evolutionary products of the hunting adaptation." A decade later his foreword to a group of studies of the gathering-hunting Kalahari San still emphasized the "fundamental role which hunting has played in human history," though he was a little less positive that the entire story could be told within its context—"*it may well be* that it was the complex of hunting-weapons-bipedalism which accounts for the evolutionary origin of *man*." His conclusion is a perfect example of the way in which the switch from the gendered to the generic meaning of the word *man* allows for ambiguity and loose thinking: "Hunting was a major factor in the adaptation of *man*. If we are to understand the origin of *man*, we must understand *man* the hunter and woman the gatherer."[8]

After all, lions, hyenas, wolves, all have hunted big game, and their brains haven't doubled in the last few million years, and omnivores galore exist—bears, boar, beaver, to name only a few—nor do their brains change considerably in the fossil record. If hunting really were (a) a male thing and (b) the one syndrome which was responsible for the evolution of hominids into humans, how is it that women are so close to men physically and intellectually, in manipulativeness and ingenuity? Why was there no specialization and how did woman, too, inherit the presumed male qualities attributed to big-game hunting?

The truth is that whatever hominids did—collected seeds, made pets, skinned animals, told stories, sang songs—as long as they did it on a human level, it would have doubled their brains. Cognition, human consciousness, is what makes the difference between us and other animals, a difference not limited to one sex. There is great variation in the size of human brains but very little known difference in the internal structure of a female or male brain.[9] And as we saw, size itself is a vague and inconclusive measure. It is the human brain organization which is significant, that famous imagination about which science knows so little and the artist so much. The enlarging brain was the human adaptation. Everything else followed.

Part III

———————————————————

SAPIENT AT LAST

Hark, Nature, hear, dear goddess hear!
—Shakespeare, *King Lear*

14

Human Like Us

The earliest member of our own species was found at Swanscombe, England, and dated to a period some two hundred thousand years ago when the climate there was semitropical.[1] Another skull of roughly the same age was excavated in Steinheim, Germany. The tools found near Swanscombe remains do not differ greatly from the handaxes and flakes found in Africa and Southern Europe with *erectus* fossils or fragments. But the skull conformations of Steinheim and Swanscombe people bear more resemblance to ourselves than they do to the well-known species today nominated *Homo sapiens neanderthalensis*, which is supposed to have lived in Western Europe from about 75,000 to 35,000 B.P. It is this last who gave rise to the folklore of Neanderthal man, the stooped and brutal caveman dragging his wife and brandishing a club, who used to inhabit comic strips and cartoons. The first Neanderthal specimen was discovered near the river Neander in Germany in 1856, before Darwin's theory of evolution had been published.

However, it was the discovery of an almost complete skeleton at La Chapelle-aux-Saints in 1908 which gave us the legend of the lumbering individual who could not stand upright, though endowed with a brain larger than most of ours today. (Remember, however, that it is not brain size but brain organization which is the determining factor in human consciousness and cognition.) To some extent, brain organization can be deduced from the conformation of the skull. In the case of Swanscombe person, the hominid who lived some hundred and fifty thousand years before *neanderthalensis*, it was possible to trace the pattern of the artery which supplies blood to the meninges —the membrane embracing the brain—by the impression left on the inside of the skull bones. The meningeal artery's form was, according to Björn Kurtén, "very advanced in comparison with that of homo erectus . . . its complexity reflects that of the brain. The pattern seen in Swanscombe *man* is of a type encountered even in some modern *men*."[2]

After considerable puzzling over the contradictory fact that fossil hip and leg bones of African finds indicated an upright posture some millions of years earlier, new investigations of the specimen from La Chapelle-aux-Saints were undertaken. In 1957 the skeleton was examined by two doctors, William L. Straus of Johns Hopkins University School of Medicine and Alex Cave of St. Bartholomew's Hospital Medical College in London. According to them, the skeleton was that of a man between forty and fifty, which at that time would have made him an old man, and he had been afflicted with severe, deforming arthritis of the jaws, spine, and, possibly, lower limbs, hence his physical peculiarities, differentiating him from his fellows and from earlier specimens.[3] So do legends and myths become promulgated as science, until a newer and more accurate version of the explanatory tale comes along to supersede the earlier one, a story which may come a little closer to the realities of the past we humans seek to comprehend.

The evidence about Neanderthals' thinking processes comes to us out of their burial practices, as well as the more sophisticated tools they left behind. While we know nothing of their family groupings, we infer a concept of humanity from the fact that their dead were reposed, sometimes folded into what is still referred to by present-day ethnographers as the "death position," legs drawn up, even bound to the trunk, in shallow graves or natural depressions with stones on or around them. The bodies were not actually buried, in the sense of interment; they were placed. "Earth to earth" and "dust to dust" are much later concepts, stemming from misconceptions and mis-

analogies which arose during the Neolithic, after the appearance of agriculture and animal breeding. Different types of
graves from this period have been found in France, Italy, South
Germany, Eastern Europe, North Africa, and Southwest Asia.

As might be expected in dealing with a period covering tens
of thousands of years and distances to be measured in the thousands of miles, the graves, the groups, and the appurtenances
vary. But the fact is that they exist: in Krapina, Yugoslavia, a
find of ten bodies that had been broken open and in some cases
burned, like the remains of animals eaten for food, suggested
the practice of cannibalism so that much is made of our peo-
ple-eating ancestors.[4] Given the hardships under which they
lived during the Ice Age, it may well be that some crisis came
along and cannibalism was a last resort. At Monte Circeo in
Italy, a Neanderthal skull surrounded by a circle of stones was
found within a cave; the way in which it had been broken open
has led some paleohistorians to perceive a resemblance to ritual
cannibalism practiced by South Sea Islanders in recent times.

Death as a long sleep is suggested by the finding of what
might have been a flint pillow under a youth buried at Le
Moustier, while the placing of a flint hand ax or other personal
possession near a dead body has been interpreted as evidence of
a belief in immortality, with the object ready for use when its
owner was reborn or arrived in a spirit land.

In other places, a body with animal skulls, horns up, ranged
around it, a burial of an individual clasping the bones of a boar;
and pieces of ocher and supplies found in and around the
graves pique the imagination, tantalizing it with questions
that may never be answered.

Joseph Campbell, who is Jungian in his orientation, feels
that the flexed position of some of the bodies from this period
represents the fetal position and a desire to return to the
womb. One asks oneself whether these people would have
known what the fetal position was, since it is only in rare instances that an infant keeps its legs drawn up, or more often
one leg, for even a brief period after birth. Moreover, graves
containing several bodies occur, as at Le Moustier, where one
person will be extended, another folded up. Grahame Clark,

who makes much of the mystique of hunting and male killing, suggests that the burial of a woman at La Férrassie with her arms folded and her legs "so tightly flexed as to suggest that the corpse may have been bound with thongs . . . may reflect a desire on the part of the living to keep the dead securely away."[5] A more literal-minded reporter says that the reason primitive people often bury their dead with legs folded up is because the more compact shape requires less digging.

In the beginning was the word, says the Bible, just as the Egyptian Ptah created Shu and Tefnut by pronouncing them. Words are symbols; they are also magic. Through words we can create equivalences for mysterious or little understood processes, substitute art for reality, and counter the physical limitations of the natural world. Actually, for most of us and in many very early creation myths, in the beginning was the mother.

> Pukwi made the country the first time. The sea was all fresh water. She made the land, sea and islands. She came out of the sky in daytime. She was as big as Karslake Island. Like an alligator she was and she was black. . . . Puriti said, "Don't kill our mother." But Iriti went ahead and killed her. He struck her on the head. Her urine made the sea salty and her spirit went into the sky.
>
> Now she travels by day from east to west and back along the Milky Way at night. At midday she makes camp and builds a big fire and causes great heat.[6]

So runs a Tiwi creation myth told to Jane Goodale by a nine-year-old.

Everywhere that ethnologists and historians probe, the myth of the Great Mother precedes the later tales of God the Father. Scholars have come up with much evidence of a female creation image prior to the almost universal male creator of historical times. Their investigations are supported by ethnographic research: Turnbull found the myth of a female generator ousted by a male god among the Mbuti Pygmies; Lucas

Bridges in Patagonia heard versions recounted by the Onas and the Yahgans; examples can be cited from classical sources, as in ancient Persia, to the above-told Australian folktale.

There is nothing in the evidence to tell about Neanderthal birth or Neanderthal woman's physiology. We cannot even prove that Neanderthals had language, though most paleontologists believe they did, placing speech as far back as *erectus*. Holloway, as noted in Part II, would assign language even to extinct branches of our genus like *Australopithecus*. One die-hard anatomist at Yale still holds out for the beginnings of language with the later *Homo sapiens sapiens*, on the basis of the presumed shape of Neanderthal's vocal cords, and a few other physical anthropologists are loath to grant speech to our Neanderthal ancestors.[7]

Whether they spoke or not, and I am inclined to believe they did, the awareness of death in European cave burials some fifty thousand years ago is the first concrete evidence we have of human consciousness as opposed to animal responses. We are all frail and anxious creatures at the mercy of forces over which we have little or no control, and death is the supreme demonstration of this fact. Humans are aware of their helplessness, and the instantaneous emotions of animals are reinforced in us, supported, increased, or dispelled by our reasoning powers. Magic, religion, and science have all developed to allay our fears, to explain phenomena which the insignificant individual cannot understand or change. Magic was the first of these, and for early humans, perhaps long into our history, magic, religion, and science were synonymous.* Hence the rituals and ceremony around that most traumatic of experiences, the loss through death of loved ones, and the development of myths to alleviate the pain experienced by the living, to appease the fear of death, or to keep the dead from taking us with them.

Women, however, had an inherent magic quality: from time to time they gave birth, and there must have been something both mysterious and normal about this capacity. Birth and death have always been associated in the human mind: "A time to be born and a time to die," "Man is born and man

---

* "I still believe they're one," said the noted architect Louis Kahn in 1972.[8]

must die," "The moment we are born we start to die." Birth is the primal metaphor, and death its first polarity; together they are the original thesis and antithesis of human thought.

In Part I we saw that the mother-child relationship is the one universal throughout the order of Primates. The mother is the whole world for the infant, and for the human child, as awareness shapes, it is primarily the mother who gives or denies food, attention, love, protection. Father and surrogate parents all come later, artificially, socially, humanly. Goodall tells of the traumatic, often fatal, effects on the infant chimpanzee in the case of its mother's death, even though an older sister may attempt, usually ineffectually, to replace or substitute missing maternal care.[9]

It is another index to the flexibility and advance over the animal condition that humanity has devised so many assists and alternatives to the original dyadic relationship of mother and child. Still, the archetype of the Great Mother, with her polarized capacity for good and evil, for birth and destruction, remains. A host of folk sayings bear witness to her primacy: "You only have one mother." "Fathers can be many, but mother is only one." If we need her so much, what will happen if she chooses not to fulfill our needs? And in our childish vision of her great powers, it is only choice that keeps her from aiding or assuaging us, never necessity or incapacity.

Females can identify with the mother and expect to achieve her power; males have had to reach outward and compensate for their inability to bear children. Womb envy precedes penis envy—which last has been well discussed by Shulamith Firestone as a symptom and symbol of an already existing power relationship.[10]

The Neanderthals, thirty-five to seventy-five thousand years ago, could not have been aware of the sequence of coitus, fertilization, pregnancy, and childbirth. We know from the work of ethnographers in Oceania and Australia that the knowledge of biological fatherhood is a recent arrival on the human scene, for the original settlers of Australia some twenty to twenty-five, possibly even forty, thousand years ago were unaware of the male role in procreation and remained unaware of it during the thousands of years that they were cut off from contact with the rest of the world.

Much has been written about male fear and envy of women's generative and sexual powers, and it is often given as a major reason for the widespread oppression of the female that confronts us today. Did womb envy originate in Neanderthal times? There is as yet no evidence to show whether or not this awareness of the female's awesome powers obtained in Neanderthal times.

Judging from present-day foraging peoples, both in the far north and under temperate weather conditions, there is no reason to believe that Neanderthal humans were as aggressive as various Freudian and Jungian projections would have them.[11] That the mother was important we may be sure; men could well have had high respect for the female without feeling it necessary to "break and control and employ" her powers, especially in conditions which put no premium on many births.[12]

Western European Neanderthals did and do capture the imagination of paleoanthropologists because it was possible—by playing fast and loose with the very sparse evidence—to fit them into the conquest-oriented, male-dominated theories which characterized prehistoric studies until the last decade, theories in large part a projection from the cultural values of the people doing the studying. They have been more studied than any group of the period, out of all proportion to their numerical representation. This is partly because of the accident of preservation in limestone caves, but also because they were found in Europe, which is where most of the people who did the studying came from.

It distorts the story of human evolution to believe, as we used to be taught, that humanity was shaped from the "cavemen" of Western Europe. David Pilbeam suggests that during mild-weather epochs there would have been anywhere from five to ten humans living in Africa for every single individual who lived in Europe. When the arctic temperatures of glacial times prevailed, the proportion would have been twenty Africans for every European.[13]

Coexistent with Western European Neanderthals were many

groups of humans in Asia and Africa who, it is now thought, were less specialized physically. Most paleoanthropologists believe that the classic Neanderthals of Western Europe constituted a genetically isolated pocket whose physical characteristics differed from those of other humans of the period. They existed for many thousands of years in the rigid conditions of the last Ice Age and in milder interglacial periods. What they do demonstrate is the new species' ability to adapt to the most extreme weather conditions, and with an extraordinarily limited range of cultural devices. Analyses of fossils and burial practices suggest extremely high mortality rates.[14] When one considers that they had no snowshoes, that the needle for sewing weatherproof clothes like those of the modern Eskimos was not invented until some fifteen thousand years ago, twenty thousand years after they disappeared, that the dog had not been domesticated, and that their hunting tools consisted of wooden spears with a simple flint or bone tip, their survival is indeed wondrous. But these "mighty hunters" either died out or were absorbed by the more modern-appearing Neanderthaloids of the Near East.

We do not know whether there was a sharp division of sex roles among the classic Neanderthals, though recent studies of their tools show many scrapers and knives which must have been used in the preparation of hides. As noted earlier, the curing of skins was traditionally woman's work in the animal-dependent cultures of modern northerly peoples like the Eskimo and the Montagnais.[15]

It makes sense to believe that the division of labor was functional: in glacial climates women had more need of shelter when they were nursing infants; they also could not travel as far or as fast as men. When they were in the late stages of pregnancy or encumbered with small children, they would have done less hunting and more preparation of hides; in a northerly climate there was little plant food to depend on.

In other parts of the inhabited world the division of labor would have been closer to that of the few remaining foragers left on earth today. However, Neanderthal humans had far more limited tools with which to encounter their environment.

Even the handax, which has been found in Western Europe and southern Africa, was not in use in southern Asia. There would have been less specialization in the mild-climate areas, with women still doing more of the gathering than men, and men doing more of the hunting than women, but with both participating according to necessity.

In the past it was thought that humans and prehumans lived mostly by hunting, but with the recent investigations of foraging diets and the new vision of tool use it is today believed that then as now plants would have provided the major portion of sustenance in mild and temperate climates, where most humans lived during the past two hundred thousand or so years. Group hunting using fire drives and traps would have been the means by which Neanderthals procured most of their meat; fire-hardened wooden spears with or without flint tips were also used by individuals.

Family arrangements cannot be demonstrated until quite late in the archaeological record. Humans, even very early humans, have the largest input of variability, a result of the many combinations made possible by their large brains. As the species with the most diverse physical endowment—with the possible exception of our earliest domesticated animal, the dog—and the widest range of behavior, we would have begun to diverge early on.

The traditional idea that there was a sharp distinction, even a clean break, between our own species and the Neanderthals is still held by some physical anthropologists. Others feel that there is not very much difference between us and our forebears of up to one or two hundred thousand years ago. Even though we were evolving, the brain was essentially the same.[16] Therefore examples from recently existing foraging peoples, in particular those who used only stone tools, may have more bearing on how our Neanderthal ancestors lived than on the lives of the previous species, *Homo erectus* and *habilis*.

It used to be taught that the nuclear family was the basic human organization, with the father providing the food and the mother and children staying at home. Later it was propounded that the basic organization of foragers—the people who used to be called hunters—consisted of bands of related men who took wives from the men of neighboring bands, giving their sisters or nieces in exchange. By this reasoning, relationships were traced through the male line and women left their own bands to live with those of their husbands. This arrangement makes for a weak position for the woman, who is among strangers, unprotected by long-term affection relationships with her own female and male relatives, as was the case in agricultural China.

Recent field work among existing foragers has provided a different picture. Wives and husbands are not anchored by property arrangements, and bands themselves split and re-form. Often a husband will stay with his wife's family for a year or two, but in the long run the determining factor is likely to be the presence of a sister or brother, of either the wife or the husband.[17] Among some groups, like the San of Africa, it is customary for husbands to join their wives' groups, where they are without influence based on blood relationships. Marriages may be planned by parents; they are made by children and unmade with comparative ease.[18]

Chastity and lifelong monogamy are rare among small-scale foraging societies today and sexual experience is allowed for in most nonliterate cultures. "There are no virgins in the villages —for every female child begins her sexual life very early," said Malinowski of the Trobriand Islanders, a statement which applies among African San, Australian Aborigines, Samoans, Arctic Eskimos, Amerindian Utes, and many other nonliterate cultures with both complex and simple material attributes.[19] Childish sexual play merges gradually into full intercourse.

In Neanderthal times, without the understanding of physical fatherhood and with much sexual freedom, the work of women and men was necessary and recognized as such. In the hardship of the European Ice Age, even in periods of mild climate, aggression against women would have been counterproductive. Judging by later developments there would have been admiration for their reproductive powers, though we cannot demonstrate it. With possessions kept to a minimum by nomadism, there would have been a certain rough equality among our forebears.

The very minimal tool kit left by our Neanderthal ancestors does not, however, preclude a rich imaginative life. In recent years a less Western-white-oriented point of view has permitted us to see that the level of technological development does not necessarily tell us much about the mental and artistic gifts of a people. The Australian Aborigines, who have a very sparse material culture and whose passing on the land leaves few marks behind, have a very complex spiritual heritage. They have a network of myths and lore connected with each hill, each rock, each pool in their horde country; they have a pantheon of heroic creatures peopling their dream time; they have dances and rituals. During twenty to forty thousand years of isolation their cultural development focused on the spiritual and the imaginative rather than the technological, which is why today they have so much appeal to poets and the other advocates of the new consciousness, rebels against the Western materialist ethos.

Moreover, the tales associated with each physical marker—soaks, springs, lakes, water holes, rocks, mounds, distinctive groups of trees—also have a functional use. They serve as geographic references so that the literary anchoring of the landscape becomes an annotated, personalized map. One water hole was formed when the turkey Gerangalgu entered the ground; at Lake Baragu the star Gigi fell down; at another lake the great Rainbow Snake emerged; he ended his travels at the rock hole which is named after him. Here the Great Mother Gadjeri sat down and rested; there she disappeared and at another point on the landscape emerged again. This knowledge is essential in the wandering of the tribes, for it tells them how long they should walk before obtaining water, where certain plants grow, or where animals are likely to come and drink. The social and economic worlds are integrated in a framework which provides a comprehensive world view. Theirs is a universe peopled by spiritual creatures of the before and after time, shape-changing and eternal, who imbued the sites through which they passed with a spiritual aura. The living people share in this essence, for they are kin to the creatures of the timeless, imaginative world whose abstract presence is grasped through an actual relationship to the land and the adventures associated with its every physical feature.[20]

Taletelling, whether it is called connecting (Forster), time-factoring (Marshack), or classifying (Chomsky), is probably as old as our species, and it is more than likely that our Neanderthal forebears had a spiritual and mythological way of integrating themselves with their natural world, though they have left little evidence for interpretation.

At three caves in the Alps remains of cave-bear skulls and bones seem to be placed ceremonially. It has been suggested that these animals played a role in the religious mythology and the subsistence of Western Neanderthal humans.[21] Hibernating cave bears might have provided a ready food supply for our European forebears during the long glacial winters—a kind of living deep freeze. In other cases humans were buried with the bones and ashes of wild cattle, woolly rhinoceroses, horses, reindeer, and bison, also animals of economic utility. In more recent times animals like these inhabit the mythic worlds of diverse foraging peoples.

Whereas Neanderthal people used to be considered a dead end in human evolution, comprising the small group of cave people in Western Europe now known as Classic Neanderthalers, the denomination today has been enlarged to include fossils of that period from many places in the world.

We saw earlier that scientists classify our past with two parallel systems: by tools and by fossils. Early in the twentieth century a horde of tools along with several Neanderthal skeletons were found at Le Moustier in the Dordogne in France. Tools like those found at Le Moustier have subsequently been found in many parts of Europe, Asia, and South Africa and are dated to the period between 100,000 and 35,000 B.P. Therefore, tools and groups of tools produced during this period are called Mousterian, after the initial find spot, and all human remains found in conjunction with them are now classified as *Homo sapiens neanderthalensis*.[22]

The Classic Neanderthals are still considered to have become extinct, while other groups of fossils from Eastern Europe and the Near East, similar to them but somewhat more generalized in form, are called Persistent Neanderthals. However, two small groups of fossils discovered in the Near East have skulls and body skeletons closer to our own bodies and heads: they are called Progressive Neanderthals.

In the Judeo-Christian tradition, which has shaped much of Western civilization, the Near East plays an important role. The Garden of Eden, first home of our mythical ancestors, and Mount Ararat, on which, at a later date, Noah's ark came to rest after the other inhabitants of the world had been destroyed by flood, are both situated in the general area. It is curious, then, that twentieth-century studies of our beginnings, and possibly those of all modern humans, keep bringing us back to the same area, for the origin of *Homo sapiens sapiens* and again at later stages in our story.

A hypothesis is, after all, an educated myth, and a recent myth proposed by science would have us descended from these Progressive Neanderthals. They are represented in the record by seventeen fossil skeletons, or fragments thereof, found in Israel: ten individuals from a small cave called Skhul in the Wadi-el-Mughara near the coastal plain and seven people from a larger cave named Qafzeh, which is located near biblical Nazareth.

Sally Binford has presented some theories in support of the hypothesis, first broached by F. C. Howell, that these fossils represent a transition between *Homo sapiens neanderthalensis* and *Homo sapiens sapiens*. Her documentation is based on an analysis and comparison of *neanderthalensis* and *sapiens* burials in Western Europe and the Near East. Though one might question whether there are enough burials to provide a representative sample, she does find more similarities between Neanderthal burials in the Near East and the later *sapiens sapiens* burials of Europe than between the Neanderthal burials in Europe and those in the Near East. She also provides support for the theory of Neanderthals' disappearance in Europe with statistics showing as many children as adults buried, whereas in the Near East as in later Cro-Magnon burials

the ratio was two adults to every child, allowing her to speculate that more children survived to reproductive age. Comparing the way of life for the Progressive Neanderthals of the
Near East with that of the Paleolithic cave people of the Dordogne in France, she theorizes that both took advantage of
herd animals.[23]

The Progressive Neanderthals were discovered in the Jordan
upland areas, and the climate was not dissimilar to today's,
though at that time the region had more wooded areas and
more contrasts of rain and dryness. Annual migrations of wild
cattle and fallow deer occurred in consequence, animals following the valleys to new feeding grounds. Since the bone waste
found in conjunction with skeletons consists chiefly of these animals, she deduces that there may have been communal hunts
to take advantage of animal migrations and acquire surpluses of
food.

Large group hunts would have required the participation of
several bands of people, like those organized by American
Plains Indians of the nineteenth century. Opportunities for
mingling of tribes would have meant encounters between
women and men of different groups, giving rise to increased
gene flow and new combinations of physical characteristics,
with a new kind of human resulting.

A more general theory suggests that the Near East was the
crossroads of the three inhabited continents: Asia, Africa, and
Europe. It would therefore be the natural meeting ground for
peoples, genes, and ideas—logical sources for the greatest di-
versification as well as the most efficient use of possibilities—so
that new human species and new inventions would indeed be
most likely to arise in that area.[24]

Before Howell and Binford outlined their theory of a Near
Eastern origin for *Homo sapiens sapiens*, the usual explanation
was that *sapiens sapiens* developed more or less simultaneously
in a number of widely separated geographical areas, a supposition which leaves much to chance.[25] Another explanation has
the "advanced" *sapiens sapiens* invading Europe and destroying
the backward Neanderthals.[26] Binford feels that since we are
one species, with *neanderthalensis* and *sapiens* as subspecies, in-

termarriage between the two was not only possible but probable, and the mingling could as easily have been pacific as warlike. The Basque language is unrelated to any other known language, and the Basques are a short, stocky people living in the remote mountain fastnesses of southwestern France and northern Spain. They still preserve a fiercely independent sense of self, and it has been suggested, not altogether in jest, that they might be descendants of the original Western European Neanderthals.

Neanderthalensis may have survived in isolated pockets while the Near Eastern progenitors were spreading into Europe, as well as into Asia and Africa. In some cases they would have died out, in others been absorbed into the better equipped Upper Paleolithic culture of *sapiens sapiens*.

The Classic Neanderthals of Western Europe were living in a rigidly cold area comparable, say, to the present-day Arctic, in climate though not in light. The first discoveries of *sapiens sapiens* remains are dated to a warm period, one of several temporary warmings during the Ice Age. This then might have been a propitious time for expansion.

It is Binford's theory that rapid population increases would have occurred during periods of relative sedentism, times when the populations were able to settle in one upland river valley awaiting the passing of the migrating herds, instead of wandering about in search of a varied supply of animals. One of the problems inherent in obtaining an almost all-meat diet in a cold climate is that meat is hard to catch, in particular with the extremely primitive weapons which are all we know for Western European Neanderthals. If for some reason the herds fail, starvation follows—whole bands and peoples may be wiped out, as happened quite recently with a band of Eskimos, the Sadlermuits, in the Central Arctic. A temperate climate allowing dependence on varied resources of plant and animal food is obviously more secure. Thus the theory of the rapid expansion and material advance of *sapiens sapiens* during the Würm Interglacial some thirty-odd thousand years ago.

Originally studied above all in France, fossils and relics are now known from a varied area across Europe and into Asia and North Africa. But the French niveau is the most thoroughly explored, partly because of the accidental discovery there of fossils, tools, and cave art during the latter half of the nineteenth century. Much of our information is still based on the long record of finds there and in adjacent areas of northern Spain, Germany, and Italy. The periods and places have been well charted; the nomenclature for various Upper Paleolithic stages now recognized in many parts of Europe and Asia is based on the early French finds, so that French place names are used for classification.

The brains and bodies of these people are loosely indistinguishable from our own. Moreover, we have clearer evidence of a common humanity in terms of bodily physique and attitudes toward procreation because, in addition to far more copious archaeological evidence—fossils, tools, even habitations—they also left visual evidence behind in the form of painting and sculpture.

15

Paleolithic Art:
What It Tells Us

Most history has been written as if women did not exist, save as passive spectators, and accounts of the Eurasian Upper Paleolithic are no exception. Everything we read assumes a male origin and male interests. Hunting magic—sympathetic and fertility—is widely accepted as the underlying motivation, with an occasional speculation about male initiation rites thrown in. Many of the facts are still unknown, and what we do know has often been presented in highly distorted fashion. Only a few faint voices have been raised to question the confident myths which often masquerade as science or history.

There is no reason to attribute Paleolithic art exclusively to male painters and sculptors, yet scholars have been doing so for generations. A vague mark at the bottom of a drawing is variously described as a spear thrower, a throwing stick, or a broken spear. Those who perceive human evolution in terms of Man the Hunter see weapons, hunting, killing.[1] Writers interested in archetype and spirit offer explanations based on religious ceremony and ritual, and they support themselves with analogies taken from ethnographic data.[2] Men are more sweeping, women more cautious, in their interpretations.

Striking examples of cave art—paintings, engraving, and bas-

reliefs—were first discovered in southwestern France and northern Spain. Several of the initial finds were made by children
roaming through the caves and passages of limestone country
in the Dordogne; others by amateur archaeologists who had
come upon examples of Paleolithic art on their own land, or
had their attention drawn to the mysterious paintings by their
daughters or sons.

Beginning with the twentieth century more and more discoveries have been made, still mostly in France and Spain,
though examples are found as far to the east as Kapova in
Siberia. They have given rise to much literature—that human
need to tell explanatory tales, to connect, and to classify—in
the fields of art and mythology as well as prehistory. Examples
of cave art—usually referred to as parietal or wall art, despite
the fact that it is also found on floors and ceilings—abound in
the Dordogne and are also found in Spain, North Africa, and
Italy. Recent discoveries in Eastern Europe and Siberia have
yielded chiefly small sculptures—animal and human figures.
Carved and decorated artifacts—tools and tool handles, peb-
bles, and seemingly ornamental or ritual objects—have been collected in both areas. It is these visualizations which give us
both explicit information and suggestions about the mental capacities, the appearance, and the interests of our ancestors.

The field for speculation is enormous, the range of those who
would fill it equally so.

In 1965 Grahame Clark was writing about Paleolithic sculpture in *Prehistoric Societies* (revised edition published in
1970):

> Others were modeled from clay and hardened in the
> fire like pottery; . . . most of those found in and
> around a hearth at Pavlov might almost have been
> produced by a hunter squatting by the fire and idly
> kneading clay into the shape of his intended vic-
> tims. . . . The *men* responsible for cave art were sub-
> ject to all the tensions of the hunter's life under con-
> ditions which evidently allowed a certain leisure
> without rendering the winning of food in any sense

easy or secure. The content of the art itself leaves us in no doubt that it was conceived in and intimately bound up with the *hopes and desires of hunters;* and *its essentially masculine character* is emphasized by the *extreme rarity of plant forms.* By the same token there is no essential conflict between the esthetic and magical aspects of cave art; it is precisely as a means of gaining some control over the wild animals on which they depended that the cave artists set out to delineate them with so much passion; and their ability to achieve authentic representations was based on a lifetime's experience watching the attitudes and behavior of their victims in the course of hunting.[3]

The "revised and enlarged edition" of John Pfeiffer's *The Emergence of Man* informed us in 1972:

The world's first great art "movement" lasted more than 20,000 years, from Aurignacian to Magdalenian times. Some of its most spectacular products are found in underground galleries, away from natural light in the passages and chambers and niches of limestone caves, and indicate in a most vivid fashion how completely *hunting dominated the attention and imagination of prehistoric man. He rarely drew people* and *never anything* that would be recognized *as a landscape,* although there are a wide variety of signs which have no obvious meaning to us. *His* overwhelming concern was with game animals seen as individuals, clearly defined and detached, and isolated from their natural settings. . . .

An important clue [to cave art] involved Cro-Magnon *man's* concern with his effectiveness as a provider. Half the battle in hunting and fighting is confidence; and if he was anything like modern *man*, he used ritual on numerous occasions to help replenish and increase his power. Perhaps he cast spells on his prey. Certain places in the depths of the cave area are covered with superimposed figures, figures drawn one on top of the other and overlapping as if the artists paid little attention to the work of their predecessors but considerable attention to where the art was located. They also represented some animals with darts or spears sticking into their sides, for example, the bison in the Shaft of the Dead Man [at Lascaux, in the Dordogne], which may have been killed ritually in revenge for the death of the hunter.[4]

In 1967 Peter Ucko and Andrée Rosenfeld had published *Paleolithic Cave Art*, an exhaustive and detailed study analyzing both art and the literature thereon, which presented convincing evidence to contradict almost every statement in the passages quoted above, as well as most other generalizations and one-note, single-theory explanations for cave art.

It is not surprising that Pfeiffer, who had earlier attributed the growth of the human brain to big-game hunting, should overlook most other evidence to continue his focus on male "exploits." But even the skeptical Ucko and Rosenfeld assumed a male origin: "There may as well be one hundred reasons why paleolithic *men* decorated caves." And, contradicting one M. Astre who felt "from the similarity in style of all Paleolithic art that painting and engraving must have been a specialist activity of the sorcerers, passing from father to son," they say, "In Australia and Africa, the available evidence suggests that anyone (at least any male) can be an artist."[5]

In 1939 Phyllis Kaberry published an account of an old woman who participated in increase ceremonies and performed the annual rite of repainting Kaleru, the sacred Rainbow Serpent of the Northwestern Australian Aborigines.[6] Shamanism has always been practiced by women and men of Siberia, the Arctic, and, in northern North America, the Ojibwa on both sides of the Canada-United States border. In Australia it is age, not sex, which determines the religious officiants. The more ancient the culture, the more likely we are to find shamanism, sorcery, magic, or priesthood practiced by members of both sexes, though customs vary widely. In modern cultures ancient or popular religions appeal to the underclasses, principally women; they also frequently involve women officiants. Spiritual yearnings and needs have never been restricted to one sex.

The picture in the Shaft of the Dead Man at Lascaux (Figure 4) is an example of the broad range of interpretations offered. Ucko and Rosenfeld describe it as "including a disembowelled bison, a 'phallic' man, a rhinoceros, and several other objects."[7]

In the passage quoted on page 137, John Pfeiffer saw it as a hunter's revenge. Grahame Clark ignores the rhinoceros to see the bison "with its entrails falling out of its side and a great single-barbed spear lying across its hind quarters and almost touching what must be either a spearthrower or the broken head of another spear; before the beast and fronted by it lies the prostrate body of a man with arms outstretched and a birdlike head."[8] The Abbé Breuil, who devoted himself to copying, studying, and interpreting cave art from the age of fourteen until his death in 1961, aged eighty-four, for a long time exercised a virtual monopoly over the field. He saw a dead hunter lying between the bison he had wounded and the rhinoceros which had subsequently killed him.[9]

Joseph Campbell approaches the painting in a more imaginative fashion, as befits the interpreter of Joyce's *Finnegans Wake*:

> The man wears a bird mask and has birdlike instead of human hands. He is certainly a shaman . . . [Australian rites provide] a plausible symbolic context for the pointing of the penis of the prostrate shaman of Lascaux—as well as for the defecation of the passing rhino, who may well be the shaman's animal familiar. The position of the lance, furthermore, piercing the anus of the bull and emerging at the penis, spills the bowels from the area between—which is precisely the region effected by the "pointing bone" of the Australians.[10]

Two female interpreters of the scene also lean toward a religious significance. G. Rachel Levy, in 1948, suggested: "The man with outstretched arms and stiff legs at Lascaux may be no corpse gored by the bison who faces him on the cave wall. His birdlike mask and his attitude may be related to the bird on the pole (if such it is) which is placed beside him. If one could imagine a hunting scene depicted in the depths of a cave, it would surely represent success and not defeat. The disembowelled bison as a separate figure would follow a fairly common precedent."[11] According to Jacquetta Hawkes, "the man appears to be birdheaded while planted beside him is a wand with a bird on its top; it is possible that this picture has totemic significance showing the human member and his totemic emblem."[12]

Actually, to interpret the myth or meaning behind this and many other cave paintings is an exercise in sheer human ingenuity. Imagine placing visitors from Mars, or even the Kalahari Desert, in front of paintings dealing with different myths in our own past, Moses and the burning bush, Christ at the wedding in Cana, or Hercules killing the lion of Nemea, and asking for an explanation. Cultural perspective and personal predilection shape the responses. We are in a better position to interpret the interpreters than the scenes interpreted.

There is no reason to insist on a male origin, as there is no reason to insist on a female origin, for Paleolithic art. Chances are that both participated, though the men may have had more leisure. Women the nourishers are more generally associated with food preparation than men. Cooking the rice and beans, getting the meal on the table—though in European Paleolithic days it was more likely to have been venison, mushrooms, and salmon—interferes with talk and thought and can be distracting. Still, in the Australian Kimberleys the men roast their catch of kangaroo, while the women attend to the food they have procured. In parts of Africa, also, hunters traditionally cook the food they have caught. As we have seen, women hunt; they also participate and sometimes officiate in religious ceremony.

Among the Vedda in Ceylon (Sri Lanka) it is the women who do the rock paintings.[13] The town of Mithila in India has a centuries-old tradition of women painters, who produce highly sophisticated work. Among the Caduveo Indians of South America women also paint, intricate decorations on ceramics and hides, as well as on the human body, while men are sculptors. There may well have been Paleolithic counterparts of our Grandma Moses, who began to paint late in life, or of Rosa Bonheur or Artemisia Gentileschi, who dedicated themselves to art from an early age. To say that only the hunter who knew the beast from the rigors of the hunt could have drawn them is foolish. It isn't the warrior who paints the battle scene, but an artist who has observed from a safe distance. Some of the peculiarities of Paleolithic animal portraits have been attributed to the fact that they may have been drawn from dead animals. Imaginary scenes based on dimly remembered reality have also been a wellspring of art.

What is true about the Paleolithic paintings and sculpture of the High Magdalenian—Lascaux is generally dated to 17,000 B.P.—is that we recognize them as art, whatever purpose or purposes they may have served at the time. It's not realism or knowledge of the wild animals' muscles and movements that the Paleolithic artists had but feeling, and a feeling which transcends the millennia, a feeling we can share. They communicate to us on a level quite different from the wonders of nature, the nest of the bowerbird, say. Even though we do not know exactly what the artists were saying, human consciousness animates their work. Though time and ruin may have added to the aesthetic force of the painting and sculpture—compare, for example, the Greek statues of the Classical period, which appeal to us for their chasteness and simplicity, but were actually painted at the time in gaudy primary colors a modern consciousness might have found off-putting—the fact that we can respond to them does tell us something about the common humanity we share with their creators.

The Upper Paleolithic period spans twenty thousand years and diverse cultures stretching from Spain to Siberia. All too often it has been treated as one unity, and the few striking pictures deep in the caves, many of which date to later periods, are usually described as typical and rule-making and are taken to represent the whole period.

Ucko and Rosenfeld have divided cave art into three categories: the first is that which is almost outdoors, in living areas at the mouths of caves and in rock shelters; the second is art which is found in corridors linked with or leading off from the above, i.e., adjacent to living areas; while the third category refers to art seemingly hidden within the recesses of enormous caves, apart from the places normally frequented by the people who made it.

The first kind, found in rock shelters and cave entrances, is analogous to art which might have existed on the walls of now destroyed houses or huts. It is art which is seen by direct light, and what remains after these thousands of years are mainly bas-relief sculptures and some engravings. This was probably the most common kind of art during the period but was the least likely to endure; destruction, weather, and subsequent diverse uses of these places made it unlikely that any trace would have come down to us. Ucko and Rosenfeld point out that the apparent scarcity of this kind of painting is undoubtedly due to conditions of corrosion. Traces of ocher on bas-reliefs, engravings, and painted blocks buried in deposits show that paintings were executed at rock shelters and cave entrances.[14]

The earliest cave art known dates back to the Aurignacian period, about thirty thousand years ago, when there had been a mild interglacial period and, presumably, the new subspecies had recently spread from the Near East and colonized Europe. Some of the oldest works known, from Aurignacian levels at the cave of La Férrassie, belong to the first category, art which is almost outside. Simple outlines of animals and "vulvas"—signs which are usually interpreted as female organs—were engraved in a single continuous deep and wide groove. As in almost all other Paleolithic stone work the limestone is too corroded to be examined for actual traces of working technique.[15]

It has always been taken for granted that these vulvas were engraved by men. And yet Lorna Marshall reports that among the San of Africa young girls draw sexual symbols, including diagrammatic representations of their genital aprons, on the smooth gray bark of trees.[16]

Phyllis Kaberry reports on women's ceremonies among the

Kimberleys and records many songs and dances which refer to sexual organs, for erotic purposes as well as in childbirth and menstruation rites. Colin Turnbull writes of the *elima* of the Mbuti Pygmies, the month-long festival during which young girls learn about love-making and take the initiative with young boys. In the last few decades—with the entry of more women into anthropology and with the spread of sexual enlightenment —we have discovered that there is far less sexual repression among women of nonliterate and noncontact societies than had been assumed by earlier Victorian-conditioned reporters. It is quite as likely that the sexual representations of Paleolithic caves were made by women as by men.

What we can be sure of is that the vulva and the sexuality and childbearing capacities of women were of the highest importance. Women's genitals have a double association, with pleasure and with birth. Many of the representations may have had to do with birth ceremonies, to ease the pains of childbirth and ensure safe delivery. The vulva is the point of origin for all of us, women and men, save those rare individuals who, like Macduff, boast of being "from his mother's womb untimely ripped." (Neither Caesar's nor Macduff's entry into the world was a likely occurrence in Paleolithic times.)

According to a woman archaeologist, there are far more representations of women's thighs and vulvas in Paleolithic cave art than has been reported in the literature.[17] Not only Abbé Breuil, who played so important a role in publishing this art, but several other early researchers in the field were members of the Catholic clergy, and they tended to ignore these disquieting reminders of the dangerous female.

One of the most striking finds in cave art belongs also to the category of exposed art and is even more directly related to the human female, as well as to the human male. At Laussel several limestone blocks which contain realistic bas-reliefs of human bodies are dated to a comparatively early period; they were executed about 23,000 B.P., during the Périgordian period. As Ucko and Rosenfeld point out human beings are represented more often than is sometimes claimed.[18] Laussel has given us five representations, of which three are female, one male, and one, a double figure of which the upper definitely has breasts, has been called either a birth scene or a depiction of intercourse. If the second, it would have to be seen as a flattened-out stylized version of the face-to-face squatting position Malinowski describes for the Trobriand Islanders. If a birth scene, even taking into account the possibilities for stylistic distortion, mother and child are of equal size, a rather unlikely proportion. Two other possibilities exist: badly preserved and hard to make out, Levy suggests it is a figure of a woman whose legs come together; and Ucko and Rosenfeld think it may have been an unfinished sculpture which was worked also from the opposite direction.

The Venus of Laussel is one of the best known of the many Paleolithic Venus figures (see Figure 3). She has an ample figure with a small head; one delicate hand rests on a full but not necessarily pregnant belly; the other arm holds an incised, single-pointed crescent, usually interpreted as a horn, above her shoulder. The hips and thighs and great pendulous breasts are all burgeoning; the legs taper away without showing the feet. Though the figure is clearly distorted in the opposite direction from a Modigliani, she is rather more to the average taste than other Paleolithic Venuses, Willendorf or Lespugue for example. (Picasso kept a copy of the latter in a special place in his studio.[19]) More fleshy even than a late Renoir or Rubens, perhaps it is the desiccation of time, which has left only traces of her original red ocher paint, that produces a general sense of awe rather than voluptuousness.

Apropos of the drooping, usually huge, breasts which characterize many Paleolithic female images, one is reminded of Turnbull's remark that the Mbuti Pygmies do not think a woman's breasts attractive until they have "descended" after childbirth, nursing, and full maturity. Compare also the Egyptian goddess Nut, apostrophized in the Pyramid Texts as "she of the hanging breasts," "the great protectress" whose body overarched the earth. Let us not confuse the Western attitude toward the breast as an erotic symbol dissociated from nutrition with that of other times and places. Whether or not the breast was a sexual symbol, the connection of the female with maternity, all-givingness, and plenty in these representations is obvious—and it is not an exclusively male image. We have all been children, and presumably all Paleolithic children would have had a recollection of the warmth, security, and sensuality of the mother's breast and body. Nor need there have been any diffidence about acknowledging the sensual components. Children would have been nursed far longer than is today customary and carried more frequently in much closer contact with their mother's bodies, given the cold weather.

The male figure, on the contrary, is smaller, shown in three-quarter profile rather than full on, neither thin nor fat, with no indicated sexual organ, and far less striking.

Art of the second category, in cave passages adjoining or leading off from the living area, may be far more extensive than had previously been thought. Ucko and Rosenfeld point out that drafts, temperature changes, and earth movements which cause passages to be blocked might often destroy the art close to the atmosphere and the open so that the deeply hidden art discovered after thousands of years may at one time have been a continuation of now-destroyed art. Most cave systems have been inadequately explored so that often we do not know the original entrances and original habitation areas of caves where "sanctuary" or hidden art has been found. Out of the hundred or so known and explored caves with Paleolithic art, Ucko and Rosenfeld document twelve which belong to this second category. They suggest that most of the caves which have usually been ascribed to category three—the hidden art which has captured the fancy of art historians and archaeologists—may originally have been connected with inhabited areas. The Paleolithic occupants would have wandered deeper into the caves to paint and sculpt and, perhaps, use the natural chambers for theatrical ceremonies.

There is a very simple reason why our Paleolithic ancestors may have chosen the deepest caverns for their most ambitious decorations and ceremonies. During the long glacial winters these would provide most protection against the cold, with an unvarying temperature. On the hottest summer days as well as the coldest winter ones, deep inside limestone caves like Lost

River Caverns of Pennsylvania the temperature stays at close to 50 degrees. Moreover, with the current energy crisis, old limestone mines and caverns are currently being put to use or proposed as fuel-saving offices and storage facilities. Two hundred feet below the earth's surface the headquarters of the Consolidated Meat Distribution Center near Kansas City, Kansas, remain at a constant 58 degrees throughout the year.[20]

The long winters may have been a leisure and ceremonial time during which Paleolithic people subsisted on meat killed earlier and kept in natural deep freeze, in the outer passages of the limestone cave networks. The inmost chambers would have served as habitations and meeting places, providing maximum protection against the severities of the Ice Age.

There is no doubt that some of the art does lie in passages and chambers difficult of access, if not necessarily completely secret. It is hard to date these representations unless organic relics—carbonized rope or other artifacts connected with daily life that can be tested by radiocarbon analysis—are found in indisputable association with them, and even then proof is not always certain. Some caves are securely dated; many are not.

One researcher has assumed that "hidden" art works are of later date than the external representations, charting a linear chronological development for the whole phenomenon of cave art. This theory is effectively criticized by Ucko and Rosenfeld, who point out that in a period covering twenty thousand years, and with several sharp climate changes, cultures must have come and gone, risen and decayed, and similarly with schools and traditions of art. They demonstrate the enormous diversities of styles, giving examples with reproductions of horses' heads in varying modes, and tear apart the attempts to sex animals by size—smaller female, larger male; delicate figures female, heavier ones male—or to see as pregnant any animal with a protruding belly. By this reasoning, and it is a reasoning much expounded in the reams that have been written about cave art, all horses by Rosa Bonheur and Paolo Uccello would be male while those of Piero della Francesca and Marino Marini would be female and pregnant.

Much of the better known cave art—animals, imaginary creatures, and, in a very few cases, scenes—is believed to have emerged from the Magdalenian period, roughly 17,000 to 10,500 years B.P. This is the period when artifacts of bone, as well as flint tools, show an increasing richness of ornamentation, and many new inventions appear. The eyed bone needle, for sewing waterproof clothing, was discovered in the late Solutrean, some two thousand years earlier, but seems to have disappeared with that culture and been rediscovered about 15,000 B.P. A wide variety of tools which would have been used by women and men, or possibly only women, begins to be developed. Harpoons and spear throwers, which we think of as used more exclusively by men, come later in the chronology of invention, after 13,000 B.P.

In the time sequence of the Upper Paleolithic epochs in Europe and Asia, Châtelperronian is the earliest; then come the Perigordian and the Aurignacian, now thought to be two parallel cultures, overlapping if not coexistent in time. The Solutrean was a relatively brief (3,000 years) and locally limited very advanced culture. The greatest quantity of evidence—art and artifact—is, not unsurprisingly, from the final period, the Magdalenian. Climatological researches show that new cultures seem to coincide with the mild-temperature periods known as interglacials. Perhaps the earlier cultures declined under the severities of harsh glacial temperatures or of shifting ecological conditions, whereas mitigating temperatures—over thousands of years—permitted resurgence and new inventions.

The Magdalenian is known best from its middle and late stages, and in western France. It is supposed to have been a period of extremely rich resources, which began during a relatively mild phase, became quite cold, and then disappeared as the Ice Age ended and woodland forests replaced the tundra over which vast herds of reindeer had roamed. During its height, climate and geography produced cool, moist conditions not all that different from the present-day habitat of the Pacific coast of northwestern North America. The Magdalenians may have lived all year round in caves as well as, on occasion, in temporary summer camps. From their food debris, we know they lived chiefly on reindeer, on migrating salmon, occasional seals, birds, hare, etc., as well as, presumably, berries, roots, tubers, nuts, mushrooms, and honey. It is a well-balanced diet, rich in protein, though not necessarily in starch, sugar, and fat. Honey and berries, with their rare sweetness of taste—and in nature sweetness is associated with much needed vitamins— would have been obtainable only in brief seasons. They would have been much prized, as indeed they were by the Indians of the Pacific Northwest coast.

One of the many misconceptions in the interpretation of Paleolithic cave art, then, regards the myth of the dangerous and difficult hunt, practiced only by males. "They weren't hunting; they were harvesting!" said Sally Binford. If the paintings of the animals were for purposes of "sympathetic" magic—to insure success in the face of danger—why are fearsome animals like cave bear and cave lion, difficult and dangerous to catch and known to have abounded during the period, so infrequently represented? And if for the purposes of fertility magic, similar to the Australian Aborigines' increase ceremonies, why are there so few paintings of reindeer, which was the staple food of the time?

It is typical of our culture's emphasis on weapons and aggression that feathered arrows, darts, and spears were so frequently perceived in the wall paintings and engravings. Featherlike signs engraved or painted on the bodies of animals are often thought to represent arrows. However, real Paleolithic bone projectile points were either not barbed or were mounted to produce only a single barb. Fully biserial barbed harpoons only appeared in the final Magdalenian—long after most of the works had been executed.[21] The interpreters of Paleolithic art works thought they were seeing weapons not yet invented at the time the works had been executed.

Ucko and Rosenfeld also find it "strange that Paleolithic *men* who lived by hunting and gathering wild fruit and berries had no interest in the increase of vegetation," another reason for considering that cave art could not have been analogous to Australian increase rites, which are performed for vegetation as well as for animals. Noting that many of the stick and line forms which have been seen as weapons fly through the air or miss their targets, they wonder why Paleolithic humans would have wanted to depict so many hunting failures.[22]

Alexander Marshack, whose book *The Roots of Civilization* speculates on the storytelling capacities of early humans, finds a simple answer. Many objects which had previously been seen as weapons look to him like plants, trees, branches, and flowers, and he deduces stories about the changing of the seasons from them and their conjunction with animals and people. Once the suggestion has been made, they do indeed resemble bare limbs, reeds, trees, leaves, and flowering plants far more than the destructive elements for which they had previously been taken.

Marshack describes a bone object, usually called a *bâton de commandement*, on which were engraved forms that resembled barbed harpoons. He examined it under the microscope, and it was clear that the engravings were impossible harpoons: the barbs were turned the wrong way and the points of the long shafts were at the wrong end. The figures were perfect plants or branches, growing at the proper angle and in the proper way at the top of a long stem.[23] He concludes that vegetation was clearly represented on the small objects and that many of the so-called "barbed signs" and "masculine objects" in the caves probably represented plant forms.[24]

The "masculine objects" to which Marshack referred come from André Leroi-Gourhan's explanation of cave art as grounded in sadomasochistic sexual symbolism. Leroi-Gourhan has spent many years charting, counting, and doing statistical analyses of the representations in the caves. He dichotomizes every image into one of the two sexes: bison, male; horse, female; weapons or barbed signs, male; holes, rounds, wounds, etc., female. It is a wild fantasy on the already fantastic perversion which is late Freudian psychology, i.e., that human sexuality consists of male sadism and female masochism. Leroi-Gourhan's theory is based on mistaken identifications, projections of our own cultural preoccupations and preconceptions onto images which are still unexplained, though it is now clear that many represent vegetation. Looking at slides and photographs of the Magdalenian animals with overpaintings of twigged branches or leaves, it is indeed startling to realize that for half a century or more these innocent figures, often feathery and delicate in outline, were seen as deadly objects.

Awareness of the Paleolithic existence of humans and human artifacts had begun in the middle of the nineteenth century in Western Europe. Explorations of Paleolithic caves, with their spectacular wall paintings, engravings, and reliefs, commenced before the end of the century. As knowledge accumulated, research was extended to surface exploration and digs. In the eastern part of the Eurasian continent, Siberian construction workers had uncovered Paleolithic bones and carved mammoth ivory as early as 1871. Though Paleolithic art works were found in European Russia and Siberia before the Russian revolution, it was not till later, in 1923, that the first entire Paleolithic sculpture was found, a mammoth-ivory Venus figure unearthed at Kostenki, on the Don River.

In the Soviet, archaeologists work within a Marx-Engels ideology based on the assumption that matriarchy preceded patriarchy, and their attitudes are somewhat different from those common in the West. Since the early discoveries much work has been done on what was essentially a mammoth-hunting culture across the frozen tundras, in contrast to the Franco-Cantabrian area, where reindeer were a chief resource. There were no limestone caverns in the Eurasian plain, and many of the settlements have been charted from the remains of hearths, huge mammoth bones, graves, and other evidence of living sites. These northern foragers who wandered across the frozen tundras during the great Ice Age lived in skin huts or other tentlike structures erected on mammoth bones. In all the Paleolithic art found in European Russia and Siberia, not a single indubitably male figure was identified, though many small statues of females and a number of animal representations exist.[25]

There were burgeoning Venus figures with the characteristic huge, hanging breasts, bulging stomachs, and enormous buttocks, small or missing hands and feet, on the order of the Venuses of Lespugue, Grimaldi, Willendorf, and Laussel. But slender figures, long, stylized, and understated, were also found. There were even five female figures from Mal'ta and Buret in eastern Siberia, which had been worked in bone or ivory to suggest sewn clothing, not dissimilar to the hide and fur trousers and parkas worn by Lapps and Eskimos of recent times.

Fewer animal figures were found and less detail was lavished on them. In the West, cave walls had lent themselves to two-dimensional art which survived by the accident of the surface on which it had been placed; so far only two or three examples of Paleolithic cave art have been found in the East.

Whatever the reason for the frequent sculpture of female figures, it is clear that the male figure is of lesser importance in the consciousness of early *Homo sapiens*. In all the Eastern representations—animal, female, and some figures which are not necessarily female or male—there are no representations of male sexual organs as such or of coitus. As in the West there were puzzling objects. For example, some stylized ivory figurines found at Mezin in the Ukraine have been variously classified: as female nudes by Abbé Breuil, as the heads of long-beaked birds by V. A. Gorodcov, while F. K. Volkov saw them as male phalli.[26] Apart from these small ivory carvings there is no suggestion of the male organ to be found in Soviet art.

In the West an occasional figure showed an erected penis in a mysterious scene with animals, as in the much debated Lascaux crypt scene—the Shaft of the Dead Man—and a few barely decipherable small drawings may have included male genitalia. As Ucko and Rosenfeld have pointed out, there are no scenes of animal copulation, very few representations of animal sex organs, and, with the dubious exception of the unfinished double sculpture from Laussel, none of human copulation. Certain isolated signs which used to be interpreted as male and female sex symbols cannot be verified as such. The ubiquity of the female genital image and the rarity of the phallus tell us something about the biological knowledge of the people who made Paleolithic art. The phallus is not important to reproduction unless it is known that the male contributes to the making of the baby. Women were still the necessary sex. Analyses of the sculpture and paintings of Eastern and Western areas show that copulation and procreation were not yet linked in the human mind.

On the basis of the evidence, then, neither in the East nor in the West is there any demonstration that Paleolithic humans connected coitus with reproduction, placed any functional value on the male sexual organ, or saw reason to emphasize it in their art. The focus was on the female—breasts, belly, thighs, and vulva.

Women's functions may also have been studied; Marshack identified bone objects with line markings as lunar calendars. It is not unlikely that these were menstrual records, with or without reference to the astronomical phenomena which are often roughly parallel to women's monthly cycles. The Venus of Laussel holds in her hand a broken crescent. Sometimes identified as an animal horn, the crescent has lines engraved on it, and it might well be a representation of the crescent moon from which the upper part has eroded or broken off. The lines could be lunar markings denoting the menstrual cycle.

Cave art shows that the woman was more important than the male and that her body was connected with fullness and plenty. There are no aggressive images connected with women, and the art itself conveys awe and wonderment rather than terror or cruelty. Animals, plants, and people are depicted. Signs formerly interpreted as weapons are representations of nature and changing seasons. Though there is much that is mysterious, there is no positive evidence for male domination, nor for certain aggressive syndromes which appear later in the human story.

——···——···——···——···——···——···——

The Mana of Blood:
Menstruation and
Menopause

In Paleolithic times one of the earliest indications of religious awareness—a constant in human existence—was the finding of red-ocher decorations tingeing skeletons and associated with burials. The sacredness of the color red predates even our own subspecies, *Homo sapiens sapiens*, for lumps of red ocher have been found in Neanderthal and other Mousterian burials.

Like the body itself, implements and ornaments were often covered with the red ocher that recent nonliterates use to simulate the blood or life energy of which it is the symbolic counterpart. The red ocher sometimes lies around the skeletal remains in cakes, steeping everything in the vicinity with its color, presumably so that all the surrounding objects may keep their living quality in the other world.[1] When she was discovered, the Laussel Venus still bore traces of the red pigment with which she had been painted some twenty-three thousand years earlier.

Even today, or at least recently, body painting with red ocher is or was an integral part of many religious and ceremonial occasions in Oceania, Australia, Africa, and the Americas.

Kaberry describes its use by the Australian Aborigines at corroborees and other celebrations including puberty and marriage. The last is a simple rite: woman and man go alone into the bush for a few days and return painted with red ocher, signifying that they are wife and husband.[2]

A prized article of trade in Australia, it was also much in demand among American Indians at the time of white contact. When the Spaniard Núñez Cabeza de Vaca was shipwrecked off the coast of Texas in 1528, he made it to the mainland. Once there he survived among the strange Indian tribes by trading. He brought snails and mussel shells from the coast inland, and returned with much desired rarities, red ocher for body paint, skins, and special stones for arrowheads.[3]

From being a sacred color red has been translated into the color of luck, of renewal, and of change. It is used in good-luck amulets in the Mediterranean and also figures as a lucky color in Chinese New Year's celebrations. Above all, it has always been the color of revolution; the red flag is not merely an incitement to anger; it signifies the overturn of present rigidities and the arrival of a newer, presumably more life-giving scheme of existence.

Very little was known about the biology of human reproduction until recent times. Women have what was long considered a mysterious, even magic, issue of this red blood of life and renewal every month save when they are pregnant and until they are past the age of childbearing. Being a woman is defined by the onset of this periodic bleeding—menarche.

Women bleed; they bleed at menstruation; they bleed at childbirth. And blood is sacred; it is the stuff of life. We bleed only while we are alive, though bleeding may cause our death. It is women, however, who bleed regularly, as well as irregularly, and who produce life.

The Australian Aborigine men had not yet invented or discovered their connection with the actual conception of children, so they created various ceremonies of equivalence to female functions—the bloody Australian initiation rites which so horrified and fascinated Western male observers. Most of the early interpreters were so thoroughly indoctrinated by Western attitudes of disgust toward female biology and female sexuality that they failed to see the emulation of woman represented by the slitting of the penis into a symbolic vulva and the reiterated bleeding. The male organ of pleasure is changed to resemble the female organ, which is both that of pleasure and of childbirth. Initiation rites transpose the actual birth of male children into a ceremonial rebirth by way of men, and the male penis is converted into a womb with a vagina. Subincision is connected with the belief in the life-giving, strengthening power of blood. Blood is sacred, and at many totem rites and other solemn occasions Aborigine men gash their arms and genitals to produce it.[4]

Several anthropologists have reported on the complex and bloody rites of circumcision and subincision. The operation is often performed in several stages, first on the adolescent boy, then at intervals of a few years to lengthen the slit and to let blood. "Cut mine, cut mine," a white observer quoted the Australian tribesmen, demanding longer and longer cuts on their penises. The wound is sometimes referred to as a "penis-womb" or "vagina."[5]

Much has been made of the cruelty and bizarre nature of these rites, in which the man seems to be demonstrating his ability to withstand pain, as the woman withstands it in childbirth or in menstruation. The blood which is collected and used in various stages of the rites competes with the blood of menstruation and childbirth. There is a strong belief among the Aborigines that blood possesses magic power. A transfer of this power takes place between men of the Walbiri tribe in a ceremony in which rivulets of blood are dripped down over a squatting man by another stooping over him.[6]

The ceremony of mingling blood engaged in by Tom Sawyer and Huck Finn is not unrelated. They became blood brothers, as though formed in the belly of the same mother. Among the Ungarinyin in the Kimberleys, the quarry must be swung round when it is killed so that its blood spatters the ground. This will cause animals to breed more copiously, another illustration of the relationship between blood and birth.[7]

Many fanciful descriptions and interpretations of the Australian ceremonies have been given. Ashley Montagu hypothesizes that the men consider menstruation to be a periodic purge and cleansing and therefore perform similar bloodletting operations on themselves. Campbell suggests that since the blood is sometimes drunk or smeared on the backs of the initiates in various stages, it is analogous to and a substitute for mother's milk. Whatever the particular etiology of the rites, which vary from tribe to tribe, the element of male compensation for woman's primary role in nature is evident. In fact, Wogeo men simulate women's monthly function by cutting their penises with a shell and allowing some blood to flow out. This is called menstruation or male menstruation. It is considered cleansing and is performed periodically, although the blood which flows and the process make the men taboo for several weeks afterward.[8]

Different cultures have different ways of mediating womb envy. Margaret Mead pointed out the symbolic rebirth compassed by adolescent initiation ceremonies, the way in which the male arrogates female biological processes to himself. She cites the womb-envying patterns of several South Sea Island cultures she studied in which the basic theme of the initiation cult is that women hold the secrets of life by virtue of their ability to make children. Since men's role is uncertain, undefined, and perhaps unnecessary, by a great effort they have hit on a way of compensating themselves for their basic inferiority. They get the male children away from the women and brand them as incomplete until the men themselves have turned the boys into men. Women, they have to admit, make human beings, but in their belief only men can make men. The imitations of birth are more or less overt: in some the initiates are swallowed by the crocodile that represents the men's group and come out newborn at the end; they may be housed in wombs, or fed on blood, fattened, have food put into their mouth, and be tended by male "mothers." Universal to the cult is the myth that somehow these rituals were all stolen from the women, sometimes that women were killed to get it. To the Westerner who comes from a society that has exalted men's achievements and depreciated women's role, it is outlandish—all the more so when one realizes that these men who depend for their manhood on a fantasy structure of bamboo flutes, played inside leaf hedges simulating artificial wombs, are not peaceful shepherds but fiercely aggressive headhunters, tall, strong, and well built and capable of magnificent anger.[9]

Only in recent years and with the growing participation of women anthropologists have we begun to realize that the widespread customs of menstrual restrictions do not necessarily represent disgust or even a low status for women; they may be connected with the mana—the magic and fearful power of the blood itself, which by a mysterious and ununderstood mechanism might become a child.

The Hebrew dictum that women are unclean—"How can he be clean that is born of a woman?" is demanded by Job in the Old Testament—was inherited by Christians and Moslems and is associated with the inferior position of women among them. The reason Judeo-Christian religion finds menstruation disgusting, unclean, is because it is a reminder of the life of the body and the supremacy of women in giving birth. This represents what Campbell calls "patriarchal inversion," the need to belittle and demean what was formerly considered sacred and awe-inspiring. The *elima* of the Mbuti Pygmies, the ceremonies of the Australian Kimberley tribes to bring on menstruation, and other celebrations of menarche demonstrate that woman's periodic issue can be admired and respectworthy: one becomes a woman and one can reproduce. Its onset may also be synonymous with the beginning of pleasure—sexual life and accessibility thereto.

In her discussion of menstrual taboos, Alice Schlegel comments that the loss of the wife's services—in sex and perhaps in cooking and household work—may be annoying to the husband, particularly in monogamous families. Where menstruating women are seen as dangerous to men, to sacred objects, and even to crops, there is also the inconvenience of guarding against accidental mischief caused by menstruating women. While traditionally menstrual restrictions among nonliterates have been taken as a mark of the inferior status of women, men suffer as much or more from these restrictions. The menstrual hut or a restriction on housework may well be a welcome monthly vacation to the woman.[10] In the Australian Kimberleys, menstruation is linked with being a woman. It has become associated with taboos and rites and has been identified with certain magical properties, in so far as it is associated with blood and the genitals. But Kaberry reported that she never detected any disgust and horror of a menstruating woman in the attitude of the men. During her period the woman camped apart and kept unobtrusively out of the way, but unless one were familiar with the general habits of social intercourse, her segregation was not noticeable except at night, when she slept on the other side of the fire some few feet away from her husband. She was not spoken of as being "dirty or unclean." She was *gunbu*—forbidden on pain of sickness or death. The blood would cause the men to sicken, so she avoided participating in activities that involved men. She herself never referred to menstruation as *kambulo*—shameful—and she did not consider herself unclean.[11]

While menstruating women are considered ritually unclean in parts of India and among Christian and Semitic peoples, there are societies where she is particularly desirable. It was believed that a Kaska man who had intercourse with a menstruating woman would pass blood in his urine so that he would sicken and die. Despite this, boys took advantage of the easy access to girls in seclusion, nor did the girls always resist their advances. When they became ill, the boys might confess such offenses.[12] Evidently it was the blood and not the woman that was dangerous, for in 1949, at the time of an ethnographer's report, modern Kaska youth had found a method of protecting themselves: they still seized the occasion to make love to menstruating girls, but they used a modern invention, the condom, to ward off the traditional dangers. Among the Hopi, on the contrary, some people feel that sexual relations may be harmful to the woman, even though she is more sexually attractive to men at this time than when she is not menstruating.[13]

When Cabeza de Vaca made his arduous trek in southwestern North America in the early fifteen hundreds, trading in the sacred red ocher, he was horrified and disgusted by the "savage customs" he observed, including, of course, segregation and special treatment of menstruating women. Schlegel finds "striking parallels, especially in American Indian practices, between restrictions placed upon menstruating women and men in a state of spiritual tension or danger, such as before warfare or the hunt, after homicide and during ceremonial periods." Practices concerning menstruation reflect a state of spiritual danger. Some cultures have used menstruation to explain and justify the inferior status of women, but if we think of the nature of menstrual taboos and of how similar they are to the restrictions many cultures apply to disruptions of normal physical or spiritual states—death, killing in warfare or the chase, ceremonial activities, and such—menstrual restrictions would seem of a like nature, differing only in that they are automatic and periodic.[14]

Menopause, the phenomenon which is limited for all practical purposes to the human species alone, probably occurred only among people located in favorable climatic conditions. Few Western European Neanderthal women might have been expected to survive past childbearing age, as few Arctic Eskimos, female and male, survived into, let alone past, their fifties.

Margaret Mead pointed out the advantage of menopause for human society, as well as for the women themselves. Those who managed to survive the rigors of childbearing—enforced in sedentary patriarchal societies, self-limited in nomadic foraging ones—were then free to give their energies in a wider range, to offer wisdom and experience to the young. In certain cultures many privileged positions become open to older women after they are no longer set apart by the mana surrounding their reproductive talents: they may become priests, shamans, village leaders (head*men*), etc.

Anthropologist Asen Balikci's film about the Canadian Arctic Netsilik Eskimos shows the old grandmother telling stories to the whole group, and one is reminded that when the Brothers Grimm assembled their monumental collection of folk tales their chief informants were certain old women. (The Balikci film depicted a remarkable tenderness and seeming mutual respect between the sexes which was very much at variance with earlier reports about the brutalities of Eskimo men toward their women.) The film also showed the division of meat according to custom. The two men who had caught a seal shared and ate the raw liver on the spot, then they dragged the animal back to the ice house where the young women reached into its innards and devoured handfuls of fresh blood, their portion, before the rest of the animal was cut up and distributed among the group.

Though much had been made in previous writings of the exclusion of women from the spiritual aspects of Australian Aborigine life, a woman ethnographer reported on the old woman who repainted the portrait of the Rainbow Serpent so that the spirit children might increase.[15] Another woman ethnographer, discussing the position of women in Northern Australia, notes that the counterpart in Tiwi language of big man, *aragulani*, is *parimarina*, menopausal woman, while the next stage for both is old age, *irula* for the old man and *intula* for the old woman.[16] In agricultural China, the pyramidal hierarchy of the extended family was arranged so that a woman endured the inferior status of daughter-in-law in her husband's home, looking forward to the time when she would become the matriarch, mother and mother-in-law, and pass over to the high side of the power relationship, tyrannizer rather than tyrannized. Reports have it that menopause depression was rare if not nonexistent in this culture, which offered actual and intangible rewards to the older woman after the oppression visited on the younger one.

Before the reaction against motherhood in this century initiated by Freudian psychology, the postmenopause woman was assured of a special devotion and loyalty from her grown children. "Who would have dreamed that a socially mature male of about eighteen years of age would still spend much time in the company of his old mother?"[17] Jane Goodall marveled at the strength of the mother-child affection relationships among the Gombe Stream chimpanzees, sentiments which used to be widely echoed on a human level.

Kaberry speaks at length about the bond between a mother and her children in the Australian Kimberleys: the sorrow when the daughter goes away to be married, the fifty-mile walk a daughter will make to see her mother, and the special loyalty and affection of both sexes for their old mothers. A *son*, too, though separated from his mother during initiation periods, cherishes a strong affection for her throughout her lifetime, giving her food and caring for her in old age. She is at great pains to present evidence counteracting the confident statements made by earlier anthropologists to the effect that there is no recognition among the Australian tribes of the physical tie between mother and child. In discussing the belief in spirit children the mother was described as merely a "domestic cow," a vessel and a medium through which the child passes. According to Ashley Montagu, "The relationship which the mother bears to the child is regarded as being, from the physical standpoint, none at all."[18]

Not so, says Kaberry. Among the tribes she studied, the child was very definitely linked physically to the mother, flesh of her flesh, blood of her blood, nursed by her milk, fed by her hands, though the father bears no such physical relationship. Thus two men with different social fathers (physical fatherhood being unknown, it is not the man with whom a woman has slept who is considered to be a child's father, but the one with whom she is living at the time the child is born, or the one who has dreamed the animal or plant or pool which will be the child's totem) and one mother will consider themselves brothers. In cases of confusing relationships resulting from "wrong marriages" under the complex Australian kinship system, tribal relatives will be named by the simple expedient of "throwing away" the father.[19]

In nonliterate foraging tribes old age is usually much respected, for old people have survived the hardships and danger of life and are, in contrast with our own attitudes, considered to have much-needed wisdom for the young. They are the walking books of Truffaut's *Fahrenheit 451*, to which the French film director thought civilization's progress might force us to return. The Kimberleys are no exception; postmenopausal and old women have much authority, in everyday affairs as well as in the religious life, where it is only they, along with old men, who can perform the increase ceremonies considered necessary to the procurement of existence.

Goodale tells in *Tiwi Wives* of the very special position of the older woman in Melville and Bathurst Islands in northern Australia. If she is a "first-wife" she wields much authority over her daughters and over co-wives' daughters, for she is their "supreme mother." Old women are treated with much respect by their sons. Not only are they looked after and cared for, their advice is often asked and often taken. In recent years, Western interference has vitiated much of the power of older women. Government and mission consider husbands the base of the domestic group, and the officials usually back up the husband's word in a family debate if some woman (usually the husband's mother-in-law or his mother) steps in to "interfere." Goodale finds it paradoxical that Western culture, the great "protector" of women's rights today, has contributed to the loss of so many of the Tiwi woman's traditional rights.[20]

In our culture, where women were valued chiefly as producers of children, they lost status once they were past childbearing age. In small-scale nonliterate societies, it was the process, not the product, which inspired respect or diffidence. Once the process had ceased, the women themselves often became important contributors in group councils, assuming official and unofficial roles.

Judging by our own recent social history, it may well be that the physiological process of menopause can be a spur to peak creativity for those women who live that long and who have managed to achieve self-expression in the arts. George Eliot, Virginia Woolf, Edith Wharton, and Kate Chopin are some of the writers who produced their greatest works from their middle forties to early fifties. The irregularities of hormone output at this time result in intense heights and surges of emotion not dissimilar to those of adolescence, but they appear at a stage in life when women artists may have acquired the wisdom and control which enable them to translate their emotions into their work.

17

Early Households

Clues to the composition of Paleolithic households are lacking in the sparse evidence so far uncovered—tools and ornaments, dwelling places, fossils, and burials—though analogy with present-day foragers suggests they would have been based on loose and shifting mutuality. The earliest living sites in Africa some millions of years ago may have been occupied for a few nights or weeks; bone waste and stone tools and chips from the manufacture of the tools were the evidence that led archaeologists to conclude that early hominids had camped there. Traces of million-year-old human habitation have been uncovered in Chinese caves, while new evidence indicates that humans might have been living in Greece some 750,000 years ago, at Vérteszöllös in Hungary perhaps 400,000. At Terra Amata, on the French Riviera, hearths and post holes and stone blocks have provided clues to human living arrangements perhaps 200,000 years ago. If the post holes are the remains of oval huts, as archaeologists infer, the space enclosed might have housed ten to twenty people in groups similar to mother-centered bands of more recent times.[1]

Among present-day gathering-hunting peoples living arrangements are fluid and changeable. When a difference of opinion or a quarrel arose among two members of a Mbuti Pygmy band, the group would often split. "When hostilities come into the open the solution is for one or the other disputant to pick

up and leave."[2] Anthropologists call this process "resolution of
conflict by fission." Similar looseness of association with frequent breakings-up and recombinations has been observed
among divers foragers—the North American Athapaskans, the
African Hadza, the Kalahari San. Richard Borshay Lee discusses the annual gatherings of !Kung San in the winter dry
season. When bands become large, people have to work harder
to procure food and more disputes arise. "This conflict usually
results in one or both parties splitting off to seek greener pas-
tures."[3] This method of solving disputes is projected for Paleolithic humans and considered instrumental in the widespread
occupation of territory by developing species. Foragers—in contrast to agricultural and urban peoples—can easily vote with
their feet. They do not wait till the food supply is exhausted to
do so; they take steps much earlier—when their patience is
exhausted.[4]

Mbuti Pygmy men, women, even children, often go off alone
to live in the forest.[5] That questing and enlarging brain, with
its omnipresent why, must also have contributed to the
diffusion of the species over much of the planet. In recent
times in North America the settling of Cape Cod and Ply-
mouth by the Pilgrims and of Rhode Island by Roger Wil-
liams' group, both of whom made friends with local Indians,
exemplify Turnbull's principle. On the other hand, most of the
white invasion of the Americas reflects the later conquest mentality, a product of a technologically more advanced state of development.

Present-day foragers do not show strong male dominance
though the interference of Western bureaucrats and the contact with settled agriculturalists often shifts the egalitarian balance between the sexes. Evidence from recent ecologically
oriented studies shows that women contribute economically
and are valued for their contribution; in consequence scholars
today question previous assumptions of strong male dominance
among Paleolithic peoples.[6] Even among northern peoples like
the Eskimos, where meat played a major role in subsistence
and was hunted chiefly by men, there is a rethinking of the old
tradition that the women were owned and given by the men,

with no voice in their own sexual experience. By the time students came upon many of the "primitive peoples" they had been subjected to exploitation, brutalization, and ill treatment by colonizers and were in a state of degradation.[7] In the north, whalers and fur traders introduced new elements which made it almost impossible to determine previous attitudes among the sexes.[8]

Male dominance as a concept may not be applicable to the interaction between the members of a band of Paleolithic humans; in severe weather conditions males and females would have had to be extremely tough and resourceful to survive; in milder climates with more abundant resources there would have been little reason or need for aggressive relations between the sexes.

As women anthropologists are now pointing out, in ethnographic studies most of the field work was done by male investigators using male informants, permitting a double element of distortion. In the male-dominated world of academia, the few women who did bring back new, unexpected, or unwelcome evidence during the past half century were liable to be contradicted, corrected, or just ignored by their male colleagues unless they phrased their material with great caution. No woman could have presented the findings of a Malinowski about active female sexuality and ignorance of blood ties to the father; she would have been ridiculed or rejected. In 1939 Kaberry's book *Aboriginal Woman* upset a good many of the previous generalizations about the degraded status of Australian women, including the pronouncement that they were excluded from the very rich spiritual life of the community. "My contention that aboriginal woman is not only profane but also sacred, may create some controversy; and some may assert that it is only in North-West Australia that the women participate to any marked extent in religion . . . they possess totems, have spiritual affiliations with the sacred past, and perform their own sacred rites from which the men are excluded."[9]

Kaberry's book had an introduction by her former professor, A. P. Elkin. Though he acknowledged the value of her work, in the very act of presenting it, he took gentle but firm exception to her statement about women's "sacred" nature and her evidence to show that they did not accept the men's superior spirituality: "Women may be independent, powerful, and spiritual, and yet be profane . . . I doubt that there is as much in another point made by Dr. Kaberry as she is inclined to think."[10] So much for the findings of women ethnographers among women subjects.

I have pointed out that chastity and lifelong monogamy are rare among small-scale societies and sexual experience is allowed for in most nonliterate cultures. Western males generally perceived this as under male control, although Malinowski himself made it clear that female repression was unknown among the Trobrianders and that sexual expression by women and men was considered normal and necessary. Reports on the Australian Aborigines as well as from Arctic ethnographers depicted the women as freely available but at the will of the male "possessor." From the work of Kaberry in the nineteen thirties and Jane Goodale in the nineteen fifties, it has become clear that Australian Aboriginal women exercise considerable sexual independence. Adultery and serial marriage are common, and when they want to sleep with a man they make it known by sending a gift of tobacco or some other message. Jealousy is a problem faced by either sex. Mutual fidelity is demanded—if not always received—and the husband's laxities are not condoned. Kaberry describes a quarrel in which the wife accused her husband of going with another woman: "Barudjil [the wife] . . . picked up her boomerang, banged him, then grabbed a tomahawk to enforce her point and pummeled him with the blunt edge on his arms and shoulders," after which the husband picked up his swag and departed, "hurling obscenities and an occasional boomerang at her which she avoided easily, but which came unpleasantly near where I was standing diligently making notes."[11]

According to Kaberry the Kimberley women had an irreverent attitude toward the supposedly sacred ceremonies of their men, regarding them chiefly as sexual objects to be admired as prospective lovers. She contrasts the male ethnographers' reports that for Australian men women were insatiable in their sexual demands with her own finding that women were all too apt to complain of the insatiability of their men.

Much of Kaberry's book is devoted to refuting, point by point, earlier generalizations about Australian Aborigine women as scarcely human, beasts of burden, helpless chattels of their husbands. The women of the Kimberleys have love corroborees, to charm new lovers or insure the faithfulness of husbands. They marry to have sexual access, not to have children. Questioned on whether she liked being married, one woman answered in pidgin English, "Me lik 'em boy; we walkabout, we *muna-muna* [have sexual intercourse]; got 'em one camp belonga twofellow; might be we catchem kangaroo, fish."[12]

After a boy's initiation festival all who have been present engage in group sex. At the conclusion of certain corroborees among the Wula and North Lunga, one woman will remain behind to have intercourse with some of the dancers. Sometimes a husband may be loath to give up his wife, and compulsion is brought to bear upon him. From their comments, the women were not unwilling. They stigmatized the reluctant husbands as "stingy," while compliant ones were praised as "proper good fellow."

Male anthropologists have reported on these customs as evidence of the degradation and subordination of women in Australian Aborigine society: "a mockery of all morals," expostulated Freudian Geza Roheim. As Kaberry points out, they can hardly be considered immoral in the Australian ethos, for they have religious sanction, and they subordinate and degrade the woman neither more nor less than the man.[13]

Among the Melanesians of Lesu extramarital dalliance is a social custom with all the force of tradition, and rape is unknown. Hortense Powdermaker reported that if a woman did not want to go with a man, she merely said no, giving an excuse or not as she pleased. It is a socially accepted custom for wife and husband to have intercourse with a number of additional partners. It would be considered abnormal if either one, when young, did not do so. A young married woman who did not have lovers would be like a young girl in our society who has no boy friends or is not invited to parties. Middle-aged women discussed their past affairs with her freely. Most of them had had so many lovers they could not remember exactly how many. One old woman asked Powdermaker rather indignantly how she could expect her to remember every man she had ever slept with. Permanent intrigues with one man were not common, for, if this occurred, the woman would divorce her husband and marry her lover.[14]

When a wedding is to take place, the women of Lesu practice their dances every night for ten days in advance. Two nights before the ceremony, they dance in a spirit of wild play, lifting their loincloths and exhibiting themselves. The dancing goes on through the night and ends with some of the women having intercourse with the men who have been watching. This is the rather promiscuous sexual intercourse which sometimes follows the wedding dances.[15] (Several extant descriptions of medieval peasant wedding festivities in Europe tell of similar scenes: wild dancing and drinking ending up in a grand free-for-all of promiscuous intercourse. Breughel's well-known painting from a later period stops just short of the conclusion.)

Polygyny, polyandry, and monogamy were practiced in Lesu. If a woman has two husbands, they are known as husband number one and husband number two. Sometimes all three sleep in the same house, three beds in a row, with the woman between the two men; other times, husband number two sleeps in the men's house, and the woman sleeps with her two husbands alternately. There seems to be no quarreling between the two men. The woman's children call both men *mum* (father). In the case of polygyny, the children of both wives call each one *nangga* (mother).[16]

The women of the African Hadza also practiced sex relatively freely, autonomously, and following their own desires. A man was married only so long as he lived regularly with his wife. Once he left her for no longer than a few weeks "his house had died"; he had no further rights over her or his children by her. She could marry as soon as she liked, and if her husband returned before she remarried she could accept or reject him as she chose.[17] The Hadza were always moving about, changing camp and the composition of the camp. Pressure was on the husband to maintain his associations with the women, not vice versa, since it was relationship to the mother, not the father, which influenced choice of residence. When a camp divided and the man's mother went one direction with a group of people and his wife's mother in another direction, he was faced with a direct and troublesome choice.

For all these people relationships correspond to the American custom of serial marriage. Ethnographers often use the words marriage and divorce somewhat loosely. Among the Eskimos and the Ojibwa marriage means a semipermanent and recognized union. Eskimo women and men switch partners frequently. People of the Ojibwa desert one another on any conceivable pretext, or on none at all. People marry where desire directs them; they remain together as long as inclination and habit dictate. One Ojibwa woman was married and divorced seven times, became a shaman at the age of fifty, and later found an eighth husband.[18]

Western observers use the conventions of our own language to phrase their descriptions of marriage in terms of male possession of women. For most foraging peoples, however, it is an economic partnership. In Western Australia, the tribespeople studied by Kaberry might come together on the basis of sexual attraction, but ultimately economic, social, and procreative needs were also involved. The Tiwi are usually considered a male-dominant society, but, according to Goodale, both male and female Tiwi viewed their culture's rules governing choice of mates as providing them with considerable freedom and variety through their life. Men achieve variety through acquisition of multiple wives, while women anticipate a succession of husbands; and both sexes manage a limited amount of sexual variety outside marriage.[19]

Among the Northern Australian Tiwi, marriage could be any one of a series of formalized contract relationships. A round-up of forms of marital and family arrangements from ethnographic sources reveals many variations. Polygyny is more common than polyandry; where the motivation is economic women desire polygyny as well as men. Among the Nayars of Southeast India, one woman is, in effect, married to a group of brothers.

A man may enter his wife's house only if she has put his sandals on the doorstep; otherwise he must wait and come back another day. There is no way of knowing who is the father of her children. Africa, known for its wide range of political forms, also turns up such customs as woman-woman marriage (a way of providing heirs for a woman landowner, who delegates a chosen male to impregnate her wife), and tribes where a pregnant bride is preferred, for she has given proof of her ability to breed. Men of the Mae Enga in New Guinea spend most of their time in the men's house and encounter women with the utmost hesitation. Arrangements where women and their children have each their own home while men live in the men's house, in a small house of their own, or with sisters or mothers, are found in Africa, in Oceania, and in Southwest North America. Hopi women are the homeowners in the pueblos, and rooms are handed down from mother to daughter. Men build houses, but they do not own them. A man feels that his sister's home is his real home though, actually, he is peripheral in both his sister's and his wife's home. Mandan, Iroquois, and Cherokee women were equally considered the owners of houses and personal property. African matrilineal societies also have odd family arrangements. In Ashanti villages, about an hour before dusk, children could be seen scurrying in all directions carrying pots of cooked food. They were bringing meals from houses where their mothers lived to houses where their fathers lived.[20] Residence groups comprised sisters and brothers and the sons and daughters of the sisters.

Perspective is everything: male and female anthropologists bring back entirely different reports. "Women see babies; men see politics," said one male anthropologist. At a May 1973 conference on women and language, Ann Bodine, an anthropologist from Rutgers, cited a male ethnographer's report on Bengali. "Basing his work on the language of the men, he came to the absurd conclusion that the language gave its speakers many ways to address men but no way to address women if they were not related."[21] In actuality, the system was balanced so that women had many ways to address women but no way to address unrelated men. The male ethnographers had reported a situation as it existed among the men and ignored the equivalent institution among women.

As Kaberry had discovered ceremonies and rights and expressions unreported by earlier male ethnographers, so Goodale's recent work among the Australian Tiwi was at variance with earlier studies. She told of the contracts women arranged with their future sons-in-law which provided the women with payments of game over periods of years, and of women's economic importance and sexual expression in Tiwi life.

Her example was given earlier of how Western civilization reinforces the man's position and weakens the woman's. This is a process which has occurred all over the world; it began with the first white contacts and has deeply infiltrated all nonliterate societies, the extent depending on the length of time during which they have had relations with patriarchal cultures. White influence usually means a loss of rights for women, whether it be among the loosely organized nonauthoritarian Navajos, the female-dominated Iroquois, African societies where women played important roles in agriculture and trade, or South American and Oceanic groups where abortion and infanticide were practiced autonomously by women as a method of birth control.

Sometimes Western white administrators insisted on the appointment of a male headman where there had been none before or where authority roles were delegated to a group of women; at others they forced the men who had hitherto hunted and played and politicked to take to farming and vested economic control in them, taking it away from the women. In the past both Christian missionary and colonial influence were male-enhancing pressures in forbidding any kind of birth control in the name of the sacredness of the unborn child's life in preference to that of the mother, as is received Christian dogma. Missionaries, administrators, and ethnologists viewed female sexual autonomy and expression as lewd and lascivious, with the missionaries seeking to enforce chastity and virginity, while administrators and colonizers introduced such civilized perversions as prostitution and rape. All assumed male possession of women and children, a concept not always applicable

among non-Western peoples. A Jesuit missionary reproached a
Montagnais Indian for not interfering when his wife slept with
other men. "How will you know that her children are your
own?" "Thou hast no sense," was the Indian's equable reply.
"You French love only your own children, but we love all the
children of our tribe."[22] Or, in the words of an African Ibo
song, "The child of one is the child of all."

In the present, new farming methods introduced into economically undeveloped areas almost invariably concentrate on
the men, who receive education in technology and are preferred
in numerous ways so that the price of improved food production and industrialization is a loss of rights and function for the
women.[23]

Just as earlier explorers saw kings and hierarchies where they
did not exist, so male anthropologists saw male dominance and
male supremacy everywhere they looked.[24] Alice Schlegel's
study of Hopi Indian women found that those who had not accepted Christianity had more autonomy and control of property and the household than was indicated in a male anthropologist's report completed some twenty years earlier.
Christianized Hopi women lost power, however, when they accepted the American kinship pattern.[25] Comparison of male
and female scholars' reports on Australian Aborigines also reveals wide discrepancies of vision. Male anthropologists exaggerated the importance of political power and technology and
minimized the Aborigine women's economic contribution, the
importance of which was fully acknowledged by the natives
themselves. Western men projected Western ideas of female
uncleanliness onto the Australians and insisted, against the
facts, that the Aborigines did not recognize the female generative principle. Male observers ignored or belittled the importance of women's ritual lives and proclaimed their subordinate
status. Women ethnographers found women and men living together in partnership, with rights, self-respect, and dignity guar-
anteed for each sex. They concluded that the Aborigine women
had complete control over their bodies and reproductive functions and that neither they themselves nor the Aborigine men
saw women as contaminating, polluting, evil, or dangerous.[26]

As we saw earlier, the old assumptions about "patrilineal hunting bands" as the earliest form of social organization are no longer accepted. The argument that slow-developing human children would create strong pressure for a nuclear family was also projected from recent Western civilizations. Human development is slower than that of the large-brained primates who are our closest animal relatives. Puberty comes between ages eleven and fifteen in a human female, at seven or eight in a chimpanzee, though neither is completely mature at that time. But a task-free childhood is far from universal, for us today, among our own forebears, and among living peasant and tribal groups. Girls, in particular, begin taking care of brothers and sisters very young—as early as age five in Samoa—and they are often helping with child care and food gathering or household chores by the age of eight. A recent study of modern American families found that on the average girls contribute more home labor—chores, housekeeping, and other daily tasks—than their brothers. In nineteenth-century Europe, Karl Marx's servant and mistress, Helene Demuth, went into service at the age of eight and was employed by Marx's wife's family, the Von Westphalens, when she was eleven. Dickens' reports on children working in factories and mines as early as age six are echoed not only in other parts of the nineteenth-century civilized world but in reports from Asia and Africa today.

In the groups with the least material culture, Australian Aborigines, Congo (Zaire) Pygmies, and Kalahari San, there is less imposition on youngsters by their elders. These children may provide part of their own food as they accompany their mothers on gathering expeditions but they are not responsible for feeding others until maturity or, sometimes, marriage. Paleolithic children would also have had fewer tasks than the children of later times.

By about ten thousand years ago humans had peopled all six continents, spreading across land connections which have since disappeared, and down to the tip of South America and the southern deserts of Australia. They seemed to aggregate in fairly small groups, and, judging by surviving gatherer-hunters, they had loose ties, flexible and subject to division and regroupings, often in flux. Band associations were probably based above all on mother-daughter and sibling relationships traced through the mother. In "marriage" the groom was likely to become attached to the bride's parents' group, for a period of years or even permanently. In seasons of hardship—dryness or cold—groups of twenty to forty would have been the rule. In summer or the season of plenty, small dispersed groups in a fairly large territory might come together for meetings of as many as one to two hundred people. Large corroborees of Australian Aborigines and African San camps embodying 100 to 150 souls are recent examples, while the annual summer encounters of Greenland Eskimos ceased almost half a century ago. At these times there would have been opportunities for exchange, resulting in the diffusion of new ideas as well as cross-group matings, bringing new inherited traits into otherwise isolated gene pools. Populations had grown, though very slowly, over a period of several million years, and cultural relics in the form of tools, hearths, and ornaments had also augmented, indicating an increase in the sources of sustenance.

The evidence for early households is still speculative, but ecological circumstance, art, and the imperfect analogies drawn from present-day foragers tell us that Paleolithic women would have had control over their own bodies, sexual expression, and full economic participation in group life. Diverse family groupings had probably begun to develop in different parts of the planet. Mother-child relationships would be the most enduring, and brothers and sisters would often retain their affinities. Over time, the sexual pull between a given woman and man might also develop, through shared experience and emotion, into a specifically human creation, the very deep communion and friendship that can be created by long-term intimacy.[27]

Part IV

HOW THE SEXUAL CONNECTION BECAME A POWER CONNECTION

I am he who made heaven and earth, who knotted together the mountains and created what is thereon. I am he who made the waters, so that the Heavenly Cow might come into being. I am he who made the bull for the cow, so that sexual pleasures might come into being.

> —*The God and His Unknown Name*
> (Egyptian texts of 1350–1200 B.C.E.)[1]

18

Gathering to Farming

The first period of agriculture is generally treated, especially by older writers, as the great period for women since practically everyone is willing to allow that plants were originally the province of females, as they still are in many ethnological contexts. Certainly woman is responsible for several of the inventions which make their appearance about this time—say ten or eleven thousand years ago—and during the ensuing four thousand years: basketry, pottery making, spinning and weaving from the fleece of sheep and goats and from the fibers of flax, the chemical experimentations which produced bread and wine and beer. There are those who would credit her with the invention of planting and reaping and with the development of all agricultural pursuits until the appearance of the plow.

However, while the beginnings of agriculture were a time of importance and respect for women, so in most places on earth were the several million years that preceded them. Recent studies indicate that agriculture was not the revolutionary invention past writers took it for and that in many respects it brought adverse consequences despite the mythical and historical accolades heaped upon it by our cultural past.

It is a part of our tradition that nomadic foragers do not cultivate the land because they are unaware of the benefits of farming, that they are ignorant and inferior. It was also believed, until recently, that they spend their time in an unceasing quest for food and that their population is limited by its scarcity. In the last decade or two, investigators have re-examined these stereotypes and they find that, on the contrary, gatherers have a sophisticated knowledge of botany. They understand the processes by which plants grow and have considerable intelligence about when and where to find an enormous variety of growing things and how to use their products. It is not for lack of knowledge that they do not farm: in many cases they live better and with less effort than the neighboring peasantry.

There have been many theories about the origins of agriculture, but the latest evidence shows that systematic cultivation of grain—wheat and barley—and first the herding, then the domestication of sheep and goats probably did arise in the land of Western white culture's mythical origins, the Near East.[1]

Let us look at the sequence of events there, beginning perhaps twelve thousand years ago. We are back in the garden, eastward in Eden, where the Euphrates and the Tigris really do rise, where, according to the Judeo-Christian Bible and the Koran, the four rivers of earth have their source. Over the previous few thousand years the pattern of existence has been shifting, here as elsewhere in Eurasia and the lands around the Mediterranean, during the final retreat of the Würm glaciation.

In the Near East, people have been coming out of caves to live in more or less permanent settlements, in skin huts first, then in houses made of rock, of pressed mud, or of mud brick. On the Anatolian plain, in Palestine, on the steppes of Iran and Iraq, and in the mountain valleys of the Zagros and of Jordan, villages exist where they had not before.

Zawi Chemi Shanidar is one of the earliest; it was inhabited at the same time as nearby Shanidar Cave, though the latter had a history of human occupation dating back some fifty thousand years. Whether these villages were at first inhabited all year round is not known; the villagers of Zawi Chemi, for example, may have sought refuge in Shanidar Cave during the cold winter, returning to open-air dwellings in milder weather.

What had been going on in this area during this period and

for a few thousand years preceding it has been called the broad-spectrum revolution. For a variety of reasons people were eating differently. There was a new interest in products of the sea and shore. Archaeologists have found evidence of the consumption of fish, crabs, water turtles, mollusks, land snails, partridges, and migratory waterfowl added to that provided by the bones of larger mammals. One group at Tepe Asiab in western Iran must have lived for some time on lizards, toads, or frogs—such was the diet revealed by their fossilized feces.[2]

This period used to be viewed as a degeneration from the Eurasian Paleolithic hunting period. But the Ice Age hunter was limited to certain parts of the planet; most people on earth had probably lived largely on plants. Based on the indications provided by recent coprolite studies, the broad-spectrum revolution may have been limited to the areas intensively studied by European archaeologists of the first part of the twentieth century. Elsewhere on earth humans have often, if not always, taken advantage of varied resources. Root cultivation—of yams and other tubers, rhizomes, and bulbs—entails less technology and developed on other continents in tropical and semitropical areas. It may have had an even longer history and a gradual integration into sedentary life and formal agricultural techniques.

Intermediate forms of cultivation had long existed. Gatherers noted when a given food would be ripe and they planned their migrations accordingly. In parts of Australia and in the Andaman Islands women dug up yams and then replaced the tops to grow again. Even more sophisticated were the Australians who forbade the gathering of certain daylilies after they had flowered. The plants were to be left to bear and to disperse seed; they were referred to as "mothers."[3]

In the Near East the new attitudes toward food, wherein everything was viewed as edible, represented imaginative ways of dealing with a changing environment. Boats and rafts were used for fishing. New methods of food preparation and cooking had been devised, as indicated by larger numbers of grinding stones and pounders.

Before the kind of agriculture we know could appear, however, people had to stay in one place long enough to gather the fruits of seeds sowed weeks or months earlier. Till recently it was thought that, with limited exceptions like the Indians of northwestern America who lived largely on products of the sea and possibly the Paleolithic hunters of the Dordogne, the first permanent settlements were linked to farming. Current archaeological studies counter this belief. Twelve thousand years ago, the Near Eastern villagers were not farmers; they lived by mixed practices, collecting, fishing, and hunting, but in areas with stable resources so that people could settle down in one place to exploit them.

Not far from the sea people took advantage of the seasonal crop of shellfish; on the shores of rivers, they harvested eels, salmon, or other salt-water fish which come to fresh water to spawn, while hunting parties went out periodically in search of larger game higher up in the mountains. As the weather warmed, stands of pistachio and oak trees appeared in upland valleys and on mountain slopes, and protein- and fat-rich acorns and nuts were added to the diet. With the exception, perhaps, of the hunting parties, women would have been playing a major role in food procurement.

People had long lived in caves in the prime upland hunting grounds. Now earlier sites like Belt and Hotu caves in northeastern Iran, the Khorramabad caves of southwestern Iran, Anatolian Palagawra where the dog was domesticated some fourteen thousand years ago, and Kebarah in Lebanon multiplied. Bands moved to river and coastal areas to take advantage of different resources.

This may have been because there were fewer large mammals available, as well as more competition for them; it may also have been because the living was easier when more resources were used and the pressure of a gradual population increase was making itself felt. In these new areas of occupation, whether or not the larger mammals were still being taken, the bulk of the food was provided by gathering. As among the Australian Tiwi, it was probably the women who brought in the major portion of protein and calories in the diet, so that their role may well have been more important than it was in the reindeer- and mammoth-hunting cultures of Europe and Siberia during the Ice

Age; it certainly was not less so. Men might still have done more of the meat hunting, but they were bringing in a luxury food; the subsistence base was provided by gathering.

It is about this time, some twelve thousand years ago, that people began to gather the seeds of wild cereal—wheat and barley—from the upland slopes and mountain valleys where they grew in profusion. On a fine spring day during the early nineteen-sixties J. R. Harlan went out in southwestern Turkey with a flint-bladed sickle of prehistoric origin, one of many which have been dug up in Mesolithic sites in the Near East, and harvested "enough wild wheat in an hour to produce one kilo of clean grain."[4] Moreover, the wild grain had almost twice the protein content of domestic wheat. This in an arid zone where, because of alternating conditions of winter rain and summer dryness, almost pure stands of wild wheat, or wild wheat and barley mixed, appear. Harlan demonstrated that in a good year, experienced plant collectors could gather in three weeks more grain than they could possibly consume in a year. Here was an explanation for the existence of certain villages whose sites had long been puzzling archaeologists.

The old books used to tell us about the uncertainties of the hunt for food before the introduction of the wondrous benefits of agriculture—the "Neolithic Revolution" Gordon Childe termed it. "Man must eat to live at all; food is perhaps the one absolute and overriding need for man. In early primitive societies the quest for food was and is the most absorbing preoccupation for all members of the group. The enlargement of the food supply was therefore presumably the indispensable condition for human progress," Childe wrote in 1944.[5] And in 1951, "The community of food-gatherers had been restricted in size by the food supplies available."[6]

More and more, the studies of recent years have created a different picture. There were those who supposed extreme male dominance as a result of the presumed scarcity of food, to be filled by the unceasing efforts of male hunters: "In the hunting period the chief contributors to the sustenance of the tribes had been the men and the role of the women had been largely that of drudges," wrote Joseph Campbell.[7] There were the slightly more sophisticated who realized that females would still play an integral role. Either way, however, we are not far from the "nasty, brutish, and short" mentality that had shaped Western thinking from Hobbes through Darwin and Freud. It was the misnamed conference on Man the Hunter which shook up this certainty.*

Ecologically oriented reports demonstrate that foragers are not on a starvation level, that, in fact, they get all the calories they need with far less labor than peasant farmers. The San of the relatively desolate Kalahari region worked only an average of three days a week to procure 2,100 calories a day. In the sixties, when Richard Borshay Lee was studying them, several years of drought occurred and farmers of the neighboring areas came to the San to learn their ways; they became foragers for a time. It is assumed that gatherers and hunters in the rich environments of prehistoric times would have had an even easier time of it.[8]

"There is abundant data which suggests not only that hunter-gatherers have adequate supplies of food but also that they enjoy quantities of leisure time, much more in fact than do modern industrial or farm workers, or even professors of archeology,"[9] says Louis Binford, himself a professor of archaeology. Marshall Sahlins goes so far as to term certain of the surviving foraging groups "the original affluent societies," since by keeping their material needs minimal they are able to satisfy them in short order with a plethora of leisure time.

If many sources of food are used, it need not be the quest for food alone which occupies the time of humans. "Why should we plant when we have so many mongongo nuts?" the San told

---

* The conference, held in 1967 with the resultant book of the same name published in 1968, overturned previous thinking about human origins. Judging by surviving gatherer-hunters, our ancestors probably lived largely on vegetable food gathered by women, rather than on game supplied by male hunters. However, "it was generally agreed to use the term 'hunters' as a convenient shorthand, despite the fact that the majority of peoples considered subsisted primarily on sources *other than meat*—mainly wild plants and fish." Just so it is generally agreed to use the generic term "man" as shorthand for women, who are more than half the world's population, and in so doing our age-old biases and misconceptions, particularly the invisibility of women, need not be unduly shaken.

Lee.† When it was suggested to the Shoshone Indians that they leave their desolate valley for richer land, they protested, "What, and leave all these wonderful mice behind?" Australian gatherers reject the European imposition as long as they can. "You people go to all that trouble, working and planting seeds, but we don't have to do that. All these things are there for us, the Ancestral Beings left them for us. In the end you depend on the sun and the rain just the same as we do, but the difference is that we just have to go and collect the food when it is ripe. We don't have all this other trouble."[10]

People do not indeed live by bread alone—or even mongongo nuts and witchetty grubs—as we can see from the elaborate imaginative systems and arts created by all human groups, not merely by the so-called advanced civilizations, though these systems do not always take material or preservable forms among the nonliterate foraging groups who used to be derogated as primitive or backward.

What the gatherers do need, however, is space, a larger area of land per person than is permitted by the concentrations of population fostered, even demanded, by agriculture. It has been supposed that the forces which kept population down in the past were the same as those today in force among foraging nomads: plant potions, abortions, infanticide, and taboos on sexual intercourse during a prolonged nursing period. After people began to settle in villages, in a period of a few thousand years, the population must have grown, for more and more village sites appear at later dates, increasing in geometric proportions.

The first villages only practiced collecting and hunting. Wild wheat and barley were gathered and stored. Evidence of subterranean pits comes from several of the early sites: Shanidar

† A half pound of mongongo nuts—the average daily portion eaten by the San in the Dobe area where Lee did his studies—provides as many calories as two and a half pounds of cooked rice and as much protein as fourteen ounces of lean beef. The mongongo tree (sometimes known as "mangetti") is drought-resistant; it gives a constant supply of nuts which can lie on the ground for months without rotting. Other San groups depend on *tsi*, beans similar to peanuts, which grow on vines, to supply their basic protein and fat needs.

Cave and Zawi Chemi Shanidar in northern Iraq, Karim Sha-hir nearby, and Mureybat on the Euphrates River in inland Syria. At Ain Mallaha on the Levantine coast, plastered pits suggest storage, while the stone-lined pits of Mureybat would seem to have been used for roasting wild grain over hot stones —necessary to remove the tough outer hulls characteristic of this form of wheat. Snails, acorns, pistachio nuts, mussels, crabs, whatever, would also have been stored in pits. At this time and in these places, agriculture was neither necessary nor desirable. The early villagers practiced empirically principles of synergy exemplified by Kent Flannery's anecdote about shar-ing a bag of caterpillar-infested pistachio nuts with his co-worker Frank Hole:

"I examined each pistachio carefully as I opened it, and as a consequence had to discard about half; but I noticed that Hole was able to eat 100% of the ones he selected, and I com-mented on his luck. To which he replied: 'I'm just not look-ing.' . . . a kilo of dried caterpillars may contain 3720 calories, 550 grams of protein, 2700 milligrams of calcium and a gener-ous supply of thiamine, riboflavine, and iron . . . the protein content is double that of the pistachios themselves, and a com-bination of the two foods probably has a synergistic effect ex-ceeding the value of the nuts alone."[11]

In other words, the protein in the dried caterpillar would complement the incomplete proteins in the pistachios, making their total protein content available to the human metabolism. In later days when people shifted to intensive concentration on grain, they paid a heavy nutritional price.

More villages appeared in the nuclear Near East. Evidently the population was increasing. We still do not know the cus-toms or familial organization of these early Neolithic peoples. There are remains of small huts and of larger ones, of round and long buildings, depending on which village site archaeol-ogists excavate. Family organization into extended or nu-clear groups is predicated on the residence shape and size, though present-day analogies allow for wide variations.

Maternal sexuality, the physical pleasure of child rearing, must surely have played a role in the increase of population which became feasible with a settled life, a hut or place of shelter for mother and child, stored food, and increasing group cooperation. Presumably, when it becomes easier to have more children, women do enjoy it. The inconveniences of carrying a tiny child are obviated, while stored food means not going out every day to forage. The decision not to abort or not to kill a newborn infant would have been the mother's, as it is now in many places where such customs exist, not that of the patriarch or the Church as it later developed. Probably nomadic peoples of the hills were still practicing measures to keep their population down. For the villagers, however, fixed homes, protection during the winter, not having to go out and collect food right after the child was born may also have decreased infant mortality.

In any event, the pleasure of nursing and caressing the child would have sufficiently outweighed the disadvantages of childbirth and child rearing so that more women permitted their infants to come to term, to be born, and to be brought up. The methods of abortion described for places in Oceania, South America, and Australia—pressure and placing hot stones on the belly—are far from comfortable, and they also involve attendant dangers. Herbal methods for inducing sterility or abortion have had some scientific investigation; they exist, but are not necessarily secure nor risk-free.

There is no reason to think that any male—the mother's maternal uncle, the mother's brother, or the man who had been living with the mother at the time of the baby's birth—would have had a say in the above decisions, especially the last since we don't know whether there was a social father, though it seems certain there was no concern with a physical father.

It used to be thought that agriculture first developed in the areas where wheat and barley grew wild. But as Harlan demonstrated, why cultivate when you can reach out and pick? In the mountain valleys of Iran and Iraq and along the slopes of the Jordanian mountains, in Syria and Palestine, people lived by collecting wild grains and legumes, fish and shellfish, and also by hunting deer, wild ass, and pig. The population increased, but the size of the settlements remained small. New groups and new villages were formed, for there was no shortage of available land.

The first steps to agriculture would not have been taken in the uplands where wheat and barley grew wild but in the outlying districts, marginal areas to which new groups had emigrated.

One such is Tepe Ali Kosh (the mound of Ali Kosh) on the Deh Luran plain of Iran, a lowland steppe near a swamp. Excavations there in the nineteen sixties have brought an intensive report on one of the first places where grain cultivation was practiced and on the sequence of events by which it became established. At first, the villagers lived chiefly by collecting and hunting, but they had also discovered farming. Analyses of seeds and bones show that cultivated wheat and barley were providing one third of their plant food while certain small wild peas, legumes no longer eaten by humans, wild grasses, pistachio nuts, and capers provided the rest. Goats and sheep were kept, but it was hunting—of wild cattle, gazelle, and wild ass—which supplied most of their meat.

With a diversified base of both collecting and agriculture and of hunting and herding, a fairly ideal food balance was reached. But this was not possible to maintain, for the introduction of agriculture and animal keeping disturbed the existing vegetation. New weeds, presumably brought down from the mountains with the seeds of wild grain, were introduced and the protein-rich peas and beans were driven out. Moreover, wild animals became fewer and farther away as their habitats were destroyed. Hunting was just as important when the site was abandoned as when it was first settled, but smaller animals were being taken, for the larger ones no longer had cover in the vicinity. It is estimated, however, that these Iranian villagers of ten thousand years ago ate more meat than present-day Iranian peasants, since they were living in a relatively unexploited environment rather than one in which intensive human occupation had disturbed, not to say destroyed, the ecological balance.

Subsequent phases of excavations at the Deh Luran site reveal that over a period of two thousand years, more and more cereals were consumed; the legumes were no longer eaten, though one of the new weeds, *shauk*, was introduced into the diet. Eventually the settlement petered out, the fertility of the land in the vicinity exhausted.

There were many and varied consequences from these first steps toward agriculture. People started depending on one or two grains and when the crop failed they were in trouble. A drought or a blight comes along, and famine results. With only a few sources of food, people are much more vulnerable to elements over which they have no control—weather failures, plant disease, and insect invasion. Alternatives are available to gatherers: certain plants will be drought resistant, and not all will succumb to sudden pest attacks or infestation by a given fungus or bacterium.

The first agricultural villages arose either in mountain valleys with high water tables or on lowland plains where there was a plentiful supply of underground water: at Tepe Ali Kosh the first planting seemed to have occurred close to the swamp margins, with little cultivation; digging sticks were all that was needed. "Dry farming" is the name for this period, before irrigation was practiced.

While the population was growing as the result of village life and the fact that women enjoyed having babies, the early cultivators were not better nourished than the food collectors before them. Though the cereal diet produces a great deal of food, by weight, on a small amount of land, the foraging diet provided a better balance. Moreover, as agricultural techniques improve, and people begin to water and fertilize their crops, the price of increased yield is decreased nutritional value, starch content is augmented while the percentage of protein is lowered.

But more important was the new element of risk that was introduced. Today, in the Deh Luran plain, the crops fail two or three years out of five when nonirrigation farming is attempted. Once the step to farming had begun, however, there was no going back to the gathering life unless the group emigrated to an unexploited area, of which there were now fewer and fewer. Though a more concentrated amount of food could be produced from a smaller area of land, farming meant more work and more risk. It called for periods of intense work countered by periods of comparative leisure, rather than the regular alternation of leisure and gathering the foragers practiced.

Moreover when people gather or hunt it feels like a game. When they farm it is seen as work—which is why so many foragers from Africa, Australia, and the Americas stubbornly resisted the change to farming imposed by colonial and other dominating powers. Since the large harvest of grain encouraged staying in one place, people settled down and became committed to property. More people living closer together produce increased tensions, and with settled living resolution of conflict by fission meant abandoning property in which they had invested labor and emotion.

Evidently human psychology was drastically changed, a process which intensified with time. Nature was personified and came to be seen as an adversary. Sometimes she was a beneficent and all-giving mother, but more often she was capricious, sending storms and blights or withholding rain. Anxiety and aggression increased, and new forms of religion arose to assuage the new insecurities. Farming people were more dependent on the vagaries of nature; with increasing fear arose also the need to dominate the elements, in order not to be in bondage to them, hence the setting up of a new order of relationships, vertical rather than horizontal.

One of the first areas to be affected was the tie between women and men. Among foragers children are loved and accepted by the group for themselves alone. With the cultivators children become useful as labor; they can watch the herds and they add needed hands for the intense moment of harvest when the food for the coming months must be gathered before it spoils or is dispersed. More population meant more labor to use but it also meant more mouths to feed, so that the process became circular. The question is when women stopped having children for their own sakes and began to produce children as tools and, eventually, as commodities.

The new risks played a significant role in the development of civilizations and in the two kinds of oppression which appear in human history after this time. One was the domination of women by men and the control of their reproductive capacities; the other resulted from the unequal distribution of food and other material goods.

During the several thousand years before written history, the population in the Near East grew more rapidly than it had in the preceding millennia.[12] If cultivation did begin because of population pressures, when did the reverse happen, and the increased labor demanded by farming create pressure for more children? Perhaps some of the answers can be gleaned by examining the phenomenon which used to be considered a precursor of farming but which is today seen as an accompaniment and a result: the keeping of animals.

19

The Discovery of Fatherhood

It has been said that the first domestication was that of woman by man, which set a pattern for later class differences.[1] On the contrary, I believe the sexual subjugation of women, as it is practiced in all the known civilizations of the world, was modeled after the domestication of animals. The domestication of women followed long after the initiation of animal keeping, and it was then that men began to control women's reproductive capacity, enforcing chastity and sexual repression. Originally, land was held in common, and individuals had rights to its use and cultivation but not exclusive ownership. Animals, on the other hand, may well have been the earliest form of private property on any considerable scale, making animal domestication the pivot also in the development of class differences.[2]

It used to be thought that animal herding had preceded agriculture, since animals can be driven or led, while fields stay in one place. The received idea was that nomadic hunters first domesticated animals, while agriculture arose second and in different areas, and that the wild Caucasian tribesmen came down like a wolf on the fold, conquering or infiltrating the peaceful agriculturalists, but were themselves absorbed by the more advanced farmers. Now, it seems that the opposite was true. Recent evidence shows that it was agriculture, or at least a settled life leading to agriculture, which appeared first and that animal keeping was a consequence of plant cultivation and exploitation, rather than its predecessor. The first villages were not farming settlements; they were villages of mixed practices —plant collecting and hunting—but with stable resources so that people could stay in one place to exploit them. There is consistent evidence for village life and the use of plant food before spotty and dubious evidence for animal herding appears in the record.[3]

When the early villagers discovered seed planting, who first had the brilliant idea of keeping sheep and goats? One theory is that cereal fields attracted grazing animals who were then captured and penned by the villagers for future use. Sheep and goats are more amenable to taming than wild cattle, and they were the earliest herd animals to be domesticated, by about two thousand years. Animal keeping is a way of storing surplus grains.[4] One can leave the sheep and goats at pasture in fields which shortage of labor and storage facilities prevent the villagers from harvesting, and then eat the fattened animals as desired.

Between nine and eleven thousand years ago villages which practiced mixed farming and collecting, hunting and animal herding, in varying proportions, developed in the Near East. Zawi Chemi Shanidar, Tepe Sarab, Çatal Hüyük, Cayonu Tepesi in Turkey, Ramad in Syria, Beidha in Jordan: these were some of the permanently occupied farming villages in existence nine thousand years ago. At this time other groups—most people on earth—still lived by collecting and hunting. The rapid expansion of population in the next four thousand years has been traced by surveys in the Middle East showing an increasing network of settlements, chiefly small villages.[5]

At the time that plant cultivation began, shortly before the keeping of animals, there would have been no reason to connect plant reproduction with humans in that pernicious analogy which resulted in the vision of the female as a passive receptacle. The Australians noted earlier saw the seed-bearing plant as a mother but made no connection between seeds and semen.[6] At Ali Kosh in the early stages goats and sheep were kept, but they would have been interfertile with the wild ones which lived in the vicinity. The observation that males were necessary for reproduction may have been loosely made during the early stages of animal keeping. It is only during the more sophisticated process of animal breeding, however, that it is essential to control the mating processes. Before that, as long as all males were not killed or castrated, it would seem natural that animals should copulate and natural that females should bring forth young, but there need be no connection between these facts as they were not connected for the Australians and the Trobrianders at the time of the first contact with Westerners.

Malinowski speaks of the distinction made between the flesh of the wild bush pigs and that of the tame village ones. Meat from the latter is considered a great delicacy while the flesh of the bush pig is taboo to people of rank in Kiriwina. Yet the female domestic pigs were allowed to wander on the outskirts of the village and in the bush, where they paired freely with male bush pigs. On the other hand, all the male pigs in the village were castrated in order to improve their condition. Thus, all the progeny were in reality descended from wild bush sires, but the natives had not the slightest inkling of this fact.[7] Malinowski also instanced "Mick's pigs," the European pigs imported by a Greek trader which were highly valued by the natives and for one of which they would gladly exchange five or ten of their own pigs. But when they had acquired it, they would not take the slightest precautions to make it breed with a male of the same superior race. They could not be made to understand, and all over the district they continued to allow their valued European pigs to misbreed.

When women were considered totally responsible for the creation of actual children, males developed alternatives to physical conception and childbirth—spiritual birth, rebirth, initiation. Through animal breeding man discovered that he played a role in creation, albeit a minor one, and his sense of superfluity was partially relieved.

On the other hand, many of the practices which developed for successful animal breeding could only sharpen his insecurities. Though his sex was necessary, the individual was competitively inessential. Only one male animal is needed to fertilize many females. A rundown of some of the practices engaged in by sophisticated animal breeders is enough to scarify any human male: a magazine article on Secretariat, a prized race horse withdrawn from the track and sold for stud, was rife with emotional overtones of competition and animal-human comparison.

"The champion thoroughbred must possess physical soundness, speed, endurance and temperament . . . not in the abstract but to a greater degree than the horses it will face on the track." Describing the mating of thoroughbreds, "There is no time for nuzzling or romancing, no exchange of neighs of passion. Whether the mare is willing or not, she is hobbled and held by three or four men while the stallion mounts. It is an ordeal that may well leave a gently bred young filly permanently unstrung . . . for stallions it's either feast or famine. For the rest of the year they are not only celibate but also fitted with a ring on the penis to prevent them from enjoying the consolation of masturbation."[8]

The insecurities of the human male in front of an incomprehensible and powerful universe were much intensified by the advances made with discoveries stemming from animal breeding. Crucial markers in the development of those most puzzling of human phenomena, sadism and seemingly motiveless malignity, can be charted therefrom.

The male desire for a harem counters the individual's fear that he will not measure up, not be good enough to be the one chosen "procreator." In practice it derives from the principles of efficient animal breeding, maximizing production of offspring. I have come across a recurrent fantasy among Western men of being the only male left on earth to fertilize all women, just as, in selective animal breeding, herd owners kill or castrate all but the one or two proven studs, slaughtering the rest for meat, or, in the case of oxen, using them for draft purposes. Females will be kept to increase the herd and for milk, but only one or a few of the males need be selected to inseminate the many breeders.

With sheep and goats, which are kept for wool and hair, more of the other sex may be spared. Wild cattle—aurochs—

were difficult to handle. In Paleolithic cave painting deer and horses are shown as friendly and unthreatening, but aurochs are perceived as frightening and awe-inspiring.[9] Until castration was practiced there was more reason to dispose of the surplus, leaving only one bull to serve.

The widespread adoption of the bull as metaphor, symbol of the potent human male, and its frequent appearance as lord and creator has led to speculation on a religious origin for this particular domesticated animal, with a utilitarian function growing out of the initial worship of a sacred bull.[10] In any event, if only one male is to be chosen to survive intact, he must be truly superior to those that are killed or castrated. The emphasis on competition and the fearfulness of the analogies are evident.

It was pointed out in Part I that modern humans introduced rape into the primate world with the so-called rape rack at the University of Wisconsin's Harlow Laboratory. Several thousand years earlier humans had begun to control animal intercourse, introducing forced coitus as animal keeping was transformed into animal breeding, perhaps before the idea of forcing females of their own species to perform the sexual act against their will occurred to them. The manipulation of sex for purpose turned the human act into an aggressive one rather than a joyous meeting. Even where the animal is larger and presumably far stronger than the female, rape does not occur in the mammal world. Because humans are sentient, human females can be bullied into submission; they can be injured and forced; they can also be killed in the act of rape, as has happened in numerous instances in human history. No observations of animal rape have been verified in the wild, though this is not necessarily true of animals kept by humans in zoos and laboratories and enclosures—the equivalent of human prisons, concentration camps, and insane asylums—or possibly even of closely confined domestic animals.[11]

It has been rightly recognized that there is some connection between dependence on animals and an inferior position for women.[12] This does not apply to a gathering and hunting society because foraging peoples do not establish dominance over anything. They live in a symbiotic relationship with the environment, in partnership with other elements of nature, as one of many.

Animal domestication involved contradictory aspects for human consciousness. Children are one lien on immortality and now men too participated in the future. To the dyad of mother and child, the father was added. The trinity emerged, later translated by man into a holy three. Still later, by that process of male inversion earlier referred to, the trinity was arrogated completely to the male, in the concept of the Father, the Son, and the Holy Ghost. The trinity of the Holy Family was metaphorized by Hegel and Marx into thesis, antithesis, and synthesis. In a later access of male arrogance, Edmund Wilson explicates the Hegelian dialectic not in terms of the basic three of reproduction, the great acquisition in human awareness, but as a symbolic rendering of the triune male genitals—testicles and penis.[13] These last, which formerly existed for pleasure, have now become utilitarian. Phallic images begin to surface in archaeology, at first debatable, later unmistakable. By historic times, the new emphasis, the new awareness, and changed worship have produced a rich harvest of mythical and visual reference. But at the time of which we speak, the first triune representation is still to come.

What had previously been for pleasure and divinity became a means of production. Comments on the historical development of animal-breeding techniques point up their effect on the human male's already shaky sense of self: "The males, either as castrates or intact animals, are killed for meat as described above since they are of *less value than females* and reach optimum value at a particular weight and time [my italics]." "The majority of the animals fall into two groups, one, predominantly of male and castrates, are killed quite young, and another group, predominantly of females, are killed in old age." "There are two ways of dealing with the problem of the male. Either the removal of the majority of males before puberty or their castration."[14] "The females would have been kept for their milk and for reproductive purposes whereas the males would have been killed while still young and only a few adults would have been kept to ensure reproduction."[15]

In gathering and hunting societies, even in some societies where animal keeping is of recent arrival, there is a sense of kinship between animals and humans. The traditional affinity with animals is reflected in totemism and in myths where animals or creatures part human and part animal give rise to the human race.

The interrelationship between the animal and human world surfaces from many mythologies and still obtains in folklore. Humans did not always make sharp distinctions between themselves and animals; they attributed to the latter qualities both human and superhuman. Shamans, as they go into their trance, tend to talk in tongues—in the language of birds and animals. In Mircea Eliade's words,

> relations of friendship and familiarity . . . are established between the shaman and the animals. . . . In one respect the animals are the bearers of a symbolism and mythology very significant for the religious life; to have contact with them, to speak their language, to become their friend and master means the possession of a spiritual life much more abundant than the simple human life of an ordinary mortal . . . animals possess considerable prestige, inasmuch as they know the secrets of life and nature and even possess the secrets of longevity and immortality. Thus in returning to the condition of the animals the shaman comes to share their secret language and enjoys the fuller life which is theirs . . . friendship with the animals and knowledge of their language represents a paradisial syndrome. *In illo tempore,* before the "fall" such friendship was an integral part of the primordial situation.[16]

Creatures who are part human and part animal and coexistence between animal and human are common in ethnographic literature. The serpent in Genesis is one of the few remaining vestiges of this kind of imagery in Judeo-Christian mythology, while the wily animals of Aesop's fables or the nineteenth-century Br'er Rabbit cycle told by African blacks transported to the American South represent folk adaptations of this tradition.

Many hunters have a sense of restraint about killing and are grateful to the animals who offer themselves for human uses. They believe that animals have a right to existence and that the relationship between animals and humans is a constant.

Among the Australian Tiwi if a baby animal pet survives overnight it is considered part of the community, given a name, and afforded burial and burial rites. Western observers were shocked to find Australian Aborigine women nursing their pet dingoes, treating them as their own babies.

Still there are manifest analogies with our own civilization, where pet cemeteries, pet food and pet clothing, antivivisection, and vegetarianism are only a few indices to deep-seated attitudes. The continuum between animals and people is felt by many. Small wonder then that the keeping and raising of animals had wide-ranging effects on the customs, art, and psyche of human society.

Whereas, in earlier times, humans had hunted and eaten animals, they now established a vertical relationship. Before that animals and humans were more or less equal. The weapons of the time—sling and stone, tipped spear, even bow and arrow—were not that deadly. Often the humans had to track for days. One way or another, hunting was a match of wits. Now humans violated animals by making them their slaves. In taking them in and feeding them, humans first made friends with animals and then killed them. To do so, they had to kill some sensitivity in themselves. When they began manipulating the reproduction of animals, they were even more personally involved in practices which led to cruelty, guilt, and subsequent numbness. The keeping of animals would seem to have set a model for the enslavement of humans, in particular the large-scale exploitation of women captives for breeding and labor, which is a salient feature of the developing civilizations.

Discussing blood and the supposed horror aroused in Western men by women's monthly courses, it has been a common

Freudian explanation that the first sight of a woman's genital aroused a castration anxiety in the small boy, an anxiety said to be reinforced by her monthly bleeding, which made him feel women were wounded and deformed. How much more sense it makes to associate man's castration anxiety with his own aggressive powers and the fear thereby engendered, the practices humans learned through animal breeding. The techniques involved were frightening enough if one imagined them turned on oneself, as one always must, given the human imagination. Later associations may have projected them onto women. The origins of selective breeding go back to prehistoric times. Castration of certain males was introduced in the late Neolithic, which meant that humans were practicing a certain selection—they selected some males for breeding and excluded others.[17]

The continents of Europe, Asia, and Africa have been in communication from prehistoric, possibly even Paleolithic times. Cranstone's descriptions of some of the animal-management techniques used by diverse peoples from this triangle tell their own story:

> The Kazak fit leather aprons to their rams in the spring [as a form of birth control], since autumn-born lambs have little chance [of survival]. The Masai practice the same method. The Tuareg divide their flocks of goats into two and arrange for the kids to be born at two seasons. . . . The prepuces of he-goats and rams which are not to be allowed to breed are bound with a cord. It seems to be rather unusual for males to be selected for breeding in order to pass on valuable characteristics. . . . The Nuer, however, choose bull-calves for breeding from the calves of the best milking cows and castrate most of the remainder, leaving one entire to about thirty or forty cows.
>
> Castration is the most usual method of controlling breeding. It has the effect, too, of rendering the animals easier to handle and affects their metabolism. The Lapps castrate most of the reindeer bucks and use them for draught and pack purposes and as bell-

reindeer which lead the herd. [In the wild, among red deer, an old female leads the herd.] The Tuareg say that castrated camels grow larger humps and fatten more quickly, and are more enduring and stronger as riding animals. They are also less dangerous, since bull-camels in rut sometimes attack people.

The method of castration in general use among cattle-keeping peoples, and applied to other animals such as camels and horses, is by opening the scrotum and removing the testicles. Some African herdsmen use a knife, others the blade of a spear. In New Guinea pigs are castrated in this way with a bamboo knife. . . .

A second group of methods involves damaging or destroying the testicles without removing them.

Sometimes the scrotum is bound with a cord beforehand so that the testicles atrophy. The Lapps wrap the scrotum in cloth and bite or chew it; the result is often a partial castration which however renders the animals docile and more easily tamed. The Sonjo of Tanzania are irrigation agriculturalists who also keep flocks of goats. They castrate all males at about six months, the only exceptions being those—apparently fairly numerous—whose testicles do not descend. The method is to strangulate the scrotum with a bow string, and then to crush the testicles with an elongated stone implement especially shaped and smoothed for the purpose. The Masai castrate rams by pounding the testicles between the two stones.[18]

One of the most surprising of understandings to emerge from the new archaeology has been the realization that there was far more trade and diffusion ten thousand years ago than had been projected. Objects traveled for hundreds and thousands of miles—cowrie shells, flint, obsidian, turquoise, carnelian, and even copper are found in areas far from their source—and must, therefore, have been obtained by trade. One is reminded of the *kula*, the trading expeditions covering hundreds of miles of island journeying, as described by Malinowski for the Trobrianders, as well as the Australian Aborigine trade network which brought rare materials and manufactured products from one end of the continent to the other. If objects traversed vast distances, ideas must have traveled also, and much farther and more easily.

Once the first steps to animal keeping and grain cultivation were taken, the complexes of settled living based on the first four—wheat and barley, goats and sheep—spread rapidly in the Near East and around the Mediterranean. On the fringes, however, people kept to earlier ways. Farming brought new material insecurities; animal raising increased psychological ones. Both techniques demanded more labor than the gathering-hunting way of life. One answer was fertility worship to produce more children; another was enslavement by conquest so that subject laborers were acquired. Material insecurities encouraged stockpiling; psychological ones led to hoarding and unequal acquisition, eventually to conspicuous consumption and the establishment of a class system.

20

The Pernicious Analogy: Sehe... Seed and Semen

The woman is considered in law as the field, and the man as the grain; now vegetable bodies are formed by the united operation of the field and the seed.
—Institutes of Manu
(Hindu text of 100–300 C.E.)

I have spoken of the need to project purpose outward, the weakness of humans at the mercy of forces over which they have no control, and the invention of magic, religion, art, and science to enable us to cope with the seeming chaos that faces us. In this disorderly universe, women do have a sense of purpose. Survival and the future of the species depend on them directly in their capacity as birth-givers.

There are obvious rewards in having children, sensual and affective ones. Anthropologists report often on the permissiveness and affection bestowed by women and men on their own and other people's children among nomadic foraging societies. We are a social and friendly species, or at least have the capacity to be so, and that tolerance for the young observed among most primate societies seems to obtain in small-scale human groups.

Children are wanted for different reasons in different societies. Cultures where women are admired for producing many

children and scorned for barrenness appear only after the inception of mixed farming. Many children are a handicap among
nomadic foragers; they are even more difficult to carry than material possessions, and birth is self-regulated. In recent times,
men may have wanted children as heirs, to bestow on them
tangible and intangible possessions, but the idea of children as
a hostage for the future, having someone to care for one in old
age, when the parent is unable to work, goes back to the earliest of times.

Women had more control over their own bodies in many
technologically deprived band societies than in the sophisticated civilizations of patriarchy. Crude methods of birth
control have always existed. The most obvious and probably
the earliest method is infanticide. Wide-ranging instances have
been reported, from the Eskimos to the Kalahari Desert people
to tribes of Oceania and Australia. Killing the second twin
and presumably two out of three triplets is a widespread custom, extending beyond foraging peoples, as indeed does infanticide, permitted and semilegal. It's an incredibly inefficient
method—think of undergoing the discomfort and pain of pregnancy and childbirth, just to dispose of the result!

The demographer Joseph Birdsell cited figures of as low as 15
per cent and as high as 50 per cent for the rate of infanticide
among Australian Aborigine tribes at the time they were first
contacted by Europeans, and he speculated that Paleolithic
humans might also have limited their populations by disposing
of newborn children.[1] In most nonliterate groups reported by
ethnographers it is women who help women. Birth groups are
composed of older women, primarily the mother of the woman
giving birth, and men are usually forbidden to appear in the vicinity. Generally the infant is not presented to the group at
large until it can be seen whether "the child has come to stay."
The Kimberley Aborigines remained apart with their newborn
infants for five days, and it was the woman who decided
whether or not to keep the child. The same is true of the
Kalahari San people and there is no preference for male over female children.[2]

After the birth of the patriarchy, however, evidence for selective female infanticide becomes common, and in many places the decision to keep or kill the infant was made by the father.[3] Though primarily an indication of the devaluing of women, killing females means there are fewer breeders and is effective for long-term population control. Where bride price is required, it raises the price of a scarce commodity, whereas if dowries are customary, poor families may feel they have no other option. Female infanticide existed into the recent past in China, India, and other parts of Asia.

In countries where infanticide is illegal, the overlap between natural mortality and willed destruction is easily blurred. In the baby farms and poorhouses of nineteenth-century England, in foundling homes and orphanages in France, systematic neglect often accomplished the desired aim without openly flouting the law. Even today underfeeding and withholding of medical attention may be responsible for suspicious sexual imbalances—high rates of male infants surviving—in parts of India and Southern Asia.[4]

Abortion also has a long history in human life—acknowledged and sub rosa. Before the discovery of the hormone-containing morning-after pill, most of us were taught that there was no effective chemical method of abortion which did not entail life-threatening dangers for the woman. Civilization has generally underrated and undervalued the intelligence, inventiveness, and ingeniousness of non-Western peoples. Reports on herbs used for abortion and contraception among nonliterate peoples are scanty and usually lack biochemical data. In recent years, however, investigation has shown that folk medicine is often empirically based on sound principles. The Ute Indians of North America were very permissive about sexual liaisons and experimentation among young people. They prevented unwanted pregnancies by using lithospermum, a plant which contained a substance since demonstrated to have a negative effect on fertility.[5]

Many groups in South America, Oceania, and Africa also use local plants to prevent or terminate pregnancy. The Bororo women of Brazil are reported to have a medicine prepared from a local plant which renders them temporarily sterile. In 1974

Marvine Howe wrote that the Christian missionaries had persuaded the women to cease taking the drug and that they were once again reproducing themselves.[6] Thirty years earlier Lévi-Strauss had found the Bororo men to be fine specimens but their women were "small and sickly, with irregular features; it is rare to find among them that bodily harmony which distinguishes their men."[7] If the women really were so inferior in appearance to the men, one wonders whether the drug they took had side effects on their general health, given the fact that men and women share a common heredity and that genetic studies have not so far revealed any sex-linked gene for physical beauty in men and ugliness in women.

Though it was known that abortion was widely practiced, when male anthropologists predominated they were less privy to women's information. In recent years many women anthropologists have brought back reports from the people concerned, the mothers, on the methods used to procure abortions. Jane Goodale tells that among the Australian Tiwi miscarriage-inducing potions are prepared from the bark of a certain tree, women jump from heights, and that they also use pressure and pummeling on the abdomen to bring on abortion. Phyllis Kaberry reports that the tribes of the North Kimberleys use hot stones and beating on the abdomen, while Janet Siskind writes of abortions accomplished by pressure among the South American Sharanahuas.

It is sometimes claimed that childbirth is less painful among "primitive" people than among supposedly tense "civilized" people.[8] In most instances, however, the reason given for inducing abortion was to avoid the pain of childbirth. Sometimes the inconveniences of pregnancy and taking care of a small child were also cited.

Goodale speaks of the Tiwi woman whose marriage has been arranged at birth, who has been living with her elderly husband and gradually introduced to sex, and who now, past puberty, is "of an age to attract the attentions of young men and to arrange meetings with them in the bush at times when she should be hunting for food for her elderly husband. If she is going to accept a lover, this is the age to do so, for as my informants commented, 'Children make such bush meetings difficult.' "[9]

Among foraging peoples living under conditions of minimum material development, the normal birth interval looks like four or five years. Kaberry said that she rarely came across a woman with more than four or five children. Siskind said that the South American women she studied generally have four or five children before they resort to abortion.

Nursing imperfectly controls conception and is much used in cultures which have been affected by the civilizations as well as in those only recently influenced. In many nonliterate societies it is aided by taboos on intercourse during the nursing period.

Given the anticontraceptive slant of most recorded civilizations, only scant evidence remains to show that methods more sophisticated than the Scylla and Charybdis of celibacy and infanticide were in use in the past. Two records from ancient Egypt—the Petri and the Ebers papyri of thirty-eight and thirty-five hundred years ago respectively—tell of contraceptive prescriptions whose operant principles are still in use: sperm-obstructing vaginal plugs or sponges, dipped in honey or olive oil to slow down sperm motility, and a local application of acacia tips, a plant containing lactic acid, the spermicide which is still the prime ingredient of modern contraceptive jelly.[10]

At the time that plant cultivation began, shortly before the keeping of animals, plant and human reproduction would not have been associated. Sophisticated animal breeding came considerably later. The progression of these discoveries was not swift, though in terms of the several million years' duration of the human species it seemed so.

Paleolithic humans did not know that semen played a role in reproduction, as they did not occupy themselves with seeds and planting and agriculture. In the evolution of consciousness, this fact must be considered as an understratum which will shape the future development of human sexual relations and human customs. The discovery of paternity has been likened to the turning on of an electric-light bulb, but it could hardly have happened that suddenly. An understanding of the reproductive process in humans is of very recent date—the mammalian egg was not discovered until 1827—and scientists are still adding to our knowledge. Several writers have detailed the misconceptions which existed in ancient times about the procreation of humans.

The commonest belief was that the child is formed entirely out of menstrual blood retained in the uterus. "Babies need blood when they're inside you, and if you're having a baby, then you don't menstruate. When you're not having a baby then you don't have to save the blood so it comes out."[11] This young girl's explanation from a modern novel by Toni Morrison is echoed on many levels from ancient and ethnographic sources. The Maori of New Zealand say, "The discharge is a kind of human being, because if the discharge ceases, then it grows into a person, that is, the 'paheke' (menstrual blood) ceases to come away, then it assumes human form and grows into a human."[12]

Once it was observed that semen was necessary for conception, the ancients were hard put to explain just how the process worked. Both Aristotle and Pliny the Elder believed the child was formed out of retained menstrual blood. Aristotle said that the male semen supplied some "impulse to movement," and Pliny amplified by comparing semen to rennet, which gathers the uterine blood into a curd so that it grows into a body. An ancient Hebrew midrash states, "The Uterus remains full of blood, which would else flow out as menstrual issue. When it is the will of the Creator, there comes a drop of white seed and falls therein, and the growth of the child at once takes place, exactly as happens when one puts rennet into a bowl of milk."[13]

Aristotle worked out his theory as a philosophical argument for the natural superiority of the male:

> Man is active, full of movement, creative in politics, business, and culture. The male shapes and molds society and the world. Woman, on the other hand, is passive. She stays at home as is her nature. She is matter waiting to be formed and molded by the active

male principle. Of course the active elements are always higher on any scale than the passive forms, and more divine. Man consequently plays the major role in reproduction; the woman is merely the passive incubator of his seed . . . the male semen cooks and shapes the menstrual blood into a new human being.[14]

This ideology proved useful and was taken on faith for more than two thousand years, translated into Catholic doctrine by way of Thomas Aquinas. Only in the seventeenth century C.E. did scientists begin to use tools to gain an actual understanding of the process of reproduction. Anton van Leeuwenhoek's use of the microscope enabled him to observe the spermatazoa in male semen in 1676. The underlying set made people theorize that each sperm contained a homunculus, a tiny person capable of growing into a human once it reached the propitious haven of the uterus.

It was Lazzaro Spallanzani, in 1775, who demonstrated that sperm were needed to make frog's eggs develop into tadpoles. Two thousand years earlier Hippocrates had traced the process by which eggs develop into chickens and compared their embryos' growth to that of humans. He believed that men and women have generating seed and that the seed of woman and man mixed together to form the child. He claimed to have seen an aborted six-day-old generating seed, though from his description it was a considerably more developed fetus than would result from a six-day pregnancy.[15] However, Hippocrates' theories did not receive wide acceptance, perhaps because women do not lay eggs. For centuries the Aristotelian doctrine held sway.

In the early sixteen-hundreds William Harvey's experiments with dissection did bring him information on embryology, and he rejected the Aristotelian theory of menstrual blood sparked by semen with the statement that all animals reproduce by eggs. Some fifty years later, one Regnier de Graaf operated on female rabbits and found that, like birds, they had ovaries, which were covered with tiny pimples, discerned by him as eggs. Actually they were ovarian follicles. Though the mammalian egg—that of a dog—was correctly identified in 1827, the actual fertilization process was not observed until 1875. Knowledge about germ cells and chromosomal union—the equal contribution of male and female—has come only in our own century.

Coincidental with these physiological gropings, however, was and is the belief that while humans may copulate and produce a body it is God who sends the soul needed to vivify an actual human being. As Briffault points out, it is not all that different from the Australian Aborigine conviction that the spirit child climbs into the womb. Some peoples believe in conception without the help of a man; others that the man is an accessory and that divine intervention is needed to assist him.

According to Francoeur, "The Pueblo Indians of New Mexico thought maidens could conceive from a heavy summer shower; the Greeks believed Aphrodite was born of sea foam; the Celtic saint Maedoc was conceived when a star fell into the mouth of his sleeping mother; the founder of the Manchu dynasty was conceived when a maiden ate a red fruit dropped on her lap by a magpie; a pomegranate placed in the bosom of the nymph Nana yielded Attis; and Longfellow records how Winonah was quickened by a western wind and gave birth to Hiawatha."[16] Pliny, Virgil, and St. Augustine believed that mares could be fertilized by the wind, and Plutarch thought the same of birds.[17] Poetry, superstition, ideology, and scientific knowledge mingle in diverse proportions for civilized as well as for nonliterate peoples in their efforts to explain natural phenomena.

Since humans had settled in villages before they began to plant seeds, there was no reason at that time to make any connection between the seed of grain and the sperm of males. The Trobriand Islanders, who planted yams, were ignorant of the function of semen or of any analogy, fancied or real, between plant and human biology. The Australian Aborigines refused to regard seeds as a source of food production even when the whites insisted. Though several of them had been introduced to gardening by white people, they rejected agriculture and the seed-semen metaphor.

All our mighty mythologies are founded on the misunderstanding of the nature of human biology and reproduction, as are the historic interpretations of them. Western religions were frankly reactionary in their effect on women's biology. Judaism vested control over a woman's body in her husband and a rabbinical court, while Christianity flatly forbade any method of birth control but celibacy and preferred the child's life to the mother's in medical emergency. Islam still takes an unequivocal stand against birth control and abortion.

The overt history of women as a force in Western civilization can be counted from the gradual expansion for popular use of birth control, beginning with the vaginal sponge in the eighteen twenties. The vulcanization of rubber in the nineteenth century led to the invention of the Mensinga cap in 1880, the earliest widely used pessary, or rubber diaphragm, as well as to the mass-produced condom. The post-World War II experiments which led to the sequential use of hormone pills have of course revolutionized man-woman relationships. Condoms for men, made originally of linen and later of animal membrane, go back to the sixteenth century—perhaps to the Romans—and they received their original approval as "prophylactics"—still their popular denomination in many languages—protection against venereal disease, to which the man might be exposed by frequenting the equally tolerated, if only semi-approved, prostitute. (The Italian euphemism for brothels, houses of toleration, reveals much about Christendom's illogical attitudes, which label male sexual desire irresistible and designate certain female human beings as necessary sacrifices to its importunacy.)

The situation is reversed in most nonliterate cultures, where it is taken for granted that women will have sex and babies; it is men who must earn these privileges. Reports from Oceania and Australia and Africa stress how this is arranged, after the birth of a girl child, and emphasize that there is no such thing as a woman who has not been married at least once in her life. Women will almost always have sex immediately after puberty; perhaps they will have experimented with it or been gradually introduced to it before their first menstruation.

For boys it is not so simple. There are cultures, like those of Samoa and the Trobriand Islands, where childish sex games turn easily into adolescent freedom before boys and girls settle down into a more stable, possibly arranged relationship. But in many places, the male must go through a complicated initiation ritual, in parts of Australia sometimes of ten or more years' duration, a period when male homosexuality is a not infrequent recourse.

He must also prove himself a hunter before he can arrange a marriage. Among the Mbuti Pygmies he must down an antelope or other large-sized game and present it to his prospective in-laws. Bride payment is common, as are continued obligations to provide the woman's family with meat. A man may have been making gifts to his future wife's mother in the case of the Tiwi, or parents or mother's brother in other cultures, for many years. By this token in most parts of Australia he will be at least fifteen, often twenty or thirty years older than the girl.

Margaret Mead thinks civilization develops out of the need to value male fields and devalue women's. Women achieve naturally and easily through childbirth, while males, seeing no such obvious purpose in the world, have had to invent compensations. Taken to its extreme, and there are some who claim as much, civilization—sometimes all culture—would be a male compensatory device, incited by male envy of the female capacity for generation. This is far from the case, for women have contributed much, though the acknowledgment of their role is scant and hard to document. However, agriculture and animal breeding did bring new anxieties. With the inception of mixed farming, male inferiority and male compensation will be a constant substratum and a constant goad in the shaping of religious and intellectual development. Male resentment at the obvious role women play in nature has led to a host of artificial and inaccurate dichotomies in later history. "Mother earth and father sky" is an early phrasing which has been translated, in more sophisticated times, to the belief that woman is body and man mind: i.e., because women can make babies, intelligence becomes masculine.[18] The one was evident, the other an invention. Man made a virtue of his defects by denying his earthliness beyond that of woman. If women were closer to nature, men must then be more spiritual, eventually closer to God. If women had the babies, it must be men who begot them, created their souls.

Whether paternity is recognized or not, fathering is pretty much a human and a social phenomenon. One of many ways in which men have tried to participate in women's experience is the *couvade*, where a man takes to his bed and simulates the pains of childbirth, for a few hours or days, at the same time his wife is giving birth. For Leacock, the basic principle of humanity is male-female reciprocity, so that men give child care when women are otherwise occupied.[19]

Fathering is extended mothering. For Mead it is a "social invention . . . under which males started nurturing females and their young . . . whether the children are believed to be his, or merely the children of a man of the same clan, or simply the legitimate children of his wife by an earlier marriage."[20] In some cases the children may be those of his sister rather than the woman or women with whom he has sex relations. While it is food sharing which is considered to be the ultimate defining characteristic of human society, there are cultures where the male contribution is slight indeed.

One such are the Malekula, a gardening people who inhabit a small New Hebrides island in Oceania, and who will come up in several contexts. Their food needs are provided by the women, who do the gardening, planting, and harvesting, chiefly of yams. Pigs are raised by the men for their circle tusks and for religious ceremonies in which women do not participate. Women do not eat pork and the men eat it only occasionally.

Sometimes, the extent to which the male participates in familial duties is insignificant: sometimes it is an exchange of services. Fathering has not achieved the importance with which the patriarchy sought to endow it; it is still a pale second to mothering. If necessity is the mother of invention, who is the father?

Another variation on the theme of mothering is the reversal of the mother-child image to apply to the sexual union, with a man in the nurturant role and the female as child. Kaberry cites the protests of an older man who had been making gifts to the parents of a girl-child since birth when the white station manager interfered with his marriage plans: "Me bin grow 'em up." This is also the expression used by the Arapesh; in a society where there is a great shortage of food, it is the husband who "grows his wife" by feeding her with gifts of food.

Since physical fatherhood is such a recent arrival on the human scene, father-daughter incest is not a particularly deep-seated taboo. It occurs far more often than its converse, mother-son incest, and is not always punished or even punishable by law. There are few myths against it; on the contrary, it is a paradigm for desirable man-woman relationships, though the father will be a guardian or father figure rather than a biological father.

When men did not know that they participated in the creative process, they arrogated it to themselves in different ways. Some of this mentality hung over in a culture lag, long after the gap in knowledge had been partially filled. Aristotle's ignorance may be some excuse for his ideology, which by the seventeenth century, about the time Leeuwenhoek discovered the sperm, had been popularized into Samuel Butler's "The souls of women are so small, that some believe they've none at all."

A comparison between the male and female views of spirit children—souls of babies waiting to be born—among the Australian Tiwi is informative here. While most Australian Aborigine tribes are—were—unaware of the connection between sexual intercourse and pregnancy, the Tiwi, who have had contact with Malay pearl fishermen over the past few centuries, have made the connection, but only recently and superimposed on older tradition. The world of the unborn children means very little to the women. If they see them or think about them at all it is as vague little birds. However, it is of vital importance to the imaginative and actual lives of the men. Their art, ritual, and many of their fantasies are bound up with it, and they see the *pitapui* (unborn children) as humans engaging in human occupations.

According to Goodale:

> Although the Tiwi recognize that either a husband or a lover can make a baby by having sexual intercourse with its mother, they also assert that such activity cannot alone create a *Tiwi* child. A Tiwi must be dreamed by its father, the man to whom its mother is married, before it can be conceived by its mother. To the Tiwi there is no conflict between the two beliefs concerning conception. In fact there is only one belief, while there may be two "fathers." . . .
>
> The *pitapui* take a human form when men see them playing on the sandbanks, and when they appear to their fathers in dreams. They not only look human, they act human, hunting and fighting as well as playing. The *pitapui* are symbolically emphasized in male ritual roles: the paternal *unandawi*'s (father's) kinship dance in the funeral ceremony, the spear dance (*tuara*), commemorate the common aspect of a spirit child when seen by its father in dreams . . . the sequence of *kakaritjui imunka* songs in the kulama ceremony may also be symbolic of the male emphasis on this world of the unborn.[21]

The male emphasis on spirit children appears to compensate for the actual fact of playing such a small, even if recognized, role in procreation.

Among the major civilizations of the world, this compensation has developed along very different lines. In general, however, since the domestication of grain and of animals began in the Mideastern heartland, although with variations and possibly in several places, and was then diffused over Europe, Asia, and Africa, certain broad trends can be traced. I shall concern myself specifically with the development of Western civilization and the major religions that come from the Near East, above all Judaism and Christianity, since it is these which have had the major control over our own world and have, in our time, influenced the rest of the planet.

Men were the original other; long before philosophers had

begun to speculate on the uselessness of woman save, in Napoleon's words, as a machine to produce babies, it was man who was useless. (Freud lifted from Napoleon the dictum "Biology is destiny.") Now he had discovered that he, too, had a place in the scheme of eternity; it was no longer woman alone who participated in the endless march of generations. Yet, the consciousness was slow in coming and always dragged along with it threads and cords of the past belief.

Feminists often speculate on what miracles might by now have been accomplished if historical energies that went into war and conspicuous consumption, culminating in the massive destructive capacities of nuclear warheads and chemical and biological warfare, had gone into constructive areas of medicine and female biology, birth control, improved techniques of infant nutrition, et al., if they had been exercised initially in these directions, rather than secondarily and often as the by-products of the former aims.

21

Çatal Hüyük and Hacilar:[1]
Early Neolithic Towns

When did the Paleolithic respect for women become translated into the Great Mother Goddess of the agricultural civilizations, the fertility figure who inspires the production of children and grain? There is no suggestion that the Paleolithic Venuses and the small early Neolithic female figurines were more than maternal symbols, embodiments of protection, warmth, and sexuality in every sense. Many children are a hindrance to a gathering-hunting people. It is unlikely that the female representations' function was to encourage the conception of children, though by ethnographic analogy they may well have protected mothers in childbirth.

The argument that a matriarchal society preceded patriarchy is often based on a hypothesis of mother-goddess worship in the Neolithic period. Yet in historical times clear reference to fertility goddesses accompanies a progressive decline in the status of women. Emphasis on fertility was an opening wedge in the debasement of the female. The power of generation was removed from the individual woman and credited to a divinity, albeit a female one at first. Fertility worship led to the forced breeding of women; more important, it signified the perversion of sex from pleasure to production.

This transformation of the sexual instinct can be traced through a study of the changes that occurred during the thousand-year occupation of a Neolithic city which came into existence almost nine thousand years ago. James Mellaart's dig at Çatal Hüyük, on the Konya plain of Anatolia in Asia Minor, was one of the most spectacular finds of recent decades.

In 1958 Mellaart spotted a mound comprising 32 acres and began excavating in 1961. As of this writing only preliminary reports have been published, and there have been many contradictions and much changing of minds. The city has been variously described as a trading center, a city of hunting shrines, religious sanctuaries linked with the Paleolithic, and proof of the existence of the matriarchy and the privileged position of women in prehistoric times.

Fourteen layers of occupation have now been uncovered, a fifteenth is visible, and virgin soil has not yet been reached. Only a one-acre portion of the entire mound has been explored, though it is not known whether the city covered the entire 32 acres during any given period of its existence. Still, if it is remembered that some five to six thousand years later historical Jerusalem during the halcyon period of the united kingdom under David and Solomon covered 10.87 acres and that sites more or less contemporary with Çatal range from ten acres (Jericho, in Jordan) to four (Jarmo, in Iraq) to one or two (Ali Kosh, in Iran), the discovery of a 32-acre city that flourished some eight and a half thousand years ago is an astonishing one. Moreover, its location on the western fringes of the Fertile Crescent was formerly considered outside the prime area of the birth of civilization.

The quarter uncovered includes many large, beautifully plastered and decorated rooms which served both ceremonial and living functions and is believed to have been the city's religious center. As yet excavations have revealed no traces of the work rooms needed to produce the intricately crafted ornaments, art, and artifacts so far unearthed.

Careful examination of published reports on Çatal (Hüyük means mound in Turkish, synonymous with Tepe and Tell in other Near Eastern languages) provides evidence for the origins of a strain of sexual repression, leading to the position which women have taken in civilized cultures, most particularly that out of which white Western European and, more recently, American civilization developed.

The earliest levels of Çatal have been scantily excavated—in four rooms the expedition brought their sounding down to Level XII, still about six feet above ground level. Since the thousand-year weight of mud-brick buildings constructed layer by layer on top of each other would press the mound below the ground, it is deduced that there must be still older levels to unearth, probably about twenty feet more of archaeological debris.

Each building level was inhabited for fifty to one hundred years, though the rooms themselves were replastered each year. The people of Çatal were quite tradition-minded, for house design and use were maintained throughout the quarter over the centuries. After one level had been abandoned, swept clean and filled in, another stratum of construction would be built on top of it, the new rooms usually serving the same purpose as the earlier ones and similarly decorated.

In the oldest occupation levels, where fewer and less ornate artifacts were found, carbonized hackberries and acorns told of plant collecting, but no evidence of agriculture remained. Later, carbonized bread wheat and six-row hulled barley demonstrated that the people of Çatal had taken up farming. Both of these plants are cultivars; they cannot reproduce themselves but must be sown by humans. Their presence indicates a long experience with agriculture, either at Çatal or elsewhere.

With the weather conditions then prevailing on the Konya plain, irrigation must have been practiced. From the evidence— remains of marsh plants found mixed in with the grain—it was of the simplest kind. Fields were near a river and the normal spring flooding was encouraged or directed onto the land to be seeded.

Over its one thousand years of existence, Çatal demonstrates the transition from collecting and hunting to planting and animal breeding. Sheep and goats were kept first, some 8,500 years ago at Level X; cattle appear two or three hundred years later at Level VII. Though there were many different animal bones, particularly in the earlier levels, in the aggregate cattle out-number all others.

The kind of cattle domestication practiced at Çatal repre-sents the first phase of animal keeping as opposed to conscious animal breeding. From the evidence, Çatal may have been one of the places where the connection was made between animal and human reproduction, for it contains early representations of the bull as a procreatory symbol. The metaphor of the po-tent, generative bull persists throughout the Bronze Age and survives in many parts of Africa and India as well as in slang references in our own world.

The people who lived at Çatal had control over their cattle. This has been deduced by analyzing and tabulating the ages at which the animals were slaughtered. A study was made of the bones from Levels VI through II, covering the four hundred years between approximately 8200 and 7800 B.P. The domesti-cation was of an archaic kind, but the fact that the bones were primarily of mature animals cannot be otherwise explained. The young of ˙wild animals are easier to kill than the wily adults; with scientific cattle breeding also there is a selection of young males for slaughter, leaving only a few bulls to service the herd. At Çatal, on the contrary, the cattle were killed only after they were full grown. Presumably they were slaughtered to provide meat after they had been bred or even when they were old. Many cattle-herding tribes in the African Sahel treasure their animals and keep them not for meat but for possession it-self, as symbols of one kind or another. The decorations and shrines at Çatal indicate that cattle, in particular bulls, were the focus of a religious cult which may have centered around the mating of a goddess of fertility with the bull of procreation. The females would have been kept for increase; the males may have been sacrificed for their horns; they may also have been used for religio-theatrical games.

The great wild cattle would have been driven into enclosures outside the city itself. Judging by the house plans, all animals, including sheep and goats, were corralled outside the living areas. Here also they were slaughtered for food, but the bulls' skulls and in particular their great curving horns were treasured for ritual and decorative purposes. If the huge aurochs were kept in pens and from them arose both the domestication of cattle and evidence through observation of male participation in the reproductory process, Çatal could be a place where the direct connection between coitus and fatherhood was made.

Judging by the sparsity of cattle bones at most village sites, they were rarely hunted during this period. "The uncomfortably potent aurochs" were difficult to handle—large, frightening, not amenable like the other ruminants—all in all, unlikely candidates for domestication on the face of it. Many archaeologists believe that the cattle were driven into large enclosures, with certain males isolated for sacrifice and the others left free to breed. It is not known whether the taming of cattle arose in Greece or in the Hungarian plains north of the Balkans and then made its way to Asia Minor or vice versa. The only other places where it is certain that cattle were raised at this time were west of Çatal—at Argissa-Maghula in Greek Thessaly (about 8500 B.P.) and perhaps a few hundred years later at Nea Nikomedia in Macedonia.

In historical times goats are associated with less threatening male sexuality—Pan, lust, goatishness—whereas the bull represents the concept of aggressive potency. Divinity is widely associated with both bull and cow in Egypt and Mesopotamia. The cow goddess disappears but the taurine metaphor remains, in Greek mythology, even in the Old Testament.

In the earlier levels of Çatal, the wall decorations showed abstract patterns believed to be based on the flat-woven Turkish rugs, called *kilims*, and various animals, most commonly leopards. In an 8,200-year-old Level VI shrine, two enormous leopards face each other. It is in the conservative tradition of Çatalian architecture, for the room underneath, dated some hundred years earlier, had also been decorated with leopards.

After Level VI leopards no longer appear; now the bull takes over, sharing primacy with a pregnant goddess. A plain undecorated room of the previous century is redecorated with a bull's head made out of plaster; actual horns were inset while the plaster was still damp. Some rooms contain great wall paintings of the bull, but more characteristic shrines are large rooms, sometimes twenty by thirty feet, with plaster bulls' heads sculptured in high relief around actual skulls and massive curving horns, which appear on the north wall. There are about fifty of these shrines and the design is the same. Facing the bull, on the south wall, is a great plaster relief of a female figure with protuberant belly, arms and legs outspread, seemingly in the act of giving birth.

Çatal is often given as an example of the peaceful woman-dominated Neolithic, but the details indicate more complexity. Once the bull and pregnant-woman juxtaposition has been made, other aggressive images also appear. There are rooms decorated by friezes of sculptures representing women's breasts; each breast is molded around the lower jaw of a wild boar. In another room a pair of women's breasts each contained the head of a griffon vulture, whose beak protruded from the open red-painted nipples. Beyond a post was a horn in plaster, evidently a male symbol; and beyond the breasts a huge bull's head crowned a red-painted niche.

Such symbolism is found neither in the Paleolithic nor in contemporary Neolithic sites—small villages and the somewhat larger Jericho. The association of the breast with the hard-pecking beak of the carrion eater contradicts all our benign images of the protective bosom, ever flowing and generous; the boar's jaw, biting not feeding, is another contradictory sadistic image.

Women at Çatal are associated with destructive power; they are also associated with death. Shrines with mural paintings of corpses under gabled shelters and huge winged figures with human feet have been interpreted as depicting religious ceremonies presided over by priestesses of death. Secondary burial has been inferred as part of the religious worship. Dead bodies were first placed outside the city on elevated platforms and left for vultures to pick. The skeletons—in varying states of decomposition—were interred beneath the floors of houses and shrines. Here is woman not only as birth-giver but as destroyer, a common ambivalence of attitudes in farming societies though not among gatherers. The Great Mother of Life and Death, the goddess Kali, Medusa and the Erinyes, Le-hev-hev and her like in Oceania—these are a few of the negative forms into which the Mother Goddess is transformed.

Whatever the role of women at Çatal, and it was an important one, by the time of Level VI, about 8200 B.P., woman is no longer friendly: these are visions of the woman denying and destroying, not in a genital sense, like the biting or toothed vagina, but in a much larger and more primitive sense of the betraying mother.

It was not always so at Çatal, however. The richness of the burials, the objects buried with individuals, and the placing of the bodies are details that can be put together to tell about the social structure of a given site. Originally women were priestesses at Çatal, but after the introduction of cattle worship, though still officiants, they no longer have the authority with which they had previously been endowed. They still have mana, the magic of blood, but now they share it with the bull in its red-painted niche.

During the gathering-hunting period some agriculture would also have been practiced. Çatal was another of those fringe settlements which may have been peopled from the rich mountains. With increasing concentration on farming, more and more labor would be necessitated. Almost nine thousand years ago there may have been a comfortable balance of nutrition. In later centuries, in order to produce the surplus indicated by the remains, trading could have been one source of riches.

At an early level of excavation, Level VIII, a special burial was found, unique for the city and elsewhere. An elaborate shrine with plastered floors painted red had an orange platform at one end. Beneath the platform a mother and a little girl were buried. The woman's body was covered in red ocher, which striped her shoulders and skull also, while the child had been partly stained with red cinnabar. The mother bore extremely elaborate jewelry for the place and period; beside her lay a macehead made of white-veined blue limestone. The little girl's skeleton, partly decayed, rested in a basket about two feet beneath the platform, and she too was richly accoutered. She wore two bead necklaces, one ornamented with mother-of-pearl pendants and deer's teeth. The beads themselves were made from varicolored stones: white, black, and blue limestone, greenstone, as well as dentalium shells. Multicolored bead bracelets encircled her wrists.

Cattle bones were located in Level VII, the stratum above that in which the priestess received her elaborate burial. After the initiation of cattle keeping, the macehead appears beside male skeletons; the priestess of Level VIII was the one female burial accompanied by such a symbol of authority.

Women who are steeped in red color, the symbol of blood and mana, are in later burials also, but they no longer have the ornate jewelry and ritual objects beside them; these now are included in male burials.

What was life like for the people who made these shrines and engaged in the religio-theatrical observances indicated by the sculptures, the wall reliefs, the paintings, and the very special arrangement of architecture? Like certain of the pueblos of Western North American Indians, there were no doors to their homes. They could be entered only through a hole in the roof, which was always on the south side and served both as a smoke hole and a doorway. A fixed ladder led from the roof down into the house; the excavator assumes a canopy or other shelter over the entrance hole and a moveable ladder on the outside leading up to the roof. People lived in the shrines and in residences next door. They cooked at hearths on the same wall as the smoke hole and baked in beehive ovens. The chief furniture seems to have been a large divan-bed, often in the center of the west wall, something like the clay *k'ang*, the couch-bed of a Chinese village home, and not dissimilar to arrangements today in Turkish villages. Underneath this large platform-bed, a woman and several children might be buried. Sometimes there were other platform-beds in the room, but there was always a smaller one in the north corner. Underneath it, a male figure might be buried, described by the excavator as the master of the house, though at this distance there is no way of knowing whether he was master, servant, or neither.

From the burials it is evident that there was a sharp distinction of sex roles in the city. In Australia and Africa men are often more highly decorated and ornamented than women;

they seem like sex objects, while the hardworking, child-raising women spend less time beautifying themselves. At Çatal, it is the women who are accompanied by cosmetic sets and copious jewelry, as well as tools. The latter include awls for sewing, bodkins for basket weaving, knives and hoes.

The men have less jewelry than the women; they have knives but they also have maces with perforated heads of polished stone, daggers and fire-making equipment: flint firestones, sometimes a piece of sulfur.

The women's cosmetics may have been for ceremonial observance: their cosmetic sets contained a palette for mixing, shells filled with powdered red ocher, a bone ointment stick, baskets containing a paste of red ocher mixed with fat, and a small spoon and fork. Obsidian mirrors were found with women's burials exclusively. One man also had a "cosmetic set," but the colors in his were blue and green; life-and-death red was reserved for women.

Many statues have been found, mostly of women, though there are occasional male figures. Several statues show a mother holding a child, and one enigmatic greenstone relief with two scenes may express the new concept penetrating human consciousness. On the left, a couple of equal size are embracing; on the right are a mother and child, possibly the results of the embrace.

There are more women than men buried at Çatal and from this fact as well as the appearance of articles which had to be procured from distant places—copper, carnelian, seashells, and mother-of-pearl are a few—it has been proposed that Çatal was an early trading city. Obsidian was a rare and much desired commodity in Neolithic times, and Çatal had a rich source nearby.

The peculiar burial arrangements at Çatal tell us that families there were not composed of a mother, a father, and their children. There is no evidence for cohabitation in the placement of the bodies under the sleeping platforms. Wives and husbands are frequently buried together, or at least side by side, in many historical excavations and in Western tradition. At Çatal the children are buried with their mothers, not at the feet of the father and mother, as one would find them, for example, in a nineteenth-century cemetery in an agricultural setting or small town in New England or Pennsylvania. Matriliny is indicated by the fact that mother and children were buried together. There are rooms where no adult man was buried. The man frequently placed under the small platform in a far corner could have been a brother, even a grown son, of the woman who lay under the large platform. Still we do not know the nature of the religious observances practiced; possibly the woman and man buried in the same house were both priests of a fertility cult celebrating female and male sex, the smaller proportion of males symbolizing the newly discovered male role in procreation, which is similarly represented in the ratio of statues with its preponderance of females and very few adult male representations.

A medical analysis of skeletons unearthed at Çatal gives much data about life as it was lived some eight thousand years ago in Anatolia. Almost all of the skeletons were from the four-hundred-year period centering about the date 8000 B.P., in particular from Levels VI and VII, the point at which, from other evidence, I have tentatively located the discovery of fatherhood by way of cattle breeding. These were the levels also where those aggressive symbols—plaster breasts incorporating boars' jaws and vultures' beaks—first appeared.

More adult women than men were buried in the only area excavated—the religious quarter. Skeletons of children are difficult, if not impossible, to sex, but the pathologist deduces, within the framework of that statement, that more male children than female children were buried. If more girls than boys survived into adulthood, it may be that boys were more susceptible to *falciparum* malaria in childhood, against which a tell-tale thickening of the skull indicated that the peoples of Çatal Hüyük had developed the protection of Cooley's anemia, as the peoples of Africa were later to develop sickle-cell anemia.

We do not know whether fewer males lived into adulthood, whether the men died and were buried away from home, or whether there were fewer male priests and therefore fewer males buried in the religious quarter.

Çatal may also be one of the earliest societies differentiated by rank, if not class, since people in other quarters—craft, market, etc.—were probably working to provide the priestly quarter with time to engage in religious and artistic activity. However, all or almost all the inhabitants of Çatal will have participated in agricultural pursuits, providing or contributing to the production of a goodly portion of their own food, as was the case in historic Sumer and in Europe down to medieval times.

Life expectancy at Çatal was fairly similar to that found in similar skeletal analyses performed on groups of Paleolithic skeletons—about thirty years. J. Lawrence Angel, the paleopathologist who analyzed the Çatal remains, felt that the women there lived one and a half to two years longer than did the women of Paleolithic enclaves whose skeletal remains he had studied. He used certain pelvic measurements to determine a woman's age at death, as well as marks of wear and scarring on the pelvic girdle to infer the number of children to which she had given birth, figures which supported the thesis of a rapidly growing population in the early Neolithic. These marks and measurements have been tested on skeletons from present-day morgues and hospitals and found to be unreliable. Still, we do know from other evidence—dated village sites in the Near East, not to say the empirical evidence of a cumulative record of geometrical increase into our own time—that village life, agriculture, and the augmentation of what we think of as civilization did result in both steady and spurting population increases, culminating in the twentieth-century explosion of planetary inhabitants.

Angel also finds a chronological trend toward reduction of males buried at home as the levels approach the date of the city's disappearance: "If this trend is valid it suggests stresses of childhood disease, hunting, war, and trading trips as forces to reduce the number of males as possible partial reasons for the end of the Early Neolithic settlement at Çatal."[2]

Not much can be deduced about infant mortality at Çatal, for there is a paucity of newborn skeletons at most of the caches found at Neolithic burial grounds, including Çatal. Ethnographic evidence shows that infants are often not counted as human souls until they have survived a given period of time, varying from five days to several months, and are not given ritual—formal—burial. A sudden drop in burials of children occurred about 8200—from Level VI on—which could indicate a change in religious practices, not inconsistent with my own conclusion that Level VI marks the point at which fatherhood was discovered and male roles in religious observances changed. Angel's conclusion is that infant dead were not given formal burial at Çatal; possibly babies who died at less than a year old were not always buried, a situation he also deduced for a later cemetery excavation at nearby Bronze Age Karatas.

Another site for cattle raising at the time of Çatal, Nea Nikomedia in Greece, had cemeteries in which the number of adult burials equaled those of children and infants, a not uncommon finding. That the ratio of adult skeletons to those of people who died before reproductive age was two to one led Sally Binford to conclude that Neanderthaloids had developed into Cro-Magnon humans while West European Neanderthals, with a one-to-one ratio of immature to mature burials, died out. Ralph Holloway used more heavily weighted statistics to conclude that the species of Homo habilis (including Australopithecus africanus) survived while Australopithecus robustus became extinct. The Çatalians had a lower ratio of immature to mature burials than the people of Nea Nikomedia. Skeletal remains from both towns show signs of endemic malaria, but in other respects the Çatalians seem to have been more healthy than the inhabitants of the European town, who suffered from a higher rate of dental disease and died younger.

Despite the combined evidence for increased population in Neolithic times, the agricultural revolution produced quantitative rather than qualitative advances. The mean life span of thirty years was more or less standard from Paleolithic times well into the nineteenth century.[3] More children lived or were allowed to live into reproductive age, but certain conditions of life were not improved; if anything they probably worsened, with longer working hours, more forced labor, poorer food. According to Angel: "The completely settled and relatively secure life of the trading settlement [of Çatal Hüyük] did not result in any real improvement in quality of diet or in health; in fact, diet and health had deteriorated."[4]

In certain respects this deterioration continued even into our own times. Children may have had a certain stability and protection in life, while childhood diseases had not yet gained a foothold in human existence—as measles and smallpox were unknown to American Indians before they were introduced by European whites. The evidence comes from a comparison of certain striae on the teeth, indications of severe emotional or physical stress caused by, say, sudden weaning or childhood disease. Among modern American whites these marks of childhood trauma are present to a slight degree in 51 per cent of child and adult skeletal remains, to a strong degree in 8 per cent; at Çatal they existed in far smaller percentages—7.5 per cent slight and 5.5 per cent strong.

The people of Çatal were comparatively tall, but slight-boned, except for the pathological thickening of skull and other bones caused by Cooley's anemia. They had more dental and gum disease than occurred in Paleolithic days, no doubt due to the increased starch and lowered protein content of their diets, though less than in modern times. They used their teeth more than we do, both for chewing and, among the women, for what Angel terms "industrial purposes," probably basketry, sewing, weaving, etc. Young children seem to have broken their legs frequently, though the breaks healed well. Despite endemic malaria, the town, estimated at over 5,000 souls, functioned for over 800 years—Mellaart claims more than a thousand. The couches with two to five sets of aurochs' horns plastered along the edges, in five of the shrines of Level VI, as well as undecorated floor benches from other levels, can be seen as healing couches. Angel compares them to the abata of late classical and Hellenistic and Roman times, which were also used during a period of newly increasing malaria. My observation indicates that the horned couches are part of a change in religious observance to worship of the horn as a potency and, possibly, life-giving symbol.

Despite the disease handicap the people of Çatal led an extremely active life. Elbows and arms showed wear and stress, while a certain number of head wounds reflect "social as well as physical wear and tear: warfare and quarrels, hunting and other accidents."[5]

One curious detail explains much and extends the picture of their lives. Almost half the thighbones analyzed show a peculiar formation at the point where the thigh joins the hip: "A special posterior development of the lesser trochanter therefore adds a little leverage in quick turning and poising as in dancing or the animal games shown in the frescoes."[6] In other words, at least half the people found in the priestly quarter of Çatal had highly developed dancer's turnout—suggesting the specific expression of religious ceremonial which was integral to their daily existence. This is not surprising, since dance is the oldest and most universal of the arts, ethnographically synonymous with religious and other festivals. However, it is not often found in the formalized and technically developed art form which must have existed at Çatal. Dancer's turnout is only achieved with much practice and difficult exercises. The tradition of the classical ballet, for example, involved apprenticeship at eight and total dedication throughout the dancer's life. The twentieth-century revolt against the long training necessary for the classical ballet was a revolt also against the discipline and repression of the earlier form, an overturning which produced modern dance and, eventually, revivified the old art. All those injuries, "the wear and tear," the children's broken limbs which Angel ascribed to "falling down the house ladder at night," the knee action and ankle flexion demonstrated by legbones are also evidence for strict athletic training beginning at an early age.

A medical study on present-day ballet dancers showed that they are subject to a wide range of athletic injuries including torn ligaments and fractured and broken bones.[7] It seems likely that the Çatalians in the religious quarter were engaged in similar severe athletic disciplines from a very early age.

On the Anatolian plain some eight thousand years ago extreme rigidity and control must have been necessary to produce a surplus for trading as well as the riches of ornamentation and art evidenced in the city itself, especially with the limited technology then existent. A puzzling feature of the sculptures and reliefs and paintings at Çatal was the absence of sexual representations. No vulvas and no male organs, though the former are prominent in Paleolithic art, and both will turn up in later Neolithic representation. Scholars have frequently interpreted the absence of sexual representation, as in Crete, as an indication of the supremacy of women. At Çatal Hüyük, Mellaart claims the absence of explicit sexual reference as proof that Neolithic woman created Neolithic religion because "emphasis on sex in art is invariably connected with male impulse and desire." The assumption that women have no sexual desire has of course been disproved by copious ethnographic evidence from nonliterate societies where women sing of the clitoris and the penis, the joys of intercourse and of sensuality. The absence of sexual representation does demonstrate the existence of sexual repression, though by whom imposed we cannot tell from this remote distance.

Wall paintings of Levels V and III recently discovered are complicated murals showing tiny figures engaged in athletic feats around and with huge animals, a kind of animal baiting resembling later illustrations of the Cretan bull games, with youths and maidens grappling animal horns, leaping onto their backs, baiting and teasing them. The Çatalian pictures were probably drawn from actual religious festivals, of dance and theater.

One injury from Angel's study indicated a deep bone infection of the left buttock, consistent with the kind of goring that occurs in bullfights—a conclusion substantiated by the animal games illustrated in Levels V and III. These murals have been interpreted as showing reverence for animals. They may tell also of sadomasochistic gamesmanship. In the importance given to animals, the difficulties of taming and killing them, there is a mingling of identification and cruelty which sheds light on the phenomenon of sadomasochism. The bull cult first illustrated at Çatal Hüyük was diffused all across the central areas of Asia, Africa, and Southern Europe. An archaeologist of the future might, indeed, admire the beauty of a bullfight painting in Spain or Mexico—matadors and picadors, brilliant capes and flourishes, the ceremony and athleticism almost a formalized dance—without taking into account the underlying cruelty and horror. Many audiences do so today, enjoying gore and sadism married to panoply and art—one symptom of the particular Spanish cultural history of inhibition, control, and torture that is an outgrowth of the basic contempt for sexuality rooted therein.

Settled life allowed for a development of art, religion, and architecture and crafts which left more complete and visible remains than did the cultures of several thousand years earlier in that area and the contemporaneous culture in other parts of the world.

The material and technological advances at Çatal have been ascribed to freedom from the pursuit of food. Art—beautiful and necessary though it be—is often achieved at the cost of life and lives. Judging by recent ethnographic evidence on the leisure of gathering peoples, there must have been less leisure, more drive and discipline—in sum more sexual sublimation— than in Paleolithic times. I would predicate sexual repression coming from animal breeding, resulting in competitive and sadomasochistic games and pursuits, as well as an early tendency toward material accumulation, read trade, as culture complexes which shaped Çatal's flowering and decline.

Where animals, and particularly the massive cattle, were of less importance, the attitude toward procreation and the position of women was somewhat different. Some 375 miles west of Çatal Hüyük was the village called Hacilar, 3,000 feet up in a well-watered intramontane valley. Very scanty remains of an early Neolithic settlement, predating Çatal, have been found; then a thousand-year gap exists—just the period during which the latter flourished. Hacilar was resettled perhaps about 7,700 years ago, about the time Çatal was abandoned. It was not a large village ever; 7,600 years ago it may have contained about 50 houses, or a minimum of 250 souls.

At Hacilar, both early and late, there is no proof that any domesticated animals except, possibly, dogs, were ever kept. In the remains of the early settlement, where a few bones of fallow deer, hare, wild cattle, and sheep or goats were found, it is felt that hunting must have been practiced. In the late Neolithic settlement, there is abundant documentation of advanced and intensive farming and no evidence of domestic animals. Judging from the sparsity of wild-animal remains unearthed and the lack of weapons, as compared to the richness of the material which told of cultivation, it would seem that the inhabitants of Hacilar were largely vegetarian. They produced a varied farming diet: naked barley and bread wheat, along with earlier forms of wheat, peas, lentils, pistachios, almonds, apples, capers, and an abundance of hackberries, the fruit which *Homo pekinensis* had enjoyed half a million years earlier at Choukoutien. They did little hunting and had to have some method of irrigation to cultivate certain of their vegetables. Religious orientation reflects their cultural and economic life. In extant excavations of prehistoric art from Crete, Greece, Egypt, and the Near East, Hacilar is one of a very few where the male figure is totally absent, while animal references are also scantier here than elsewhere.[8] Surely it is no coincidence that in a village where animals were not kept and hunting was a peripheral activity, all the statues are of women—at every age and stage of maturity: standing with the pointed breasts of youth, reclining with full breasts and distended pregnant bellies, women seated in the birth position, standing women with huge drooping breasts, or, frequently, with hands cupped offering breasts, in a gesture which will turn up again and again, in art and life, in history and ethnography. Among the many statues of baked clay are only two, or possibly three, which show the woman (goddess or talisman) associated with another figure.

One enigmatic fragment is an ample woman with missing arms, a portion of the lower half of a child at her midsection, its leg curled over her thigh. It is described as "Young Woman Playing with Her Son," but the child might just as well be a daughter. Another small unbaked clay figure which shows a woman clasping a fragment of a small animal to her chest and seated on a larger animal is nominated "Mistress of the Animals Holding a Leopard Cub and Seated on a Leopard." And one seated figure with hands cupping breasts who has a portion of what seems to be the long curving tail of an animal across her back is dubiously reconstructed as "Mistress of the Animals Seated on Two Leopards."

This is not to say that no notice is taken of animals alone. A few pottery containers are shaped in the form of animals—theriomorphic vases is the archaeologists' description. The copious finds of richly ornamented pottery are decorated chiefly in geometric patterns, but some of these stylized forms—probably derived from the limitations imposed by earlier ages' basketry patterns—would seem to represent animals and plants. There are even a very few fragments of clay figures and heads of animals. But the "male principle" is conspicuously absent. There are no representations of men or phalli, nor of animal horns or of massive frightening beasts; no association seems to be made between potency and aggression; the concept of potency has yet to appear. Nor is there any emphasis on the Great Mother as a figure of terror and death—surely a projection of male anxiety and hostility.

Hacilar may well exemplify the myth of the peaceful female-dominated early agricultural community. Large rooms in the excavated buildings point to an extended family rather than a nuclear organization. Life was sunnier in this rich valley between mountains than in the malarial Konya plain where Çatal Hüyük developed. With its small population, every inhabitant at Hacilar would have been able to partake of the fruits of the soil in a basic model of an egalitarian society.

Different strains and different cultural emphases existed at the same time and in nearby locations. Çatalians may have been more quarrelsome and competitive than the peaceful Hacilarians to the west. There is no need to assume matriarchy per se for Çatal or Hacilar even if households centered around the mother. Numerous statues of women have been excavated at Jericho, Beidha, Jarmo, Sawwan, and other sites of the period, both rich and poor. The ambiguous evidence from Çatal is the only positive indication that the male role in generation had been recognized. Judging by the grave goods, it is probable that there was less emphasis on possession, more on sharing, and more sexual freedom in the smaller communities than existed in the larger city of Çatal Hüyük.

Is the myth of the matriarchy a justification for the imposition of the patriarchy? Surely the idea that the patriarchy was preceded by the matriarchy is not only a reverse image of the power wielded by men, but also a metaphor, a childlike phrasing of the power of the Great Mother. We all desire a great all-giving mother—to suck at the ever-flowing breast—but what poor mortal female can possibly live up to the demands of the infant when closely spaced, forcible breeding has begun to be enforced? Thus we resent weaning, we resent younger siblings, we resent the adult male who sleeps with the mother. Daughters, as well as sons, will harbor all these and more against the also beloved mother. The ambivalence of our feelings, the love that becomes transformed to hate, is more prevalent under the patriarchy and under the heavy socializing of the earlier civilizations; a substratum capable of development may be hidden in looser and more simply organized societies.

22

Sadism and Masochism: Inherent or Acquired?

Are sadism and masochism inherent in the human animal? Sadism is defined as "a perversion in which gratification is obtained by torturing the loved one" or, in a larger sense, as "a love of cruelty, conceived as a manifestation of sexual desire." Masochism, the obverse of sadism, is the "abnormal sexual passion in which one finds pleasure in abuse or cruelty from his or her associate; hence, any pleasure in being abused or dominated."[1]

The words themselves are of recent origin. *Sadism* derives from the Marquis de Sade, who lived in the second half of the eighteenth century and on into the nineteenth, dying in 1814. *Masochism* comes from the novels written by Leopold von Sacher-Masoch, who died in 1895. Though the human history of torture and cruelty goes back thousands of years, evidently no need was felt to identify the sexual components of these phenomena until the last century or so. Writers on sexuality—Krafft-Ebing and Freud and his followers—brought the words into wide usage, so that in our own time they are familiar if not completely understood concepts.

Freud took it for granted that aggressive impulses were inborn and rooted in sexuality. In his version, the first "crime" was committed when the son killed the father because he desired the mother. A follower of Freud's, Gregory Zilboorg, changed the facts but kept the emotional tenor. He said the initial crime was not the murder of the father, it was the rape of the mother. Both men assumed innate violence and active sadistic sexuality in men and passivity in women, who are being acted upon rather than acting in both cases. (Until recently, there was little room for daughters in psychoanalytic formulations of this kind.) Freud's thinking was shaped by Greek myths, which themselves reflect fairly late stages of political development. When studies of matrilineal societies were published, like that of the Trobriand Islanders by Malinowski, they disproved the Freudian thesis. In these societies, it was the mother's brother who had authority over the son's presumed object of desire so that Bertrand Russell could imagine the Oedipal myth reframed with supreme power vested in God the Maternal Uncle, rather than in God the Father.

Is rape, for example, a sadistic perversion? And if so, does its seeming ubiquity make a case for the inherently sadistic nature of men?*

In the same way are woman naturally masochistic? Freud's initial view of women as incomplete men, feeling themselves deformed or castrated because they lacked penises, led him to see them as essentially passive. When they were active, they were being "masculine"—a view that has been disproved by ethnographic researches. Masochism as a biological female trait was only implicit in Freud's earlier writings; he made it explicit in his later work. It was his followers, among them Sandor Rado, Geza Roheim, and Helene Deutsch, who further developed the thesis of woman as inherently masochistic.

The wish to inflict suffering develops, I believe, from sexual energy deprived of outlet. It may also be caused by a need to control, anxiety projected onto others. But nobody chooses to suffer unnecessarily. Masochism is an alternative to a worse suffering, physical or psychic. Sadism can exist in the aggressor

---

* There are cultures where neither rape nor the concept itself exists—from the peaceful Arapesh described by Margaret Mead to the Lesu of New Ireland, to the newly discovered Tasadays of the Philippines.

without masochism in the victim. There is a component of masochism, however, in the sadist's identification (conscious or unconscious) with the object of his or her cruelty.

In his study of Paleolithic art mentioned in Chapter 15, André Leroi-Gourhan divided the representations into male and female. He explicated many mysterious markings in sexual terms, inventing a complicated set of equivalences which made lines, sticks, and plants into weapons, then phalli; rounds, triangles, and other enclosed shapes into wounds, then vulvas. The man-horse-spear image was complemented by that of woman-bison-wound; the male spear and the female wound were seen as symbols of sexual union and death.

Associating the vagina with a wound comes from the Freudian thesis of castration anxiety, in which the small boy takes his and his father's bodies as universal models and assumes that the shape of his mother's and sisters' genitals is the result of castration, that the vagina is a wound, a "gash" in popular terminology, rather than a normal biological manifestation. But this identification is a projection of a violent and terror-filled culture in which the body is hidden so that the first sight of nakedness comes as a shock and everybody's genitals are shameful. It is symptomatic of a recent historic mentality to connect sex with wounds and sadism and to link animals thereto. This comes from the direct linkage between war and sexual oppression in the history of civilization.

In Freud's Vienna, woman's position was manifestly inferior to that of man, so that one might make a case for the penis as a symbol of male power. In the Upper Paleolithic period, however, where there were more representations of females than of males, we cannot prove that a similar situation was already in effect. Morever, as was discussed earlier, Leroi-Gourhan's categorization was based on mistaken identification to begin with, since many of the so-called weapons were probably leaves, branches, and other vegetation. There is no proof that sado-masochistic syndromes were present in the paintings and sculpture or in the people who made them. When war, cruelty, and torture do surface—some millennia after the adoption of agriculture and animal breeding—there is little doubt about their existence. They can be traced in the architecture, the visual decorations, and eventually in the literature, in which last the sexual elements are also revealed.

Many of the factors contributing to sadism and to masochism need not have functioned in the Paleolithic. Psychoanalysts have differed in their views on human sexuality. Freud predicated civilization on its repression. Wilhelm Reich, one of his most gifted students, felt that repressed sexuality was responsible for civilization's deformities rather than civilization itself and broke with the master over this point.

Reich's basic humanity was outraged in particular by the work Geza Roheim had attempted, mixing psychoanalysis with anthropology in a book called *Psychoanalysis of Primitive Cultures*, based on a trip to Australia and New Guinea in the spring of 1929. He quotes Roheim's reactionary outlook on life: "In the purely physical sense their manner of carrying out intercourse seems to be more genital than the Europeans'. They *penetrate more deeply*, work with stronger physical stimuli; with a slight exaggeration, one might even say the woman is only satisfied if after intercourse she feels ill with an inflammation." How can he know?

Reich expostulates, "With a *slight* exaggeration? Has psychoanalysis been founded, the existence of the unconscious discovered, and the morbid sadistic concept of coitus revealed, in order that an official representative of psychoanalysis may summon up the courage and narrowmindedness, to assert such things with authority?"[2]

This was written in 1931. Since then, the expansion of Freudianism, particularly during and after World War II, has given a sanction of seemingly advanced views to what were essentially nineteenth-century ideas on sexuality, and not only in esoteric studies like the work of Leroi-Gourhan. In 1968 Erik Erikson asserted that in every *normal* sexual relationship there was probably some element of sadism, while Irving Singer, writing in 1973, confidently assured us that women need to be banged on the cervix to achieve a preferred kind of orgasm![3]

Reich pointed out "that in the authoritarian patriarchy the genitality of men is considered a proof of potency, while the genitality of women is considered a disgrace." For him, genitality was all, and he saw "a disturbed capacity for gratification" as the pathological basis of sexual aggression.[4] He thought in terms of a primeval age "when love life was free and unrestricted" and traced a line of development which combined Marx-Engels' thinking with the reports of Malinowski on the Trobriand Islanders to project an economic origin for sexual repression:

> With the economic interests of a developing social stratum and the suppression of the sex life of children and adolescents, the sexual experience of the whole community changed. Sexual disturbances and neuroses appeared—sadistic attitudes in the sex life of men and sex negation in the women. . . . Sadism is as prevalent as it is today only when the natural genital functions are hindered or disturbed; in other words, *inhibited genitality changes not only into anxiety but also into sadism and perhaps this is the sole origin of sadism.* . . . Roheim and most analysts view sadism as a natural manifestation in the area of sex, and its origin is therefore biological.

Reich quotes Roheim, declaring that the deepest human sadistic attitudes are linked to the first eruption of teeth and that sadism signifies the desire to devour one's sexual partner. Why, he demands, do not Roheim and the other analysts take account of the differences among peoples in different places since sexual sadism is nonexistent in some cultures and prominent in others.[5]

Of female masochism, directly, Reich does not speak since he feels that women are the forced victims of male sadism rather than the willing receptors. His theory of forcible inhibition—"sex negation in the women" is his rather judgmental expression—would mean that their masochism is sadistic aggression turned on themselves. Reich clearly acknowledges the sexuality of women: "There is, in this respect, no difference between the healthy man and the healthy woman."[6] Essentially, however, he sees women in relation to or as analogues of men rather than as wholes, with their own specific biology, nature, and history.

Karen Horney and, somewhat later, Clara Thompson also took exception to the view of sadomasochism as inherent in human and animal biology, but from rather different points of view. They focus more on the female, i.e., the masochistic, side of the proposition: male equals aggression equals sadism; female equals passivity equals masochism—and they place more emphasis on cultural conditioning of women under patriarchy.

Horney discusses women's "lowered self-esteem of centuries duration." She points out the factors in Western culture which "predispose to the appearance of masochism in women," including "blocking of outlets for expansiveness and sexuality . . . the estimation of women as beings who are, on the whole, inferior to men (insofar as it leads to a deterioration of female self-confidence.) . . . economic dependence of women on men or on family, inasmuch as it fosters an emotional adaptation in the way of female self-confidence . . . [and] surplus of marriageable women, particularly when marriage offers the principal opportunity for sexual gratification, children, security and social recognition." She concludes "that in our culture it is hard to see how any woman can escape becoming masochistic to some degree, from the effects of the culture alone."[7]

Both Horney and Thompson are cautiously critical of Freud's and his followers' Oedipally based physiological theory of female masochism as the result of penis envy. "Sadism and masochism have fundamentally nothing whatsoever to do with intercourse, but the female role in intercourse (being penetrated) lends itself more readily to a personal misinterpretation (when needed) of masochistic performance; and the male role, to one of sadistic activity."[8]

Writing some years later, in a work not published until after her death, Thompson took an even stronger stand against Freudian "biology":

> Culturally we have been educated to think of women as having less sexual drive than men. . . . Observation of animals does not seem to confirm this, accord-

ing to Ford and Beach. The sexual drive of the female in heat is *insatiable*. . . . *One female at that time can exhaust several males* . . . psychoanalysis thus far has secured extensive acquaintance with the psychology of women in only one type of culture. Facts observed by Freud in a particular part of the Western world have been interpreted as an adequate basis for an understanding of female psychology in general and as evidence for a particular theory about specific biological factors in the nature of woman. I have pointed out that characteristics and inferiority feelings which Freud considered to be specifically female and biologically determined can be explained as developments arising in and growing out of Western woman's historic situation of underprivilege, restriction of development, insecure attitude toward the sexual nature, and social and economic dependency. *The basic nature of woman is still unknown.*[9]

Both these women were practicing psychoanalysts, trained by students of Freud, working with male colleagues whose feelings and male bias had to be considered, if not catered to, else they risked total isolation, with a resultant inability to practice their already touch-and-go profession.

It is difficult enough for any artist, thinker, or scientist to be a revolutionary, but a woman is in double jeopardy, assailable because of her sex as well as her ideas. Horney and Thompson pointed out many of the male-oriented ideas in psychoanalytic theory, but they were often forced to adopt a temporizing tone. Like Reich, Horney tended to attack the master's theories by way of his followers' interpretation; it did neither of them any good, for both suffered expulsion from the society of the faithful. Writing after Freud's death, Thompson was able to attack Freud's essay "Economic Theory of Masochism," which was based on studies of male homosexuals: "What a passive male homosexual imagines about the experience of being a woman is not necessarily similar to female sexual experience."[10]

Where in history does the phallus cease to be an organ of enjoyment and become an organ of conquest? How far back can we trace the concept of aggressive sexuality, leading to sadism? One step is the worship of the animal horn as a symbol of male potency. Animal horns are like fingernails, bony growths consisting largely of keratin. Their purpose in animals is largely ornamental, with a secondary function of offense or defense. The phallus is of course made of flesh; blood is responsible for its erection; it is rich in nerve endings and sensation.

Only after humans have begun to control and breed animals, in particular the massive wild cattle, does the horn alone and unmistakably appear in conjunction with fertility worship. The new ideology—envisioning the human penis as a hunk of horn—denies the pleasurable aspects of sexual congress to focus on an ideal of the ever-ready breeder. In a positive view the phallus would be valued in all stages from the excitement of erection to the happy shrinking of realized satisfaction. The whole misplaced construct of the phallus as plow, harrow, sword, or gun begins in sadomasochistic imagery of fertility worship. Women are enslaved by being worshiped as mothers, more specifically as breeders. Men are enslaved to the religion of a massively erect phallus as weapon or producer. Nowhere in these metaphors is it acknowledged that the penis is an organ of exquisite pleasure. Even today, the horn survives as a symbol of luck, or procreation, and of male power. In the Mediterranean countries, one can still buy a good-luck amulet, a twisted horn, usually of red coral—the red, of course, relating to the red ocher used in burials from Paleolithic times on, the red of blood and of life, the whole being an amulet of fortune. On the other hand, when the ascetic antisex Christian religion entered the popular consciousness, the pagan horns of procreation were assigned to the devil, along with the satyrs' goat feet. A man became a cuckold wearing horns when his wife was "unfaithful"; he was reduced to a beast as his wife indulged in sex like the beasts, indiscriminately and without regard to capitalist or Christian possession. The two-finger sign of Mediterranean countries—extended forefinger and little finger signifying the horns which ward off the evil eye and ill luck generally—is another survival of the early religious propitiatory significance of the cattle symbol of male power and potency derived from the great discovery brought about by animal keeping and breeding.

A parallelism between cruelty and animal breeding shows up in many cultures. Pigs were domesticated in Europe and Asia, probably in several places, and are widely used today as food animals. Yet there are islands in Oceania where they figure in special religious worship and their primary importance is hardly for food. The men of Vao, the island off the coast of Malekula referred to earlier, worship an evil female deity, Le-hev-hev, in ceremonies which exclude women. Part of the worship centers around the breeding of boars raised for their circle tusks. Women do not participate in the raising or the eating of pig meat, and the men do not eat the sows—they eat only the male porkers. These animals are, however, reduced to sorry condition by the cruel practices which produce the most highly prized deformations—tusks which may be trained, ideally, to circle twice, even thrice, around, piercing the hapless animal's cheeks and jaws in the process.

The deformation is produced by knocking out the boar's upper canines so that the lower-jaw tusks, which grow in a curve, pierce the cheek flesh and re-enter the jaw. Sometimes they keep growing to form another complete circle, while those which produce a third circle have the highest value. The circle-tuskers are used in religious feasts, the only time they may be eaten. Not surprisingly they produce little meat. Therefore some of the boars are gelded and sacrificed before the tusks re-enter the jaws. According to Cranstone:

> Their value is much less but they provide more meat. For this reason pigs are often killed in pairs, a circle-tusker and a gelding. The circle-tusker is of value only while alive, and only if the tusks are in good condition; if a tusk is broken the pig is worth little. Its physical condition does not affect its value, but after death its tusks are worthless. . . . Tusked boars . . . become almost a form of currency, and a complex network of obligation comes into being. It appears too that the importance of pigs is such that land which

might be used for cultivation is left to provide foraging ground for them.

Sows are not eaten by either sex. Women may not, because pigs are killed only in the context of ritual in which women have no part. Men may not, because sows being female are ritually dangerous to them. Layard says of the cultivation of tusks: "This practice lies at the base of the natives' whole overt religious life, gives rise to the chief form of currency, and so largely regulates all their economic activities . . . and permeates every aspect of life."[11]

An effort has been made to link the Megalithic culture of certain islands in Oceania—including Vao and the larger Malekula, settled from Southern Asia in waves beginning about two thousand years ago—with the dolmens of Malta, Spain, and Britain. Direct or indirect though the connections may be, the parallelism between sadomasochistic practices and selective animal breeding is found in widely separated areas of human settlement.

Throughout the Mediterranean the history of sadistic animal games is an ancient one. From Çatalian rituals to Cretan bull-vaulting to the Iberian bullfight, there are overlappings of sexual repression, animal-human analogies, and proof of potency. In Crete women and men participated in the games; in Spain and Portugal the contest in cruelty is a demonstration of male courage and ritualized torture.

"Murder is never asexual," said Norman Mailer, and the butchering of animals we have befriended is also a form of murder, recognized in the Italian curse, "Go die, slaughtered."†

† "Va a morire, ammazzato."

Part V

CIVILIZATION AND THE BIRTH OF THE PATRIARCHY

Be fruitful and multiply, and replenish the earth, and subdue it: and have dominion over the fish of the sea, and over the fowl of the air, and over every living thing that moveth upon the earth.

—Genesis 1:28

!Kung San mother and child. *(Photograph Melvin Konner/Anthro-Photo)*

Montagnais-Naskapi woman hunter setting snare. *(Photograph Richard Leacock)*

Venus of Laussel. Paleolithic relief sculpture, circa 24,000 B.P.
(*Photograph Jean Vertut*)

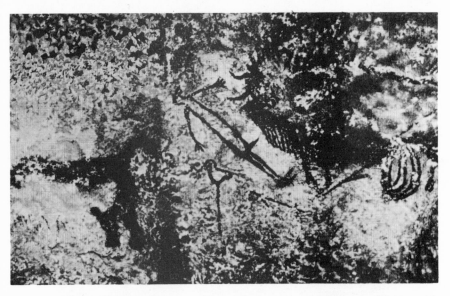

Shaft of the Dead Man at Lascaux. Cave painting, circa 12,000 B.P. (*Photograph Jean Vertut*)

The triune male genital and woman as a potential. Potsherd from Choga Mami, circa 7000 B.P. (uncalibrated radiocarbon date). (*Photograph Joan Oates*)

Uruk vase, circa 3200 B.C.E. Front view showing nude worshipers bringing gifts to the goddess Inanna. (*Courtesy Directorate General of Antiquities, Baghdad, Iraq*)

nze Age goddess from the bog at Viksø, Denmark. *(Courtesy P. V. Glob, Arch-logical Society of Jutland)*

The Goddess of War, central European ceremonial sculpture, circa 550 B.C.
(Photograph Fürböck, Graz, Austria)

Defeated Britons—Roman soldier riding down women and children. Stone relief from the Antonine Wall, circa 150 C.E. (*Reproduced by courtesy of the National Museum of Antiquities of Scotland*)

Attis emasculating himself. Bronze statuette, circa 200 C.E. (*Courtesy of the Archaeological Museum of Split, Yugoslavia*)

23

———ıı———ıı———ıı———ıı———ıı———ıı———

The Power of Procreation:
From Matriliny to Patriliny

Four key factors are pivotal to the development of civilization, cities, and class society. These are plow agriculture, the castration of the bull to produce oxen for drawing the plows, irrigation, and increasing population. To a greater or lesser degree they have been accompanied by the rise of the patriarchy and the economic and sexual subjugation of women. The connections between the four are manifold: the ox is needed for large-scale agriculture made possible by canal irrigation, as well as for moving earth in the construction and control of the canal network, and the encouragement of childbirth results from the need for more labor to work the fields intensively, to watch and feed the animals, and to produce a surplus for the few people at the top of the pyramid which now begins to take shape in organizing human societies. Plow agriculture calls for animal raising and generally results in a switch from female to male cultivators using ox-drawn plows, from matriliny to patriliny, from community ownership to individual ownership of land, which is passed on from father to son.

These four phenomena make their appearance in the three thousand years between the disappearance of Anatolian Çatal Hüyük and the rise of cities in southern Mesopotamia, the home of the first "high civilization" in the history of human-kind. Different observers link the four phenomena in different causal relationships as they attempt to trace their origins. It is not known which appeared first and where, nor which was cause and which was result.

So far, representations of plows and draft animals date back only some 5,200 years ago, though it can be assumed that the animals and tools themselves existed considerably earlier. The earliest known vestiges of canal irrigation have recently been located in central Mesopotamia at a point more or less midway between pre-existing agricultural settlements to the north and the ancient Sumerian cities where it is believed that written history and the state began. Choga Mami is the name of a dig where archaeologists Joan and David Oates believe they have found traces of artificial water channels. These canals were in use over seven thousand years ago. And at the same time they find that population density was also increasing, as evidenced by the size and number of settlements in the immediate vicinity of these first earthworks. The presence of wooden plows and dredges and of oxen to draw them cannot be demonstrated at the site, but the existence of canals and of comparatively large populations supported by a small amount of land is presumptive evidence for their use, as is the fact of a gradual increase in the number of cattle bones—1 per cent at the most ancient layers of occupation, increasing gradually to 9 per cent several hundred years later, at a time when an ambitious canal some fifteen feet wide ran past the largest settlement in the vicinity. Canalization entails digging ditches, moving large masses of dirt, and eventually controlling the flow of water over fields by means of dikes and sluice gates, all calling for an increased investment of human and, possibly, animal labor.

A curious fragment of pottery dated to the same period—some seven thousand years ago—was dug up in this settlement of Choga Mami: a potsherd whose design may shed some light on the causes and interrelationship of the above-mentioned pivotal factors. It shows three geometricalized figures, a woman, a man, and a woman, linked arm in arm, and all display very specific genital areas (see Figure 5). The upper body of the

male comprises a large inverted triangle whose point reaches
the center of a horizontal bar, and from the bottom of the
body triangle append three prongs, the outer ones shorter than
the middle one. It looks for all the world like an unbalanced
pitchfork and is the first indubitable extant representation of
the triune male genital.

In Paleolithic painting and sculpture the emphasis had been
on the penis, usually erected, not on the testicles; it was the excitement and activity of the male sex organ which drew attention, not its generative capacity. Clay cylinders from Paleolithic
caves, stone cylinders from Siberian mammoth-hunting sites, as
well as Neolithic cylinders from Jarmo and Tepe Guran in the
Middle East, are often referred to as phalli by the excavators.
Any long rolled shape can be seen as a phallus, and, to paraphrase Freud's "Gentlemen, sometimes a cigar is just a cigar,"
sometimes a cylinder is just a cylinder, a grinder, a spreader, a
finger, or an unknown tool or ornament. Cautious investigators
refer to these infrequently located artifacts as "possible penis objects."

A nine-thousand-year-old cylinder surfaced at the Deh Luran
digs (discussed in Chapter 18) where early transitions between
gathering and farming have been traced. A seven-thousand-
year-old level produced a small sculpture, a flat-based oval on
which a round and a cylinder shape join, looking rather like
a clenched fist and upright index finger. A few similar sculptures were excavated at a dig near Choga Mami and contemporaneous with it—Sawwan—where about fifty alabaster sculptures of women were also found. The excavator at Sawwan had
no hesitation about terming the six alabaster artifacts penises,
though, if they are indeed phalli, it would seem that these
early Near Easterners pictured themselves as having one tes-
ticle.

At Choga Mami, however, the three-in-one male sexual appa-
ratus is complete and unquestionable. The emphasis on the testicles provides evidence for the new understanding which must
have come from animal observation. The connection of the
semen producers with reproduction, animal and human, may

have been made through experiments in animal castration to produce tractable draft animals.

The two female figures also focus on increase, or at least the capacity for same. The plump little sculpture known as the Venus of Willendorf has a small but distinct mons veneris with the cleft of the vulva clearly incised; in other Paleolithic sculpture the vulva and female sexual triangle might be delineated. But in the clay fragment from Choga Mami, each woman is drawn with a large open diamond-shaped figure between her thighs, seemingly the original portmanteau of womb and vulva, the confusion which causes so many problems in later history.

Throughout the Near East many Neolithic sculptures portray women in every phase of life and maturity. Opulent "mother goddesses" from Çatal Hüyük and nearby Hacilar offer their breasts, embrace children, give birth, and possibly, as in the unique instance of the Çatal plaque, tell a story in two episodes—the embrace of two figures followed by its consequence, a mother and child. On the Choga Mami shard from a shallow bowl, however, where the women are schematically depicted with small upper-body triangles—one of which may have breasts—atop blocky, large-thighed lower halves, woman is seen as a potential, open, empty, waiting to be filled up, not bursting with life and sexuality as earlier and elsewhere. The emphasis in male and female figures is on reproduction rather than fulfillment.

It cannot be a coincidence that this suggestive drawing dates from a time when, according to site surveys, a population explosion was taking place in northern and central Mesopotamia and just before the same thing happens to the south. The emphasis on human increase combines with the results to which this emphasis led. The "penis objects" found at Sawwan and elsewhere may or may not demonstrate a knowledge of the male role in reproduction, but with the potsherd from Choga Mami, the concept of male seed and insemination enters human thought.

Though village life may have lowered the infant mortality rate, population growth was gradual and in certain areas, like Western Europe and much of Africa, barely noticeable for several millennia after the introduction of agriculture. There is a distinction between safe childbirth and survival and the worship of fertility for its own sake. The desirability of the first is unarguable; the second is open to debate. For the woman doing the bearing, many children are a dubious benefit. The more children, the more work; increased fertility of women is not a liberating factor, even if the children themselves are put to work at ever-earlier ages. Archaeological data demonstrate this proposition, showing the unceasing effort entailed by Neolithic peasant life. Where querns or grinding stones and pestles and handstones were found in small quantities during the earliest stage of Ali Kosh—in the Deh Luran excavations discussed previously—they have become omnipresent grave goods at neighboring Tepe Sabz some four thousand years later. Gordon Childe lauded this agricultural revolution, but Bertrand Russell remarked of it, "With the introduction of agriculture *man*kind entered upon a long period of meanness, misery, and madness, from which they are only now being freed by the beneficent operation of the machine."[1]

Here then is an explanation of the demographic fact of geometrically increasing population during the last several thousand years. It has been said that among primates there is an equal division of labor except for childbirth. It is a very unequal division.[2] In most languages, the words we use for reproduction of the species recognize that biology imposes an extra burden of work on women: *labor, carrying, nursing, bearing* . . .

Beginning several thousand years ago in the "fertile crescent," women of the ensuing civilizations and in many parts of the Afro-Eurasian triangle have been selected for fertility. This was not so in Oceania, Australia, and the Americas and may be a partial explanation for the "period of adolescent sterility" which puzzled anthropologists like Margaret Mead and Ashley Montagu. They could not understand why in Australia, the Trobriand Islands, and Samoa, despite seeming sexual freedom, girls did not usually conceive during the first few years after menarche. In Oceania and the Americas the religion of fecundity was not practiced, and women were not pushed into or selected for maximum exploitation of their reproductive tal-ents. They make more ecological sense than we do. Among Australian Aborigines, for example, menarche occurs at about age fifteen, and women do not usually have their first child until age eighteen or nineteen, in contrast to our own society where twelve, eleven, even ten-year-old girls become pregnant and eighteen- and nineteen-year-old women may have already given birth to four, five, or more children.[3]

Animal breeding and its consequences, literal and analogous, were one side of the story; the fertility goddess is the other. Emphasis on fertility and on the mother goddess does not nec-essarily demonstrate the power of women in Neolithic society. When woman is worshiped for her "natural" powers, woe be-tide her humanity. Forced breeding and sexual repression go to-gether. Limitations in the area of male-female sexuality led to the overdevelopment of maternal sexuality, and this in turn led to the subjugation of women as it is practiced in the historical Western patriarchy. As Adrienne Rich wrote, "Male domina-tion has been founded on male control of female sexuality and reproduction, on institutionalized male ownership of women and children."[4] From the Near Eastern locus it spread through-out five continents, by a process of diffusion and conquest and in varying forms, superimposed on earlier traditions and with contradictory beliefs surviving or peering through the earlier scheme.

In the past, as in certain existing cultures, it was women who made the decision to prevent or abort pregnancies and to kill newborn children. When did they relinquish the decision-mak-ing function? We are taught that people do not willingly give up power. Did women decide to have more children or were they constrained to? How did the sensual and affective pleasure of maternal sexuality become transformed into the brutal insti-tution of forced breeding?

Till recently it had been assumed that geometric population increases were a result of first the invention and then the devel-opment of more efficient agricultural methods, technological advances—that, in effect, humans are logical and efficient, and as civilization advances more people are born and survive. This is a hangover from nineteenth-century confidence which saw human evolution as a linear progression of conquest over nature, with industrialized Western white males in the vanguard. Actually, human populations have increased for many reasons: biological, medical, political. They have also been controlled and kept from increasing by women and by women and men in agreement. The demographic problem did not begin in this century, though Malthus' vision of it was a narrow and distorted one, his approach brutal and unnecessarily cruel.

We saw that the adoption of agriculture enabled more people to eat less well, from a small area, if they worked longer hours than the foragers had. Moreover, a gifted United Nations agronomist, Ester Boserup, deduced that, just as foragers spend fewer hours and less labor on feeding themselves than do farmers and modern industrial workers, in the same wise each technological advance in farming has required a higher input of labor per person for the corresponding increase in food production. From long-fallow cultivation using slash-and-burn techniques, through short fallow with hoe culture, plow agriculture using draft animals, and irrigation, under preindustrial conditions each new step necessitates more individual hours per person working and more people working. Only when there are more hands available for a given area of land will people voluntarily adopt the method which requires more labor.

The common impression is that by producing more food farming enabled more people to survive and that the agricultural revolution was the cause of geometrically increasing world populations. New information indicates that it was the increased labor attached to farming that demanded more people. The establishment of fertility worship resulted; it differed from the previous respect for women's generative powers. The breeding of animals suggested the control of women's reproductive capacities. Slaves were also captured to fill the need for more labor.

A steady natural increase of humans occurred during the foraging period of our existence, so small as to be barely perceptible in a ten-thousand-year slice of the whole, but humans did people all six continents before the adoption of farming. Beginning about ten thousand years ago, social factors—religion, politics, and imposition from above by rulers of conquering groups —led to sudden spurts in specific areas, eventually to the perilous condition in which we find ourselves today. The history of women's subjugation is shaped by changing attitudes and knowledge about human procreation. Where fertility is not valued, and birth control is practiced by women, population will not increase substantially. Because of distorting cultural and sexual traits, semistarvation and overpopulation appeared in specific areas thousands of years ago while others were unpopulated or well below their carrying rate, even for foragers, who need access to large areas of land.

Women are more specifically and immediately involved with population increase than are men. Discussants of the demographic problem often overlook this significant fact, given the confusion engendered by the English language's double use of the word *man*, as a generic term and as a specific sexual reference. Birth control and birth attitudes were originally regulated by women. We can trace society's increasing domination over reproduction as social, religious, and political institutions changed.

The linkage of the generative bull and the fecund woman at Çatal Hüyük is an early example of new religious emphasis; the three-pronged male and womb-containing females from Choga Mami are another. From a period several hundred years closer to us (about 4500 B.C.E.) come some provocative finds in cemeteries of two of the most ancient cities in Sumer. In Eridu, traditional home of Enki, the Sumerian god of water and wisdom, a lizard-headed figure with clearly delineated testicles and penis was unearthed in a woman's grave, while in Uruk, later known as the home of the goddess Inanna, several female figures with similar elongated reptilian heads were found.[5]

Peter Ucko, that gadfly of generalizers, has supplied data on the incidence of female and male sculptures found in Mediterranean and Near Eastern excavations during the prehistoric period, including these finds at Eridu and Uruk, sculptures often taken to be indicative of the worship of female or male deities. The great majority of figures are clearly female either with breasts or with "sexual triangle," many are sexless, and a few are male "as indicated by clear secondary sexual characteristics of male beard."[6] Male figures with penises are extremely scarce, while the lizard-headed male with full genital appurtenances from Eridu, like the drawing on clay from Choga Mami, is almost unique. Evidently and in spite of the example of animal breeding, the awareness of male procreatory function, as symbolized by sperm-producers, was indeed slow in arriving. That its arrival coincides with an awareness of property and property rights is not remarkable, since animals were the first self-propelling portable property whereas land stayed in one place and rights to its use would be vested in a communal clan or extended family.

One area where population increased suddenly and irregularly some five to six thousand years ago was ancient Mesopotamia, the land between the rivers. Scholars wonder whether the population increased intentionally so as to have more labor or whether a natural population increase created the new villages which led eventually to the civilization of Sumer. Why do large cities appear first in the unpromising area of southern Mesopotamia rather than in rich wooded areas, mountain valleys with large vegetable resources and much game? Why didn't the upland gatherers with more access to food expand their populations, especially if a few methods of food storage were used? Or, from another aspect, why is it that gatherer-hunters who today regulate their populations did not do so ten thousand or so years ago when the first farming societies began to develop?

The demographic problem goes back to the adoption of agriculture. With the coming of animal breeding and planting came also new concepts. State and religious ideology fosters the worship of possessions and fertility and accumulation. Progeny, both animal and human, are seen as wealth, and the accumulation of wealth becomes desirable only under certain forms of social development. In foraging societies, women controlled their own bodies and there was relatively little emphasis on material accumulation. Nomadic people have to travel light and possessions become a burden. Moreover, foragers know their environment well and have little insecurity about tomorrow's food; they feel no reason to hoard; they may not even have to store.

The insecurities of agriculture produce the emphasis on private possessions, while animal breeding, in telling the human male about his role in procreation, suggests the worship of the male sexual organ. In the domestication of cattle and the discovery of castration lay the roots of a religious development which both solved and caused problems. As I have noted, one bull, many castrates, and many cows set a pattern which influences human psychology for millennia to come. In Sumerian writings of later periods the king is a wild bull who mates with a goddess cow; temple personnel vowed to sexual sacrifice abound, be the sacrifice gelding, chastity, or ritual mating.

The misplaced analogy of seed and semen assigned generation to men. The worship of fertility in animal, plant, and human and the glorification of the phallus as seed producer: these are the religious and utilitarian vectors which influenced the rise of the patriarchy.

The metaphor of mother earth, reducing the female to passivity, was particularly damaging. Earth is soil, a mixture of minerals, air, water, and dead organic matter—hardly the same as the live body of a human woman, with its contribution of 50 per cent of the genes as well as a hospitable active environment which feeds the fetus through a shared circulatory system. In the absence of biological knowledge male semen, actually analogous to pollen, was credited with the power inherent in the fertilized egg; the female became a passive gestator receiving a fertile seed rather than the producer of one of two gametes which must unite, combining reproductive cells in order to produce an embryo, the animal equivalent of the fertilized seed which grows into a plant.

A difficult distinction should be emphasized: that between fertility as generation, the magic of creation, and fertility as production. The one was arbitrarily reassigned to man, the second left to woman in her capacity as childbearer. This was the doctrine used to subjugate the female of the species in most known civilizations. We treated ourselves as breeders treat animals, ignoring psychological, aesthetic, and human and natural principles.

Recent studies claim that a man's sexual capacity is more limited than a woman's, yet civilization has usually assumed the opposite. In absolute terms of physical-aesthetic considerations, the sexes are probably equal in their capacity for sensual enjoyment. Though the ancient Greeks did not think so— Tiresias was blinded by Hera when, having spent time both as a woman and as a man, he testified that women enjoyed the sexual act nine times more than men—I am inclined to agree with Keats: "Who shall say between Man and Woman which is the more delighted." By all accounts, delight is more frequently allowed for in nonliterate, small-scale societies than in our own tradition. Males and females have active physical sexuality, and both can be controlled volitionally. The repressed sexual energy finds outlet either constructively in artistic expression or destructively in sadomasochism. To some extent the sublimation must be voluntary else there is paralysis, numbing, and deadening. Why have women not contributed artistically and creatively in greater measure to historical civilizations? Though some of their contributions are masked behind anonymity or credited to male relations, they have also had their creativity enormously damped by the more rigid restrictions which have been their lot throughout Western, not to say world, history, the written story which begins at the same time as the arrival of severe sexual repression. It is also coeval with the authoritarian state and the patriarchal family, which I see as the state in microcosm rather than as its model.

Early indications of an emphasis on human reproduction are found in the area in which the first historical civilization arose. This is just before major population increases occur in lower Mesopotamia, in Egypt, and in the rest of the nuclear Near East.

Before the domestication of animals sex had been primarily an erotic pastime, though there must always have been some sense of its mystic nature. From the postfestival orgies of the Australian Aborigines to the Dionysian rites of the Greek matrons of classical times, from the sacred prostitution and temple rites of Near Eastern and Oriental religions down to today's gropings in the form of group-sex societies, etc., there has always been some recognition of the potential for transcendence inherent in orgasm. The way in which physical release can take us out of our conscious self and give us an illusion of union with the infinite is related to the human striving of religion, art, theater, ritual experience of various kinds. This is the curious ambivalence which makes sex the highest and the lowest, the most elevated as well as the most profane, of human experiences, the source of life-energy which permeates all nonmaterial and many material creations. It is this that makes orgasm the prototype for all mystic ecstasy (recognized intuitionally perhaps by Wilhelm Reich when he created the artificial construct of the orgone as the mysterious substance, source of healing and creative power for humans). Even when sex is renounced as the direct road, we seek to be transported outside the boundaries of the self, to erase our consciousness in orgies, drunkenness, drugs, religion, art, and varied mystical experiences.

Havelock Ellis recognized this numinous quality, terming it "the miraculous flame of sex." A sacred source of energy, it is connected with religion and art, in festival and in search of the divine. Originally sex was not a means, to be used in fertility rites, but a mystery—one facet of that human striving for transcendence, the which is inherent in orgasm but which is sought and achieved in many other ways, too, that need to escape the conscious self and merge with something larger which characterizes all religious, mystic, and artistic strivings. It is the paradox of humanity that our human, as derived from primate, nature is to be social, but to think is to be alone, and we are always striving to reconcile the conflict.

In the earlier times, as in many non-Western societies today, babies were something a woman produced from time to time, as sex was something a woman engaged in from the earliest age —sometimes even before puberty. In Melville Island and parts of Africa, for example, it is considered that sexual intercourse is considered necessary for the maturing of the female, to bring on puberty, while the Eskimo children who play at "putting out the lights," the Trobrianders, and the Samoans all engage in sexual play long before they are capable of reproducing themselves. Inhibitions about sex might well be one result of the knowledge that intercourse brings with it babies, so that a woman can choose to be childless by refusing to engage in sex, especially if birth-control methods are suppressed. On the other hand, if a premium is put upon having babies, then a situation may arise where the woman is validated chiefly by producing children.

When women and men discovered that sex was connected with reproduction, things changed for both of them. Once it became connected with children, it took on a different dimension. Woman became a producer of children, not automatically but through her capacity for intercourse, and children themselves, in a settled agricultural community, became a source of wealth. According to Sandor Bokonyi, "Neolithic *man* recognized quite early that domesticated stock was the basis of 'wealth.' "[7] The analogies between possession of animals and their young and possession of women and children could only come about after the development of farming and animal keeping, and the exploitation of the labor of children as well as the exploitation of women as producers. Hence the beginnings of the materialization of sex and of the objectification of the female.

In a culture where it is taken for granted that all women will bring forth children we can see where women would be more sexually aggressive. Later on, with the results of sexual intercourse being manifest, there is more likelihood of women's being shy—the traditional attitude of civilization with man the aggressor and courter and woman the courted, the hesitant. The enjoyment of sex for the woman is now shadowed by the foreknowledge of its result—feared or desired.

We saw earlier that there is little emphasis on lineage among foragers, though the mother's (the uterine) family has the stronger pull. When people settled down on land, however, there was more reason to be concerned about hereditary rights. It seems likely that the inhabitants of Çatal Hüyük and Hacilar, as well as other villages of the period, traced their lineage from a common feminine ancestor, by way of mothers, the system commonly found among matrilinies in existence in Africa and the Americas.

In the nineteenth century, with the Western white rediscovery of peoples who traced descent through the mother and did not take account of the father's role in procreation, what is today called matriliny was dubbed matriarchy and Bachofen predicated it as a necessary, primitive form of family from which the more advanced and admirable patriarchy had developed. In the more sophisticated twentieth century it was observed that matriliny did not necessarily mean the power of women, and that in cases where descent was traced through the maternal line a woman might often be under the authority of her brother rather than of her husband, but she did not have *political* power herself.

Surviving matrilineal cultures take many forms, and women do not necessarily, nor even often, have what looks like real power in them. In her study *Male Dominance and Female Autonomy*, Alice Schlegel explains that she uses the term *autonomy* rather than *power* because she is not referring to "women's equivalence to men but rather to a woman's control over her person and her activities and her meaningful contribution to society beyond breeding and feeding."[8]

However, the very fact that descent is traced through the female line, rather than the male, gives woman a sense of her own identity in a way that the patriarchal system cannot. The magic of names alone is important. In the Western world a woman gives up her earlier self to shelter behind her husband's for the greater part of her life. In the case of Mrs. Richard Smith, as Dorothy Hage remarked, "it is as if her entire identity is summed up in that 's' tagged onto the man's name."[9] And in the novel *Small Changes*, Marge Piercy describes a woman searching for a woman friend, now married, who must seek her under a new name in the telephone book: "She had to find out that strange name before she could find her. Miriam Berg was no more. Abolished. Women must often lose a friend that way and never be able to find each other again."[10]

Contrast the advanced West with the Australian Tiwi culture, wherein each human being has her or his own name—a name carefully chosen which belongs only to that person, has never before pertained and never will pertain to any other Tiwi. Name magic exists everywhere—from the San to the Iroquois—though with us it would seem to be an evil magic which serves to erase the female. Only under special aristocratic circumstances is the name of the female line preserved. Spanish and Italian systems may include the names of both parents in the surname, postponing the erasure for one generation. Afterward, the mother's name is dropped, the father's perpetuated. (In Italy, it is customary to merge a woman's name into that of her husband when she marries: Maria Barone in Gambino.)

Under matriliny, however, the woman has both concrete and abstract perpetuation of the species vested in her and in the fruits of her belly. Even in male-dominant societies where, by Schlegel's criteria, female autonomy is low, it would still be higher in a matrilineal culture than in a patrilineal one. Comparing the better position of Ambo women with the generally low status of women among the patrilineal Herero, neighboring peoples in South-West Africa, Schlegel reasons that when women are the link between the past and the future they have a dignity which is otherwise lacking and that both men and women must think differently about the status and importance of women in such cases. Descent systems thus are influential in setting up the image of oneself as a woman or as a man and determining how one behaves to one's fellows, of whichever sex.

From the long millennia of Neolithic agriculture, we have only tantalizing archaeological hints—the burial arrangements at Çatal Hüyük, the size of the houses at Neolithic Jericho, the finding of so many female figurines, the composition of the grave goods—on which to base speculations about Neolithic households. Imperfect as they may be, analogies are often made with recently existing matrilineal groups. One of the most thoroughly studied matrilinies was the group of American Indians banded together as the Iroquois League. They provided evidence for the nineteenth-century anthropologist Lewis Morgan, and the book he wrote in turn influenced Engels and in consequence the way in which Marxists today think about early groupings. Certainly women among the Iroquois did, at the time of the first contact with whites, have enormous power and prestige. Even after their economy had been influenced by the introduction of alien elements like the gun and fur trapping—both of which strengthened the male role at woman's expense —these women continued to retain their influence.

In questions of economy and inheritance Iroquois women were more important than men, in religion their equals. Skilled agriculturalists in a fertile region with ample land to draw on, although men helped in the forest-clearing of the fields, it was the women who did the planting, cultivating, and harvesting of crops. This was accomplished by means of "mutual aid societies" consisting of all of the women of the village. The women managed the households, and were in charge of the succession of family titles. They were matweavers, carvers of bark utensils, and makers of clothing. Men had different specialties—they made weapons and were warriors (although war seems to have arrived chiefly with white conquest), and they carved wooden ornaments. In religion and ceremony, offices were divided equally between the sexes. Some of the medicine societies were composed exclusively of men, some of women, while in others equal numbers of women and men participated.

The matrilineal Iroquois family consisted of a head woman (the matron) and her daughters and sons, the daughters and sons of her daughters, and so on. There were matrilineal families consisting of three or four living generations which numbered fifty or less, while others were composed of one hundred and fifty or more members.

With women taking care of the economic responsibilities, it is believed that the men were free to engage in political organization, which may have led to the founding of the Iroquois League of the Six Nations. As for hunting, a Jesuit observer wrote in 1653, "The Hurons and other peoples distant from the sea, who are sedentary, hunt only for pleasure, or on extraordinary occasions."[11]

As with so many other American Indian peoples, our view of the Iroquois has been colored by the Western white conquest mentality as well as by changes wrought in their culture and the impetus to war introduced by the European conquerors. The Neutrals, a tribe of Indians bordering the League's western territories, state that Iroquois women "held political offices alternately with men." It seems more probable that it was the women, the elder matrons, who appointed the sachems—the peace chiefs—who were the prime political powers before the expansion of the warrior complex that occurred during the hundred years between 1650 and 1750. Buell Quain wrote:

> Coming to a unanimous agreement the women of the maternal line chose the child successors to a series of names which might culminate in high administrative titles of community or nation . . . in former times women carefully watched and censured the behavior of their titled men. If a sachem expressed opinions contrary to what they considered the general welfare, and persisted in his misbehavior, they removed him from office. . . . At marriage it was the principle matrons of each participating family who arranged and decided the matches.[12]

It is the contention of the same author that, as with so many other nonliterate peoples, it was white contact which destroyed the Iroquois, not only by direct conquest but also by corruption of their earlier pattern of existence. By the time of the Revolutionary War the importance of the class of warrior chieftains had so increased that sachems, or civil chiefs, were little more than honorary titles. The rise of militarism, if not completely dependent on European contact, did receive a powerful stimulus from it. The two sets of ideals—peaceful co-operation toward national ends and competition for individual war glory—oppose each other. The growth of the latter was a symptom of the former's decay. Military emphasis was a mutation which grew in inverse proportion to the decline of the old order.

Only at the end of the nineteenth century did the United States Government succeed in breaking the men's resistance to agriculture. Before that, the Iroquois women, with their mutual aid societies, enjoying the pleasure of group work, their co-operative living, and group councils, would seem to have been a

prime example of women's talent for leadership and co-operation, the nonexistence of which was claimed in a book that had
a certain popular success some years ago.[13]

The Iroquois women were not the only Indian women to
own property and houses and to delegate power. This is true of
the Hopi women to this day, and was true of Eastern woodland
Cherokees and of the Mandans, who were farmers and bison
hunters on the Missouri before the introduction of the horse
on the North American continent completely changed the
economy and psychology of many Amerindian groups. Though
anthropologists who studied North American Indians during
the nineteenth and twentieth centuries found both matrilineal
and patrilineal groups, there is evidence that bands which had
been matrilineal often changed to patriliny under white
influence and as a result of changes created by the European
market for furs.[14]

Despite the flourishing economies created by Amerindian
groups like the Iroquois and the Cherokee, there is a widely
prevalent view today that matriliny exists only in stagnant agricultural backwaters similar to the earliest periods of Neolithic
agriculture, while patriliny is a necessity for growth and
efficient use of resources. Mary Douglas questions this assumption in an essay examining matriliny and patriliny in recent
ethnographic contexts. Equating growth with increase of
wealth, differentiation, and inequality, she notes that anthropologists believe descent is traced through the mother only in
poor, egalitarian economies. Matrilineal groups are organized to
recruit members by means other than direct inheritance. The
Ashanti have ranking systems and hierarchies, but they emphasize descent from a common womb rather than close lineal connections. Douglas finds that in matrilineal systems the emphasis is on alliances between groups rather than on exclusiveness
of individual groups. Matriliny does not, of itself, provide a
strong authority system. Leadership by achievement is encouraged. An open authority system is not necessarily disad-
vantageous. If it encourages achievement in some circumstances, it can have great adaptive value.[15]

One would think that the qualities inherent in matrilineal groups, "open recruitment of talent and *man*power, strong intergroup alliance, scope for achievement," would indeed be of great adaptive value, and yet a majority of groupings in the last five thousand years of the planet's history have been in the opposite direction. How did this happen? Patriliny, we note, is commonly found with the plow, with the raising of animals, with the herding of animals. Animal breeding set off a chain of events, an unhappy and augmenting combination of psychological and economic elements, with the result that civilization was based on an economy of scarcity in the same wise that the Pyramids were built on the backs of slaves, of laborers forced or convinced to donate their time.

Patriliny is more effective for growth only where things are more important than people and where people are produced as things, tools to be used for the aggrandizement of others, be they priests, warrior kings, or fathers. This is the etiology of patriarchy, and of all known civilizations, using *civilization* in the narrow technical sense of societies embodying cities and technology and writing, not in the broad idealistic sense with which the upper-class beneficiaries of these factors have often endowed the word.

Patriliny maximizes possession; matriliny maximizes group co-operation and recruitment of hands. Patriliny is effective for growth where there is a shortage of food and other resources. Combined with polygyny it produces maximum increase of population, who are then available to hierarchical powerholders for increased production of goods inequitably divided. Matriliny opens up the authority system and makes more effective use of human initiative and ingenuity. It would probably have been more flexible than patriliny, but once males discovered their role in fathering children, an overcompensation developed. In a mistaken notion of biology, seed and semen were equated. Male seed then came to be worshiped as a source of prosperity, of grain, animals, and above all children. Patriliny and its concomitant, patriarchy, are more efficient for producing a large number of children than either matriliny, even with men wielding power, or matriarchy, if such ever existed. The system in use today in our own society, bilateral inheritance, is weighted in favor of patriliny through names, preferential inheritance, and other prerogatives, but it incorporates some advantages of the earlier system.

24

Women in Sumer

Sumerology, a study that began only in the last fifty years, has shown that the Sumerian network of city-states—Uruk, Nippur, Lagash, Ur, Eridu, Umma, and Kish are a few of them—was the first truly urban civilization, as opposed to the castle ruling over the countryside of ancient Egypt or Crete. Many of our laws and customs are incipient in the Sumero-Akkadian state, and a direct line can be traced by way of the Old Testament, which reflects and borrows from Sumero-Akkadian writings— laws and business transactions and literary works—as well as from subsequent records in other areas of the ancient Near East.[1] Sumer in the south was the earliest urban center; Akkadia in the north developed subsequently and merged with the older civilization.

Sumer is axiomatic, not because it necessarily represents the first civilization—we do not know what was going on elsewhere at the same time—but because a clear line can be traced through Sumer and Babylon to the Hebrews and certain neighbors of the Sumerians, the Hittites, the Greeks, and other Indo-European nomad tribes, leading to our own civilization and customs. Hence my focus on extant details of Sumerian writings, mythology, and archaeological finds. Most of history is known through the viewpoint of those in power, and Sumer is no exception. The story of the decline of women and of the underclasses is written between the lines; often it must be deciphered in reverse, like mirror writing.

The role of women in early Sumer compared favorably with that of women in later history: Hebrew, Greek, even Victorian women could not avail themselves of many of the rights of the Sumerian woman. She could be a religious officiant, own property, sign contracts, engage in business, be a witness. Compare this with Jewish law, where one hundred women do not equal one male witness, or the English common-law concept of *feme covert*, which made married women nonexistent, their legal status encompassed by the phrase "married women, infants, and lunatics." Her position was strongest in the earliest period and progressively deteriorated.[2]

On the face of it, Mesopotamia was an unpropitious land for the developments which there occurred, lacking in raw materials like lumber and metal, subject to sudden severe storms, extremes of heat and cold, swirling dust clouds and drought, and generally unpredictable weather. Complex irrigation systems, the use of ox-drawn plows and dredges, and a large supply of labor were needed to produce the twice-yearly returns of barley which formed the basis of its economy. It rose to preeminence through a combination of trade, conquest, and sheer organization.

Essential to this development was an expanding population, today seen as a prerequisite for rather than the result of Sumerian technological advances.

By the middle of the fourth millennium, about 3500 B.C.E., the southernmost part of Mesopotamia, the land of Sumer, was a network of small fishing, herding, and agricultural villages, of modest material development, governed by an assembly of elders, women and men, with one self-appointed leader who had to be careful in asserting authority not only to shape but also to reflect the will of the assembled townspeople.[3] This is "primitive democracy," the system used by many small-scale gathering and horticultural societies, and it is believed that the earliest governing bodies in the southern cities grew out of these first councils.[4]

Within the next two or three centuries a sudden change took

place. Throughout the Near East population had been gradually increasing over the thousands of years—sixteenfold in 4,000 years in the area of the early Deh Luran villages. In Sumer, however, site surveys show that about 3300 B.C.E. the number of inhabitants doubled within a very brief period—say, a hundred years. The reasons for this sudden spurt are not known. People from agricultural villages like Choga Mami and Sawwan may have emigrated south, bringing with them their knowledge of irrigation and cattle raising, mixing with or swamping the local inhabitants. Gathering nomads may have taken up farming and animal keeping. Herdspeople may have settled down in the area in some symbiotic relationship with existing villages or combined the herding way of life with complementary means of subsistence such as fishing.[5] Or a combination of two or more of the above factors may have led to economic, political, and ideological change.

Shortly after this change, another shift in population density took place, possibly as the result of the first increase. This was the growth of cities, unrelated to increasing population.

Uruk is characteristic. Around 3500 B.C.E. it was a ceremonial center with two temples, the Eanna (house of the goddess Inanna) and the White Temple, surrounded by many small towns and villages of equal importance. Within the next few hundred years Uruk's population grew from 10,000 to 40,000. This did not represent a regional increase; it resulted from the abandonment of outlying settlements during these centuries. A defensive wall requiring "prodigious labor" was built at the turn of the millennium, and villages were either "compelled or persuaded" to move within its precincts.

Elsewhere in Sumer similar events were taking place. Whole districts outside the city centers were seemingly abandoned: in Nippur, several hundred miles to the north, perhaps even earlier; in Larsa, in Ur, in Umma and Lagash, several hundred years later and by slightly different processes. After 3000 B.C.E. intercity warfare, kingship, and class differentiation can be traced—for the first time.

The earliest form of government for the cities of Sumer was theocratic; the city was organized around a temple, for it was the gods who brought protection and ensured fertility. Reflecting the common tendency toward teleological reasoning, most historians say that the theocracy in Mesopotamia, the rule of priests and a temple, arose in part from physical hardship since the temple was a storehouse of food, given the chancy nature of farming in the southern Mesopotamian flood plain. However, Sumerian religion early focused on reproductive plenty—of harvest, of animals, of humans. With the increase of anxiety after agriculture, it seems to me that once the hoarding mentality occurred, the development of fertility worship was a response, a syndrome which led to expanding power.

Fertility worship set the stage for the temple as an institution—and the Sumerian cult of fertility worship goes back into the fourth millennium. The Uruk vase pictured in Figure 7, dates from that era and is a three-foot-high alabaster vessel. It shows the city goddess Inanna, or a priestess representing her. Clothed and crowned, she welcomes a procession of naked men bearing gifts to the village storehouse. Behind her is the temple, signified by the reed gateposts, the altar with its vases, animals, and fruits, and, on lower registers, the cattle, sheep, and grain that represent material plenty.

Two essays of Thorkild Jacobsen set forth the evidence enabling us to project "primitive democracy" as the governing system of the southern cities. Jacobsen looks to the myths written down more than a thousand years later in his explanation, but he supports his assumption with archaeological findings from the end of the fourth and the beginning of the third millennia. In the myths the gods and goddesses are organized into a bicameral assembly: sometimes it is the fifty senior deities and seven lawmaking gods and goddesses who meet; at other times the fifty elders constitute an upper house and the rest of the gods and goddesses the lower house. In any case, it is an assembly in which "goddesses as well as gods played an active part."[6]

In researching the archaeological evidence, Jacobsen points out that the Sumerian word *unkin*, meaning a general assembly of all the citizens, occurs in the earliest documents, the Uruk tablets from protoliterate times (before 3000 B.C.E.). Another word appearing in these earliest texts, in which only individual words, not records or sentences, can be distinguished, is *en*, which in later days means priest or priestess, sometimes lord or delegate. The word for the autocratic military leader, which came to denominate the hereditary office of king, is *lugal*, and this word does not appear until several hundred years later, in the Early Dynastic I tablets found at Ur. The words for the king's palace and for the earliest forms of military organization —soldiers, sergeants, company, and colonels—also appear for the first time on these Ur tablets, whereas the cuneiform symbol for a temple has been a constant since the very first appearance of written words.

The first control was that of elders over youngers, which could and can verge on tyranny. While decisions over general welfare were probably made by a council of elders (note, however, that among the Iroquois it was a council of women), it is likely, both from literary mythic references and from ethnographic analogy, that marriages and sexual unions had been arranged by mothers, who could be expected to have some degree of understanding for their children, and that fair amounts of choice and experimentation were allowed for. As the landholding and property-accumulating system developed, control became fiercer, especially when centered in an autocratic head rather than in a council of wise elders. These latter would have some understanding of the foibles and desires of youth, even if they insisted on respect for their own privileges. They might also exercise tolerance, since their own positions were not achieved by force but derived from mutual respect and were subject to the will of the group. A regime dependent on the pleasure of the ruled—one in which the leaders follow the wishes of the group almost as often as they impose their own— differs in essence and application from one supported by armed force, and the latter appears only after about 3000 B.C.E.

In the south records attest to clan ownership of land. Farming was made possible only by large-scale reclamation, diking, and clearing of land, necessitating community co-operation. Marsh dwellers in reed huts and island settlements lived largely on fishing, with hunting and gathering as supplements, though cattle herding came to be practiced later.

According to Sumerian tradition, their oldest city was Eridu, located on a fresh-water lagoon in the southernmost part of Mesopotamia, a tradition supported by archaeological findings which have traced Eridu's temple building to before 4000 B.C.E. Eridu's population and importance had already begun to decline by the time Nippur and Uruk had achieved temporal status, but it kept its prestige as the home of Enki, the god of water and wisdom, and of his mother, Nammu, the goddess of pools and of the deep, the fresh water beneath the land. In third-millennium cylinder seals, Enki is depicted with streams of fish cascading from his head, and a layer of fishbones on an early temple altar substantiates the hypothesis that Eridu was originally a fishing village. Nammu figures in myths which were written down only after 2000 B.C.E., and there is good reason to believe that she originally played a much more important role than those ascribed to her in the myths.

The earliest indications of private property, in the form of individual seals dated to circa 4500 B.C.E., came from northern Mesopotamia. This was the land which had had the earlier development of mixed farming—animal keeping and grain cultivation. On the fringes of the settlements, sheep and cattle herders, recently converted from foraging, may have had symbiotic relationships with the farmers. Patriliny is the likely form of social organization in either case.

In the south, communal ownership of land, later attested by contracts and inheritance records, hung on long into the third millennium. The earliest development of cities in south Mesopotamia may have come out of group co-operation and out of group ownership of resources centering on matrilineal clans with the temple as organizer.

By historical times northern private ownership had combined with southern organization to produce the league of city-states known from tradition and record. Initially it was a league of states centered around the city of Nippur, whose god Enlil became important in the Sumerian pantheon. This league broke up into competing warring states. Eventually, temporary rulers appointed by the council seized power and achieved domination over other city-states.

Mesopotamian history used to be given as a record of conflict between Sumerians in the south and Semites, peoples of the northern agricultural and mountainous part of Mesopotamia as well as of the western deserts of Syria and Canaan, who spoke languages belonging to a common family—Akkadian, Assyrian, Babylonian, and the later Aramaic and Hebrew. Some scholars felt that the Sumerians were more democratic and more pro-woman than the Semitic peoples. Thorkild Jacobsen has demonstrated, however, that Sumerians and Semites had lived peacefully together from the earliest times, with conflict breaking out only as the city-state develops. The north is earlier associated with animal keeping and private property, the south with group ownership.

The causes of the shift were probably economic rather than racial. The imposition of a superstructure, first theocratic, then military and monarchical, led to demands for the expansion of tribute. The surplus for this tribute was not inevitable; it was an artificial exaction, requiring either force or ideological imposition by the state, which demanded labor and goods. Hence the change from matriliny, which utilizes talent, to patriliny, which maximizes possession and production and control.

This change in the status of women in Sumer is taking place during the third millennium, the time when the first kingdoms arose.

In the words of 1066 and All That, was civilization "a Good Thing"? Until recently, with a few exceptions, the answer was always positive.* Even now we hear of the great inventions of

---

* Tacitus saw clearly how civilization functioned for the conquerors: "To induce a people, hitherto scattered, uncivilized, and therefore prone to fight, to grow pleasurably inured to peace and ease, Agricola gave private encouragement and official assistance to the building of temples, public squares and private mansions. . . . He trained the sons of chiefs in the liberal arts. . . . The result was that in place of distaste for the Latin language came a passion to command it. In the same way our National dress came into favor. . . . And so the Britons were gradually led on to the amenities that make vice agreeable—arcades, baths, sumptuous banquets. *They spoke of such novelties as 'civilization,' when really they were only a feature of enslavement."* Or, in Engels' words: "From its first day

writing, metallurgy, urban configurations, trade, etc. But, looking at the record, it would seem that it was a good thing for a
relative few. Robert M. Adams remarks on the increasing emphasis on militarism, as reflected in the construction of fortifications, in the mustering and equipping of large bodies of soldiers, in the emphasis on martial equipment in the "Royal
Tombs of Ur," and in the many myths, epics, and historical
inscriptions which tell of fighting and battle among the city-
states themselves. He concludes that the early Mesopotamian
cities were "amalgams brought together to increase the economic well-being and offensive and defensive strength of a very
small, politically conscious superstratum." For the vast majority, he adds, the advantages of the city—protection for one's
personal and household goods within the walls, as well as access
to the temple stores of food in case of enemy siege or natural
disaster—had to be balanced against heavy demands on the individual for taxes and military and work (*corvée*) service. Most
of the population was tied to the city only under varying degrees of duress and was only marginally affected by the most
characteristically urban institutions.[8]

The war leader appointed by the council of the earliest times
—perhaps about 3000 B.C.E.—was transformed into a king some
hundred or two hundred years later. One of the early kings,
Gilgamesh, entered literature as the hero of a group of tales
describing his adventures. He is credited with having built the
huge walls encircling Uruk, Inanna's city, and in the epic
that bears his name the warfare between Inanna and Gilgamesh—the female deity and the semi-divine or later deified
male—reflects the decline in status of the female, both goddess
and mortal.

The institution of kingship took shape over the next few
hundred years. Our information comes from the Sumerian
King List, which often attributed reigns of obviously mythical

---

to this, sheer greed was the driving spirit of civilisation; wealth and again
wealth and once more wealth, wealth, not of society but of the single
scurvy individual—here was its one and final aim. If at the same time
the progressive development of science and a repeated flowering of supreme
art dropped into its lap, it was only because without them modern wealth
could not have completely realized its achievements."[7]

length—36,000 years to one of Gilgamesh's forerunners, Dumuzi, who turns up in mythology as the husband of the goddess Inanna and is subsequently worshiped as a dying fertility god. Though the data in the King List are fictionalized, building inscriptions demonstrate that most, if not all, of the people named were based on historical personages. There was one queen on this list—Ku-Baba, who reigned for a hundred years and founded the dynasty of Kish, in the north. As "a woman of wine"—a tavern keeper and wine seller—who became queen, she was the legendary patroness of the alehouse, the wineshop, and of alcoholic beverages. Though Ku-Baba may have been a real queen, she is sometimes identified with the later Anatolian goddess Cybele, worshiped with wine and revelry, as well as with the fertility goddess of Çatal Hüyük.

Sometimes, leaders or would-be kings would seize power by claiming to restore justice to the people. One such was Urukagina of Lagash, whose *apologia pro vita sua* has been preserved and translated. It provides further evidence to suggest that matrilineal egalitarianism preceded patriarchal hierarchy. Claiming inspiration from Nanshe, the goddess of justice and mercy, the king boasts of restoring freedom—*amargi*—in relieving the people from encroachments and impositions which had developed in recent times.[9] As pointed out by Adam Falkenstein and reiterated by Samuel Kramer in accepting his translation, the word *amargi* means literally "return to the mother." But, says Kramer, "we do not know why it came to signify freedom." Feminists have no problem with this concept. The return to the mother is a return to the mother-centered family of matriliny.[10] I would theorize that it refers to a folk memory of a time when there was a preclass, prepatriarchal society—a golden age with no slavery, no kings, no employer in the form of temple or private landowner, no forced labor or forced military service, no heavy produce appropriations (taxes) by temple or king.

It has been pointed out that there is a certain amount of distribution even in egalitarian economies, when the food gathered, hunted, or grown by one or several individuals is shared out around the hearth or among close relatives. It does not, however, grow more complex than the pooling and reallotment of stored food for an extended family—the presumed matrilineal clan of Neolithic days. The key role in the initial form of redistribution is often played by the oldest woman in the active generation, since she usually administers the household and runs the kitchen.[11] On the Uruk vase of the fourth millennium the woman who stands at the temple gate welcoming the procession which bears grain and fruit and animals to the storehouse is a personification of this woman, the guardian of the stores.

Thus freedom would have been associated with the weak and open authority system that, as Mary Douglas pointed out, is a characteristic of matrilineal society, rather than with the tight restriction of the first hierarchies, which produced the early forms of civilization in Mesopotamia. Return to the mother did not mean freedom in any absolute or modern sense. *Amargi* referred to the relative freedom that had existed under the theocracy and under the extended-clan family system that preceded it, as both preceded the war-leader-turned-king of the dynastic stage. This evolution—from village, to temple state, to monarchy—began in the middle of the fourth millennium, a thousand years before Urukagina's edict, and was substantially completed some five hundred years later at the time of the building of the Uruk city wall during the legendary reigns of the first kings.

Sumero-Akkadian royal edicts and law collections tell about their mores and the changes which took place over the millennia. Urukagina's *Reform* is the earliest extant record, currently dated to about 2450 B.C.E. One is reminded that when Hitler took power his initial speech proclaimed, "We must have law and order!" In the same way, Urukagina claims to have triumphed over the power of the priests. He tells of lands unfairly appropriated, of high taxes, and of other abuses, from all of which he has relieved the people. One provision makes it seem likely that selective monogamy, bearing more heavily on the woman than on the man, was a fairly recent development in third-millennium Sumer. It would seem that in the fourth millennium both serial monogamy and polyandry existed, as well as polygyny, as they often do in non-Western small-scale societies. Urukagina forbids women to take two husbands, as they had been wont to do in previous times, on pain of being stoned to death.

After Urukagina, a progressive deterioration occurs in the rights and role of women. Sumerian myth usually has the goddess refer to her mother's house or ask her mother's permission in marriage; the later Akkadian myths refer to a father's permission, though the house may still be the mother's. In third-millennium writings, too, one reads of fathers and mothers arranging marriages, while later law collections refer only to fathers.

Divorces were obtainable in Urukagina's time; his edict eliminates the fee demanded by the chief priest in granting them, without specifying other conditions. Four hundred years later, a collection of laws testifies to the value placed on women: men pay for the privilege of marriage with bride price, and a man who divorces his wife must also give her alimony—"a mina of silver."[12] Two hundred years later, in another set of laws both bride price and dowry exist and a man who leaves his wife for another woman must continue to support the wife.[13]

By the time of Hammurabi, the Babylonian king who reigned from 1785 through 1759 B.C.E. (circa), a husband could divorce his wife at will, though he had to return her dowry.[14] (Five hundred years later, under the Middle Assyrian laws—applying to the northern Mesopotamian kingdom of Assyria—he could divorce his wife at will, and "if he wants, he may give her something."[15])

There are instances in Sumer of women acting as regents for their sons or ruling by themselves for brief periods, but nowhere near as many as in ancient Egypt, where, for example, Queen Hatshepshut ruled for some forty years. Her rule was an exception even in Egypt, however, as shown by sculptures where Hatshepshut is depicted with a long, curled beard, the symbol of male authority. Though female autocracy is not necessarily better than male autocracy, for ordinary women the rule of queens and the worship of goddesses allows for a stronger self-identity.

In the earliest times women and men were high priests, with political and religious power. Sometimes a man would be priest for the goddess, a woman for the god. By historical times, in the period when the kingship had evolved, the office of high priestess was an honor reserved for the daughter or wife of a king. Her duties would be chiefly ceremonial, though there were exceptions. Sargon of Agade, the first Akkadian ruler, unified north and south Mesopotamia about 2400 B.C.E. and built the capital city of Agade, from which came the name Akkadian. His daughter Enheduanna was a poet whose work was copied down and transmitted through the centuries. As high priestess, she may have played a political role in her lifetime. In general, however, it was the priests who wielded temporal and administrative authority in the goddess' service, or the king might hold the offices of king and priest together. About 2000 B.C.E., under a later king, Shulgi, there were many women appointed to administrative duties in the collection of animals for the temple, a form of taxation. A few hundred years later, by the middle of the second millennium, however, the custom of appointing priestesses as high officiants seems to have disappeared; only high priests figure in the service of goddesses and gods.

The participation of women in work is not to be taken as an index of equality. In Sumer and Akkadia as elsewhere women worked hard and along with men, in the fields and in manufacturing. By the middle of the third millennium certain humble occupations had a predominance of women workers. Women invented and specialized in producing barley beer and later wine, made in southern Mesopotamia from dates, and are cited as keeping wineshops and taverns.[16] In palace and temple there were probably always more women in service than men. Many women were employed in the temple industries connected with the main needs of food and clothing, in the stores and kitchens, in the flour mills and as spinners and weavers in the cloth factories, most of whom appear to have been slaves. If they had children, they received a small allowance for these helpers or dependents. A superior order of attendants—personal maids, hairdressers, nurses, and cooks—waited on the chief priest's wife and children.[17]

A provocative article by Sumerologist I. J. Gelb[18] gives some indication of the minimal existence of these workers, slave and semislave, from about 2500 to 2000 B.C.E. on, and what it meant to be a woman captive, slave or "semi-free." During that epoch, women received half as much food as men; both were paid in monthly rations of barley, yearly ones of wool, and regular—perhaps four times a year—distributions of oil, and occasionally paid also in peas, dates, and fish. During the period before Sargon's conquest of Sumer, during his reign, and later, in the Sumerian revival known as the Third Dynasty of Ur, the systematization of rations applied in widespread areas of Mesopotamia and neighboring Elam. Forewomen received more than did ordinary slaves and "semi-free" workers.† The former received forty "quarts" of barley per month as opposed to thirty for ordinary workwomen, though less than the sixty commonly allotted to men, both ordinary workers and foremen. Peasant farmers—free men—received 125 quarts of barley a month as pay, in addition to the normal food allotment. Old men received less than other adult men but more than ordinary women, who in turn received more than old women. Sometimes male children were allotted more food than female ones, but not always.

In the dispute over which came first between the sexes, larger size and strength for males or differential feeding, Gelb, like most male historians, opts for the former by stating that those who did harder physical work received more food. However, the Mesopotamian ration system would certainly result in selection of females for smallness. In this scheme, which is followed, if less rigidly and systematically, in many parts of the world today, genetically tall women would be less likely to survive to reproductive age on minimal rations than those whose inheritance demanded less protein and caloric intake for full

† The phrase is Gelb's and the distinction is not clear, for the same word, *geme*, literally "mountain woman," is variously translated "captive," "slave," and "worker" attached to a household, temple, workshop, or palace.

growth. All women would have been stunted in comparison to men, since the difference in size between male and female humans is not 50 per cent, but more like 10 or 11, similar to that between female and male chimpanzees but unlike, say, the hamadryas baboons.[19] Small wonder that femininity and femaleness became synonymous with weakness, softness, tenderness, while the dictionary defines male as "robust, strong."

The first authoritarian and controlling governing bodies, centered on matrilineal clans, with marriages arranged first by mothers and later by mothers and fathers, were, then, over a period of centuries perverted to the service of individual strong leaders. As class stratification set in, women could, in the beginning, keep up with their males and achieve positions on their own, though usually on a somewhat lower or more insecure footing. The categories of class and caste with regard to women —you're always in the caste of women no matter how high you rise on the ladder of class—are taking shape in this period.

25

The Decline of the Mother Goddesses

Life-giving semen, life-giving seed,
King whose name was pronounced by Enlil,
Life-giving semen, life-giving seed,
Ninurta whose name was pronounced by Enlil.
—Sumerian hymn (circa 2000 B.C.E.)[1]

Most of us were brought up to believe that monotheism was a great advance over polytheism, while for some of us atheism was the next step forward. Leaving aside the question of theology and comparative religion, it strikes me that as there is no progress in art so there is no progress in religion (matters of the spirit), which can be seen as an intensely serious aspect of art if not its original expression.

Before it could be said that God created *man*, humans had to conceive of God. We invented divinity, not vice versa. The mother goddess was imagined not by one or the other of the sexes but by women and men locating the power of creation outside the material body of the human being on earth who was born, fucked, gave birth, and died.* That the deity was

* It is a measure of our English language and attitudes that there is no simple matter-of-fact verb like the Australian Aborigine *muna-muna*—apart from the biological "copulate"—only awkward circumlocutions like "have sexual intercourse" or harsh and male aggrandizing vulgarisms. (In Partridge's Dictionary of Slang, we are told that a woman can be fucked, she

female meant that woman herself partook of some divinity as childbearer identified with a female creator, though it was a divinity that hedged and circumscribed her activities. Whether the worship of the supreme mother goddess everywhere preceded the worship of the father god is impossible to determine at the moment. It is certain that there was a mother goddess, that she was worshiped, and that her worship declined, not to say disappeared, with the rise of patriarchal religion, though it was never possible to stamp it out completely.

It seems likely that before the concept of a queen or king of heaven appeared, some few thousand years ago, the universe was viewed as a pantheistic collection of forces inherent in nature, forces that were female and male, animal and human, and combinations of both. The Mesopotamian pantheon of the fourth millennium showed the gods as immanent in nature, not rulers but expressions. There were the mountain range, Hursag; the sky, An (sometimes female, sometimes male) with its flowing breasts, the clouds; the plenty within the storehouse of dates, Inanna, later the storehouse itself; the divine cow, Ninsun or Nintur; Nammu, the goddess of the deep; and a host of other goddesses—nourishing, fostering, birth-giving, human- and animal-creating.

In the later ordering of the pantheon the goddesses and gods were paired; still later most of the goddesses fade or disappear, leaving only the questionable Inanna, of whom more later. In protohistorical and into historical times, each village or town had its own goddess or god or a pair of tutelary deities.

Changes in Sumerian religion reflect changes in Sumerian politics. Following, paralleling, perhaps symbolizing the shrinking status of the earthly woman in Sumer and Akkadia is the gradual disappearance of the mother goddesses and the elevation of the gods in hierarchical order, culminating in the victory of Marduk over Tiamat, a version of Nammu, in what was essentially a state political instrument, the late Akkadian creation myth *Enuma elish*.

Mesopotamian religion can be schematized in outline over

can fuck, but she cannot fuck a man, though he can fuck her: "fuck" is defined as "verb, intransitive, transitive only with a male subject.")

the millennia. In the earliest time—the fourth millennium—it was a celebration of fertility and production, enduring aspects that were to be incorporated into later religious development. In the third millennium there was a struggle between the diffuse mother goddess image and the ruler god, between loose authority, self-achieved or assumed, seconded by the unanimous endorsement of the village council, and pyramidal hierarchy. At the beginning of this millennium or the end of the previous one, women may have been eliminated from earthly decision-making groups, though goddesses still participate in the divine assembly.[2]

In early times the creation of life was separate from the sexual meeting. During the third millennium the gods were paired in marriage, and male imagery and male metaphors of vitalizing powers and generation became common though the birth-giving and nourishing female deities struggled for expression. By the second millennium the male god had prevailed over the female. The mother goddesses were reduced in role, supplanted by a daughter god, who owed her existence to a father. Her image was contradictory: sometimes she embodied the loving and life-giving qualities of the earlier goddesses; more often she was wilful sexuality seen as betrayal, cruelty, destruction. She represented procreation through intercourse.

The early polity disappeared; one god became prominent. The first images of the male god were as ruler of the state, receiving his authority from the divine assembly of gods, in particular from An, the sky, and Enlil, Lord Wind, though Enki, Lord Earth, was also prominent. Not fatherhood was emphasized as much as lord, master, ruler, and the heavens were administered like a feudal estate, with various gods and goddesses assigned their tasks by the rulers, just as the worldly administration of the temple estates was arranged.

During the second millennium the autocratic ruler god was translated into the powerful but caring father. The God we know from Hebrew and Christian sources was taking form, though as yet he merely ruled, he did not create. To this millennium also can be traced the constitution of the extended family wherein the father derived his authority from the model of the king, the family is the state in miniature. We who have been brought up on the tradition of the ruler at the top of the pyramid of authority see monotheism as an advance over other religions, for it reflects historical forms of government centering on the rule of one male.[3]

Monotheism is authoritarianism. The worship of a single male ruler is a cultural projection of specific historical events. This does not constitute progress over the earlier beliefs in immanent and transcendent natural forces. Even if the Old Testament God of Wrath can sometimes be seen as the God of Love, he is still paternalistic and we are dependent on his character and whim.

Returning to the fourth millennium, we can trace the evolution of the fertility theme in the festivals and traditions centering around Inanna.

Originally Inanna was the goddess of the date palm, which grew well in the brackish soil of southern Mesopotamia, wherein her city Uruk was located. An early representation of Inanna appears on the Uruk vase described in Chapter 24 and illustrated in Figure 7.

The worship of Inanna ensured both vegetable and animal procreation, and the sacred marriage rite—ceremonial intercourse enacted by the king as Dumuzi and a priestess who represented the goddess—was to ensure plenty for the coming year. Plants, animals, produce spring from it, and the people's rejoicing in the gifts of the land is a much repeated theme. When Inanna is angry all mating ceases, the ewe does not bring forth lambs, the cow does not calve, the land is bare of vegetation. The sacred marriage rite was practiced in other cities, and with other goddesses and gods, but in its development the relationship between female and male is gradually reversed. Eventually generation is credited exclusively to the male, whether he is envisioned as the central spathe of the date palm, the bull of heaven or earth, or the human himself.

The female then becomes a passive instrument of production fecundated by the male, and Inanna is often referred to in the literature as a storehouse heaped up with fruits and grain. After the act of coitus, a banquet would be offered to the city's citizens; slaves would have extra rations—fish, oil, fruit—distributed to them. It is during this period that the distinction between fertility as generation-creation and fertility as fecundity-production is becoming confused in human thought.

Inanna was wedded to Amash or Amaushumgallanna, the central male spathe in the palm whose pollen must be dusted on the flowers to make them fruitful. It was during the third millennium that heavy irrigation and intensive cultivation made it impossible to grow wheat in the southern part of Mesopotamia. Eridu may have been the first city to become deserted as a result of the exhaustion of the soil. From about 2700 B.C.E. on, barley, which is more tolerant of increasing salt levels, had become the principal crop in the south. After it was no longer possible to raise barley, date palms were still practicable. A wine was made from the fruit, and dates in their natural state provided a concentrated supply of sugar and calories. To cultivate dates it is necessary to understand and practice the principles of plant cultivation. The union of the goddess with the god in the sacred marriage rite symbolized the process of plant reproduction.

Eventually Amash was seen as the shepherd-god of sheep, Dumuzi, as Damu, the power of growth in trees and vegetation. He was also identified with the historical king, Dumuzi, mentioned in the King List as having reigned some time before the legendary Gilgamesh, i.e., shortly after 3000 B.C.E. These male gods, Dumuzi, Damu, Amash, have in common that they are always referred to in song and myth as husband, son, or brother; the male parent is unnamed and unheeded. In true matrilineal tradition there is no concern over a father. This is the original view of the male role, and it is perpetuated in popular religion. The cult of Damu or Dumuzi is a curious blend. There is the official fertility rite, the sacred marriage; there is also a masochistic cult wherein the remaining goddesses—mother, sister, wife—mourn a dead god.

This element appears again and again in transmuted form in future history. The mourning for the dead King Dumuzi, who later becomes Tammuz, is related to the worship of Orpheus,

Osiris, Dionysus, and Christ—sacrificial male figures originally worshiped above all by women.

The best-known sacred marriage rite was that between the goddess Inanna, played by a human woman as priestess, and the king, Dumuzi (probable date, circa 2800 B.C.E.), who had married Inanna in legend, and whose role was enacted by later kings as his earthly incarnation. Other parties might also be the principals. After the Akkadians became prominent, Inanna and Dumuzi were translated into Ishtar and Tammuz, Akkadian counterparts, as the protagonists of the yearly drama in which the king took on the god's identity, a priestess that of the goddess.[4]

One early text describes Inanna, the bride, decorated for her wedding with freshly harvested date clusters—her jewelry and personal adornments—standing at the lapis lazuli door of the *giparu* (the storehouse within the temple which, in later centuries, becomes the sacred cult chamber). She goes to receive her bridegroom Dumuzi at the door of the *giparu*—the opening of the door for the bridegroom was the main symbolic act of the Sumerian wedding—and he is led into the *giparu*, where the bed for the sacred marriage has been set up.[5]

From the earliest records—in cylinder seals dating to the middle of the fourth millennium—celebrating the participation of the male in nature's round to the sacred marriage rite of Neo-Babylonian days, about 700 B.C.E., is a jump of some three thousand years, longer than the total duration of Christianity. Not surprisingly the transformation is enormous. Just as the Roman Catholic mass changed over two millennia and varied in different places where it was celebrated, so the *hieros gamos* (the sacred wedding) must also have evolved and changed in the two or three, perhaps even five, thousand years in which it existed. (A present-day report by Elizabeth Colson on the Plateau Tongas, a matrilineal group from Southeast Africa, tells of the ritual coitus performed once yearly by the headman and his wife, which ensures fertility for the coming spring.[6])

In a poem known as the "Herder Wedding Text," of about 2000 B.C.E., the role of the woman—maid, goddess, queen, priestess—is clearly delineated; she is a seducer in a drama which admits of no self, for she exists only to rouse the male and effect the act which will bring plenty to the land. The literal translation by Samuel Noah Kramer contrasts with the more chaste version by Thorkild Jacobsen. In the former, Inanna baldly describes her vulva, "the piled-high hillock," and asks who will plow it for her, the maid? Her vulva is well-watered ground for men, she says, who will station his ox there? The chorus replies that the king, Dumuzi, will plow it for her and, seemingly content, she asks the man of her heart to plow her vulva, not a happy thought, certainly, in contemporary terms.[7]

Jacobsen has Inanna praising "her parts," the entire pubic area. She describes her sexual triangle as a ceremonial barge, and as the cosmic barge of heaven that is the new crescent moon. She then uses a series of landscape metaphors that culminate in fields, hillock land bordered by levees and moist lowland, both ready for plowing. Here the agricultural imagery is more specific and more convincing. Inanna's body is land waiting to be cultivated, and, the translator explains in a note, since a woman can own land but does not operate the plow, she needs the king to be the plowman and to bring his oxen to the fields.

Apart from the varying interpretations, it must be remembered that the English language has a built-in prejudice which tends to make male sex active and female passive. There is no way of knowing how far back these attitudes go. The songs of Australian Aborigine women, which hymn the clitoris, as well as African and American Indian ethnographic material, provide a manifest contrast. That the eminent organ of female pleasure should be ignored in a hymn to sexual joy would be indeed strange, but these are not odes to pleasure, they are official politics, in male versions, exhortations to male potency and the material produce it is deemed to symbolize. The "Herder Wedding Text" ends on the same note as earlier agricultural texts. Inanna rejoices in the great abundance that Dumuzi brings; she has asked Dumuzi the Wild Bull to bring her rich yellow milk, and so he does. Before that, however, Dumuzi's response to Inanna's love-making produced a monster erection, according to Jacobsen, with salutary effects on nature: "With the exalted rising of the king's loins rose at the same time the flax, rose at the same time the barley, did the desert fill as with delicious gardens."[8]

We stand witness at the birth of the phallarchy, the origins of phallus worship, the pernicious effects of which are still with us, operating to the detriment of women and men. Though "plow my vulva" may be the imagination of the twentieth-century translator, the image of utilitarian sex and women's passive role is implicit in both versions.

Shulgi, the Sumerian ruler mentioned earlier in connection with the employment of women tax collectors, has left many hymns which describe the sacred marriage rite specifically in its state form. Presumably written by males attached to the court, several are in the king's own voice, as though he himself had composed them. Shulgi was the son of Ur-Nammu, the first king of the newly reconstituted line of Sumerian rulers (the Third Dynasty of Ur), who had recaptured control of Sumer and Akkadia about 2100. Described by historians as a fulsome braggart, Shulgi left many self-glorifying hymns—about thirty are extant in whole or in part—and some of their extravagant praises may have been written by the king himself.[9] In these texts, and in several from succeeding Sumerian reigns, the goddess still has powers to bestow, a contradictory hangover from the past. Her gifts reveal the values of the period, however, in their mingling of the sexual act with the warlike leadership powers that now result from the consummation of the sacred mating between the priestess-goddess and mortal king.

In one sequence, Shulgi has gone by boat from his city of Ur to Inanna's shrine at Uruk. Inanna describes how Shulgi will caress her, bringing life to her with his hands, taking her on the bed. In return, she says she will embrace him and decree his fate—he will be the faithful shepherd, a figurative title for the kings of Sumer, and receive the shepherdship of all the lands. In battle she will be his leader, in combat always present. She pronounces him fit to hold his head high on the dais and to sit on the lapis lazuli throne, validating his realm through their act of coitus. Hence he bears the crown on his head, carries the mace and the weapon, guides straight the long bow and the arrow, fastens the throwstick and the sling at his side. These and many other powers are his because Inanna holds him dear. The hymn ends with a ritual exordium, stating that he is the beloved also of the moon goddess, Ningal.[10]

In later epochs, Hebrews, Christians, and Moslems also invoke their deity, Jehovah or Allah, to sanctify bloody deeds and repression. The situation is more ambiguous in Sumer and early Mid Eastern theology. The goddess is both over and in the service of the king, to whom she is object and for whom she does all: "When for the wild bull, for the lord, I shall have bathed/ . . . When in his fair hands my loins shall have been shaped . . ."[11] The poet put the all-powerful Inanna into the service of the mortal king, who receives his office and temporary godship through being her spouse. By 2000 B.C.E. Sumerian religion was entwined with politics and, like Sumerian society itself, vertically organized.

Though the king received his power from the goddess, she was a woman and therefore ambivalently viewed. Several other compositions, from this period and shortly afterward, reflect this fact: "Inanna, most deceitful of women," runs a line from a song to Inanna in which Dumuzi, the "wild bull," is himself counseling Inanna to deceive her mother.[12] And in one of the several versions of the epic of Gilgamesh, this one written in Akkadian, Inanna, here Ishtar, is taunted by the hero-king, Gilgamesh: "What lover did you ever love constantly?"[13]

The subjugation of female sexuality was in process of accomplishment during the thousand years before these texts were written down, and it is delineated in the myths.

The Sumerian tale of Inanna's descent into hell reflects the ambivalence of attitudes toward her. Inanna's sister Erishkegal ruled in the nether land, the home of the dead. When Inanna ventured into her sister's domain, Erishkegal had her seized, stripped naked, and hung from a stake like a side of rotting meat, there to stay. Inanna was finally released through the agency of wily Enki, her grandfather, but she had to provide a substitute. This substitute turned out to be Dumuzi, her husband. Till fairly recently it was thought that Inanna had gone down to the land of the dead to bring Dumuzi back to life, but newly translated tablets have proved differently. She had not gone down to rescue Dumuzi; rather she had had him captured and brought to hell as her replacement when she discovered that he was not mourning her death but seated high on a throne celebrating. This rivalry between divine female and semidivine or deified male will culminate over the millennia with the (seeming) disappearance of the female and the reign of male divinity. But more than a thousand years before monotheism has emerged, the battle between male and female elements in the divine pantheon is still being played out.

Women have a worse time of it in Akkadian mythology, which stems from a later period. A late Akkadian tale tells how the Queen of the Underworld was brought to bed and dominated by a man, who then came to rule as Nergal, the King of the Underworld. Originally autonomous and independent, Erishkegal was undone by sex, dragged from the throne and forced into coitus. It is the beginning of a long literary tradition describing the humbling of female pride and self-expression, best exemplified perhaps by *The Taming of the Shrew*.

In the exordium to the sacred marriage text quoted earlier, Inanna's invitation to Dumuzi was variously interpreted by different translators. A chaste metaphor drawn from the farmer's experience in one version became an encouragement to sexual athletics in another. The myth called "The Marriage of Enlil and Ninlil" has been presented as a case of rape.[14] Careful examination of the various translations raises doubts about the episode and larger questions about translators' ability to penetrate the Sumerian material. I have mentioned that Sumerology dates back only half a century. The study of one dead language, accessible only through faint wedge marks left on ancient clay, and reached through three other dead languages—Akkadian, Elamite, and Old Persian—poses enormous difficulties. *Traduttore-traditore*—"translator-traitor"—is an Italian saying about live languages; how much the more so in this instance where so little is known about the peoples whose work and lives we presume to interpret.

Two versions of the myth have been published. In Jacobsen's, a maiden goddess, Ninlil, is warned by her mother *not* to walk by the stream, for she might be seen by the god Enlil, and "forthwith, he will embrace thee, he will kiss thee!" In the better-known version by Samuel Noah Kramer, whose popularizing books on Sumerian culture and mythology have received wide circulation since *From the Tablets of Sumer* was first issued in 1956, Ninlil's mother expressly sends her to walk by the stream (or canal), a more unlikely occurrence. In any event Ninlil is approached by Enlil as her mother, Ninshebargenu, has predicted. She protests her inexperience: "My vagina is too little, it knows not how to copulate; my lips are too small, they know not how to kiss."[15]

Whether he persuades her or rapes her, she is impregnated by him. This is deduced from a passage also under debate, in which Enlil strolls through the Kiur, the assembly in which the fifty great gods and the seven lawmaking gods meet. These cause Enlil to be arrested and sentence him to banishment, terming him *uzug*, and it is on the strength of this word that both scholars deduce the rape of Ninlil. *Uzug* appears in different contexts and is translated variously as ravisher, rapist, immoral one, sex criminal, and menstruating woman. Jacobsen tells us that *uzug* means "one who is under a sexual taboo, who is sexually unclean . . . dangerous to the community. This term may be used of a menstruating woman or—as here—of a person who has committed a sex crime, rape."[16] Since Ninlil follows Enlil after his banishment and since only the word *uzug* (menstruating woman, sex criminal, rapist!) and Enlil's banishment testify to the act, the rape is not proven. My interpretation is that the taboo Enlil broke was that of having intercourse with, and marrying, Ninlil against her mother's wishes— that the word *uzug* refers to the fact that marriages were to be arranged by the mother, as was customary among matrilineal peoples like the Australian Tiwi and the American Iroquois.

Most translators assume that the taboo of menstrual uncleanliness, so strongly regulated by Hebrew, Moslem, and Hindu law, goes back to Sumerian days. From the temple archives at Ur, about 2500 B.C.E., tablets referring to the employment of women as weavers are translated: "Payments for the sick, for the days of absence (when unclean [*uzug?*]) and sundry expenditures of female workers for one month."[17] That women did not work while menstruating is likely, but to call the menstrual period unclean is probably a projection from later days. In similar wise, Egyptologists influenced by Judeo-Christian prudery write that the god Atum created the world through *self-pollution,* though the actual text of the fairly late myth reads, "I copulated with my fist; I masturbated with my hand."[18]

Though neither scholar boggles at the thought, I find it difficult to believe that the same word would be used for a rapist and a menstruating woman. Even the phobic Hebrews, who equated menstruation with disease—it was "an issue," as were pus from leprosy, running sores, and other signs of infections—and who ordained similar ritual cleansing after "pollution" by childbirth, did not go that far. (Sexual fluids were also considered "polluting," but the measures of purification were less stringent and of shorter duration.) Jacobsen does question Kramer's characterizing as a "delightful myth" a story which "tells how Ninlil's mother deliberately makes her daughter expose herself so that she may be raped by Enlil, how Enlil abandons her as soon as he has raped her, how she follows him and is seduced three times in succession by men whom she meets on the road—all of them, as it turns out, Enlil in disguise."[19] Evidently the myth of Enlil and Ninlil still escapes our Western understanding.

Much about Sumer must, of necessity, escape our Western understanding, especially since the culture continuum summed up under the rubric Sumero-Akkadian, Assyrian, and Babylonian was constantly changing during its three-thousand-year existence. In an early Sumerian tradition the sky is female and male. An the sky god is married to An the sky goddess. In the earliest times the sky may have been female alone or female and male combined; in Akkadian translations, however, Anu the sky god is married to the goddess Antum. This can be compared to the conflicting and coexisting Egyptian traditions where, in the one, the sky goddess Nut overarches the earth and, in the other, the sky goddess named Hathor is the divine cow, whose teats send down the milk of heaven. In Sumer An is often referred to as the bull of heaven or the fecund breed bull, with his wife An as the divine cow. A later tradition reflecting the agricultural image has An the sky god married to Ki the earth. On the other hand, Enki, the god of wisdom and water, is also seen as Lord Earth, produced by An's marriage to his mother Nammu. In other Sumerian traditions An married Ninhursag, the goddess of birth, and eventually he is named as the husband of Inanna (the only goddess permitted to survive into the late historical period), although, following earlier genealogy, she would have been An's great-granddaughter.

The persistent tradition of a female sky identifies Inanna as the rain goddess—her breasts are the clouds pouring out the beneficent rain—overlapping with visions of her as the thunder goddess and her later evolution into the patron of war. "I step onto the heavens and the rain rains down/I step onto the earth and grass and herbs sprout up," says one hymn.[20] She is shown riding a lion or in a chariot drawn by seven lions; sometimes she is herself the lion. Enheduanna, the poet daughter of Sargon the Great, writing circa 2350 B.C.E., invokes her as the destroyer of mountains: "O my lady, at your roar you made the countries bow low. . . . With the charging storm you charge,/with the howling storm you howl."[21]

A series of myths found on many different tablets reflects the competition between gods and goddesses for the creation of humanity, a competition that ended with the decline of the mother goddesses and the assignment to the males of the major role in both power and creativity. The myths have been arranged by Jacobsen to present a sequential origin story, giving both a chronological and etiological picture of the Sumerian world view.

The initial myth tells of the gods' reluctance to labor. Tired of working so hard, they appeal to Enki's mother Nammu for relief. Nammu instructs Enki on what to do, and working in combination with Ninmah, the goddess of birth, they create humans to do the gods' work. People are made from the clay of the deep—Apsu—the source from which Enki himself had issued, engendered on it by Nammu. In one version Ninmah, lit-

erally August Lady, a variant of Ninhursag—Lady Mountain—
or Ki, the earth goddess, stands over Nammu to receive the
child, made of silt, when Nammu gives birth, while Enki is a
helper, representing the sweet water that moistens the clay.[22]

In a more complex tablet of later date, Enki instructed his
mother to have two womb goddesses pinch off pieces of the
clay for her. She then put limbs on each lump and thus gave
birth to human beings, assisted by Ninmah and eight other
goddesses.

Afterward there was a feast to celebrate the delivery. The
Sumerian gods and goddesses were an uproarious lot, given to
celebrations and to drinking, sometimes too much. At this banquet, Ninmah and Enki both drank heavily, and they began to
exchange boasts. Ninmah said she could change humanity's
form at will from good to bad. Enki dared her to do her worst;
he would find a role for whatever warp of nature she could
create. Ninmah began to make all kinds of strange and defective creatures—a giant, an incontinent person, a barren woman,
a human with neither male nor female genitalia, and so on, six
in toto. Enki found a place and a livelihood for all. The creature who had no genitals became the eunuch he set to wait
upon the king; the barren woman a lady-in-waiting to the
queen, and each freak Ninmah had created he inserted into the
Sumerian social order.

Then Enki proposed that they change places. He would
create the imperfect beings; let Ninmah fit them into society.
He proceeded to make a creature so warped and distorted that
life was barely present: his eyes were diseased, his liver and
heart hurt, his hands trembled, he was too feeble to take nourishment. His creation was so ailing—prematurely senile, unable
to eat and to move—that Ninmah was unable to do anything
for it. Helpless to alleviate this epitome of human misery, she
was horror-struck. She shrieked with rage and despair. So it
turned out that Enki was more efficient at evil than Ninmah.
As Jacobsen puts it, when the goddess decides to create imper-
fection, something can still be made of the warped humans she
molds, but when clever Enki decides to be malign, he wins the

contest. Thus the goddess makes life but the god excels at misery and death.[23]

The male takes center stage, and male imagery predominates, in the writings that date from 2000 B.C.E. on. The same word, *nummum*, served the Sumerians for water and semen, as in the "life-giving semen, life-giving seed" referred to in the epigraph to this chapter. Enki lifts his penis and ejaculates, and the Tigris River is filled with sparkling waters. The verse from the sacred marriage hymn in which Dumuzi's mighty erection produced the harvest was cited earlier. Elsewhere, rain from the mountains is seen as seminal water, bloodied in a deflowering, according to Jacobsen.

The evolution of Sumerian customs is reflected also in the description of the king's antecedents which prefaced royal edicts and announcements. In the third millennium kings did not name a father, they boasted of their descent from a goddess; but they named their gods as patrons, proclaiming themselves servant of a god. Ur-Nanshe was the son of Ninsun, the goddess of justice; Gudea the son of Ninmah, the good cow; and Ur-Nammu was the son of Nanshe, goddess of mercy. Eventually this ritual exordium would tell of a king whose mother was the goddess of justice or of mercy, who was nursed at the breasts of Ninhursag, the dairy goddess, beloved of Inanna, and was sustained by An and Enlil of Nippur, with other gods who were patrons of individual cities. The goddesses represented the king's moral and fecundating qualities, the gods the worldly authority conveyed on him by the rule of the different cities necessary to validate his reign over the kingdom.

Further evidence of the decline of the mother goddesses comes from the change in personal names over the millennia. Matrilineal references were frequent in the third when goddess names were incorporated into the kingly appellation. Ur-Nanshe was an early ruler of Ur named after a goddess of mercy and justice; Ur-Nammu was the first of the newly reconstituted dynasty of Ur, which sought to return to earlier tradition.

The last king to use a goddess name was Lipit-Ishtar, shortly

after 2000 B.C.E. In the second and first millennia, both kings
and male commoners use god names only. Ninurta of the plow,
Suen or Sin the moon god, Dagan and Adad the Assyrian
weather gods, Asshur and Nabu—these were some of the royal
favorites.

In the third millennium Nammu and other mother goddesses were giving place to Inanna, the goddess of fertility
through sexual intercourse. In cylinder seals of the period the
fertility goddess is on top in depictions of ritual mating.[24] Later
representations show her facing her consort; finally she is dominated by him. Thus Inanna's uneasy union with Dumuzi.

Where early kings had boasted of their goddess mothers, in
the millennia to come the creating goddess is reduced; Nammu
—"she who gave birth to heaven and earth"—becomes the
housekeeper of Enlil, Ninhursag a mere wet nurse. Inanna-Ishtar remains, but the ambivalence of need-resentment is always
present and ever stronger; eventually the whore overpowered
the virgin-madonna aspects.

From the time of the first unification of Mesopotamia in
mid third millennium, Inanna is associated with Ishtar, the
Akkadian goddess of war and harlotry and sexuality, and by
the first millennium the warrior-conqueror god Marduk has
achieved primacy.

For the Sumero-Akkadians, the Babylonians, the Assyrians,
and other associated Near Eastern religiocultural groups, there
was no need to dichotomize woman into madonna and whore.
Inanna-Ishtar combined the two in one envelope, though she
was conceived more as virgin whore than as madonna mother.
She is the type of daughter goddess who remains a virgin because she never gives birth. Initially the term *virgin* can be seen
as a synonym for *maid* or *young girl*. It refers to the original
sexual freedom—the permissive customs that preceded the patriarchal period and were characteristic of so many of the small-
scale cultures to which I have earlier referred. *Milady* persists as
a form of address in Sumero-Akkadian and Babylonian prayers
and invocations, but to read into it the significance and associations of the Catholic Madonna (*ma donna*—my lady) is a projection of a later cultural ethos.

Inanna is not an all-giving mother, she is a questionable and irritating necessity to *man* in the peopling of the world and the consequent acquisition of material goods through production or conquest. Later on, Hebrew and Moslem religion will attempt to do without her; they do not succeed, for she sneaks into the folk religion in several guises, as the Shekhina, as the Matronit, and, in her most negative aspects, as Lilith. In Christian mythology Mary was made a mere vessel, a passive recipient for the son of God, but future generations idolized her anew in the cult of Mariolatry, while a whole pantheon of gods and goddesses crept back into worship in the form of saints. Then Protestantism came along and firmly cleaned house, expelling saints, sometimes the Virgin herself.

26

The Authoritarian State and the Family

> I will create man. Let him be burdened with the toil
> of the gods that they may freely breathe.
> —Akkadian myth (circa 1500 B.C.E.)[1]

The father-headed family was a relatively late development in Sumer, preceded and suggested by the authoritarian state. Selective monogamy, permitting concubines and second wives to men while demanding chastity for women, arose during the third millennium, the period when the authoritarian state was taking shape. The battle for male supremacy was symbolized by myths showing an uneasy battle between the goddesses and the gods, in which the gods established precedence and a pyramidal organization centering on An, the sky god. Matrilineal egalitarianism disappeared, but, judging from the subtext of historical inscriptions and myth, matrilineal descent with males holding power probably hung on well into the millennium. The authoritarian state was the model from which individual fathers derived power. Present-day observations of surviving foraging peoples and simple groupings support this hypothesis, based on analysis of Sumerian religion and writings.

Nineteenth- and early-twentieth-century thinkers assumed that the authoritarian family preceded and set the pattern for the stratified state. Historically, they come on the scene together; but there is today more evidence for the authoritarian state preceding the power of fathers—patriarchy—than vice versa. We are more aware of just how much anthropological evidence of the nineteenth and twentieth centuries was skewed by Western observer bias, preconception, and misconception. In the early nineteenth century, theorists were still conditioned to think of the Old Testament as describing ancient history, with some leavening from Greece and Rome. Later nineteenth-century political philosophers based their theories on the historical civilizations of Greece and Rome. Only recently has information on the earliest states become available.

Just as the Sumerian king lists began in the dim past with mythology and then recorded actual reigns as the chroniclers came closer to their own times, as Herodotus and Tacitus preface their histories with mythical geneses, so Old Testament beginnings in the mists of myth, proceeding through historically recognizable events, were generally accepted as the preface to our own past. Hence our acceptance of the wandering-shepherd patriarch as prelude to the state ruled by a father-king, the world ruled by a father-god. Most of nineteenth-century and much of twentieth-century thinking is still underlain and influenced by these assumptions of history and prehistory, despite the facts and principles made available by the natural sciences—physics, biology, astronomy, archaeology, et al.—during the past few centuries.

One Sumerian myth in which the gods grew tired of labor and created humans as slaves to do their work was cited in Chapter 25. Several other Sumerian and Akkadian myths iterate the motif of people made to serve the weary gods.[2] This was a convenient explanation, an ideology which justified the power of priests, who were the earthly representatives of individual divinities. Originally kingship had been a temporary office, received as an appointment from the council. The soldier king who represented himself as the chief priest of the city god either created or adapted this world view and built a bureaucracy around it. Whether it justified the theocratic rule, the power of priests, and was perverted to the king's use or was the creation of the war leader himself cannot be stated with the information on hand. Since written material is late, after the process itself had begun to take form, we can only speculate on just how it happened. However, the way in which Sumerian and, later, Akkadian mythology was ordered, along with its transformation over the centuries, does demonstrate the three-thousand-year shaping of power in Mesopotamia.

The ruler metaphor—humans created to serve the gods—appears later than the fertility motif and is related to social and political forms which develop only after 3000 B.C.E. If one believes that form follows function, the progressive changes of religion in Sumer and then in Akkadia, Babylonia, and Assyria tell something about their social structure and the directions in which they evolved.

The process began in the third millennium. By the beginning of the first millennium, religion was constructed as a militarist state, and it was indeed inextricably mingled with the worldly state, metaphor, model, and justification for its form and functioning.

We saw how the sacred marriage rite came into the monarchy's service by the time of the Third Dynasty of Ur, about 2100 B.C.E. The mother goddess disappeared or became a nurse, and the battle was joined between Inanna-Ishtar—goddess of sexuality—and the male gods. These last changed as the kings of different cities achieved power over the country. Since state ideology is supported by religious observance, the king was the temporal embodiment of the chief god, just as in later epochs emperors and kings often wore the mantle of divinity, claiming election by God through his worldly representative, the pope, partaking of the aura, sometimes the actuality, of godship. The king was his city god's earthly representative, taking his place in festivals, and while some kings validated themselves with official religion, later ones brought their own city gods into prominence, finally changing the order of the pantheon as the power center shifted.

Initially, the religious festival of which the Akkadian creation myth became an integral part was probably a simple harvest festival. A version in which the king participated has been traced back to the middle of the third millennium. It centered around the city god's visit to a temple in the open country outside the walls and his return home to the city temple.[3]

Near Eastern culture was being shaped in increasingly warlike, materialist, and inequitable directions: the religious ceremonies reflect what was happening in the state. By 700 B.C.E. the sacred marriage rite of the New Year had been combined with the harvest festival, but the festival had become a complex ritual celebrating the victory in battle of one warrior god over the whole pantheon, but above all over the mother of all living things—Tiamat, an Akkadian name for our old friend Nammu, she of the primeval waters, the watery deep, who was originally a leading element in the fertility cult, now enslaved and put to use. "Don't kill our mother," said the Australian myth, and yet in genesis after genesis, tale after tale, from every quarter of the world, the mother is slain, reduced, consumed, yet never dies.

The creation battle and the sacred marriage rite were one long ten-day festival which culminated in the union of Marduk, conqueror of the great mother Tiamat, with Ishtar, who had added the patronage of war and of harlotry to her original fertility powers. The focus of the festival was the recitation and re-enactment of the Akkadian creation myth, sometimes cited as a decisive station on the road to patriarchal religion.[4] Actually the steps had been charted in the previous millennia, beginning in the third, when the female deities were espoused and reduced. The tale is usually referred to as *Enuma elish* from its opening words: "When above." It continues, "the heavens had not been named/below the earth had not been called by name" and recounts the victory of Marduk, the young warrior god, over the old order, led by Tiamat, the mother of all the gods and goddesses. Tiamat is a transmuted version of Nammu, the goddess who begot Enki, wisdom god of Eridu, that early city of Sumer long since disappeared.

During the early third millennium An was the most important god in the Sumerian pantheon. Though he always retained the shadowy aura of authority he was gradually supplanted in decision-making by his son Enlil of Nippur, probably at the time Nippur became the leading city and meeting place of the Early Dynastic (2800 to 2400 B.C.E.) league of Sumerian cities.

Nippur remained the ceremonial center of Sumero-Akkadia long after the dwindling of its temporal importance.

The version of the Akkadian creation myth which has come down to us is a late one, found in the library of Assurbanipal of Nineveh (660–638 B.C.E.), and the tone and content are far removed from Sumerian genesis. myths. Fragments of copies of the myth have been found in other cities, including Assur in Assyria, where the Assyrian storm god is substituted for Marduk, but none of them predates the first millennium. When the festival began, probably about the middle of the third millennium, it may have been Enlil, the Sumerian air god of Nippur, who was represented by the king.

Scholars feel that though it may have been Sargon the Great —the first Sargon—who began the transformation of the harvest festival into a battle celebration, it is more likely to have been Hammurabi, a Semite king descended from Amorites (West Syrians), who re-united North and South Mesopotamia about 1850 B.C.E. and who made his capital at Babylon, where Marduk was city god. In the surviving account, dating about a thousand years later, "the king in symbolic action fought and won as the embodiment of Marduk the battle against chaos which established the ordered cosmos for the new year as it had done primevally."[5]

The symbolic battle justifies the warlike rule of a single leader, unifying the disparate parts of the land under a strict bureaucracy. It is a tale of bloody combat resulting in established order. *Enuma elish* probably dates from the second half of the second millennium; it is a cautionary tale glorifying the rule of Babylon in the south, Assyria in the north, or whatever regime chose to adapt it for its own uses. Two descriptions give details of the ritual, the sacrifice of first a sheep and on another day a bull (white in Babylon and black in Assur, where Assur, the storm god, was the male protagonist), the recitation and acting out of the myths, culminating in the creation of humans, no longer from clay vitalized by water nor from sexual intercourse, but from the blood of Tiamat's consort Kingu.

Marduk's decisive victory over Tiamat is told in all its gory detail:

Tiamat became as one possessed. She lost her reason; uttered wild piercing screams; trembled; shook to the roots of her limbs; pronounced an incantation; and all the gods of the battle cried out. Then Tiamat advanced; Marduk, as well: they approached each other for the battle. The Lord spread his net to enmesh her, and when she opened her mouth to its full, let fly into it an evil wind that poured into her belly, so that her courage was taken from her and her jaws remained opened wide. He shot an arrow that tore into her, cut through her inward parts, and pierced her heart. She was undone. He stood upon her carcass and those gods who had marched by her side turned for their lives. He encircled them with his net, destroyed their weapons, made them captive, and they wept.

The poisonous monsters to which Tiamat had given birth and assigned splendor, Marduk flung into fetters, arms bound behind, and trampled underfoot . . . returning to the carcass of Tiamat, mounting upon her hinder quarters, with his merciless mace [he] smashed her skull. He cut the arteries of her blood and caused the north wind to bear it off to parts unknown . . . Marduk now paused, gazing upon the dead body, considering the foul thing, to devise an ingenious plan. Whereafter he split her like a shellfish, in two halves; set one above, as a heavenly roof, fixed with a crossbar; and assigned guards to watch that her waters above should not escape.[6]

Marduk takes the lower half of Tiamat's body for the earth, establishing the zenith in her belly. The warrior-god has created the universe from the body of the conquered goddess.

Enuma elish is a decisive recounting of the victory of the male world of battle over the female world of creation, with Marduk treating Tiamat as raw material, making humans himself, not by generation but by killing, out of the blood of a slain enemy. The form in which it endures was written down long after the appearance of another Sumero-Akkadian phenomenon, the ambivalent and peculiar institution whereby woman's sexuality is a sacrifice, a prize which she no longer enjoys for its own sake. Along with its other inventions, Sumero-Akkadian civilization may have invented the phenomena of sex for money, sex for sacrifice, and the sacrifice of sexuality by men as eunuchs and by women vowed to chastity as high priestesses.

The origins of prostitution lie in the destruction of woman as an active entity. She is neuter, existing for the enjoyment of men. "The attitude of a society toward prostitution," says Eleanor C. M. Laughlin, "can be seen as a barometer of the degree to which woman is reduced to mere instrumentality."[7] At this stage and place in history most people are being reduced to instrumentality, women as breeders, men as soldiers, both as workers, witness the myth in which human beings are created by the gods as their slaves, which enables kings to treat their subjects as the gods treat kings. There are degrees, however, and as the priestess is to the king, the wife to the husband, the slave girl to her mistress, the "harlot of the square" is the instrument of lowest grade, the bottom rung in a series into which each human is now slotted.

Popular tradition of prostitution has it that it is the oldest profession and pimping the second oldest. Marx, Engels, G. B. Shaw all took prostitution as a paradigm of modern capitalism, on the basis that if you could sell sex for money, you could reduce anything to material terms. How indeed did it come about that the man was the buyer, the woman the seller? In sacred prostitution, sex is a symbolic act; each time the man has intercourse, he is planting his seed, ensuring a material return. The prostitute takes the risk: she may become pregnant, whether the children are wanted or not. Children are a commodity, and sex itself has become a symbol of production, with the woman's sexuality promising a delivery, never mind that it is not necessarily or perhaps not at all desired in a specific instance. The seeds of Western materialism are sown in Sumer, which is why we study their culture for causes and explanations of present-day sexual, familial, and economic phenomena. The sale of one's sexual charms and attractions, in various guises, still influences all of female life in Western culture. Prostitution was used as a metaphor for the situation of women, who had the choice of selling their sexual services in the respectability of marriage or on the open market in prostitution, with many intermediate degrees of life and half-life interposed, both hidden and recognized.

In literature about the origins of prostitution, tracing a religious etiology to the sacred marriage rite in honor of Inanna or some other goddess of sexual love, procreation, and harlotry, male writers tend to express a prurient joy or a puritanical horror at the supposed sexual freedom—what has been called the school of history as pornography. Actually, it should be seen as the invention of woman as object, a literal sacrifice on the altar of male desire, rather than any kind of equal meeting of desires. In the chicken-egg controversy of which came first, monogamy or prostitution, the prevailing male viewpoint has always called prostitution a necessary sop to male desire, given the tradition that male sexuality is irresistible and uncontrollable, whereas females either have none or are essentially passive respondents to male importunacy. In fact, it is women not men who have the greater physiological capacity for active sex. But if sex is practiced as a symbol for reproduction, not for pleasure, even in prostitution, then the woman becomes an instrument. And with the help of oil, saliva, or other lubricant, time is the only limitation on the number of tricks she can accommodate, and instances are told of soldiers lining up, being allowed a few minutes apiece for what has to be the merest shade of expression on the male side as well. By Goodall's account chimpanzees manage better, while Kate Millett's sculpture "The Brothel," with its pairs of female legs extending from a row of urinals, makes a metaphoric point about human sexual debasement.

In the class society which evolved in Sumer and Akkadia, the temple had been organized to serve the gods, the people served the temple and the king. I spoke of the validating myths which had it that humans were created as slaves to the gods, so that the gods could enjoy themselves while people labored, a metaphor which was applied all the way down the hierarchy. In exchange for labor the gods—and their worldly surrogates, priests, kings, and designated representatives—offered fertility and protection in the form of food, clothing, and other material appurtenances, in severely regulated amounts. In the temple there were many grades of priests and priestesses, several of which involved sexual functions. Eunuchs and priestesses were employed in large numbers, though it is not known exactly what their duties were.

The sacred marriage rite, with its emphasis on female fertility and male generation, was quite different from the earlier participatory sexual celebrations, which may well have continued in rural areas. The orgiastic festivals described for Grecian women may not differ all that much from periodic group sexual experiences which are written about by Malinowski (the *katayausa*), Phyllis Kaberry, and others cited in earlier chapters. The ritualized coitus of king and goddess before a passive audience is an early spectator sport, while phallus worship and glorification of male seed become more and more insistent with ensuing millennia. Every act of male coitus becomes a symbol of the fructifying religious one.

Thus male sex is deemed necessary and good while female sex is evil, inasmuch as it threatens inheritance, male dominance, and other characteristics of the patriarchy. Moreover, if a woman experiences many men, she has a standard of comparison and can criticize the sexual adequacy of the one to whom she is chained in a marriage based on materialist-accumulative considerations.

Did the people feel that they participated vicariously in the sacred marriage rite, so that each man who went to a prostitute was enacting the rite with each act of coitus and each woman seduced the man with conscious arousal as the prostitute-harlot-courtesan's role developed over the ages? It is as if the male must be courted to produce the people, the animals, the grain so desperately needed for an accumulative society whose surplus—often exacted and more artificial than actual—paid for conquest and for the conspicuous consumption of a ruling elite. It was an ideology in which it was the product that counted, not as formerly the enjoyment, and it was reinforced by the distribution of luxury items—fish, dates, extra oil rations—to slaves, semislave workers, and peasants that was a feature of the annual or semi-annual holiday.

In the second and third millennia before Christianity the class of sacred prostitutes may have lived in a brothel on the temple precincts. In Neo-Babylonian times, during the first millennium, prostitutes were permitted to live near the temples of Ishtar in Uruk, according to Leo Oppenheim, who describes the streets of the cities of Babylon as "teeming with domestic animals, cripples and prostitutes."[8]

Temple prostitution had begun as sex servicing the religion of procreation. In a materialist religion, the next step put copulation into the service of the material. Thus temple prostitution and common prostitution evolved out of a similar etiology: sex put to service—of the gods and of the religion of procreation. The fertility of land and animals and people depended on the religious rite.

The highest priestess, who played the role of Inanna or, earlier, the local city goddess, was often the daughter—sometimes the wife—of a king. Her role was highly circumscribed. She was vowed to chastity except for the one yearly ceremony, which at some periods may have been unconsummated. There were other, lesser priestesses who were also enjoined to chastity; they came from the upper classes and might be married but evidently did not have children, for their marriage contracts mention both their inheritance and other rights and that they might supply concubines to their husbands in order to produce children. At the lower levels were prostitutes available in brothels or in their own premises to anyone who paid—the poor man's concubine, according to H. W. F. Saggs.

The earliest known reference to prostitutes is in the *Laws of Lipit-Ishtar* (circa 1934–1924 B.C.E.): "If a man's wife has borne him no children but a prostitute from the street has borne him children, he shall provide for that prostitute her corn, oil, and clothing, and the children which the prostitute has borne him shall be his heirs; but as long as his wife lives the prostitute shall not reside in the house with the wife."[9] In the same code, reference is made to the marriage of prostitutes —"If a man marry a harlot . . ."; but the conclusion is indecipherable. While historians state that no stigma attached to the resort to temple prostitutes or to the keeping of concubines, both occupations certainly meant low status for the women themselves. In advice to a son, a father says: "Do not marry a temple prostitute or make a slave-girl mistress of your house, for besides being accustomed to accepting other men she would make an unsympathetic and intractable wife." Elsewhere a father advises his son not to go with "a harlot of the square."[10]

In other texts, the classes of temple prostitute—literally, hierodule or sacred slave—vary from the hierodule of heaven, Inanna herself, through several gradations of priestesses vowed to chastity and priestesses of the lower class, vowed to the service of male sexuality. What all these provocative references have in common is that chastity and sex on demand are linked, which is not as strange as may first appear, since both preclude any spontaneous sexual activity of the woman's own choice and for her own pleasure. One might add eunuchs as a depressed group, since they would seem to have taken part as actors, possibly in female dress, in cult performances and were equally deprived of sexuality, exemplified by a text referring to "the Kurgarru and Issinu whose virility Ishtar has changed into femininity to wear the mask before the people."[11]

Much has been made of the libidinous activity permitted women in Sumero-Akkadian life.[12] This is a misinterpretation of the formal chains put on them by the time of written history, about 2000 B.C.E., which probably developed during the preceding thousand years. The symbolic union of king and priestess did not result in children, as far as we know. In certain surviving contracts, provision is made for the children of priestesses. Again, we do not know what were the rules governing their sexual relations. In later centuries it was assumed by Roman and Hebrew literature and tradition that prostitutes practiced birth control, sometimes equated with movements in intercourse. Documents like one from first-millennium Babylon providing for the adoption of a prostitute's child, not to mention the afore-cited law of Lipit-Ishtar, demonstrate that whatever methods were in use, they were far from foolproof.[13] Despite the law, infanticide, abortion—self-induced or midwife-administered—and folk remedies of more or less efficacy and threat to life have been and still are widely used, be it in present-day Italy and Morocco, Ancient Greece and Rome, or medieval Denmark. No doubt they were employed in Sumer and Akkadia also.*

By 2000 B.C.E. Sumero-Akkadian civilization registers its fear of free sexuality in strict rules controlling the priestess and in contempt for the prostitute.

This is the nub of the ambivalent attitudes—alternating reproaches and supplications—toward Inanna-Ishtar which characterize the mythic and epic texts from 2000 B.C.E. on. Originally Inanna was a free maid. Inanna chose and Inanna enjoyed, an intolerable situation in the development of a hierarchy characterized by a male warrior class directing a primarily male bureaucracy.

The temples themselves began as economic institutions. Over the millennia they developed into huge bureaucratic and parasitic organizations which engaged in symbolic theater—rituals of conspicuous consumption—as a means of uniting and controlling the cities' inhabitants, of assisting the military in enforcing inequity.

Several writers have commented on the materialist, joyless ethos of Mesopotamia and the ambivalence of the temple as holy and practical. Certainly it gave an organized shape to life, as slavery is organized. Why was this ethos accepted, to the extent to which it was? Freud predicated the existence of civilization on sexual repression and sublimation. Succeeding theorists amplified or modified his original dicta. It was pointed out that the relationship is not a direct one; i.e., you don't produce more civilization or more art in direct proportion to the amount of sublimation. I have noted that the sublimation must be volitional to some extent. Psychoanalytic scholars as diverse as Reich and Marcuse and Fromm all observed that authoritarian and militaristic regimes always base themselves on severe sexual repression. The repressive nature of civilization

* Abortion became legal in Italy in 1978.

produces alternate responses of numbing paralysis and a chain of self-perpetuating tyranny, whereby each level of the ranking pyramid passes on to a lower level the cruelty and domination received from the one above. The thousands of years of Mesopotamian history are a clear example of the linkage between militarism and war and the division of people into classes of more and less privilege, more and less prosperity, more and less sexual expression. Sexual deprivation of women is combined with the invention of a class of women who exist only to serve male sexual desire, to provide sex on demand or as propitiation, regardless of their own wishes. The mass of men are also controlled by difficulty of access to women or by the price which is put on them, in marriage or in fleeting encounters.

27

War and Sex and Animals

For a nation to be civilized, it has to abolish its standing army.

—Immanuel Kant

Inanna—better known under her Akkadian name Ishtar—is the Sumerian goddess who has most penetrated Western consciousness, the only one to survive into later times and the commonest in writing. The character and functions of earlier female deities were assimilated to her Akkadian name so that the word *ishtar* became a synonym for *goddess*. Essentially, however, she was "the goddess of war and whore," her chief concerns being battle, also known as the dance of Inanna, sexual love, and procreation.

Inanna is often confused with the prototype mother goddess. Actually she is quite different from Nammu, Ninhursag, Nintu, Nanshe, and a host of other mother figures who originally gave birth on their own, unaided by male impregnation, who suckled gods and kings, and were powerful as mothers without heterosexual undertones. Though Inanna, too, was probably a mother goddess in earlier times, when we encounter her in myth and poetry from 2000 B.C.E. and later she is a daughter not a mother, born of the union of male and female, and is characterized by her relationship to male gods—her grandfathers Enki and Enlil, her husband Dumuzi—while her mother is present but peripheral. She represents the fertile impulse involving a male and is regarded with mixed feelings. Other daughter goddesses from neighboring countries relate to her: Anat, Antit, Anath, Astarte, Ashtoreth, and Isis overlap many of her functions. Her Akkadian version brought in the battle aspects; indirectly Ishtar may come from the Hittite Arinna, Lady and Queen of Heaven and Earth. It was Ishtar who marched before the Assyrian armies in battle; on one occasion she is said to have manifested herself bodily to the whole army. Anath, known as the "Violent Goddess"—the Hebrew Ashtoreth—was regarded with awe and fear and distaste, in contrast to her mother.

These daughter goddesses descend from the supreme god, but they still have a mother, Asherah in the case of the Canaanite goddess of harlotry and war combined. Later Greek goddesses will be born asexually from the father alone, Athena springing from the brow of Zeus while Aphrodite was born of the water out of Uranus' sperm awash in the billowing wave— the old sea metaphor which appears in dreams and poetry as a symbol of sexual intercourse. For the Greeks war was perhaps too important to be entrusted to the goddess of profane love; it became the department of Aphrodite's brother Ares. Our own nonrationalist Western ethos, however, has comfortably assimilated the juxtaposition of war and love under one heading; we have a romantic tradition which equates love, sex, pain, suffering, and death, as in the line by Ronsard, "*Car l'amour et la mort n'est qu'une même chose* (for love and death are the same thing), or the description of orgasm as *la petite mort*.

We saw in Chapter 25 that by about 2000 B.C.E. Inanna had conferred the prerogatives of kingship on Shulgi including the appurtenances of office and the weapons of war, and that she was his leader in battle. She had become the patron of war only after she was synthesized with Ishtar a few centuries earlier, when Sargon I unified northern and southern Mesopotamia as the kingdom of Agade—Akkadia—and greatly extended its hegemony.

I mentioned that the concept of the peaceful Sumerians conquered by warlike Semites was disproven by the researches of Thorkild Jacobsen. He demonstrated that Sumerian and Se-

mitic names were mingled in the historic inscriptions of the
Sumerian city-states long before the first recorded conquests by
Semitic rulers—Sargon I in the third millennium and Hammurabi of Babylon in the second. There is still a tendency,
however, to think of the advanced culture of Sumer invaded by
warlike pastoralists of a lower material level of culture, the
"haves" conquered by the "have-nots."

It is a part of Western tradition to give high marks to any
culture which produces bigness and material objects—be it the
Moguls, the Incas, the Chinese, the Babylonians, the Assyrians,
or the Egyptians—and to dismiss as primitive those cultures
whose legacy is measurable only in abstract terms of imagination. The ancient Hebrews are a curious exception: their history has been much distorted, the ambivalent relationship with
the dominant cultures which owed existence to their gift—the
Book or what is usually termed the Judeo-Christian heritage—
alternating between persecution and uneasy tolerance or appreciation.

In the twenty-five hundred years before Babylon fell to the
Persians, waves of conquest back and forth between north and
south Mesopotamia and neighboring countries brought the
northern Assyrians, the northeastern Kassites, the western
Syrians, as well as descendants of the Akkadians into prominence in Mesopotamia, with interim periods of anarchy,
fighting, or alliances (including, by 1000 B.C.E., with the Hebrews), in which vassal kings pledged themselves with tribute
to one ruler or another. There were attacks not only by the
Semitic Akkadians and Amorites and Assyrians, but by the
Lullus and the Gutians, the Indo-European Kassites, Hurrians,
and Hittites, the Mitanni and the Urartu. The chronicles of
Sumer and Akkadia, and later Babylonia and Assyria, speak
about the lawless invaders; the Gutians, for example, are characterized as stinging serpents of the north.

But history is written from the point of view of those writing
it. It may well be that the invasions were provoked by preda-
tions and demands made for tribute in the form of goods and
labor, as well as conflict over immigration and boundaries.
Translators point out that the Sumerian word for slave, *geme*,

meant, literally, mountain woman, meaning that women were
taken from the mountains to serve in temple workshops, in
king's palaces, and eventually on private estates.[1] A temple record from Lagash during the third millennium shows that
women and children were brought back from war expeditions.[2]
Male war prisoners may have been killed or women, particularly young women, and children may have been more vulnerable to capture, and could always be put to use—sexual or otherwise.[3] In any event, the incursions were not a one-way street.

In some instances the conflicting interests of herdspeople
and farmers may have been involved. Foraging peoples may be
converted to animal raising by choice, merely by contact with
the farmers and exposure to their knowledge, but frequently necessity enters. It was shown earlier that as people of mixed
practices—farming and animal keeping—settle on the land,
they change the ecology, so that it is no longer possible to live
by foraging—gathering and hunting. Different plants grow,
game is killed or unable to graze; the wide range of land necessary for the foragers' subsistence is occupied and enclosed so
that the previous round of wandering is no longer possible.
Herdspeople are more dependent, however, than either
foragers or mixed farmers. Like the former, they need a wide
area of land, but they are also constricted by the demands of
their animals. They must travel where the grazing is good.
Moreover, theirs is a specialized way of life; they cannot exist
autonomously. They obtain some of their own food, raw materials, and manufactured goods from the settled peoples.[4]

Whether the pastoralists were already herders or were forced
to turn to animal keeping during the late Neolithic and Bronze
Age, the herding way of life demanded access to pasture lands.
The basically agricultural organization, with clan or temple or
private ownership of land, in Sumer, Akkadia, and the northern
part of greater Mesopotamia later known as Assyria impinged
on this access. The herdspeople were forced to change their
ways. They either had to settle down on land of their own or
develop symbiotic relationships with the farmers, as happens
much of the time. On the other hand they might take to raiding, given the development of different psychological values en-

gendered by animal breeding. The stress of conquest and insecurity fostered by the new relationships between animals and humans gave rise to accumulative values that encouraged raiding and warlike traits. This turn was further encouraged when central governments appropriated tribute and labor.[5]

Myths about the competition of the shepherd and the farmer for Inanna's favors show that the Sumero-Akkadian story is not a history of settled farmfolk against warlike herders. The final outcome makes it clear that there are no hard feelings: Inanna chooses the farmer, but she needs the shepherd too. In good times, agricultural and herding peoples combined in symbiosis, until the balance was disturbed by aggression-predation on one side or the other.

The history of the back-and-forth movement of nomadic herdspeople, whose waves of invasion press on the "peaceful advanced civilizations," is a stereotype commonly presented by historians influenced by conventional Western thinking, as in the recounting of the Mesopotamian story. In truth, incursions were made by kings and city-states for produce, for military service, for labor; wanderers and immigrants were captured and enslaved, women carried off as booty. Long before we hear about their successful conquests, historical references are made to Amorites and Gutians in lowly occupations, employed in the temples as fishermen and weavers, and to the other "semi-free" persons whose rations were so parsimoniously doled out.

Recent history has left detailed accounts of the chain of events set off when a culture with advanced technology swamps people who live by simpler means.

It was, for example, the invasion of whites and the pressure of land expropriations which transformed the American plains into a welter of warring tribes in the nineteenth century. The initial step had occurred several hundred years earlier when horses and guns were introduced into North America by the Spaniards, elements which set off a new pattern of bison hunting on the Great Plains. As noted earlier, the introduction of simple animal keeping introduces sadistic patterns into human lives. In this case, a lethal weapon and the animal most closely associated with the waging of war were introduced by mounted conquistadors. Not surprisingly, new warlike traits, raiding, sadistic cruelties, and changes in sexual relationships also developed among the Amerindians.[6] Changes not completely dissimilar can be found in ancient history also.

On the North American continent, gathering tribes like the Navajos and the Comanches were transformed into raiders and warriors in less than one generation. The Comanches had lived for unknown centuries on the northern plains, subsisting on wild vegetables and small game. They were famous for their cowardliness; their response to threatening strangers was to run away with all possible speed. After they obtained guns and horses from the Europeans who entered the plains, they moved southward and changed tactics. They became a scourge, harassing other Indian populations and Europeans, inflicting terror from the Mexican frontier to Louisiana.[7]

Agricultural or semi-agricultural Indians were driven out of forest lands by white invaders, pressing on the gatherer-hunters who had inhabited the Great Plains. Formerly these tribes trapped buffalo in periodic group hunts, in which women, children, and men participated. When men were mounted and equipped with guns, in imitation of the whites, hunting methods changed and new patterns of sexual relations emerged.

Under the new brutalizing pressures, religious cult centered around cruelty, sacrifice, self-mutilation, and deeds of vengeance. Sexual restrictions and emphasis on chastity were also part of the complex which followed on the adoption of the horse, animal castration, the lasso, the saddle, and the stirrup.[8] Scalp-taking had been a restricted practice existing chiefly in eastern North America. This barbarous custom—used here in the literal Greek sense, since the first known scalp takers were the Scythians of the Eurasian plains, barbarians because they spoke a language which sounded to the ignorant Greeks like *bar-bar* or the barking of dogs—was encouraged and spread by the whites, who paid a bounty for each Indian (or enemy white) scalp taken. Scalping was incorporated into the new masculine mystique taking shape in the period after white penetration of North America. We are more aware today that the white stereotype of cruel and bloodthirsty Indians developed in a time when they were fighting a desperate and losing battle in defense of their homelands.

Though we have sparse evidence of the events taking place several thousand years earlier when Mesopotamian culture began to radiate out and interact with peoples to the north and west and east in Europe and Asia, similar processes may have been set in motion. Male bureaucracy was established during the third millennium in Sumer and Akkadia. To what extent neighboring egalitarian foragers were influenced cannot be determined, but another recent example from the North American continent indicates what could happen. In recent years anthropologists have studied American Indian groups and documented the change-over from loose authority systems to stricter male-headed ones imposed by male-dominant conquerors. The gathering Navajos had retained their tradition of loosely ascribed authority, egalitarian female roles, and sexual permissiveness among young people even under the influence of the Spaniards and the Catholic Church and after the adoption of sheepherding. There was even more pressure on them to take up Western ways in the second half of the nineteenth century when they came under the aegis of American governmental authorities, who preferred to deal with one male leader and lamented "anarchic" Navajo customs.

Sumerian influence reached out without gunpower and the other post-Renaissance developments brought into the Americas by Western white conquerors. It did radiate in all directions, though ideas flowed in as well as out. Sumerian cylinder seals have been discovered in ancient Egypt, and the Egyptian system of hieroglyphs, formerly thought to be the oldest method of writing, is now believed to have been suggested by cuneiform, which predates it by a few centuries. Contacts between the two cultures became increasingly frequent during the pre-Christian millennia, though they were basically different in aspect and outlook. In both cultures writing was a tool of the elite. In Sumer it was initially and primarily an instrument of economic order, not to say enslavement, used by the bureaucracy, whereas in Egypt originally it served a formal and ritual religious function in tomb inscriptions and on palace walls.

Materials were exchanged between Mesopotamia, Arabia, and the Indus Valley during the third millennium. Fourth-millennium stones with sign writing that looks like cuneiform have been unearthed in Romania. Discoveries in Turkmenia of third-millennium buildings resembling the Mesopotamian temple (the ziggurat), of bronze implements, and of four-wheel carts, as well as of traces of writing, were recently announced by Soviet archaeologists.[9]

As in the earlier case of cattle domestication it is not always known which of the areas originated a given culture trait. The fifth-century historian Herodotus pointed out that the Eurasian-African land mass is, in effect, one continent, and, as I noted in earlier chapters, contact and exchange have been maintained within it from the earliest beginnings of the human story. Some discoveries began in nonliterate areas and were adopted and expanded by literate ones, the lands we call civilized, then re-exported into the nonliterate areas of their first utilization. Thus ironworking and horse breeding, which began to the north of the first states, were integrated into the repressive order of civilization and influenced the conduct of war.

In the history of civilization animals and war became increasingly entwined in a causal crescendo of power and domination, act and symbol. The first use of oxen was for plows, but close on the heels of the plow was the ox-drawn cart, to be followed by the war chariot—described by militarist historians as the first tank. The wheel may have been invented in northern Mesopotamia, where private property seals first surfaced—the area later known as Assyria—on the presumptive evidence of clay disks from Tepe Gawra (circa 4000 B.C.E.); clay models of wagons and chariots appear in Tepe Gawra levels of about 3000 B.C.E. The first clear evidence of the use of carts in Sumer is in pictograms from Uruk of about 3100 B.C.E. From about 2900 on vehicles appear frequently, as models, in paintings on pottery, and in chariot burials at Ur, Kish, and Susa. These carts were drawn both by oxen and by onagers, an almost extinct wild ass which was domesticated at some period in the fourth millennium and used as a draft animal until the introduction of the horse some thousand years later. The onager was a difficult animal to use, not well adapted for draft purposes. Those in use must have been either castrated males, or females, judging by the history of the more tractable horse.[10]

Horses were domesticated on the Eurasian steppes, as draft animals initially. Introduced into Mesopotamian patterns of war by the Hittites, they were substituted for the onagers and oxen that draw the battle carts of third-millennium sculptures.

Tribes who combined a nomadic pastoral way of life with horseback riding emerged on the central Eurasian steppes almost a thousand years after the first records of large-scale warfare in Sumer. The Scythians are the first people known to have ridden horses; they were mistaken for man-horses by Mesopotamians, probably laying the basis for the fabled centaur of Greek mythology. With the spread of warlike traits, the riding horse was integrated into the new patterns of life. In the developed states of the Mid East, it was, at first, a treasured show animal, traded and bred for kings, but not ridden by them. Only stableboys and trainers are shown mounted on horseback in, for example, second-millennium Egyptian art.

Mounted horsemen played an important role in the Kassite conquest of Old Babylonia in the late second millennium. The Assyrians picked up the use of the animal from the Kassites, and swift war carts and mounted cavalry subsequently enabled them to expand their conquests and impose power over large domains.

Proudhon's proposition "Property is theft" has been amended by latter-day anarchists to "Property is murder." The connection works two ways. Trade, the nineteenth-century dictum had it, follows the flag; four thousand years ago, as today, all too often it was the flag and murder which followed trade. Long lines of caravans were characteristic of the earlier period, and trade networks linked much of Europe and Asia, even Africa, to the Near Eastern heartland. Individual settlements of traders in Kanesh, in Bogazhkoy, and in other far-flung outposts of Mesopotamian culture preceded conquest. Exchange of mores, demands for tribute, and murder in the form of warfare and captured slaves followed. References have shown that the custom of capturing and selling human beings goes back at least five thousand years. Historians write that slavery was minimal, with the slaves limited chiefly to women and children, whether describing Sumer or Amerindians of the Pacific Northwest, but it is hard to see what was minimal about it for the human beings involved.

As mentioned earlier, historians concluded that male war prisoners in Sumer five thousand years ago must have been killed, judging by Old Testament and Greek references to similar customs. In later days, Sumerians seem to have blinded male war prisoners, to discourage running away, another practice followed also by the Greeks. While slavery was different in these ancient times from the eighteenth- and nineteenth-century European and American enslavement of blacks, as well as from, say, the widespread Roman use of slave labor, it cannot ever have been a good life. One difference is that in ancient times many people seem to have sold themselves into slavery, permanent or for a term of years; the custom of parents' selling their children because they couldn't feed them was also widespread, testimony to the increased hardship brought about by the spread of agriculture. Judging from art and literature, Bronze Age life expectancy would seem to have been considerably shorter than it was during both the Paleolithic and the early Neolithic.[11] It has been speculated that seventeen years was the average life span. I noted that analyses of skeletons at Çatal Hüyük and of various Paleolithic group burials gave roughly thirty years as the average life expectancy for those periods. If these figures are indicative, they are a remarkable verification of the effective substitution of quantity for quality engendered by civilization and its concomitant, forced breeding.

Organized warfare and the cruelty it brings in its wake began some five thousand years ago in Mesopotamia, as documented by the presumptive evidence of city fortifications, like the walls of Uruk and Nippur. More exact testimony comes from the Vulture Stele of Eannatum of Lagash (circa 2500 B.C.E.), a large limestone marker which describes and illustrates Eanna-tum's victory over the neighboring state of Umma. Sculptural reliefs show him leading his soldiers over the enemy dead and riding in his chariot, with dead bodies caught in a net and armed soldiers in phalanx. An inscription of his nephew En-temena tells of the slaughter of 3,600 Ummaites.

Scenes of warfare were pictured perhaps a century earlier on the Standard of Ur. This ivory panel inlaid with shells and lapis lazuli consists of several registers, telling the story of a suc-cessful battle charge. The king rides in an onager-drawn cart; he is followed by carts bearing armed soldiers; after the victory, armed foot soldiers drive the defeated—soldiers and captives, bound, wounded, and in disarray—before them.

Literary works from the following millennium fill out the bare historical evidence of earlier times. Epics and laments de-scribe the war campaigns and the hostilities, the famine and suffering inflicted on the people: dead bodies melting in the sun, people not brought to burial, those who died on the roof, and those who died inside the house, the blood which flowed, of the brave and the fearful, of the loyal and the treacherous, the people who starved and those who resorted to eating their children. War and siege know little discrimination.

One commentator has compared the Sumerians in their ma-terialism with present-day Americans, noting that they valued "rich harvests, well-stocked granaries, folds and stalls filled with cattle large and small, successful hunting on the plain and good fishing in the sea."[12] Sumerian materialism spreads in exagger-ated form all over the Near East and thence westward, east-ward, southward. Shylock's "My daughter! O my ducats! O my daughter!" is foreshadowed in the second millennium by many of the Sumerian lamentations. A passage from "The Destruc-tion of Ur" wails, "My possessions like heavy locusts on the move have been carried off, O my possessions I will say/ My possessions, who comes from the lands below, to the lands below has carried off . . . O my possessions, I will say,/ My precious metal, stone and lapis lazuli have been scattered about,/ O my possessions I will say."[13]

The Babylonian creation story discussed in Chapter 26 recorded the final hardening of the state, as exemplified by the victory of one permanent leader, the young battle god Marduk. *Enuma elish* was a martial tale ending in mass slaughter; it reflected a battle mentality. The Gilgamesh epic may have earlier roots than Marduk's victory over Tiamat; fragments of this string of tales go back to Sumerian days, and the Sumerian version differs from the later Akkadian recensions. One substory, "The Taming of Enkidu the Martu"—the Sumerian word for Amorite—tells about the conflict between the gatherer-hunters and the grain producers and reveals how so-called civilized countries' attitudes toward women were involved in this clash of cultures. Schematized, it may be a prototypal unfolding of how foraging people changed their ways after contact with the Sumero-Akkadians.

Both Akkadian and Sumerian versions are told from the very male viewpoint of the second millennium B.C.E., but within their contradictions are echoes of earlier popular tales. The Akkadian epic is confused and contradictory, with much switching of viewpoints. Male friendship—that of Enkidu and Gilgamesh—is glorified, and women are ambiguously viewed. Undoubtedly, many separate folk tales and myths are here combined; archetypal explanations hint at earlier themes and ethical problems, and substories interject. In the prior, Sumerian recension, Enkidu was not the friend but the loyal servant of Gilgamesh, his leader.

Enkidu is an early characterization of the "noble savage," who gives up the freedom of the primal way of life for the attractions as well as the corruptions of civilization; he pays with his life. He lives in harmony with nature, an *enfant sauvage* who lies down with the beasts and sucks of their milk, who knows not bread or alcohol. Initially, the city folk send out a harlot to entrap him; she wraps her legs around him and they bed down for several days, after which the beasts will no longer tolerate him, for he is ruined by his contact with a woman. She is a softening civilizing influence. He goes back to Uruk with her and there makes friends with Gilgamesh, the legendary builder of the Uruk city wall. They go off on a series of adventures, as a result of which he is killed in punishment for his part in a fight with the Bull of Heaven. The archetypal story has been repeated ever since: the effete joys of civilization soften and destroy; but the myth has it that the delights of culture are worth the price, which is to die for one's conquerors.

Mortal women are instruments or are absent from this fable. Only the goddess Inanna-Ishtar appears, and she is powerful, independent, and treacherous. Gilgamesh turns her down because of her sexual freedom, because she has been to bed with so many others, all of whom he says have come to a bad end. However, while he resents a powerful and independent woman, as will all men in subsequent history, it is still dangerous to flout her. Because he has refused her, Inanna asks her father Enlil to send out the Bull of Heaven to do battle against him. Gilgamesh and Enkidu kill the bull. In consequence sterility falls on the land, the trees do not fruit, animals stop bearing, and the people are punished for Gilgamesh's sin. Inanna-Ishtar is allowed to retain traces of her earlier compassion. She weeps for her children, shrieking like a woman in childbirth, though it was through her intervention that this early bullfight took place and she had participated in the divine decree that resulted from the animal's death.

Though mortal women are subservient, weakening, or instruments of corruption, they are necessary. Gilgamesh's faithful and loving mother appears in one of the final episodes; and toward the end the temple harlot reconciles Enkidu to his approaching death.

Buried within the many themes and incidents of the Gilgamesh epic is an adolescent-male myth of the wonderful world without women which still surfaces in male writings. It is the earliest extant tale of male bonding and the diabolic influence of women, describing a string of individual feats of heroism and posing moral questions about the inevitability of death, not only for the human Enkidu but for the hero-king himself.

Enuma elish was ancient agitprop in support of a martial king. The Gilgamesh epic has mingled elements of folklore and philosophy; it is a comment on nature and civilization and mortality, the unconquerable powers of the ancient gods. In the battle of Enkidu and Gilgamesh against the Bull of Heaven we get a foretaste of the Greek hubris, and of brutal animal games which carry over into the sadistic competitive pursuits to which males are still encouraged. The references are to actual events, the change of Enkidu from forager to shepherd, and the development of *friendship* as a form of pledging and subservience, perhaps even vassalage, since by Akkadian times Enkidu had been transformed from a servant to a friend.

By the next millennium, with the destruction of Tiamat, all traces of woman as the supreme creator disappear from official state religion. Never will woman in the Western world have the primary importance even of an Inanna, though she may sneak in as a kindly suffering mother in the stories of Isis and Osiris, Mary and Jesus, and as a beneficent spirit in the medieval Shekhina.

The changing stories show the threat posed by woman's sexuality and how she was tamed. Enkidu feared the harlot and cursed his original entrapment by her, though at another point she was admiringly compared to the wife. There was fear of Inanna-Ishtar, and the way in which that fear was handled demonstrates what has happened to sexuality. From a peaceful and joyous encounter it was translated into a symbol of warfare. This curious mixture of attitudes toward women is a constant in Western culture, and its roots can be found in the perversion of sex into war and killing and sadism for man, while the basic stratum of masochism is set for woman.

The average man was forced as well as encouraged to participate in actual warfare; the violence of outlet there provided was a perverse compensation for the restrictions on activity, long labors which took away leisure and spontaneous sexuality. In military service, men were deprived of women for long periods of time, with the promise of booty in compensation—concubines and possessions, or simply rape and rapine. Sex becomes one of a series of material rewards. Prostitution increases at this period, for life is reduced to labor, possession, reward, rather than participation. Necessity and psychological impetus combined in a particular way to suggest the exercise of sadistic power to some and to facilitate its imposition on and acceptance by masses of others, both male and female. No wonder freedom meant return to the mother!

The kind of sexual repression which was demanded of great numbers of humans at this time and which was to become the rule throughout the course of "civilization" (*pace* Freud and his followers) has no counterpart in ethnographic data from foraging peoples, or even great numbers of simple small-scale societies. In the degree to which it was accomplished (always imperfectly), it could never have been enforced on or accepted by women, had it not been for the existence of maternal sexuality. For most women, that aspect was strengthened at the expense of adult sexual expression. This shifting of focus was originally imposed from outside and always with a most uneasy balance. As for men, their acceptance of severely repressive structures was based on a transference of sexual energies directly into the perverse expression of violence and cruelty which is necessary to wage war and to establish dominion over others. A chain of suffering is created: pass it on, pass it on. This deflection of sexual energies is not basic to humanity: it grew out of a given cause-and-effect which, once established, tends to be self-perpetuating.

At this time in history, possession has entered the arena as a substitute for feeling. Despite ambivalent historicoreligious efforts to establish spiritual and affective dimensions in life, it remains a constant throughout five thousand years of Western history.

The confusion between sexuality and war and the introduction of daily violence into relations between men and women are everywhere demonstrated—in large scale by the goddess; in small by beatings, tearing off of ears, and other brutalities specifically referred to in the kingly edicts which have been preserved. The Middle Assyrian Laws of about 1300 B.C.E. are particularly harsh. Mention was made earlier of self-abortion; the punishment decreed for the woman who has taken the liberty of regarding her body as her own possession is to be impaled on a stake and left unburied. In marriage, apart from punishments prescribed for adultery, when wives go out with their heads uncovered the husband is given carte blanche to flog his wife, pull out her hair, split and injure her ears. "There is no legal guilt in it." Commentators point out that these laws are crueler than those promulgated by Hammurabi four hundred years earlier, with many of the penalties involving mutilation: a slave girl who presumes to wear a veil shall have her ears cut off; if a husband does not choose to kill his adulterous wife and her lover, he may cut off her nose and should then castrate her lover and slash his face. If a man's daughter was raped, the father might then violate the despoiler's wife; if the rapist was unmarried, he might merely force him to marry the daughter; small comfort to either of the women involved.

A few hundred years earlier, the laws of Hammurabi had also provided for death and mutilation in several of the punishments. In line with earlier statements about uterine relations and paternal ones, we note that mother-son incest is punished by a fiery death at the stake for both, whereas for father-daughter incest the penalty is comparatively mild—exile for the man. Can this be put down to patriarchy, the power of fathers, with daughters considered as only one more possession to dispose of? I think not. Despite the overcompensating importance being given the male at this period, the visible facts of biology still have greater influence. (On the contrary, among the Hittites, the Indo-European people who introduced not only draft horses and horse chariots but also iron technology and the spoked wheel into the Near East, the punishment for incest with mother, daughter, or son was death to the man; sodomy with sheep, pigs, or dogs was also accounted a capital crime, though permissible with horses and mules.)

All the law collections had class distinctions—lighter penalties for offenses against common men and women than for those against gentlemen and gentlewomen, and still lighter ones where slaves were concerned. The sins of the father are visited on the daughter—"if a gentleman strike a pregnant gentlewoman, causing her to miscarry, and she dies as the result, his daughter shall be killed—and on the son: if a builder's work is defective, with the result that the house collapses and the houseowner's son is killed, the builder's son shall be put to death."[14]

The usual explanation for the increasing severity of laws from Urukagina's reforms through Ur-Nammu and Lipit-Ishtar of Sumer and Akkadia to Hammurabi of Babylon and, lastly, to the Middle Assyrian Laws is that each nomadic herdspeople introduced their barbarian cruelties to the civilized Sumerians; but the actualities are more complex. The salient point may not be whether Sumer or Akkad or Assyria is responsible for the progressive drop in the status of women. Examination should be made, rather, of the way in which forcibly colonizing states developed, for warfare is dependent on the perversion of sexuality into sadism and violence, a linkage that is made increasingly evident as we look at the spoils of war—booty and rape and concubinage.

Part VI

—¤¤——¤¤——¤¤——¤¤——¤¤——¤¤——¤¤—

THE FATHERLAND

The common want of logic . . . this merciful provision of nature, this buffer against collisions, this friction which upsets our calculations but without which existence would be intolerable, this crowning glory of human invention whereby we can be blind and see at one and the same moment, this blessed inconsistency, exists here as elsewhere.

—Samuel Butler, *Erewhon*

28

Gifts from the Greeks

About five thousand years ago the first hierarchical, exploitative societies arose in Mesopotamia. They spread out over the next few thousand years and made their influence felt in much of the Afro-Eurasian land mass. Integral to the success of the first organized bureaucracies was the distortion of human sexuality into actual and symbolic production, the repression of female sexuality, and the linkage of war and sex for men. With the worship of material accumulation, people were reified to be used as tools and frequently were treated as possessions themselves. In autocratic societies children were the possessions of their parents; women were first valued as producers of children, later transformed into property. The sexual nexus became an expression of the dominance hierarchy, perhaps the most widespread, the most pervasive, and the most difficult to root out.

Before the middle of the second millennium, the Near East was parceled off into spheres of influence, owing tribute to warring central powers, which built cities and temples and administered a heavy bureaucratic and military superstructure based on the surplus production engendered by that mixture of technology and organization which we call civilization. Agriculture and animal breeding, bronze and copper casting, writing, the ability to construct huge buildings, and above all the imagination and means to utilize human and animal labor—for the benefit of a very few—were among the techniques invented or adopted. All this was accomplished—and we, the products of a materialist society, have been brought up to admire it—on the sweat, the blood, the deprivation of a great many people, who lived fewer years, labored longer, and ate less well than the smaller number of people who occupied the area before these developments.

By 1000 B.C.E. ancient societies incorporating diverse elements from these earliest stratified societies are located around the Mediterranean and feed into what eventually becomes our own tradition, the Western world. Christian antecedents are found in ancient Israel—the land of the Old Testament—and in the Greco-Roman area; what we call the Judeo-Christian tradition can be seen as an amalgam of ethical Hebrew monotheism, late Greek and Egyptian mystery religion, Greek philosophy, and Roman law.

In a world where acquisition was a supreme value, war was viewed as a legitimate means toward this end. Odysseus' description of his raid on Ismarus—"I sacked the city and killed the men; taking the women and many goods, we divided them"[1]—is echoed by many passages in the early books of the Old Testament, which view the land of Canaan as a place to be exploited, where slaves, polygyny, and the accumulation of goods were taken for granted as the divinely ordained organization of the world. If a city does not surrender the Israelites are to besiege it, "smite every male thereof with the edge of the sword: But the women, and the little ones, and the cattle, and all that is in the city, even all the spoil thereof, shalt thou take unto thyself . . ."[2]

Attitudes toward women were well established by the time the Greeks came on the historical scene, shortly after 1000 B.C.E. A collection of city-states often at war with one another, though capable also of alliance to fight foreign invaders, they resemble the much earlier Sumerians in that they think of themselves as one people, the Hellenes (the Sumerians had called themselves the Blackheads). Basically the Greeks are in the mainstream of the development we have so far been tracing: warlike, slave-based, male-dominant, with an increasing strain of misogyny. The good life is outlined for a male upper class; it includes slaves and cattle as basic necessities. Women are objects, whether for the production of children or for sexual diversion. Speakers of an Indo-European language related to that of the Hittites before them, in some cases they may have merged with the earlier inhabitants of the peninsula; in others, as in Sparta, they would seem to have made the indigenes a subject class, the helots, who worked the land while Spartan overlords occupied themselves with war.

The position of women varied from state to state; the harshest laws may have been in Athens, associated for us with the early development of philosophy, science, and history. Paradoxically, Spartan laws, which served as the model for Plato's *Republic*, were kinder to women, allowing them education, athletics, and an equal start in life, and as much food for female as for male children. (In Athens, boy babies were nursed twice as long as girls, and there were differentials in feeding throughout childhood.) This anomaly, whereby a constant state of war, efficiently waged, may result in more strength, more self-expression, and more autonomy for women, will be examined again when we look at the peoples of northern Europe and the Eurasian steppes.

Athenian women were kept sequestered; they were not educated and were under the complete control of fathers, brothers, and eventually husbands. They were not allowed to own or inherit land, to sign contracts, or to engage in business. Married, ideally, at about fourteen to men of about thirty, their role was to produce a male heir. Athenian attitudes toward women produced two cultural phenomena which later gave the Greeks a reputation for liberal sexuality: male-male relations and a complex system of institutionalized, state-licensed prostitution.

State and private prostitution flourished in many Greek states. In classical Athens, the polis maintained brothels staffed with slave women, both in the city itself and in the nearby port of Piraeus; they were a tourist attraction and a high-yield source of government income. Individual harlots were registered and subject to a special tax; these might be non-Athenian citizens born in another Greek state or in a foreign state or former slaves who had been manumitted or had accumulated enough money, sometimes with the help of former clients, to buy their freedom. There were severe fines for inducing Athenian citizen women to become prostitutes, indication that it did happen. Some of the poorest Athenian women whose families had been unable to arrange dowry marriages for them might well prefer the more lucrative trade of prostitution to the occupations otherwise open to them: spinning and weaving wool, washing clothes, selling food or articles of clothing or ornamentation produced in the home, nursing, and midwifery.

In an early instance of the victim being punished for the crime, a married Athenian woman who had been raped or seduced was equally disgraced; her husband had to divorce her and she was returned to her family to live in seclusion, though surely some women must have escaped to the underworld. The rapist was less severely punished than the seducer, who had breached the family's confidence. In classical Athens, the rapist merely paid a fine while the seducer's life was at the disposition of the offended husband.

Custom and law were less severe in two other parts of Greece, particularly in earlier times. In Sparta adultery seems to have been regarded with a tolerant eye. Male citizens were often away at war, and a chief concern may have been increasing the supply of soldiers. Spartan women were much derogated by later Athenian writers for their licentious ways and promiscuity. Spartan husbands were also accused of lending their wives to friends, in order to produce heirs for them. Analogizing with modern Western white views of relaxed Eskimo and Indian sexual customs, it is quite possible that many of the women's escapades may have been undertaken on their own initiative. In one instance, during the eighth century, they undoubtedly took advantage of their husbands' absence on campaign to have relations with their helot laborers, an episode which produced numerous offspring euphemistically recorded as "children of unwed mothers." These were not, however, admitted to full Spartan citizenship; they were sent off to southern Italy, where they founded the colony of Tarentum, today's Taranto.

The law code of Gortyn, on Crete, dated to the sixth or seventh century B.C.E., treated women in some respects with a liberality equal to or exceeding that of Sparta. In Gortyn adulterers were fined, as were rapists of men or women, though if the adultery had been committed in the home of the woman's husband, father, or brother, the fine was doubled.

As a means of free enterprise, one of the few open to women in Ancient Greece, the sale of one's person was then, as later, an avenue of social mobility. From a common prostitute, a woman of intelligence and talent might become a hetaira, companion to men, the equivalent of *les grandes horizontales* of the late nineteenth century. But though the hetairai emerged in public and become known through the important men they influenced, as respectable Greek wives did not, their position was a risky one, subject to restraints different from those on the sequestered wife and not unfamiliar to women of later periods. Lose your protector or your looks, tread on officialdom, and all is lost. No wonder they had a reputation for being grasping and mercenary, since money was the sole protection that endured.

Infanticide was common practice in Greece, as later in Rome. In Sparta the object was eugenic; boy babies were examined for physical defects and unfit infants disposed of. All girl children seem to have been kept, however, for Plutarch merely reports that newborn females were consigned to the women's care. In Cretan Gortyn, the child was presented to the mother's husband and the decision as to whether it should be kept or exposed was his. In Athens the purpose may have been birth control. On the basis of demographic statistics, scholars believe that selective female infanticide was practiced from very early times; studies show a preponderance of male children in classical Athens. In one instance the ratio is five males to every female, though the lesser importance given to women probably led to their being underreported as well.[3]

Exposed girl children had a special economic value. Young girls could be bought or abandoned children adopted to be reared as hostages for the future, prostitutes whose earnings would support the superannuated whore or the independent merchant willing to make a long-term investment. Aspasia was a foreign-born hetaira who lived for some years with Pericles, orator and political leader of fifth-century Athens, then with an Athenian citizen named Lysicles, and ended her days as a brothel keeper.

Rare prostitutes who achieved favor as hetairai have been recorded by history; the great majority must have lived bleak and unrewarding lives. Feminists note that there are no records of citizen wives desiring to become hetairai, but there were women of the latter class who attempted to live as respectable wives, confining though that status was.

Historians have often romanticized Greek attitudes toward sexuality. Erotic paintings on wine cups date from the sixth century B.C.E. on. Frequently they show scenes of group sex, either the satyrs and maenads who formed the wine-god Dionysus' entourage or depictions of the men and women who attended the parties at which the wine cups were used. These would have been upper-class men and prostitutes; the wives, daughters, and sisters of privileged men were never invited to these *symposia*. A wide range of male sexual activity is portrayed on these cups, some homosexual, but more heterosexual. Intercourse in many positions is illustrated. Numerous scenes show women giving pleasure to men in fellatio, very few show its analogue, cunnilingus, while there are no extant portrayals of the two acts performed together, in the position popularly called "sixty-nine."[4] Anal sex occurs frequently with women and men as object. There is little reason to believe that Greek sexual freedom was concerned with women's satisfaction. According to Plutarch, the lawgiver Solon, himself a homosexual, advised the husbands of heiresses to have marital relations with their wives three times monthly. Plutarch endorses this recommendation, extending it to marriage in general, on the ground that it takes off petty differences and keeps small quarrels from growing into large breaches.

Greek misogyny is well documented, beginning with Hesiod in the eighth century B.C.E.: "Do not let a flaunting woman coax and cozen and deceive you; she is after your barn. The man who trusts womankind trusts deceivers."[5] The seventh-century poet Semonides of Amorgos was perhaps the coarsest of woman's vilifiers. In *On Women*, he catalogues their vices, describing the characteristics of the different kinds of women Zeus created from divers animals, including the sow, the donkey, the weasel, and the fox, from soil and from the shifty sea. The one made from the sow wallows in the mud, rolls on the ground, and keeps her house like a pigsty; the weasel woman is insatiable in her sexual demands—"she is wild to make love, but her husband wants to vomit when he comes near her." The one from the monkey "has the ugliest face imaginable, hardly any ass, and skinny legs. She knows every kind of monkey trick and routine and doesn't mind being laughed at." He concludes that, despite rare exceptions, Zeus designed women as the greatest of all evils, especially to their husbands, even if they seem to be useful in some way.[6]

In the fifth century B.C.E. Aristotle considered the female state as being, as it were, a deformity, though one which occurs in the ordinary course of nature. Prefiguring Freud, he pronounced the female a mutilated male and declared it inappropriate in a female character to be manly or clever.

Plato is often considered to be more friendly to women, but on closer examination he turns out merely to be less hostile than his compatriots. As Sarah Pomeroy puts it:

> A chasm gapes between the beastlike women in the verses of Semonides and the female watchdogs of Plato's Republic; yet, upon closer analysis, the attitudes of one of the most celebrated misogynists and one of the greatest philogynists of antiquity show more similarities than differences. Even Plato—of ancient authors the most sympathetic to women—found that one sex was in general inferior to the other, although he allowed for exceptions. . . . the views of Aristotle were more representative; he elucidated in detail the range of woman's inferiority, from her passive role in procreation to her limited capacity for mental activity.[7]

It was from the Greeks rather than the Hebrews that Christianity received its strongest antiwoman impetus, while Greek misogyny also influenced the Romans. The patriarch honors women in their place, while the misogynist dislikes and fears them whatever they do. The worst fault a woman can have is to have none at all. Thus, Juvenal, writing shortly after the beginning of the Christian era, asks, "Who could endure a wife that possessed all perfection?"[8]

As elsewhere, we know more about what well-to-do Greek men did and thought than about the practices of the uneducated, which includes women of all classes in Athens, if not in Lesbos or Sparta. What little we know of Greek popular religion has come to us filtered through literature, as in the *Bacchae* of Euripides, in which Pentheus, King of Thebes, suspects the women of sexual license on their annual expedition to the country to celebrate the feast of Dionysus.

Jane Ellen Harrison, the famous classical scholar at Cambridge University, wrote about Greek popular rites by carefully picking her way through allusive references in Greek drama and prose, supplemented by her interpretation of vase paintings. Her *Prolegomena to the Study of Greek Religion* was first published in 1903; in the three quarters of a century since then, new information enables us to see links between Greek and Hittite mythology, as well as adjacent Near Eastern religions. Harrison examines ancient harvest festivals allowing for sexual license and traces the development of several cults over the centuries, culminating in the eventual asceticism of the late Orphic rites, just prior to and contemporaneous with early Christianity. In a world of increasing differentiation between classes, with the enormous mushrooming of slavery under the Roman Empire, with little free outlet for women of any class and men of the lower classes, the appeal of puritanism and of a belief in a future world where the unhappiness of the present will be redeemed was manifest and widespread. Orphism was only one of several mystery religions which arise at almost the same period, the prelude to our own epoch. These religions emphasizing ecstatic rites appeal to women of all classes and to men of, above all, the underclasses.

Many of the cults centered around fertility worship, death, and resurrection. Interpreters usually claim that they recapitulate the round of nature in agricultural society. However, the particular form of worship for a dead god-child-man—Attis-Adonis, Tammuz-Dumuzi, Orpheus, Osiris, Dionysus-Bacchus, Christ, as the case might be—frequently showed strong elements of masochism and of sadism. The ecstasies of sorrow and of joy provided much needed outlet in a severely repressive society. In the beginning, the cults of Dumuzi-Tammuz, of the related Attis-Adonis, of Dionysus, and of Osiris were especially popular with women. Adonis was the beloved of Aphrodite, as Attis was loved by Cybele, and Tammuz by Ishtar; the goddesses are usually linked as goddesses of fertility. While Cybele and Inanna-Ishtar were directly invoked as war deities, I noted in Chapter 27 that Aphrodite occupied herself with love and beauty, leaving bellicose activities to Ares, her sometime brother and sometime husband.

Characteristic of the festivals is the celebration of a sacred marriage rite, whether of actual sexual union or of symbolic merging in mystic oneness, and a period of great weeping and mourning for the death of the god. Relationships are confused; though the god is beloved, he is frequently seen as a child, and he may be invoked as brother-son-husband. It is hardly surprising that with such strong restrictions on man-woman relationships women's affective energies are expressed in terms of mother-son love. Thus in Christianity we hear of the beloved Christ child, or Baby Jesus, who is worshiped like Tammuz, the darling of his mother, yet at the same time the ideal of mystic union is celebrated when a nun becomes the "bride of Christ."

The Dionysian cult is one of the earliest popular religions. An ecstasy cult practiced chiefly by women, it spread from northern Thrace over all of Greece. The women left their houses and work and roamed about in the mountains, whirling in the dance, swinging thyrsi and torches. At the height of the ecstasy they seized upon an animal or, according to the myths, even a child, and tore it into pieces, which they devoured raw and bleeding. This is the so-called omophagy—a sacramental meal. The maenads incorporate the god and his power within themselves by devouring the animal's parts.[9]

In a world of exceeding cruelty, religion was equally extreme. There were cults of weeping, mourning celebrations of death, pain, and deprivation. Other masochistic cults, for men, involved sacrifice and self-mutilation, as in the castration practiced by the priests of Attis.

From the period around the turn of the Christian epoch, descriptions of the Hellenist cult of Isis have come down to us with more concrete information. The mingling of asceticism and eroticism documented for the cult of Isis was probably characteristic of many of the mystery religions. Isis herself was supposed to have been a prostitute in Tyre for ten years. When her brother-husband Osiris was killed and dismembered by Set, Isis searched for the various parts of his body and found everything except his penis. Osiris was often represented by his missing part—as a phallus. The temples of Isis were located in the popular neighborhoods, near brothels and marketplaces, and were reputed to be meeting places for prostitutes. Vows of abstinence, from given foods and from sexual intercourse, were a feature of the worship. These vows were made for brief periods or for life; women might dedicate themselves to perpetual virginity in the service of Isis. Her cult was an egalitarian religion open to all. There were slaves who converted their owners, but though it spread to the upper classes the Isis cult always retained its associations with lower classes. At the time of the Mysteries of Isis, the celebrants enacted first the lamentations of Isis and then her joy when she found Osiris' body, exchanging embraces, dancing in the streets, and inviting strangers to dinner parties.[10]

At the beginning of the first millennium before our epoch the Greek world was confined to a small corner of the Balkans and a few toeholds on the Anatolian coast of the Aegean Sea. Greek colonies spread out, but they were always centered around the Mediterranean—"Our Sea," the Romans called it. "We inhabit a small portion of the earth, from Phasis [on the east coast of the Black Sea] to the Pillars of Heracles [Strait of Gibraltar], living around the sea like ants and frogs around a pond."[11] When Greek culture merged with and was incorporated into Roman civilization, the degree of domination and the extent of hegemony spread widely. By the time of Trajan's death, in 117 C.E., the Roman Empire stretched from the Atlantic Ocean to the edge of the Caucasus, nearly 3,000 miles; from Britain and the Rhine in the north it extended south to a line running more or less along the border of the Sahara Desert and thence to the Persian Gulf.[12]

One part of this world was the small area at the time known as Judea, the Roman colony which had previously owed allegiance to Assyria, Babylonia, Egypt, and Persia and which for a very brief time, perhaps a little over a century, had its own hegemony and empire.

29

The Puritan Strain

The Hebrews' written literature is an exception to that of the Near East and the Mediterranean. For the first time we are permitted to catch glimpses of the other side of civilization, the underclass who are the people encroached upon. The Greeks, like the Sumerians before them, lauded agriculture and had only contempt for those people in their eyes too incompetent or too ignorant to practice it. Not so the Hebrews; they remembered their own past too vividly. The picture of the Garden of Eden, where food is gained without toil, is like a folk memory of a foraging people. Not long before they turned to the wandering shepherds' way of life described in the middle chapters of Genesis, they may have been nomadic foragers, dispossessed from a part of their range or otherwise forced to abandon their earlier way of life. Abraham's father, Terah, was an idol maker, who came originally from Ur of the Chaldees—that is, southern Mesopotamia. Abraham sojourned for a long time in Haran, a caravan station on the route between Syria and Babylon.

It took three thousand years before science corroborated the biblical tale—a metaphor for the preagricultural human adaptation—by studying the leisure and pleasures of recently existing gatherer-hunters, with the results described in earlier chapters.

After the expulsion from Eden, and the compressed history of human origins, Genesis depicts the early Hebrews as an underclass of nomads, living on sufferance among the Canaanites,

sometimes permitted to camp and draw water, at others forced
to move on. When Abraham left Haran for Canaan he took
his wife "and all the substance he had gathered"—slaves, cows,
tents. The descriptions of the Hebrew way of life in the early
books, in which kine and women and children are valued as
wealth, is reminiscent of many African cultures in the Sahel—
the Masai, the Watusi, the Fula or Fulani. As was pointed out
earlier, it is almost impossible for nomadic pastoralists to be autonomous; they must have symbiotic relations with settled
neighbors from whom they obtain commodities not supplied
by their own way of life. Sometimes it is peaceful coexistence
on more or less the same level; more often the relations are vertical. In the biblical description of the Israelites' conquest of
Canaan, with the Israelite tribes wandering, living in tents, allowing some of their neighbors to live as bondspeople, servants,
and concubines, but killing many, one is reminded of the class
structure which recently fell apart in Zambia. The Watusi, now
called the Tutsi, were invaders who had conquered the Hutu,
while the Twa were at the very bottom. These last were evidently the indigenous occupants of the area into which first the
Hutu and later the Tutsi had penetrated. It is a pattern which
emerges in many other places. In Britain the Saxons, themselves conquerors of the native Celts, become the lower classes
to the Norman invaders. Earlier the Royal Scyths and the Cim-
merians in their migrations probably established similar relations with the indigenes they encountered in their wanderings
on horse and in wagons.

The Israelites conquer the land of Canaan, shortly before
1000 B.C.E., and are briefly an overclass, still living among local
indigenes but with the power relationship reversed, now landowners and agriculturalists as well as herdspeople. Five hundred years later they are subjects again, the ruling oligarchy ex-
iles in Babylon, many others in flight to Egypt, and the
remnant still on the land paying taxes to the Babylonian Empire instead of to their own monarchy. And their great contribution, the Old Testament, was written down and edited after
the Babylonian exile (586–538 B.C.E.) when they are once more
an underclass, though it included earlier writings and reflects

events from the previous millennium until about three hundred years before the birth of Christ.

Scholars date the composition of the diverse material—tales, rules, preachments, proverbs, and poems—to a period between 1200 and 300 B.C.E. The actual writing down probably occurred between 900 and 300 B.C.E., with the earliest surviving text, one of the first five books only, dated to a fifth-century Samaritan version. Other early versions are the Greek Septuagint of the third and second centuries B.C.E., fragments of the Qumran texts (the Dead Sea scrolls), and the Masoretic Hebrew texts of many centuries later.

This sequence of powerlessness and power and again powerlessness influences the special contribution of first the Hebrew and then its much more powerful offshoot the Christian religion. Concepts like "Blessed are the poor" were alien to Greco-Roman thinking. The preachings of the reforming Jewish rabbi were an outgrowth of the Hebrew concern for fair dealing and charity, initially among themselves, but also in their relations with the outer world. The ethical approach of Judaism was expanded in Christianity, in principle, if not in practice. Paradoxical strains were set up: fierce acquisition was countered by asceticism and holy poverty, and conquest had to be justified by conversion.[1]

Like the Greeks the Hebrews shared in the common values of the Near East. Recent scholarship has traced how many of the law codes and customs and myths of earlier Near Eastern societies were incorporated into the Bible.[2] The Song of Songs is probably a version of a Canaanite sacred marriage hymn which slipped through almost in toto—and in contradiction to most of their writings on marriage and sexual relations. What the Jews added to the existent Near Eastern and Mediterranean ethos was an emphatic rejection of sex as a numinous activity and a certain distaste for it even in its profane aspects. They also introduced a revolutionary concern for ethics. "An eye for an eye" reflects Near Eastern laws of long standing, but "Thou shalt not kill" was new.

In a world where sexuality was already being defined from the male viewpoint so that women were, at best, highly suspect and, at worst, completely ignored, a world where women had been reduced to instrumentality, the puritanism of the Hebrew religion, combined with the Hebrews' concern for fairness, was not completely nocuous. Within the framework of a male-oriented society, paternalistic kindnesses toward women were invoked.

On the other hand, sex is profane and polluting in the two books of ritual law, Leviticus and Deuteronomy, both of which were recorded when the Hebrew religion was shaping as an expression of identity against oppression, notwithstanding its own inegalitarian attitudes. Barbarous punishments are decreed along with milder restrictions. Women are defined as unclean in their biology; in fact, the word "unclean" tolls out repeatedly in an almost orgiastic rejection of all the creeping and crawling things that are abominations, in the complex prohibitions on what can be eaten and what can be used, and with regard to the pollutions which deny one access to the community.

The Old Testament is a man's book: a compendium of writings from a male-dominated society. It portrays a man's world and describes activities and events conducted primarily or exclusively by males—war, cult, and government. It tells of a jealously singular God, who is described and addressed in terms normally used for males.[3] Its injunctions are to men, and when it speaks of the people, it uses the Hebrew term *Am*, meaning men, not men and women.

Ethical rules—"Thou shalt neither vex a stranger nor oppress him for ye were strangers in Egypt"—are intermixed with sexual and health regulations.

Leviticus, the first book of the law, dated somewhere between the eighth and fifth centuries before Christianity, but written down after the return from Babylon, expresses the priests' distaste for the female, as well as for biology itself. With Chapter 11, we begin to get the particular insistence on clean and unclean, pure and impure, the search after holiness which will set aside the humiliated people, make them superior inside to those who oppress them outside. And part of this self-depriving search is the antibody part. We are often told that the Christians introduced the ascetic element into the Judeo-Christian tradition, but scripture does not entirely support this thesis. From the first word "unclean," to be cried after lepers, there is a paranoid intensity: "Every swarming thing . . . is an abomination; it shall not be eaten . . . I am the Lord your God; consecrate yourselves therefore and be holy, for I am holy. You shall not defile yourselves . . ."[4]

Natural body processes are lumped indiscriminately with sickness, menstruation with illness: "This is the law for him who has a discharge and for him who has an emission of semen, becoming unclean thereby; also for her who is sick with her impurity; that is, for any one, male or female, who has a discharge, and for the man who lies with a woman who is unclean."[5]

The strictures on sexual intercourse and menstruation follow directly on the prohibitions on lepers and the definition of a running issue: "Whether his flesh run or his flesh be stopped from his issue it is his uncleanness."[6] Sexual intercourse is also polluting: "If any man's seed of copulation go out from him then he shall wash his flesh and every garment and be unclean until the even."[7] Menstruation makes a woman unclean during, and for seven days after, her monthly period—i.e., twelve days out of each twenty-eight-day cycle. Combined with the longer period of uncleanness enjoined after childbirth, this meant that for much of her adult life a woman was not allowed to participate in religious ceremonies or enter the temple. Small wonder that Ezekiel found women weeping for Tammuz at the entrance to the holy place. With such restrictions they may well have been attracted to more welcoming local cults.

A man who lay in the same bed with his wife during her menstrual period was unclean for seven days, and intercourse "with a woman having her sickness" was punishable by exile; "if she has uncovered the fountain of her blood; both of them shall be cut off from among their people."[8]

Women are not addressed directly but through fathers and husbands. "*You* shall not lie carnally with *your* neighbor's wife . . . *You* shall not lie with any beast and defile *yourself* with it, neither shall any woman give herself to a beast to lie with it, it is perversion."⁹

It is made clear, through the differential rules for purification after childbirth, that girls are more defiling than boys. A mother is unclean for seven days after the birth of a male child, but for fourteen days after that of a female. Moreover, to the initial uncleanness in the case of a male child's birth, another thirty-three days are added for further purifying before a woman is allowed to "touch any hallowed thing, or come into the sanctuary."¹⁰ For a female child, the additional purification rites take twice as long, sixty-six days after the earlier fourteen. (This regulation has been compared to Aristotle's pronunciamento that it took forty days for a male fetus to develop a soul, but ninety days for a female "ensoulment," since both demonstrate a belief in female inferiority.)

While there are precedents from nonliterate societies for isolation during natural processes, for the dangerous power of menstrual blood, the particular emphasis on disgust, uncleanness, impurity belongs to civilization, be it Hebrew, Moslem, Christian, or Hindu.¹¹

Many of the laws of earlier times are repeated—some, like the regulation about the ox that gores, almost verbatim from Hammurabi's Code. The Hittite law on rape is also that of the Hebrews: when a woman is raped in the city, she is adjudged guilty of co-operating with the attacker, for she could have cried out and gotten help, and both are to be stoned to death. If the rape, however, occurs in the country, "then the man only that lay with her shall die: But unto the damsel thou shalt do nothing . . . For he found her in the field, and the betrothed damsel cried, and there was none to save her."¹²

In premonarchic days, virginity may not have been valued as highly as in later times. In Exodus, "If a man entice a maid that is not betrothed and lie with her, he shall surely endow her to be his wife. If her father utterly refuses to give her unto him, he shall pay money according to the dowry of virgins."¹³

By the time Deuteronomy, the second book of laws, was recorded, several centuries later, there is no longer a question of enticement. A man may demand proof of his bride's virginity,

and if she is not a virgin, she is to be stoned to death. Therefore, all unmarried women are by definition virgins and it is
only rape which is legislated. "If a man find a damsel that is a
virgin and is not betrothed and lay hold on her and lie with
her, and they be found; Then the man that lay with her shall
give unto the damsel's father fifty shekels of silver, and she
shall be his wife, because he hath humbled her, he may not put
her away all his days."[14] The law reflects earlier law codes,
Hammurabic and Assyrian, with the slightly more kindly addition of an injunction against divorce.

In all cases, however, the woman is not consulted; it is the father who decides how to dispose of his daughter. Life does not
always follow the law; one instance in the Bible where a daughter contrived to marry at her own desire occurs in the first book
of Samuel: ". . . Michal loved David: and they told Saul, and
the thing pleased him."[15]

The injunctions against prostitution—"Thou shalt not sell
thy daughter to be a whore"—were later extended into analogy
with Israel abandoning the true Jehovah and playing the whore
with strange gods. The Hebrew condemnation of intercourse
outside marriage, for men as well as for women, was in contrast
to most of the cults surrounding Israel.

I have pointed out that prostitution, sacred or profane, is to
not be equated with women's self-expression. We saw how the
introduction of the sacred marriage rite as a symbol of production led to the worship of male sexuality and the instrumentality of the female. Temple prostitution was practiced in
many cities of the Near East and the Mediterranean. In Israel,
particularly in the later writings, whores and whoring are constantly being held up as an abomination. But it is clear from
many biblical references that the prostitute existed on the margins of society, tolerated if not encouraged. It was sin for a
daughter of Israel to be a whore (as Athenian citizen-women
were not to be sold into prostitution) but the hero Jephthah,
"a mighty man of valor," was the son of a harlot. Rahab, the
whore who hid the Hebrew spies from Jericho's king, played a
helpful role in Israel's destiny. In gratitude, when the city was
taken, she and her family alone, of all the inhabitants of Jeri-

cho, were spared, "and," in the chronicle's words, "she dwelleth in Israel unto this day." Samson visited a whore before being undone when he fell in love with the foreign harlot Delilah. The prophet Hosea was married to Gomer, a prostitute, though he was abasing himself as an example to Israel: "The Lord said to Hosea, Go take unto thee a wife of whoredoms and children of whoredoms; for the land hath committed great whoredoms departing from the Lord."[16] Still, on the face of it, the only opportunity a woman had for sexual initiative was to play the part of a whore; Tamar, in the Book of Genesis, had no choice but to pose as a sacred prostitute in order to entice her father-in-law into making her pregnant.

Though Tamar was a foreign woman, sacred prostitution was practiced in the Temple of Solomon at various times, probably by Hebrew and foreign women. The Hebrews had adopted many of their neighbors' customs—they worshiped idols, practiced Baal worship, and prostrated themselves to both Asherah and Ashtoreth. What we know as Jewish religion emerged only after the return from the Babylonian exile, under the aegis of a fierce male priesthood. The Old Testament's frequent injunctions against idol worship are *ex post facto* explanations for Israel's misfortunes; the priests reproved the people and pointed to their sins in the attempt to enforce their harshly exclusive monotheism.[17]

30

Shall He Treat Our Sister as a Harlot

In a patriarchal society, rape and prostitution can be seen as
two sides of a coin, conjoined through the glorification of virginity and chastity. The Old Testament and Greek literature
tell of many rapes, though the act of violence itself is usually
inferred. Only the brutal gang-rape by the Benjamites, which
resulted in a concubine's death, has realistic details. Even here,
it is like a war report: she is abused all night and in the morning has the strength left only to stagger to the doorstep and die.
As a concubine "who had played the whore" she was sacrificed
when the rowdy Benjamites threatened homosexual rape of her
master, the Levite. The old man who was his host, mindful of
the duties of hospitality, enjoined them not to do "so vile a
thing." In place of the Levite, a member of the priestly clan, he
offered the rioters his own virgin daughter, along with his
guest's concubine, but they satisfied themselves with the
woman who was the lowest of all three on the social scale. A
whore—loosely, any woman who has been accused of sexual
misconduct—is always fair game.

Rape is so institutionalized in Western tradition that
women's responses are not recorded.[1] It is a crime against the
man who has authority over her, not against the woman.

When Zeus wanted a woman, he took her; the myths do not distinguish as to whether a mortal woman is raped or accepting of divine love; we are more likely to hear about her husband's displeasure, as Amphitryon resented Alcmene's visits from Zeus. Yet, in the Sumerian tale Shukalletuda and the Shade Garden, when the goddess Inanna lies down to rest and wakes to find that the gardener has "taken advantage of her in her sleep," she is furious and punishes humans in consequence.[2]

In Genesis 34:31 the answer of Jacob's sons, "Shall he treat our sister as a harlot?" when Jacob remonstrates with them after their treacherous attack on the Shechemites points up the intimate association of rape and prostitution. If a whore may be raped, since there is no man to protect her, a woman who has been raped automatically becomes a whore. Once her virginity has been breached she loses value on the marriage market. Women, being passive and possessions, are déclassé if they have relations with a man other than the one who has been given authority over their sexuality, never mind whether with or without their consent. In Hebrew law, as in most other Near Eastern law codes and in Mediterranean custom until very recently, the only remedy open to an unmarried woman after rape was to marry the criminal. If a woman refused to obey her family, she had few options; often prostitution was her only recourse. In the mass rapes of Bangladesh a few years ago, many women were disowned by their families; this is prefigured by the European servant girls of the nineteenth century who were first abused by the son or father of the family, then dismissed without references for profligacy. In Sicily until the early nineteen seventies it was common to kidnap and rape a young woman, who then had no choice but to marry the perpetrator of her dishonor.

In another sense, also, rape and prostitution become allied once a market value has been placed on sex. A woman may sell her sexual services in prostitution; a man may steal them in rape. In the world of the early civilizations theft was recognized and honored in war, as long as one stole not from one's fellow nationals but from another group, the speakers most likely of another language—in Deuteronomy described as "all the cities which are very far off from thee." Rape is also socially approved; it is getting something for nothing. When the men of the cities conquered by the Greeks or the Hebrews are put to the sword, the women are taken as concubines or bondswomen; probably the difference is that upper-class women like Cassandra are concubines, the servants are subject to the will of the men though not dignified by concubine status. By extension therefore rape is a sign of manliness; to the victor belong the spoils, to the conqueror the women, and to take a woman by force means being a conqueror.[3]

Deuteronomy does, however, have kindly instructions about how the captive is to be treated. She is to be given a month to mourn her parents before she is forced into sexual relations. If she does not please her master, she is to be allowed her freedom. "Thou shalt not sell her for money, thou shalt not make merchandise of her because thou hast humbled her."[4] What other recourse she would have besides prostitution is difficult to imagine. Women in this cruel and authoritarian society are given Hobson's choices: give in to rape or be dishonored in prostitution. No doubt some chose the latter, with its illusion of freedom, while others would have settled for the protection of the former if the master were at all tolerable.

With woman as instrument, we saw how the physical gratification in prostitution is reduced to a minimum. The woman is performing a service, not expressing her needs and feelings, and the man is deprived of a truly reciprocal and therefore participatory experience. What then is the gratification in rape? It is perversion in the most literal sense; instead of pleasure, the gratification is in the conquest. Like the imprisoned animal who diverts his or her sexual energy into attack, so does the human, only in this case civilization has made the outrage a convention. Many a nineteenth-century Western white thought that rape was the savage way of making love. This is not true. Recent studies have shown that rapists are often sexually impaired; they suffer from disfunctions, such as impotence and delayed ejaculation. The realization that rape is a crime of violence and has little to do with sexual gratification is just beginning to penetrate the popular consciousness.[5] Though the male organ is envisioned in macho fantasies as an extension of man's other weapons—sword, gun, or club—the living penis is quite inadequate to such a purpose. In individual rape, the injuries to the woman are usually wrought by the arms—literal or otherwise—not by the precious male triune. The Deuteronomic law which forbids "taking a man by the secrets"—a woman who does so in order to help her husband in a fight is to have her hand cut off—must have had an inhibiting effect in other cases, too, an effective injunction against the most potent self-defense a woman has, as cinematographer Nelly Kaplan demonstrated when she had her heroine kick an assailant in the genitals to fend off attempted rape.[6]

A common way to force a woman into prostitution, past and present, was to kidnap and rape her, once or repeatedly, to break her will and deprive her of her sense of self, as well as to impress on her that her sexuality is not hers but at the disposition of others. If it's going to be taken by force, it might just as well be sold at a profit, though as we noted in Greece, the profit might not accrue to the woman herself.

It is not clear whether Dinah, the sister to whom Jacob's sons referred, was raped or seduced by Prince Shechem. It is an index to these warrior societies' indifference to women as human beings that we know so little about the woman's feelings. As with Ninlil, who became Enlil's loyal wife, so with Dinah and the many mortal women taken captive and carried home in the victors' train: not only is woman a passive field to be plowed, she is also portable. As the tale tells it, while Jacob and his family were camped outside Shechem, Dinah went out to visit with the daughters of the land and "Shechem the son of Hamor the Hivite saw her, he took and lay with her and defiled her." According to the Hebrews' own laws, Shechem did what was legal after the rape or seduction of a virgin: he sent his father with a marriage proposal and generous bride gifts. Moreover, Hamor proposed that Hebrews and Hivites exchange wives, that the Hivites marry the daughters of the Hebrews—unspecified sisters and nieces of Dinah—and the Hebrews the daughters of the Hivites. When the Jews insist that their kin must be circumcised, the Hivites undergo the painful opera-

tion, and "on the third day, when they were sore," Dinah's
brothers "came upon the city boldly, and slew all the males."
Not only do they repossess themselves of their sister, now living
with Shechem, but they "spoiled the city . . . took their sheep,
and their oxen and their asses . . . all their wealth, and all
their little ones, and their wives took they captive," subjecting
the Hivite women to worse treatment than Dinah's.[7] Their response to Jacob points up the lack of distinction which prevails
when women's active sexuality is forbidden.

And yet there were strong women in the Old Testament. Jael
was one, the wife of a Kenite not a Hebrew, who offered Sisera
a sup of milk after the battle and then took a nail and ham-
mered it into his head. This was before the monarchy, when Israel was ruled by judges, and "Deborah a prophetess judged Israel at that time." Deborah's stirring song of victory, believed
to date from the eleventh century, is one of the earliest extant
poems in the Bible.[8] And Jael's action was cited only recently
as the inspiration for a black woman prisoner who killed the
prison guard attempting sexual liberties with her.[9]

Judith's assassination of Holophernes, when she entered his
tent in the guise of a seductress and then proceeded to behead
him, is, however, relegated to the Apocrypha, while Esther, the
dutiful daughter of Israel who won Ahasuerus' love on her uncle's instructions and then saved her people from destruction, is
in the canon itself, a less fiery example. In either case, they are
acting as sex objects, using their sexuality as a prostitute does,
though the end was to the Hebrews' advantage. From a
woman's point of view, the real heroine in the Book of Esther
is Ahasuerus' first wife, Vashti, who refused to come at the
King's command. The women who served the chroniclers' purposes were written about. Other women must have resisted patriarchal imposition, as Chinese women were wont to commit
suicide in the bridal chair rather than be married against their
wishes, but we hear nothing of them.

Once a woman's "virtue" has been lost, whether involun-
tarily or by her own actions, she is damaged goods. No more is
said about Dinah after the episode with Prince Shechem. Presumably she was kept in isolation, like a Greek wife who had

been divorced by her husband. If she did escape, there were few occupations open to an unprotected woman; her choice might have been to become one man's servant or a harlot. And the latter path must have been taken by many, for there was no dearth of prostitutes.

Ancient society was based on war, on exploitation, on greed. According to Aristotle one of the reasons why statesmen should know the art of warfare was "in order to become masters of those who deserve to be enslaved."[10] These attitudes were as true of the earliest Hebrews as of the Greeks and the Romans. They were, however, less successful empire builders than either of the latter. In consequence, it was only after the return from Babylon that they formulated an ethic which went beyond the materialism of the ancients, that showed a concern not only for their fellow Hebrews, but even for non-Hebrews.

By the time the laws were written down, Jewish society had long passed its material apex. The United Monarchy of David first and then Solomon (circa 1000–930 B.C.E.) had broken into northern and southern kingdoms after Solomon's death. The Assyrian conquest in 721 permanently dispersed the larger fragment, and Nebuchadnezzar's infestation of Jerusalem destroyed the southern portion—all that was left of Solomon's empire, in 586 B.C.E.

Thus on the basis of a tribal ethos which served to unify a small kingdom that broke down within a century is constructed a book which has lasted for two thousand years, a book created out of defeat and dispersal and conquest. Somewhere within this book a new synthesis was created, which took the concepts of the power kingdoms—conquest, bureaucracy, and naked force—and added another, more viable, dimension. One aspect was sexual puritanism, superimposed on the sadomasochistic underpinning of the previous two or three thousand years. While rape and booty were taken for granted in the versions whose composition was earliest in time, in later editings rules were formulated, not only for the treatment of captives, as we saw, but for that of bondservants, Hebrew and stranger, for fairness in business dealings, and for charity. In contrast to earlier Near Eastern law codes, class distinctions were elimi-

nated in the Bible, except for the blanket one between Hebrews and foreigners. Frequent is the reminder "because ye
were slaves in Egypt" or "because ye were strangers in a strange
land." It is this feeling for the underclass, initiated in the Old
Testament and developed further in the New Testament, the
book created by a reforming sect of Jews, which has made
Christianity effective in its broad appeal to subject peoples
over the past two millennia.

Where women are concerned, the Hebrew record is mixed.
Their laws and attitudes were kinder to women than those of
the Assyrians if harsher than those of the Sumerians. Some
commentators make a case for women being stronger and more
active in the earliest period, before the monarchy and the establishment of a bureaucratic government, which would be consistent with observations made elsewhere in the Near East and
the Mediterranean.[11] The Greeks and the Romans recognized
prostitution and slave concubinage as legitimate for men. They
licensed the former and made money for the state from it. The
Old Testament appears to disapprove of sex outside marriage,
but it accepts polygyny, concubinage, and, in the sending in of
Rachel's and Leah's maids to Jacob, the master's sexual rights
over all the female servants, common practice throughout the
Near East. It does not explicitly forbid prostitution—only the
selling of one's own daughter as a whore, and the practice of
prostitution on temple precincts.

The transported Africans in nineteenth-century America
adopted Old Testament tales for their own self-esteem. If
looked at in the light of compensatory literature, when the
"chosen people" were powerless slaves, tolerated and allowed to
exist but no more, at the impressive court of Nebuchadnezzar,
the boastful and self-righteous tone of the historical books becomes less offensive. The insistence on seed and multiplicity
and on their apartness and identity was shaped to fit the needs
of an oft-conquered people. The sources for "Let My People
Go" and "Joshua Fit the Battle of Jericho" were wishful parables to the Jews long before they spoke to enslaved blacks.
Their actual history in relation to the powers around them is
somewhat different from the dramatic tales of the book. They

built no huge cities like Babylon and Uruk and Assur, left few splendiferous ruins. Babylon's two thousand five hundred acres under Nebuchadnezzar are in sharp contrast with the ten acres compassed by the Jerusalem city walls under Solomon (circa 970–930 B.C.E.).[12]

During the diaspora, attitudes changed and influences were now received from Hellenist and Roman Christian sources, as earlier they had come from Near Eastern neighbors. Concubinage disappeared, though polygyny was practiced well into the Christian era in the West, even into the nineteenth century in Moslem countries. Adultery was forbidden with the punishment of death for man and woman, but the judgment was based on the violation of property rights, not sexual equality.

Men were literally valued more than women. One example is that the payment to release a male from religious vows is almost twice that for a woman. The general distaste for the body cited earlier, the almost phobic attitudes about life processes, comes down much more heavily on the childbearers, the producers of life. The exclusion of any female reference in religious imagery—where formerly it was Inanna who had prevented all bearing and fertility in the land, now it is the Lord who has "fast closed up all the wombs of the House of Abimelech" at the time the latter took Sarah into his harem—had to have an effect on the way men and women thought about themselves.

On the other hand three references to earlier matrilineal tradition remain in Genesis, the first book of the Old Testament, and one hung on into the recent past, in the rabbinical definition of a Jew as the child of a Jewish mother. On the face of it, this judgment seems to show the rabbis' mistrust of women, since only the woman knows for sure who is her child's father. I believe it reflects the heritage of foraging times, possibly retained on a pragmatic basis, since Old Testament Hebrew men had a tendency to marry out. Though the practice was frowned upon initially, they were always bringing in the daughters of neighboring groups. Tamar is only one of several examples. Sarah and Abraham sent back to Haran for a cousin to marry their son Isaac, but Esau displeased his parents by marrying an Edomite. Jacob went back to Haran and there fell in love with his cousin Rachel, though Laban trapped him into marrying both sisters. Moses, it will be remembered, married the daughter of a Midianite priest, and there was conflict back and forth about the problem, since the Jews' exclusiveness was at odds with the emphasis on increasing their numbers—especially in latter days.[13]

The customs accepted by their Near Eastern and Mediterranean neighbors were anathema to the Hebrews. Homosexuality, typified by anal sex, was an abomination punishable by death and, as we saw in the story of the Levite's concubine, in practice considered a worse sin than the rape of a virgin. Moreover, the injunctions against "unnatural ways" and the sin of Onan—masturbation or coitus interruptus—became a rigorously restrictive, not to say anti-sexual, code, which was further developed in Talmudic times, the centuries just before and for several hundred years after the birth of Christ, when the interpretation of religion was hardening into dogma. The strict rules were a prohibition on experimentation and elaboration in heterosexual practice also. Women were not to approach their husbands to initiate sex, because of their modesty and Eve's sin: "Thy desire shall be to thy husband and he shall rule over thee."

Positions in marital intercourse were legislated by the Talmudic rabbis. In one part of the Talmud, "A man may do all that he will with his wife," but most other sources condemn "intercourse not in the usual way." One second-century rabbi issued a fiat against intercourse where the woman is above the man.[14] In line with Jewish emphasis on multiplying the people, however, marital relations were approved—in fact, the number of times per week, as well as the length of time a husband could stay away from his wife, was legislated according to the husband's profession. Only Talmudic study excused the man from *onah*, the wife's right to sexual intercourse. On the other hand, the woman was to satisfy her husband's sexual needs.

The Talmud assumed that an unmarried man would be unable to resist sexual temptation. The wife's function was to give him pleasure, thus helping him to resist his natural tendency to commit immoral acts. Even after marriage, however, he is thought of as waging a continuous battle against his sinful desire for extramarital sex.[15]

The precious male seed was believed to be equivalent to humans, and the Babylonian Talmud (500 C.E.) has a strong condemnation against masturbation. One third-century rabbi felt that "whoever emits semen in vain deserves death."

Though Christianity would carry the sexual bind much further, the ascetic strain was prefigured by the dissident Hebrew sect known as the Essenes. (Recent archaeological discoveries indicate that this group may have been the actual as well as the spiritual source of the new synthesis that, in later centuries, would become the Christian religion.) Writing about 100 C.E. the Jewish historian Josephus describes two orders of Essenes, the one practicing celibacy, the other marital restraint, which included avoiding intercourse when wives were pregnant since, according to Josephus, their purpose in marriage was reproduction and not "self-indulgence."

The first-century Jewish philosopher Philo also believed that intercourse should be only for procreation, explicating thus the biblical condemnation of homosexuality and of intercourse during menstruation, when, he thought, conception would produce deformed infants. Philo criticized immoderate and insatiable desire, deeming unchaste "the rage for sexual intercourse," even with one's own wife, and condemned the "passion of love."[16] As with most other patriarchal pronouncements on sexual impulses, he writes from the male viewpoint, ignoring any feelings or desire a woman might have. Her contribution was to receive the male seed and to give it shelter and sustenance.

Because of these attitudes Jewish men were not allowed to practice birth control, but women, by their very inferiority, were spared certain prohibitions. Moreover, as the emphasis on survival under outside domination increased, there was a tendency to encourage all practices that would increase the people. This meant that the woman's life was preferred over that of the fetus—you don't kill the cow to save the calf. On occasion, the rabbis permitted sterilization or the use of a *mokh*—a sponge or wool tampon inserted into the vagina to occlude the opening of the uterus—for married women: when the woman's life would be endangered by pregnancy or when she suffered excruciating pain in delivery. It is assumed that there are certain other conditions under which a woman will use a *mokh*. The slave, the convert, and the captive, who do not know what fate is in store for them, are described in the Talmud as having recourse to contraception. And Rabbi Naman, a teacher in Babylon at about 330 C.E., quotes another rabbi who permitted the use of a *mokh* in three cases: for minors—that is, girls under twelve—nursing mothers, and pregnant women.[17]

The Gemara, a part of the Babylonian Talmud, which probably dates back to the first or second century C.E., makes an oblique reference to coitus interruptus during a mother's two-year nursing period, taking it for granted that the man "will thresh inside and winnow outside." The severe and literal emphasis against the spilling of male seed, inferred from the story of Er and Onan, the brothers who practiced coitus interruptus with Tamar and died shortly thereafter, may postdate this particular passage. In medieval days the demon Lilith was blamed for even such unconscious sins as nocturnal emission, a possible reflection of the more intensely antibody, antifemale, and antisexual attitudes of the dominant Christians, who surrounded the small sect of Jews, now struggling to survive the persecutions of their more powerful offspring.

It was assumed that harlots practiced birth control, either with a *mokh* or by moving during and after the act of coitus, which is interpreted as serving to expel the seed.[18] In effect, this may have meant that a married woman was expected to lie still, just as the Latin writer Lucretius averred that the customs of prostitutes were not fitting for Roman wives. According to him movements in intercourse made it difficult to conceive; surely, he counseled, our wives have no need of such effeminate movements.* The equation of female sexual pas-

* Lucretius advises that the proper position for conception is *a tergo*, from the rear, "after the manner of wild beasts and quadrupeds because the seeds in this way can find the proper spots in consequence of the position of the body. Nor have wives the least use for effeminate motions; a woman hinders and stands in the way of her own conceiving when thus she acts; for she drives the furrow out of the direct course and path of the share, and turns away from the proper spots the stroke of the seed. And thus

sivity with respectability seems to predate the Victorian era by at least two thousand years. The entire male domination of sexual acts must have had severely inhibiting effects on spontaneous expression for woman, a heritage that is still with us.[19] Love was directed toward children; woman's functions in marriage were "to grind corn, suckle children, be a beautiful wife, and bear children."[20]

Even more than in the Old Testament, Talmudic quotations can be found to justify diverse conclusions about the position of women. The patriarchal tradition in Jewish heritage needs no exegesis—women's inferiority is a given within and without the Hebrew world. What is specific to Hebrew theology is the bind in which the Jews found themselves once they rejected female imagery in creation, despised the body and its functions, and at the same time emphasized the value of fair treatment, charity, and kindness. They were caught in ambivalences which in Christianity turned into almost pathological double binds. Talmudic Judaism developed rabbinical courts which decided on all questions of life, from the most intimate to the most formal. The heritage of puritanism is passed on to the Christians and there combined with asceticism to produce an even more body-hating schema. The Jewish tradition decrees marriage for all; only a rare prophet or rabbinical scholar was excused from this obligation. In practice, the usage was to arrange early marriages for men and women.

If the Greeks hated women, the Hebrews had contempt for them. But the patriarchal problem is that no one has yet figured out a way to eliminate women from actual life, despite the theoretical ascription of holiness and spirituality to men, the innumerable inventions of myth which ascribed creation to men, seduction and sin and evil to women.

In the Old Testament we see an early dichotomization, which underlies two thousand years of patriarchy and which is still operant in our cultural tradition—the profane and the holy. The spirit is considered superior to and separate from the body. Women, however, are more nakedly connected with the

---

for their own ends harlots are wont to move, in order not to conceive and lie in child-bed frequently, and at the same time to render Venus more attractive to men. This our wives have surely no need of."

body's role in maintaining life—and the process of patriarchal inversion is spelled out in a series of prohibitions and punishments, rules and taboos. It is only one of a series of dichotomies which have formed the bases for much of Western thinking and are accepted by women as well as men. With the Jews, nature is profane, worship holy. This dichotomy of spirit and body is peculiarly unworkable in the case of women, who are necessary and yet inferior and suspect. The Talmud expresses it thus: "With the Jews one great consideration of life is to have children and more especially male children; because when a boy is born all rejoice over him, but over a girl they all mourn. When a boy comes into the world he brings peace with him, and a loaf of bread in his hand, but a girl brings nothing." The tractate *Niddah* (The Menstruous Woman), says: "It is impossible for the world to be without males and females, but blessed is he whose children are boys, and hapless is he whose children are girls."[21]

The attitudes of the Talmudic writers were passed on to the early Christians. The Jews were harshly patriarchal, but they valued women too highly as wives, producers of children, preferably sons, to permit themselves the total misogyny in which several Greek writers indulged. Katherine Rogers points out that the Bible itself is most misogynistic where it has been influenced by Greek thinking in the apocryphal books of Ecclesiasticus and Esdras and in the writings of Paul. Later Christian commentators distorted the Old Testament to make it more misogynist than it was. St. Paul harped on the Adam and Eve story as the basis for women's inferiority. In the original Old Testament tale of David and Bathsheba, the emphasis was on King David's adulterous desire when he accidentally saw Bathsheba naked as she was bathing and on his murder of her husband. The Christians shifted the blame onto Bathsheba, so that she has come down to us as a seductress.[22]

Moreover, where the Jews were concerned with numerical survival, the new religion no longer felt it necessary to increase by sexual means. In the first place, the end of the world was imminent; the coming of the Kingdom of God was expected at any time. Christianity increased by conversion; it reached out rather than forward. So the new emphasis was on chastity for both women and men; marriage was good, but virginity was better. Celibacy as a choice for women was one road away from the impasse which has been made of the male-female meeting, a rather drastic one.

The new religion was never revolutionary. From "Render unto Caesar the things that are Caesar's" to "Servants, obey in all things your masters," it preached accommodation to the external powers. But within itself the initial impetus was toward egalitarianism.

The early organization was informal and there were many women among the first converts. Women, in the beginning, enjoyed positions of leadership, as prophets, deacons, and patrons who provided shelter and a meeting place. Acts, particularly, has many references to single women and wife-husband teams who worked for the new religion.[23]

By the end of the first century c.e. it was clear that the Parousia—the end-time or the second coming of Christ—was not imminent. The Church reverted to some of the Jewish and Greek feelings about women. The pseudo-Pauline letter to Timothy, with its clear definitions of men's authority over women, is generally dated to the early part of the second century.† In Paul's letter to the Colossians, husbands were to love their wives, but wives were to submit to their husbands. It was not that the first Church planned to revolutionize men-women relations—it was just that relative status on earth would be of no importance in Paradise, so that Paul could say, "There is neither Jew nor Greek, there is neither slave nor free, there is neither male nor female, for you are all one in Christ Jesus."[24] But Jesus Christ had not returned, and the microcosm which was the persecuted Church, home of slaves and women, began to imitate the macrocosm around it. More and more, the early egalitarianism gave way to an accommodation with the forces around it. The process was, of course, enormously facilitated when Constantine converted to Christianity in the early fourth century.

† Paul's first letter to Timothy is believed by modern scholars to have been written after Paul's death.

31

The European Connection

To the north of the "civilized world" of the ancients, in Europe and Asia, lived the people lumped together by the Greeks and Romans under the name "barbarians." Their forebears had indeed given rise to the classical states of Greece and Rome, in the various waves of post-Minoan invaders, as well as to the Aryan invasion of India and to the languages, if not the peoples, of most of Europe and eventually the Western white world. By the middle of the first millennium B.C.E. a complex society had taken shape, influenced by earlier developments in the area as well as by the technologies of the ancient civilizations.

At this point the distinction between nomadic foragers of the earlier periods of human existence and herdspeople—pastoral nomads—should be restressed. Foraging peoples still existed in Eurasia as recently as one thousand years ago—a very few exist even today in remote parts of India and Southeast Asia.[1] By three thousand years ago, however, the majority had been converted to agriculture and/or animal keeping. I explained earlier that animal breeding did not precede agriculture and that pastoral herding was not a primitive state of development, a bridge between food collecting and farming. On the contrary, nomadic herdspeople utilize complex systems, choosing a mixture of animals matched to the different kinds of grasslands they encounter: cattle, horses, and camels need long grass, while sheep and goats crop close.

As agriculture and animal breeding spread through much of Europe and Asia different combinations developed, to take advantage of the different ecologies found there. The horse was domesticated during the third millennium, somewhere in the region of the Hungarian plains, the south Russian steppes, and the Caucasus. As noted in Chapter 27, it had been introduced into the civilized Near East from the north by about 2000 B.C.E. In the meantime, a complex system of pastoralists who knew agriculture but lived mainly on animals was taking shape across the steppes of inner Asia and Central Europe. In the development of the specialized mode of existence which characterized the Indo-European herdspeople, the use of horses was a necessity. They developed the technology for full utilization: harnesses, bits, even carts, and finally iron stirrups. Their subsistence, largely based on pastoral nomadism, stemmed from the invention of horseback riding.[2]

True nomadic pastoralists are limited in their material equipment. Like foragers, they must travel light. They rarely use pottery, have very few metal containers, and possess only the simplest of household goods. Their homes are portable, and they are unlikely to have ritual or decorative art objects. Clothing and artifacts are often made from animal products of horn, bone, wool, and skin. On the open plains which provide grazing land for their animals, wood is scarce. Many of their tools are of perishable materials. For these reasons, it is difficult to trace their history by archaeological methods. They do not own land and they cannot afford concubines, servants, and the conspicuous consumption which characterized the established bureaucracies in the Near Eastern kingdoms. In the beginning at least, the nomad tribes of the Eurasian steppes could not bring to bear the efficiency of domination exercised by their civilized neighbors.[3]

I spoke earlier of how the horse was integrated into the practice of war and of how horse breeding facilitated the expansion and the efficiency of warfare, while, at the same time, it strengthened the underlying psychological motivation. In the case of Greater Mesopotamia and Syria, Palestine, even Egypt, what had happened was that already settled warlike, materialist, accumulative peoples adapted to their own uses the techniques introduced by the nomadic herdspeople. The Hittites, who lived in Anatolia during the third millennium, used horses for draft purposes and knew iron technology. The first people to use the riding horse as a war machine may have been the Kassites, who lived in the mountains to the northeast of Greater Mesopotamia and conquered the Old Babylonian kingdom founded by Hammurabi shortly after the middle of the second millennium.

E. D. Phillips has shown how the aggressive way of life fostered by horse riding spread throughout Europe and Central Asia. Horsemen went south, conquering the Near East; the Kassite wave was the first; the Persians were later Indo-European invaders. Other mounted warriors went north, plundering the pastoralists of the steppes, who did not usually ride. Helpless against cavalry attacks, the latter either gave up their flocks and herds to the invaders or paid tribute. The only way to resist was to adopt the enemy's methods and to take to the horse themselves.

Thus raiding complexes were transmitted to the steppes, wherein arose communities of mounted warriors who controlled subject tribes and huge flocks and herds. The more people took to the steppes, the more nomadic they became. Horses needed extensive pasture, so there was more reason to conquer more areas. The herdspeople spread in all directions. Where the steppe would not support agriculture, they adapted to life on the open land; elsewhere, as in South Russia, they exacted tribute from the settled agriculturalists. Forest people who lived by gathering and hunting were recruited or converted to a different way of life—by example or necessity—when the pastoralists encroached upon areas from which the foragers had previously drawn sustenance at certain times of the year; mass migrations occurred only when folk were driven from their lands by invading groups.[4]

Within this complex mixture of interrelationships are comprised the peoples variously described under the names Scyths and Teutons, and eventually the Celts, all of whom spoke Indo-European languages. They are not usually considered civilized, for although they had complex technologies, they did not use writing and they had no centralized dominating bureaucracies; their settlements never become cities on the scale of Babylon, Assur, Athens and Rome.

It is difficult to trace their movements over the millennia before they enter written history, during the conflicts with the Greeks and the Romans and the later conversion to Christianity.

First source of information is Herodotus, writing in the fifth century before our epoch. Variously termed the "father of history" and the "father of lies," he is today recognized as the world's first anthropologist, a rousing tale-teller whose work still provides confirmatory material for archaeologists, anthropologists, and historians. He jumbles many tribes together under the general name Scyths, though he also gives specific tribal identities and explains that there were Scyths who were settled agriculturalists and others who were horse-riding pastoralists living in the special way of life described above. In one place he describes them as "a people without fortified towns, living in wagons which they take with them wherever they go, accustomed one and all, to fight on horseback with bows and arrows, and dependent for their food not upon agriculture but upon their cattle."[5] Elsewhere, however, he mentions the agricultural Scyths, the nomadic Scyths, and the Royal Scyths. These last had picked up conspicuous-consumption customs from the Middle Eastern and Mediterranean civilizations: they practiced a form of suttee, with sumptuous royal burials in which wives, horses, and chariots were interred with the dead king; they were also the dominators of subject agricultural tribes, occupying the extreme high side of the vertical interrelationship that usually existed between the settled agriculturalists and the horse-and-cattle raisers.

At the extremes of the Scythian territory were peoples Herodotus called hunters, the Thyssagetae and the Iyrcae, though we imagine that in today's terminology foragers or gatherer-hunters would be a more accurate description. Beyond them, to the north and east, was another Scythian tribe, the Argippaei, described by the historian as living on fruit from a tree he calls ponticum—a kind of cherry. They strained the ripe fruit through cloths and got from it a thick dark-colored juice, which they lapped up with their tongues or mixed with milk for a drink, making cakes from the remaining sediment. He writes further:

> They have but few sheep, as the grazing is poor. Every *man* lives under *his* ponticum-tree, which *he* protects in winter with bands of thick white felt, taking them off in the summer. These people are supposed to be protected by a mysterious sort of sanctity; they carry no arms and nobody offers them violence; they settle disputes amongst their neighbors, and anybody who seeks asylum amongst them is left in peace.[6]

The different peoples varied in organization as in subsistence techniques. A careful reading of Herodotus on Asian peoples, and of Tacitus, writing about the Germans some six hundred years later, brings evidence of peaceable egalitarian band societies—with the equality going across sex lines—existing in northern reaches of the Europe and Asia of their times.

The Fenni described by Tacitus are clearly egalitarian gatherers and hunters. They have "neither arms nor homes; their food is herbs, their clothing skins, their bed the earth . . . the men and women are alike supplied by the chase; for the latter are always present and demand a share of the prey."[7]

In some places the social organization was what we would call "rank society," with some people owning more than others, but no real stratification.[8] Tacitus describes the German moots, which are typical of this form of government, one of the bits of evidence which gave rise to the theory of primitive democracy deduced by Jacobsen for early Sumer: they are a sort of town meeting where "the final decision rests with the people . . . the chief is heard more because he has influence to persuade than the power to command."[9]

In other places class societies like that of the Royal Scyths took shape. Graves with treasure hoards of gold ornaments and weapons and rich tumulus burials appear throughout Eurasia, from England to the steppes, by the middle of the second millennium before our epoch. In some areas, as under the Scyths of Central Eurasia, agricultural tribes were kept in subjection by mounted peoples; in others, groups lived by fishing (Northwest Europe, particularly Scandinavia), by gathering and hunting (parts of the forest lands of Germany and Poland), or by mixed practices of farming and animal raising (the Swiss lake dwellers).

Trade connections were, however, maintained from one end of Europe to the other, not only within the "barbarian" area but between the barbarians and the civilized peoples. The Scyths had Greek craftsmen working for them, and Greek, and later Roman, objects are found as far away as Germany and Scandinavia, just as amber found its way south to the Mediterranean. Technologies were also passed in both directions; it took almost a thousand years for the wagon to travel from Mesopotamia to England and Holland, while I have noted that the use of the horse and of iron was transmitted in the opposite direction.

In all these societies, ancient writers were surprised to find the position of women rather different from the repressive situation typical of their own worlds. Herodotus explained the Sauromatae, eastern neighbors of the Scyths, as being descended from the union of a group of Amazons with some of the free Scyths. The women had been shipwrecked within Scythian territory, at Cremni on the shores of the Sea of Azov (Lake Maeotis). When the Scyths discovered, after a battle, that their opponents were women, they sent out an equal number of their youngest men to make acquaintance with the Amazons. "Neither party had anything but their weapons and both lived the same sort of life, hunting and plundering." They struck up friendships, using sign language, and the young men and women paired off. The Scyths never managed to learn the language of the Amazons, but the women learned to speak that of their husbands. "Ever since then the women of the Sauromatae have kept to their old ways, riding to the hunt on horseback, sometimes with, sometimes without their menfolk, taking part in war and wearing the same sort of clothes as their men."[10]

The Sauromatae are believed to be the same people mentioned centuries later by Tacitus as the Sarmatians. By the time he wrote, they had migrated westward from the shores of the Sea of Azov in Asia to what is now Bulgaria, on the eastern fringes of the lands of the Germani, but they still lived in wagons and on horseback. (A modern writer believes the customs of the Sarmatians are—or were until recently—still extant in the lives of the Gypsies or Romany.[11]) Tacitus also reports on the Veneti, who, though they have fixed habitations, "have borrowed largely from the Sarmatian character; in their plundering expeditions they roam over the whole extent of forest and mountain."[12]

Also like the Sauromatae are the Issedones, who allowed equal authority to women and men. Herodotus mentions the peculiar sexual customs of the Massagetae, whose queen, Tomyris, led them to a victory over Cyrus the Persian: "Though each person has a wife, all the wives are used promiscuously . . . if a man wants a woman, all he does is hang up his quiver in front of her wagon and then enjoy her without misgiving." Greek fashion, Herodotus makes the sexual choice at male initiative; with our newfound awareness of how much ethno- and androcentric views have colored nineteenth- and twentieth-century writings about foreign cultures, we can safely conclude that Massagetae women enjoyed more sexual freedom than was allowed to the women of the Greeks. Similarly, he speaks of the Agathyrsi who "live in luxury and wear gold on their persons. They have their women in common so that they may all be brothers and, as members of a single family, be able to live together without jealousy or hatred."[13] The Agathyrsi remind us of the Nayars of India, discussed earlier as a warrior caste who practice a form of polyandry in which a woman is, in effect, married to a group of brothers, any of whom may cohabit with her.

According to Herodotus, the Scyths' chief deity was the goddess of fire and the hearth—the Greek Hestia—whom they called Tabiti. They also worshiped Zeus, under the name Pa-

paeus, and the earth—Papi—believed by them to be the wife of
Zeus.

The German tribes had been under Roman attack for more
than two hundred years at the time Tacitus wrote about them.
Since he was writing a moral tract for the benefit of Roman
readers, some of his strictures on German chastity are today
viewed with distrust. However, his statement, "They even believe that the sex has a certain sanctity and prescience, and
they do not despise their counsels, or make light of their answers," is supported by other sources, ancient and modern.[14]

In recent years archaeologists have turned up increasing
confirmation for these and other ancient writers' observations
on the relative freedom enjoyed by women among the barbarians. Silver cups and fragments of pottery depicting women on
horseback have been found at several places in Central Europe.
Male and female burials at a site in Saarbrücken dated to 450
B.C.E., were accompanied by grave goods of equal richness.
Several cemeteries in Czechoslovakia, the earliest dated to 700
B.C.E., yielded wagon burials in which women and men were
found inside or on top of four-wheeled vehicles.[15]

More recently several burials have confirmed the ancients' reports that women of the Germans were trained and fought as
soldiers along with their men. A grave dating to 350 B.C.E. containing the bodies of three women and eight men was excavated in Tecklenburgh, Westphalia. All the bodies were buried
with shields, swords, and spears. The women had died of
wounds; they also had bows beside them. Other graves with
women warriors dressed in trousers and bearing arms, who were
killed by sword strokes, have been found in various places in
West and East Germany and Czechoslovakia.[16]

Tacitus, when telling of Queen Boadicea's revolt against the
Romans in Britain, explains that the royal line admits of no
distinction of sex. Celtic warrior tales tell of queens who participate in war and decide whom they will bed, who are in every
sense mistress of their own persons. Queen Maeve boasts to her
husband of her position before she married him: she was mistress of one of the provinces of Ireland, had her own castle and
her own, exaggeratedly large army at her disposal. She married

him only on condition that she retain her sexual freedom, and she makes use of this freedom when it serves her purpose, as in the tale about the Brown Bull of Cooley, to whose owner she offers "the freedom of her own upper thighs" in exchange for the use of the bull for one year.[17]

Keeping women in inferior positions has always been inefficient. Thus in Sparta, the women managed the estates while their husbands were away at war. Tacitus reports that the management of the household, the home, and the land was left to the German women even when the men were not fighting: "They [the men] pass much of their time in the chase and still more in idleness, giving themselves up to sleep and to feasting, the bravest and most warlike doing nothing."[18]

In our own country, in World Wars I and II, mobilizing the country's full resources enabled women to enter occupations previously reserved for men. Sometimes, after the war, women were forced back into their previous isolation in the home; in other instances they retained newly acquired participatory social roles.

In the loose societies of Europe before Christianity, class differentials seem to have been more strongly enforced than sex restrictions. Increasingly, theories which see the subjection of women as the basic one from which other class stratifications arose are being called into question.[19] New tools of science and scholarship have produced imaginative researches into previously masked areas of our nonliterate past. A picture of increasingly complex caste-class relationships emerges from them, substantiating the strength and breadth of roles exercised by women in barbarian Europe. Ruby Rohrlich-Leavitt deduces a class society in Minoan Crete, with women playing leading roles.[20] Evidently class identification transcends sex loyalty. Women also enjoyed stronger and more autonomous positions in the "uncivilized" pre-Christian parts of Europe than were permitted them after the benefits of Roman Christianity had been extended to the whole of Europe.

——ɪɪ——ɪɪ——ɪɪ——ɪɪ——ɪɪ——ɪɪ——ɪɪ——

The Christian Contradiction

It was the first time I could do something I could respect myself for. Until that time I was nobody. If God had wanted me to die because I saved Jews, I was ready to go on the cross, like Jesus.

—Katarzyna Kalwinska, explaining why she had sheltered Jewish fugitives from Nazi death camps at the risk of her own life. *New York Times*, April 20, 1978.

The period of ferment during which Christianity began to spread throughout the area of Roman domination, comprising what had previously been Hellenistic civilization in Asia Minor, Egypt, and Greece, was, as I have said, characterized by many other-worldly cults. Women were prominent in many of these as worshiper and worshiped, from the religion of Isis, who was mother and wife and who had been a whore, to a wide variety of syncretistic Gnostic sects.

In *The Golden Ass* of Apuleius, Isis introduces herself: "The Phrygians, first born of men, call me Mother of the Gods, goddess of Pessinus; the inhabitants of Attica, Minerva of Cecrops' city [Athens]; the Cypriots living amid the sea, Venus of Paphos; the arrow-bearing Cretans, Diana of Dictynna; the triple-tongued Sicilians, Proserpina of the Styx; the original Eleusinians, Ceres of Attica, some call me Juno, others Bellona, some Hecate, others the One from Rhamnus."[1]

Isis here has assimilated many of the great mother goddesses, though they also retain their own special qualities. She was named first the Mother of the Gods, otherwise known as Cybele, who has been identified with the first goddess of birth represented on the walls of Çatal Hüyük. In the form known in Classical times she was worshiped as Cybele, the great goddess of nature, mother of all living—plants, animals, gods, and humans. She did not rule but she created new beings.

By the second century C.E. she is described as a daughter goddess, child of Uranus and wife of Cronus. Originally, in Asia Minor she had been wild and savage, like Dionysus himself, and her cult was celebrated with dance and tambourine. Two hundred years before the beginning of the Christian era, during the Hannibalic Wars, her image and her cult were brought from Pergamum in Asia Minor to Rome, and she became a national Roman goddess, who granted victory and protected the state. Over the centuries image and rites changed. She became associated in myth with Attis, a young shepherd, who castrated himself for love of her. In consequence Cybele's priests performed the same operation on themselves, becoming eunuchs in her service. Statues of Attis performing the sacrificial act, with his belly exposed and a flint or knife held high in his right hand, are found all the way from Asia Minor to as far west as England. It was under the Roman rule that cults of this sort, focusing on pain and deprivation, spread throughout their provinces.

I have pointed out that Christianity can be seen as a combination of Hebrew and late Greek and Roman mystery religions. Jane Ellen Harrison showed how much Christianity owed to the Greek mystical cults—Dionysian rites and the later development of Orphism. We saw that the tradition of masochistic women's cults went back to Sumer, at least, and was perhaps intensified under the Akkadian impact with the increasing severity of male dominance and class and sex oppression. These cults provided outlet and ecstasy. They stem from the first harvest festivals, which in turn relate to the still earlier and universal traditions, documented from ethnographic records, of celebrations allowing for ritualized sexual promiscuity. After agriculture and animal breeding had fostered anxieties and, with the first civilizations, created property and class differentials, these orgiastic celebrations were often translated into the masochistic cults referred to earlier—Inanna-Dumuzi, Ishtar-Tammuz, Cybele-Attis, Isis-Osiris, et al. The cultic rituals, which usually involved the weeping of the mother for the lost child who is also husband-son-brother, took different forms in different countries, allowing for more or less self-expression and more or less aggression or weeping and self-laceration.

Dionysus of Thrace and the Bacchanales came from a central European tradition and seemed to permit more expression and a fiercer outlet, whereas in the heavily socialized civilizations the cults were "gentler," focusing on sacrifice and self-reproaches and suffering.

As the worship of Attis developed over the centuries, taking away from Cybele's influence, a blend of both traditions evolved. In Rome the rites of Attis were celebrated in March, over a period of weeks. Nine days of fasting and sexual abstinence preceded the enactment of Attis' fatal deed. The pine tree under which Attis collapsed and died after he had emasculated himself was brought into the city. Then came a Day of Blood during which the priests ran through the streets flagellating themselves till they drew blood and the celebrants wept and tore their clothes. The tradition of self-attack and mourning exists in other sects, and the medieval *penitentes* need not be in a direct line of descent from Attis worship; they were, however, an expression of similar psychological needs.

In some sects women were the chief participants—in the Greek and Roman traditions the only ones permitted to join in certain celebrations. However, during the first centuries of the Roman Empire the masochistic strain intensifies. Civilizations extend their bureaucratic and hierarchical organization, and sexual deprivation as well as class and caste domination increase. More democratic cults arose, which allowed slaves and lower-class men to participate along with women of every social stratum. Upper-class men also were attracted to them. Eventually the Orphic and Isis streams merged with Gnosticism and flowed into early Christian tradition. The Attis custom of self-emasculation was emulated by the early Christian monks who also castrated themselves in the ultimate act of sexual renunciation.

How Christianity prevailed eventually, to be adopted as the official religion of the Roman Empire in 320 C.E., is outside the scope of this book. Some say that Constantine made it the state religion in response to the conversion of many of his troops, conquered barbarians impressed into the Roman army of domination, though it is his mother, Empress Helena, who is officially credited as the instrument of his conversion.

The counterrevolution by which the initial impetus toward class and sex equality was subverted had occurred almost two hundred years earlier. During the second century after Christ a male bureaucracy had already emerged. The first- and second-century orthodox tradition produced the pseudo-Pauline letter to Timothy: "Let a woman learn in silence with full submissiveness. I do not allow any woman to teach or to exercise authority over a man; she is to remain silent."[2] It also produced a political structure which claimed to have the authority of God —the familiar figure of the Lord, King, Ruler, Master, Judge, and Father.

As Elaine Pagels points out, it was no coincidence that the orthodox insisted that this father-god figure could be represented only by men. Furthermore this devolution occurs just at the time—about 140–200 C.E.—when some churches were developing a hierarchical structure of organization. At the head of this orthodoxy stood the bishop, described in orthodox sources as God's representative. Below him were the priests—all men— and beneath them the third order in the hierarchy, the deacons, who by this time were exclusively male. A striking correlation now exists between the exclusively masculine image of God, the social structure of domination, and the political structure of the community.[3]

The fatherland is well-trodden ground for mainstream historians, and feminists, too, have usually begun their explorations of the hidden story with the period on which there is the largest body of accessible record. I have chosen to highlight specifics

I felt were specially relevant to the points I have been discussing.

Almost a thousand years ensued before Christianity penetrated the whole of barbarian Europe. Scanty reports on the position of women during the Dark Ages—the early medieval period—tend to confirm the observations of Herodotus and Tacitus from earlier times.

Women appear frequently in the record in a wide variety of occupations. Their position seems to have been strongest in the period between 700 and 1200. Although it is a sparsely documented era, David Herlihy has made a case for the significant role they exercised in the economy. In southern France and Spain Burgundian and Visigothic laws allowed women to administer their own property, to participate in the administration of family property, and, when widowed, to act for their families. Women were landowners and managers elsewhere in Europe; they were also heads of families. The wives of warriors and of priests were prominent in the records; they acted in their own names, managed estates and businesses, and their children were often known by their mothers' names rather than their fathers'. Since early medieval laws gave even married women personal title to property, they figure frequently in the documents. Many of the surviving sources refer to women's public acts. They do not seem to have been relegated to domesticity, nor were their activities determined by or subordinated to their sexual functions, and this holds true well into the medieval period.[4] In France women kept relatively equal status with men until the entry of Christianity. In England women of the feudal classes functioned in a considerable number of public capacities almost to the end of the Middle Ages. They appear in manorial registers as property owners, brewers, bakers, cultivators, weavers, and as plaintiffs or defendants in business matters.[5]

During the Middle Ages, moreover, both before and after the conversion to Christianity, a war society existed within Europe, and the wars continued for centuries, with brief periods of truce or relative peace. There were wars between nations; there were wars against "infidel" invaders and rebellions after conquest. The eighth century saw the Arab conquest of Spain. The Moslem—Saracen—penetration of France provided a rallying point; Charlemagne united his country in the battles which stopped the Moorish penetration into Europe, after which the Crusades were organized. Expeditions in the opposite direction took men away from their homes in Christian holy wars, by which kings and popes attempted to expand their domains under the emblem of the "true faith."

I spoke earlier of the anomaly by which a state of war can lead to a strong position for women, as in Sparta, and of the relative autonomy enjoyed by women in the Scythian lands and under the Germani at the time of the Roman invasions. As a consequence of the endemic conditions of war which prevailed during the Middle Ages, women also had to perform a variety of functions on the home front, especially in view of the limited energy sources available in a preindustrial society.

Partly as a result of the spread of Christianity, Roman law, and with it Greek philosophy, came to influence the barbarian kingdoms of Europe. The Roman concept of the family strengthened male power and the paterfamilias governed the position of women in Christian Europe. The tradition known as the "Perpetual Tutelage of Women" comes from early Roman law. The concept that women are perpetual children and only men are adults has had its ups and downs and has been more or less enforced. In essence, however, the definition of women as minors who never grow up has been perpetuated, in modified form, to this day; vestiges of it can still be seen in our legal system. Perpetual tutelage means that woman's relation to man is designated by the concept of *manus* (hand), under which the woman stands (*feme covert*). Women do not exist under the law—they can only go from under one hand to another—hence the still extant practice of "asking for a woman's hand in marriage." Technically it is the father who is being asked. Some of the most restricting aspects of Roman law were incorporated into canon law—the rules of the Church —whence they passed into English common law.[6]

The contrast then was of a class society where women enjoyed economic participation and varying degrees of social autonomy with the more strictly enforced Mediterranean attitude inherited from Greeks, Romans, and Jews. Christianity took the Jewish mistrust for women and added its own repressions, in a much stricter interpretation of Hebrew mores. Significant was the fact that the idealization of chastity was transformed into a loathing for the body and a severe condemnation of sexual acts.

The Christian distaste for the female and her physical functions went far beyond the already phobic attitudes of the Hebrews. Sex was rarely accepted even as a profane activity. The establishment of a celibate male hierarchy gave an added prurience to the authority the Church assumed over people's private acts.

The history of the early Church Fathers' *pronunciamenti* against masturbation, against coitus "not within the fit vessel," turns up extremes which make the Talmudic judgments mild indeed. Comparisons of penances for sexual and criminal offenses inflicted from the sixth to the eleventh century show some extraordinary equivalences. Some bishops ordered equal penalties for intentional homicide, for abortion, and for oral intercourse; seven years of fasting on bread and water, along with renunciation of marital relations, was typical. One ecclesiastic, in office from 690 to 710 C.E., decreed penances of seven years, fifteen years, even life for such sins as oral and anal intercourse, but only seven years for intentional homicide. Even if the punishment's duration was reduced through prayers, the value scheme is manifest.[7]

The principle which sacrificed the mother's life to that of the fetus is early set forth and long maintained. In twelfth-century Paris a theologian named Peter Cantor is asked about a woman who has suffered "a rupture of the navel (umbilicus) in a previous childbirth. The doctors say that if she bears another child she will die. May she 'procure sterility' for herself?" Peter gives a brusque negative. "This last thing is not at all lawful, because this would be to procure poisons of sterility; that is prohibited in every case."[8]

In the twelfth century the Augustinian doctrine of original sin based on the line in Psalm 51, "In iniquity my mother conceived me, in sin was I born," was carried even further. Ecclesiastics like St. Albert decreed that a husband who was too ardent a lover of his wife treated her as a harlot.[9] Intercourse should be only for procreation; to delight in the sexual act was a mortal sin.[10]

The doctrine of the Church changed over the centuries, but not for the better till much, much later. It was sin "when a woman is known in a different way from what nature requires." In the thirteenth century Thomas Aquinas condemned any semination "outside the vessel," any departure from the normal mode (the missionary position), and equated coitus interruptus, the most accessible method of birth control, with sodomy. The fit way according to Thomas was with woman beneath the man, because of man's natural superiority to woman. Moreover, it was believed that this position facilitated conception. If the woman was above the man, the seed "would pour out of the matrix."[11] After Thomas, any other position was condemned as unnatural and adjudged mortal sin. Authority was found in the Old Testament, the New Testament, and Aristotelian theories of women's inferiority, which Thomas Aquinas adapted to Christianity.

The Talmudic writers had been troubled by sexual desire, the distinction to be made between lust and procreation. Christianity carried the sexual bind much further. With many Christian theoreticians sexuality was lust; all intercourse carried some degree of sin.

The twelfth-century bishop Huguccio said that coitus "can never be without sin, for it always occurs and is exercised with a certain itching and a certain pleasure; for, in the emission of the seed, there is always a certain excitement, a certain itching, a certain pleasure." His pupil Innocent III amplified: "Who does not know that conjugal intercourse is never committed without itching of the flesh, and heat and foul concupiscence, whence the conceived seeds are befouled and corrupted."[12] Husbands, love your wives was translated as pure spirit; sex was best avoided. A small undercurrent admitted the possibility of husband-wife love expressed also in sexual relations.

Christianity attempted to apply a single sexual standard to men and women, which can be summed up in the word *no*. Husbands were told what to do; wives were addressed chiefly by being asked to report any "unnatural practices"—usually assumed to be anal intercourse—to their confessors.

In later centuries priests were instructed to question their parishioners as to whether they used forbidden means of intercourse, but they were cautioned to couch their questions in a form that would not suggest to the confessant methods effective for birth control (or pleasure) of which she or he was unaware. They were to avoid "imprudently questioning the young of either sex, or others, about matters of which they were ignorant, lest they be scandalized and learn thereby to sin."[13]

When Christianity adapted Greek philosophy and tied it to Jewish theology, the dichotomization of mind and body was enormously strengthened; it was the culmination of a process that had begun several thousands of years earlier. In the philosophical system based on dualities, mind, spirit, objectivity were usually assigned to men; body, emotion, and subjectivity to women. If woman is all body she is of course incapable of resisting her body's impulses. As the weaker vessel she cannot bring to bear the strength of her missing intellectual and spiritual qualities and therefore easily succumbs to lust, being at the mercy of her passions, her desires, above all her bodily functions. In this respect, the derogation of sex involved also an enormous increase in the derogation of women.

Goddesses were now represented by the mother of Christ, who was not God the Mother but a mere vessel for the gestation of the divine child, in accordance with already well-established belief about women's role in reproduction. In Catholic theology, Mary had never known sex. Her impregnation by God's Holy Spirit was an ethereal process with no bodily—that is, sexual—connotations. Even the suggestion that she had subsequently had sexual relations with Joseph in order to produce the siblings referred to in the early Gospels aroused great rage among the Church Fathers.[14] Medieval Christian dogma insisted that Mary was *virgo intacta*. "Clean maiden that she is/And with man never did amiss," runs a couplet in a mystery play of the period.

This is the official side, recorded in religious writings, in church documents. We saw earlier that the Old Testament spoke, above all, to a propertied class, to the masters, men who had bondservants and possessions. And yet, it was noted in Chapter 29, scholars believe that until the Babylonian exile the Jews engaged in local cults, worshiped the fertility gods of their neighbors, and practiced sacred prostitution, as evidenced by archaeological discoveries and by the constant condemnations in the Bible. In the same way, the fact that priests are condemning the poisons of sterility, unnatural practices and positions, harlotry and fornication throughout the Church's history indicates that they never succeeded in stamping out these practices. Fornication was considered less sinful than practicing unnatural methods of coitus in marriage: in principle contraception equaled murder so that in the sixteenth century Pope Sixtus V decreed the same penalties for both acts.[15] The realities, however, differed from the written ideal, the practices from the *pronunciamenti*.

In similar wise, a constant duality existed between the antimaterialism of Christian philosophy and the materialist power of worldly authority, papacy and monarchies. Like most successful religions the new faith was elastic enough to permit of varying interpretations and to be adapted by many power structures for their own uses. What was constant was the sexually repressive, sadomasochistic underpinning, with religious devotion offered as an outlet. The identification with Christ's suffering on the cross and with Mary's loss of her beloved son, the otherworldly rewards in the New Testament, promised in exchange for the pains of this one, had—have—a universal appeal, given the oppressive syndromes that characterize the war civilizations.

The people themselves never really accepted official doctrine. Though the Church—official Catholicism—was male-run and misogynist at its center, the clerics could not stamp out certain pro-woman tendencies in popular worship. Women, in particular, identified with the Virgin as a suffering mother and addressed special prayers to her. Moreover, one of the strengths of Catholicism—like Roman religion before it—has been its ability to accommodate to diverse tendencies among the various peoples it proselytizes and to follow as well as to lead, enabling it to merge with or absorb local religions like those of Bahia in Brazil and various African meldings. In southern Europe, particularly in Italy, paganism was integrated into the Church by way of the institution of sainthood. On a regional level, local miracles and saints could be comfortably assimilated. Temples to the Great Mother, as at Paestum, could incorporate churches for Our Lady, and towns and shrines dedicated to Venus were renamed in honor of "St. Venus." The Feast of the Assumption, a special day to celebrate the taking up of the Virgin Mary into heaven, originated in the East and came to Rome through Byzantine influence. It was universally celebrated by the end of the Middle Ages, though only in 1950 did Pius XII declare that the doctrine was "revealed."

To those who had no privilege over their own bodies, women who must obey fathers and husbands, slaves who must obey masters, Christianity did offer the dual ideal of celibacy and chastity.

For women, celibacy was a fairly new concept. Under the Hebrews women and men could vow themselves to God for brief periods of time. In Sumerian religion a few upper-class women were priestesses and hierodules dedicated to chastity during their reproductive years only, or to the once yearly intercourse of the sacred marriage rite. The vestal virgins of Rome were twelve women from noble families who tended a sacred flame and on whose abstention from sex Roman honor and prosperity depended. In both Rome and Sumer these were positions open only to a few women from aristocratic strata, and the obligation ended at menopause. In the cult of Isis and in other mystery religions of the period just before and after Christ's birth women—and men—of all classes might vow celibacy for shorter or longer periods, occasionally even for life.

Christianity, however, recognized and encouraged lifelong celibacy—for men and for women—although the latter were always subject to the former.

In actual practice, however, celibacy, as well as voluntary chastity, even monogamy, tended to be luxuries available above all to the propertied classes, and within them to men more than to women. Daughters were subject to fathers and often could not enter convents without dowry payments. In slave society also control over one's own body had been reserved for middle- and upper-class males. The great underclasses of the past are little recorded, be they slaves or bondspeople, serfs or peasants.

The woman slave was at the disposition of her master, and the man slave had to satisfy himself with the leavings. When Odysseus returned to Ithaca, he was more concerned with the damage Penelope's suitors had wrought on his house than he was with the rape of the maids. Where property considerations were not involved, provisions for marriage were often sketchy; the records of marriage contracts tell about the customs of the upper classes, those who were disposing of property along with women. Imaginative Greek and Roman studies today can sometimes infer, from lists and dates and gravestones, bare statistics of birth, death, occupation, and number of children of slaves, even their marriages. Of their feelings we know less. Similarly, in the sparsely documented medieval era, scholars today examine church records, notarial archives when they first appear, available tax rolls, and estate censuses.

Like the slave, the serf was lucky to be able to have a wife. In feudal times it was unlikely that he could worry about whether his wife was virgin or not, especially since the *droit du seigneur* gave the lord of the estate sexual privileges over the women serfs as previously the Hebrew, Greek, or Roman slaveowner had enjoyed sexual rights over his or, among the Romans and then rarely, her human possessions.

Sexual deprivation was the rule, not the exception, for many members of the war society that characterized Christian Europe. Serfs were disposed of by their lords; soldiers might be away from home for months or years. The feminist scholar

Heath Dillard has deduced that in one area of Europe, northern Christian Spain, throughout the Middle Ages marriages lasted on the average ten years, and that half the combined population and over 60 per cent of the men never married.[16] Men died in war, women in childbirth, made much less safe by enforced breeding; both died of disease and malnutrition.

In two Spanish towns studied by Dillard, rape and adultery were the subject of severe and complex legislation. Of all the crimes a woman could commit, interracial—that is, interfaith—sexual intercourse was the most harshly punished. It was not an offense for a Christian man to sleep with a Moslem or a Jewish woman, but Christian women who slept with Moslems or Jews were sullied by the contact and the whole Christian community was disgraced thereby. In line with my earlier comment about male sex as conquest, intercourse between Christian men and Jewish and Moslem women was justified as an insult to inferiors and a demonstration of Christian prowess. Sexual conquest of Jewish and Moslem women was thus a legitimate form of aggression, an expression of Christian superiority. It was legal to strike the shameless woman (*muger mala*) who insulted or verbally dishonored a reputable person, and if it was discovered that she had slept with two or three men she might be killed without penalty. Public prostitutes were totally without honor and could be defamed or raped with impunity.[17]

These were harsh times for Spain, but the legacy of sadism in the interconnection of war and sex, rape and prostitution reached out to affect all of European, not to say Western, mores.

At the lower levels of society, however, people could sometimes come together out of mutual need, even affection. The ideal of chastity and arranged marriages applied chiefly to the propertied classes, perhaps the upper two thirds of the population.

Comparing the family lives of rich and poor, historian Diane Hughes studied the copious notarial archives of Genoa. She examined records of notarial acts such as marriage contracts, dowry pledges, divorce proceedings and legitimizations, wills, estate inventories, and apprenticeships and guardianships, beginning in 1156 and continuing through 1400, in order to extrapolate information about the life styles of artisans and aristocrats. At this time in Genoa, particularly in the earlier period covered by her study, the artisans were chiefly humble folk, with modest holdings and little property. Artisan women's lives were often based on a working partnership with their husbands; wills show that the business was not infrequently left to the widow rather than to the male offspring. Such was not the case with aristocratic women. Property considerations were primary in their marriage arrangements, and when husbands died, the property would be left to sons or peripheral male relatives, and widows often returned to their natal families.[18]

Affection was also more likely to develop between children and mothers in poorer families, where children were nursed by their mothers, often for several years, and infancy was spent in the home. The aristocratic custom of sending children away to nurse at the breast of a countrywoman seems to have been common not only in upper-class Florence and Genoa but in several other parts of Europe.[19]

Among the lower classes the actuality of life asserted its own pressures. Society sets up a theoretical norm, but the practice is influenced both by the exigencies of everyday life and by the refusal of humans to fit themselves into the abstractions society tries to impose. Similarly we saw in Chapter 1 that the complexities of the Australian horde system of marriage, which so intrigued anthropologists Radcliffe-Brown and Lévi-Strauss, were found by later field anthropologists to be observed largely in the breach. When they did a statistical rundown of actual marriage arrangements there was very little correspondence with the postulated rules, just as few Western people observe the Ten Commandments religiously in their daily living. In the same way, human beings contrived to evade the excessive rigidities of Christian morality erected on the basis of Roman law. In Genoese documents, the mamma, the affection name for the woman with whom a small child might spend anywhere from one to four years, was often mentioned in a will; bequests of money, property, or a treasured article were made to their wetnurses by both women and men.

Prolonged nursing—up to four years—continued into the early twentieth century among peasant and lower-middle-class households of Europe, serving also as a partial birth-control measure, thus enabling poor European women to approximate the normal birth interval of nonliterate foraging peoples mentioned earlier.

When the custom of putting aristocratic children out to nurse was discarded and poor women were brought into the home to breastfeed the offspring of the well-to-do is not clear from the records. Whether children were sent away or wet-nurses brought into the home, the fact that wealthy women did not nurse their own children meant that they often became pregnant again almost immediately after giving birth. Forced breeding resulted from the combining of Christian morality and normal human sexual desire.

In fourteenth-century England a confessor writing to his bishop explained that among his flock the men fornicated because they could not afford to set up homes and to have children.[20] It is probable that some form of birth control was practiced by these couples; coitus interruptus or abortion, self- or midwife-administered, would have been the most effective and accessible means.

Poor women could—and often did—take the fullest advantage of the partial protection offered by lactation; well-to-do women were deprived not only of this safeguard, available to the poor, but also of the sensual pleasures involved in breast stimulation and mother-child contact. These gratifications were all the more important in women's sensual and affective lives, given the shambles the Church had made of sexuality between adults.

The idealization of the seemingly innocent joys of nursing—of mother love—in the Madonna image and in the worship of Mary offered women a guilt-free outlet, though their pent-up passion might well prove suffocating to the children. The boy, in particular, was likely to be laden with all his mother's starved sexuality since society valued males more than females, and the projection of the woman's feelings about herself might well work to the detriment of the mother-daughter relationship. In addition, a mother's biological pull toward the opposite sex was more easily transferred to the infant male. The idealization of the Madonna and the infant Jesus incorporates characteristics from many of the pagan mother-son cults referred to in earlier chapters.

The religious life did offer some refuge from a martyrdom of incessant pregnancies, to the more prosperous classes particularly. It was one way to avoid being literally bred to death. The grandmother of the famous French letter writer Madame de Sévigné had entered a convent after her husband's death, abandoning her four young children to the care of others. Sévigné herself, widowed at twenty-six, with two children, prudently refused to remarry. She lived her full complement of threescore and ten years—hale and hearty and productive—dying at seventy and then as a result of a fever caught nursing her daughter through one of her innumerable illnesses. Françoise-Marguerite, the beloved child to whom most of the letters were addressed, survived her mother by only seven years, her health ruined, her beauty destroyed by numerous pregnancies, many of which miscarried. She had been a great beauty, but when she died, she must have been much reduced. The letters frequently refer to her lamentable situation. Sévigné was criticized for her coldness, but, once safely widowed, she seems rather to have decided to spare herself the kind of martyrdom that was to be inflicted on her daughter.

The Comte de Grignan married Françoise-Marguerite de Sévigné in 1669; she was twenty-two and he was forty-one. By 1670 she had already had one miscarriage, and a daughter, Marie-Blanche, was born in November of that year. (Marie-Blanche entered a convent young and survived until 1745—the longest lived of the Sévigné-Grignan progeny.) A son was born in 1671, and another daughter, Pauline, adored by her grandmother, in 1674. Between and after the successful pregnancies there were many miscarriages, as well as poor wizened infants who did not survive their first year. Throughout this period Madame de Sévigné frequently refers to Françoise-Marguerite's ill health and to the disfigurements suffered by her beauty. Her letter of March 4, 1676, is written a week after she has congratulated the countess on being safely over her lying-in:

I am addressing myself to you, dear Count, for you are reported to have said that my daughter's confinements were the models of what confinements should be, and the oftener she does it the better. Dear God! She never does anything else. I must, however, warn you that unless you call a halt to this business out of common humanity, and if this poor machine is never allowed a pause, you will destroy it utterly, which would be regrettable. I am putting this to you for your serious consideration—the subject can scarcely be called hilarious.[21]

In 1678 she refers to "my daughter's weakness and emaciation . . . the loss of weight is due to the condition of her lungs . . . if this should continue she is not long for this life . . ."[22]

The Comte de Grignan had already killed off two wives before he inflicted those incessant pregnancies on Françoise-Marguerite. Later centuries deduced that the cause of this havoc was syphilis. The count is believed to have infected Françoise-Marguerite and the children, which accounts for the many illnesses and frailty of the son, who survived only into his twenties, for the beloved Pauline's "blemishes," which so greatly troubled her grandmother, and for all those miscarriages and infant deaths.

In England, Ann Fanshawe bore twenty-one children in the twenty-three years and twenty-nine days during which her marriage lasted. Her childbearing career was brought to a close only by the death of her husband in 1666, and she survived to write an autobiography that describes her many activities as well as the births, deaths, and burial places of her children, only five of whom outlived their mother.[23]

The custom of forced breeding was continued, not to say exaggerated, by later centuries. The composer Pleyel, founder of the still existent French piano-manufacturing establishment, was one of forty-some children of his father, though history does not tell us on how many wives these infants were wrought. Enrico Caruso was the fifteenth child of his mother, the first to survive.

33

Women Have Always Worked

The arrival of Protestantism, with the Reformation, did little to ameliorate the situation of women and the expression of sexuality between adults. The single authority of God was stressed, replacing the papal hierarchy. There was a renewed focus on the Old Testament, strengthening the master-ruler father-god image. As the ruler was God's earthly representative on earth, so the father of the family represented supreme authority in the home. Individual autocracy was strengthened. The king ruled his country in the name of God; the father repeated the pattern in a smaller scale. In Wilhelm Reich's words, "The authoritarian state had its representative in every family, in the figure of the father, and the family became the most important instrument of power."[1]

Like the Hebrews before them, Protestants dispensed with the female image in religion, minimizing the importance of Mary and, in most cases, eliminating the saints. Obedience to males was further stressed. Moreover, many Protestant sects rebelled against the ritual and aesthetic splendor of Catholicism, leaving their practicants free to focus on materialist aims —the business of making money in the world. Protestants often rejected the golden visions of a future life implicit in

Catholic mythology, as well as the theatrical, artistic element in Catholicism which, even if translated into material terms, did allow for a certain expression of sublimated sexuality.

In England, for example, pagan festivals had slipped into the official Church, with church-ales, periodic drinking fests and gatherings held in connection with church festivities—"when the sweet bagpipe doth draw forth the damsels to frisque about the maypoles." Even before Puritan times, English Protestantism legislated against this kind of spontaneous expression: in 1572 the Elizabethan canons ordered that "the church wardens shall suffer no plays, feasts, banquets, suppers, church-ales, drinkings to be kept in the church."[2]

The celebration of the First of May with the dance around the Maypole is, of course, a relic of pagan fertility rites. The orgiastic rollick around the phallic pole is an agricultural society's adaptation of the more universal periods of promiscuity characteristic of human beings both before and after the adoption of agriculture and animal breeding.

Despite the seventeenth century's prohibitions against church-ales, in 1743 they still exist, but are described as occasions "when people go from afternoon prayers on Sundays to . . . some publick house where they drink and be merry."[3] One wonders whether, at this time, the people include the "damsels" of earlier centuries.

Beginning about 1500, the father's authority was strengthened, and his power over both wife and children increased. Lawrence Stone has found overwhelming evidence of the change in parent-child relationships and of attitudes whereby children were seen as little animals whose will must be broken and who must be kept in total subjection to the authority of elders and superiors—primarily the parents, father first, then mother. More interest was taken in the rearing and education of children, but the process was considered similar to that of breaking in a horse or training a hunting dog.

Even in the Middle Ages, education—consisting chiefly of the learning of Latin—had been a forced process. The schoolmaster's equipment was a rod or a bundle of birch twigs rather than a book. However, very few children received these benefits, whereas, by the late fifteenth century, more children of all classes were being taught to read and write. In the beginning of the sixteenth century, flogging became routine punishment for schoolchildren regardless of rank or age. Severe physical punishment was used in the home, the school, and the university. Whipping was so common that when, in 1671, a didactic clergyman wished to characterize hell to young people, he described it as "a terrible place, that is worse a thousand times than whipping. God's anger is worse than your father's anger."[4]

This institutionalization of sadism and cruelty and violence meant that the children who had been maltreated themselves internalized the maltreatment and later passed it on to those over whom they had power, creating that chain of oppression earlier referred to, in which the wife and the children of the brutalized male become the victims of the victim, the phenomenon which we today call battered wives and children. In the sixteenth century both wife-beating and child-beating seem to have been accepted practices.[5]

To these trends in family relationship should be added the weight of guilt felt by children whose mothers bore child after child at the cost of health and life. Sévigné describes the death of the Dauphine after childbirth: "She blessed her little ones, adding, 'I bless you as well, my little Berry, although you are the cause of my death.' "[6] Similarly, an orphan of my acquaintance who was asked when his mother died answered, "I killed her. I mean she died borning me." In adulthood, this guilt and its consequent shame are often transformed into brutality and incorporated into the sick, sadomasochistic heritage of civilized heterosexual relationship.

We saw earlier that the dictum "No lady moves" was prefigured in Talmudic and Roman sources. An aspect of civilized Europe's attempts to deny women's active sexuality is the belief that movement or enjoyment by women in sex will always have a negative effect, whatever the desired end. If she wants to conceive, Musitanius, writing on the diseases of women in 1709, advises:

Passionate coitus is to be avoided, for it is unfruitful. Sometimes the woman does not draw back her buttocks, and conquers, as is the custom of Spanish women, who move their whole body while they have intercourse, from an excess of voluptuousness (they are extraordinarily passionate), and perform the Phrygian dance, and some of them passionately sing a song, which in Spanish is called Chaccara, and on account of this Spanish women are sterile.[7]

On the other hand several folk traditions decree that if a woman wishes to avoid pregnancy, lying still and holding the breath during intercourse will prevent conception.[8]

The full weight of Christian sexual repression and European materialism was probably felt less in the lower levels of society, though the prohibitions filtered down in somewhat attenuated form.

The custom of living together without benefit of marriage was common among the very poor—perhaps the lower third of society—from the time of the Middle Ages and the introduction of Christianity. It continued in many parts of Europe, enduring at the bottom of the social scale into the comparative present.* Just as the exigencies of life did not always permit of the legitimization of marriage, so the ideal of parental power and premarital chastity was not always enforceable under the disorganized conditions of poverty. When there was no money or land to leave, no professional preferment to use as a club, it was more difficult to exercise authority over children. "We poor men must marry where we love," Mozart wrote to his father in the eighteenth century, explaining his marriage to the penniless Constanze Weber.

These same poor men brought—bring—their damaged psyches and the internalization of society's double standard

---

* In Partinico, Sicily, in the early nineteen sixties, young couples who could not afford the *corredo*—trousseau and housekeeping equipment—that local mores required as a prerequisite to marriage would elope, run away, and then return and live together unmarried for years, producing children and raising a family, always planning to be married in church when circumstances permitted.

into their relations with the opposite sex. It is more difficult to trace the harm done to women, since their responses and reactions are for the most part reported by male sources, strained through male eyes, and Church and state assume they are passive in love, the respondents to importunate male needs, despite or perhaps because of the Christian contradiction which makes them all body and no body.

Before industrialization, on the lower levels of society—among the peasants and laborers—all members of the family contributed work to eke out their meager subsistence. New opportunities arose with the spread of technology, but women often continued their traditional pursuits under different circumstances. The occupations named in Chapter 28 as open to women in classical Greece—the manufacture of textiles and clothing, the service trades of laundry and food preparation, the fabrication and sale of items of ornament—were still filled largely by women, sometimes translated into factory labor or piecework done at home. They were always ill paid, and if the woman lived at home or kept contact with her natal family, she was expected to contribute the major portion of her earnings to the common funds to help support the household.

By the eighteenth and nineteenth centuries, poor families were in movement, and there was less stability and less control of young people. The old tradition of living together before marriage was brought with them by young girls who went to cities to work—in service or in the new factories.[9]

When women left their families to earn money, emigrating from country protection to city anonymity, opportunities and pressure to engage in "illicit" sex increased, but there was no family or community support to assist the young woman in gaining the protection of the legal ceremony. Servants were victimized as they had been throughout history, but by the nineteenth century, with the growing middle class, there were more of them, and they were more likely to be cast adrift, seduced and impregnated by the sons of the house, fired for immorality by the elders. Working-class women who took up with men of their own class, thinking that the liaison would, as in earlier times, be a stable one, with or without marriage, often found themselves abandoned by their lovers, unable or unwilling to maintain their promises.[10]

The contradiction between Judeo-Christian moral attitudes and Western materialist ones carried less weight among the very poor. The only commodity the poor man had to sell was his labor, while the poor woman had two, her labor and her sexual services. Prostitution was always an alternative, a corollary of women's inferior economic opportunity. Female sexuality had more market value than other skills or labor. Women prostituted themselves to feed their families and to feed themselves. Asked if she let men fuck her for sausage rolls, one young girl replied, "Yes, meat pies and pastry, too."[11]

One way or another sexuality was sold or bartered for property, in arranged marriages and on the open market.

In nineteenth-century England it was felt that women's employment in the new industrial system, as instanced by fourteen-hour days in cotton mills and dragging coal cars underground in mines, disturbed the order of nature, and reform commissions took up their cause, with the idea of keeping women in the home. But the majority of women had always worked alongside men. That they were so ill paid made prostitution attractive, for as long as their physical attributes endured. Among the poorest classes chastity hardly existed after the age of fourteen. Social attitudes deprived women of their own physical expression, whether among the respectable middle- and upper-class women who were, by Victorian days, considered to be without sexual feelings or among the lower-class women who were believed to be all body and made contemptible thereby. In the eyes of the women who practiced it, prostitution was a legitimate road away from poverty and exploitation.[12]

In the nineteenth century lower-class women crossed over the line from respectability and back again fairly easily, particularly in the anonymity of cities. The popular idea that "the harlot's progress is short and rapid, and that there is no possible advance moral and physical and once abandoned she must always be profligate" was contradicted by the researches of Henry Mayhew and William Acton.[13] Women grew old in prostitution and, according to Acton, himself a practicing physician, they were rather more healthy than their socially approved sisters, who slaved fourteen hours a day in the factory and bore endless children. Mayhew's and Acton's writings show that for the poor there was no sharp distinction between respectable society and the "depraved underground." There were women who prostituted themselves on occasion or in addition to other work, merging inconspicuously with the respectable poor. Prostitution was often a stage in a woman's life or a part-time profession with which she added to her bare earnings as a shopgirl, a factory worker, a housemaid, or a needlewoman. In Acton's words, "poverty, evil training, and seduction" drove women into prostitution; its consequences forced them to resort to infanticide, baby-farming, and abortion.

The ambivalence of attitudes about women's sexual expression and the peculiar contradictions which have made the most transcendent physical act into a commodity continue into the present. Prostitution of women and young men is presumably based on the principle that women do not need sex enough to pay for it on the market and that men need it so much they are willing to buy it. It is also premised on the idea that sex is a service unilaterally offered by the female or by males playing a female role and bought by the male rather than a participatory process involving two human beings. On the one hand prostitutes are despised as the lowest rung on the social ladder, as they were back in Sumerian days. On the other, hustling has become the master metaphor of our materialist society where we are all measured for sale in business, profession, even marriage, and tempted to treat ourselves as commodities in a vertical climb for advancement. Hustle is used variously to mean straight prostitution, pimping, hurrying, selling oneself, pulling off a confidence trick, or using devious methods and charm to gain one's end.

Only in our own century have we finally begun to shape new concepts about women's and men's sexual rights. The result is the ferment and confusion in which we now find ourselves, with five thousand years of the materialization of sex hanging over us. We may doubt whether civilization has entailed progress over the so-called savage state in several abstract senses. But any woman who looks back to her grandmother and great-grandmother cannot doubt that within Western society some advances have been made, imperfect as they may seem. The more we penetrate the past roots of oppression, and its result-ant superstructure, the more we shall be able to build toward a future of true human intercourse.

Epilogue and Prologue:

The Machine Stops

. . . I accept the Universe.
—Margaret Fuller

. . . she'd better.
—Thomas Carlyle

In the course of writing this book, I suddenly understood the meaning of the myth of Medusa. To look into her face was to be turned to stone. When Perseus cut off the gorgon's head, Pegasus, the winged horse of poetry, leaped upward out of the blood spurting from her neck. And as a particularly exciting thought hit me, I realized that Medusa was reality, and I felt the terror of single awareness. Similarly, to face the position of women over the last several thousand years can be paralyzing. Only in art, and then infrequently, have poets been able to approach its awesome injustice.

Even though she gave in eventually, Margaret Fuller was right to question the universe. Almost a century later Ellen Glasgow wrote that she had never been able to accept the universe. Her novels were her answer to the givens with which she was confronted.

In the late nineteen sixties and early nineteen seventies women came together in the new feminist movement. We shared our insights and realized that we are right not to accept the universe, at least as it has been presented to us by male authority, in terms corrupted by a greed-based civilization. Shored up by our sisters, we were able to face the extent of our disadvantaging, to see the metaphors based on mistaken biology, to strain out some of the assumptions that masquerade as science. Our intellectual world was full of misnomers and mis-analogies which have shaped poetry, philosophy, thought itself. The tool of thought, language, was suspect, based on premises of aggression and false dichotomies, so that a serious and useful agricultural scientist could say that scientists seek power over nature as politicians seek power over men when in truth science must seek penetration and understanding of, collaboration with the forces of the natural world to which we humans belong, rather than domination over them.[1] The great dichotomizing tradition of Western civilization begins with the supposed passivity of the female, with woman as earth and man as vitalizer. From thence come the others: dominance-submission, body-spirit, mind-body, etc.

History and writing emerge with the reification of people and of sex, with vertical relations. In the state it was the king who ruled subjects, the subjects who ruled slaves; in the family, the father who ruled wives and children. Five thousand years of the substitution of acquisition for feeling and of the glorification of aggression have entered our very marrow. The most beautiful form of communion is described in smirched and derogatory terms and used as an execration: so-and-so is a slimy fuck, a cunt; he screwed me; she sucks.

That initial impetus fell apart. We've gone off, some into oblivion or survival enclaves, others into well-paid niches, which may make their explorations less compelling. Many just got tired. For one thing, the times did not immediately improve. The parousia has not arrived; on the contrary.

Feminism has survived and entered the mainstream of American culture, but no longer is there any implication of sweeping political or societal changes; reformism is the order of the day. There were always many strains in the movement, and in a competitive, materialist world it is not surprising that more and more women are attracted to the idea of grabbing power for themselves. If the choice is between being pushed around and pushing other people around, one would prefer to be the pusher not the pushee. During the nineteen seventies, as political change became ever more illusory, more and more women settled for the individual line of self-advancement.

Statistically, the new feminism of the late sixties and early seventies did not change the economic situation of women. There are a few more women in high places. Some professional barriers have been breached. The distribution of money has become even more unequal and more concentrated in the hand of an elite than it was some thirty years ago. Income figures still reflect lowest incomes for black women, then white women, and then black men, and the proportions have improved only slightly in the last decade.[2] Many women have entered the labor force but primarily in the lower-paying jobs. They form a pool of low-paid workers, those with the least skills, and they serve rather to shore up the inequities of the system. The gap between the earnings of women and men has also increased. A report of the Labor Department published toward the end of 1976 showed that men earned 75 per cent more than women today, whereas twenty years ago the difference was 50 per cent.[3]

"Are you a feminist?" I asked a woman of my acquaintance recently.

"Who has time to be a feminist! With my job, three children, and all I have to do in the house. When I retire, I'll be a feminist." This particular woman lives in Pennsylvania and has a full-time job, her pay raised, in 1978, from $3.50 to $4.00 an hour. She has three children ranging from eleven to eighteen years in age. I have seen various estimates of the American woman's work week—those employed outside the home and those whose work entailed *only* housework, cooking, and child-raising—placing their work load as high as one hundred but never less than seventy hours a week. Compare these with the life of the Australian Aborigine woman of the Pitjandjara, described in 1933 as arduous drudgery sometimes consisting of as much as four to six hours a day—a work week of twenty-eight to forty hours.[4] Which, if either, is the liberated woman I leave to the reader to decide.

The most hopeful thing to come out of the women's movement has been the larger percentage of women in graduate schools, in medicine, in law, in disciplines of the humanities and science. The insights that were so blinding to us have been taken up by women in academia. At many levels they are turning the magnifying glass on the human story as it used to be taught, removing the male prism. On the other hand, once graduated, they are still subject to a discriminatory system. Despite the showy individuals, the new Ph.D.s and M.D.s earn less and advance more slowly than their male counterparts. And five years after the Federal government issued an order against discrimination in educational institutions, the percentages of women faculty members remain dismally low.[5]

Meanwhile the world outside has moved farther away from idealism. The uneasy balance of material acquisitiveness and aspiration toward ethical behavior has tipped decisively toward the materialist side. "If I can't take it with me, I ain't going," said a bumper sticker I saw the other day. In an exploitative society people are advised to get ahead by beating on someone else. Interpersonal relations have broken down. Everything is for sale: warmth, support, and understanding from therapists or self-help books; instant riches from state lotteries; anodynes in the form of alcohol, marijuana, tranquilizers; individual salvation in a wide range of new and old religions. The media package and sell politicians and ideas; abstract concerns are translated into purchases, as in the *Whole Earth Catalogue*, the *Jewish Catalogue*, and the Buycentennial of 1976. Feminism is no exception. Solutions are individual—up the organization (the corporate woman), self-assertion, freedom through underwear, devices for masturbation, the joys of gay sex—everything is marketable. Salesmanship is the means, power-through-possession the end by which feeling and caring are subverted. The pathology of loneliness increases. Business and personal relations are like a constant state of war.

An early slogan of the movement was, "None of us are liberated until all of us are liberated." Magazines and newspapers may talk about the new sexual freedom, describe individual women as liberated, but there are only varying degrees of personal accommodation and personal expression. Given the heritage of five thousand years of treating sex as a power relationship, with male sex as aggression and female as submission, it is not surprising that the new relaxation of attitudes brought with it more libertinism than liberation. Ever increasing numbness is countered by sensation and violence in the popular arts. The sexual revolution has meant money in the pocket for entrepreneurs.

The whore issue is still very much with us. That prostitution exists, despite the relaxation of attitudes, shows that it is still a power symbol. "The enslavement of women lies simply in the fact that people desire, and think it good to avail themselves of her as a tool of enjoyment." Thus Tolstoy in the eighteen-sixties.[6] Where men used to take women, now women are being instructed to do the same with men. Fortunately not many of them can. Most of the women who answered *The Hite Report* questionnaire felt that the sexual revolution is a myth.[7] It has left them free to say yes but not to say no. The double standard is still with us. The quantity of sex has gone up; the quality has not. We are encouraged to use each other as masturbatory devices; the new emphasis on sexual prowess further dehumanizes physical intimacies.

It was Reich who introduced the revolutionary yet obvious concept that not all orgasms are alike, that some sex is better than others. Today, when orgasm for women is recognized as a desirable end, few of us acknowledge that orgasm has a wide variation, for women and for men. (Ejaculation is not synonymous with orgasm.) In line with our other materialist attitudes, we go by the numbers instead of by the depth of the experience. In the past and for much of Western history, it would seem that deep and gratifying sex was not of common occurrence.

In a period where women are granted more expression, sexual acts still retain the aura of conquest and violence; rape increases; hustling is omnipresent as image and reality.

On a very different scale the social breakdown can be translated into economic dilemma. At the very moment we reach an apogee of materialism, the profit motive is becoming untenable. It was like a vast chain letter, promising things that were taken from other people; it cannot be indefinitely extended. Space may be infinite—there are questions about this—but our planet is finite. The profit motive could function on conquest and expansion till we reached the limits of earth and of material resources. We are close to these limits now. The debate about whether human ingenuity and imagination in the form of technology will be outrun by human greed will be resolved by the events of the next thirty or forty years.

The principles of sharing and caring are our only hope, in the large sense as well as in the small, in the relations between individuals, as in the relations between nations. Autocratic control increases internationally, and live or die becomes a world alternative. Reports from Chile, from Argentina, from Iran, to mention only a few, show how sadistic tactics are used to control people against their will.

Socialist claims that woman's subjection to man is a function of capitalism and that destruction of the class system under socialism would solve problems of male-female inequality have not been validated by existing socialist states. In the two largest, the Soviet Union has a class system based on a bureaucratic elite, and as of 1978 China was moving in that direction. In both states, women have come nowhere near achieving parity in political and economic institutions and still do double work, in the home and outside. There are no indications that they have gained sexual equality, nor signs pointing toward positive change in the near future.

In 1964 Mao Tse-tung told André Malraux that the Chinese Communists were the first group in China to address themselves to women, to the young, and to the peasants and that in consequence every one of them felt involved. Since his death Maoism has been largely abandoned; a return to earlier Chinese hierarchical attitudes is reported. In the country, arranged marriages and wife selling still exist.[8] In the cities, late marriage, sexual abstinence, and hard work had been the Maoist solution to the ages-old degradation of women in

China. Even if temporarily effective, no permanent restructuring of society can be achieved by this kind of imposition from above. As with early Christian ideals, new forms of repressive sadism will emerge. Puritanism and asceticism inevitably lead back to dominance and control and materialism again. Sex cannot be repressed and eliminated; it finds outlets, usually destructive. It must be incorporated. The answer is to integrate. Only when the power nexus is removed, when the whore issue disappears from attitudes and language, can we hope for an approximation of equality between the sexes. An approach must be made toward seeing sexual meetings as equally body and mind-spirit, toward valuing active female and male sexuality, toward achieving a holistic philosophy.

I have tried to shed some light on the sexual roots of sadism and the desire for dominance which spread throughout the world beginning at a given moment not too long ago in human existence. Solutions must be multilevel, but there will be no solutions, only increasing hierarchy and lack of freedom if we do not get at the causes, the oppressive principle growing out of the relation between man and woman which has mushroomed to be the greatest danger to the world's survival. As I see it, the dominance hierarchy is the underlying problem.

We cannot go backward; we must start from where we are. And where we are could be the beginning; we may be in the infancy of civilization. There is, for example, uncultivated land which can be developed to feed the hungry people in Asia, Africa, and Latin America. On the bases of wasteful aims, we have created complex technologies. How much further we could go if instead of power domination, with its pump-priming of war and armaments, we could achieve co-operative forms of social encounter! If even a portion of the almost 300 billion dollars the world spends annually on armaments were diverted into agricultural and educational improvements for the earth's four billion inhabitants, food could be produced, suffering relieved, relations between people and nations transformed.

It may take a quantum leap. What we are working for is the time when out of a sufficiency of material things—as once out of a minimal amount—sharing and living, doing rather than accumulating, will once again become modes of behavior. Then the process, not the end; the journey, not the arrival; the experience, not the possessing will be paramount.

If we consider that our species existed for some two hundred thousand years without imposing burdens on a subject class, and that the phenomena discussed in these pages have existed only for a little over five thousand years, during which survival has been rocky and imperfect, it is clear that the stages traced in Parts IV, V, and VI were not inevitable in form. At the moment, it looks as if even the liberality of the evolutionary process has been stretched. Not only were the divisions into caste and class, by sex and occupation, respectively, unnecessary ones —they were antiproductive and the catastrophic results are upon us. Imminent destruction threatens from several sides— nuclear explosion, pollution, expanding population, et al. Patriarchy had a long run for its money. Human ingenuity devised all kinds of compensations for its seemingly intolerable customs, but the point of no return is close. Apocalypse or change are our only alternatives. Given the long prehistory of our species, I imagine the second will prevail.

In the nineteenth and early twentieth centuries, most writers assumed that the stages of human social development— whether the horde of Darwin, Spencer, and Freud or forms of matriarchy postulated by Bachofen, Engels, Briffault, Neumann, etc.—were predetermined and a progression from a lower to a higher state. In our twentieth-century sophistication, and with the help of comparative ethnography, we know these were not inevitable stages. Social developments were a combination of happenstance, and of vectors of environment and psychology. They were unnecessarily cruel. If our sexual and social evolution had happened along other lines—and limited cases exist, refuge areas in the face of hostile odds, where some material advance and, above all, survival were accomplished in opposition to the prevailing trend toward hierarchy—it would have been quicker, easier, more productive. One problem, however, is the self-perpetuating nature of aggression and conquest, the killing off, subjection, or conversion to dominance-submission ideology of the gentler peoples when they are exposed to the hierarchically organized dominators. There is hope for humanity, however, if we acknowledge that patriarchy, sadism, and fighting are not inherent in the nature of either civilization or the species.

We have had five thousand years of war and hierarchy; ten thousand years of anxiety leading to sadomasochism, dominance-submission, and power through possession; and, on a conservative estimate, two hundred thousand years of being a sharing and friendly species. The prognosis is not an easy one. We must change characters and change society. Multilevel goals—inner and outer, objective and subjective—are involved. But the possibilities exist, within ourselves in our brains, our nervous systems, and our genes, and outside, in the planet's resources. I have hope of human survival and amelioration given our spread under such inimical circumstances as were created by the first civilizations. Both direct voice and social pathology indicate increasing awareness of the dead ends that face us if we continue on our doomsday path. The incentive for change is there, and adaptation has been the hallmark of the human genus throughout its several-million-year existence.

Nothing ever ends: the end is the beginning.

Source Notes

CHAPTER 1 SCIENCE IMITATES SOCIETY

1. Schlegel, *Male Dominance and Female Autonomy*, p. 21.
2. See Briffault, *The Mothers*; Campbell, *The Masks of God*; Graves, *The White Goddess*; Neumann, *The Great Mother* and *The Origins and History of Consciousness*; others influenced by Jungian concepts.
3. See Davis, *The First Sex*; Diner, *Mothers and Amazons*; et al.
4. Wickler, "Socio-sexual Signals and Their Intra-Specific Imitation among Primates," in Morris (ed.), *Primate Ethology*, p. 109.
5. Goodall, "A Preliminary Report on Expressive Movements," in Jay (ed.), *Primates*, pp. 351–52; Jay, "The Common Langur of North India," in DeVore (ed.), *Primate Behavior*, p. 226.
6. Lévi-Strauss, *The Elementary Structures of Kinship*.
7. Cf. L. R. Hiatt, "Gidjingali Marriage Arrangements," M. J. Meggitt, "Marriage Classes," A. Yengoyan, "Demographic and Ecological Influences," F. Rose, "Australian Marriage," in Lee and DeVore (eds.), *Man the Hunter*, pp. 165–208.
8. Rose, op. cit., p. 205.
9. Meggitt and Yengoyan, op. cit., pp. 171, 187–88; see also Goodale, *Tiwi Wives*; Kaberry, *Aboriginal Woman*.

CHAPTER 2 THE IDEA OF DOMINANCE

1. Jay, "The Common Langur of North India," in DeVore (ed.), *Primate Behavior*, p. 221.
2. K. Yoshiba, "Local and Intertroop Variability," in Jay (ed.), *Primates*, p. 228.
3. Imanishi, "Social Behavior in Japanese Monkeys," in Southwick (ed.), *Primate Social Behavior*, p. 77.
4. Cited in Kolata, "Primate Behavior," p. 55.
5. Darwin, *The Descent of Man*, p. 225.

6. Lorenz, *On Aggression,* p. 271.

7. J. P. Scott, "Agonistic Behavior of Mice and Rats," in Southwick (ed.), *Animal Aggression,* p. 110.

8. Kolata, op. cit., p. 55.

9. Carpenter, "The Howler Monkeys of Barro Colorado," in DeVore, op. cit.

10. S. Eisele, quoted in Hahn, *On the Side of the Apes,* p. 82.

11. Tiger and Fox, *The Imperial Animal,* p. 31; Hall, "Behavior and Ecology," in Jay (ed.), op. cit., p. 83.

12. Goodall, *My Friends the Wild Chimpanzees,* p. 21; Goodall, "Chimpanzees of the Gombe Stream Reserve," in DeVore (ed.), op. cit., pp. 425–73; Goodall, "A Preliminary Report on Expressive Movements," in Jay, op. cit., pp. 313–14; Goodall, "Mother-Offspring Relationships," in Morris, op. cit., p. 325.

13. William Greulich's experiment has been reported widely: see Judy Fireman (ed.), *Cat Catalog* (New York: Workman Publishing Co., 1976), p. 173, for a recent account.

14. Morris, *The Naked Ape,* pp. 78–79.

15. See Chevalier-Skolnikoff, "Male-Female, Female-Female, and Male-Male Sexual Behavior," for comprehensive data on laboratory observations of orgasms in female monkeys.

16. Herschberger, *Adam's Rib,* pp. 11, 201.

17. Weisstein, "Psychology Constructs the Female," in Gornick and Moran (eds.), *Woman in Sexist Society,* pp. 138–39.

CHAPTER 3   OUR PRIMATE RELATIVES

1. The Gombe Stream Research Center in the Gombe Stream Reserve, Tanzania, was closed in 1975 because of local terrorist action and reopened in 1977 (see *New York Times,* May 22, 1975, and Oct. 15, 1977).

2. Goodall, *My Friends the Wild Chimpanzees;* Goodall, "Chimpanzees of the Gombe Stream Reserve," in DeVore (ed.), *Primate Behavior,* p. 429.

3. V. and F. Reynolds, "Chimpanzees of the Budongo Forest," in DeVore, op. cit., pp. 415–16.

4. Pilbeam, "An Idea We Could Live Without," p. 68.

5. *New York Times,* May 7, 1975.

6. Goodall, *My Friends the Wild Chimpanzees.*

7. Goodall, "Mother-Offspring Relationship," in Morris (ed.), *Primate Ethology,* pp. 287–337.

8. V. Reynolds, *The Apes,* pp. 270–74.

9. Engels, *The Origin of the Family, Private Property and the State*, p. 44.
10. Briffault, *The Mothers*, Vol. 1, pp. 119–20.
11. Schaller, *The Mountain Gorilla*, pp. 283–84.
12. Tanner and Zihlman, "Women in Evolution," p. 594.
13. Fossey, "More Years with Mountain Gorillas," p. 580.
14. Zuckerman, *The Social Life of Monkeys and Apes*, (London: K. Paul, Trench, Trubner, 1932), pp. 233–34.
15. Hall and DeVore, "Baboon Social Behavior," in DeVore, op. cit., pp. 71–72.
16. DeVore and Washburn, "The Study of Primate Behavior," in DeVore, op. cit., pp. 1–13.
17. Eaton, "The Social Order of Japanese Macaques," pp. 97–106.
18. Goodall, *In the Shadow of Man*, pp. 112–15. See *New York Times*, Apr. 20, 1978, for Goodall on chimpanzee war, and *New York Times*, May 2, 1978, for Montagu's response.
19. Kropotkin, *Mutual Aid*, p. 3.
20. "Monkeys, Apes, and Man," CBS Television Network, Oct. 12, 1975.
21. Pilbeam, op. cit., pp. 66–67.
22. Hall, "Behavior and Ecology of the Wild Patas Monkey," in Jay (ed.), *Primates*, pp. 32–119.
23. J. S. Gartlan and C. K. Brain, "Ecology and Social Variability in Ceropithecus aethiops and C. mitis," in Jay, op. cit., pp. 253–92.

CHAPTER 4 AGGRESSION AND MALENESS

1. Lore and Flannelly, "Rat Societies," p. 113.
2. Moss, "A New Image for Hyenas," p. 38–45.
3. D. E. Davis, "Physiologic Factors in Aggressive Behavior," in Southwick (ed.), *Animal Aggression*, p. 148; R. Blier, "Bias in Biological and Human Sciences: Some Comments," *Signs*, Vol. 4, no. 1 (Autumn 1978), p. 160.
4. Ibid., p. 150.
5. Kolata, "Primate Behavior," p. 55.
6. Eaton, "The Social Order of Japanese Macaques"; see also Lore and Flannelly, "Rat Societies," p. 115.
7. Blier, op. cit., pp. 160–61; see also H. H. Lambert, "Biology and Equality: A Perspective on Sex Differences," *Signs*, Vol. 4, no. 1 (Autumn 1978), pp. 99–102.

CHAPTER 5   MATERNAL SEXUALITY

1. N. Newton and M. Newton, "Psychological Aspects of Lactation," p. 1180.
2. Rossi, "Maternalism, Sexuality and the New Feminism," p. 25.
3. See Imogen Howe, letter to the *New York Times Magazine*, Apr. 1, 1973, p. 69.
4. Rossi, op. cit., p. 26.
5. Ibid., p. 27.
6. Goodall, "Mother-Offspring Relationships in Free-ranging Chimpanzees," in Morris (ed.), *Primate Ethology*, p. 302.
7. Briffault, *The Mothers*, Vol. 1, p. 133.
8. Jay, "Primate Field Studies and Human Evolution," in Jay (ed.), *Primates*, p. 495.
9. Eaton, "The Social Order of Japanese Macaques"; Kolata, "Primate Behavior."
10. Pilbeam, "An Idea We Could Live Without," p. 66.
11. Horney, *Feminine Psychology*, pp. 60ff.
12. J. B. Miller, *Psychoanalysis and Women*, p. 10.

CHAPTER 6   FROM MAN THE HUNTER TO WOMAN THE GATHERER

1. W. S. Laughlin, "Hunting: An Integrating Biobehavior System and Its Evolutionary Importance," in Lee and DeVore (eds.), *Man the Hunter*, p. 304.
2. Lee, "What Hunters Do for a Living," in Lee and DeVore, op. cit., pp. 40–48.
3. Holloway, "Australopithecine Endocasts," pp. 195–200; Holloway, quoted in the *New York Times*, Sept. 26, 1975.
4. Quoted in Montagu, *Man and Aggression*, p. 5.
5. E.g., the illustration of a small male monkey evolving into a taller ape man carrying a stone dagger and then into a tall bearded muscular male with a spear that was featured in the brochure for a 1976 course on evolution at the American Museum of Natural History in New York City.
6. Cited in Balikci, "The Netsilik Eskimos: Adaptive Processes," in Lee and DeVore (eds.), op. cit., p. 81.
7. Buettner-Janusch, *Origins of Man*, pp. 359–60.
8. Pilbeam, *The Evolution of Man*, p. 33.
9. Leakey and Ardrey, "Man the Killer, a Dialogue," pp. 73–85.
10. Jolly, "The Seed-Eaters," pp. 4–24.
11. Turnbull, discussions, in Lee and DeVore, op. cit., p. 341.
12. J. D. Clark, *The Prehistory of Africa*, pp. 66–67.

13. Montagu, op. cit., pp. 9–10.
14. Chomsky, *Language and Mind*, p. 82.

CHAPTER 7 THE CARRIER BAG THEORY OF EVOLUTION

1. Laughlin, "Hunting: An Integrating Biobehavior System," in Lee and DeVore (eds.), *Man the Hunter*, pp. 304–20.
2. Lee, "What Hunters Do for a Living," in Lee and DeVore, op. cit., pp. 41–43.
3. J. D. Clark, *The Prehistory of Africa*, pp. 76–79.
4. Tanner and Zihlman, "Women in Evolution," p. 597.
5. Bryant and Williams-Dean, "The Coprolites of Man," pp. 100–10.
6. Tanner and Zihlman, op. cit., p. 600; Lancaster, "Carrying and Sharing in Human Evolution," pp. 85–87.
7. Cf. J. D. Clark, op. cit.; Lancaster, *Primate Behavior and the Emergence of Human Culture*; Slocum, "Woman the Gatherer: The Male Bias in Anthropology," in Reiter (ed.), *Toward an Anthropology of Women*; Tanner and Zihlman, op. cit.
8. Simons, "Ramapithecus," pp. 31–32.

CHAPTER 8 WOMAN THE POTTER

1. *New York Times*, Dec. 12, 1975.
2. Laughlin, "Hunting: An Integrating Biobehavior System," in Lee and DeVore (eds.), *Man the Hunter*, p. 318.
3. J. D. Clark, *The Prehistory of Africa*, pp. 69–70.
4. Tanner and Zihlman, "Women in Evolution," p. 590.
5. J. D. Clark, op. cit., p. 91.
6. Ibid., p. 99.
7. Harlan, *Crops and Man*, p. 29.
8. Boserup, *The Conditions of Agricultural Growth*, p. 12.
9. Abramova, "Paleolithic Art in the U.S.S.R.," p. 170.
10. Leacock, introduction, in Engels, *The Origin of the Family, Private Property and the State*, p. 39.

CHAPTER 9 WOMAN THE HUNTER

1. J. D. Clark, *The Prehistory of Africa*, p. 72.
2. Yellen and Lee, "The Dobe-/Du/da Environment: Background to a Hunting and Gathering Way of Life," in Lee and DeVore (eds.), *Kalahari Hunter-Gatherers*, pp. 32–46; L. Mar-

shall, "The !Kung Bushmen of the Kalahari Desert," in Gibbs, *Peoples of Africa*, pp. 249–50.

3. Pilbeam, "An Idea We Could Live Without," p. 69.
4. Goodale, *Tiwi Wives*, pp. 151–82.
5. Landes, *The Ojibwa Woman*, pp. 135–43; J. Mirsky, "The Eskimo of Greenland," in Mead (ed.), *Cooperation and Competition Among Primitive Peoples*, pp. 54, 83–84.
6. J. D. Clark, op. cit., p. 73.
7. Teleki, "The Omnivorous Chimpanzee," p. 36.
8. Tanner and Zihlman, "Women in Evolution," p. 600.
9. Reid, *A Law of Blood*, p. 68; B. Quain, "The Iroquois," in Mead, op. cit., p. 269.
10. Herbert Basedow, quoted by Meggitt, "'Marriage Classes' and Demography in Central Australia," in Lee and DeVore (eds.), *Man the Hunter*, p. 176.
11. Silberbauer, "The G'wi Bushman," and Watanabe, "The Ainu," in Bicchieri (ed.), *Hunters and Gatherers Today*, pp. 305, 469–71; Woodburn, "An Introduction to Hadza Ecology," in Lee and DeVore, op. cit., p. 54.
12. E. F. Gombrich, "Zebra Crossings," *The New York Review of Books*, Vol. XVIII, No. 8 (May 4, 1972), p. 35.
13. Jobson and Moore as quoted in Grant, *The Fortunate Slave*, pp. 13, 22.

CHAPTER 10   THE FIRST TEACHERS

1. A. Jolly, *The Evolution of Primate Behavior*, p. 212.
2. Tanner and Zihlman, "Women in Evolution," p. 597.
3. J. D. Clark, *The Prehistory of Africa*, p. 72.
4. Lancaster, *Primate Behavior and the Emergence of Human Culture*, p. 80; Tanner and Zihlman, "Women in Evolution," pp. 585–608.
5. J. D. Clark, op. cit., p. 71.

CHAPTER 11   EARLY STAGES OF EVOLUTION

1. *New York Times*, Nov. 10, 1972.
2. Bordes, *The Old Stone Age*, p. 47.
3. *New York Times*, Dec. 5, 1975.
4. *New York Times*, Oct. 31, 1975.
5. *New York Times*, Apr. 12, 1975.
6. Reported in "Science and the Citizen," *Scientific American*, Vol. 234, No. 2 (Feb. 1976), p. 54.

7. Holloway, "Australopithecine Endocasts"; Holloway, quoted in *New York Times*, Sept. 26, 1975.
8. Leacock, personal communication; see *New York Times*, Sept. 12, 1976, for report on Fore.

CHAPTER 12 SEX AND CONSCIOUSNESS

1. Tiger and Fox, *The Imperial Animal*, p. 76; Sherfey, *The Nature and Evolution of Female Sexuality*, pp. 96–100.
2. Singer, *The Goals of Human Sexuality*, pp. 159–94.
3. Freud, *The Basic Writings of Sigmund Freud*, pp. 612–13.
4. Money and Ehrhardt, "Gender Dimorphic Behavior and Female Sex Hormones," p. 736.
5. Sherfey, op. cit., pp. 141–42.
6. Salzman, "Psychology of the Female: A New Look," in J. B. Miller (ed.), *Psychoanalysis and Women*, pp. 204–6.
7. A. Jolly, *The Evolution of Primate Behavior*, p. 200.
8. Jay, "Primate Field Studies and Human Evolution," in Jay (ed.), *Primates*, pp. 487–503.
9. A. Jolly, op. cit., p. 186.
10. Kolata, "Primate Behavior," pp. 55–58; Pilbeam, "An Idea We Could Live Without," pp. 63–70; Rohrlich-Leavitt, *Peaceable Primates and Gentle People*, pp. 3–4.
11. Eaton, "The Social Order of Japanese Macaques," pp. 97–107; Goodall, *In the Shadow of Man*, pp. 82–88, 182.
12. Tanner and Zihlman, "Women in Evolution," pp. 606–7.
13. Wickler, "Socio-sexual Signals," in Morris (ed.), *Primate Ethology*, pp. 77–78.
14. Jay, "Primate Field Studies and Human Evolution," in Jay, op. cit., p. 492.
15. Pfeiffer, *The Emergence of Man*, p. 160.
16. Goodall, *In the Shadow of Man*, p. 191.
17. Sherfey, op. cit., p. 138.
18. Smith, *The Brain*, p. 320.
19. Ibid., p. 260.
20. Ibid., p. 30.
21. P. Breggin, "The Return of Lobotomy and Psychosurgery," *New York Times*, Feb. 24, 1972; B. Roberts, "Psychosurgery: The 'Final Solution' to the 'Woman Problem'," *The Second Wave*, Vol. 2, no. 1 (1972), pp. 13–15, 43.
22. *New York Times*, Nov. 1, 1975.
23. Morris, *The Naked Ape*, p. 63.

24. C. R. Carpenter, *Naturalistic Behavior of Nonhuman Primates* (University Park: Pennsylvania State University Press, 1964); Wickler, op. cit., pp. 69–147.

25. Goodall, "A Preliminary Report on Expressive Movements," in Jay, op. cit., pp. 313–74.

26. Slocum, "Woman the Gatherer: The Male Bias in Anthropology," in Reiter (ed.), *Toward an Anthropology of Women*, p. 44.

27. Marshall, "Sexual Behavior on Mangaia," in Marshall and Suggs (eds.), *Human Sexual Behavior*, p. 110.

28. Holloway, "Australopithecine Endocasts," p. 194.

CHAPTER 13   THE BRAIN IS THE HUMAN ADAPTATION

1. Chomsky, *Language and Mind*, p. 83.

2. *New York Times*, Sept. 26, 1975.

3. Holloway, "Culture: A Human Domain," p. 404.

4. Holloway, "Australopithecine Endocasts," pp. 196–200, 201–2.

5. E.g., Ralph Solecki, "Neanderthal–Worthy Ancestor," in Fried (ed.), *Explorations in Anthropology*, pp. 182–88.

6. Cf. Ardrey, *The Hunting Hypothesis*.

7. Pfeiffer, *The Emergence of Man*, p. 221.

8. Washburn, foreword, in Lee and DeVore (eds.), *Kalahari Hunter-Gatherers*, p. 4.

9. Holloway, "Australopithecine Endocasts," p. 187.

CHAPTER 14   HUMAN LIKE US

1. Kraus, *The Basis of Human Evolution*, pp. 243–44.

2. Kurtén, *Not from the Apes*, p. 115.

3. W. Straus and A. Cave, "Pathology and Posture of Neanderthal Man," *Quarterly Review of Biology*, Vol. 32 (1957), pp. 348–63.

4. G. Clark and Piggott, *Prehistoric Societies*, p. 50.

5. G. Clark, *The Stone Age Hunters*, p. 42.

6. Goodale, *Tiwi Wives*, pp. 3–4.

7. Dr. E. S. Crelin, cited in Hahn, *On the Side of the Apes*, p. 217; Ralph Solecki, "Neanderthal–Worthy Ancestor," in Fried (ed.), *Explorations in Anthropology*, p. 187.

8. Kahn, personal communication.

9. Goodall, *In the Shadow of Man*, pp. 226–31.

10. Firestone, *The Dialectic of Sex*, pp. 53ff.; G. Rubin, "The

Traffic in Women: Notes on the 'Political Economy' of Sex," in Reiter, *Toward an Anthropology of Women*, pp. 185ff.

11. E.g., G. Zilboorg, "Masculine and Feminine: Some Biological and Cultural Aspects," in J. B. Miller (ed.), *Psychoanalysis and Women*, pp. 96–131.

12. Campbell, *Primitive Mythology*, p. 315.

13. Pilbeam, *The Ascent of Man*, pp. 74ff.

14. S. R. Binford, "A Structural Comparison of Disposal of the Dead in the Mousterian and the Upper Paleolithic," pp. 139–48; also personal communication.

15. Brace, *The Stages of Human Evolution*, pp. 90–92.

16. Kurtén, *Not from the Apes*, p. 129; Brace, op. cit., pp. 63–64, 66–67, 89–90; etc.

17. J. Helm, "The Nature of Dogrib Socioterritorial Groups," and J. Woodburn, "The Stability and Flexibility in Hadza Residential Groupings," in Lee and DeVore (eds.), *Man the Hunter*, pp. 118–31, 99–102; Lee, "Male-Female Residence Arrangements and Political Power in Human Hunter-Gatherers," pp. 167–74.

18. M. Shostak, "A !Kung Woman's Memories of Childhood," in Lee and DeVore (eds.), *Kalahari Hunter-Gatherers*, pp. 275–77; Leacock and Lurie (eds.), *North American Indians in Historical Perspective*.

19. Malinowski, *The Sexual Life of Savages*, pp. 56–57.

20. R. Berndt, "The Walmadjeri and Gugadja," in Bicchieri (ed.), *Hunters and Gatherers Today*, pp. 182–88.

21. Campbell, *Primitive Mythology*, pp. 339–41.

22. S. R. Binford and L. R. Binford, "Stone Tools and Human Behavior," p. 78.

23. Discussion based on S. R. Binford, "A Structural Comparison of the Disposal of the Dead," "Late Middle Paleolithic Adaptations," and personal conversations.

24. Suggested to me by Ellen Harold in 1972; see also Birdsell, *Human Evolution*, pp. 523–25.

25. Brace, *The Stages of Human Evolution*, pp. 3–6.

26. G. Clark and Piggott, *Prehistoric Societies*, pp. 89–104.

CHAPTER 15 PALEOLITHIC ART

1. E.g., G. Clark, *The Stone Age Hunters*; G. Clark and Piggott, *Prehistoric Societies*; Pfeiffer, *The Emergence of Man*.

2. J. Hawkes in Hawkes and Woolley, *Prehistory and the Begin-

   nings of Civilization, pp. 283–86; Levy, *Religious Conceptions of the Stone Age*, pp. 3–28; Campbell, *Primitive Mythology*, pp. 286–89, 299–312, 374–83.

3. G. Clark in G. Clark and Piggott, op. cit., pp. 70, 78–79, 84.
4. Pfeiffer, op. cit., pp. 251, 265.
5. Ucko and Rosenfeld, *Paleolithic Cave Art*, p. 135.
6. Kaberry, *Aboriginal Woman*, p. 206.
7. Ucko and Rosenfeld, op. cit., p. 52.
8. G. Clark in Clark and Piggott, op. cit., p. 84.
9. Cited by Ucko and Rosenfeld, op. cit., p. 43.
10. Campbell, op. cit., pp. 303–4.
11. Levy, op. cit., p. 21n.
12. Hawkes in Hawkes and Woolley, op. cit., pp. 276–77.
13. Hays, *The Dangerous Sex*, p. 30; Y. Véquaud, *The Women Painters of Mithila* (London: Thames and Hudson, 1977); Lévi-Strauss, *A World on the Wane*, pp. 155ff., 161ff., 173ff.
14. Ucko and Rosenfeld, op. cit., p. 42.
15. Ibid., p. 52.
16. Marshall, "The !Kung Bushmen of the Kalahari Desert," in Gibbs (ed.), *Peoples of Africa*, p. 275.
17. S. R. Binford, personal communication.
18. Ucko and Rosenfeld, op. cit., p. 39.
19. A. Savelli, personal communication.
20. *New York Times*, Mar. 3, 1977.
21. Ucko and Rosenfeld, op. cit., p. 100.
22. Ibid., pp. 174–95, 229.
23. Marshack, *The Roots of Civilization*, p. 173.
24. Ibid., p. 219.
25. Abramova, "Paleolithic Art in the U.S.S.R."
26. Campbell, op. cit., pp. 327–28.

CHAPTER 16 THE MANA OF BLOOD

1. Levy, *Religious Conceptions of the Stone Age*, p. 68.
2. Kaberry, *Aboriginal Woman*, p. 94.
3. Birket-Smith, *Primitive Man and His Ways*, p. 59.
4. Ibid., p. 51.
5. Hays, *The Dangerous Sex*, p. 13; Weideger, *Menstruation and Menopause*, pp. 105–7; see also B. Bettelheim, *Symbolic Wounds* (New York: Collier Books, 1962).
6. Birket-Smith, op. cit., pp. 16–17.
7. Ibid., p. 48.

8. Hogbin, *The Island of Menstruating Men*, pp. 88ff.
9. Mead, *Male and Female*, pp. 103–4.
10. Schlegel, *Male Dominance and Female Autonomy*, p. 25.
11. Kaberry, op. cit., p. 238–39.
12. Schlegel, op. cit., p. 90.
13. Schlegel, op. cit., p. 93n2.
14. Ibid., p. 93.
15. Kaberry, op. cit., pp. 204, 206, 207.
16. Goodale, *Tiwi Wives*, p. 226.
17. Goodall, *In the Shadow of Man*, p. 237.
18. Kaberry, op. cit., pp. 54–60.
19. Ibid., p. 122.
20. Goodale, op. cit., pp. 228–29.

CHAPTER 17 EARLY HOUSEHOLDS

1. Pfeiffer, *The Emergence of Man*, p. 141.
2. Turnbull, "The Importance of Flux in Two Hunting Socie-ties," in Lee and DeVore (eds.), *Man the Hunter*, p. 135.
3. Lee, "Work Effort, Group Structure and Land-Use in Con-temporary Hunter-Gatherers," in Ucko, Tringham, and Dim-bleby (eds.), *Man, Settlement, and Urbanism*, pp. 182–83.
4. Ibid., p. 182.
5. Turnbull, discussions in Lee and DeVore, op. cit., p. 156.
6. Lee, "Male-Female Residence Arrangements and Political Power," p. 173; Leacock, "The Changing Family and Lévi-Strauss."
7. Leacock, introduction, in Engels, *Origin of the Family, Private Property and the State*, pp. 36, 38.
8. Ibid., p. 31; see also Leacock, "The Changing Family and Lévi-Strauss," in Leacock and Lurie (eds.), *North American Indians in Historical Perspective*.
9. Kaberry, *Aboriginal Woman*, pp. xi, 277.
10. Ibid., p. xxx.
11. Ibid., p. 144.
12. Ibid., p. 103.
13. Ibid., pp. 152–53.
14. Powdermaker, *Life in Lesu*, pp. 244–45.
15. Ibid., p. 144.
16. Ibid., p. 227.
17. Woodburn, "Ecology, Nomadic Movement and the Composi-

    tion of the Local Group Among Hunters and Gatherers," in
    Ucko, Tringham, and Dimbleby, op. cit., pp. 196–97, 203.

18. Landes, *The Ojibwa Woman*, pp. 91–94.

19. Goodale, *Tiwi Wives*, pp. 335–36.

20. M. Fortes, cited in Bohannon and Middleton (eds.), *Family and Residence*, p. 322.

21. Reported in *Off Our Backs*, June 1973.

22. Leacock, introduction, in Engels, *Origin of the Family, Private Property and the State*, p. 38.

23. Cf. Boserup, *Women's Role in Economic Development*.

24. Fried, *The Evolution of Political Society*, pp. 86–87. Goodale compares her findings in *Tiwi Wives* with those in earlier studies and discusses discrepancies.

25. Schlegel, *Male Dominance and Female Autonomy*, pp. 143–44.

26. Rohrlich-Leavitt, B. Sykes, and E. Weatherford, "Aboriginal Woman: Male and Female Anthropological Perspectives," in Reiter (ed.), *Toward an Anthropology of Women*, pp. 123–24.

27. Anthropologists who write of the freedom with which foragers and some horticulturalists change partners in their early adulthood also note the existence of long-term sharing relationships among older couples.

PART IV

1. Translated by J. A. Wilson, in Pritchard (ed.), *Ancient Near Eastern Texts Relating to the Old Testament*, p. 4.

CHAPTER 18   GATHERING TO FARMING

1. See Harlan, *Crops and Man*; Isaac, *Geography of Domestication*.

2. Mellaart, *Earliest Civilizations of the Near East*, p. 22.

3. Harlan, op. cit., p. 23.

4. Cited in K. Flannery, "Origins and Ecological Effects of Early Domestication in Iran and the Near East," in Ucko and Dimbleby (eds.), *The Domestication and Exploitation of Plants and Animals*, pp. 80–81.

5. Childe, *Progress and Archaeology* (London: Watts and Co./Thinkers Library, 1944), p. 12.

6. Childe, *Man Makes Himself* (New York: New American Library/Mentor Books, 1951), p. 61.

7. Campbell, *Primitive Mythology*, p. 139.

8. Lee, "What Hunters Do for a Living," in Lee and DeVore (eds.), *Man the Hunter*, pp. 30ff. (One of the earlier statements of a situation since extensively discussed; cf. Flannery, op. cit., p. 75.)

9. L. R. Binford, "Post-Pleistocene Adaptations," in S. R. and L. R. Binford (eds.), *New Perspectives in Archeology*, p. 328.

10. Lee, op. cit., p. 33; F. Eggan, discussions in Lee and DeVore, op. cit., p. 95; quoted in Harlan, op. cit., p. 49.

11. Flannery, op. cit., p. 98, n. 71.

12. Site surveys are cited by Hole, "Social Organization in Western Iran 8000–4000 B.C.," in S. R. and L. R. Binford, op. cit., pp. 253–56. See also Adams, *Land Behind Baghdad*; Adams and Nissen, *The Uruk Countryside*; Hole, Flannery, and Neely, *Prehistory and Human Ecology of the Deh Luran Plain*.

CHAPTER 19 THE DISCOVERY OF FATHERHOOD

1. Lévi-Strauss, *The Elementary Structures of Kinship*, p. 14.

2. Though the timetable is reversed, this Marx-Engels thesis still holds up. Cf. Harlan, *Crops and Man*; Isaac, *Geography of Domestication*; Joan Oates, "Prehistoric Settlement Patterns in Mesopotamia," in Ucko, Tringham, and Dimbleby (eds.), *Man, Settlement, and Urbanism*, pp. 299–310; Sacks, "Engels Revisited," in Reiter (ed.), *Toward an Anthropology of Women*, pp. 215–17.

3. Harlan, "The Plants and Animals that Nourish Man"; D. Perkins, "Prehistoric Fauna from Shanidar, Iraq" (*Science*, Vol. 142, pp. 1565–66), the one report with early evidence of domesticated sheep.

4. Flannery, "Origins and Ecological Effects of Early Near Eastern Domestication," in Ucko and Dimbleby (eds.), *The Domestication and Exploitation of Plants and Animals*, p. 87.

5. See note 12, Chapter 18, above.

6. Cf. Kaberry, *Aboriginal Woman*, pp. 42ff.

7. Malinowski, *The Sexual Life of Savages*, pp. 190–91.

8. Tom Buckley, "When Secretariat Stands at Stud," *New York Times Magazine*, Sept. 23, 1975, p. 94.

9. S. R. Binford, personal communication. See also Piggott, *Ancient Europe*, p. 36.

10. E. Isaac, "On the Domestication of Cattle," pp. 195–204; Isaac, *Geography of Domestication*, passim.

11. Lorenz reported rape among enclosed greylag geese. More recently it has been claimed for mallard ducks at the University of Washington Arboretum, "a seminatural suburban environment." Barash, "Sociobiology of Rape in Mallards," p. 738.

12. Cf. Sacks, "Engels Revisited," in Reiter, op. cit., pp. 211–34.

13. E. Wilson, *To the Finland Station*, p. 223.

14. R. E. Chaplin, "The Use of Non-morphological Criteria," in Ucko and Dimbleby, op. cit., pp. 240–41.

15. P. Ducos, "Methodology and Results of the Study of the Earliest Domesticated Animals," in Ucko and Dimbleby, op. cit., p. 272.

16. M. Eliade, "The Yearning for Paradise in Primitive Tradition," in H. A. Murray (ed.), *Myth and Mythmaking*, p. 65.

17. S. Bokonyi, "Archaeological Problems and Methods of Recognizing Animal Domestication," in Ucko and Dimbleby, op. cit., pp. 219–27.

18. B. A. L. Cranstone, "Animal Husbandry: The Evidence from Ethnography," in Ucko and Dimbleby, op. cit., pp. 255, 256, 257, 258.

CHAPTER 20 THE PERNICIOUS ANALOGY

1. Birdsell, "Predictions for the Pleistocene Based on Equilibrium Systems Among Hunter-Gatherers," in Lee and DeVore (eds.), *Man the Hunter*, pp. 236–40.

2. Kaberry, *Aboriginal Woman*, p. 242; Marshall, "The !Kung Bushmen of the Kalahari Desert," in Gibbs (ed.), *Peoples of Africa*, p. 263.

3. Rich, *Of Woman Born*, pp. 119–20; Mead, *Sex and Temperament*, p. 49; Firth, *We, the Tikopia*, p. 374; Pomeroy, *Goddesses, Whores, Wives, and Slaves*, pp. 164–65.

4. Boserup, *Woman's Role in Economic Development*, p. 49.

5. Noonan, *Contraception*, p. 12.

6. *New York Times*, Aug. 2, 1974.

7. Lévi-Strauss, *A World on the Wane*, p. 200.

8. N. Newton, quoted in Rossi, "Maternalism, Sexuality, and the New Feminism," p. 28.

9. Goodale, *Tiwi Wives*, p. 130.

10. Himes, *Medical History of Contraception*, p. 64.

11. Toni Morrison, *The Bluest Eye* (New York: Holt, Rinehart and Winston, 1970), p. 31.

12. Quoted in Briffault, *The Mothers*, Vol. 2, pp. 413ff.

13. Ibid., p. 417.
14. Translated in Francoeur, *Utopian Motherhood*, p. 9.
15. Hippocrates, *Diseases of Women 1*, translated by A. E. Hanson in *Signs*, Vol. 1, no. 2 (Winter 1975), p. 582.
16. Francoeur, op. cit., p. 7.
17. Briffault, op. cit., p. 418.
18. Cf. Briffault, op. cit.; Neumann, *The Origins and History of Consciousness*.
19. Leacock, introduction, in Engels, *The Origin of the Family, Private Property, and the State*, pp. 33, 39.
20. Mead, *Male and Female*, p. 189.
21. Goodale, *Tiwi Wives*, pp. 138ff.

CHAPTER 21 ÇATAL HÜYÜK AND HAÇILAR

1. This chapter is based on Angel, "Early Neolithic Skeletons from Çatal Hüyük"; Helbaek, "First Impressions of the Çatal Hüyük Plant Husbandry"; Mellaart, *Çatal Hüyük, Excavations at Hacilar*, "A Neolithic City in Turkey," "Excavations at Çatal Hüyük, 1962," "Excavations at Çatal Hüyük, 1963," "Excavations at Çatal Hüyük, 1965."
2. Angel, op. cit., p. 90.
3. Brothwell, "Human Nutrition," in Ucko and Dimbleby (eds.), *The Domestication and Exploitation of Plants and Animals*, p. 540.
4. Angel, op. cit., p. 94.
5. Ibid., p. 92.
6. Ibid., p. 93.
7. Reported in *New York Times*, December 4, 1975.
8. See Ucko, *Anthropomorphic Figurines*.

CHAPTER 22 SADISM AND MASOCHISM

1. Definitions from Webster's New International Dictionary of the English Language, 2d Ed., unabridged (Springfield, Mass.: G. & C. Merriam, 1959).
2. Reich, *The Invasion of Compulsory Sex-Morality*, pp. 192–93.
3. Erikson, *Gandhi's Truth*, p. 236; Singer, *The Goals of Human Sexuality*, p. 94.
4. Reich, op. cit., p. 36.
5. Ibid., pp. 193–94.
6. Reich, *The Sexual Revolution*, p. 7.
7. Horney, *Feminine Psychology*, pp. 229–31.

8. Ibid., p. 232.
9. Thompson, On Women, pp. 22, 141.
10. Ibid., p. 144.
11. Cranstone, "Animal Husbandry: The Evidence from Ethnography," in Ucko and Dimbleby (eds.), The Domestication and Exploitation of Plants and Animals, pp. 248–49.

CHAPTER 23   THE POWER OF PROCREATION

1. Russell, The Conquest of Happiness (New York: Horace Liveright, 1930), p. 152.
2. Engels, The Origin of the Family, Private Property, and the State, p. 58n.
3. Reports in the New York Times, Jan. 12, 1976.
4. Rich, New York Times, Nov. 20, 1976, Op Ed page.
5. M. A. Mallowan, "The Development of Cities from Al 'Ubaid to the End of Uruk 5," in Cambridge Ancient History, Vol. I, Part 1, Ch. VIII, pp. 348ff.
6. Ucko, Anthropomorphic Figurines, p. 174.
7. Bokonyi, "Domestication and Exploitation of Animals," in Ucko and Dimbleby (eds.), The Domestication and Exploitation of Plants and Animals, p. 222.
8. Schlegel, Male Dominance and Female Autonomy, p. 23.
9. Hage, "There's Glory for You," p. 7.
10. Piercy, Small Changes (Garden City, N.Y.: Doubleday, 1973), p. 344.
11. Quoted by Quain, "The Iroquois," in Mead (ed.), Cooperation and Competition Among Primitive Peoples, p. 241n2.
12. Ibid., pp. 243, 258, 259.
13. Cf. Lionel Tiger, Men in Groups (New York: Random House, 1969).
14. Leacock, introduction, in Engels, The Origin of the Family, Private Property, and the State, p. 36.
15. Douglas, "Is Matriliny Doomed in Africa?" in Douglas and Kaberry (eds.), Man in Africa, pp. 123–37.

CHAPTER 24   WOMEN IN SUMER

1. Extensively documented in Pritchard (ed.), Ancient Near Eastern Texts Relating to the Old Testament. Cf. Kramer, The Sumerians, and Jacobsen, The Treasures of Darkness.
2. Saggs, The Greatness That Was Babylon; M. A. Mallowan, "The Development of Cities," in Cambridge Ancient History,

Vol. I, Part 1, Ch. VIII, and C. J. Gadd, "The Cities of Babylonia," ibid., Part 2, Ch. XIII.

3. Saggs, *The Greatness That Was Babylon*, p. 37; Fried, *The Evolution of Political Society*, p. 161; Tacitus, *The Agricola and the Germania*, p. 47.
4. Jacobsen, *Toward the Image of Tammuz*, pp. 139ff.
5. Adams, "Patterns of Urbanization in Early Southern Mesopotamia," in Ucko, Tringham, and Dimbleby (eds.), *Man, Settlement and Urbanism*, pp. 735–50; Adams and Nissen, *The Uruk Countryside*.
6. Jacobsen, *Toward the Image of Tammuz*, p. 164.
7. Tacitus, *The Agricola and the Germania*, pp. 72–73; Engels, *The Origin of the Family, Private Property, and the State*, pp. 235–36.
8. Adams, op. cit., p. 743.
9. Gadd, op. cit., pp. 141–42.
10. Kramer, *The Sumerians*, p. 79; Rohrlich-Leavitt, "Women in Transition," p. 40.
11. Fried, "On the Evolution of Social Stratification and the State," p. 716.
12. *Laws of Ur-Nammu*, in Pritchard, op. cit., p. 524.
13. *Laws of Lipit-Ishtar*, in Pritchard, op. cit., p. 160.
14. *Laws of Hammurabi*, in Pritchard, op. cit., p. 172.
15. *Middle Assyrian Laws*, in Pritchard, op. cit., p. 183.
16. Hawkes, *The First Great Civilizations*, pp. 104–7.
17. Gadd, op. cit., p. 129.
18. Gelb, "The Ancient Mesopotamian Ration System."
19. Lancaster, *Primate Behavior and the Emergence of Human Culture*, p. 82.

CHAPTER 25 DECLINE OF THE MOTHER GODDESSES

1. Translated by Kramer, in Pritchard (ed.), *Ancient Near Eastern Texts Relating to the Old Testament*, p. 576.
2. Saggs, *The Greatness That Was Babylon*, pp. 37–39.
3. This development is traced in Jacobsen, *The Treasures of Darkness*, though his interpretation differs from mine.
4. Jacobsen, *Toward the Image of Tammuz*, p. 94.
5. Ibid., pp. 375–76.
6. Colson, "Plateau Tonga," in Schneider and Gough (eds.), *Matrilineal Kinship*, p. 50.
7. Kramer, *The Sacred Marriage Rite*, p. 59.

8. Jacobsen, *Toward the Image of Tammuz*, p. 95.
9. Gadd, "Babylonia c. 2120–1800 B.C.," in *Cambridge Ancient History*, Vol. I, Part 2, Ch. XXII, pp. 605ff.
10. Kramer, op. cit., pp. 64–65.
11. Ibid., p. 63.
12. Kramer, *The Sumerians*, p. 251.
13. Jacobsen, *The Treasures of Darkness*, p. 143.
14. Kramer, *History Begins at Sumer*, pp. 84–88.
15. Kramer, *The Sumerians*, p. 146.
16. Jacobsen, *Toward the Image of Tammuz*, pp. 207, 356.
17. J. Hawkes, *The First Great Civilizations*, p. 115.
18. J. A. Wilson, in Pritchard, op. cit., p. 6.
19. Jacobsen, *Toward the Image of Tammuz*, p. 153.
20. Jacobsen, *The Treasures of Darkness*, p. 136.
21. Loc. cit.
22. Jacobsen, *Toward the Image of Tammuz*, p. 117; *The Treasures of Darkness*, pp. 80, 131–32.
23. Jacobsen, *The Treasures of Darkness*, pp. 113–14.
24. Cf. Frankfort, *Cylinder Seals* (London: Macmillan, 1939); Campbell, *Oriental Mythology*, pp. 41–44.

CHAPTER 26 THE AUTHORITARIAN STATE AND THE FAMILY

1. Jacobsen, *The Treasures of Darkness*, p. 181.
2. Ibid., pp. 116–18, ccp. 180–82.
3. Saggs, *The Greatness That Was Babylon*, pp. 383–84.
4. Campbell, *Occidental Mythology*, pp. 75ff.
5. Jacobsen, *Toward the Image of Tammuz*, p. 9.
6. Campbell, *Occidental Mythology*, pp. 82–83.
7. E. Laughlin, "Equality of Souls, Inequality of Sexes," in Ruether (ed.), *Religion and Sexism*, p. 226.
8. Oppenheim, *Ancient Mesopotamia*, p. 141.
9. Translated by Kramer, in Pritchard (ed.), *Ancient Near Eastern Texts Relating to the Old Testament*, p. 160.
10. Quoted in Saggs, op. cit., p. 442.
11. Quoted in Saggs, op. cit., p. 348.
12. Kramer, *The Sumerians*; Hawkes, *The First Great Civilizations*.
13. Translated by Kramer, in Pritchard, op. cit., p. 547.

CHAPTER 27 WAR AND SEX AND ANIMALS

1. Gadd, "The Cities of Babylonia," in *Cambridge Ancient His-*

tory, Vol. I, Part 2, Ch. XIII, pp. 127, 129ff.; Saggs, *The Greatness That Was Babylon*, pp. 169ff.

2. Gadd, op. cit., pp. 129–30.

3. Ibid., p. 152.

4. Cranstone, "Animal Husbandry: The Evidence from Ethnography," in Ucko and Dimbleby (eds.), *Domestication and Exploitation of Plants and Animals*, pp. 248–62.

5. Oppenheim, *Ancient Mesopotamia*, pp. 82–83.

6. Birket-Smith, *Primitive Man and His Ways*, pp. 66ff.

7. Fried, "On Human Aggression," in C. M. Otten (comp.), *Aggression and Evolution* (Ann Arbor, Mich.: Xerox College Publishing, 1973), p. 360.

8. Birket-Smith, op. cit., p. 68.

9. *New York Times*, Dec. 7, 1974.

10. Nobel, "The Mesopotamian Onager as a Draft Animal," in Ucko and Dimbleby, op. cit., p. 483.

11. Cf. Brothwell, "Dietary Variation and the Biology of Earlier Human Populations," in Ucko and Dimbleby, op. cit., p. 534.

12. Kramer, *The Sumerians*, p. 263.

13. Ibid., p. 263.

14. Pritchard (ed.), *Ancient Near Eastern Texts Relating to the Old Testament*, pp. 164ff.

CHAPTER 28 GIFTS FROM THE GREEKS

1. Quoted in Finley, *The Ancient Economy*, p. 126.

2. Deut. 20:13, 14 (King James).

3. Pomeroy, *Goddesses, Whores, Wives, and Slaves*, pp. 40, 46, 69–70.

4. Ibid., pp. 142–43.

5. Quoted in Rogers, *The Troublesome Helpmate*, p. 24.

6. Pomeroy, op. cit., pp. 49–52.

7. Ibid., p. 230.

8. Quoted in Harold, "More Thinking About Feminism," p. 57.

9. As described in The Oxford Classical Dictionary, 2d ed. (Oxford: Clarendon Press, 1970), p. 352.

10. Pomeroy, op. cit., pp. 222–23.

11. Plato's *Phaedo*, quoted in Finley, op. cit., p. 30.

12. Ibid., p. 29.

CHAPTER 29 THE PURITAN STRAIN

1. Cf. Finley, *The Ancient Economy*, p. 29.

2. E.g., Pritchard (ed.), *Ancient Near Eastern Texts Relating to the Old Testament.*

3. Bird, "Images of Women in the Old Testament," in Ruether (ed.), *Religion and Sexism,* pp. 41ff.

4. Bible quotations in this chapter were originally taken from an old family Bible, the American Standard Version of 1901, based on the 1881–85 revision of the 1611 King James Version. I have retained certain of these quotations, either for euphony or as having influenced our view of sexuality and the female; others I have conformed with the 1952 Revised Standard Version of the Old Testament, indicating in the note which source I am using. Lev. 11:41–44 (RSV).

5. Lev. 15:32–33 (RSV).

6. Lev. 15:3 (ASV).

7. Lev. 15:16 (ASV).

8. Lev. 20:18 (RSV); cf. ASV's "with a woman while she is in her menstrual uncleanness."

9. Lev. 18:20, 23 (RSV).

10. Lev. 12:4 (ASV).

11. Cf. Hogbin, *The Island of Menstruating Men,* wherein menstruation is considered a necessary cleansing, despite the pollution it brings, and where its analogue is artificially induced by men.

12. Deut. 22:25–27 (ASV).

13. Ex. 22:16–17 (ASV).

14. Deut. 22:28–29 (ASV).

15. I Sam. 18:20 (RSV).

16. Hos. 1:2 (ASV).

17. Cf. Patai, *The Hebrew Goddess;* Russell, *A History of Western Philosophy;* et al.

CHAPTER 30 SHALL HE TREAT OUR SISTER AS A HARLOT?

1. See Brownmiller, *Against Our Will,* and Griffin, "Rape," for complete exegeses of this institutionalization.

2. Kramer, *The Sumerians,* pp. 162–63.

3. Brownmiller, op. cit., and Griffin, op. cit., both stress the ways in which historical society encouraged rape.

4. Deut. 21:10ff. (King James).

5. Rougemont, *Love in the Western World,* p. 298; *New York Times,* Oct. 6, 1977.

6. *A Very Curious Girl,* a film written and directed by Nelly

Kaplan. The passage in Deuteronomy reflects earlier Assyrian and Hittite laws.

7. Gen. 34:13–29 (King James).

8. Patai, *The Hebrew Goddess.*

9. Joan Little, reported in the *New York Times*, Jan. 7, 1975.

10. Quoted in Finley, *The Ancient Economy*, p. 136.

11. Bird, "Images of Women in the Old Testament," in Ruether, *Religion and Sexism*, pp. 61, 68; Patai, op. cit., *passim.*

12. Oppenheim, *Ancient Mesopotamia*, p. 140; Kenyon, *Archaeology in the Holy Land*, p. 121.

13. In Books of Ezra and Nehemiah the taking of strange wives is anathematized; on the other hand, the convert Ruth is praised, in the book named for her.

14. Cited in Noonan, *Contraception*, pp. 50ff.

15. Hauptman, "Images of Women in the Talmud," in Ruether, op. cit., p. 198.

16. Noonan, op. cit., pp. 50–55.

17. Noonan, op. cit., pp. 10–11, 50–55; Himes, *Medical History of Contraception*, pp. 72–78; see also Feldman, *Birth Control in Jewish Law.*

18. Himes, op. cit., p. 75.

19. Cf. testimony cited in Hite, *The Hite Report.*

20. Quoted by Parvey, "The Theology and Leadership of Women in the New Testament," in Ruether, op. cit., p. 120.

21. Cited in *Hebraic Literature*, p. 14.

22. Rogers, *The Troublesome Helpmate.*

23. Parvey, "The Theology and Leadership of Women in the New Testament," in Ruether, op. cit., pp. 137, 142–46.

24. Gal. 3:28 (RSV); cf. Pagels, "What Became of God the Mother?"

CHAPTER 31 THE EUROPEAN CONNECTION

1. The Birhors and the Paliyans of India are described in Bicchieri, *Hunters and Gatherers Today*, pp. 371–447, with passing reference to other foragers of Southeast Asia.

2. Piggott, *Ancient Europe*, p. 182.

3. Bridget Allchin, "Hunters or Pastoral Nomads" in Ucko, Tringham, and Dimbleby (eds.), *Man, Settlement and Urbanism*, p. 115–19; Cranstone, "Animal Husbandry: The Evidence from Ethnography," in Ucko and Dimbleby (eds.), *The*

Domestication and Exploitation of Plants and Animals, pp. 260–62.

4. E. D. Phillips, "The Royal Hordes: The Nomad Peoples of the Steppes," in Stuart Piggott (ed.), *The Dawn of Civilization* (New York: Holt, Rinehart and Winston, 1961), pp. 303–28.

5. Herodotus, *The Histories*, p. 286.

6. Ibid., p. 278.

7. Tacitus, *The Agricola and the Germania*, p. 46.

8. Fried has developed this concept in his paper "On the Evolution of Social Stratification and the State," and the subsequent book *The Evolution of Political Society*.

9. Tacitus, op. cit., p. 111; cf. Reid, *A Law of Blood*, for a description of Cherokee society, in which women and men participate in the governing body.

10. Herodotus, op. cit., pp. 306–8.

11. Piggott, *Ancient Europe*, p. 196.

12. Tacitus, op. cit., pp. 140–41.

13. Herodotus, op. cit., pp. 128, 305.

14. Tacitus, op. cit., p. 108; cf. Julius Caesar, Suetonius, and other Roman historical commentaries, as well as modern archaeological findings.

15. Piggott, *Ancient Europe*, pp. 179, 181, 196–99.

16. *New York Times*, July 26, 1976.

17. Campbell, *Occidental Mythology*, pp. 36–40, 303.

18. Tacitus, op. cit., p. 114.

19. E.g., Stewart and Winter, "The Nature and Causes of Female Suppression"; Lewis, *Psychic War in Men and Women*, Ch. 8, 10; Sacks, "Engels Revisited," in Reiter (ed.), *Toward an Anthropology of Women*, pp. 211–34.

20. Rohrlich-Leavitt, "Women in Transition," pp. 10–29.

CHAPTER 32   THE CHRISTIAN CONTRADICTION

1. Apuleius, *The Golden Ass*, p. 264; quoted in Vermaseren, *Cybele and Attis*, p. 10.

2. 1 Tim. 2:11–12 (ASV).

3. Pagels, "When Did God Make Man in His Image?", p. 38.

4. David Herlihy, "Land, Family, and Women in Continental Europe, 701–1200," in Stuard (ed.), *Women in Medieval Society*, pp. 13–42.

5. Catherine Silver, personal communication; Barbara Hanawalt,

"The Female Felon in Fourteenth Century England," in Stuard, op. cit., p. 127.

6. Jo Freeman, quoted in Harold, "More Thinking About Feminism," p. 61.

7. Noonan, *Contraception*, pp. 143–70.

8. Ibid., p. 177.

9. Ibid., pp. 287–88.

10. Ibid., pp. 240ff.

11. Ibid., pp. 76–77.

12. Ibid., p. 194.

13. Ibid., p. 375.

14. Rogers, *The Troublesome Helpmate*, p. 18.

15. Noonan, op. cit., p. 362–63.

16. H. Dillard, "Women in Reconquest Castile," in Stuard, op. cit., p. 73.

17. Ibid., pp. 80–89.

18. Hughes, "Domestic Ideals and Social Behavior," pp. 115–43.

19. Ibid., p. 131; see also Piers, *Infanticide*.

20. Noonan, op. cit., pp. 229–30.

21. Sévigné, *Letters*, p. 150.

22. Ibid., p. 205.

23. D. M. Stenton, *The English Woman in History* (New York: Schocken, 1977), pp. 153–55.

CHAPTER 33 WOMEN HAVE ALWAYS WORKED

1. Quoted by Stone, "The Rise of the Nuclear Family," p. 25.

2. Ibid., p. 29.

3. Quotations in this and an earlier paragraph from Oxford English Dictionary description of church-ales.

4. J. Janeway, quoted in Stone, op. cit., p. 37.

5. Stone, op. cit., pp. 34–57.

6. Sévigné, *Letters*, p. 364.

7. Quoted in Himes, *Medical History of Contraception*, p. 172.

8. Ibid., pp. 21, 22, 118n, 121, 161.

9. Scott and Tilly, "Woman's Work and the Family in Nineteenth Century Europe," pp. 152ff., 161–65.

10. Basch, *Relative Creatures*, pp. 103–40, 195–209; Scott and Tilly, op. cit., pp. 166ff.

11. Quoted in Scott and Tilly, op. cit., p. 170.

12. Basch, op. cit., pp. 198–206.

13. Cf. Walkowitz, "Notes on the History of Victorian Prosti-

tution," pp. 107ff.; Marcus, *The Other Victorians*, pp. 137–38, 141ff.; Scott and Tilly, op. cit., p. 170; Basch, op. cit., pp. 123–40, 195–209.

EPILOGUE AND PROLOGUE

1. R. Revelle, quoted in *New York Times*, Oct. 26, 1975.
2. *New York Times*, May 31, 1976; Mar. 6, July 24, 1977.
3. Ibid., Nov. 29, Dec. 5, 1976; Apr. 3, 1977.
4. Tindale, "The Pitjandjara," in Bicchieri (ed.), *Hunters and Gatherers Today*, p. 261.
5. *New York Times*, Jan. 26, Dec. 6, 1977.
6. L. Tolstoy, "The Kreutzer Sonata," in E. J. Simmons (ed.), *Short Novels* (New York: Modern Library, 1966), p. 147.
7. Hite, *The Hite Report*; see also review of *The Hite Report* by E. Jong, *New York Times Book Review*, Oct. 3, 1976.
8. *New York Times*, Sept. 12, 1977.

Bibliography

Bibliographies can serve two purposes. They buttress the writer's findings, documenting research and telling scholars and professionals what one's sources were and how much study went into the book. The other purpose is to point the way for interested readers so they can find out more about specific areas which have stimulated their curiosity. I have settled for a selected bibliography showing some of my sources and pointing also to books and papers where readers may find more information on material I have been unable to treat in as much detail as I would have liked. Books, articles, and papers I found particularly exciting in the shaping of my theories are starred: sources where the reader will find useful detail and amplification I was unable to include are double-starred. Some sources referred to in the notes are also in the Bibliography, not necessarily because they are good, or even useful, but for the record, since they were much used.

BOOKS AND PAMPHLETS

Adams, R. M., *Land Behind Baghdad*. Chicago: University of Chicago Press, 1965.

——, and H. J. Nissen, *The Uruk Countryside*. Chicago: University of Chicago Press, 1972.

Ardrey, Robert, *The Territorial Imperative*. New York: Atheneum, 1966.

——, *The Hunting Hypothesis*. New York: Atheneum, 1976.

Bachofen, J. J., *Myth, Religion and Mother Right* (1861), trans. Ralph Manheim. Princeton, N.J.: Princeton University Press/Bollingen Series, 1967.

**Basch, Françoise, *Relative Creatures: Victorian Women in Society and the Novel*. New York: Schocken, 1974.

Beard, Mary R., *Woman as Force in History: A Study in Traditions and Realities*. New York: Collier, 1971.

Beauvoir, Simone de, *The Second Sex*. New York: Bantam, 1961.

Benedict, Ruth, *Patterns of Culture*. Boston: Houghton Mifflin/ Sentry, 1959.

*Bicchieri, M. G. (ed.), *Hunters and Gatherers Today*. New York: Holt, Rinehart and Winston, 1972.

Binford, S. R. and L. R., *New Perspectives in Archeology*. Chicago: Aldine, 1968.

Birdsell, J. B., *Human Evolution*. Chicago: Rand McNally, 1975.

Birket-Smith, Kaj, *The Paths of Culture: A General Ethnology*, trans. Karin Fennow. Madison and Milwaukee: University of Wisconsin Press, 1965.

*——, *Primitive Man and His Ways*. Cleveland, Ohio: World, 1960, 1961.

Bohannon, Paul, *Africa and Africans*. Garden City, N.Y.: Doubleday/Natural History Press, 1964.

——, and John Middleton, *Marriage, Family and Residence*. Garden City, N.Y.: Doubleday/Natural History Press, 1968.

Bordes, François, *The Old Stone Age*. New York: McGraw-Hill/ World University Library, 1970.

Borun, Minda, Molly McLaughlin, Gina Oboler, Norma Perchonock and Lorraine Sexton, *Women's Liberation: An Anthropological View*. Pittsburgh: KNOW, Inc., 1971.

*Boserup, Ester, *The Conditions of Agricultural Growth*. Chicago: Aldine, 1965.

**——, *Woman's Role in Economic Development*. New York: St. Martin's Press, 1970.

Boston Women's Health Book Collective, *Our Bodies, Ourselves*. New York: Simon and Schuster, 1973.

Brace, C. Loring, *The Stages of Human Evolution*. Englewood Cliffs, N.J.: Prentice-Hall, 1967.

Briffault, Robert, *The Mothers*, 3 vols. New York: Macmillan, 1927.

**Brownmiller, Susan, *Against Our Will: Men, Women, and Rape*. New York: Simon and Schuster, 1975.

Buettner-Janusch, John, *Origins of Man*. New York: Wiley, 1966.

Bullough, Vern L., *The Subordinate Sex*. Urbana: University of Illinois Press, 1973.

Calverton, V. F., and S. D. Schmalhousen (eds.), *Sex in Civilization*. New York: Macaulay, 1929.

Cambridge Ancient History, Vol. I, Part 1: *Prolegomena and Prehistory*, and Part 2: *Early History of the Middle East;*

Vol. II, Part 1: *History of the Middle East and the Aegean Region, c. 1800–1380 B.C.* London: Cambridge University Press, 1970, 1971, 1973.

Campbell, Joseph, *The Masks of God*, 4 vols. New York: Viking, 1968, 1970, 1971. Editions used: Vol. I, *Primitive Mythology*, 1970 (Compass); Vol. II, *Oriental Mythology*, 1968; Vol. III, *Occidental Mythology*, 1971 (Compass); Vol. IV, *Creative Mythology*, 1968.

Chance, Michael R. A., and Clifford Jolly, *Social Groups of Monkeys, Apes and Men.* New York: Dutton, 1970.

Chiera, Edward, *They Wrote on Clay: The Babylonian Tablets Speak Today*, ed. George G. Cameron. Chicago: University of Chicago Press/Phoenix, 1938, 1962.

Childe, V. Gordon, *New Light on the Most Ancient East.* New York: Praeger, 1953.

Chomsky, Noam, *Language and Mind.* New York: Harcourt, Brace & World, 1968.

——, *Problems of Knowledge and Freedom.* New York: Random House/Vintage, 1971.

Clark, Grahame, *The Stone Age Hunters.* New York: McGraw-Hill, 1967, 1970.

——, and Stuart Piggott, *Prehistoric Societies.* Harmondsworth, Middlesex, Eng.: Penguin, 1970.

Clark, J. Desmond, *The Prehistory of Africa.* New York: Praeger, 1970.

Clark, W. E. LeGros, *History of the Primates.* Chicago: University of Chicago Press/Phoenix, 1964.

Cohen, Ronald, and John Middleton (eds.), *Comparative Political Systems.* Garden City, N.Y.: Doubleday/Natural History Press, 1967.

Contenau, Georges, *Everyday Life in Babylon and Assyria.* London: Edward Arnold, 1954.

Crawley, Ernest, *The Mystic Rose: A Study of Primitive Marriage and of Primitive Thought in Its Bearing on Marriage*, revised and enlarged by Theodore Besterman. New York: Meridian, 1960.

Darwin, Charles, *The Descent of Man.* New York: Appleton, 1927.

——, *The Origin of Species.* New York: New American Library/Mentor, 1958.

Davis, Elizabeth Gould, *The First Sex.* New York: Putnam, 1971.

Day, Clarence, *This Simian World.* New York: Knopf, 1921.

Delaney, Janice, Mary Jane Lupton, and Emily Toth, *The Curse: A Cultural History of Menstruation*. New York: Dutton, 1976.

DeVore, Irven (ed.), *Primate Behavior: Field Studies of Monkeys and Apes*. New York: Holt, Rinehart and Winston, 1965.

*Diamond, Stanley, *In Search of the Primitive*. New Brunswick, N.J.: Transaction Books, 1974.

Dimbleby, G. W., *Plants and Archeology*. London: John Baker, 1967.

Diner, Helen, *Mothers and Amazons: The First Feminine History of Culture*, ed. and trans. John Philip Lundin. New York: Julian Press, 1965.

Dobzhansky, Theodosius, *Genetics of the Evolutionary Process*. New York: Columbia University Press, 1970.

——, *Mankind Evolving*. New York: Bantam/Matrix, 1970.

*Douglas, Mary, and Phyllis M. Kaberry (eds.), *Man in Africa*. Garden City, N.Y.: Doubleday/Anchor, 1971.

Du Bois, Cora, *The People of Alor*. Cambridge, Mass.: Harvard University Press, 1969.

Ehrenreich, Barbara, and Deirdre English, *Complaints and Disorders: The Sexual Politics of Sickness*. Old Westbury, New York: The Feminist Press, 1973.

**Engels, Frederick, *The Origin of the Family, Private Property and the State*, ed. and with an introduction by Eleanor Burke Leacock. New York: International, 1972.

Erikson, Erik H., *Gandhi's Truth: On the Origins of Militant Nonviolence*. New York: Norton, 1969.

Feldman, David M., *Birth Control in Jewish Law*. New York: New York University Press, 1968.

Fernea, Elizabeth Warnock, *Guests of the Sheik: An Ethnography of an Iraqi Village*. Garden City, N.Y.: Doubleday/Anchor, 1969.

Finley, M. I., *The Ancient Economy*. New York: Viking Press, 1973.

——, *Aspects of Antiquity*. New York: Viking Press, 1968.

——, *The Use and Abuse of History*. New York: Viking Press, 1975.

—— (ed.), *Slavery in Classical Antiquity*. Cambridge: Heffer and New York: Barnes and Noble, 1968.

Firestone, Shulamith, *The Dialectic of Sex*. New York: Bantam, 1972.

Firth, Raymond, *Tikopia Ritual and Belief.* Boston: Beacon Press, 1968.

——, *We, the Tikopia: Kinship in Primitive Polynesia.* Boston: Beacon Press, 1970.

Ford, C. S., and F. A. Beach, *Patterns of Sexual Behavior.* New York: Harper, 1949.

*Forde, C. Daryll, *Habitat, Economy and Society: A Geographical Introduction to Ethnology.* New York: Dutton, 1963.

Fox, Robin, *Kinship and Marriage.* Harmondsworth, Middlesex, Eng.: Penguin/Pelican, 1967.

Francoeur, Robert T., *Utopian Motherhood: New Trends in Human Reproduction.* South Brunswick, N.J., and New York: Barnes/Perpetua, 1973.

Frankfort, Henri, *The Birth of Civilization in the Near East.* Garden City, N.Y.: Doubleday/Anchor, n.d.

*——, Mrs. H. A. Frankfort, John A. Wilson, Thorkild Jacobsen, *Before Philosophy: The Intellectual Adventure of Ancient Man.* Baltimore: Penguin, 1968.

Frazer, Sir James George, *The Golden Bough: A Study in Magic and Religion* (1890). Abr. ed. New York: Macmillan Paperbacks, 1960.

Freud, Sigmund, *The Basic Writings of Sigmund Freud,* trans. and ed. A. A. Brill. New York: Modern Library, 1938.

*Fried, Morton H., *The Evolution of Political Society.* New York: Random House, 1967.

—— (ed.), *Explorations in Anthropology: Readings in Culture, Man, and Nature.* New York: Crowell, 1973.

Friedan, Betty, *The Feminine Mystique.* New York: Dell, 1975.

Gibbs, James L., Jr. (ed.), *Peoples of Africa.* New York: Holt, Rinehart and Winston, 1965.

Glob, P. V., *The Bog People: Iron-Age Man Preserved.* New York: Ballantine, 1971.

**Goodale, Jane C., *Tiwi Wives: A Study of the Women of Melville Island, North Australia.* Seattle: University of Washington Press, 1971.

Goodall, Jane (Jane van Lawick-Goodall), *In the Shadow of Man.* Boston: Houghton Mifflin, 1971.

—— (Baroness Jane van Lawick-Goodall), *My Friends the Wild Chimpanzees.* Washington, D.C.: National Geographic Society, 1967.

Gornick, Vivian, and Barbara Moran (eds.), *Woman in Sexist Society*. New York: Basic, 1971.

Grant, Douglas, *The Fortunate Slave: An Illustration of African Slavery in the Early Eighteenth Century*. London: Oxford University Press, 1968.

Graves, Robert, *The Greek Myths*, 2 vols. Baltimore: Penguin, 1955.

——, *The White Goddess: A Historical Grammar of Poetic Myth*. New York: Random House/Vintage, 1960.

Hahn, Emily, *On the Side of the Apes*. New York: Crowell, 1971.

Harding, Thomas G., and Ben J. Wallace (eds.), *Cultures of the Pacific*. New York: Macmillan/Free Press, 1970.

**Harlan, Jack R., *Crops and Man*. Madison, Wis.: American Society of Agronomy, Crop Science Society of America, 1975.

Harrison, Jane Ellen, *Prolegomena to the Study of Greek Religion* (1903). New York: Meridian, 1957.

Hawkes, Jacquetta, *The Dawn of the Gods*. New York: Random House, 1968.

——, *The First Great Civilizations: Life in Mesopotamia, the Indus Valley, and Egypt*. New York: Knopf, 1973.

——, *Man on Earth*. New York: Random House, 1955.

——, and Sir Charles Leonard Woolley, *Prehistory and the Beginnings of Civilization*. New York: Harper & Row, 1962.

Hays, H. R., *The Dangerous Sex: The Myth of Feminine Evil*. New York: Pocket Books, 1972.

Hebraic Literature: Translations from the Talmud, Midrashim and Kabbala, ed. Maurice H. Harris. New York: M. Walter Dunne, 1901.

*Heiser, Charles B., Jr., *Seed to Civilization: The Story of Man's Food*. San Francisco: Freeman, 1970.

Henriques, Fernando, *Stews and Strumpets*. London: MacGibbon and Kee, 1961.

*Herodotus, *The Histories*, trans. Aubrey de Sélincourt, revised edition. Harmondsworth, Middlesex, Eng.: Penguin, 1972.

**Herschberger, Ruth, *Adam's Rib*. New York: Pellegrini & Cudahy, 1948.

*Himes, Norman E., *Medical History of Contraception*. New York: Schocken, 1970.

Hite, Shere, *The Hite Report: A Nationwide Study of Female Sexuality*. New York: Macmillan, 1976.

Hogbin, Ian, *The Island of Menstruating Men: Religion in Wogeo, New Guinea.* Scranton, Pa.: Chandler, 1970.

Hole, Frank, Kent V. Flannery, and James A. Neely, *Prehistory and Human Ecology of the Deh Luran Plain.* Museum of Anthropology, Memoir No. I, University of Michigan. Ann Arbor, Mich., 1969.

Horney, Karen, *Feminine Psychology,* ed. Harold Kelman. New York: Norton, 1973.

——, *The Neurotic Personality of Our Time* (1937). New York: Norton, 1964.

Iglitzin, Lynne B., and Ruth Ross (eds.), *Women in the World: A Comparative Study.* Santa Barbara, Cal.: Clio Press, 1976.

*Isaac, Erich, *Geography of Domestication.* Englewood Cliffs, N.J.: Prentice-Hall, 1971.

*Jacobsen, Thorkild, *Toward the Image of Tammuz and Other Essays on Mesopotamian History and Culture.* Cambridge, Mass.: Harvard University Press, 1970.

*——, *The Treasures of Darkness*: A History of Mesopotamian Religion. New Haven: Yale University Press, 1976.

Jay, Phyllis C. (ed.), *Primates: Studies in Adaptation and Variability.* New York: Holt, Rinehart & Winston, 1968.

Jeanniere, Abel, *Anthropology of Sex.* New York: Harper & Row, 1967.

*Jolly, Alison, *The Evolution of Primate Behavior.* New York: Macmillan, 1972.

Josephus, *The Jewish War,* trans. G. A. Williamson. Baltimore: Penguin, 1960.

*Kaberry, Phyllis M., *Aboriginal Woman: Sacred and Profane.* London: Routledge, 1939.

Kapelrud, Arvid, *The Violent Goddess.* Oslo: Scandinavian University Books, 1969.

Kenyon, Kathleen, *Archaeology in the Holy Land.* New York: Praeger, 1970.

Kramer, Samuel Noah, *History Begins at Sumer* (original title *From the Tablets of Sumer,* issued in 1956). Garden City, N.Y.: Doubleday/Anchor, 1959.

——, *The Sacred Marriage Rite.* Bloomington: Indiana University Press, 1969.

——, *Sumerian Mythology.* New York: Harper & Bros., 1961. (Philadelphia: American Philosophical Society, Memoir No. XXI, 1944).

——, *The Sumerians: Their History, Culture, and Character*. Chicago: University of Chicago Press, 1963.

—— (ed.), *Mythologies of the Ancient World*. Garden City, N.Y.: Doubleday/Anchor, 1961.

Kraus, Bertram S., *The Basis of Human Evolution*. New York: Harper & Row, 1964.

Kropotkin, Peter, *Mutual Aid*. New York: Knopf, 1918.

Kurtén, Björn, *Not from the Apes: A Study of Man's Origins and Evolution*. New York: Random House/Vintage, 1972.

*Lancaster, Jane B., *Primate Behavior and the Emergence of Human Culture*. New York: Holt, Rinehart and Winston, 1975.

Landes, Ruth, *The City of Women*. New York: Macmillan, 1947.

——, *The Ojibwa Woman*. New York: Norton, 1971.

*Leacock, Eleanor Burke, and Nancy Oestreich Lurie (eds.), *North American Indians in Historical Perspective*. New York: Random House, 1971.

**Lee, Richard B., and Irven DeVore (eds.), *Kalahari Hunter-Gatherers: Studies of the !Kung San and Their Neighbors*. Cambridge, Mass.: Harvard University Press, 1976.

**——, *Man the Hunter*. Chicago: Aldine, 1968.

Lévi-Strauss, Claude, *The Elementary Structures of Kinship*, rev. ed. Boston: Beacon, 1969.

——, *The Savage Mind*. Chicago: University of Chicago Press, 1970.

——, *Totemism*, trans. Rodney Needham. Boston: Beacon Press, 1963.

——, *A World on the Wane (Tristes Tropiques)*, trans. John Russell. New York: Criterion, 1961.

Levy, G. Rachel, *Religious Conceptions of the Stone Age and Their Influence upon European Thought* (originally published 1948 under title *Gate of Horn*). New York: Harper Torchbooks, 1963.

*Lewis, Helen Block, *Psychic War in Men and Women*. New York: New York University Press, 1976.

Lorenz, Konrad, *On Aggression*. New York: Bantam/Matrix, 1970.

——, *King Solomon's Ring* (1952). New York: Crowell/Apollo, 1961.

Malinowski, Bronislaw, *Argonauts of the Western Pacific* (1922). New York: Dutton, 1961.

——, *Magic, Science and Religion and Other Essays*. Garden City, N.Y.: Doubleday/Anchor, 1954.

——, *The Sexual Life of Savages in North-Western Melanesia* (1929). New York: Harcourt, Brace & World/Harvest, n.d.

Marcus, Steven, *The Other Victorians: A Study of Sexuality and Pornography in Mid-Nineteenth-Century England*. New York: Basic, 1966.

**Marshack, Alexander, *The Roots of Civilization*. New York: McGraw-Hill, 1972.

Marshall, Donald S., and Robert C. Suggs (eds.), *Human Sexual Behavior: Variations in the Ethnographic Spectrum*. Englewood Cliffs, N.J.: Prentice-Hall/Prism, 1972.

Mead, Margaret, *Coming of Age in Samoa* (1928). New American Library/Mentor, 1949.

——, *Growing Up in New Guinea* (1930). New York: Dell, 1968.

——, *Male and Female*. New York: Morrow, 1949.

**——, *Sex and Temperament in Three Primitive Societies* (1935). New York: Dell/Laurel, 1971.

*—— (ed.), *Cooperation and Competition Among Primitive Peoples*. Boston: Beacon Press, 1961.

Mellaart, James, *Çatal Hüyük*. New York: McGraw-Hill, 1967.

——, *Earliest Civilizations of the Near East*. New York: McGraw-Hill, 1971.

*——, *Excavations at Hacilar*, 2 vols. Edinburgh: Edinburgh University Press, 1970.

**Miller, Casey, and Kate Swift, *Words and Women*. Garden City, N.Y.: Doubleday/Anchor Press, 1976.

**Miller, Jean Baker (ed.), *Psychoanalysis and Women*. Baltimore: Penguin, 1973.

Mitchell, Juliet, *Woman's Estate*. New York: Pantheon, 1971.

Money, John, and Anke A. Ehrhardt, *Man and Woman, Boy and Girl*. Baltimore: Johns Hopkins University Press, 1972.

Montagu, M. F. Ashley (ed.), *Man and Aggression*. New York: Oxford Paperback, 1971.

Morris, Desmond, *The Naked Ape*. New York: McGraw-Hill, 1967.

—— (ed.), *Primate Ethology*, Chicago: Aldine, 1967.

Murray, Henry A. (ed.), *Myth and Mythmaking*. Boston: Beacon Press, 1968.

Myrdal, Jan, *Report from a Chinese Village*, trans. Maurice Michael. New York: Random House/Pantheon, 1965.

Neumann, Erich, *The Great Mother: An Analysis of the Archetype*, trans. Ralph Manheim. Princeton: Princeton University Press/Bollingen Series, 1972.

——, *The Origins and History of Consciousness*, trans. R. F. C. Hull. Princeton: Princeton University Press/Bollingen Series, 1970.

Newman, Lucile F., *Birth Control: An Anthropological View*, Addison-Wesley Module 27. Reading, Mass.: Addison-Wesley, 1972.

*Noonan, John T., Jr., *Contraception: A History of Its Treatment by the Catholic Theologians and Canonists*. Cambridge, Mass.: Harvard University Press/Belknap Press, 1965.

Oakley, Kenneth P., *Man the Tool-maker*. Chicago: University of Chicago Press/Phoenix, 1964.

*Oppenheim, A. Leo, *Ancient Mesopotamia: Portrait of a Dead Civilization*. Chicago: University of Chicago Press, 1972.

Patai, R., *The Hebrew Goddess*. New York: Ktav, 1967.

Pfeiffer, John E., *The Emergence of Man*, rev. and enl. ed. New York: Harper & Row, 1972.

Piers, Maria, *Infanticide*. New York: Norton, 1978.

Piggott, Stuart, *Ancient Europe from the Beginnings of Agriculture to Classical Antiquity*. Chicago: Aldine, 1965.

*Pilbeam, David R., *The Ascent of Man*. New York: Macmillan, 1972.

——, *The Evolution of Man*. London: Thames and Hudson, 1970.

Plato, *The Symposium*, trans. Walter Hamilton. Harmondsworth, Middlesex, Eng.: Penguin, 1974.

Plutarch, *Lives of the Noble Greeks*, trans. and ed. Edmund Fuller. New York: Dell, 1959.

Polanyi, Karl, *Primitive, Archaic and Modern Economies*. New York: Doubleday/Anchor, 1968.

——, Conrad M. Arensberg, and Harry W. Pearson, *Trade and Market in the Early Empires*. Glencoe, Ill.: Free Press, 1957.

**Pomeroy, Sarah B., *Goddesses, Whores, Wives, and Slaves*. New York: Schocken, 1975, 1976.

Powdermaker, Hortense, *Life in Lesu: The Study of a Melanesian Society in New Ireland*. New York: Norton, 1971.

Pritchard, James B. (ed.), *Ancient Near Eastern Texts Relating to the Old Testament with Supplement.* 3rd ed. Princeton: Princeton University Press, 1969.

Raphael, Dana (ed.), *Being Female: Reproduction, Power, and Change.* The Hague: Mouton, 1975 (distr. in U.S. by Aldine, Chicago).

Rawson, Philip, *Primitive Erotic Art.* New York: Putnam, 1973.

Reed, Evelyn, *Problems of Women's Liberation.* New York: Merit, 1969.

*——, *Sexism and Science.* New York: Pathfinder, 1978.

——, *Woman's Evolution from Matriarchal Clan to Patriarchal Family.* New York: Pathfinder, 1975.

Reich, Wilhelm, *The Discovery of the Orgone:* Vol. 1, *The Function of the Orgasm* (1942, 1948), trans. Theodore P. Wolfe. New York: Farrar, Straus and Cudahy/Noonday, 1961.

——, *The Invasion of Compulsory Sex-Morality* (1931, 1934, 1951). New York: Farrar, Straus and Giroux, 1971.

——, *Sex-Pol: Essays, 1929–1934,* ed. Lee Baxandall; trans. Anna Bostock, Tom DuBose, and Lee Baxandall. New York: Random House/Vintage, 1972.

——, *The Sexual Revolution,* 4th ed., rev., trans. Theodore P. Wolfe. New York: Farrar, Straus and Giroux, 1970.

*Reid, John Phillip, *A Law of Blood: The Primitive Law of the Cherokee Nation.* New York: New York University Press, 1970.

**Reiter, Rayna R. (ed.), *Toward an Anthropology of Women.* New York: Monthly Review Press, 1975.

Renfrew, Colin, *Before Civilization.* London: Cape, 1973.

——, *The Emergence of Civilization.* London: Methuen, 1972.

Reynolds, Vernon, *The Apes: The Gorilla, Orang-utan, Chimpanzee, and Gibbon.* New York: Dutton, 1967.

——, *Budongo: An African Forest and Its Chimpanzees.* Garden City, N.Y.: Doubleday/Natural History Press, 1965.

**Rich, Adrienne, *Of Woman Born: Motherhood as Experience and Institution.* New York: Norton, 1976.

Rogers, Katherine M., *The Troublesome Helpmate: A History of Misogyny in Literature.* Seattle: University of Washington Press, 1966.

*Rohrlich-Leavitt, Ruby, *Peaceable Primates and Gentle People: Anthropological Approaches to Women's Studies.* New York: Harper and Row (Harper Studies in Language and Literature), 1975.

—— (ed.), *Women Cross-Culturally: Change and Challenge*. The Hague: Mouton Publishers, 1975 (distr. in U.S. by Aldine, Chicago).

Rosaldo, Michelle, and Louise Lamphere (eds.), *Women, Culture and Society*. Stanford, Cal.: Stanford University Press, 1974.

Rougemont, Denis de, *Love in the Western World*. New York: Harcourt, Brace, 1940.

Ruether, Rosemary Radford (ed.), *Religion and Sexism: Images of Woman in the Jewish and Christian Traditions*. New York: Simon and Schuster, 1974.

Ruitenbeek, Hendrik M. (ed.), *Psychoanalysis and Female Sexuality*. New Haven: College & University Press, 1966.

Russell, Bertrand, *A History of Western Philosophy*. New York: Simon and Schuster, 1945.

Sabloff, Jeremy A., and C. C. Lamberg-Karlovsky (eds.), *The Rise and Fall of Civilizations*. Menlo Park, Cal.: Cummings, 1974.

Saggs, H. W. F., *Everyday Life in Babylonia and Assyria*. New York: Putnam, 1965.

——, *The Greatness That Was Babylon*. London: Sidgwick and Jackson, 1969.

Schaller, George, *The Mountain Gorilla*. Chicago: University of Chicago Press, 1963.

*Schlegel, Alice, *Male Dominance and Female Autonomy*. New Haven: HRAF Press, 1972.

Schneider, David, and Kathleen Gough (eds.), *Matrilineal Kinship*. Berkeley: University of California Press, 1961.

Sévigné, Marie de Rabutin Chantal, Marquise de, *Letters from Madame la Marquise de Sévigné*, sel. and trans. Violet Hammersley. New York: Harcourt, Brace, 1956.

Sherfey, Mary Jane, *The Nature and Evolution of Female Sexuality*. New York: Random House, 1972.

Shneour, Elie, *The Malnourished Mind*. New York: Doubleday/Anchor, 1976.

Singer, Irving, *The Goals of Human Sexuality*. New York: Norton, 1973.

*Smith, C. U. M., *The Brain: Toward an Understanding*. New York: Putnam, 1970.

Southwick, Charles H. (ed.), *Animal Aggression*. New York: Van Nostrand-Reinhold, 1971.

—— (ed.), *Primate Social Behavior*. Princeton: Van Nostrand, 1963.

Stuard, Susan Mosher (ed.), *Women in Medieval Society*. Philadelphia: University of Pennsylvania Press, 1976.

Suetonius, *The Twelve Caesars*, trans. Robert Graves. Baltimore: Penguin, 1957.

Tacitus, *The Agricola and the Germania*, trans. H. Mattingly, rev. S. A. Handford. Harmondsworth, Middlesex, Eng.: Penguin, 1970.

Thomas, Elizabeth Marshall, *The Harmless People*. New York: Random House/Vintage, 1959, 1972.

Thompson, Clara M., *On Women* (1964), ed. Maurice R. Green. New York: New American Library/Mentor, 1971.

Thomson, George, *Studies in Ancient Greek Society*, Vol. I: *The Prehistoric Aegean*. London: Lawrence and Wishart, 1949.

Tiger, Lionel, and Robin Fox, *The Imperial Animal*. New York: Holt, Rinehart and Winston, 1971.

Tringham, Ruth, *Hunters, Fishers, and Farmers of Eastern Europe, 6000–3000 B.C.*, London: Hutchinson, 1971.

Turnbull, Colin M., *The Forest People: A Study of the Pygmies of the Congo*. New York: Simon and Schuster, 1961.

———, *Man in Africa*. Garden City, N.Y.: Doubleday/Anchor, 1976.

Ucko, Peter J., *Anthropomorphic Figurines of Predynastic Egypt and Neolithic Crete with Comparative Material from the Prehistoric Near East and Mainland Greece*. Royal Anthropological Institute Occasional Paper No. 24. London: Szmidla, 1968.

*———, and G. W. Dimbleby (eds.), *The Domestication and Exploitation of Plants and Animals*. Chicago: Aldine, 1969.

*———, and Andrée Rosenfeld, *Palaeolithic Cave Art*. New York: McGraw-Hill/World University Library, 1967.

*———, Ruth Tringham, and G. W. Dimbleby (eds.), *Man, Settlement and Urbanism*. Cambridge, Mass.: Schenkman, 1972.

Van Lawick-Goodall, Jane, *In the Shadow of Man*. Boston: Houghton Mifflin, 1971.

Vermaseren, Maarten J., *Cybele and Attis: The Myth and the Cult*. London: Thames and Hudson, 1977.

War: The Anthropology of Armed Conflict and Aggression. Supplement Based on Plenary Session in Washington at 66th Annual Meeting of American Anthropological Association. New York: Museum of Natural History, 1967.

Weideger, Paula, *Menstruation and Menopause*. New York:
    Knopf, 1976.
Wilson, Edmund, *To the Finland Station*. New York: Farrar,
    Straus and Giroux, 1973.
Wollstonecraft, Mary, *The Rights of Woman* (1792), and John
    Stuart Mill, *The Subjection of Women* (1869). Everyman's
    Library, No. 825. New York: Dutton, 1955.

PAPERS AND PERIODICALS

*Abramova, Z. A., "Palaeolithic Art in the U.S.S.R.," *Arctic An-
    thropology*, Vol. IV (1967), No. 2, pp. 1–179.
*Angel, J. Lawrence, "Early Neolithic Skeletons from Çatal Hüyük:
    Demography and Pathology," *Anatolian Studies*, Vol. 21
    (1971), pp. 80–95.
Barash, David P., "Sociobiology of Rape in Mallards: Responses of
    the Mated Male," *Science*, Vol. 197 (August 1977), pp. 788–
    89.
Barker-Benfield, Ben, "The Spermatic Economy: A Nineteenth-
    Century View of Sexuality," *Feminist Studies*, Vol. 1, No. 1
    (Summer 1972), pp. 45–74.
Binford, Sally R., "A Structural Comparison of Disposal of the
    Dead in the Mousterian and the Upper Paleolithic," *South-
    western Journal of Anthropology*, Vol. 24, No. 2 (Summer
    1968), pp. 139–54.
——, "Apes and Original Sin," *Human Behavior*, Vol. 1, No. 6
    (November–December 1972), pp. 65–71.
——, "Early Upper Pleistocene Adaptations in the Levant,"
    American Anthropologist, Vol. 70, No. 4 (August 1968), pp.
    707–17.
——, "Late Middle Paleolithic Adaptations and Their Possible
    Consequences," *BioScience*, Vol. 20, No. 5 (March 1, 1970),
    pp. 280–83.
——, "The Significance of Variability: A Minority Report," in
    The Origin of Homo Sapiens. Paris: Unesco (Ecology and
    Conservation 3), 1971.
——, and Lewis R. Binford, "Stone Tools and Human Behavior,"
    Scientific American, Vol. 220, No. 4 (April 1969), pp. 70–
    72, 77–82.
Birdsall, Nancy, "Women and Population Studies," *Signs*, Vol. I,
    No. 3, Part I (Spring 1976), pp. 699–712.
*Bryant, Vaughn M., Jr., and Glenna Williams-Dean, "The Cop-

rolites of Man," *Scientific American*, Vol. 232, No. 1 (January 1975), pp. 100–10.

Chevalier-Skolnikoff, Suzanne, "Male-Female, Female-Female, and Male-Male Sexual Behavior in the Stumptail Monkey," *Archives of Sexual Behavior*, Vol. 3, No. 2 (March 1974), pp. 95–117.

Dworkin, Andrea, "Pornography: The New Terrorism," *The Body Politic*, No. 45 (August 1978), pp. 12–14.

El-Wailly, Faisal, and Behnam Abu es-Soof, "The Excavations at Tell Es-Sawwan: First Preliminary Report (1964)," *Sumer*, Vol. 21 (1965), pp. 17–32.

Eaton, G. Gray, "The Social Order of Japanese Macaques," *Scientific American*, Vol. 235, No. 4 (October 1976), pp. 97–107.

Fayerweather, Mary, "Women of the Medieval Towns: The Interaction of Familial and Economic Roles in the Late Middle Ages," unpublished paper.

Fisher, Elizabeth, "Hustlers All: A Speculation," *APHRA*, Vol. 2, No. 2 (Spring 1971), pp. 2–14.

Fossey, Dian, "More Years with Mountain Gorillas," *National Geographic*, Vol. 140, No. 4 (October 1971), pp. 574–85.

Fried, Morton H., "On the Evolution of Social Stratification and the State," in S. Diamond (ed.), *Culture in History* (New York: Columbia University, 1960).

Fritz, Leah, "Is Pornography Gynocidal Propaganda?" *Review of Law and Social Change*, in press.

Gardner, Howard, "The Loss of Language," *Human Nature*, Vol. 1, No. 3 (March 1978), pp. 76–84.

Gelb, I. J., "The Ancient Mesopotamian Ration System," *Journal of Near Eastern Studies*, Vol. 24 (July 1965), pp. 230–43.

*Griffin, Susan, "Rape: The All-American Crime," *Ramparts*, Vol. 10, No. 3 (September 1971), pp. 26–35.

Hage, Dorothy, "There's Glory for You," *APHRA*, Vol. 3, No. 3 (Summer 1972), pp. 2–14.

Harlan, Jack R., "The Plants and Animals That Nourish Man," *Scientific American*, Vol. 235, No. 3 (September 1976), pp. 88–97.

Harold, Ellen, "More Thinking About Feminism," *APHRA*, Vol. 3, No. 3 (Summer 1972), pp. 56–71.

———, "Thinking About Feminism," *APHRA*, Vol. 2, No. 3 (Summer 1971), pp. 14–24.

446 BIBLIOGRAPHY

Harrell-Bond, Barbara, "The Influence of the Family Caseworker on the Structure of the Family: The Sierra Leone Case," *Social Research*, Summer 1977, pp. 193–215.

Helbaek, Hans, "First Impressions of the Çatal Hüyük Plant Husbandry," *Anatolian Studies*, Vol. 14 (1964), pp. 121–23.

Herman, Judith, and Lisa Hirschman, "Father-Daughter Incest," *Signs*, Vol. 2, No. 4 (Summer 1977), pp. 735–56.

Holloway, Ralph L., Jr., "Australopithecine Endocasts, Brain Evolution in the Hominoidae, and a Model of Hominid Evolution," Ch. 8 in *The Functional and Evolutionary Biology of Primates*, ed. Russell Tuttle (Chicago: Aldine, 1972).

——, "Culture: A Human Domain," *Current Anthropology*, Vol. 10, No. 4 (October 1969), pp. 395–412.

——, "New Australopithecine Endocast, SK 1585, from Swartkrans, South Africa," *American Journal of Physical Anthropology*, Vol. 37, No. 2 (September 1972), pp. 173–86.

Hughes, Diane, "Domestic Ideals and Social Behavior: Evidence from Medieval Genoa," in Charles E. Rosenberg (ed.), *The Family in History* (Philadelphia: The University of Pennsylvania Press, Inc., 1975).

Isaac, Erich, "On the Domestication of Cattle," *Science*, Vol. 137 (1962), pp. 195–204.

Isaac, Glynn, "The Food-Sharing Behavior of Protohuman Hominids," *Scientific American*, Vol. 238, No. 4 (April 1978), pp. 90–108.

——, and Garniss Curtis, "Acheulian Tools," *Nature*, Vol. 249, No. 5458 (June 14, 1974), pp. 624–27.

Jolly, Clifford J., "The Seed-Eaters: A New Model of Hominid Differentiation Based on a Baboon Analogy," *Man*, Vol. 5, No. 5 (1970), pp. 3–25.

Jacobsen, Thomas W., "17,000 Years of Greek Prehistory," *Scientific American*, Vol. 234, No. 6 (June 1976), pp. 76–87.

*Kolata, Gina Bari, "Primate Behavior: Sex and the Dominant Male," *Science*, Vol. 191, No. 4222 (January 9, 1976), pp. 55–58.

Lancaster, Jane B., "Carrying and Sharing in Human Evolution," *Human Nature*, Vol. 1, No. 2 (February 1978), pp. 82–89.

Leacock, Eleanor, "The Changing Family and Lévi-Strauss, or Whatever Happened to Fathers?" *Social Research*, Summer 1977, pp. 235–59.

——, "Women, Social Evolution, and Errors, Crude and Subtle." Unpublished paper.

*Lee, Richard Borshay, "Male-Female Residence Arrangements and Political Power in Human Hunter-Gatherers," *Archives of Sexual Behavior*, Vol. III, No. 2 (March 1974), pp. 167–73.

Levine, Seymour, "Sex Differences in the Brain," *Scientific American*, Vol. 214, No. 20 (April 1966), pp. 84–90.

Leakey, Louis, and Robert Ardrey, "Man the Killer, a Dialogue," *Psychology Today*, Vol. 6, No. 4 (1972), pp. 73–85.

Lore, Richard, and Kevin Flannelly, "Rat Societies," *Scientific American*, Vol. 236, No. 5 (May 1977), pp. 106–16.

Mellaart, James, "A Neolithic City in Turkey," *Scientific American*, Vol. 210, No. 27 (April 1964), pp. 94–104.

——, "Excavations at Çatal Hüyük, 1962," *Anatolian Studies*, Vol. 13 (1963), pp. 43–103.

——, "Excavations at Çatal Hüyük, 1963," *Anatolian Studies*, Vol. 14 (1964), pp. 39–119.

——, "Excavations at Çatal Hüyük, 1965," *Anatolian Studies*, Vol. 16 (1966), pp. 165–91.

Money, John, and Anke A. Ehrhardt, "Gender Dimorphic Behavior and Fetal Sex Hormones," *Recent Progress in Hormone Research*, Vol. 28 (1972), pp. 735–63.

Monter, E. William, "Women in the Economy of Calvinist Geneva, 1580–1780." Unpublished paper.

Moss, Cynthia, "A New Image for Hyenas," *Smithsonian*, Vol. 6, No. 4 (June 1975), pp. 38–45. Later published in Cynthia Moss, *Portraits in the Wild: Behavior Studies of East African Mammals* (Boston: Houghton Mifflin Co., 1975).

Newton, Esther, and Paula Webster, "Matriarchy: As Women See It," *APHRA*, Vol. 4, No. 3 (Summer 1973), pp. 6–22.

Newton, Niles, and Charlotte Modahl, "Pregnancy: The Closest Human Relationship," *Human Nature*, Vol. 1, No. 3 (March 1978), pp. 40–49.

——, and Michael Newton, "Psychological Aspects of Lactation," *New England Journal of Medicine*, Vol. 277, No. 22 (November 30, 1967), pp. 1179–86.

*Oates, Joan, "Goddesses of Choga Mami," *The Illustrated London News*, April 19, 1969, pp. 28–30.

*——, "New Perspectives from Iraq," *The Illustrated London News*, April 5, 1969, pp. 30–33.

Pagels, Elaine H., "What Became of God the Mother? Conflicting Images of God in Early Christianity," *Signs*, Vol. 2, No. 2
(Winter 1976), pp. 293–303.

——, "When Did Man Make God in His Image? A Case Study
in Religion and Politics," paper presented at the Scholar and
the Feminist III Conference, Barnard College Women's
Center, Columbia University, New York, April 10, 1976.

Pilbeam, David, "An Idea We Could Live Without—The Naked
Ape," *Discovery*, Vol. 7, No. 2 (Spring 1972), pp. 63–70.
Later published in D. Hunter and P. Whitten (eds.), *An-
thropology: Contemporary Perspectives* (Boston: Little,
Brown, 1975).

——, "Rearranging Our Family Tree," *Human Nature*, Vol. 1,
No. 6 (June 1978), pp. 38–45.

Rakoff, Vivian M., "The Family: An Ethological Imperative,"
Social Research, Summer 1977, pp. 206–34.

Revelle, Roger, "The Resources Available for Agriculture," *Scientific American*, Vol. 235, No. 3 (September 1976), pp.
164–78.

Rohrlich-Leavitt, Ruby, "Women and the Origin of the State of
Sumer," revision of paper presented at the annual meeting
of the American Anthropological Association, Washington,
D.C., November 1976.

——, "Women in Transition: Crete and Sumer," in Bridenthal
and Koonz (eds.), *Becoming Visible: Women in European
History*. Boston: Houghton Mifflin Co., 1977.

Rossi, Alice S., "The Biosocial Side of Parenthood," *Human Nature*, Vol. 1, No. 6 (June 1978), pp. 72–79.

——, "Maternalism, Sexuality and the New Feminism," in Joseph
Zubin and John Money (eds.), *Contemporary Sexual Behavior*. Baltimore: Johns Hopkins University Press, 1973.

Scott, Joan, and Louise Tilly, "Woman's Work and the Family
in Nineteenth-Century Europe," in Charles E. Rosenberg
(ed.), *The Family in History*. Philadelphia: The University
of Pennsylvania Press, Inc., 1975.

Sidel, Victor W., and Ruth Sidel, "The Delivery of Medical Care
in China," *Scientific American*, Vol. 230, No. 4 (April 1974),
pp. 19–27.

Silver, Catherine Bodard, "Salon, Foyer, Bureau: Women and the
Professions in France," *American Journal of Sociology*, Vol.
78, No. 4 (January 1973).

Simons, Elwyn L., "Ramapithecus," *Scientific American*, Vol. 236, No. 5 (May 1977), pp. 28–35.

Smith, Cyril J., "History and Rape Laws," *International Bar Journal*, May 1975, pp. 33–40.

Snitow, Ann, and Ellen Harold, "Her Daughter Was Her Muse," *APHRA*, Vol. 2, No. 4 (Fall 1971), pp. 40–52.

Stewart, Abigail J., and David G. Winter, "The Nature and Causes of Female Suppression," *Signs*, Vol. 2, No. 3 (Spring 1977), pp. 531–53.

Stone, Lawrence, "The Rise of the Nuclear Family in Early Modern England," in Charles E. Rosenberg (ed.), *The Family in History*. Philadelphia: The University of Pennsylvania Press, Inc., 1975.

**Tanner, Nancy, and Adrienne Zihlman, "Women in Evolution," *Signs*, Vol. 1, No. 3, Part I (Spring 1976), pp. 585–608.

Teleki, Geza, "The Omnivorous Chimpanzee," *Scientific American*, Vol. 228, No. 1 (January 1973), pp. 32–42.

Walkowitz, Judith, "Notes on the History of Victorian Prostitution," *Feminist Studies*, Vol. 1, No. 1 (Summer 1972), pp. 105–14.

Index

About the Author

ELIZABETH FISHER is one of the pioneers of the current feminist movement. In 1969 she founded the first feminist literary magazine, *APHRA*. Her articles have appeared in the *New York Times*, the *Nation*, the New York *Post*, and other newspapers and magazines, and she has written and translated fiction and drama. She was visiting professor at the Women's Writers' Center at Cazenovia College, Cazenovia, N.Y., and has taught Women's Studies at New York University.

/301.412F533W>C1/